Mexican Popular Art

Clothing and Dolls

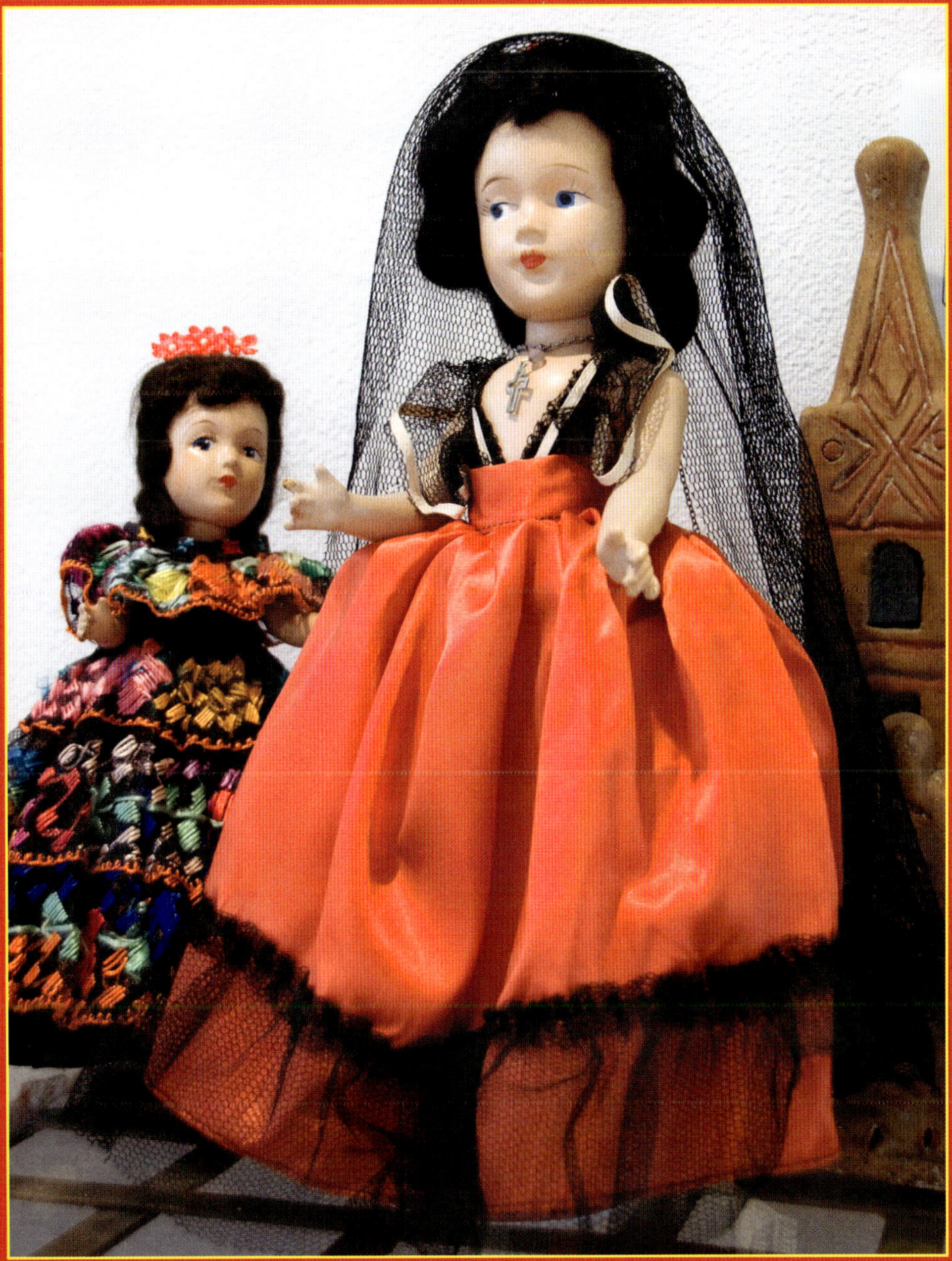

Wendy A. Scalzo

Photography by John & Wendy Scalzo

Contributing Editor Sarah N. Balzac

Schiffer Publishing Ltd

4880 Lower Valley Road, Atglen, Pennsylvania 19310

Please note:
All the dolls shown in the photographs are in the author's collection, unless otherwise credited.

Disclaimer: No part of this book may be reproduced or utilized in any form or by any means, electronically or mechanically, including the photographs without permission from the author. The author has gathered material through her own independent experiences, purchases and study. The author acknowledges that all of the data gathered in the book could be impartial to others research and does not dispute or negate any other findings based on substantiated studies other than her own. The research was not sponsored by any manufacturer, museum, company or other entity. Photographs were from the author's personal collection and all others were contributed with permission from the originators. The author will credit all those resources taken from any contributors past or present at the back of the book in the bibliography.

The values given within this book are intended as a value guide rather than arbitrarily set prices. The author claims no definitive source in pricing the dolls; it is purely based on dealers, customer sales, auctions, shows, and past and present sales. The price range given for each doll is from fair (body intact may have mild crazing, clothing may be dirty) to excellent condition (sometimes including original tags and boxes). All values are quoted as accurate as possible, but in the case of errors--- typographical, clerical, or otherwise--- the author and publisher assume no liability for any loss incurred by users of this book.

Other Schiffer Books on Related Subjects:
San Miguel's Mexican Interiors, Sandy Baum
Popular Arts of Mexico, Donna McMenamin
Mexican Folk Art from Oaxacan Families, A. & A. Rothstein

Photography by John & Wendy Scalzo
Library of Congress Control Number: 2007939781

Designed by "Sue"
Type set in Dutch809 BT/Aldine721 BT

ISBN: 978-0-7643-2887-9
Printed in China

Schiffer Books are available at special discounts for bulk purchases for sales promotions or premiums. Special editions, including personalized covers, corporate imprints, and excerpts can be created in large quantities for special needs. For more information contact the publisher:

Published by Schiffer Publishing Ltd.
4880 Lower Valley Road
Atglen, PA 19310
Phone: (610) 593-1777; Fax: (610) 593-2002
E-mail: Info@schifferbooks.com

For the largest selection of fine reference books
on this and related subjects,
please visit our web site at **www.schifferbooks.com**
We are always looking for people to write
books on new and related subjects.
If you have an idea for a book please contact
us at the above address.

This book may be purchased from the publisher.
Include $3.95 for shipping.
Please try your bookstore first.
You may write for a free catalog.

In Europe, Schiffer books are distributed by
Bushwood Books
6 Marksbury Ave.
Kew Gardens
Surrey TW9 4JF England
Phone: 44 (0) 20 8392-8585; Fax: 44 (0) 20 8392-9876
E-mail: info@bushwoodbooks.co.uk
Website: www.bushwoodbooks.co.uk
Free postage in the U.K., Europe; air mail at cost.

Dedication

I dedicate this book to my adorable husband, John R. Scalzo,
who always encouraged me to do what I love.

Acknowledgments

I acknowledge my father and mother, Roland J. Reaux and Zulma Delgado Colom, for if it weren't for my father's unrelenting savor of tequila and Mexican *cabrito* (goat), or my mother's Spanish heritage, I may never have learned to love the beauty of Mexico. I also recognize my three wonderful children: Roland, Nicole, and John Michael; without them I am nothing but a hoarder of Mexican dolls.

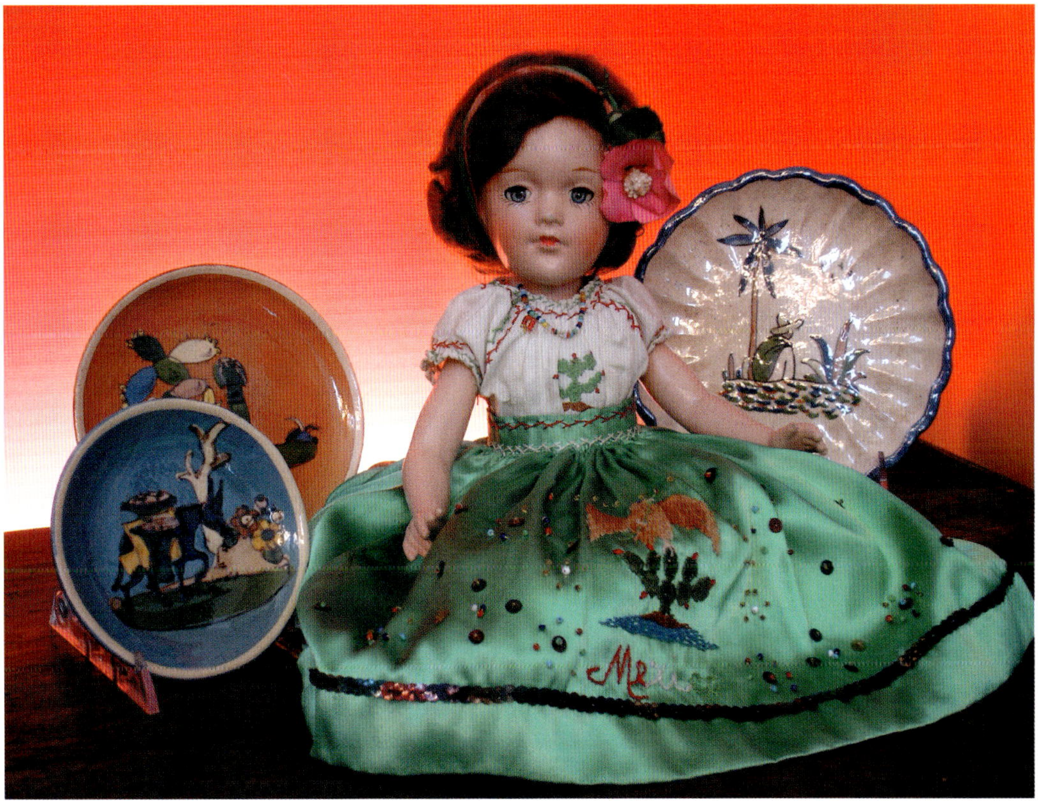

Tonita, a rare 16 in. composition doll. She is wearing a "*China Poblana*" dress with an embroidered cotton blouse. The skirt is in a vibrant green silk satin accented with glass beads and sequins. Mexico's national emblem of the eagle and snake in its mouth is centered at the front of the skirt. "Mexico" embroidered along the border around the skirt scattered w sequins and trimmings. She wears an under slip made of crepe silk. Open leatherette shoes that tie, a glass beaded necklace. Stung with movable parts, mohair wig accented with flowers. All original. Made in the USA. Tlaquepaque pottery, 1950s. Doll $450 to 800

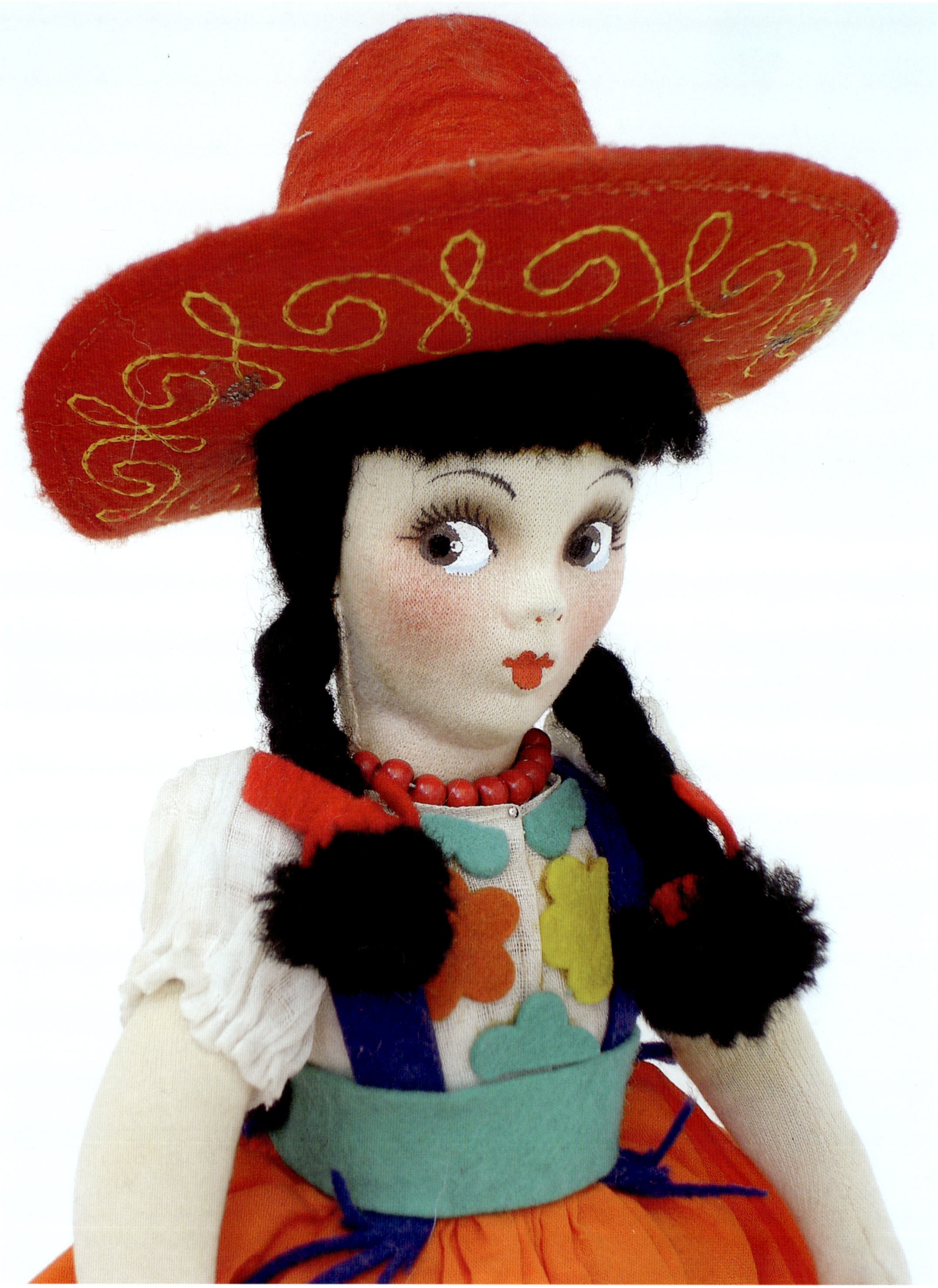

Contents

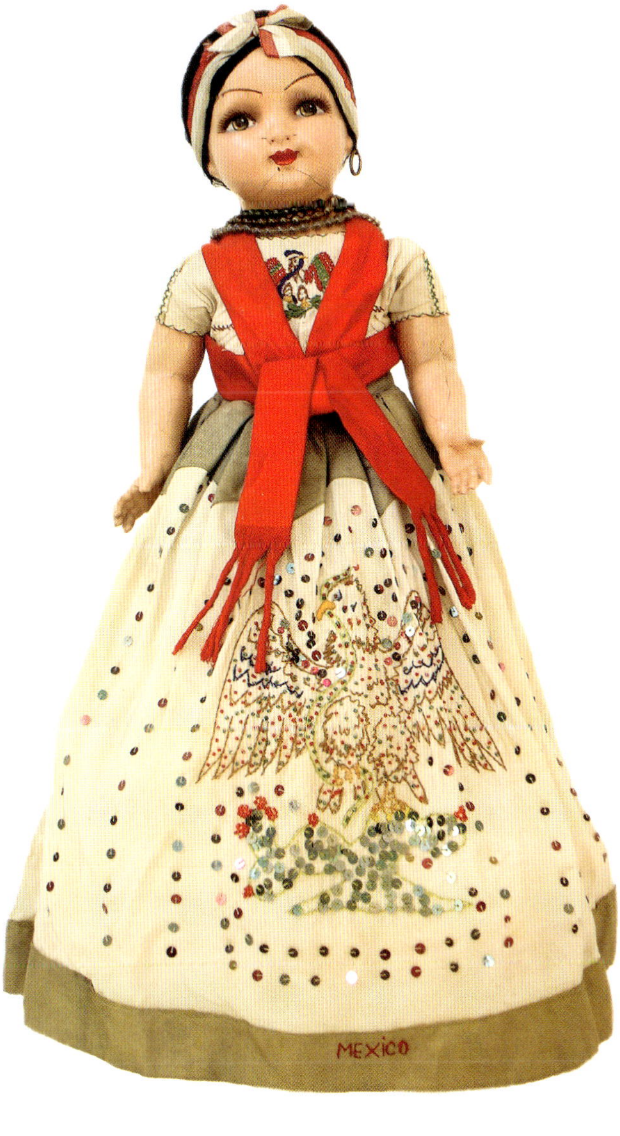

Preface

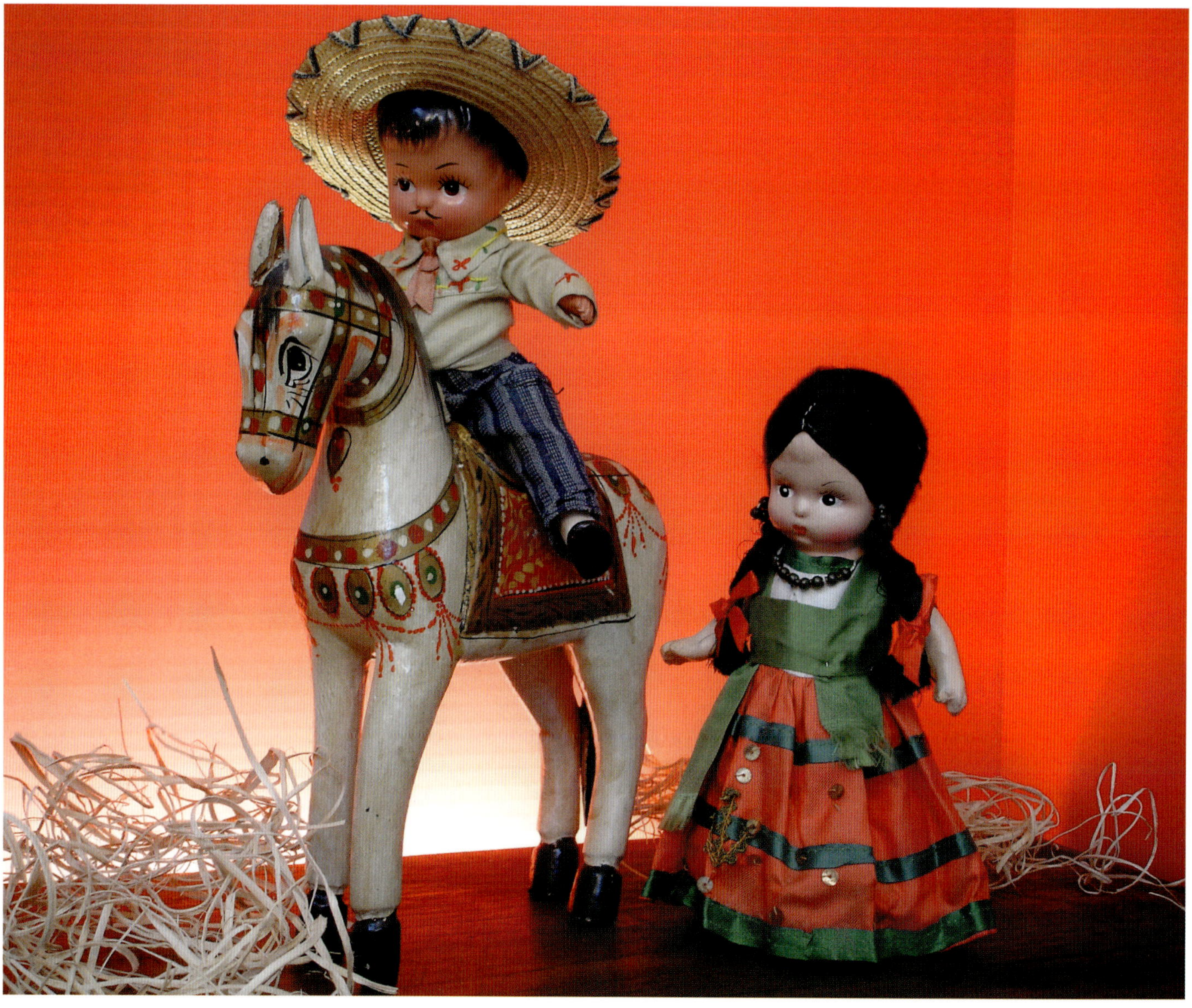

Carlito and Maria with a horse, c.1950s. Two 10 in. composition tourist dolls mint with box. Carlos is a *campesino* with his wife Maria as a charra. He is wearing a white cotton shirt that ties at the waist with embroidery and *chapa* style pants. Molded features all hand painted detail and a *petate sombrero*. Maria is wearing a *zagalejo* style skirt and a green *rebozo* over a white top. Cotton black threads create a beautiful braided wig. $75 to 150

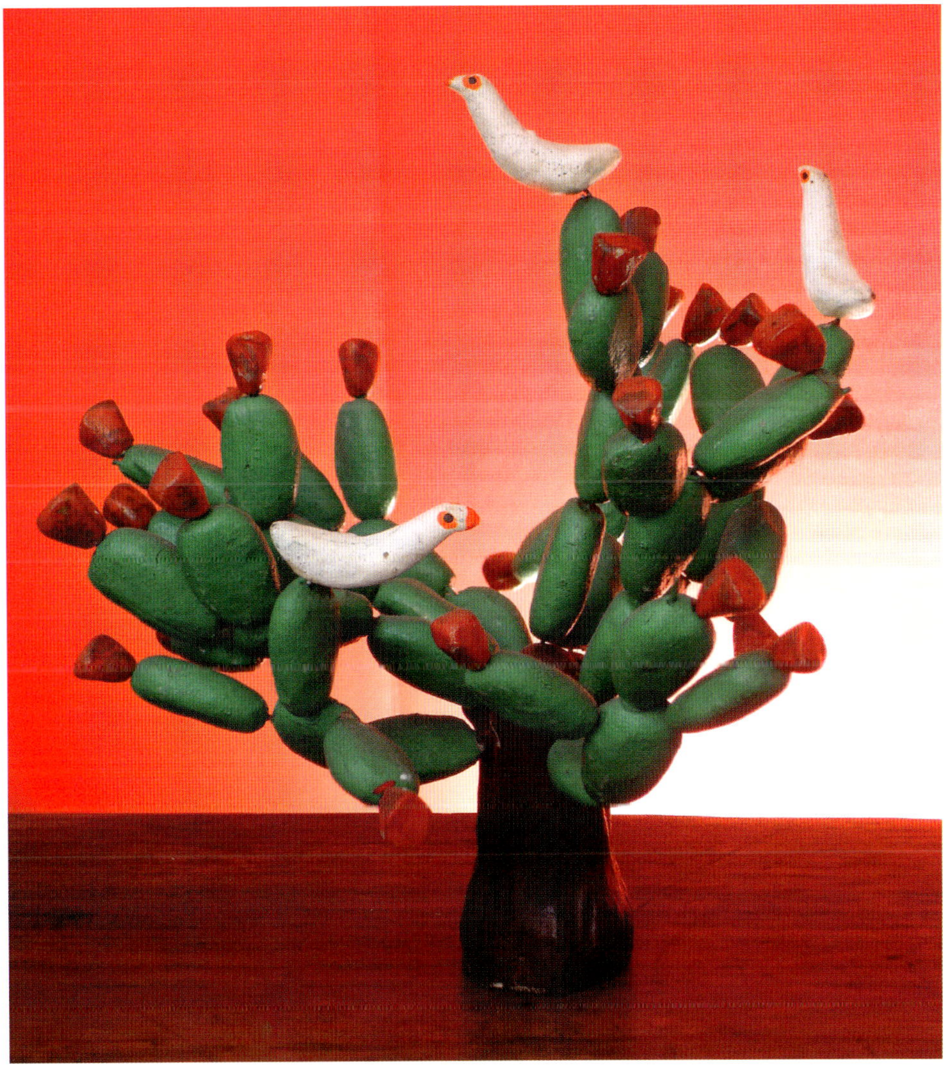

Red and green polychrome painted ceramic over wire Mexican cactus with *pajaros* (birds). Made in Mexico, c.1950s, 10 in

The satisfaction I feel about Mexico's popular arts is one of pure delight. Through art and costumes I can inhabit the strong Mexican traditions, especially through my "niche," the costume doll.

After many years of collecting Mexican dolls and consuming countless hours of empty research into their origin and costumes, I realize how important it is to document what I learned and share my dolls with the rest of the world. Very few, if any, of Mexico's popular arts books acknowledge Mexican-made dolls, and there is no publication that has exclusively recognized them. Mexico's folk art has sustained the integrity of its culture during the 20th century. Most Mexican costume dolls encompass all the attributes of folk art. This was my inspiration to write this book, which is a heart-felt tribute to the dolls and their beautiful costumes. I hope to promote their importance to costume, doll, and art collectors of the past, present, and future. The majority of the dolls date from the late 1890s to the early 1960s, with the exception of a few by current folk art doll makers. There are examples of the most recognizable costumes from some of the predominant regions of Mexico. The dolls were made by native artisans and foreign makers, with inherent detail to authenticate their clothing.

Through the 20th century, a revival of Mexican appreciation of their indigenous clothing emerged. It was a union and acceptance of new trends, methods, and implements. The native Indians as well as Spanish and European settlers' influences altered Mexico's indigenous clothing. The blended talents of these cultures and urban life began to modify centuries of customs into what is now a predominantly a *mestizo* ethnic nation (mixed Indian blood). Those Indians who were neither swayed by colonial domination nor modernization refused to sacrifice their heritage and have clung to the traditional values of their birthright. Convinced to sustain their place in the progression of tradition over cultural extinction they fled to the more remote regions of Mexico. Although there has been a marginal Indian existence near the cities they have managed to retain much of their grounded traditions. So what may appear to be a costume to a foreigner or to even some urban Mexicans are remnants of the original clothing.

The Mexican doll preserves a visual story through its costumes that shows variations from decade to decade.

These dolls have been profoundly overlooked in the many different genres of doll collecting and as Mexican folk art. Not only are they exceptionally beautiful, they exemplify changes in their clothing that took place from the end of the 19th and into the 20th century.

It has been an incredible challenge to accurately document each doll's costume and their relative market values. For the most part, the lack or bits of information that I found was unclear and polluted. I cannot emphasis this enough, and this is why I felt it was time to trace all the data that I could find and make a documentation. Each doll presents a skilled or trained "*pintor*" (painter) and "*costurera*" (costume maker). Some might call the dolls unrefined or provincial, and just another tourist souvenir that was mass-produced, but that is certainly not true. They are pieces of Mexico's popular art culture and have residual value along with other acclaimed tourist pieces. Mexican pottery, as well as costume, consumes color and tradition into its ornamentation that mimics regional traits of the local style. The dolls are remarkable and invoke the same credibility as any present-day collectible doll. Their costumes submit to a lineage of Spanish and Indian influences and credit changes that led up to 20th century culture. Lively accents and indigenous traits make these among the most popular costumes in the world.

I received my first Mexican doll when I was eight years old. I named her Maria. She was dressed as an 8" *charrita* (little cowgirl), with long black braids made from cotton threads finished at the ends with red bows. Her face and body were of a solid *muñeca de irrompibles* (unbreakable composition dolls); delicate hand-painted details gave her a precious expression on her face. Her dress was handmade woven cotton, beaded and embroidered with flowers. She wore a little red sombrero tied tightly around her face. I played with her for many years and never forgot about my little "*chulita*" (cute little girl).

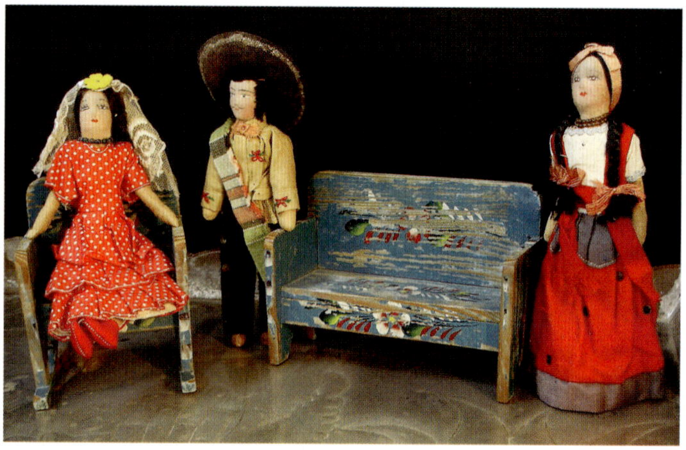

A trio of 6 in. tall cloth *mestizo* dolls, tiny detail, with authentic early 20th century painted wood doll house furniture. $15 to 35

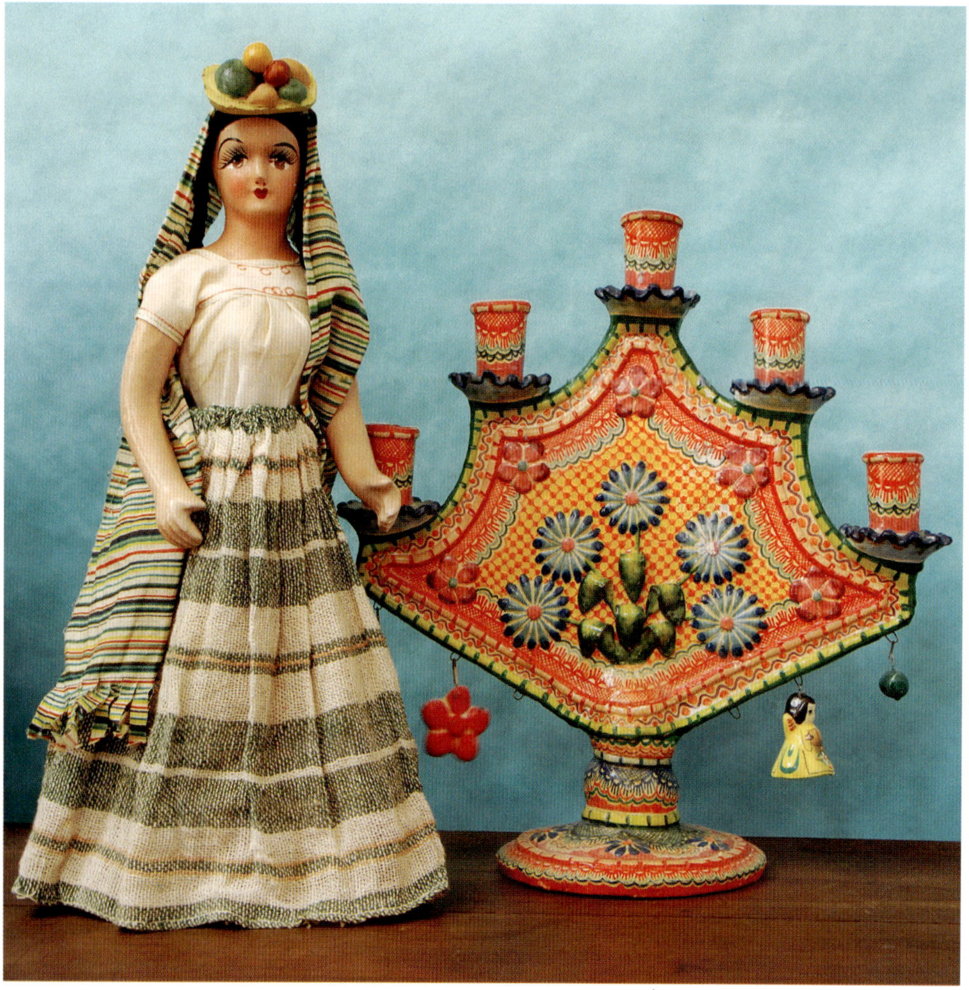

A pristine 17 in. *mestiza* from the 1950s. Made inMexico, composition 5 pc. strung body with an embroidered top and open weave full skirt. Long braids and colorful *rebozo*, she is carrying fruits in a compo basket on her head, standing next to a popular arts grand polychrome Pueblan *candelabra*. Doll $175 to 375

I hope you enjoy the dolls & some of my Mexican folk art . Most are from my private collection, no longer seen at typical retail shops. I purchased them over the years in antique or thrift stores, garage sales, doll shows, private sales and online auctions. I have given some of them names, as you will notice in the captions. This was strictly a personal notation, they did not come with names. Other dolls in the book were generously shared or loaned to me and are credited to the contributors. They are rare and beautiful examples of Mexican dolls, hand made from cloth, composition, plaster, or other materials. Some are from specific regions and periods and others are a credit to their artistry and medium. It is difficult to definitively date them or ascertain the precise city they may have been made in, but observation is the key. I trust that I have summarized their origins practically. Their traditional clothing, condition, construction, and regions are sometimes the only source available when researching their provenance. This can lead to many dead ends; regardless, I will do my best.

Other pieces of Mexican art shown throughout the book were not used only as props, but also as a point of reference. It was important to point out similarities among the many different Mexican folk arts. Some of the folk art pieces do correlate with the dolls costumes by origin and age. Just as Mexican souvenir pottery was at the peak of its popularity, so were the costume dolls.

I have added a glossary at the back of the book that will help you become familiar with some of the Mexican, Indian, and Spanish words as well as other important words I used in the descriptions and text. If you see a word in *italics,* most likely it is in the glossary.

There are certainly many Mexican dolls that do not appear in this work. I have yet to discover every one, although that would be nice and I am always searching for more. I will be dedicated to the progression and recognition of any significant find. As a collector for more than 25 years, my knowledge is a reliable and definitive source, but who isn't always interested in learning more. Through the years, my collection grew and so did my ambition for writing this book. Never has the subject been presented in a format worthy of their significance, until now, and I am honored to present you with some fine examples.

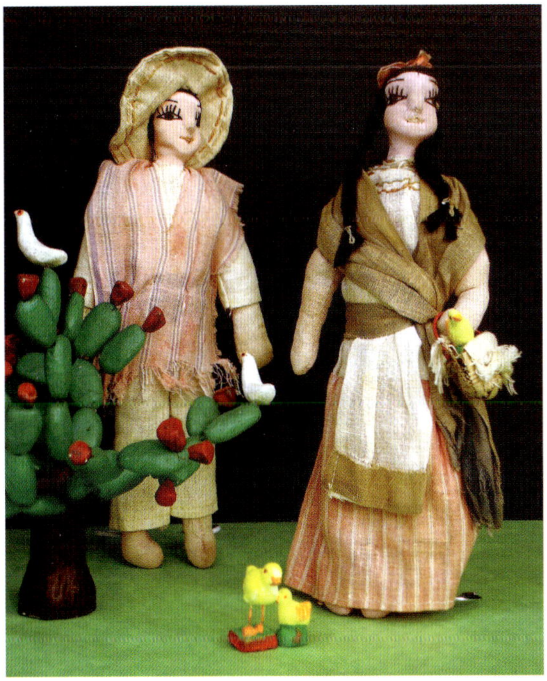

Attributed to Ravca, typical costumes c.1940s. A 13 in. needle molded facial features, great detail and traditional clothing of the *mestizo* Indians. Import $75 to 150

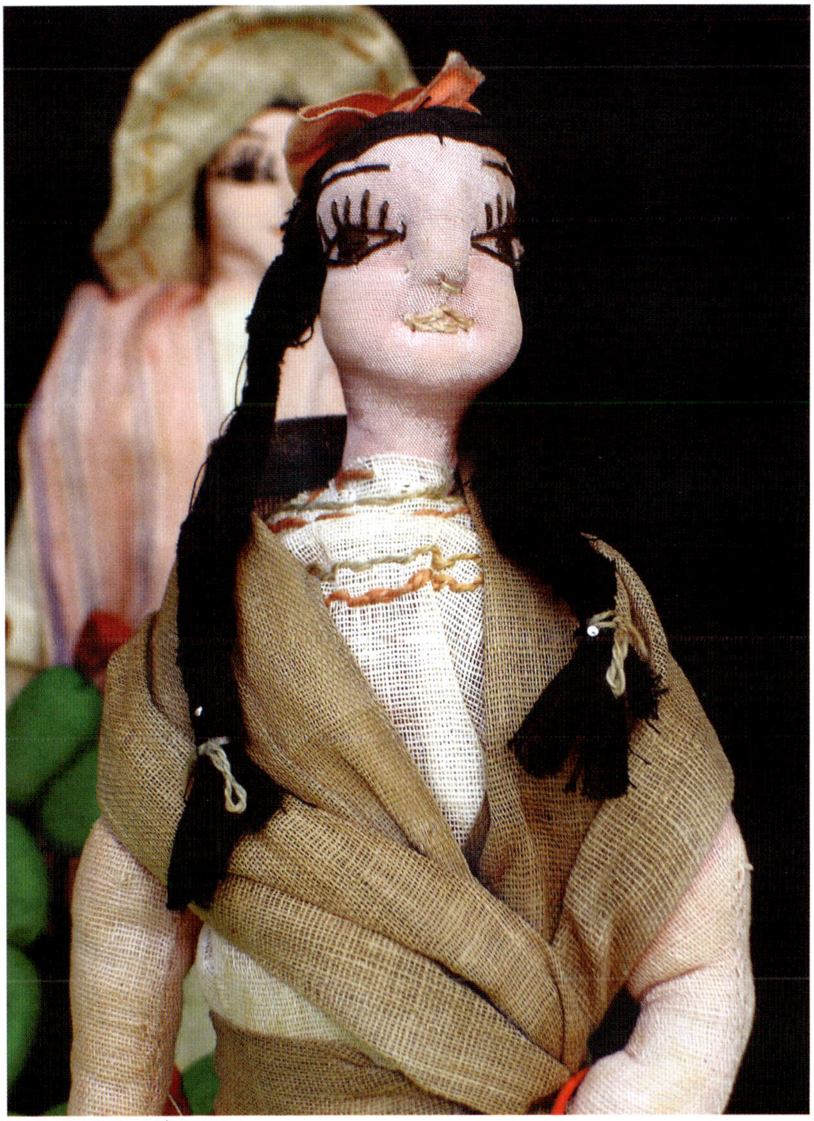

A closer look at the Ravca Mexican Indian. Her face is needle molded with stocking cloth. Long braids made of ribbons for her hair and a brown *rebozo*. Made in France $75 to 150

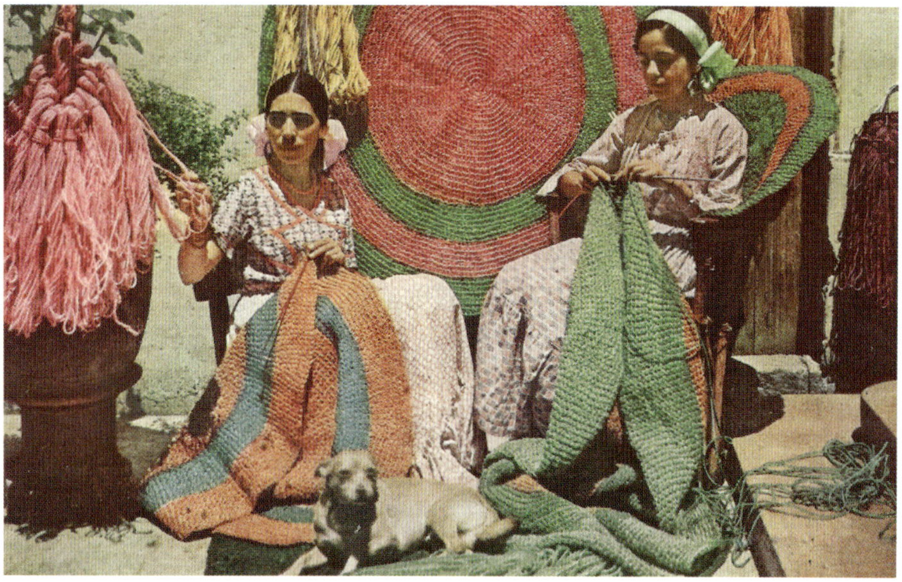

A spectacular color print of *mestizas*, generational Indian skills of weaving and sewing rugs, making their traditional folk art, 1934.

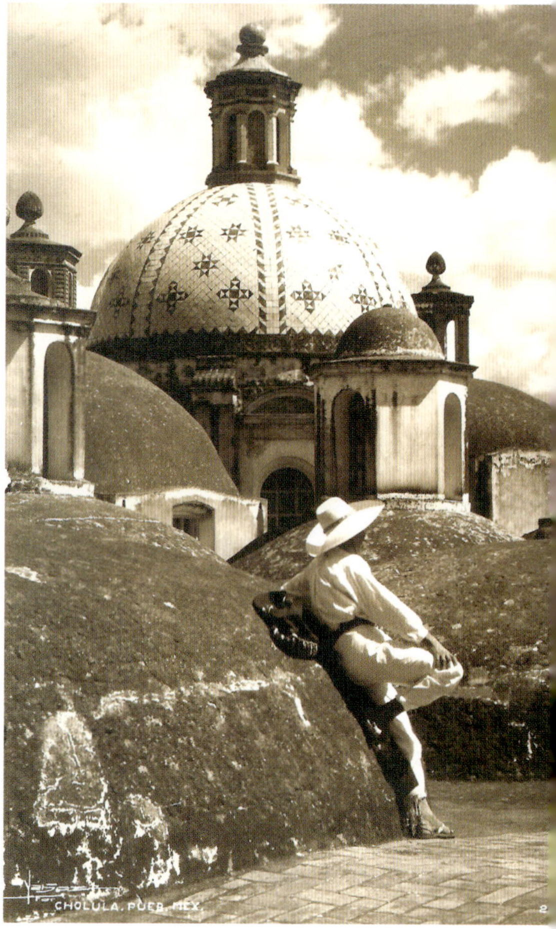

Postcard, black and white photograph, "Mexican in Puebla " wearing the *tipica calzone blanco*, c.1930 Mexico D. F. 4 x 5 in. $15 to 40

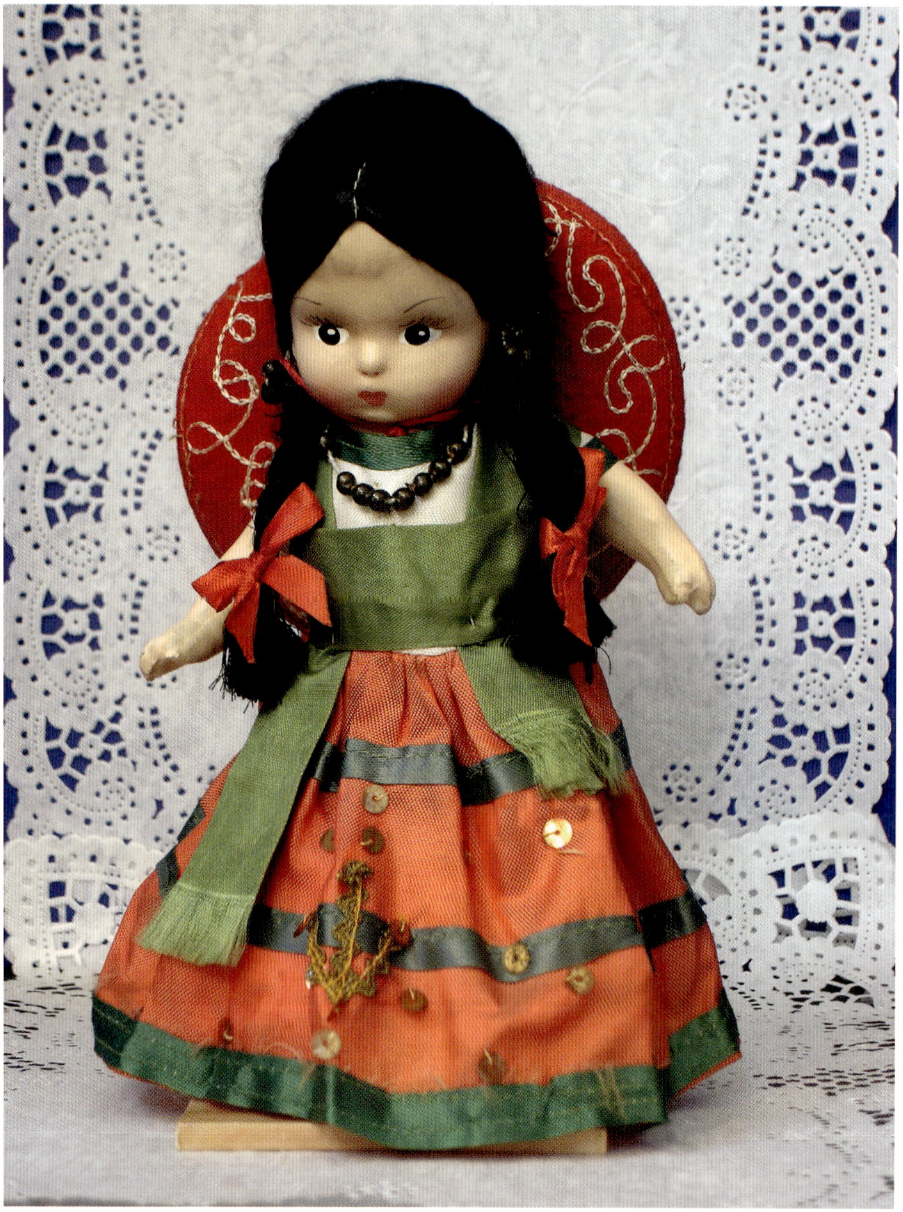

Maria is a 8 in. *muñeca de irrompible* made in Mexico. Dressed as a *charra* in her full skirt. A rayon skirt trimmed with green ribbon and sequins. Molded composition 5pc body with movable legs and arms. Wig braids, bows, ribbon and a large red felt sombrero. Souvenir doll made c.1950. Mint condition. No markings. $50 to $80

Introduction

Art is a central part of Mexico's daily life: it is found along the streets, in their cooking, on their costumes, and in every Mexican home. They are a race of natural artists and instinctively they have preserved their culture. Their pottery "*una cazuela*" (cooking pot) hangs on the wall or may be arranged in a way to compliment the kitchen as well as be utilized to cook "*frijoles*" (beans).

Huge "*ollas de aqua*" (earthen water jars) are painted with glorious patterns and colors to pay tribute and "*corriente*", a common term among the Mexicans that expresses the common use, its beauty and personal intention of purpose. A beautiful long red scarf is draped over an Indian woman's shoulder, then under her arm, and tied tightly to the opposite side of her body. It is her *rebozo* and in it she holds her baby---warm, safe, and beautiful. They want the things they use in everyday life to be useful and beautiful. Not only does it serve as a utilitarian object but it could also present itself as an aesthetic piece. Their choice of color, method, and traditions exemplify the Mexican culture as one of the most recognizable. The connection between their ageless past and present is mirrored clearly in all their folk art, and I find these same ambitions in vintage Mexican costume dolls.

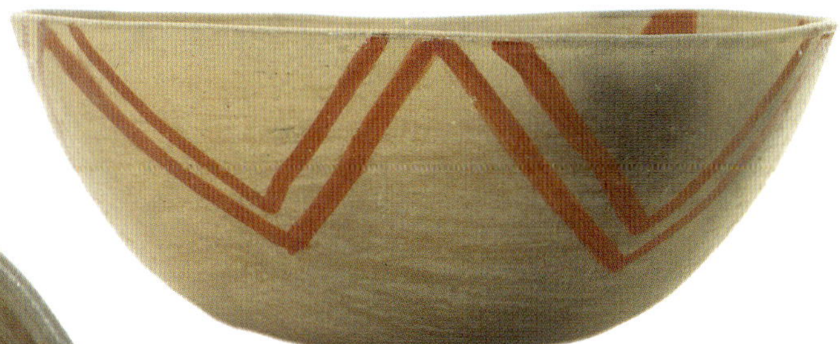

A stunning example of Mexican popular arts is seen in this original Pueblan bowl. Wood fired, burnished and brushed with an oxide slip floral design. 13 in. diameter, 6 in. tall, 1890s. $150 to 400

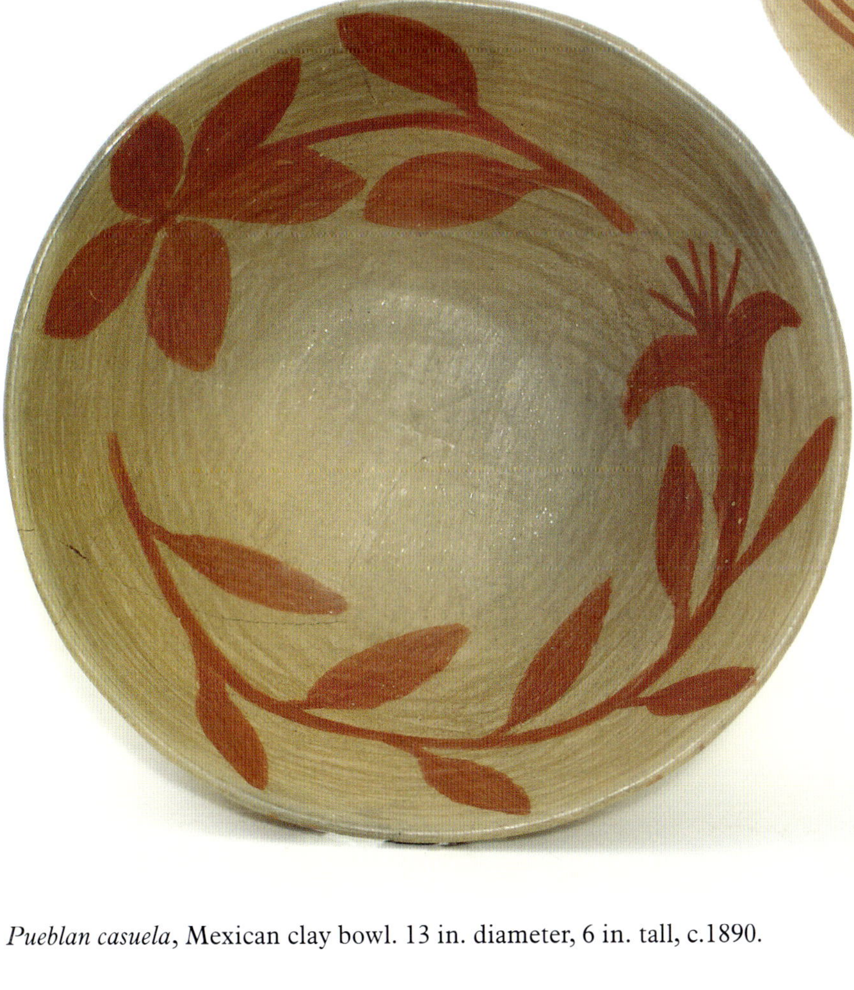

Pueblan casuela, Mexican clay bowl. 13 in. diameter, 6 in. tall, c.1890.

Through the dolls you will find the diverse inheritance of Mexico in how they encompass European, tribal, and regional traditions in their costumes. Influences by way of Europe, Asia, and particularly Spain enriched the Indians of Mexico with new ideas and techniques in the early centuries. The traditions form the foundation of Mexican culture in the "*mestizo*" (of European and Indian blood) people. Their customs, language, music, and folk art is an ethnic mix, a blending that is wholly Mexican and now its national culture. It was a blueprint that gave the progressive Mexican a venue of expression while keeping their spirits connected to their roots. Their passion as well as their dedication evokes affection and respect, while creating art or doing any task. They connect so strongly to their beliefs and heritage that it is prevalent in everything they do.

I believe the *mestizo* is Mexico's triumphant force in their art and the reason it has evolved into a country so profoundly skilled in all facets of art. In a colorful utilitarian object to a fine art, folk art, and "arte popular," you will find traces of the Mexican who created it. Their heritage as well as their innate skill is truly a gift. I hope this work will serve as an informative and visual source for those who have admired Mexican dolls and their beautiful costumes. I try to give a useful reference of the clothing and costumes they wear so that you can appreciate and learn about each one. I also include some current Mexican dolls that I feel carry on traditional value and quality. Their excellence is evident, surpassing current mass-produced souvenir Mexican dolls that are on the market.

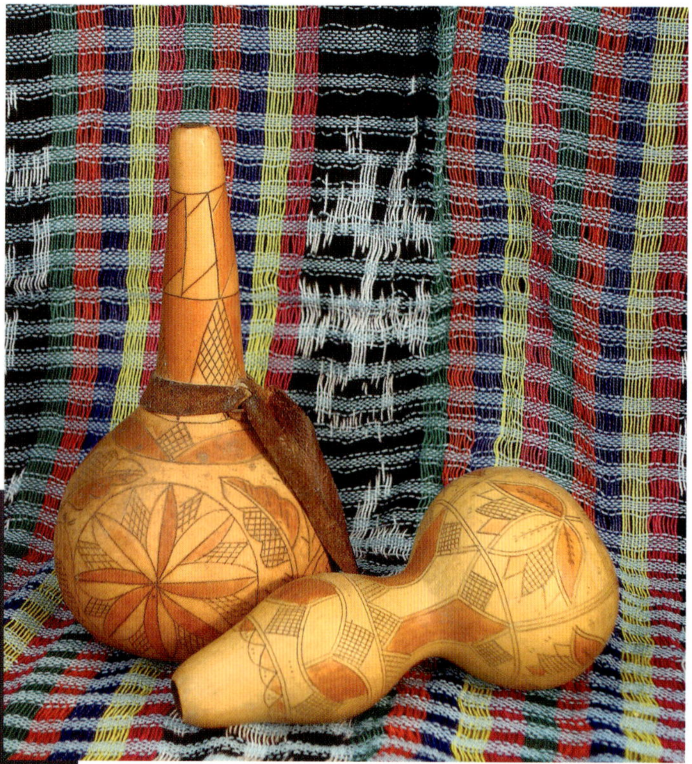

Small gourds, scored with intricate motifs of peyote and flowers. They show natural ageing with some tinting. Behind is an open weave cotton *rebozo*. Made in Mexico 20th c.

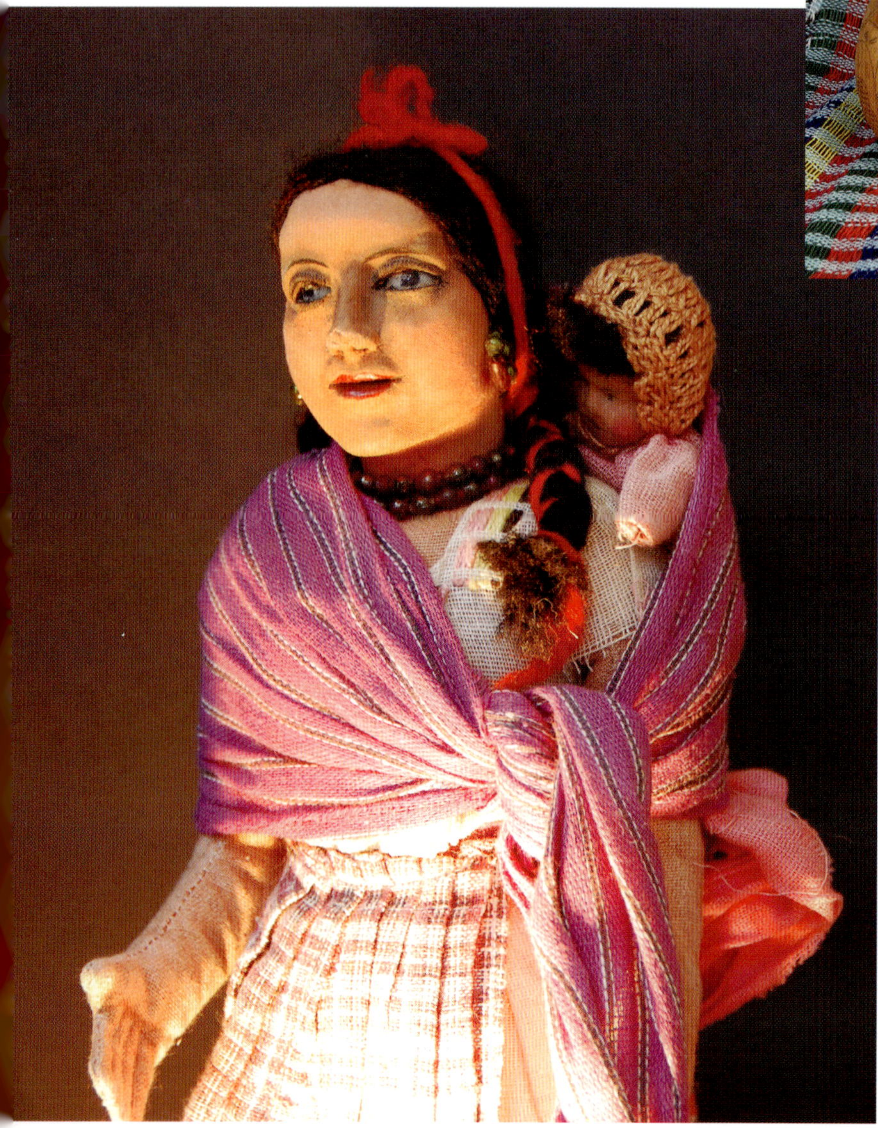

A close look at the large 18 in. cloth doll c.1930s, with her baby wrapped in the *rebozo*, Sanborns tag, Mexico D. F $75 to 150ea

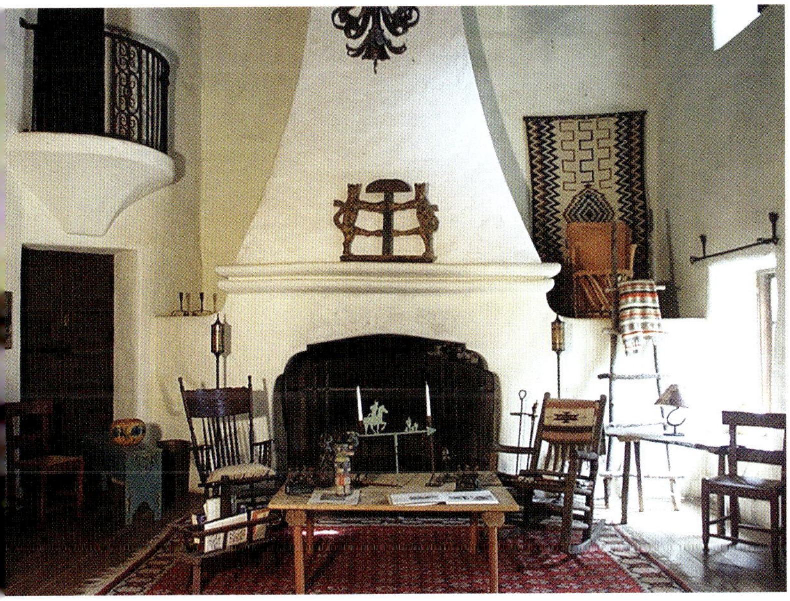

Spacious open areas with white walls as a canvas, vintage serapes and hand woven rugs, along with pottery.Surrounded by iron work and colonial wooden pieces, all hand crafted in a Mexican Rancho, 2006.

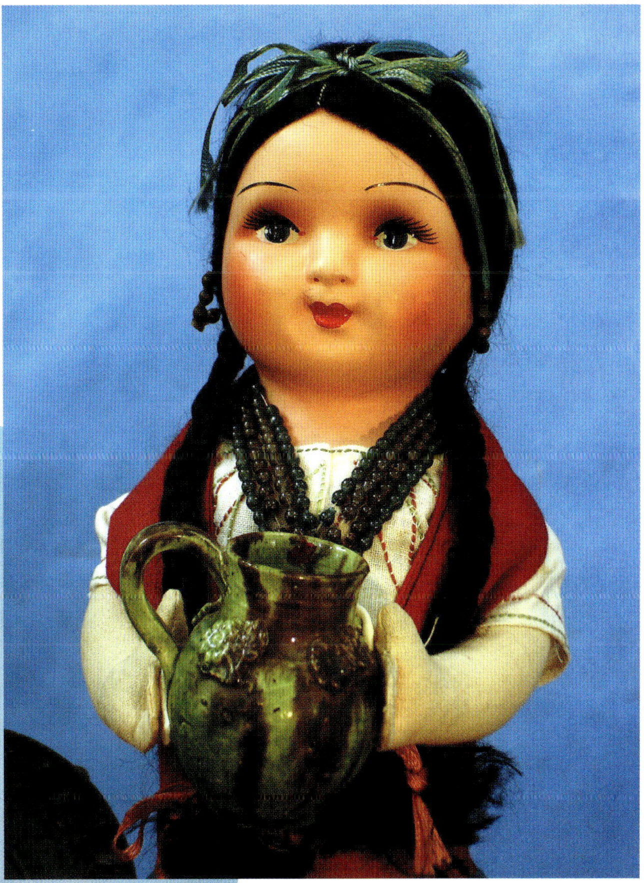

A charming close-up of the large old Mexico composition and cloth doll, remarkable condtion, c 1940s, holding her green tourist drip ware pottery. $150 to 225

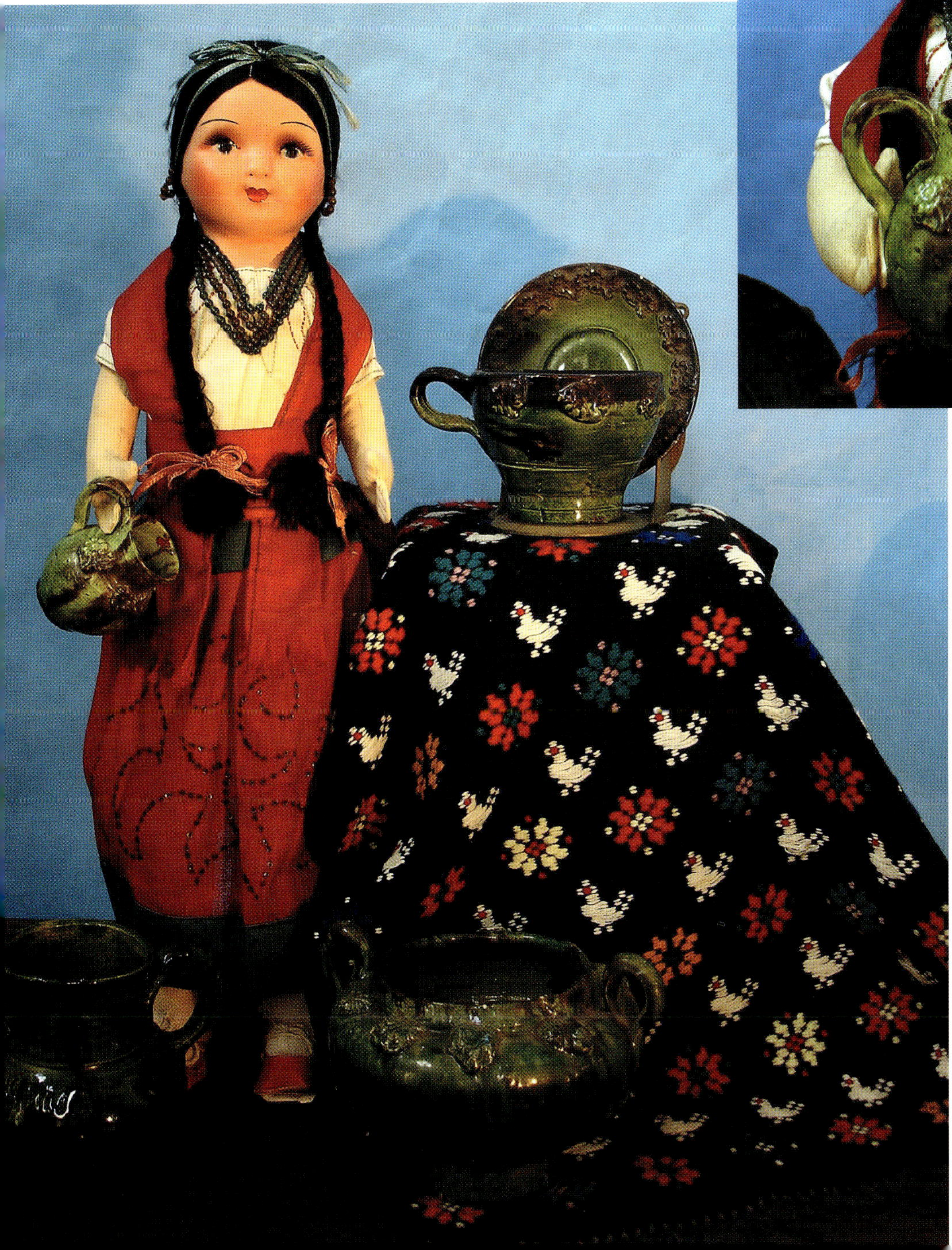

A large composition and cloth doll, made in Mexico, c.1940s. Hand applied polychrome facial features, long braids in black wool threads, glass beaded necklace, in a red and green *castor* skirt with white *blusa*, a white stiff slip underneath of *manta*. Red paper shoes and white cotton socks. Beautiful detail in mint condition. Standing next to an old wool textile and green tourist drip ware. $150 to 225

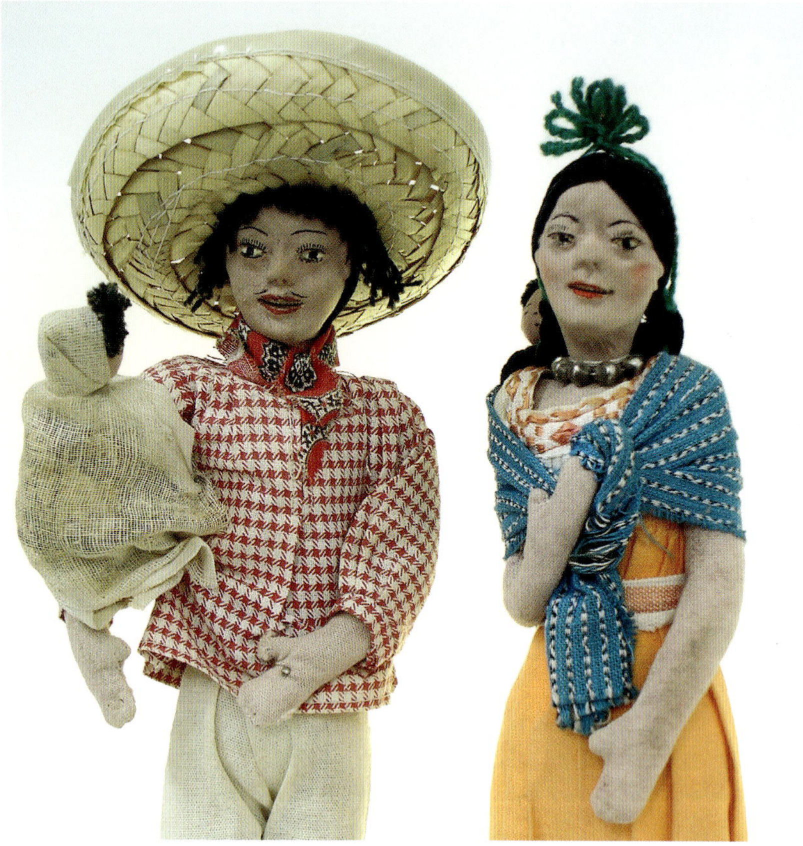

The close-up of the cloth Mexican couple from the 1930s, demonstrates patterns and weaves of their *manta* cloth garments. $100 to 150

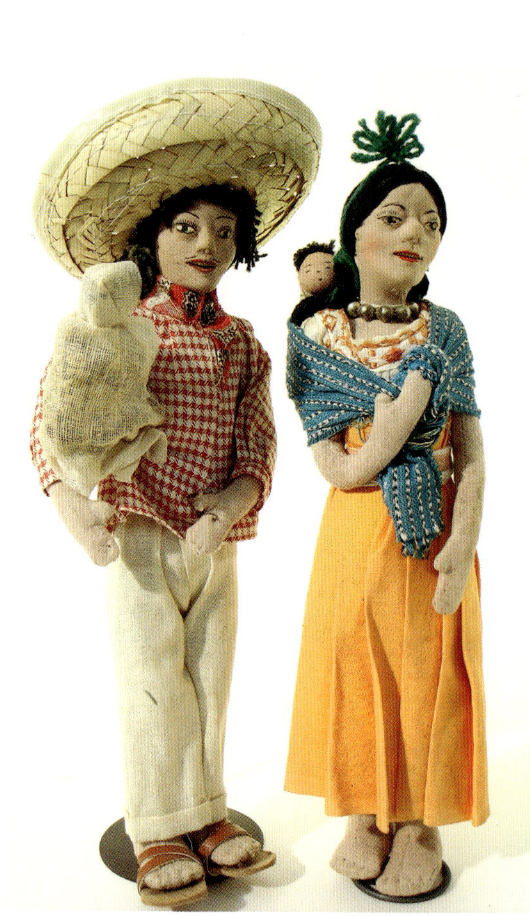

Hard cloth stuffed Mexican dolls from the 1930s . A 13 in. special Indian couple with twins, the "Sanchez Family." A red and white woven shirt and *moño* around his neck, white pants with an oversized woven *sombrero*. She is wearing an orange skirt, an embroidered off white *huipil* with a woven turquoise *rebozo* that holds her child, barefeet. Black braids of wool yarn, mitten hands and molded facial features. He wears leather huaraches. $100 to 150

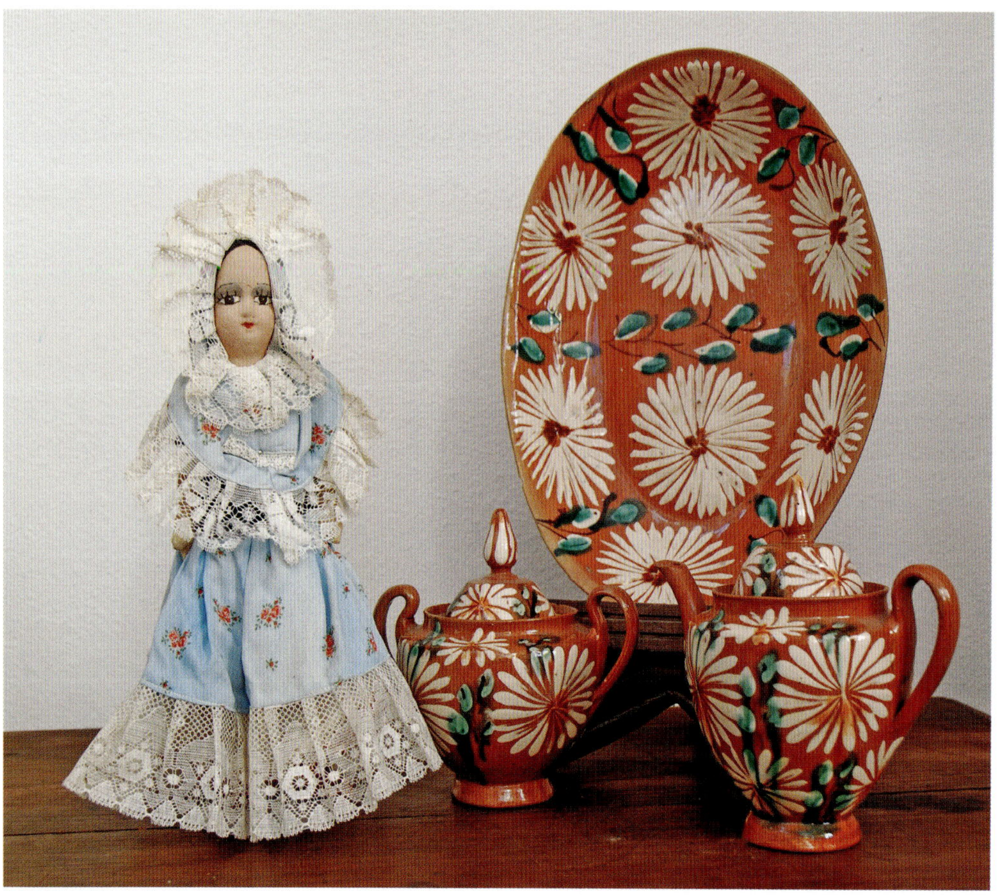

A stunning Tehuana cloth doll 1930s An 11 in. *mestiza* in a traditional dress made in Mexico. Her *resplandor* (head scarf) is a magnificent piece. Doll made of cloth and pressed felt molded face, painted features. $100 to 175

PART 1
Traditional Clothing

The traditional costumes of Mexico have sustained a chronological homage to their country's heritage. The many regions support local differences unique to their particular beliefs, origin, and climatic conditions. An indigenous society blended with centuries of European, primarily Spanish, contact has provided influences that filtered into the lineage of their clothing. You can enjoy various pieces that are distinctively Mexican; they provide keen preservation of their society. The clothing personifies 20th century Mexican culture.

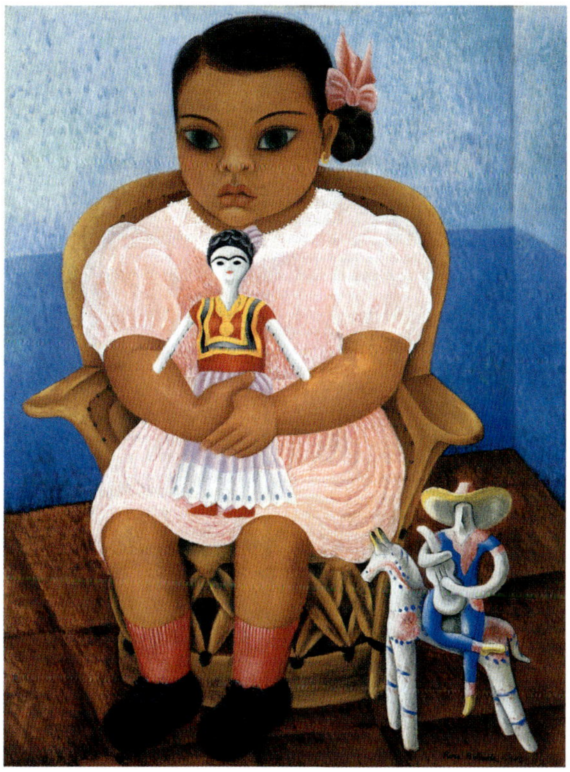

A beautiful oil painting by Rosa Rolanda (1895-1970), *Niña de la muñeca*, Colección Andrés Blaisten, México, Universidad Nacional Autonóma de Mexico, 2005. Courtesy of museoblaisten.com

Original Mexican clothing is recognizable by its countrymen, but may be more challenging for the student or foreigner to discern. The clothing offers clues that can help you recognize where they come from, but even these can be confusing. Although the costumes are often more provincial, they may include characteristics of a particular region. Today, many native Mexicans combine their regional items of clothing and it is hard to rigidly identify where they come from. Typical Indian and *mestizo* clothing shares traditional traits that have become diluted. They blend pieces and by doing so they compromise some of the exact determination of the costumes. Costume dolls can provide legitimate documentation of a culture and how it's clothing transforms from decade to decade. Sociologically, toward the end of the 19th century Mexican regional clothing began to conform to contemporary standards. A lot of the Indians were nomadic and married into other tribes or sought economic stability that in turn diffused their customs. Regardless, the clothing and costumes of Mexico still defines their people worldwide.

Through the dolls' garments you can admire a millennium of enriching changes and influences. Most of the costume dolls in this book were marketed for tourist or doll collectors. The costumes they wear are national costumes or the typical clothing that accurately represents the many different Mexican garments.

There are noticeable differences between the two most prevalent styles of clothing: the *mestizo* and the indigenous Indians. These two styles of clothing feature common and recognizable garments of Mexico's costumes, especially those of the *mixteca* people of central Mexico. Many centuries of influences are projected through their costumes and will be noted in the captions with the pictures. The *mestizo's* costumes show significant differences. As the *mestizo* group grew with more Spanish influence, variations in their clothing also established a social structure. The "*peon*" (farm laborer) and the "*campesino (a)*" (country farmer) had a more humble dress than the more urban Mexican *mestizo*, such as the more affluent charro (a) and the *haciendados* (land owners). Clothing worn by the *mestizo* upper classes were much more elaborate than those of the lower classes.

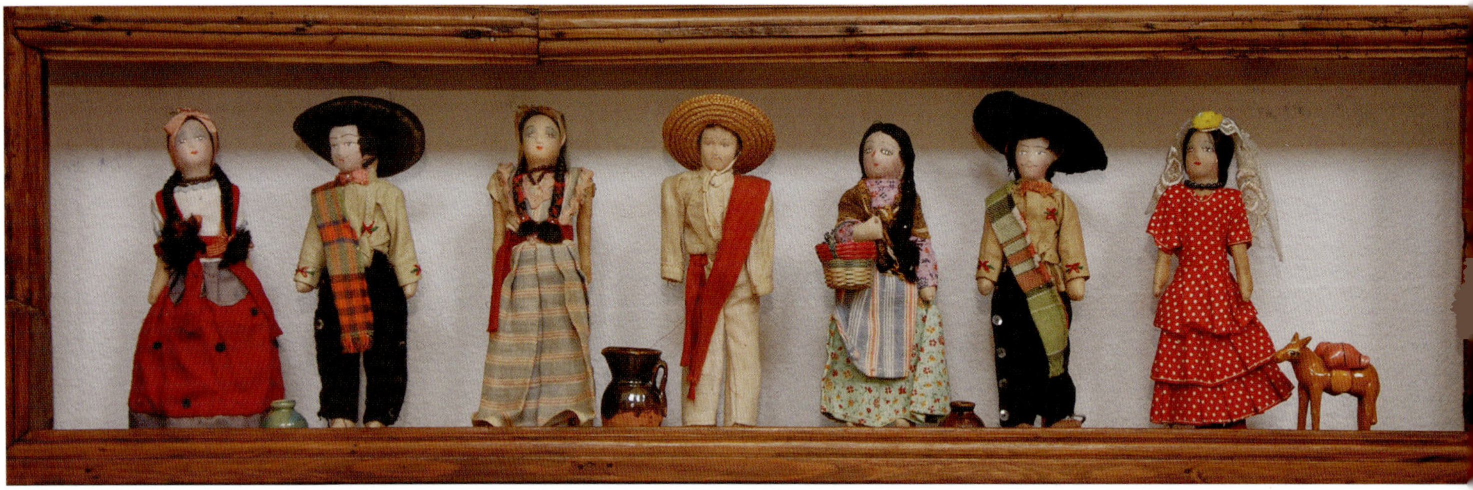

A collection of 6 in. souvenir cloth dolls, c.1940s. Wearing all the many different popular costumes that have defined Mexico's people. Indian and *mestizo*. Made in Mexico $15 to 40ea

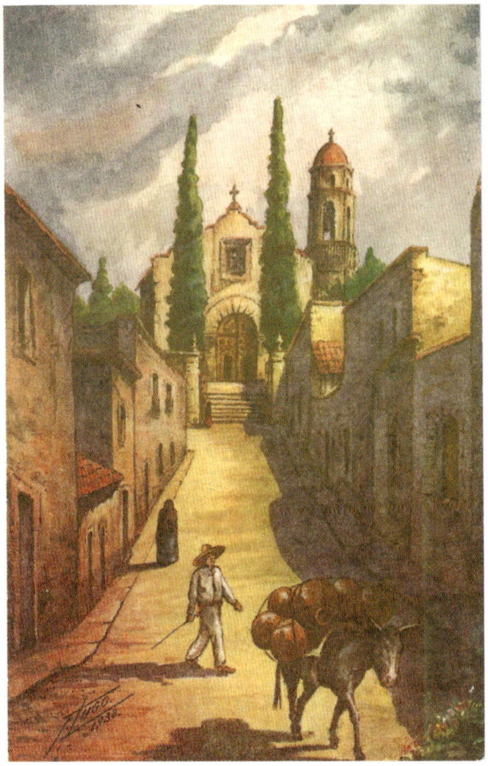

A color tinted paper litho postcard, "*Tipo Vendedor de Ollas,México,*" The pot seller, CIA. MERC. Fema, S. A. Mexico c.1930s, 5 x 3 in. $15 to 25

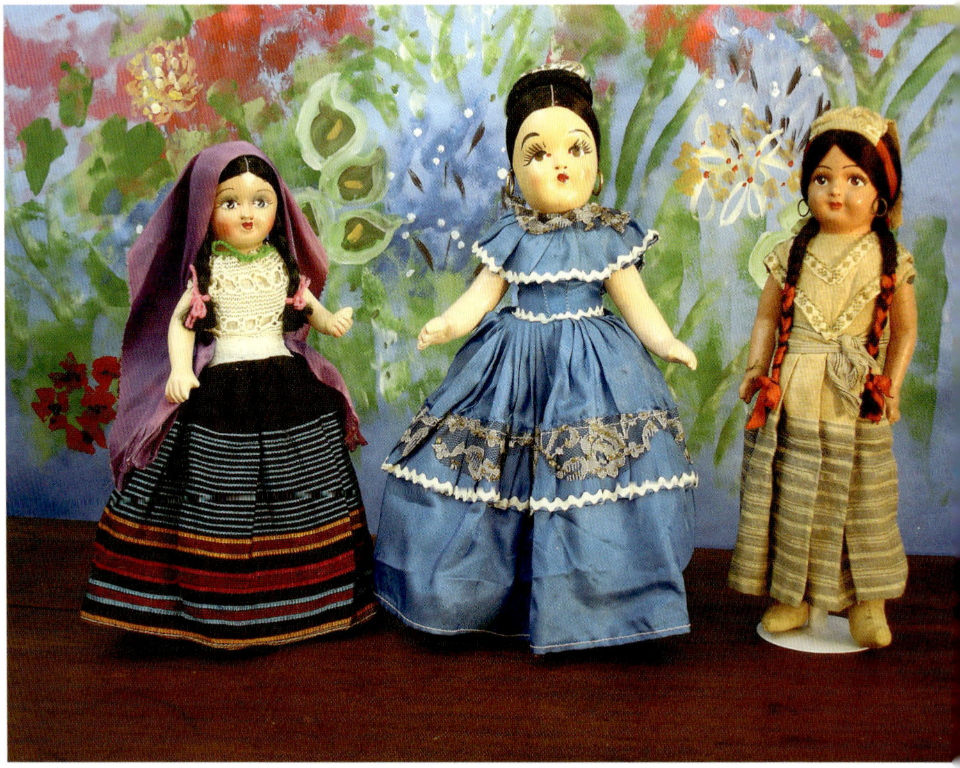

Old Mexico tourist dolls from three different social classes, made in Mexico from 1930s to 1950s. From left to right, a 13 in. composition *Michoacán mestiza*, a 14 in. composition Colonial Señorita, and a 14 in. cloth and composition indigenous Indian woman $100 to 225

Postcard, color photograph, "*Las Chinas Muchachas*" two beautiful young *mestiza* with their full skirts on the grass, c.1940s Mexico D. F. 4 x 5 in. $15 to 40

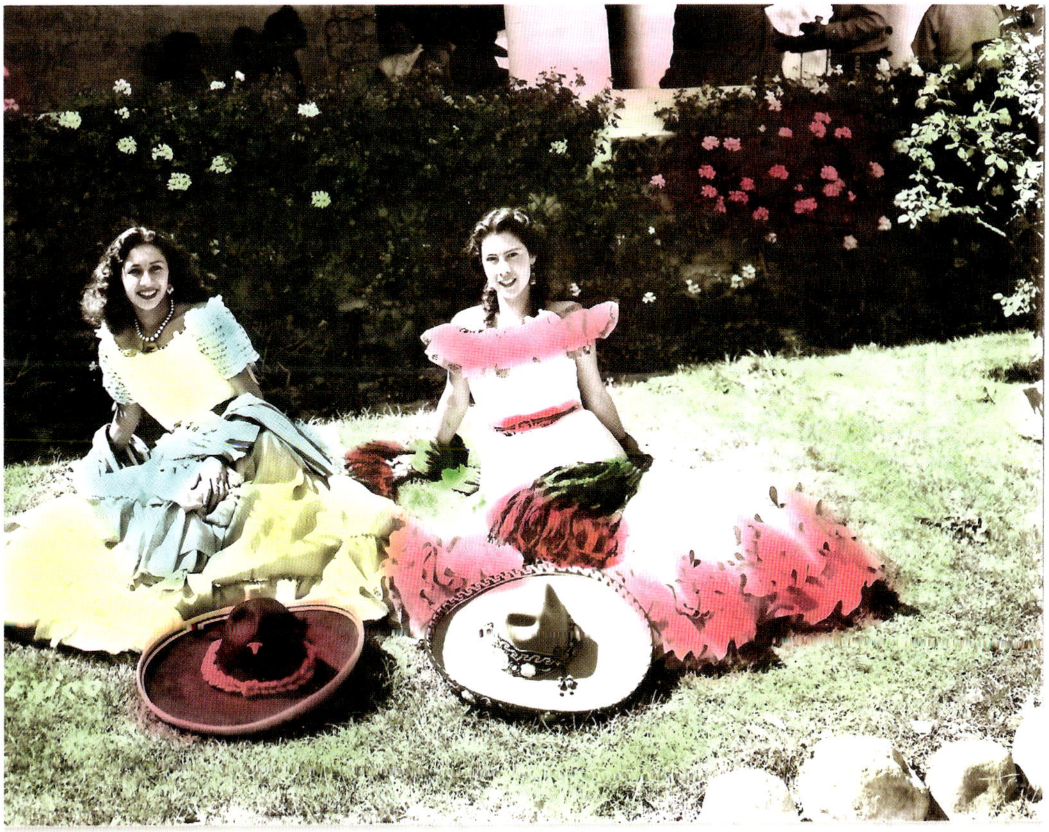

Below:
Polychrome painted faces, darling expressions of a country couple, old Mexico, chubby cheeked 9 in. composition dolls. A *campesino* and his wife with their pet donkey. Stamped on back EIH. Made in the USA by E.I. Horseman Toy Co., imported and dressed in Mexico, c.1940s. $50 to 75

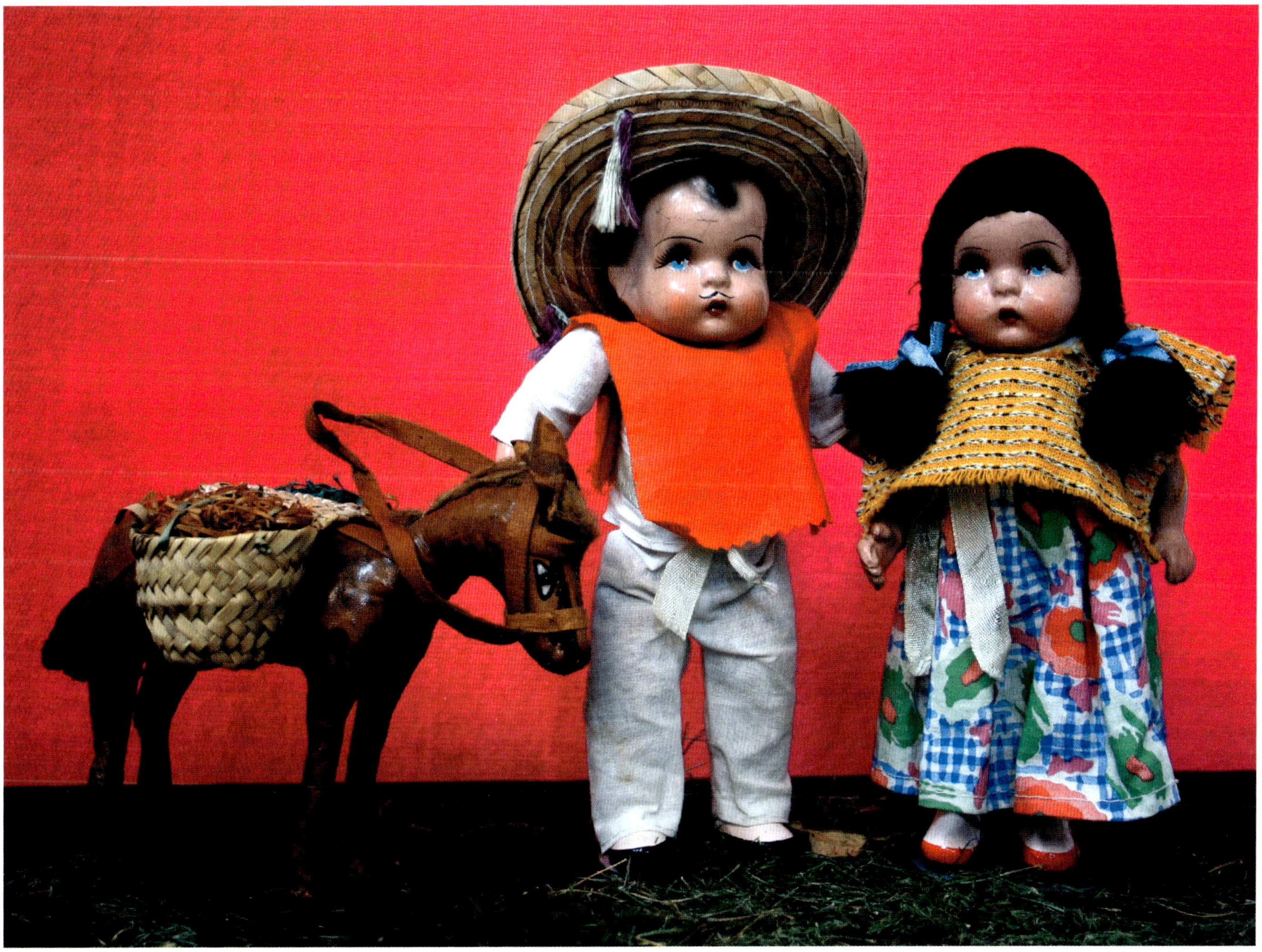

Indian costume dolls illustrate a timeless loyalty to their original traditions. They demonstrate tribal customs and developed weaving techniques. Weaving is one of the oldest forms of Mexican art and some of the dolls wear woven pieces. The Spaniards were amazed with the quality and beauty of the Indians' skills. It would take many hours to make some of the native dolls. The combined talents of old techniques and regional traits were conserved skillfully by the doll makers, but unfortunately the dolls were never signed, marked by their makers, or labeled. This creates a challenge when distinguishing their exact origin. I cannot guarantee that 100% of the native dolls are from the apparent designated regions, but I provide an accurate probability that they were. Indian dolls were often sold to local vendors in the main tourist cities. The vendors would order or buy the dolls to sell to tourists. It was also highly plausible, as well as more profitable, that the Indians sold their own dolls. They would make them in their village, then travel hundreds of miles to sell them on city streets to tourists. Just as all other artisans, doll makers spread *el petate* (a woven mat) on the ground and displayed their dolls.

Many of the same garments worn by the *mestizo* still reveal obvious influence from their Indian roots, so there is definitely "*syncretism,*" the blending of traits from different cultures into one.

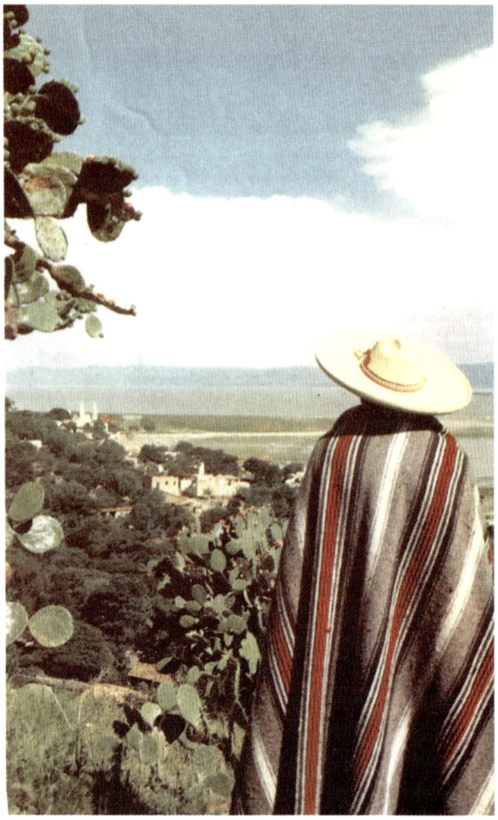

A color copy photograph, a Mexican and his colorful *serape*, 8 X 5 in., c.1940. Puebla, Mexico.

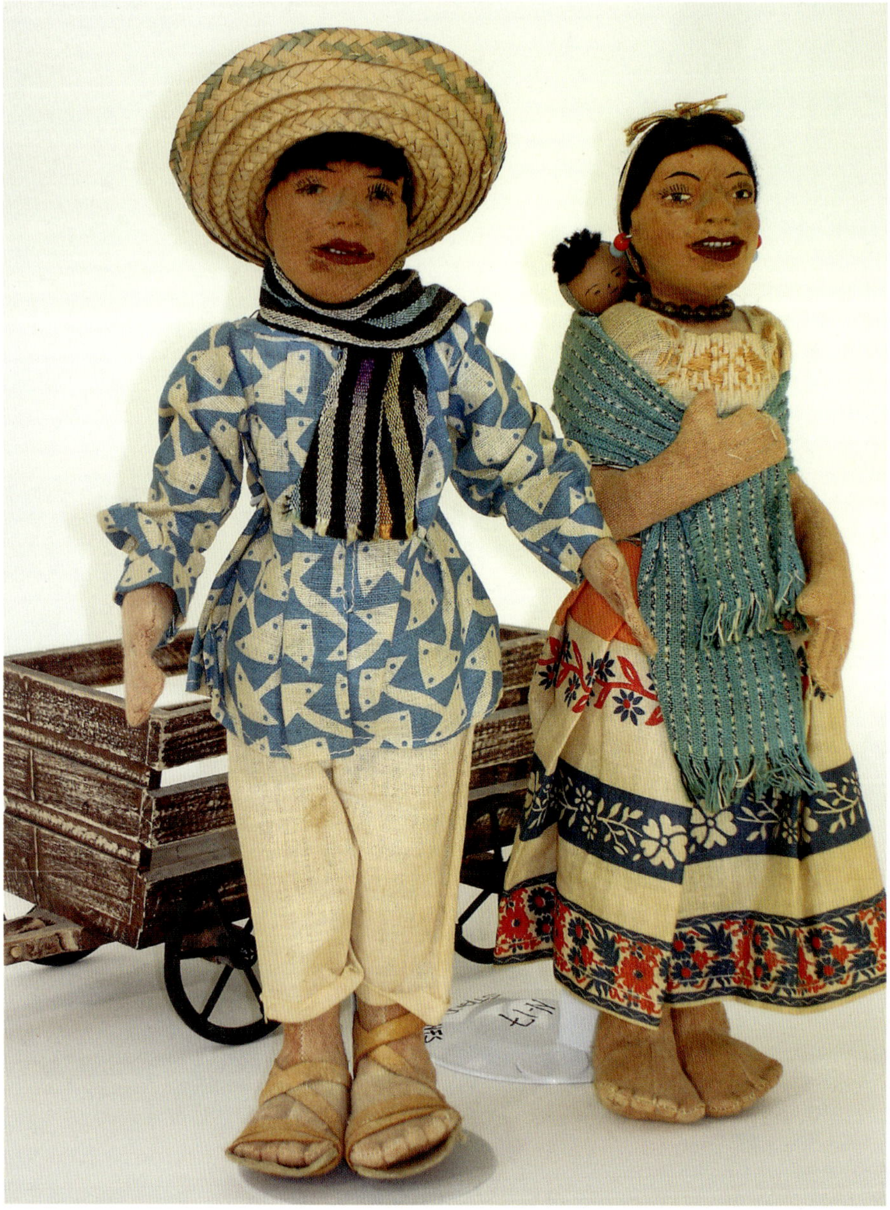

The Vazquez family, 15 in. all-cloth dolls, made in Mexico, likely Kimport Dolls. Not marked. Hard muslin cloth filled body. Made c.1940s, with molded features, inset eyes and teeth. Remarkable detail, exaggerated features and the skin coloring of an indigenous Mexican clothed *mestizo* Indian style. Their hair is made of wool threads. $75 to 150
Descriptions of costumes:
The dolls are wearing muslin clothing, store bought cloth referred to as *manta*. The man's pants are the typical *calzone blanco* style, light weight that ties at the waist, and rolled up at the hem. His long shirt is loose fitting, button less and worn outside the pants. His leather *huaraches* (sandals) are traditional shoes or bare feet. The *sombrero* is made of palm reeds and has contrasting dyed green reeds that create patterns. His wife is definably beautiful in her customary hand embroidered *huipil* top, a full skirt of a printed cloth that shows color and beauty. A hand loomed *rebozo* supports her baby as well as adds warmth. A beaded necklace of seeds and earrings and a rayon ribbon holds her long braids at the back.

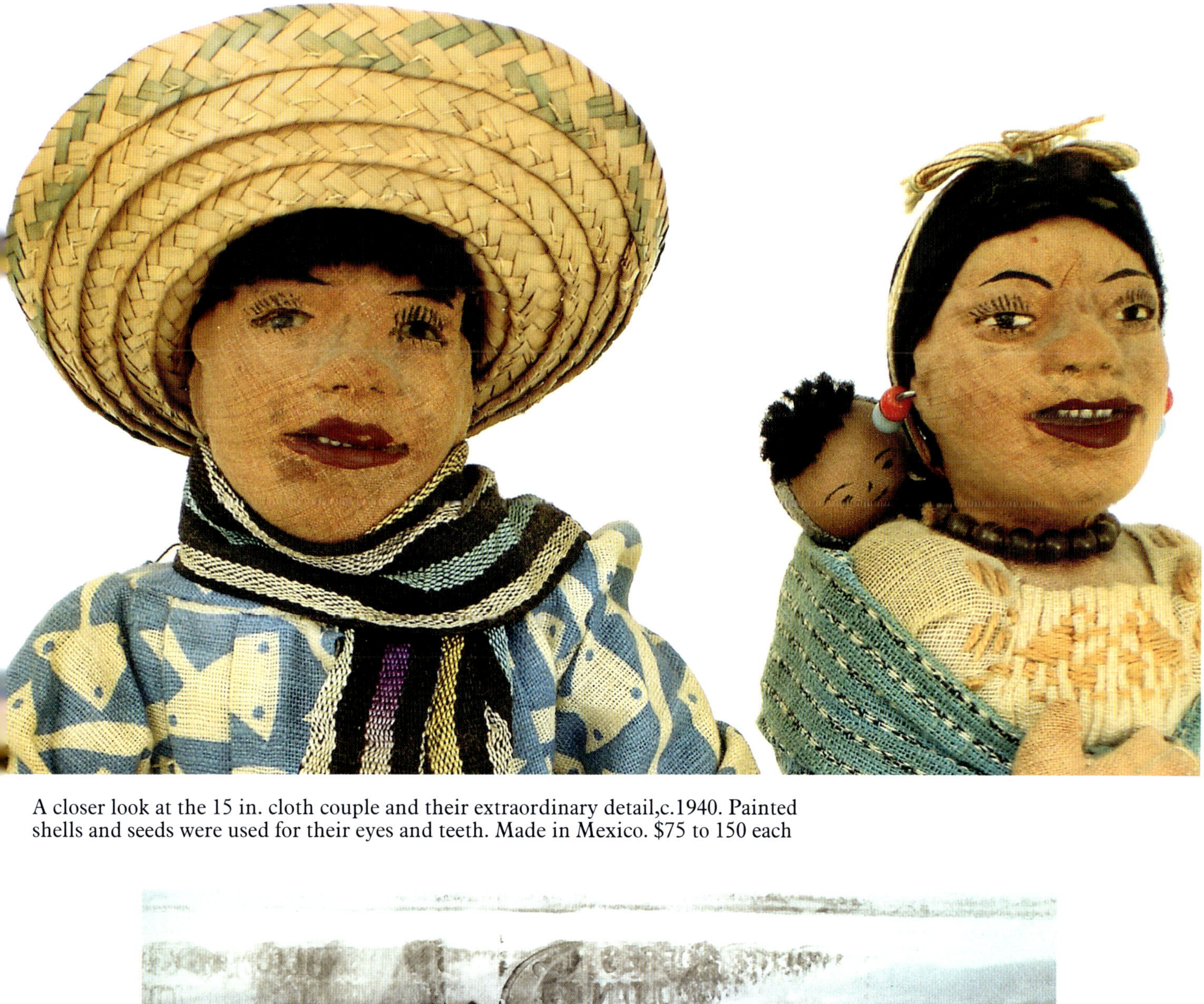

A closer look at the 15 in. cloth couple and their extraordinary detail,c.1940. Painted shells and seeds were used for their eyes and teeth. Made in Mexico. $75 to 150 each

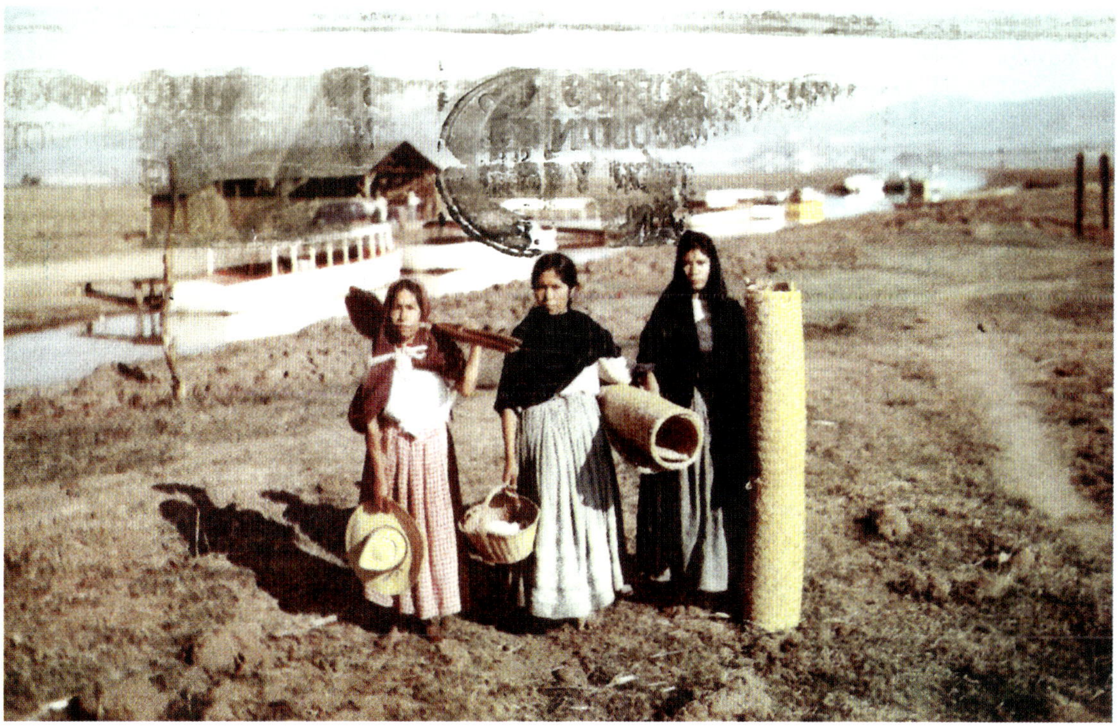

Postcard, color postcard photograph, *Nativas Isla Janitzio Patzcuaro*, Mich. Mexico, Fema stamped c.1954 3 x 5 in. $15 to 40

Two locals, on right a 12 in. *mestiza* and on left a 14 in. Indian cloth dolls, early tourist souvenirs handmade by locals, dolls dressed in two of the most common styles of costumes, c.1930s. $75 to 150 ea.

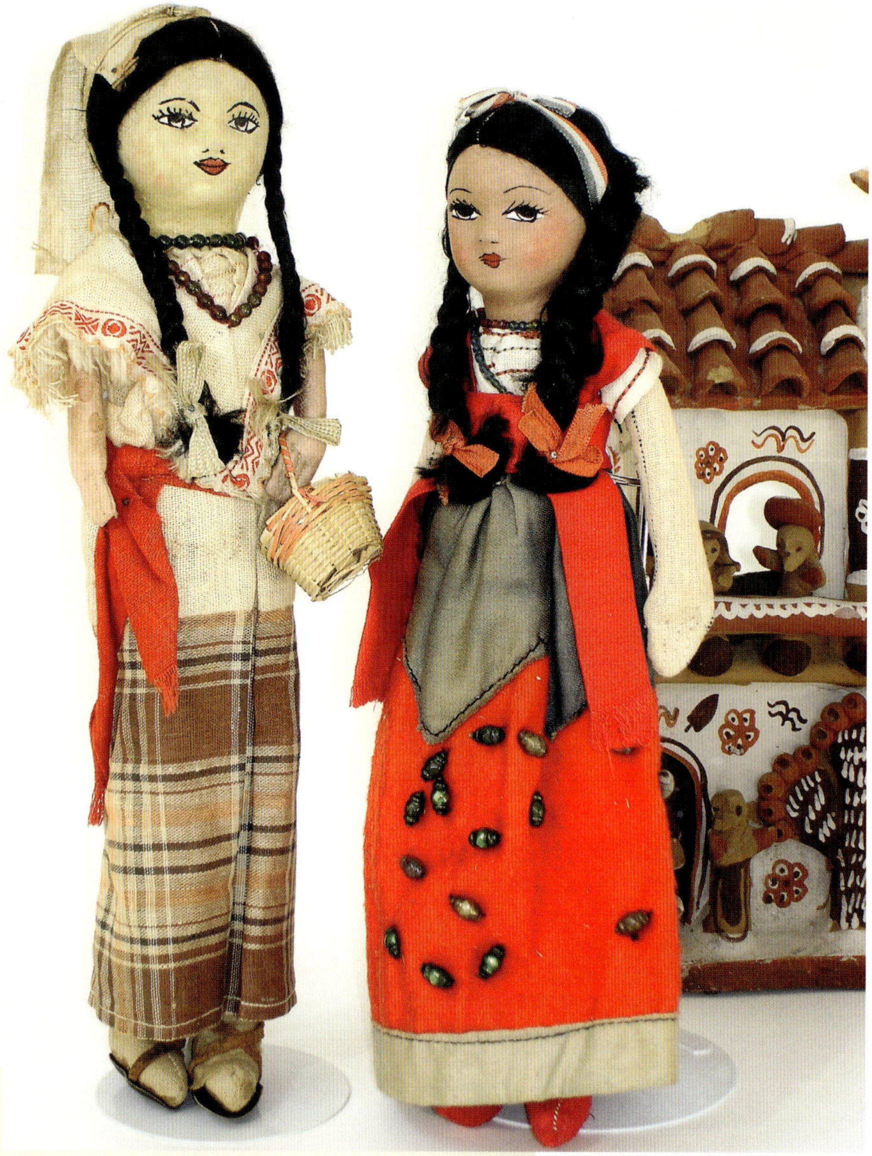

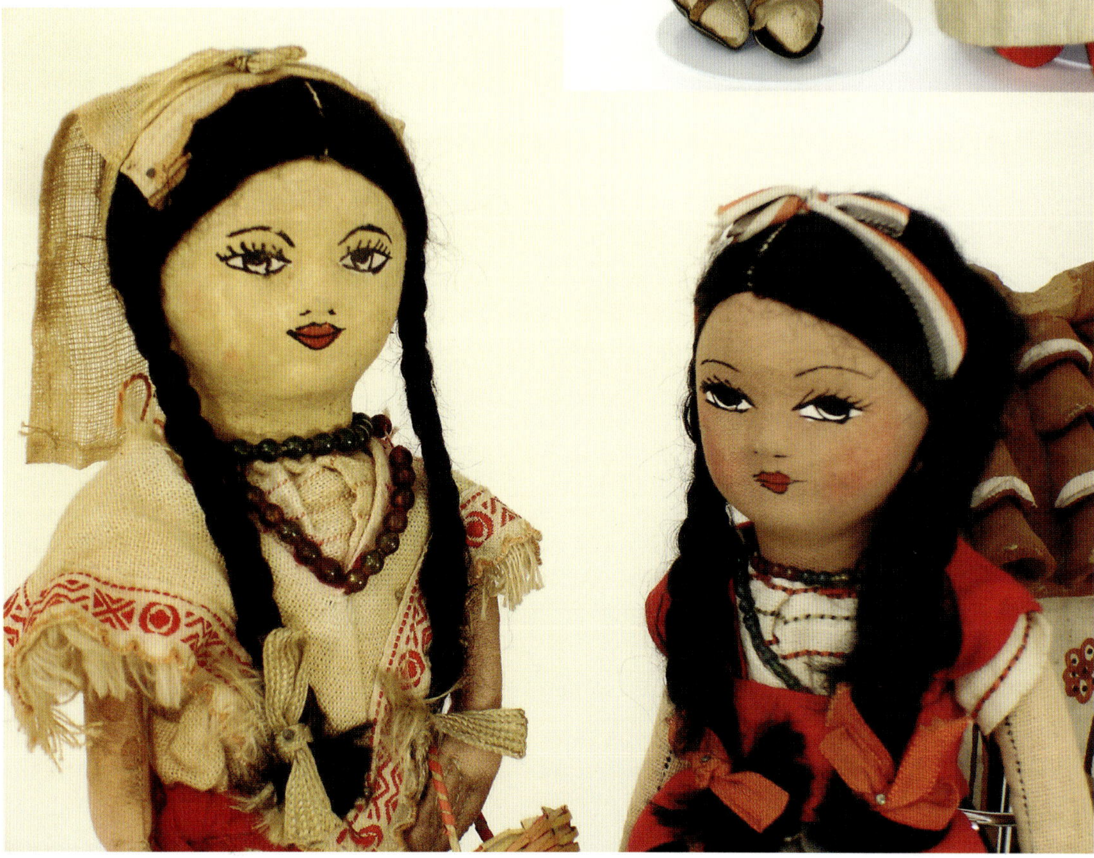

A close view at the detail of the a *mestiza* and Indian cloth dolls, careful rendering with indigenous traits. $75 to 150 ea.

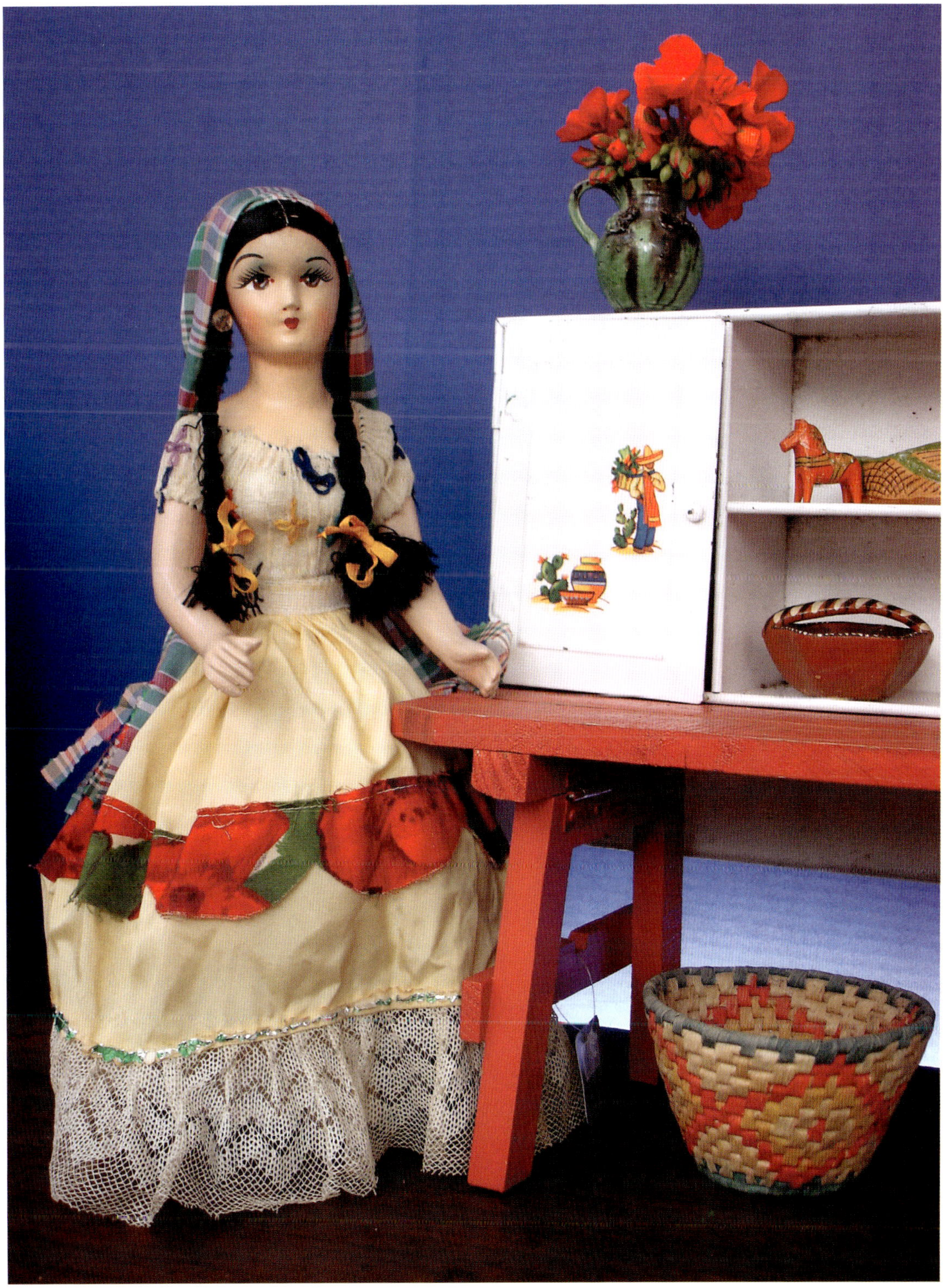

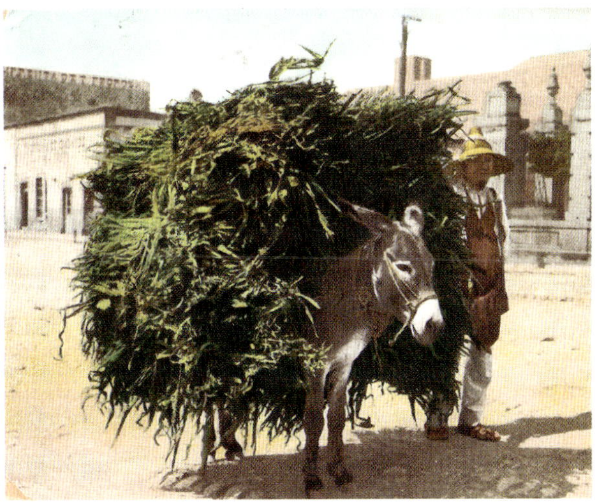

A large 17 in. strung composition doll, made in Mexico c.1950. Standing next to a wood table and an old enameled decaled cupboard with small native souvenirs. $150 to 350

Postcard, color tinted, "Loaded Burro", JG Hatton, Stamped c.1909, 3x5 Mexico $15 to 40

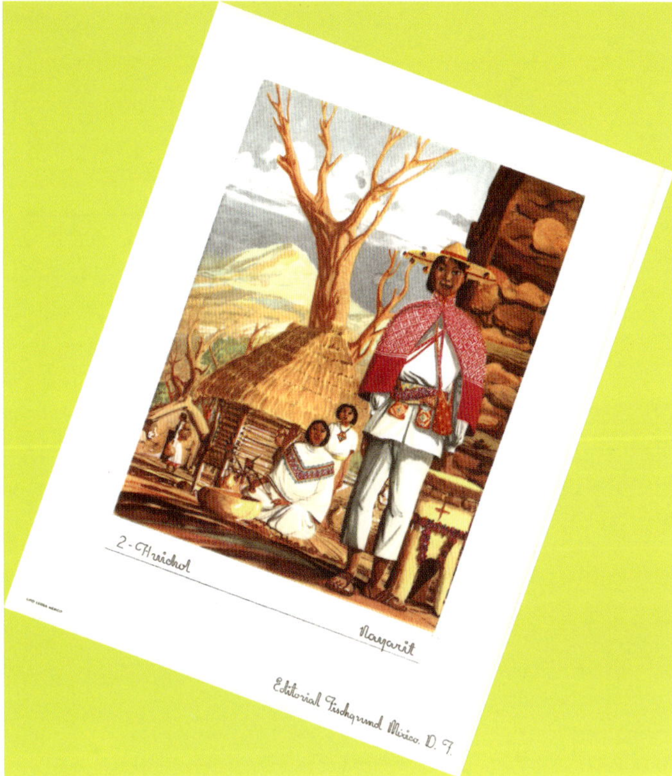

A colored plate of *Huichol of Nayarit*, by Ramon Valdiosera. Editorial Eugenio Fishgrund Mexico, D.F. c.1940s, Small booklet with 12 plates litho. $40 to 75

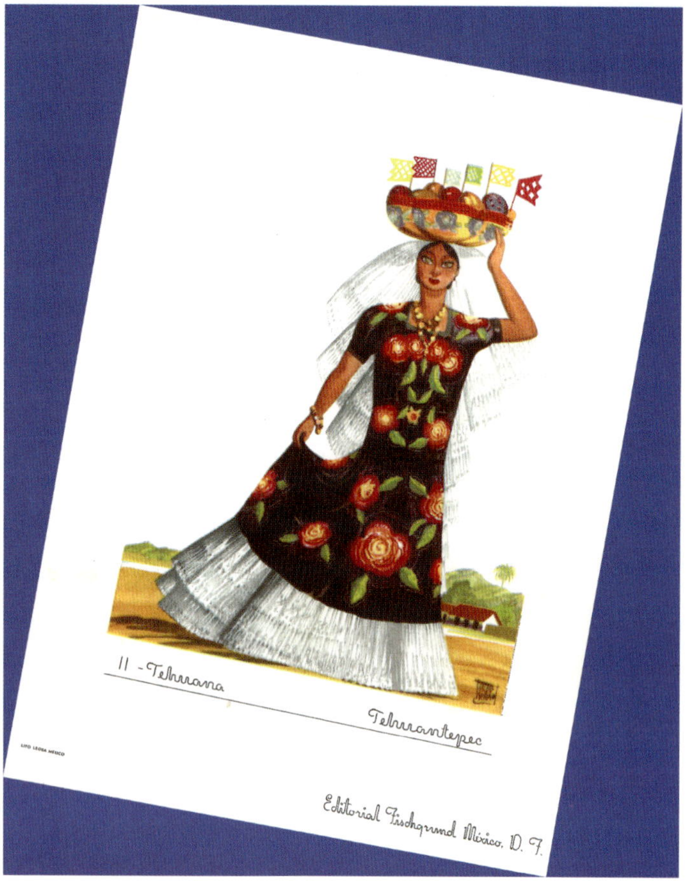

A colored plate of *Tehuana of Tehuantepec*, by Ramon Valdiosera. Editorial Eugenio Fishgrund Mexico, D.F.c.1940s, Small booklet with 12 litho plates. $40 to 75

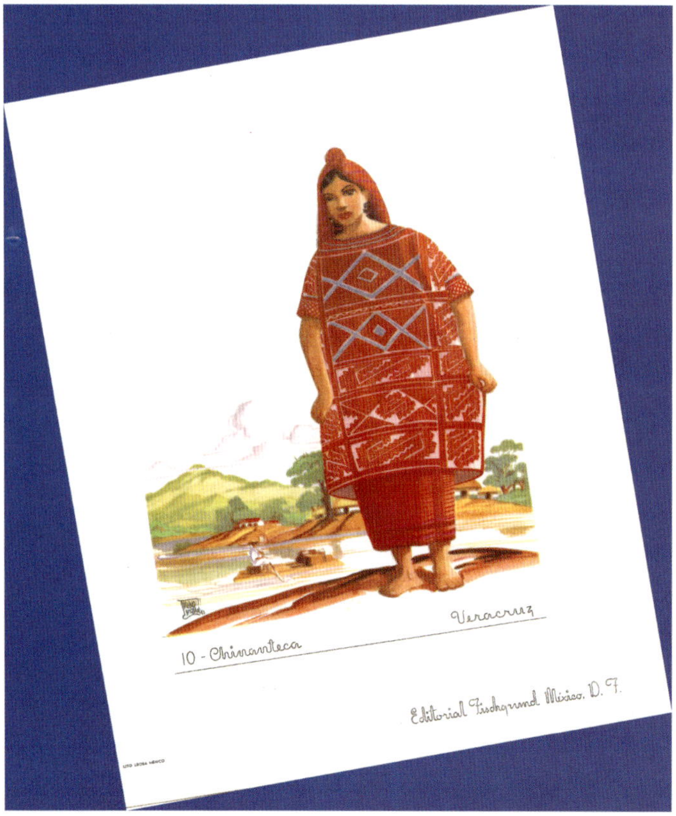

A colored plate of *Chinanteca of Veracruz*, by Ramon Valdiosera. Editorial Eugenio Fishgrund Mexico, D.F.c.1940s, Small booklet with 12 litho plates. $40 to 75

Mexican clothing captures period clothing trends and regional changes of the time. The most identifiable pieces of clothing noted are (1) the *serape* (a woven shawl), also known as the "*sarape*," (2) *el sombrero* (the wide brim hat), (3) *el rebozo* (the long rectangular scarf), (4) *la falda*, or *el enredo, el corte* (the skirt), (5) *faja* (belt or sash), (6) *el quechquémitl* (poncho-style shawl), and (7) *el huipil* (the woven top or tunic).

Remarkably, many of these garments have sustained importance, and in remote regions they are still preferred. However, visibility of the more original Indian costumes are seen less in metropolitan areas today.

Some of the clothing has modifications that are exceptional, and each artisan captures their own interpretation of a costume. A lot of the original garments have changed, but through the dolls they have been conserved. Photographs, paintings, remnants of clothing, and vintage dolls are usually the only conservation of a culture's clothing. We can appreciate Mexican festive holidays because through their traditional dances and parades you can witness a variety of costumes from the villages they represent.

Mexican clothes comprise much variation from region to region, with bright colors and designs that have purpose to validate their ancestry. Just as *tlaquepaque* pottery exposes a continuous emphasis to their humble culture, so too does their clothing. The Indians' intrinsic techniques that are tied with the Colonial period denote the blended characteristics. Although Mexican textiles derive from their ancient civilizations, the Spanish encouraged profound influences as well. Every item of their costumes has progressed in a wide range of design and function. A brief synopsis of each of the most important items of clothing is offered here. The dolls provide a wonderful view of the variety of some of Mexico's most prized costumes.

Mexico consists of 32 districts (similar to states). Within the districts numerous native costumes were once or are still worn by the native people. In the district of Oaxaca alone, there are over fifteen different indigenous variations; you can imagine what a challenge it would be to document the costumes of the more rural and remote regions. All of the Indian costumes are not found on the vintage dolls, but I did include many that were.

In an exceptional book by Donald and Dorothy Cordry, *Mexican Indian Costumes*, you can discover differences in the Indian costumes and textiles. It certainly would be of assistance to those interested in the variations of Mexico's indigenous costumes and their differences from village to village. There was no rhyme or reason why villages so close in proximity had entirely different costumes or why some villages had almost identical costumes that were thousand of miles apart. This is something that I have left up to future research and those who have earned concrete recognition on the study of Mexican Indian clothing and textiles. Another fabulous book that goes into deep discussion of their clothing is *Mexican Costume*, by Chloë Sayer. I have recognized that although the costumes on vintage dolls may not always be an actual version of the garment they represent, it is the closest we can get tangibly. They are small representatives and a testament of traditional clothing, which collectively explains the Mexican culture and its role in documenting Mexican clothing.

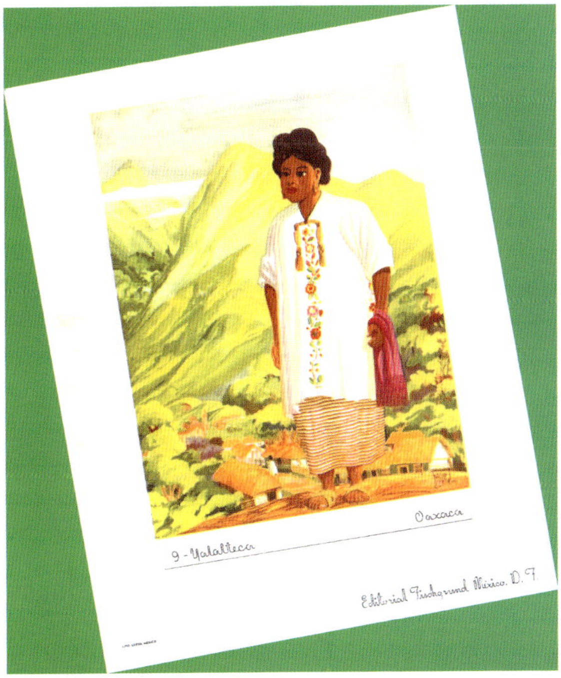

A colored plate of *Yalalag of Oaxaca*, by Ramon Valdiosera. Editorial Eugenio Fishgrund Mexico, D.F.c.1940s, Small booklet with 12 litho plates. $40 to 75

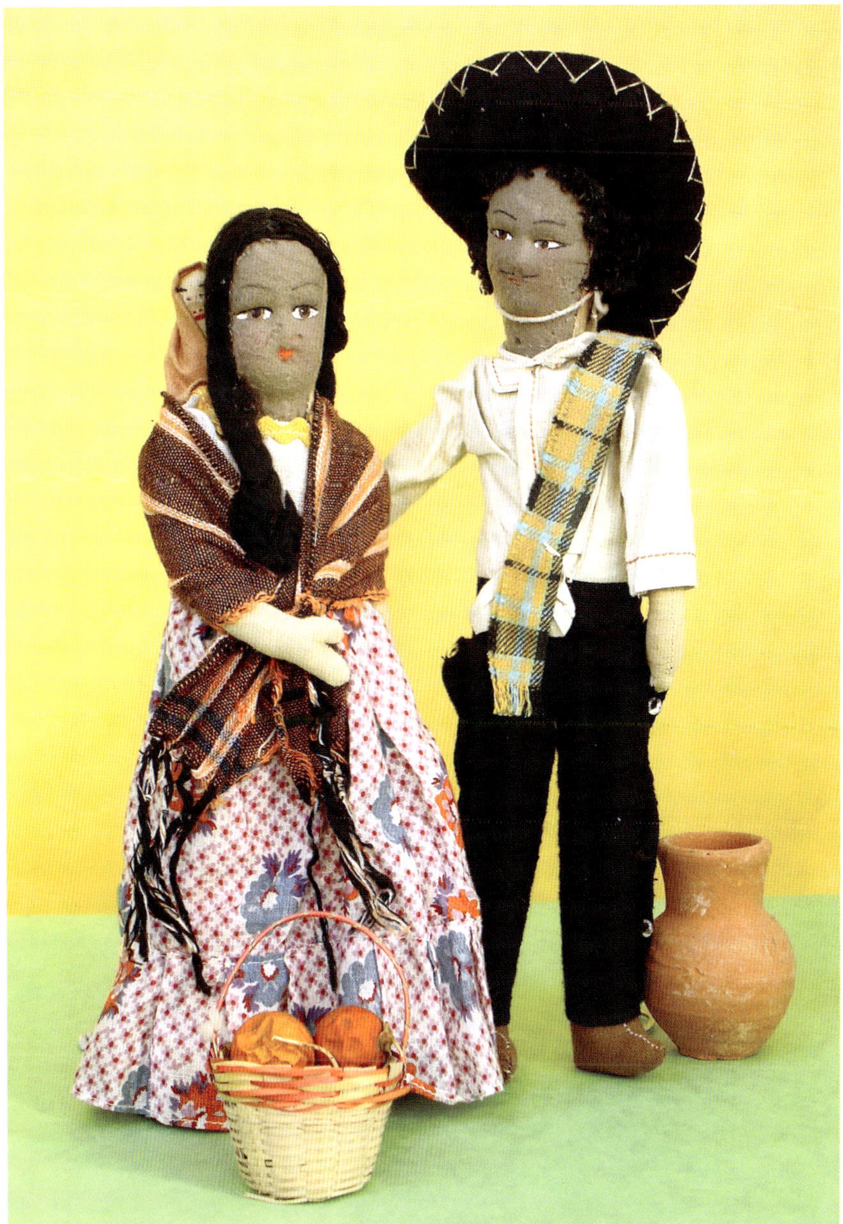

A colorful *mestizo* 12 in. family made of cloth with felt molded faces, c.1930s. She is carrying her baby on her back in a *rebozo*, a full *enagua* calico long skirt. He is a *campesino* dressed with a traditional white shirt and studded trousers. Simple detail but quality craftmanship $45 to 125ea.

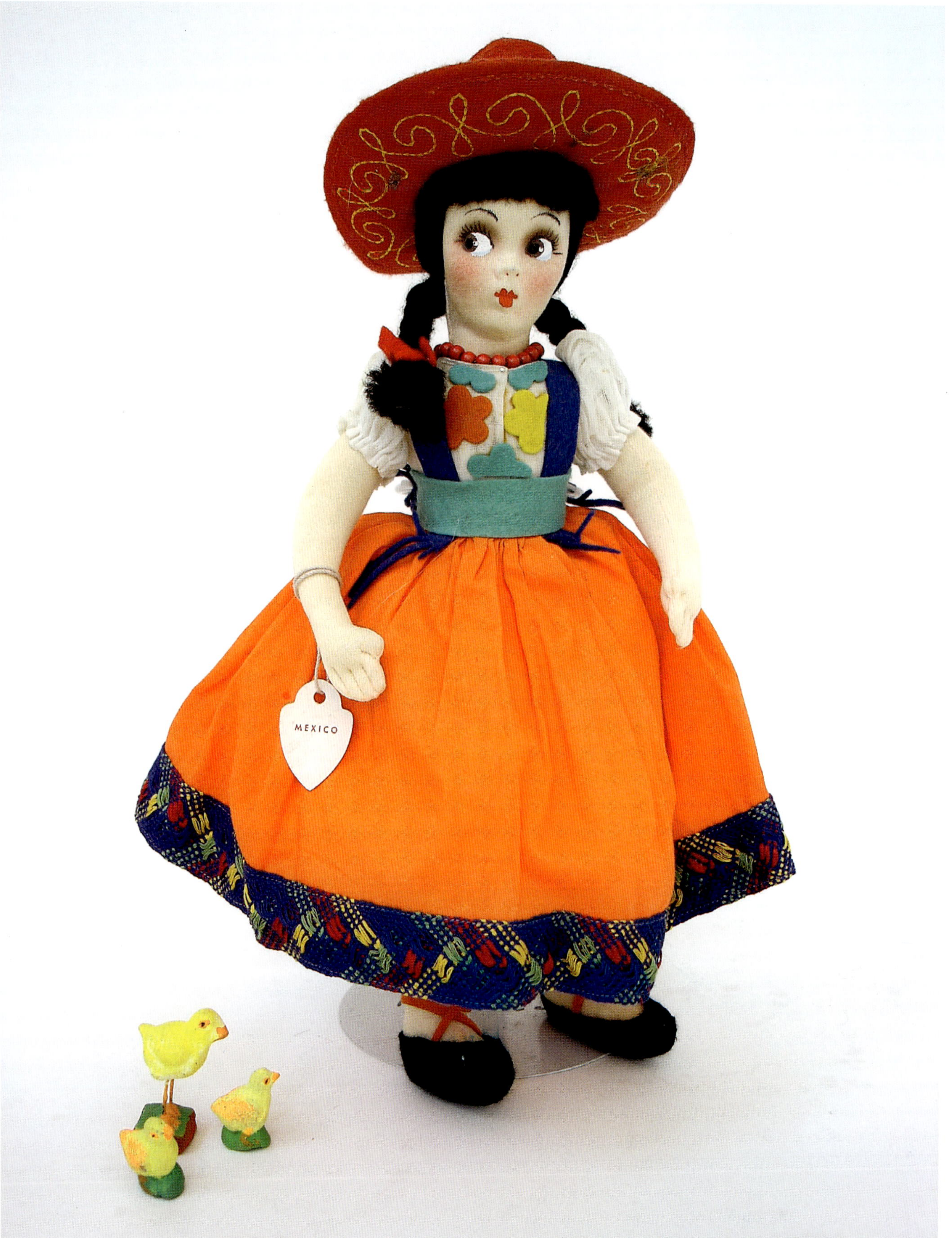

Attributed to the Lenart Toy Co. A 14 in. colorful cloth doll, c.1948, jointed at the head and legs. A felt molded facial features with a sweet google eye expression. Made in New York. Tag on wrist attributes the costume "México." White cotton top, red orange skirt with mock embroidered trim. Wood red beads around her neck and a red *sombrero* felt hat. $45 to 90

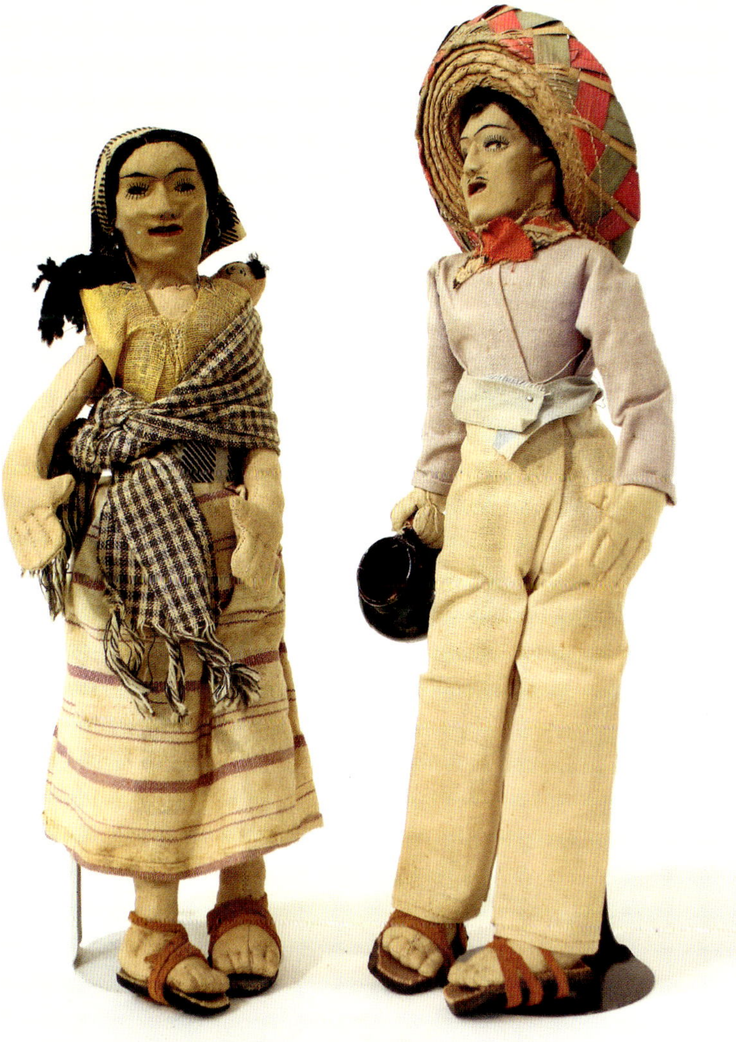

The cloth dolls "*Cortez Family,*" stamped Mexico, c.1920s. A typical Indian couple, 14 in. made of cloth, hard stuffed with straw. The female is carrying her baby in a woven *rebozo*, she has a black wool braided wig. A yellow *huipil* and a lavender and white woven skirt, leather *huaraches*. Stitched fingers and feet. He is wearing *manta* clothing with a red *moño*, holding a green *Metepec* water jug. $75 to 200

Below:
"Cortez Family" demonstrates the inset features under their molded faces. Stamped Mexico, c.1920s. Their faces reveals a ghostly complexion with realistic molded facial features. Painted eyelashes, moustache and eyebrows. His sombrero has dyed colorful maguey border. $75 to 200

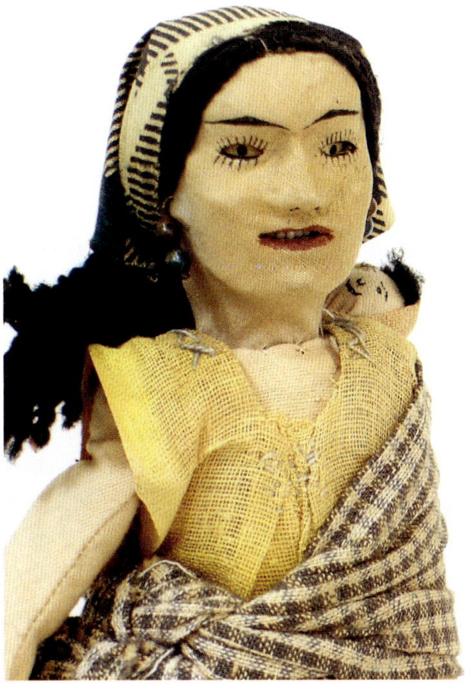

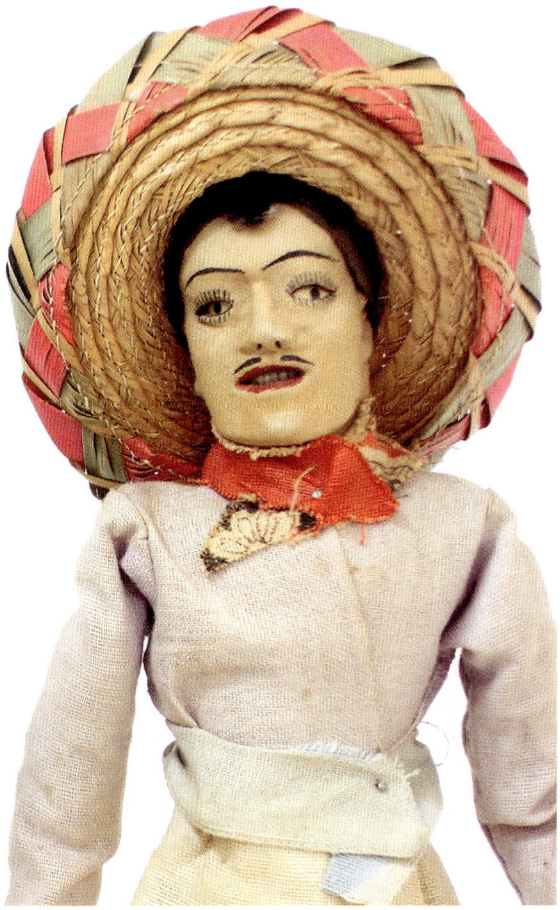

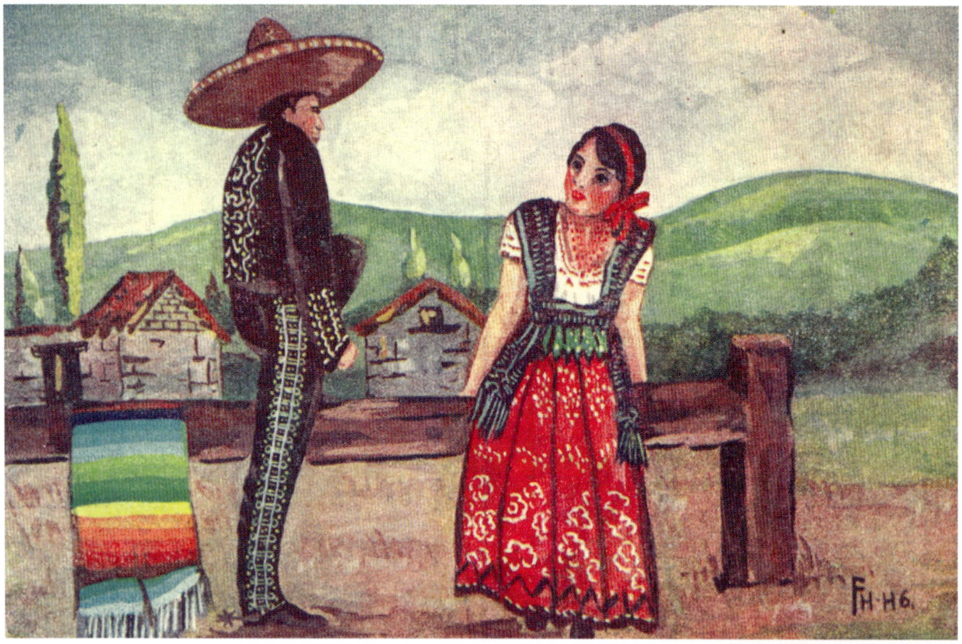

Postcard, color postcard photograph, "*Tarjeta postal*" two *mestiza* at the fence c.1937 Fred Liebig, Mexico D. F. 4 x 5 in. $15 to 30

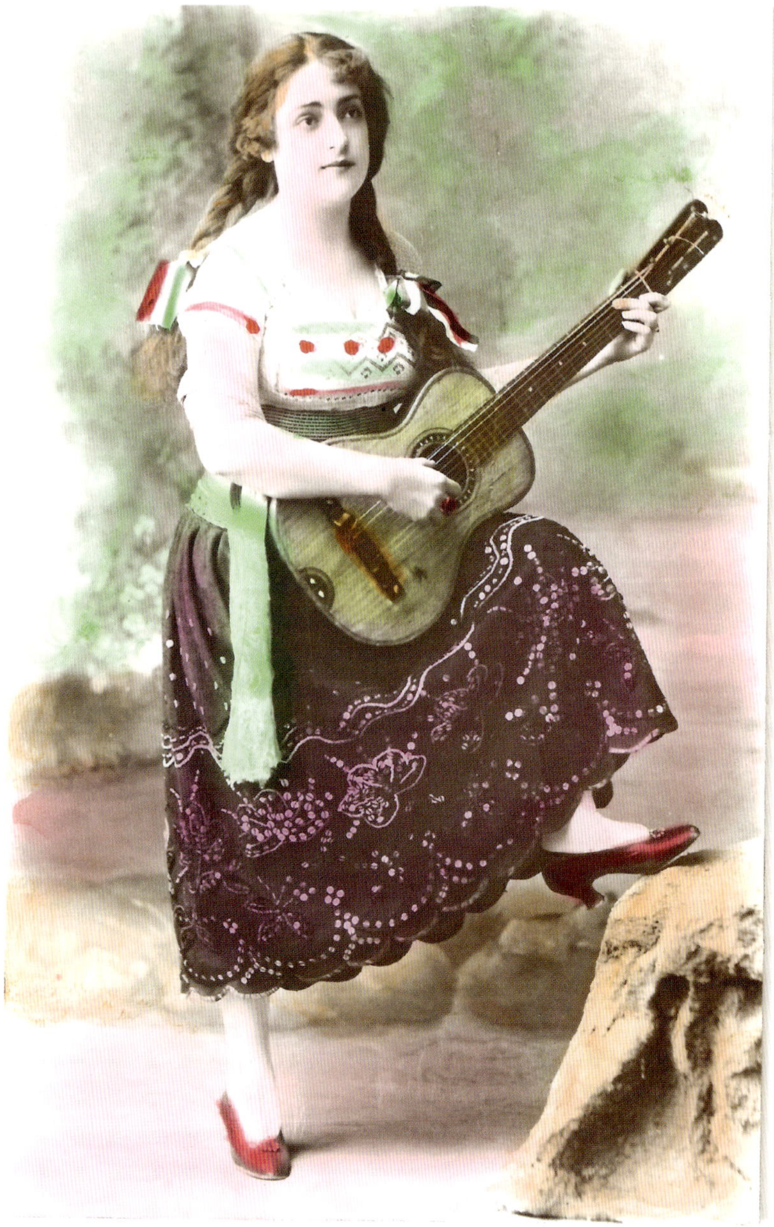

Postcard, color postcard photograph, "*Guitara*" a healthy *mestiza* with her guitar, c.1930s Mexico D. F. 4 x 5 in. $15 to 20

Popular Arts of Mexico

"Popular arts are those which spring spontaneously from a people as an immediate consequence of their family, civil or religious needs. When they are cultivated under an artistic or commercial influence foreign to these needs they cease to be true popular arts." Gerald Murillo, pseudonym Dr. Atl, an accomplished painter as well as philanthropist for Mexican popular arts. It was a true passion of his to conserve the recognition popular arts deserve.

After Mexico's many revolutions in the early 1900s, hardships caused many cultural changes in Mexico. The indigenous people's lifestyles had residual influences forced upon them by Spanish leaders, and their priorities were not of their own making. The many social classes were central during these times at setting trends that encouraged the wearing and using of imported clothes, while abandoning their own country's treasured garments. Thankfully, those interested in holding onto their culture's attributes began to acknowledge an appreciation for their original Indian traditions. Patrons of the arts began a renewal of gratitude for their own civilization and indigenous foundation. Exhibits and social gatherings inspired artist and people throughout the country. An exhibition of popular arts was patronized by the Ministry of Commerce, Industry and Labor in 1921. The Executive Committee with the help of Dr. Alt arranged for a premier indigenous exhibit on September 19, 1921. This exhibition celebrated 100 years of the end of Mexico's independence from Spain. An appreciation of their Mexican arts was finally realized as a significant turning point in sustaining and protecting the original customs of the Mexican population.

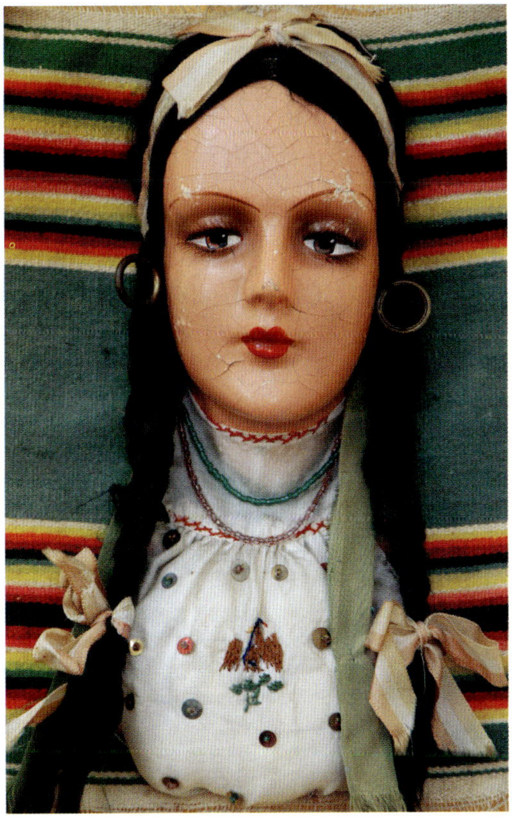

A beautiful vintage composition head of a *China Poblana*, 9 in. *mestiza* boudoir doll, c.1940s made in Mexico. Hand painted molded features, black mohair braids. Her top is silk with sequins and embroidery, placed on a vintage wool *serape*. $99 to 150

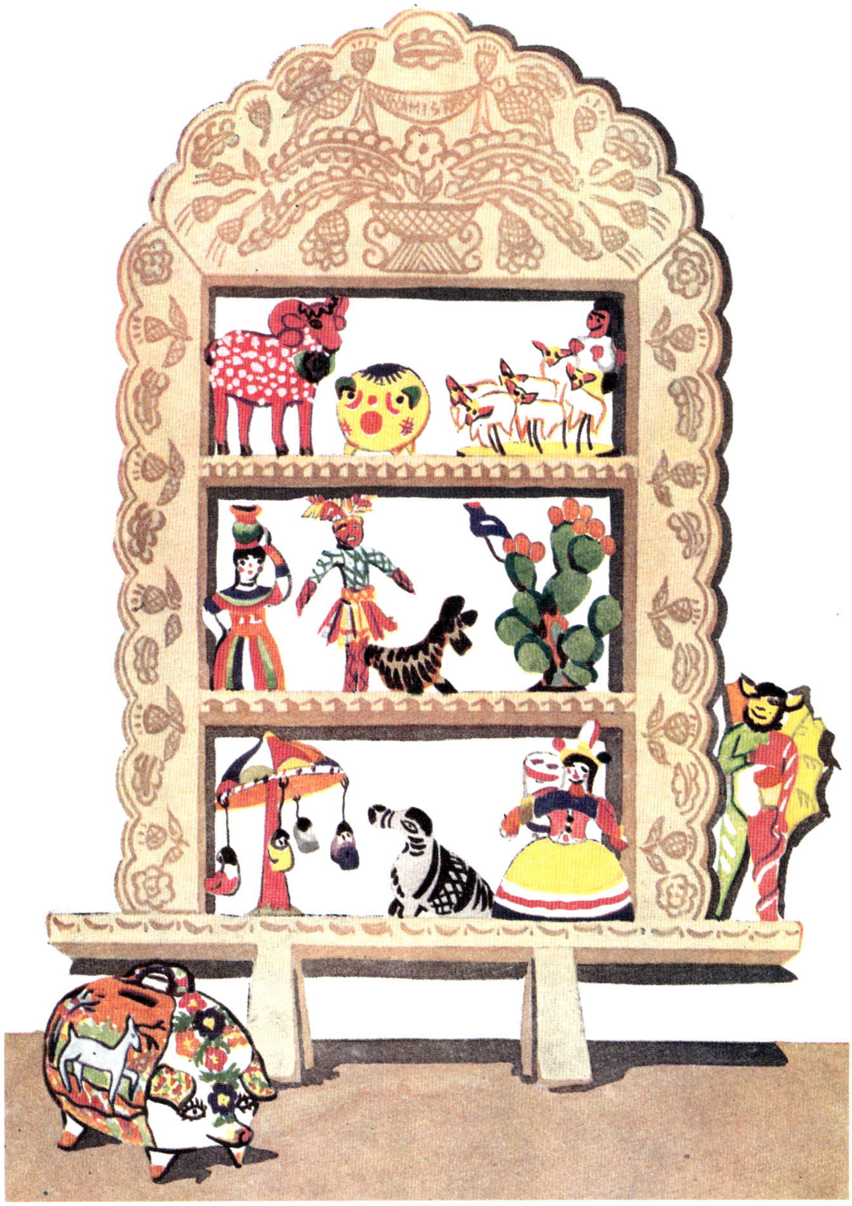

A color litho plate of a variety of vintage clay toys "*Trastero*," Michoacán Style, by L. Alice Wilson, 1939

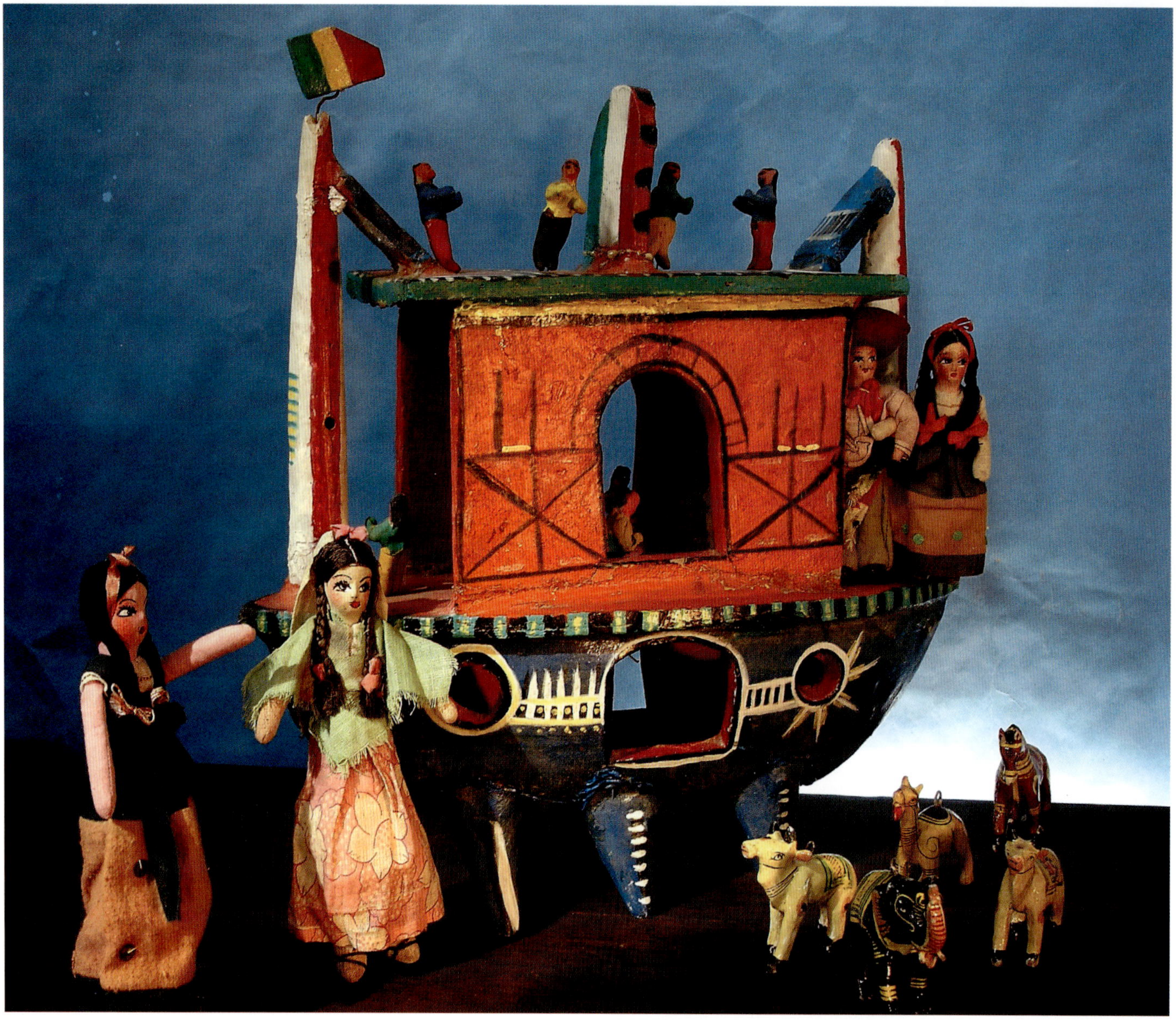

Folk artist, *Candelario Medrano* large polychrome sculpture ferry boat, c .1940s-50s. Surrounded by 3 in. and 6 in. old Mexican cloth dolls on the boat and standing at the stern and bow. Made in Mexico. Dolls valued from $15 to 40 ea.

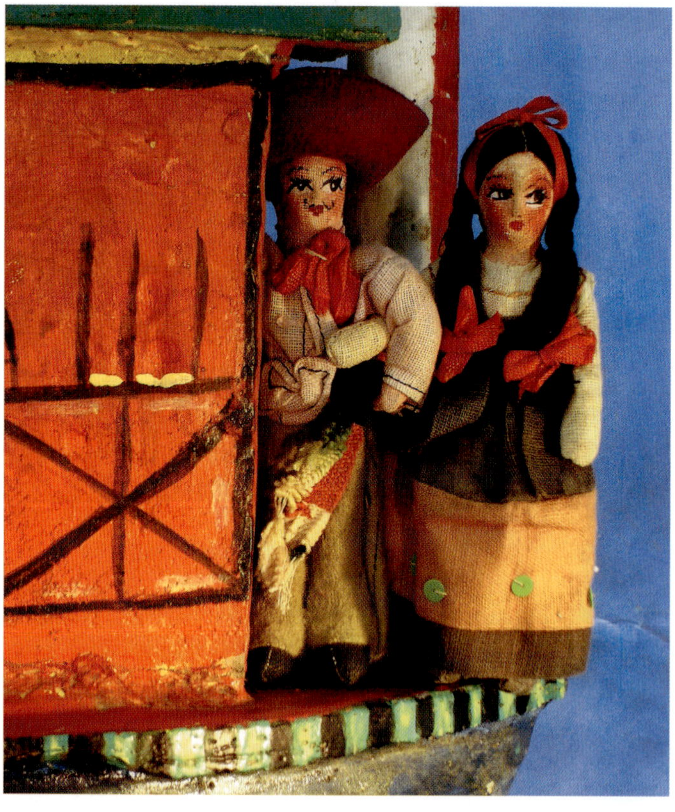

Small detail but very special miniature Mexican dolls at the bow of the ferry, c 1940s/50s. Made in Mexico. Dolls valued from $15 to 40 ea.

The Ministry of Commerce exhibition impelled a revelation to elite Mexicans who had overlooked their magnificent artistic history. Soon they began to try to reestablish what they had almost destroyed. Dr. Atl published two beautifully illustrated volumes on Mexico's popular arts, *Las Artes Populares,* around the same time. This publication and others increased Mexico's tourism, driving interested travelers to their country. Before long, their folk arts as well as their fine arts were being recognized throughout the world. Diego Rivera, Jose C. Orozco, and David A. Sigueiros constituted a few of the pioneering modern painters and muralists. Through them was revealed the struggle between the classes and Spanish domination; it was surely the inspiration for some of their work.

The revival triggered a domino effect at all levels of Mexican society, that many resented and some embraced. Nevertheless, the exhibition cultivated a renewed interest in Mexican arts and textiles, especially those that were worn by the people of Mexico. Visitors were awed by elaborately woven or embroidered clothing that rural Mexicans wore. Their admiration gave many Mexicans pride and more reason to hold onto their traditions. A lot of the indigenous costumes had already disappeared by 20th century, but there was clearly a grounded culture to be explored. Although Europeans had influenced the *mestizo* Mexicans, ties to their Indian traditions from their elders and ancestors were still existent. Mexicans are very proud of their heritage, as it is evident in their popular arts as well as their costumes.

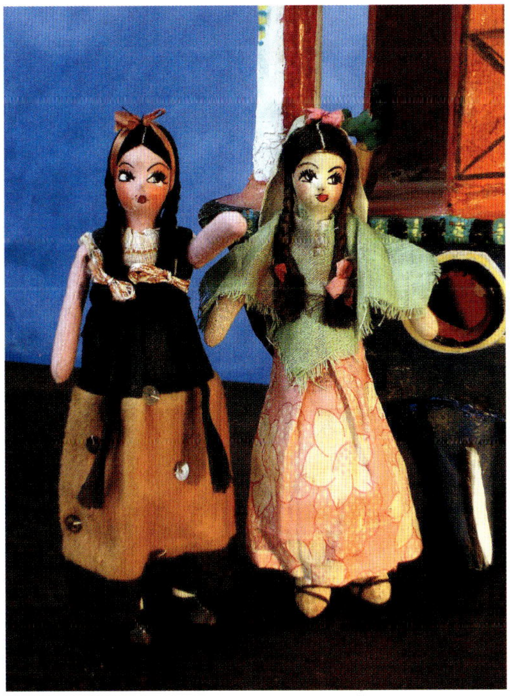

Mestiza 6 in. tourist cloth dolls, c.1940s/50s, made in Mexico. Dolls valued from $15 to 40 ea.

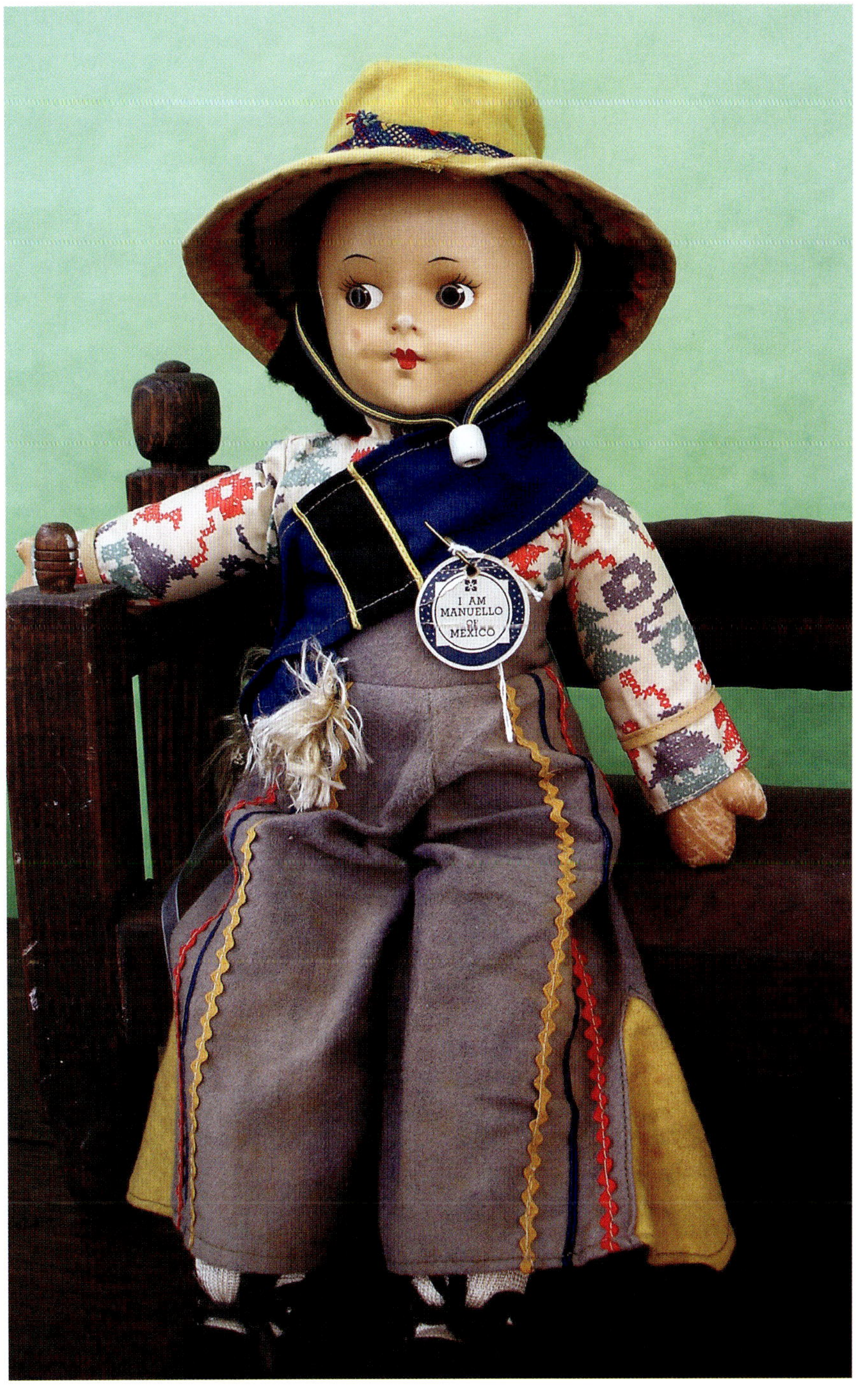

Attributed to the Junel Novelties, rare 18 in. doll of celluloid and cloth body, c.1930s. Original tag, and adorable clothing, Averill style. USA $100 to 150

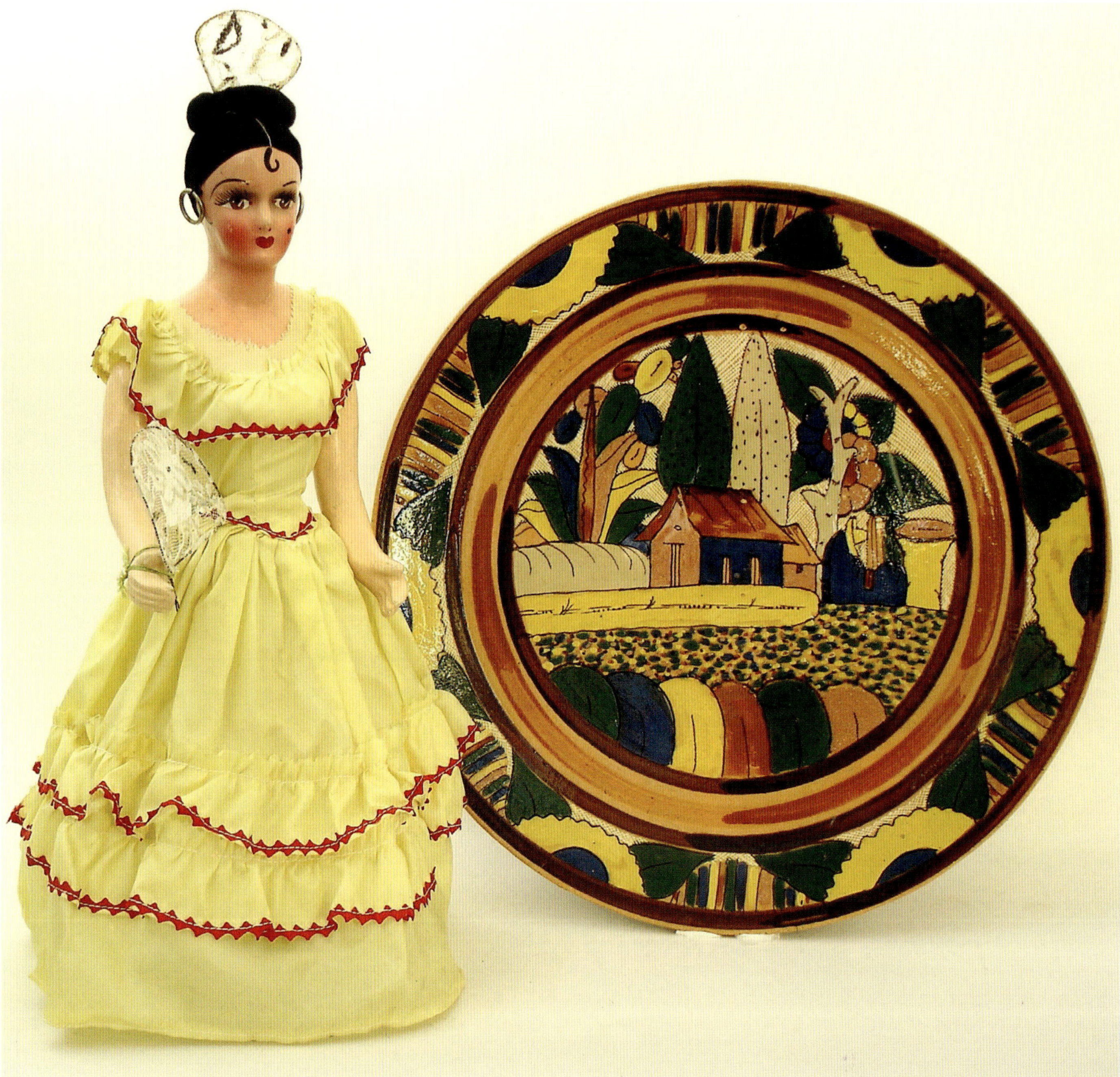

A stunning *mestizo* Señorita, in her yellow dress. She is a 16 in. tall, a 5 piece composition female doll, the body is cloth filled with sawdust. A popular tourist piece during the 1950s and 60s. She is made in Mexico of a hard composition known as "*muñeca de pasta*." Hand painted detail and mohair wig. Next to the doll is an Old Mexico late 1940s- 50s' *Tlaquepaque* platter, 16 in. diameter. A *petatillo* grained patterned in excellent condition. Not signed, marked Made in Mexico. Doll $75 to 275

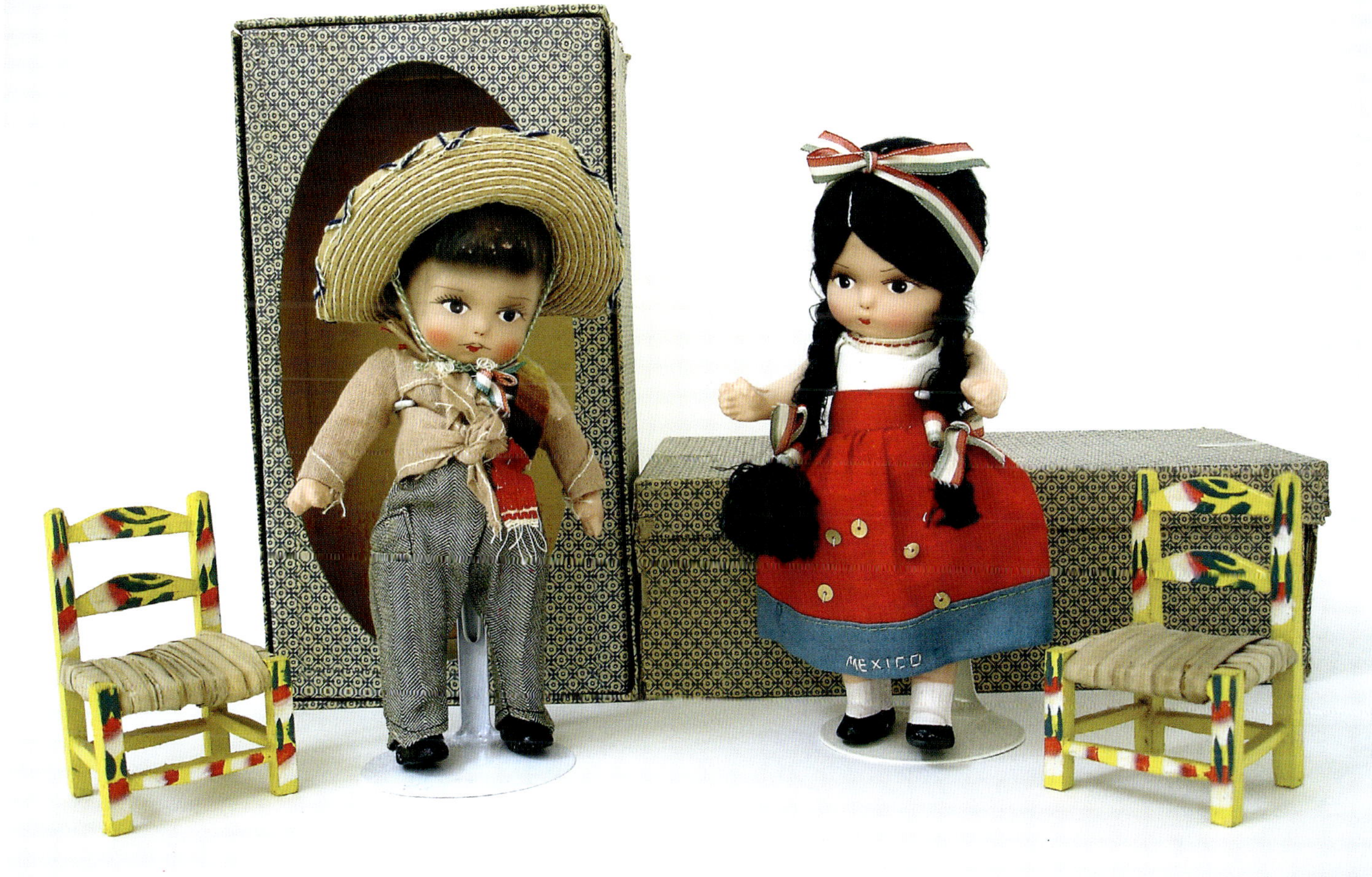

A mint cameo boxed set "*Ricardo and Amelia*," 10 in., made c.1940s-50s. All composition, 5 parts, legs and arms move freely, strung with rubber bands or string. Maker possibly Reliable Toys of the composition body parts, molded hair under the wig is indicative of these companies' imports. Hand painted detail with authentic detailed clothing of the Mexican *mestizo campesinos*. $75 to 150 pair
Descriptions of costumes:
They were costumed in old Mexico. Ricardo is wearing the typical clothing of a *campesino*, an urban dweller but worker. His black and white woven pants tie at the waist as well as his muslin shirt. He has painted black boots and wears a large sombrero made of *petate* straw. Amelia is dressed in a *castor* red skirt with little embellishments. She wears a petticoat, painted black slippers, a white top, and a satin hair ribbon in Mexico's national colors. The expression on her "*irrompible*" face is sweet and clean and her cotton threaded hair is braided. The photo reveals the remarkable condition as well as the hand-stitched collar of her *blusa*.
Ricardo's clothing is typical of the Mexican *campesino*, especially those from c.1940s. His clothing was suitable to work in as well as be part of the new *mestizo* styles that was influencing all of those living near or in the city. He carries his *serape*, something you rarely see a Mexican without.

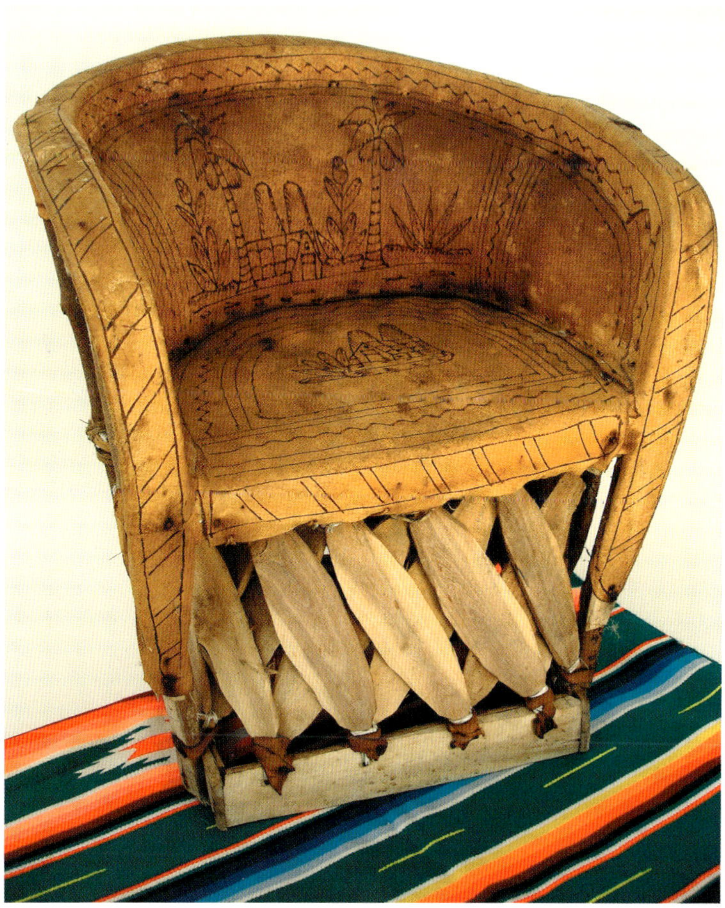

A child's vintage *equipale* Mexican handmade chair. All original, 1940s woven pigskin and *ixtle*, a fiber from the maguey plant. Stud nails around the wooden braces. Burnt etched cactus and palms design. Shown with the chair is a border town *serape* from old Mexico, chair 1950s.

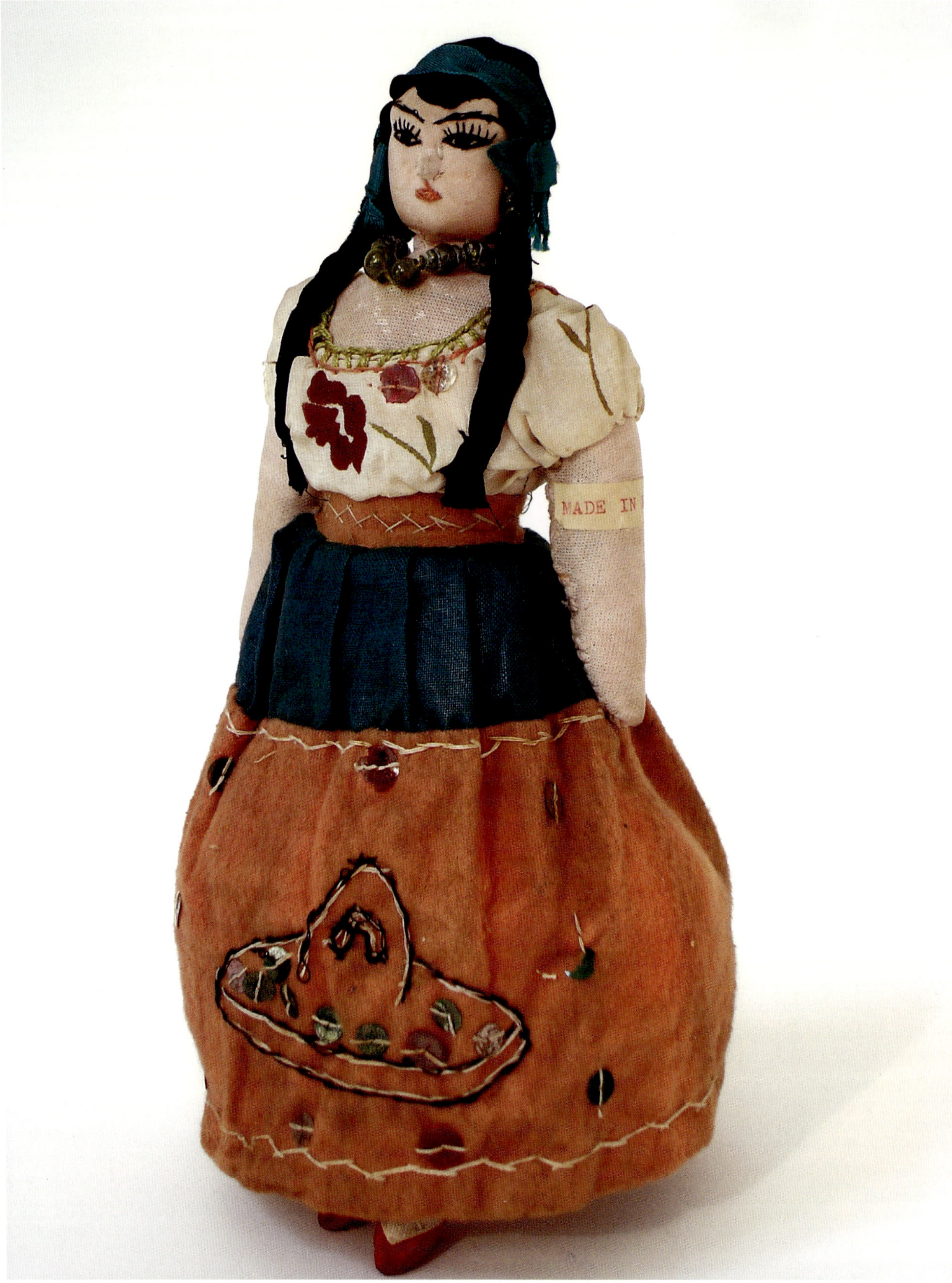

New York Worlds Fair Mexican Doll, dated 1940. She is a piece of history as well as a tribute to the Mexican folk doll artistry of the time, 11 in., hard stuffed cloth body hand-stitched of muslin. Great detail with a molded nose and embroidered facial features, needle embroidery. Her hair is black silk ribbon turned and stitched to appear like long braids topped with a green sash. Around her neck is a glass beaded necklace. A silk *huipil* is carefully embroidered with flowers and some fish scale sequins. She is wearing a full long skirt of cotton also embellished with a *sombrero* and sequins. Her shoes are sewn red fabric to the foot. A sticker Made in Mexico is on her arm and the original seal from the New York Worlds Fair is under the skirt. Skillfully done and a certified representation of the Mexican tourist doll of her time. Very hard to find with this concrete provenance. $100 to 250

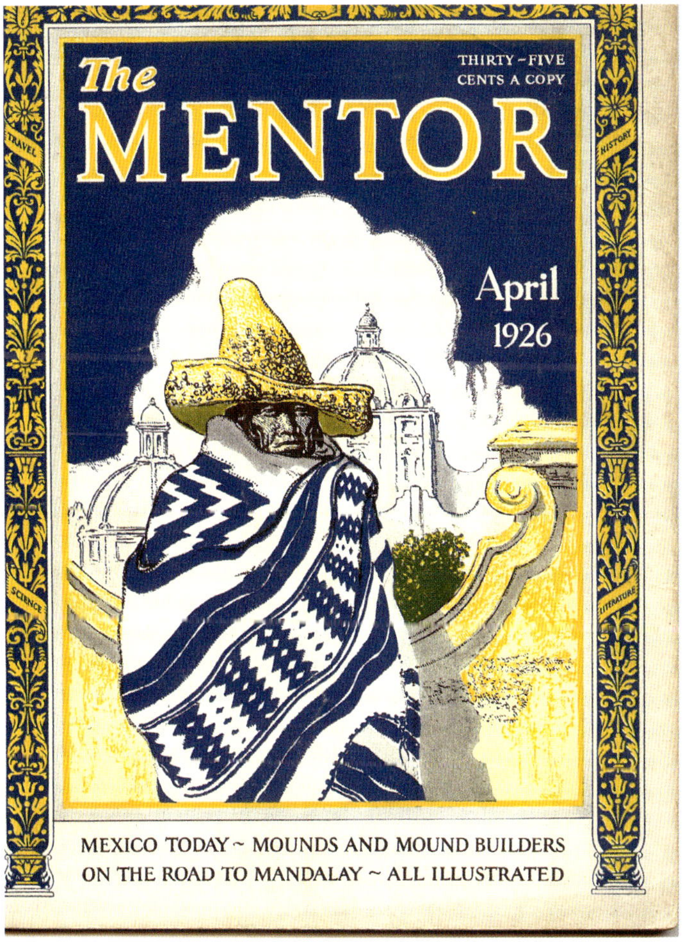

The Mentor, April, 1926, magazine cover features Mexico and its thriving tourism, a spectial tribute to famed artist Diego Rivera. The Crowell Publishing Co., Ohio, USA. $25 to 60

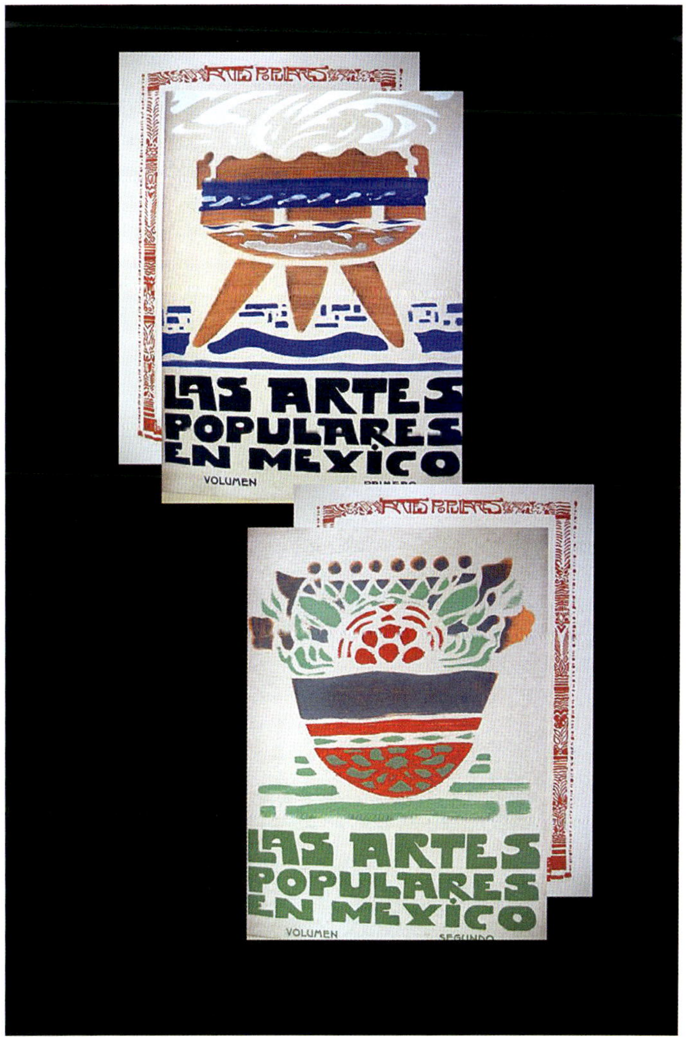

Two volumes by Dr. Atl (G. Murillo), *Las Artes Populares de Mexico*, 1922 editions. The books are rare and measure approx. 12 in. x 9 in. Text in Spanish, plates and photographs of popular arts. 2nd ed. Made in Mexico

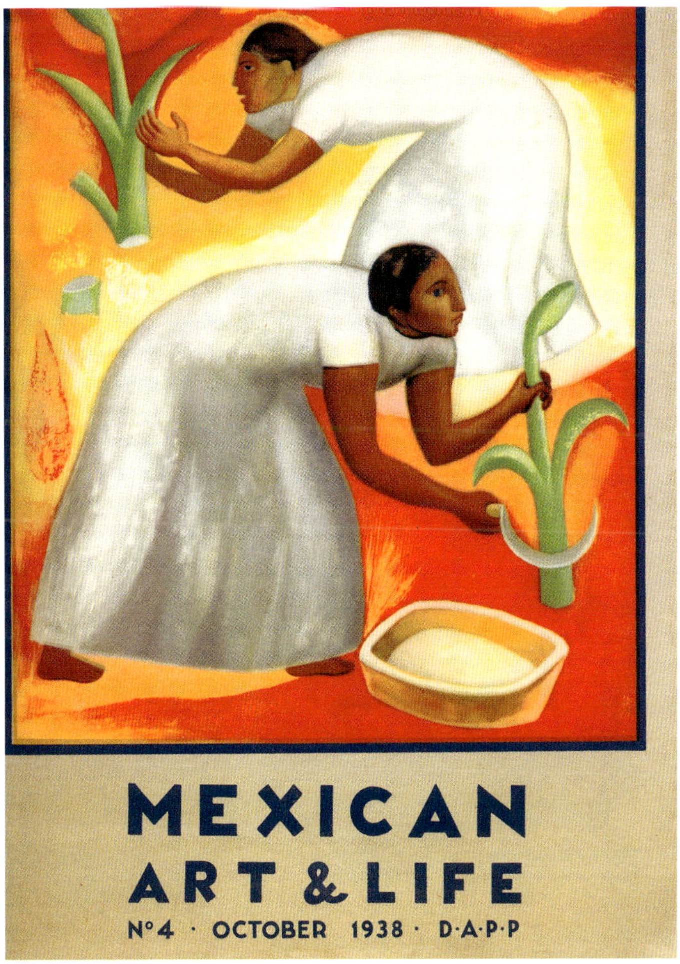

Mexican Art and Life magazine cover, No. 4, October, 1938, published by D.A.P.P., Mexico City $40 to 75

Mexican native costumes contain a visible history fashioned from both European and Indian techniques. New fashionable customs from the Spanish were blended beautifully with indigenous garments, adding colorful motifs without sacrificing conventional tradition. In some rural regions, the women's clothing shows little change. They still wear ancient garments, such as the *quechquémitl* and wrap-around skirts, *enredos*. Some *mestiza* women preferred the peasant blouse, *blusa*, introduced by the Spanish, and the full, cord waist, gathered skirt, *la enagua*, a little shorter in length. It was an integral part of the mixed nation and a progressive change toward modernization. Their clothing explains diverse changes that took place during the 20th century, just as with all of the Mexican popular arts. Vintage costume dolls are the tangible evidence of Mexican communal compromises.

A color painting of a *serape*, 1939, by L. Alice Wilson.

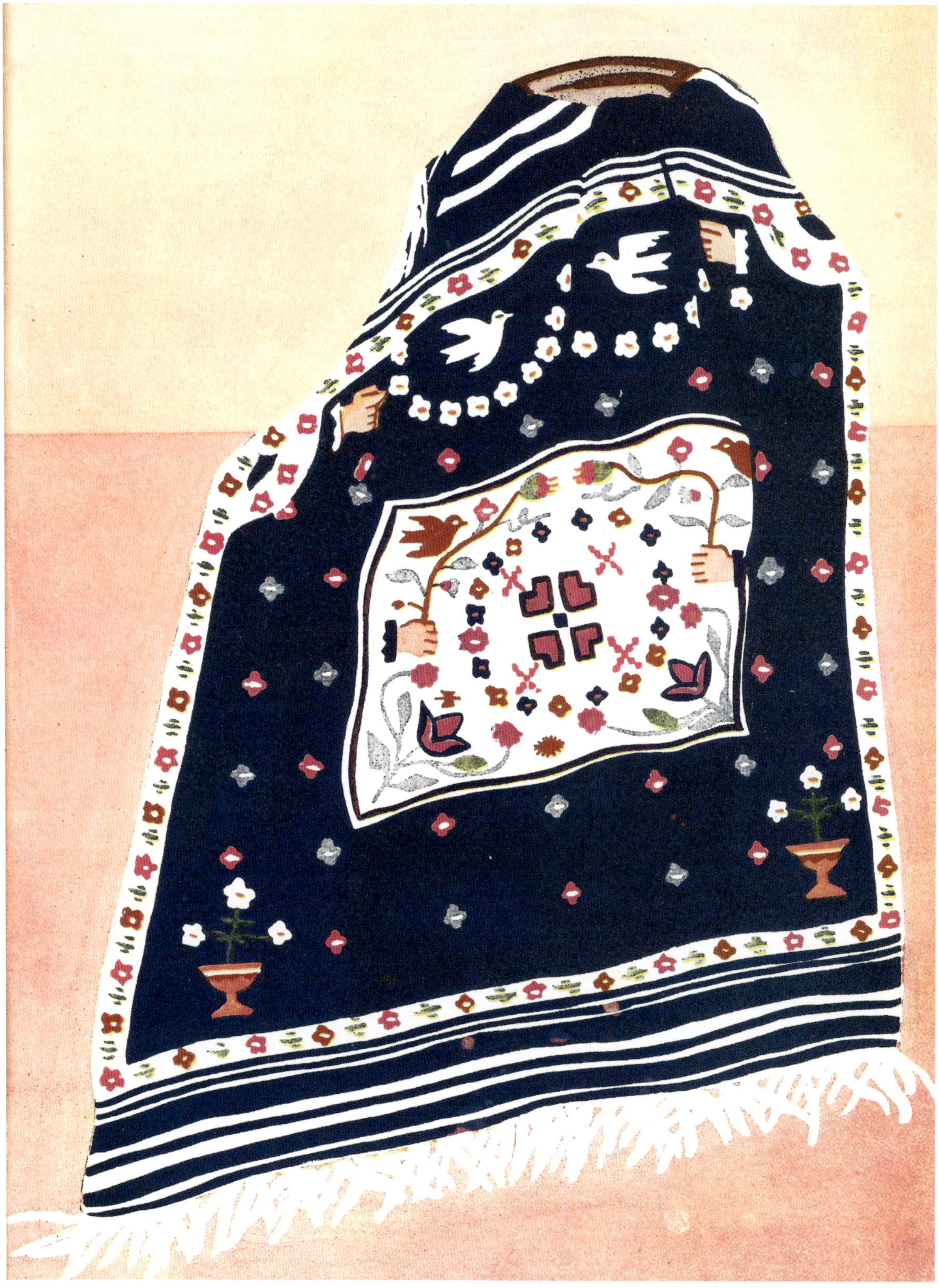

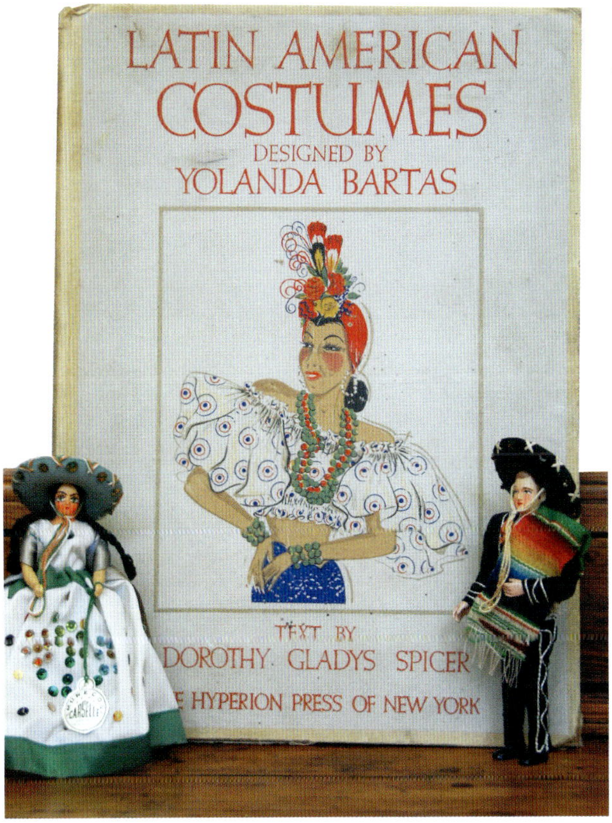

Latin American Costumes, by Yolanda Bartis. A large cloth board book with exceptional original prints of costumes throughout South America. 11 x 16 in., 1941, The Hyperion Press of New York $150 to 250

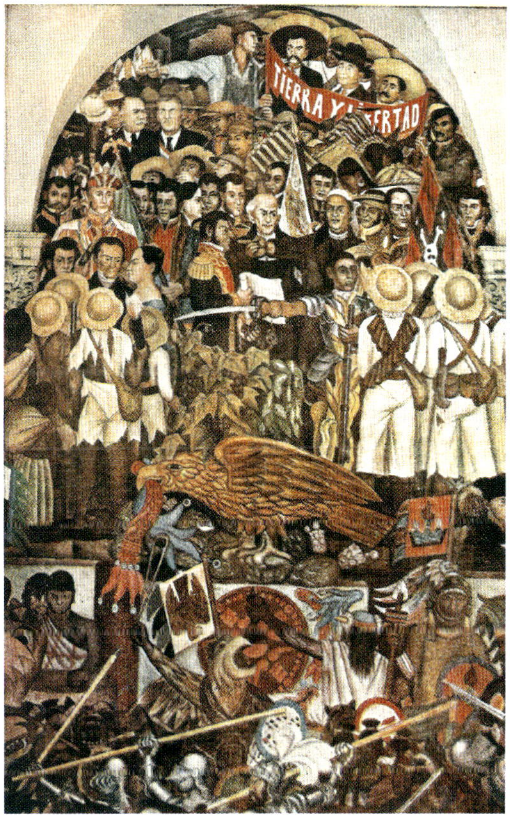

Postcard, *Palacio Nacional De Mexico*, fresco by Diego Rivera. The Independence War of Mexico (1810), scenes of the conquests, c.1930s, printed in Mexico D. F. 3 x 5 in. $15 to 40

17 in. tourist dolls, c.1940s. Polychrome painted, a plaster composition, made in Mexico. They are standing among some fine *tonalá* and *talavera* plates and vases. Dressed in a calico *manta* and a *castor enagua* skirts with embroidered *huipils* and *blusas*. Their features resemble those of Frida Kahlo, with flowers and indigenous jewelry. $150 to 350

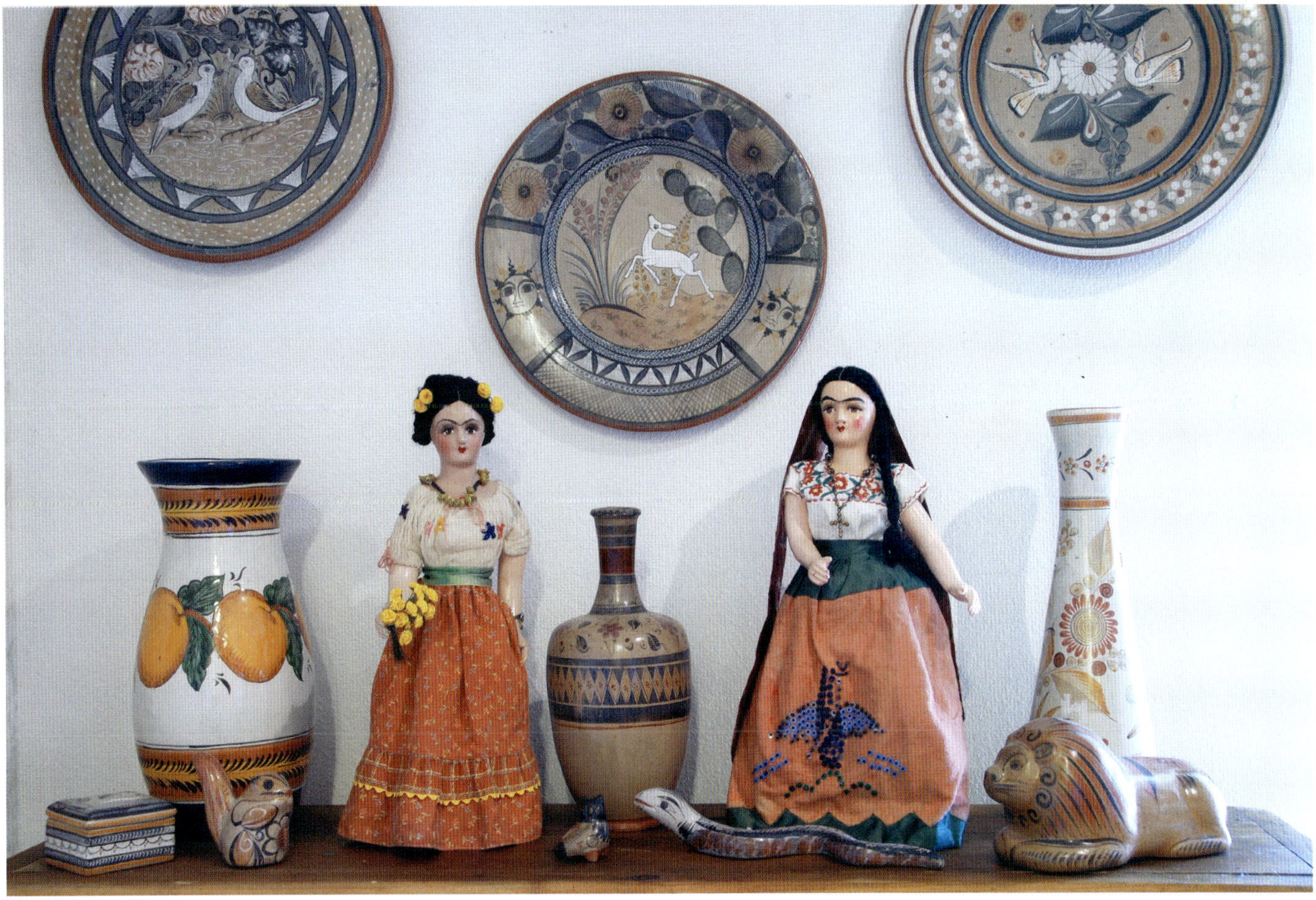

Popular Costumes of Mexican Regions

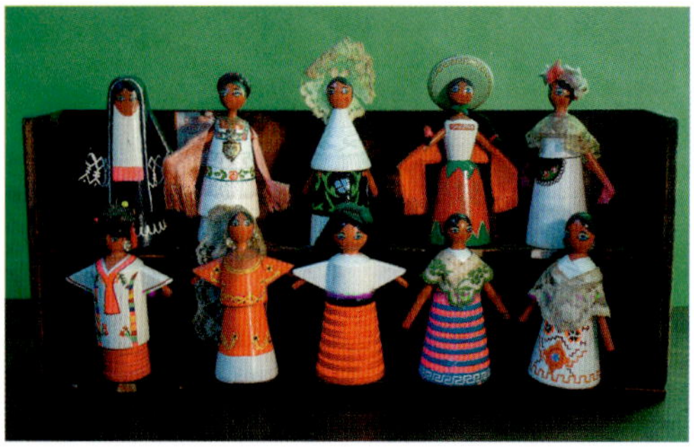

Angeles Pre-Hispanicos de Mexico, c.1960. Ten rare examples of wooden Mexican women dolls in their regional costumes. Pegged and removable from the rectangular wooden stand, the original sticker from the Lincoln Center gift shop. The dolls are 4.5 in. x 3 in. wide. The stand is 15.5 in. x 7.8 in. x 3 in deep, with two tiers. $150 to 250 set
From left to right, the regional costumes are as follows: *Serrana, Mestiza, Zandunga, China Poblana, Jarocha, Yalalteca, Tehuana, Tarasca, Totonaca, Otomi*. Each doll is handmade, painted with the traditional traits of its region, and trimmed with lace and beads.

...*"more and more costumes are left at home when trips are made to the larger towns and cities. Fear of being laughed at by mestizos cause the Indian to wear nondescript clothing."* --
-Donald and Dorothy Cordry, *Mexican Indian Costumes*

This thought holds much truth, as the modern civilization had subsequently settled its standards throughout Mexico with extreme affect on their Indian costumes. Their clothing had been influenced by commercial cloth, economical priorities, and convenience. Although many of the original indigenous textiles were threatened, the people managed to sustain a globally identifiable costume, particularly through distinctive pieces, such as the *serape, rebozo, sombrero* and the *huipil*. All of these colorful and distinctive garments represent a true expression of the country's struggle to cling to traditional values. Their adaptations from region to region demonstrate a mixed intermingling of items. Mainly because of nomadic blending, but also because they were admired, the styles were adopted from one tribe to another. Traditional dress still ignites a creative means of self-expression for the wearer, even though the lively costumes are seen today only in festivals or performances.

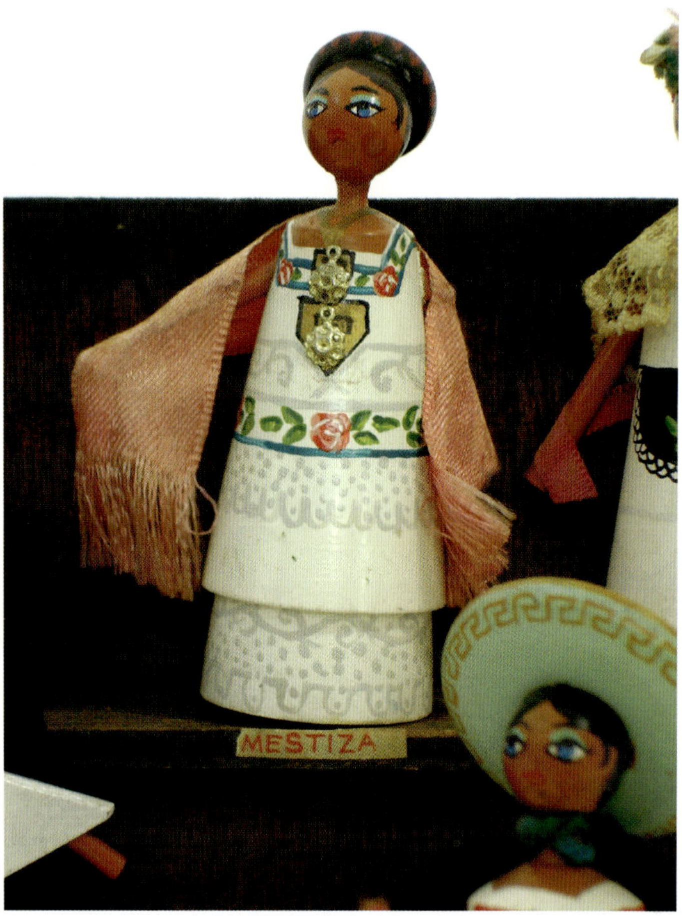

The *Mestiza*, Angeles Pre-Hispanicos de Mexico Doll. A detail of the wooden 4.5 in. doll. See description of the other dolls together.
Description of costume:
The costume on the *mesitza* wooden doll is painted with particular detail to the Spanish influences. Delicate little flowers on a white *huipil* dress, a proud pink *rebozo* covers her shoulders. Her jewelry discloses her status.

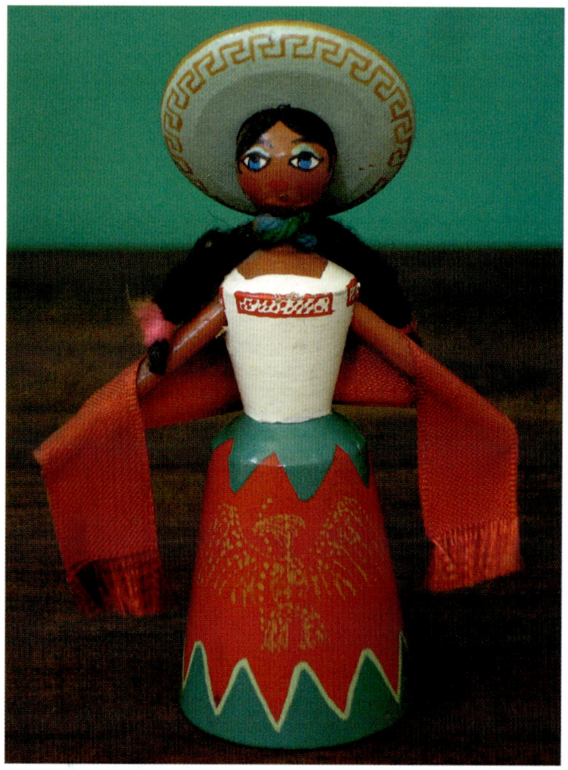

The "*China Poblana*," Angeles Pre-Hispanicos de Mexico Doll. A close-up of one of the wooden 4.5 in. dolls. See description of the other dolls together.
Description of costume:
The costume of the *China Poblana* doll is considered the women's national costume of Mexico. Painted with delicate folk art style, great detail. Her red skirt accented with green is centered by Mexico's eagle emblem; she wears a Spanish blouse, red *rebozo*, and matching *sombrero*.

The popular regions listed here are in alphabetical order, with brief descriptions. Discerning the Indian costumes to a particular region is extremely difficult because many of the dolls wear those distinctive pieces mentioned with variations of diluted provenance. The regions are categorized sensibly, identifying only those that were popular and with discernable characteristics. Some of the costumes from the other regions have been added, as they were an essential part of 20th century Mexican clothing. Some vintage pictures and postcards are also included. The women's costumes are the most prevalent on the dolls, after all, they were the most spectacular. The regional costumes noted are those found predominantly on vintage dolls; there are hundreds of other indigenous as well as regional costumes, but they are not apparent on the vintage dolls that were studied for this work. The most recognized costumes exhibit an impressive quality that characterizes the typical Mexican clothing of the 20th century.

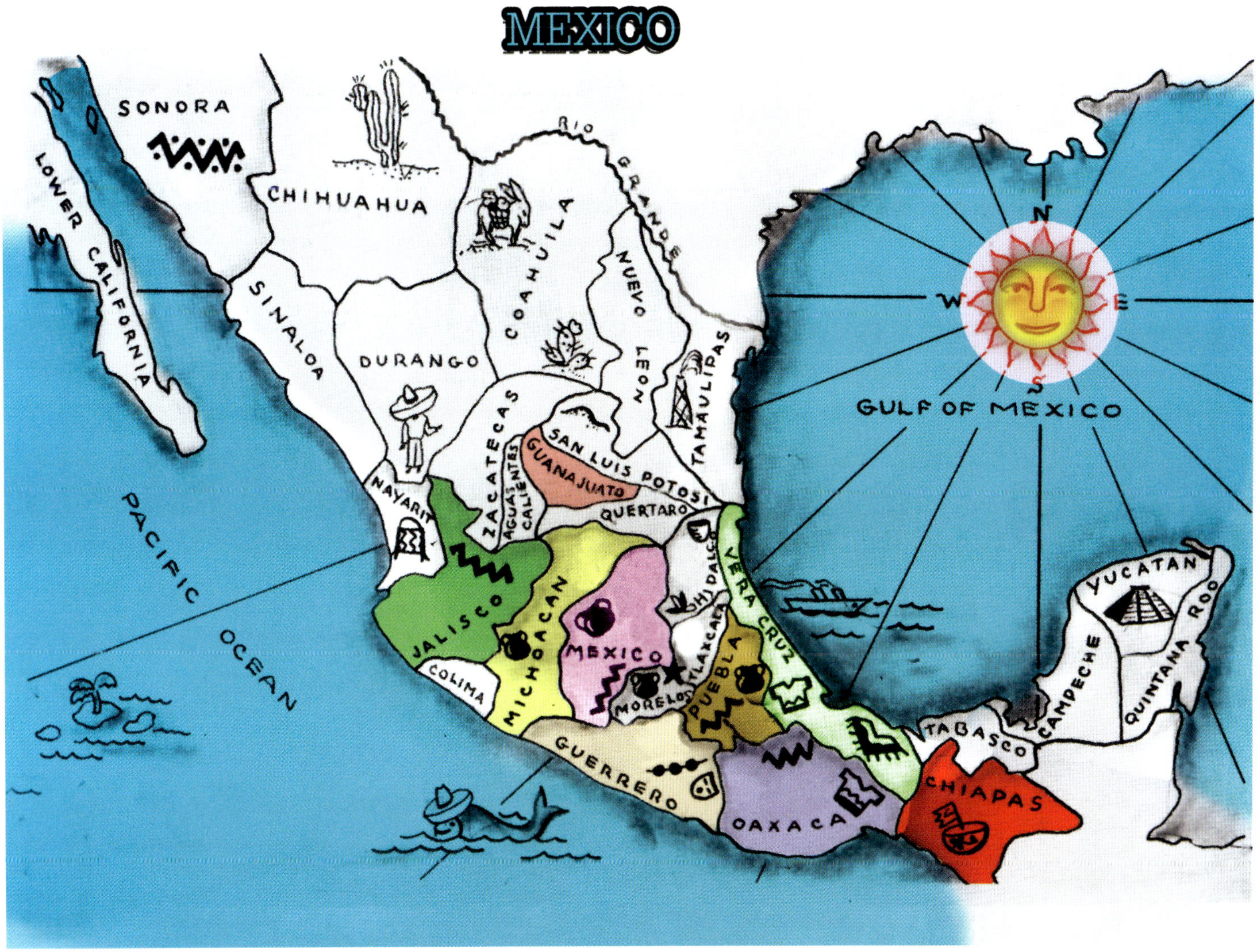

Map of Mexico showing the many districts (states) in color. These were popular tourist regions during the 20th century.

Chiapas

Beautiful Chiapas, located on the southern tip of Mexico, is the home of many Mayan ruins. In the highlands of Chiapas, Indians may wear long diamond symbolic *huipils* and the wrap-around *enredo* skirts. Banded bold colors trim the border with ruffled ribbons, and profuse embroidery shows traces of their Mayan ancestry. Both pre-Columbian and European influences can still be seen in their costumes at festivals of the highlands. In Chamula, the women wear a dark head cloth and grey colored *huipils*. The Chiapanecan *huipils* are woven of colorful cotton or wool threads in complex designs. One of the most beautiful *mestiza* festive dresses is that of the traditional *Chiapaneca* dress. It is a flamboyant costume that has vivid colors of local flora against a dark black background. The fabric is now a synthetic commercial netting blend with profuse embroidery added by hand or machine. The costume consists of a peasant blouse of banded flowers in a Spanish style, with a matching full skirt with tiers of the same, banded, embroidered flowers. They are used in folkloric dances, wearing their hair in a bun accented with flowers and satin *rebozos*. The women look like flowers when they are dressed, as they are absolutely gorgeous.

Attributed to Abelardo Ruiz, a Chiapas woman, painted papier mache doll 13 in., colorful surface of the Chiapaneca costume with ribbons and flowers, c.1960s. $45 to 75

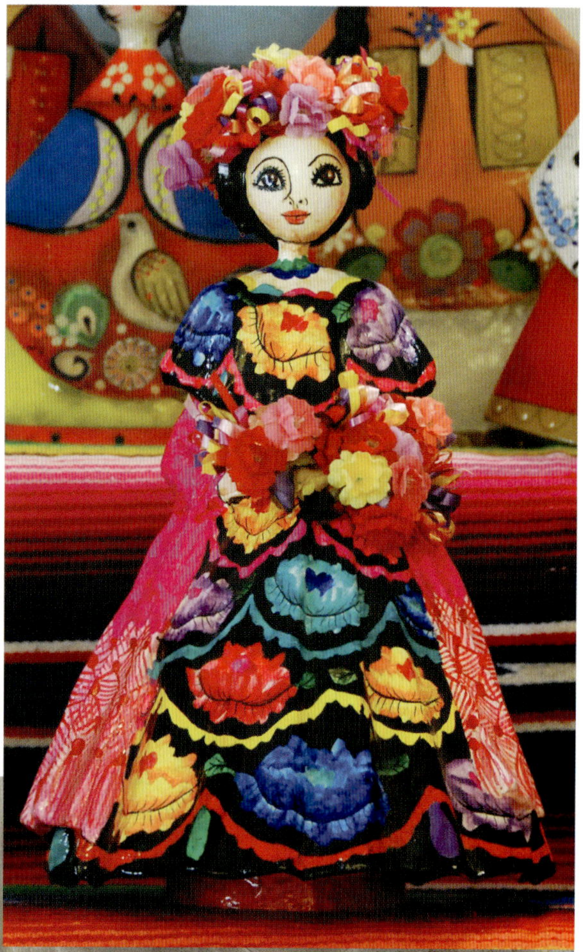

A 13 in. Chiapas beauty, in her "*Chiapaneca*" gala gown. Made in Mexico, c.1950s. Popular arts Olinala chest of drawers with indigenous pots. $100 to 200

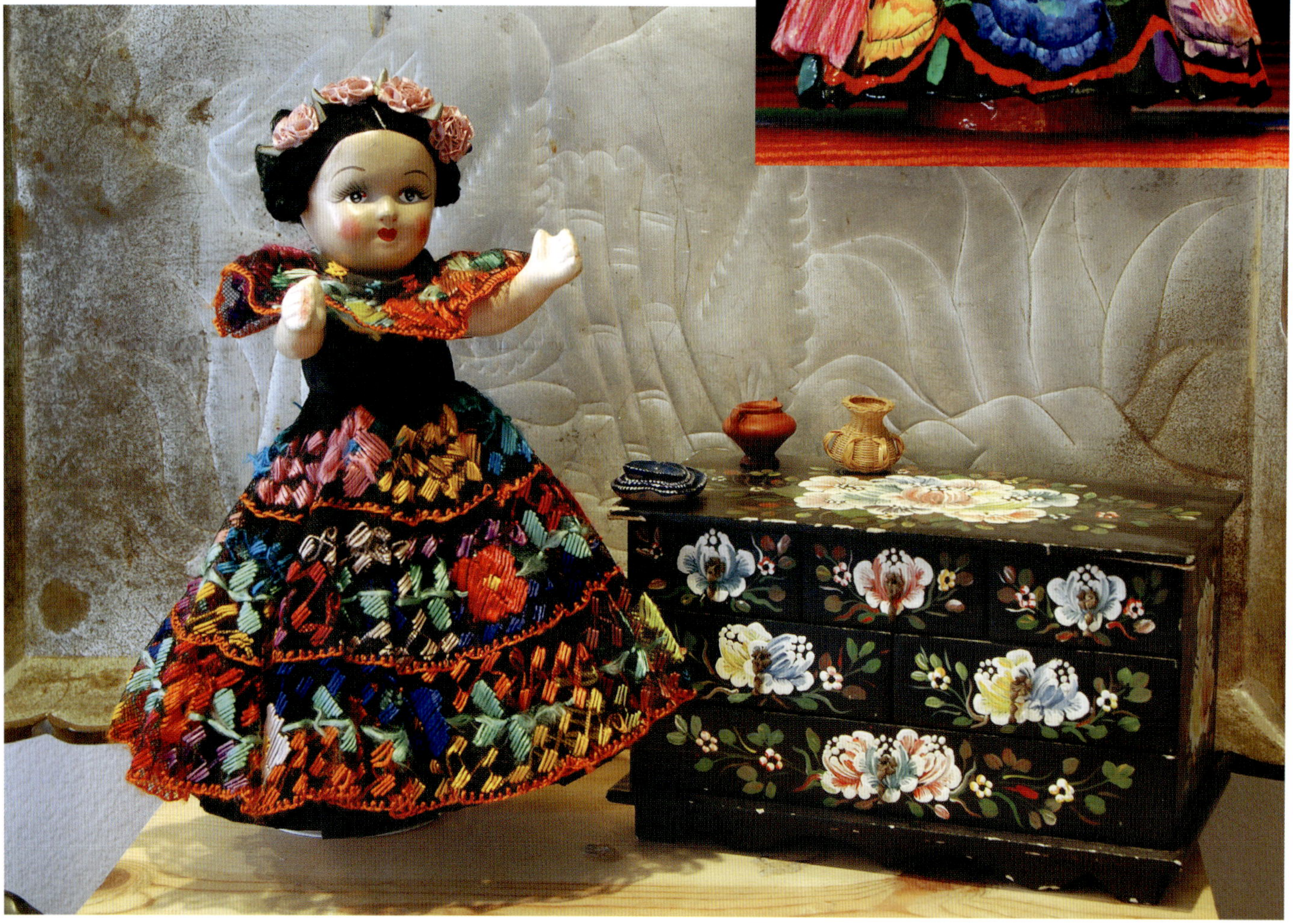

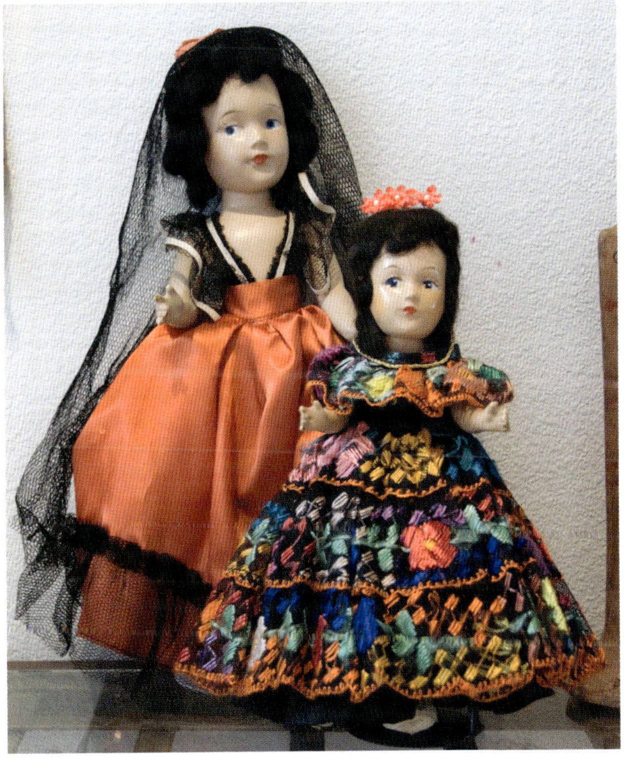

Dream World dolls, all composition jointed bodies and black mohair wigs, c.1940s. A 16 in. colonial Spanish girl and a 13 in. Chiapaneca costumed beauty. Made in the USA. $100 to 150

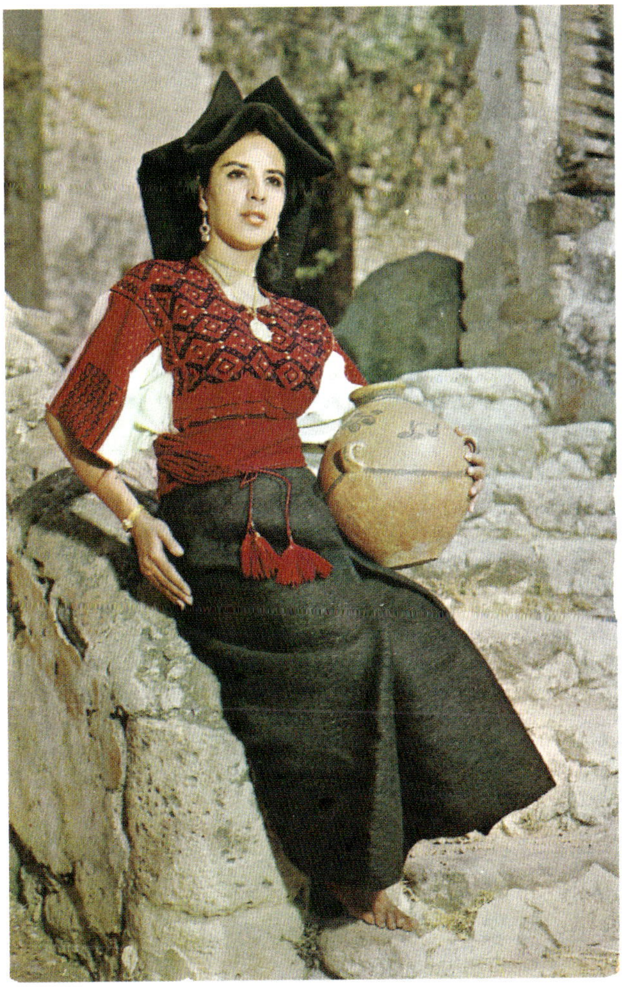

Postcard, color photograph, "Chamula Indian from Chiapas" *enredo* indigenous costume with *servilleta* head piece. Cristacolor, Lito Juventud, c. 1950, Mexico D. F. 4 x 5 in. $15 to $20

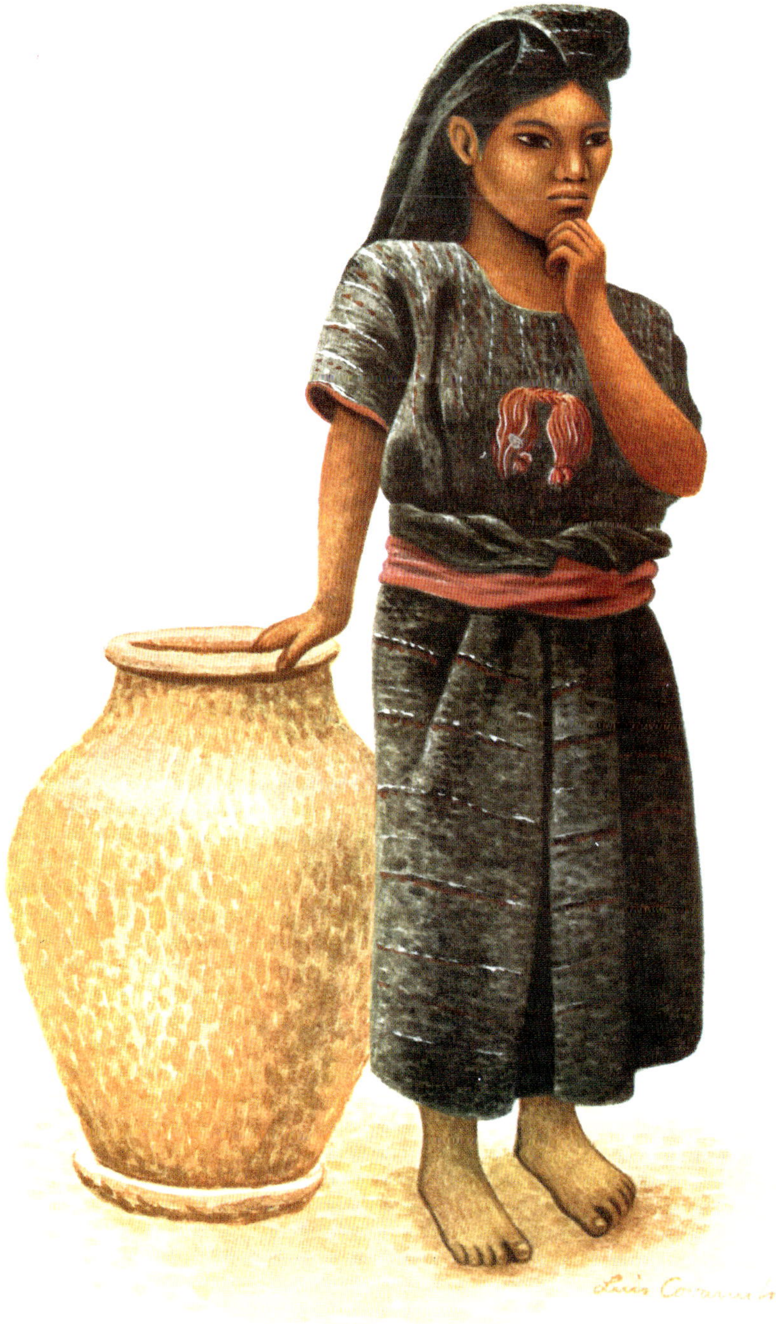

A color chrome picture, c.1940s.

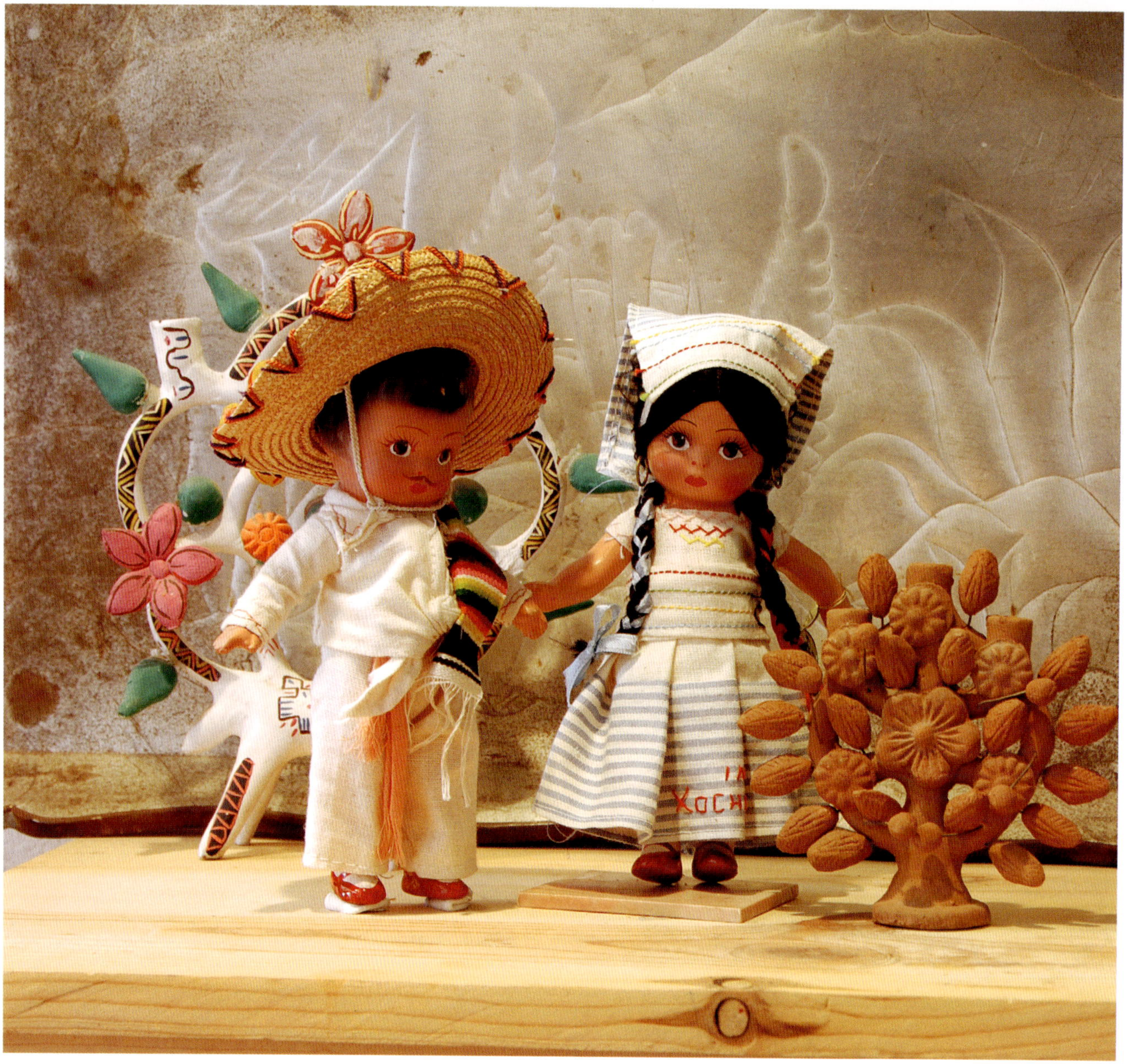

Two old Mexico tourist 9 in. composition dolls, jointed with hand-painted details, c.1950s. The strung *caballero* is a peon from Xochimilco with his *mestiza* wife, standing next to *arboles de vida* ceramic pieces. $125 to 200 pr.

Estado de Mexico

Costumes and indigenous garments from many regions can be seen in the state of Mexico. Many rural Mexicans travel to visit the modern capitol city, built on the ancient Aztec capitol, Tenochtitlan. They travel from economic need or curiosity to Mexico City, where modern civilization is booming. It is economically and culturally the most important city at this time. The boroughs are composed of hundreds of *colonias* (large neighborhoods) with diluted mixed Indian and *mestiza* groups. The Metepec is famous for their hand painted, brilliant colored *candelabras*, *arbol de la vida* (tree of life) ceramic sculpture in a polychrome pottery or solid colored dried terra cotta style. The Otomi women from Toluca create a distinctive style of skirt known as the *chincuete*. The skirt is hand woven in white and blue or as a purple background with white stripes. Their tops are usually a white cotton *blusa* and/or with the *quechquémitl*. One of their identifiable *quechquémitls* is dark navy blue with a white loop border at the bottom and floral cross-stitching at the neckline. The Indian doll in her blue and white cotton woven costume exemplified an urban Mexican Indian girl living near the city. Some of the finest *rebozos* are made on the traditional strap loom as well. *Xochimilco* is an extraordinary city on the southern outskirts of Mexico City. There the region is known for its canals and the *chinampas* (floating gardens), a popular tourist attraction with colorful *trajineras* (Xochimilco boats) that carry people along the canals. The floating gardens are beautiful, but they were once a primary place to grow the crops of corn or beans, since it was the main water source for Mexico City. The *mestiza* woman was certainly everywhere. Her clothing was lively with rich embroidery and urban flair.

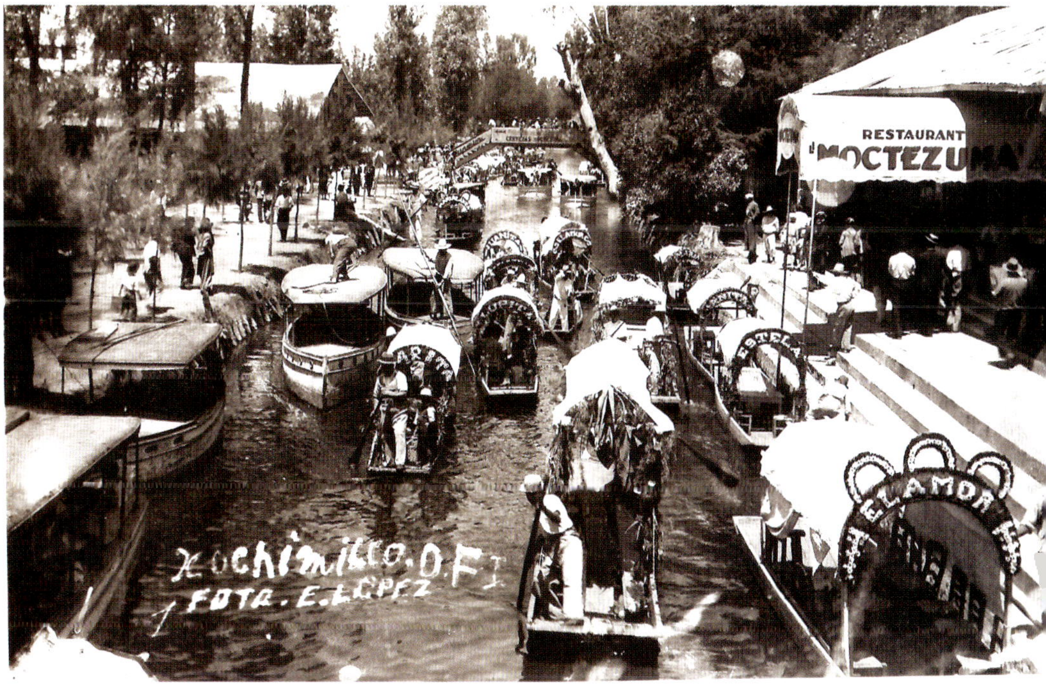

Postcard, "Xochimilco, D. F.", Foto, E. Lopez, c.1950s, 3x5 in. Mexico $15 to 30

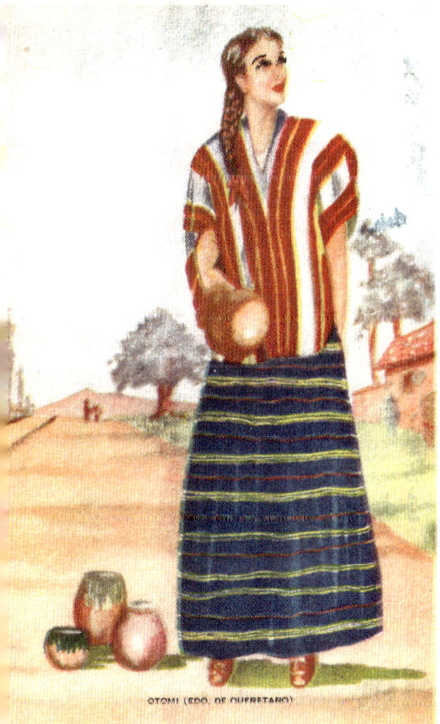

A color tinted paper litho postcard, "Otomi Indian Woman," Edo. De Gueretaro Tarjeta postal, Mexico c1930s, 5 x 3in Mexico $15 to 25

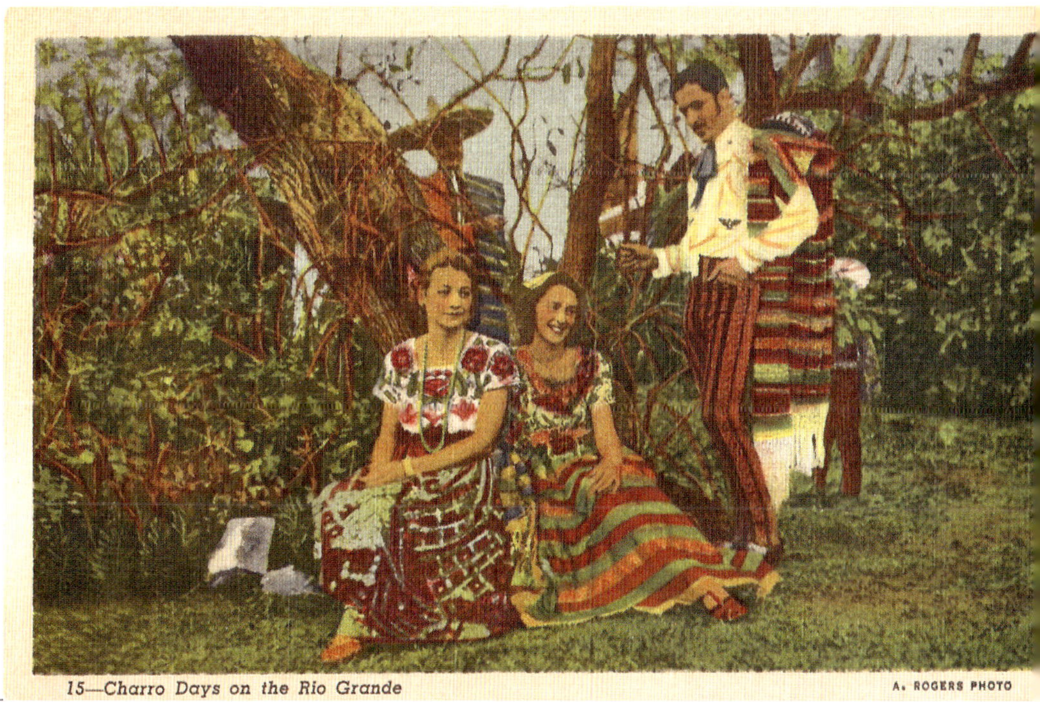

Postcard, color tinted, "*Charro* Days on the Rio Grande," Rogers Studio, 3x5 in. USA $15 to 30

Guanajuato

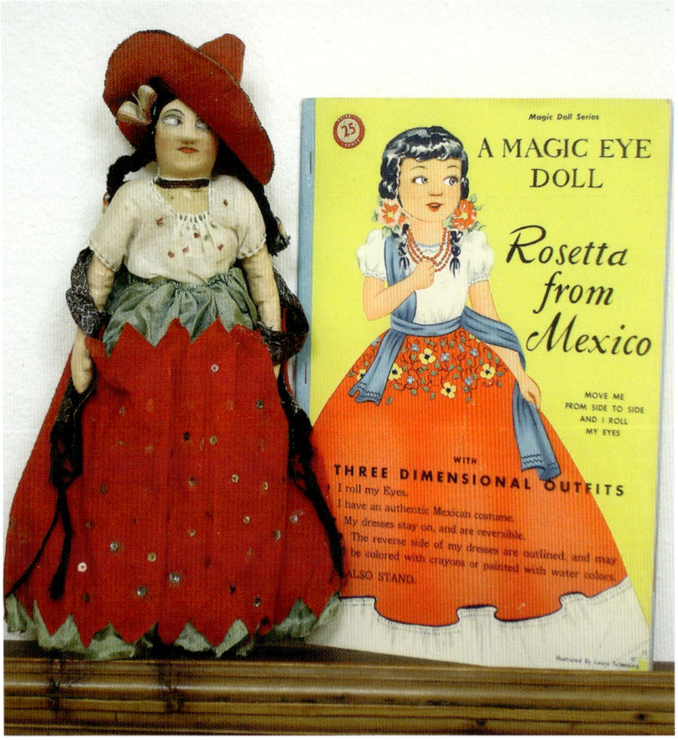

Rosetta from Mexico book and doll with moving eyes, c.1950s. Made in USA. The 13 in. cloth doll *mestiza* dressed in a red castor and sequined *enagua* skirt, c 1930s, white embroidered top, and glass beaded necklace. Hand-painted gazing eyes similar to the Magic Eye book, doll $75 to 150

Nestled in the Sierra de Guanajuato is the beautiful colonial capital city of Guanajuato. It is located in central Mexico, just north of Michoacán. Every year the famed International *Cervantino* Festival is held here, in honor of Miguel de Cervantes, the author of *Don Quixote*. Another beautiful town is San Miguel de Allende, with its Gothic style colonial cathedral and structures. This state exhibits a plethora of European influences in its architecture, with many plazas and cobblestone allyways. The 20th century costume most associated with Guanajuato is the *mestizo Galereña*. In the city of Dolores Hidalgo, polychrome plates with Spanish *majolica* influences are very popular collectibles, and the city is also known for wood *bateas*. Their beautiful women wear traditional white embroidered peasant Spanish influenced tops and a full gathered, red flannel skirt, with triangular borders in green at the top and bottom, often referred to as the *zagalejo.* Sometimes they layer skirts with one over another, one of a calico print and then an apron; under her skirt is white slip and pantaloons. Tradition states this was so that the women could work in one skirt, then step out of it to reveal the other and go into town to do shopping for dinner. They would wear a colorful cotton or rayon *rebozo* and glass-beaded necklaces. Their long braids were finished with colored ribbons.

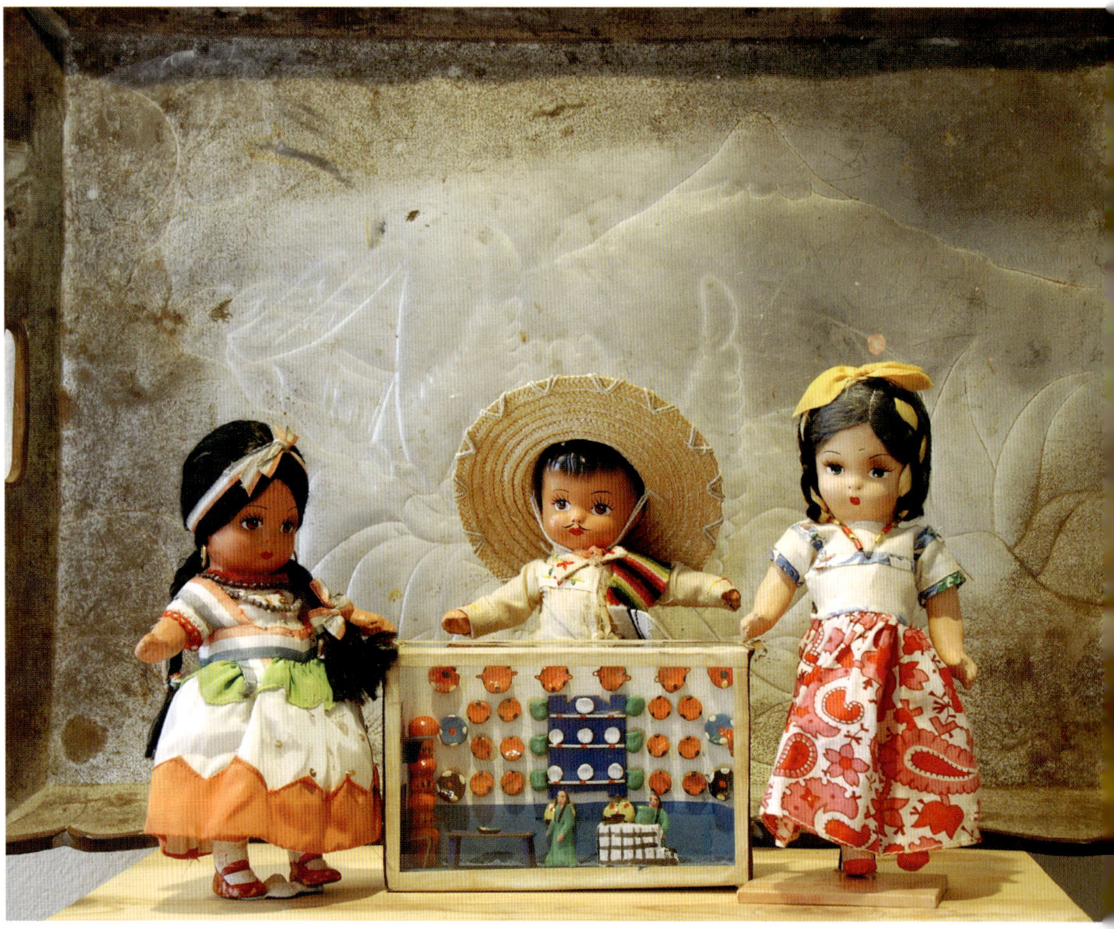

A trio of 9 in., old Mexico composition tourist dolls, all dressed from their region of Guanajuato, as a *Galareña* or in her *zagalejo* skirt, and the *caballero* costumed as a *campesino.* A glass case protects the tiny pottery scene, a popular souvenir. $75 to 125 ea.

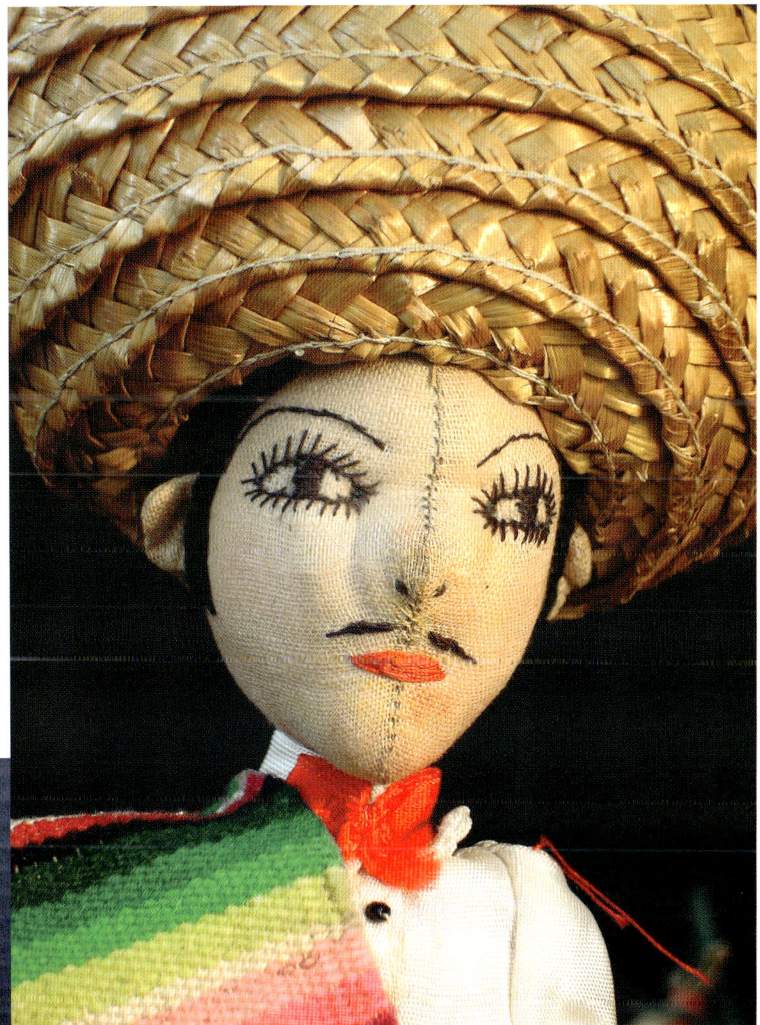

Detail of the European male cloth doll dressed as a Mexican *campesino mestizo*. Center stitched down the face, needle embroidered. Fantastic color and detail

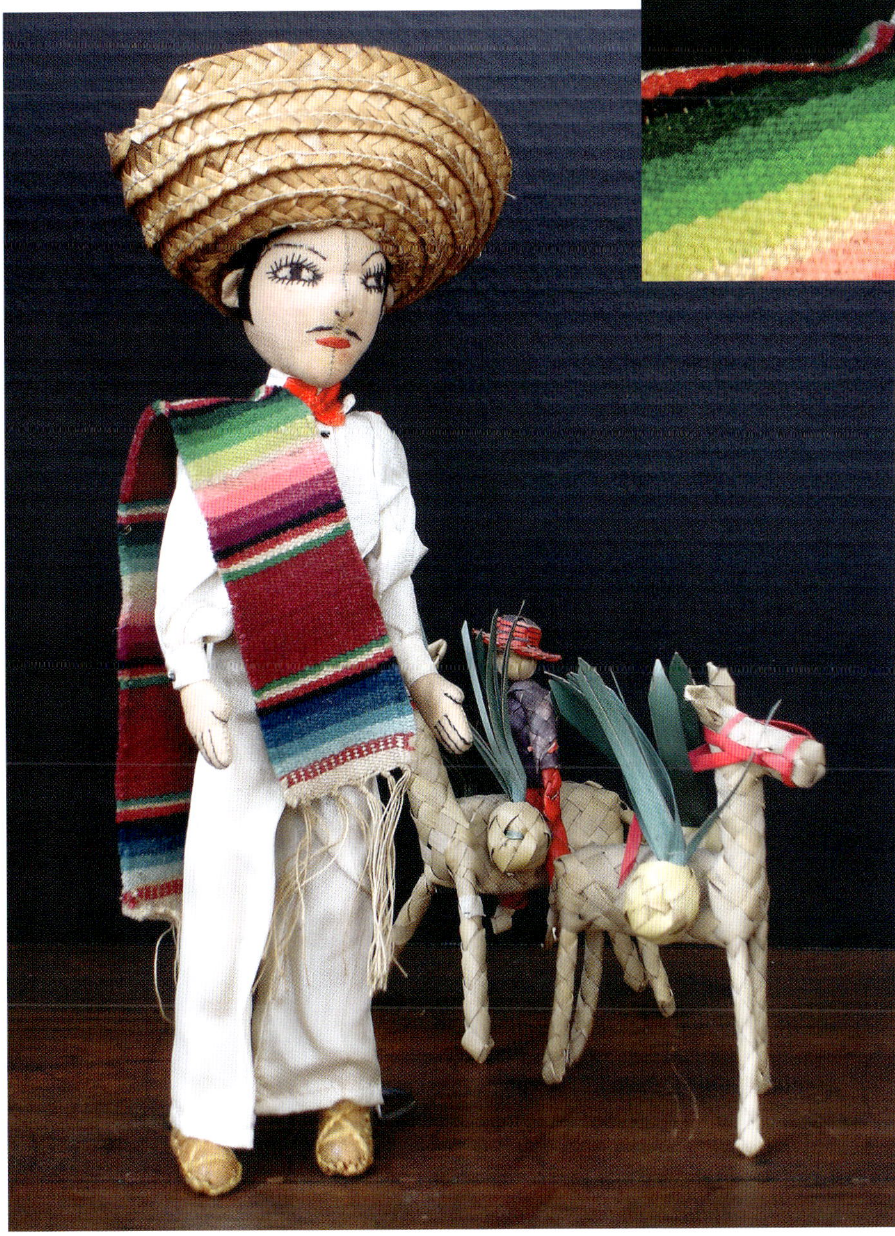

An import, European cloth doll dressed as a Mexican man *mestizo*. Made in Mexico, 13 in. Similar to a Steiff doll, no markings. Stitched facial features, wool *serape*, and large straw woven *sombrero*. $80 to 200

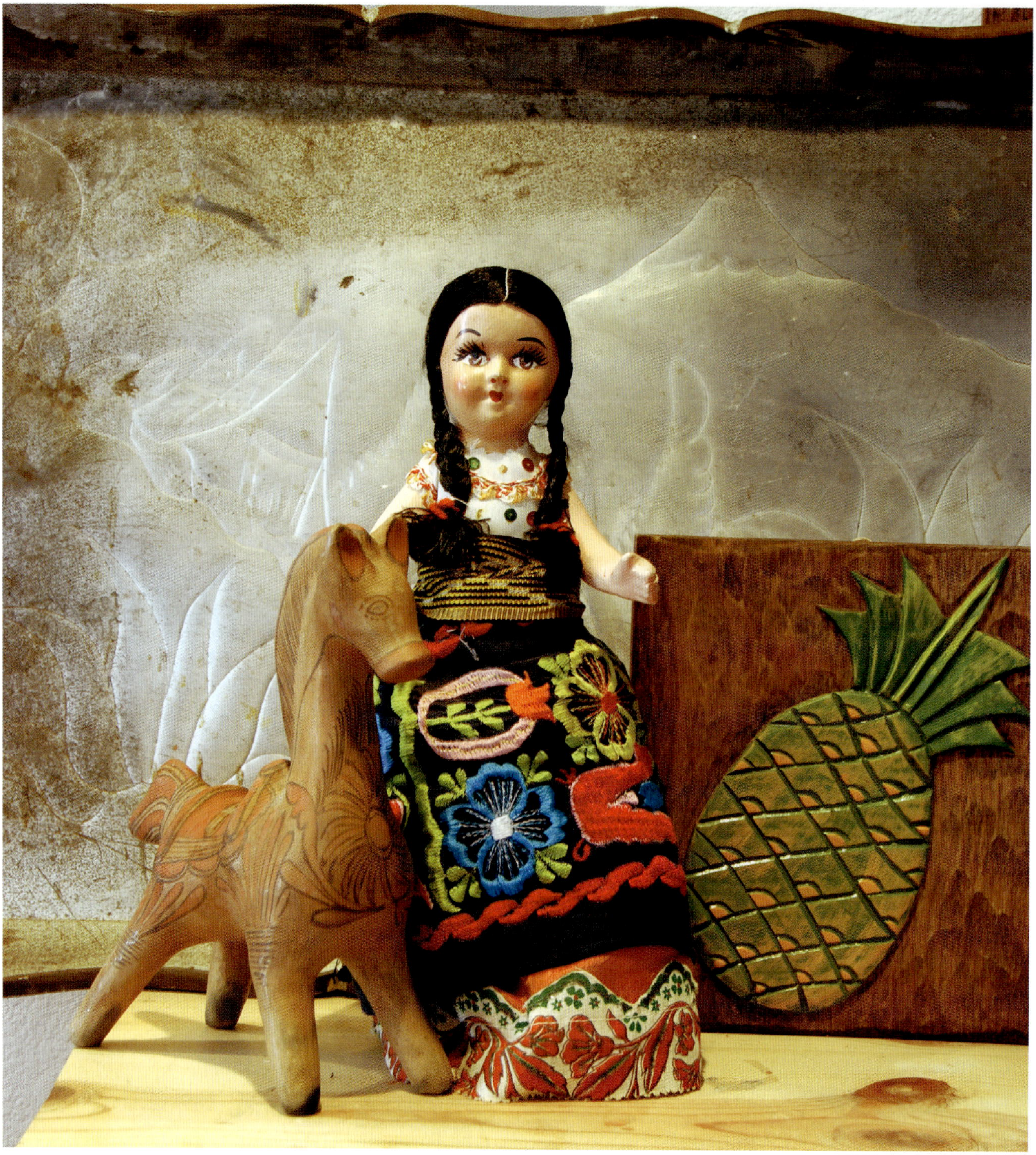

Attributed to the costumes of Guerrero. The skirt's bands of embroidery tell a story on this 14 in. composition doll, c.1950s. Strung with black mohair wig, hand-painted polychrome detail. Shown with an old Mexico, red clay bank, c.1930s. All made in Mexico $100 to 200

Guerrero

A very impressive district of western Mexico is that of Guerrero, a tourist destination for it's silver at Taxco and beautiful beaches at Acapulco. The people are known for their costumes in folkloric dances, such as the *La Chilena*, the dance of the handkerchief, and for sepia and brown terracotta pottery. The designs of their pottery show many of the same influences as well. The urban *mestiza* costumes in the early 20th century were a full skirt with colorful tops and lace; they have a very Spanish colonial look to them. Nestled in the hills is Olinalá, one of the most prized cities and the birthplace of the most important pre-conquest style lacquer ware. Decorative motifs of flowers, animals, and landscapes are applied in a unique process. Fine woven *enredos* and other articles of

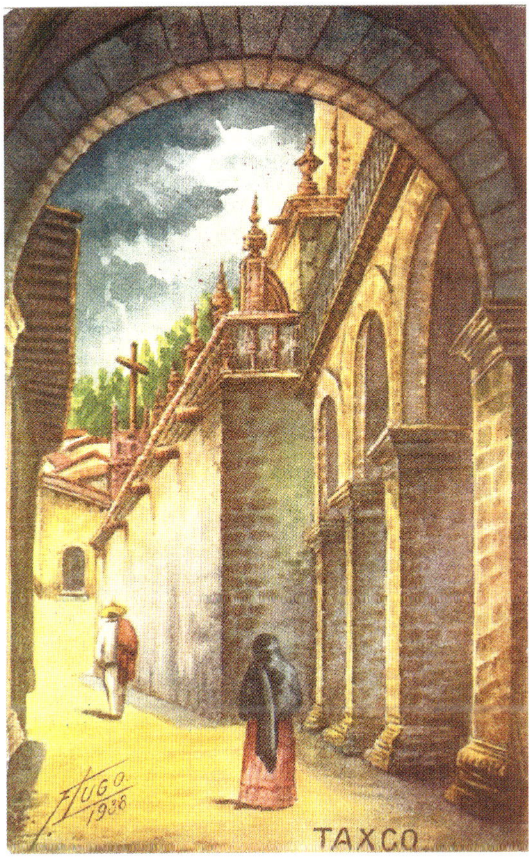

A tinted litho postcard, 5 x 3 in, Taxco Street Scene, colonial Mexico, *HUGO*, 1938, printed in Mexico by Frederico Liebig $15 to 30

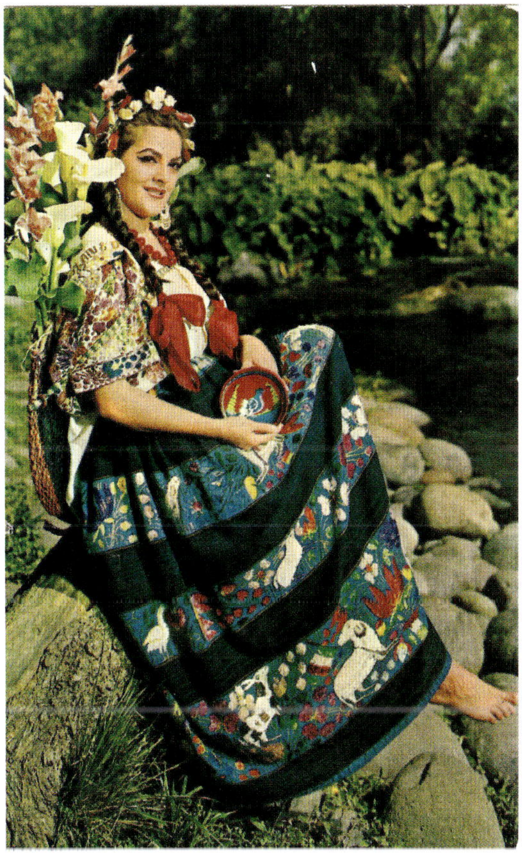

Postcard, color photograph, "Guerrero Woman, Acateca Costume," Cristacolor, Lito Juventud, c.1950, Mexico D. F. 3 x 5 in. $15 to 40

dress are produced with the same integrity as their *olinalá*. Their local tops are bordered with reverse satin-stitch embroidery in vivid detail, as well as their skirts. It is a Nahua town and their traditional *enredo* skirts are famous for the story-telling embroidery, much like that of the *olinalá* lacquer ware. Spectacular bands around the entire skirt incorporate writing into their embroidery designs, with every conceivable creature and flora. It is truly a breathtaking textile and rare to see them in this century.

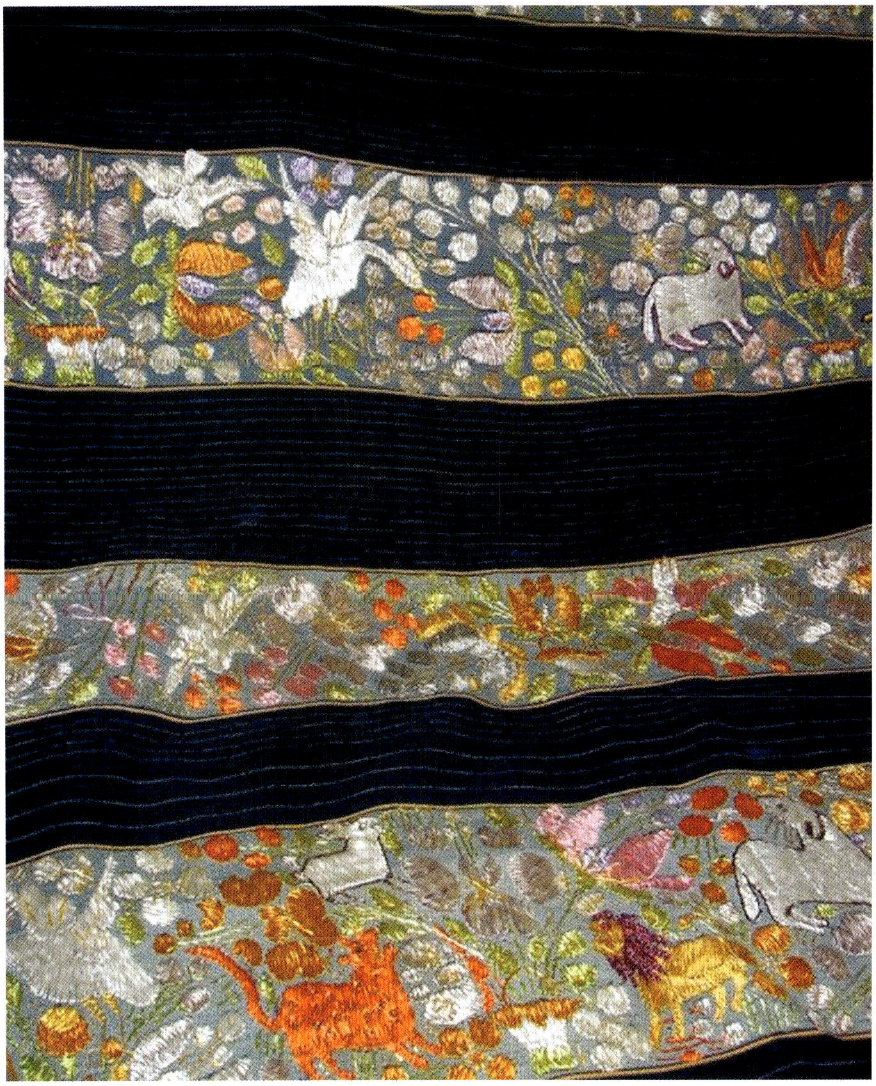

A stunning piece of a section of an *enagua* skirt from the Nahua of Guerrero. Natural dyed indigo blue cotton, with rich embroidery and profuse stitching that creates bands of story telling through their motifs. 80 x 30 *Courtesy of Lydia Delgado Colom*

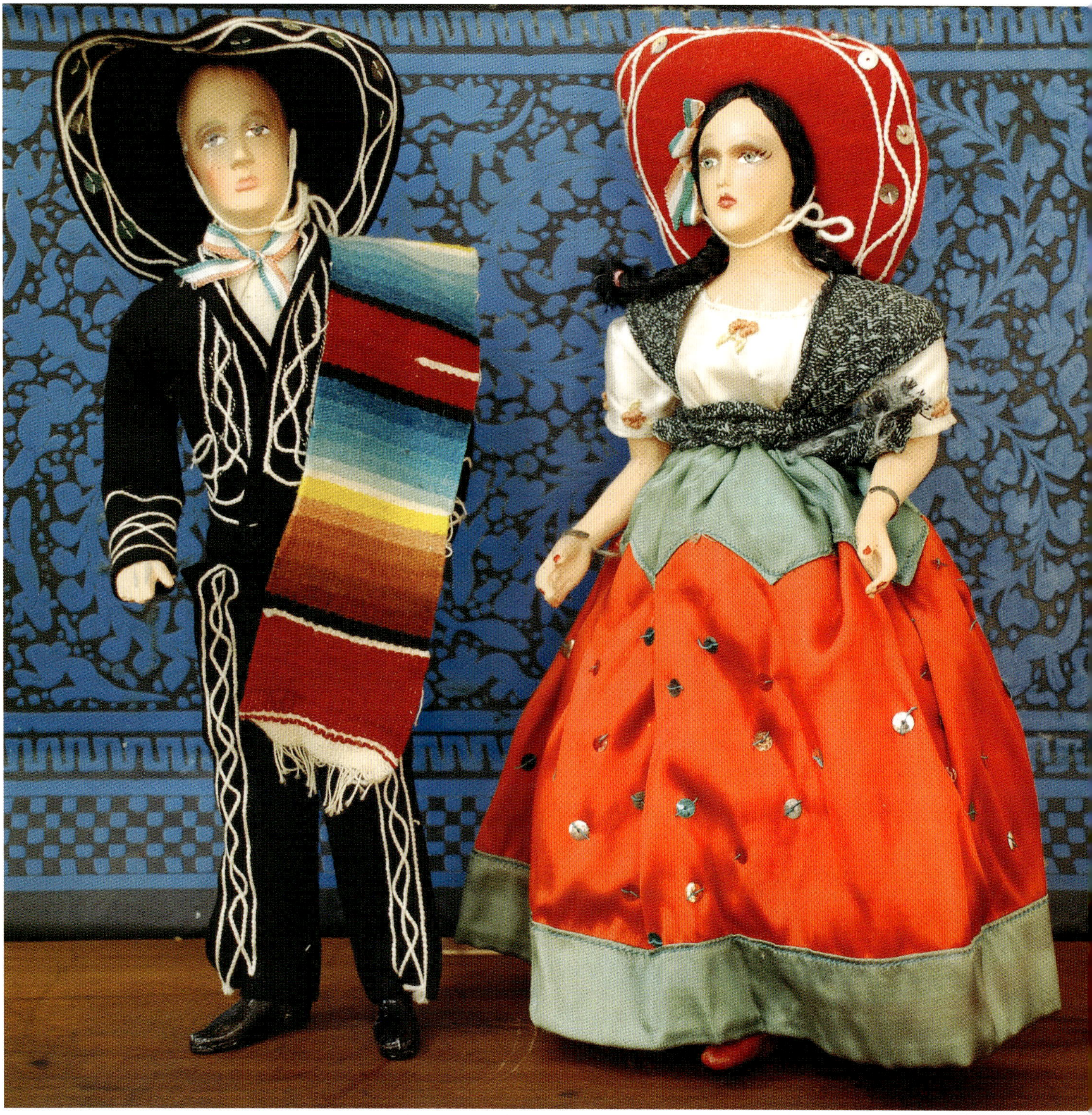

El charro and *la charra*, old Mexico, c.1930s composition dolls. Tourist souvenirs popular in the *curios*. They are 13 in. dressed in authentic clothing of the upper class *mestizos*. Hand-painted detail and clothing. Very well made, jointed arms, solid torso and legs. Spanish style wool suit with elaborate stitching, a large *sombrero* and colorful *serape*. *Charra* with her crossed *rebozo* has beautiful detail and is wearing a full *enagua* skirt like that of the *China Poblana* or *Galareña*. Made in Mexico. $75 to 150 ea.

Jalisco

The state of Jalisco is an important place for Mexico's popular arts, with towns named after distinctive pottery techniques, such as Tonalá and Tlaquepaque . Also, the city of Guadalajara is where many of the large cloth dolls were sold and bought. Notable detail and accuracy was captured in these amazing dolls, authenticating their indigenous clothing and features. These particular dolls truly identify a part of their civilization. The unpretentious clothing the Indian dolls wear portrayed their actual clothing accurately. A flamboyant and festive costume is that of the *adelita* (ad-de-lee-ta). The name of this costume is adapted from the legend of a *soldadera,* the Mexican woman soldier during the time of the Mexican Revolution. The *adelita*'s dress is a popular costume worn in the folkloric Mexican dances and also in their *Escaramuza* event, in which eight women show their horse showmanship while riding sidesaddles during a special Mexican event known as the *Charrería.* They wear a wide-ruffled dress, tight at the bodice and waist, with tight long sleeves or puffed in the upper part; the skirt is circular to have movement and the length reaches the calf. White or bold solid colors are accented with underskirts also with ruffles and pantaloons. They usually wear their hair pulled back with a bow of ribbon trimmed with flowers. Sometimes the performers may wear a felt *sombrero.* A *rebozo* is worn over her shoulders, or crossed if walking on foot, or around the waist when riding, next to the sash of the dress. This dress is a common costume for 20th century Mexican *mestiza* women and you see them frequently as part of all Mexican festivities.

A picturesque costume for both the male as well as the female is the *traje de charro* and *charra.* The *charro* costume is now primarily a part of Mexican exhibitions known as the *charreria* and the *charreda,* two very important shows that demonstrate traditional forms of Mexican horsemanship. This costume has also been associated with the flamboyant *Mariachi*s, the acclaimed Mexican musical groups. Worn in their performances, it was an ideal costume because of its pretentious appearance. The *charro* men's costume is an interpretation of a Spanish suit or military uniform. The suit is made of cotton, wool, or leather embellished with no limitations. It was the clothing of the important and the wealthy men, the urban *mestizos* or *haciendados.* They wore this fine suit around town and while riding their horses. It was made of the best cloth ornamented with *plateados* (silver) buttoning along the legs and or on the cropped jacket. A white cotton shirt was open at the neck to show a tie that was his *moño,* a cravat made of silk or rayon

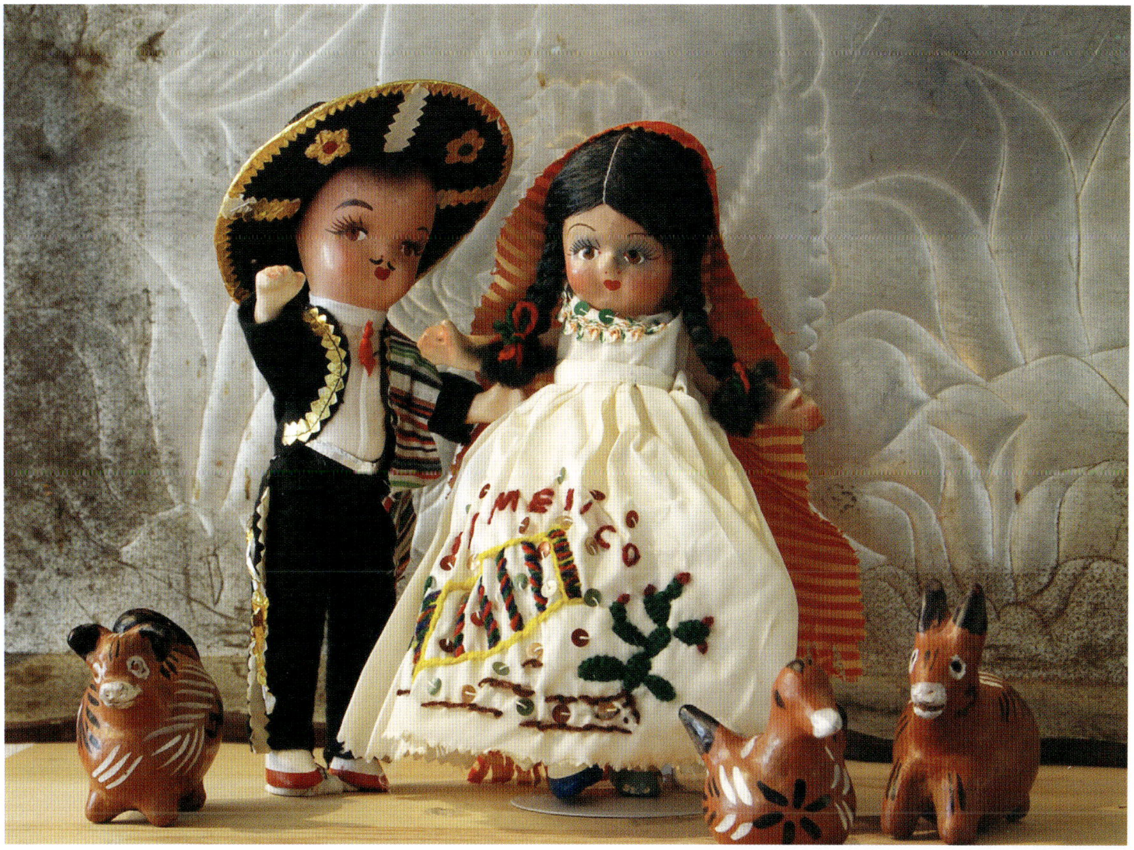

A *mestizo* couple from Jalisco, 11 in. composition dolls c.1940s, Mexico. Dressed as a *charro* and *la Señorita* in her stunning white skirt. Beautifully embroidered, surrounded by miniature animal pottery banks. $80 to 125

and usually red in color. A broad-rimmed *sombrero* with a high crown, pinched and banded, was ornamented with silver thread cording. His pants are close-fitting, custom made of the same cloth as the jacket; they are bordered with a one-inch flap on the sides studded with *plateados.* The crotch of his trousers is wider and accommodates him comfortably while riding his horse. Sometimes he will wear *chaparreras*, leather chaps that cover the trousers. His shoes are leather boots with iron and silver spurs. The *charro* costumes represented nobility and an elite social class. It has been declared that the *charro's* merit of valor is what enabled him to wear this costume, not his wealth.

The *charra* woman accompanies the *charro* in these exhibitions and will wear her own stunning suit. Her jacket is almost identical, but shorter, like that of a Spanish *bolero*. She will also wear a white top that may be finished with lace and her *moño* around her neck. Instead of pants, she wears a long skirt with ornamental borders and finishes. Her hair is tied tightly in a ponytail or braids, with a large, elaborate sombrero custom-made for her. She is impressive and demonstrates a strong presence for the serious Mexican horsewoman.

Jalisco is also the home of Huichol Indians, a highly religious tribe. They are dedicated to their indigenous costume and gratefully they have managed to sustain their way of life to some degree. You can find the Huichol tribes in other regions of Mexico, such a Nayarit. The Huichol men's clothing has the most colorful decorative costume of all of the Mexican Indian men. They wear wide cropped, cotton trousers finished with cross-stitch embroidery and a loose, open-sided shirt with colorful wool sashes and numerous small multi-colored wool bags in various sizes and motifs. They also will wear a colored embroidered cape and will paint their faces during fiestas. The designs on their garments are instrumental to their beliefs and stem from nature. The men's hats are low and ornamented with colorful bands of wool or feathers. The Huichol women's costume consists of a gathered embroidered skirt, a short white long-sleeved *manta* top, and a large *quechquémitl* cape. Necklaces of shells, sandals, and beaded earrings are just a few of their many accessories. Their pieces of *manta* are hand-sewn together and embellished with mystic and symbolic motifs in colorful, intricate patterns. The contrast of embroidered colored motifs against the white cloth highlights the beauty of their garments.

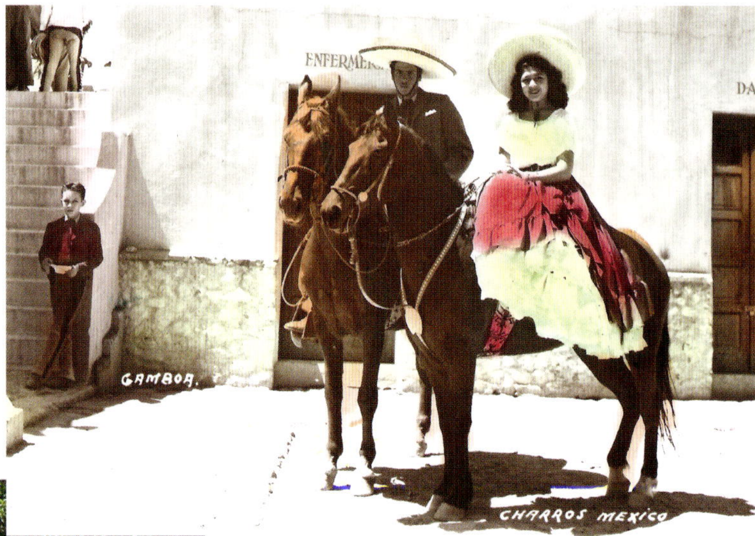

Postcard, color photograph, "Charros " on their *caballos* (horses). A *mestizo* couple dressed in traditional clothing of the period, c.1930s, Mexico D. F. 4 x 5 in. $15 to 40

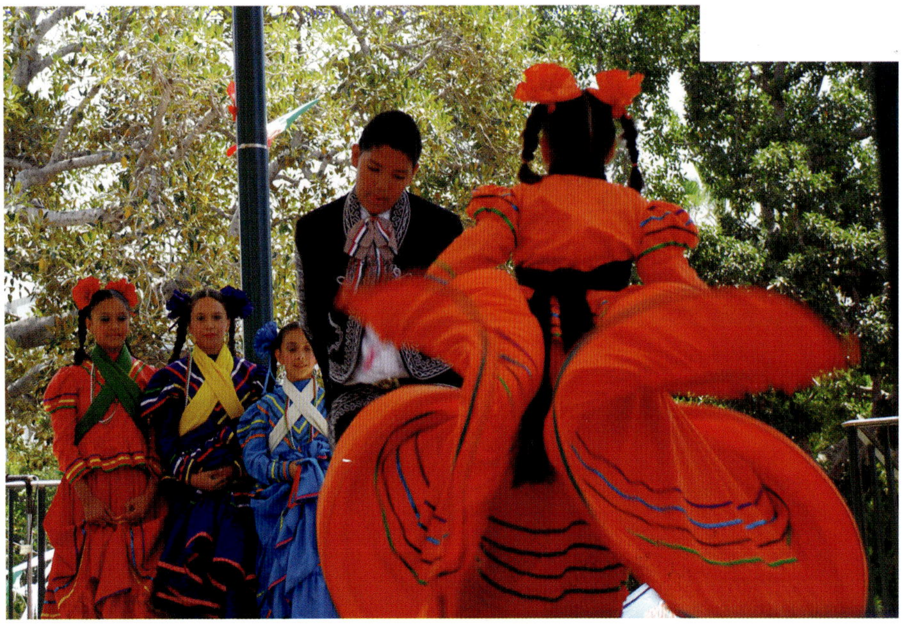

Cinco de Mayo Folorico, "The Mexican Hat Dance," 2007, on Olvera Street in Los Angeles, an *Adelita* dancing with her *charro*. Layers of vibrant colored material creates this flamboyant woman's costume of the *Adelita*.

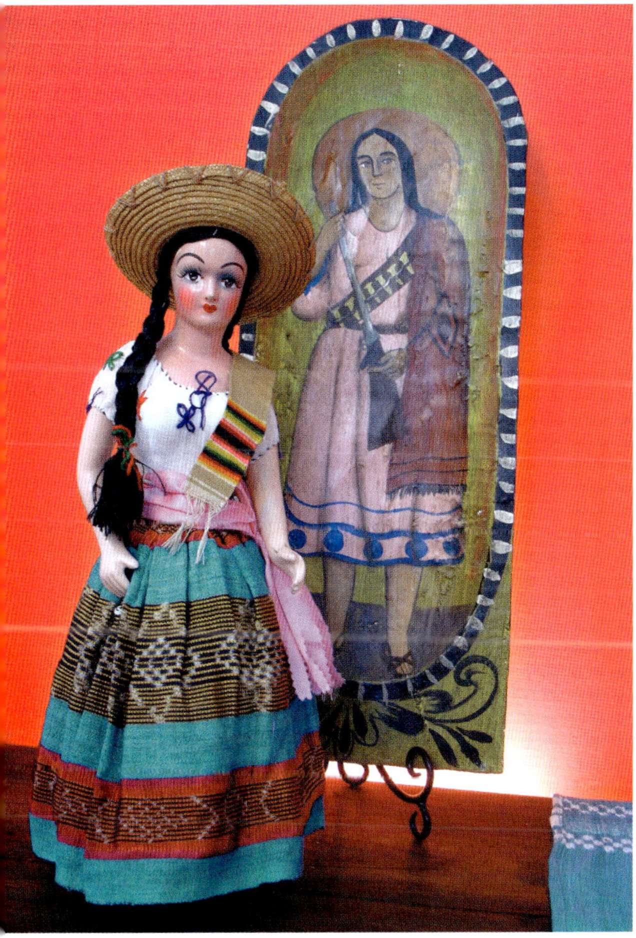

Attributed to the "*La Soldadera*," the women of the Revolution, c.1950s. A 17 in. Mexican composition paste doll. Her head, arms and legs are composition with a cloth stuffed body. She is joined together by hooks. Dressed in a long woven cotton skirt in teal, red, black and gold threads. She wears a white Spanish peasant blouse and sash, with a *serape* and *sombrero*. Next to a hand painted folk art piece on an original antique Mexican *batea* bowl. Made in Mexico, artist unknown. $125 to 350

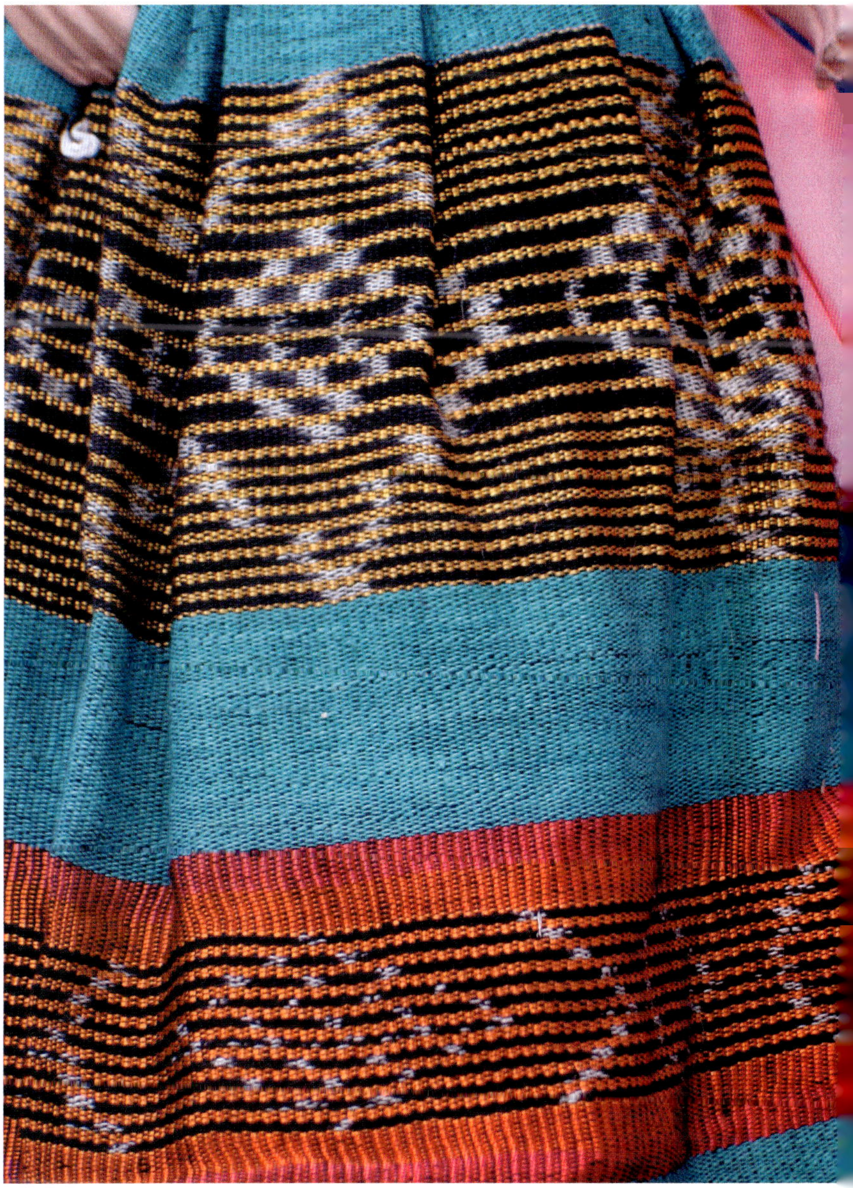

This beautiful colorful pattern on the skirt is repeated throughout the weave and in excellent condition. A cotton and rayon weave in teal, red, black, and gold threads. Made in Mexico.

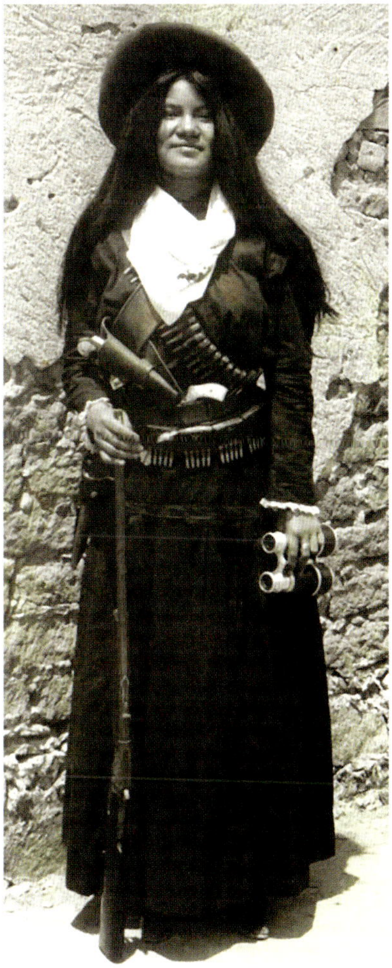

A picture postcard of a *Soldadera* from the Mexican revolution $10 to 30

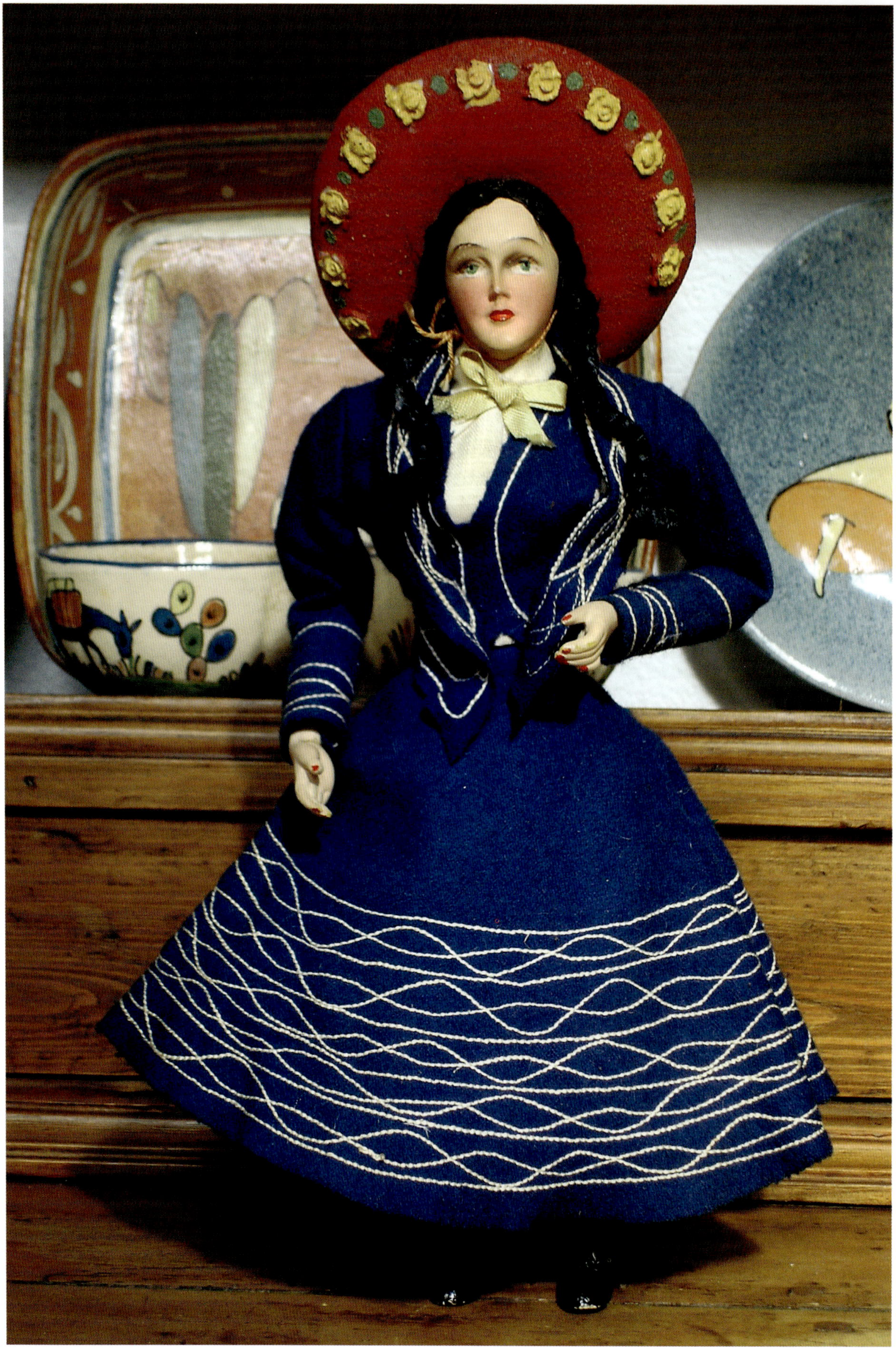

A 14 in. *charra* composition doll, maybe early Poveda, dressed in an indigo wool *charra* woman's wool suit and a polychrome compo *sombrero*. The *greca* soutash roping around her *bolero* style jacket is an authentic trim still used today. Trimmed with embroidered detail and painted features. $75 to 150

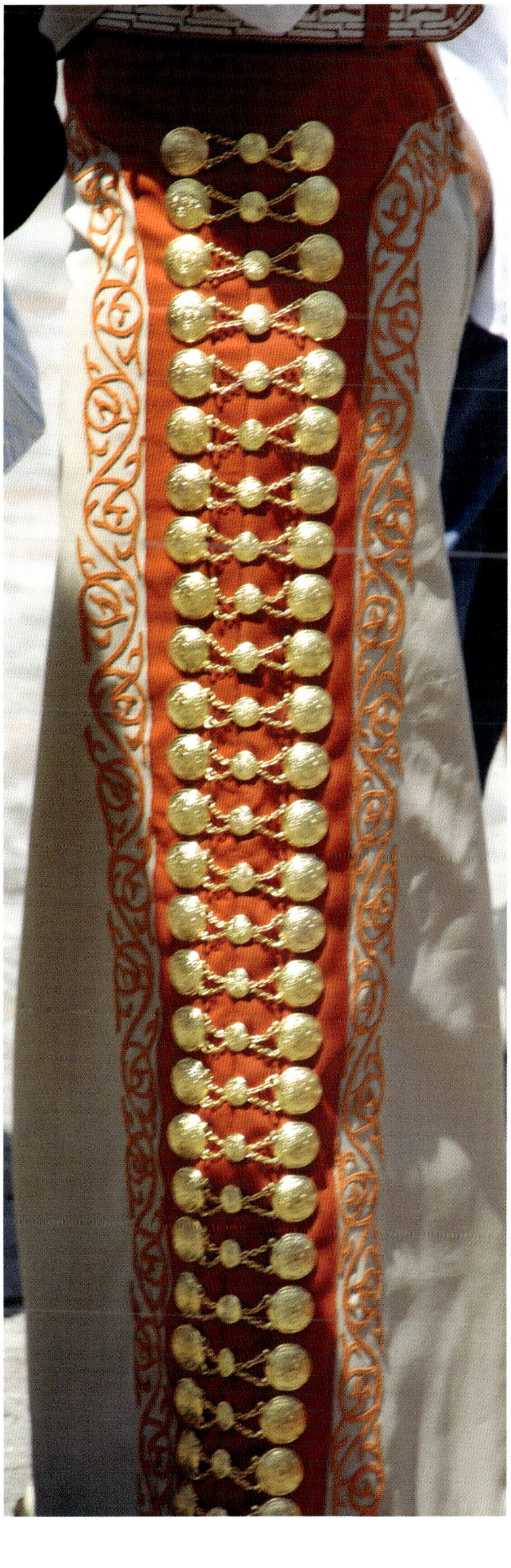

Cinco de Mayo, 2007, on Olvera Street in Los Angeles, a close-up of the *charra* folklorica costume. The side of her skirt is embellished with hundreds of gold buttons and *greca* embroidery by machine.

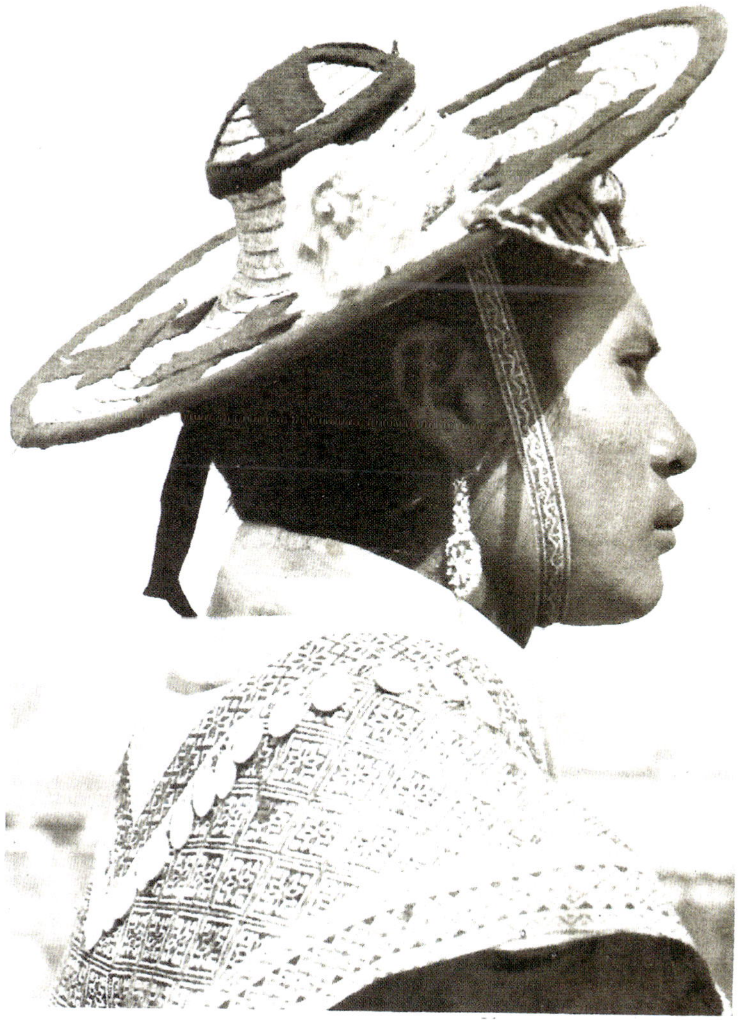

A Huichol Indian with strong indigenous features and authentic clothing, c.1934.

Michoacán

The *Michoacános* has a large *mestiza* society with a grounded, pre-Hispanic civilization. It is a Mexican state with one of the most desirable weather conditions, situated on the central western pacific coastal region of Mexico, with *Jalisco* to its north. *Michoacán* is the home of the *Tarascan* or the *Puerpécha* indigenous Indian groups. The beautiful *Tarascan* women wear long black or indigo striped skirts, sometimes with frilly aprons and dark striped *rebozos*. Their long braids are tied off with bows and they wear white or colored *huipils* tops. They have always produced high quality, hand-embroidered fabrics and are known for their rich and distinctive patterns with colorful dyed cottons woven in a multitude of designs. The regional woolen skirts are in dark colors gathered in folds at the back. One of the most popular pre-Columbian dances is the *La Danza de los Viejitos*, dance of the old men. A mask and cane dance, it is commonly done by the men wearing the *moral* bag and a *sombrero* with colorful strands of ribbons. The *mestiza* woman wears beautiful embroidered blouses, usually white with a squared or rounded peasant neckline. Their full skirt is gathered like those of the *zagalejo*, in dark solid colors, stripes, banded colors and embroidery. They always wear their beautiful *rebozos* that are spectacular in design and quality. Jewelry and beautiful lace is often part of their ensemble.

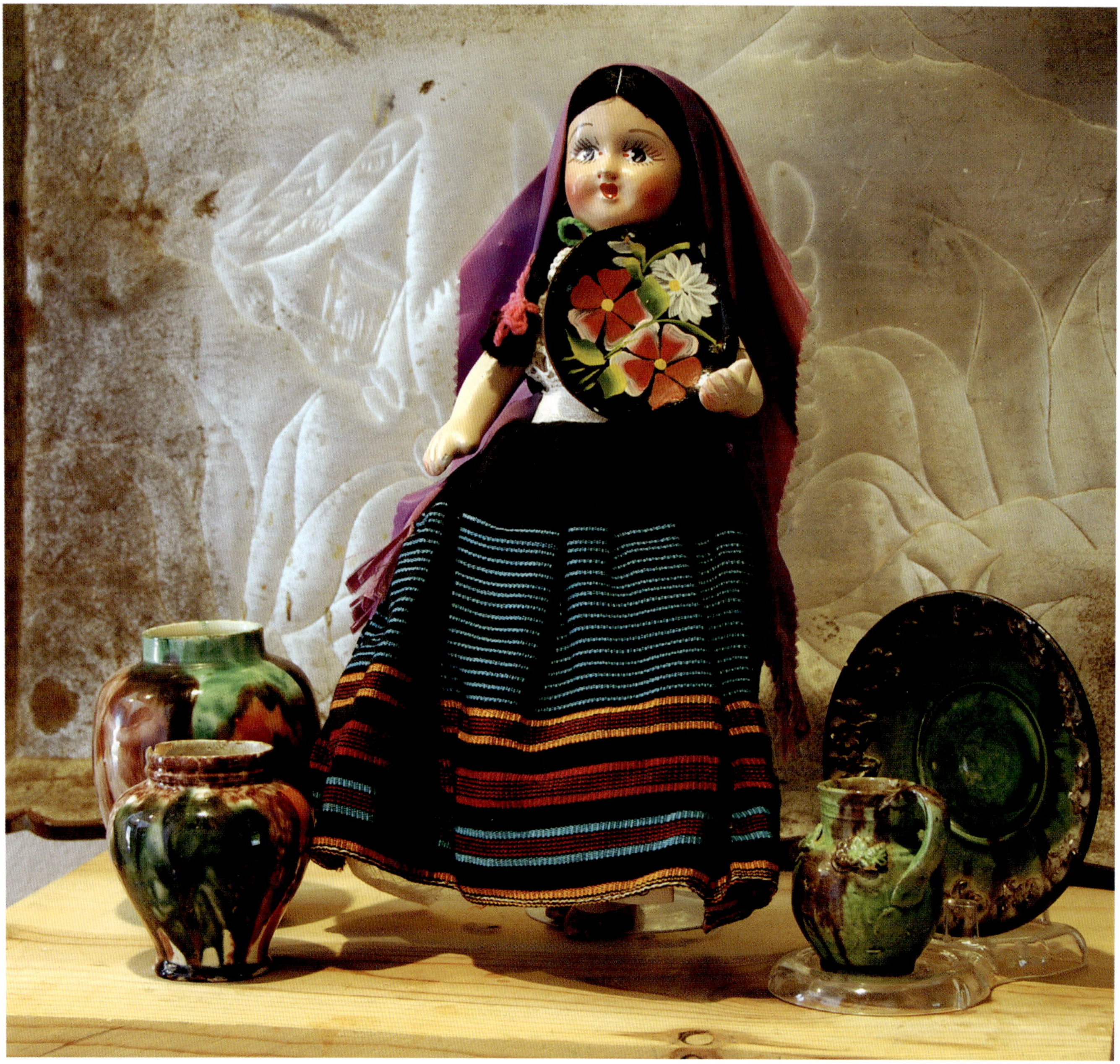

A 14 in., solid composition doll from the district of Michoacán, c.1940s. She is holding a *batea* platter and surrounded by tourist miniature popular drip ware. Made in Mexico $125 to 200

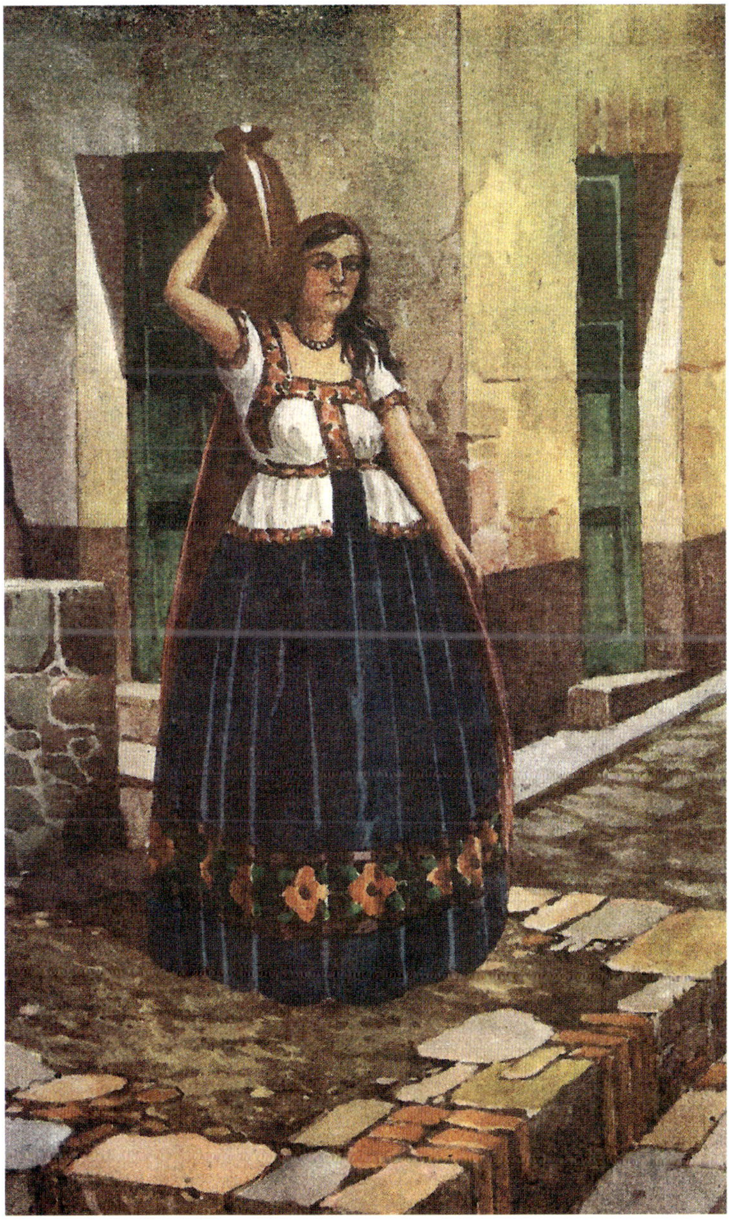

Postcard, color photograph, "Michoacána " walking through the streets. She carries a large *olla* on her shoulder, stamped c.1943, Mexico D. F. 4 x 5 in. $15 to 40

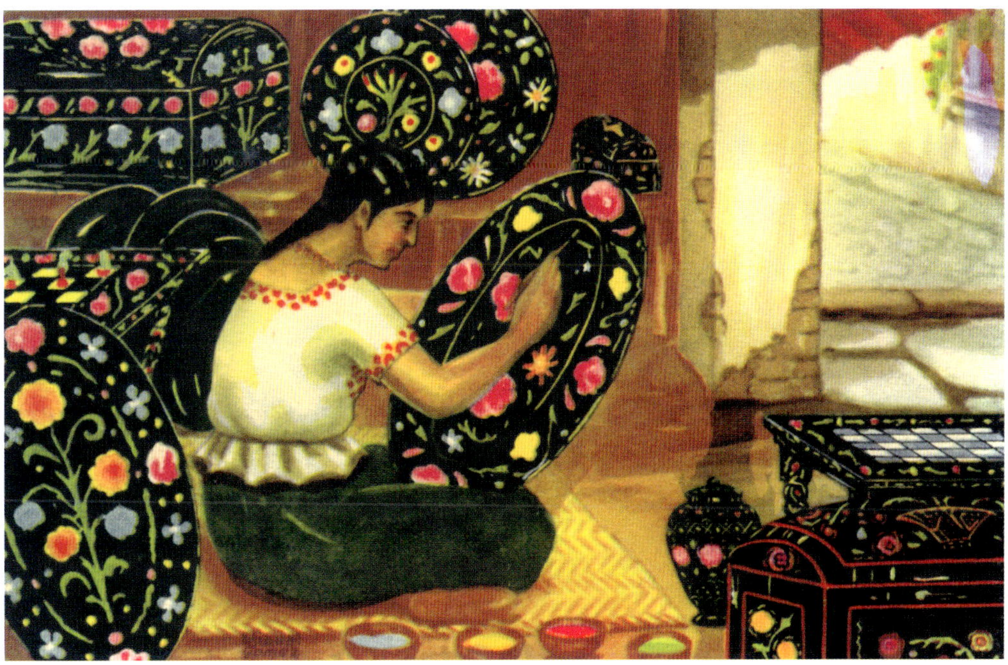

Postcard, Uruapan Laquer, Made by Fishgrund, Apartado Mexico D. F. 4 x 5 in. $15 to 40

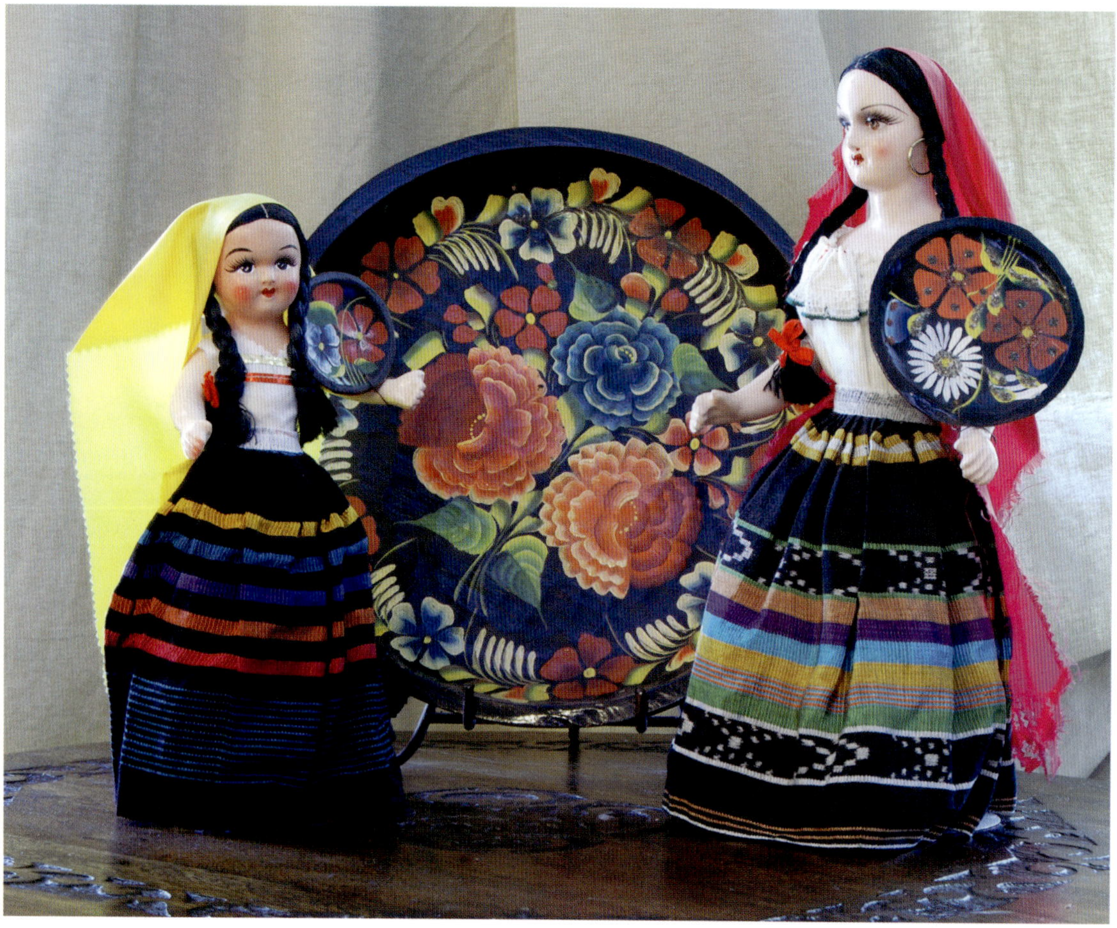

Two *Michoacán* dressed composition dolls holding *batea* platters, made in Mexico, 17 in. and 14 in. A large *batea olinala* platter centered. $100 to 325ea

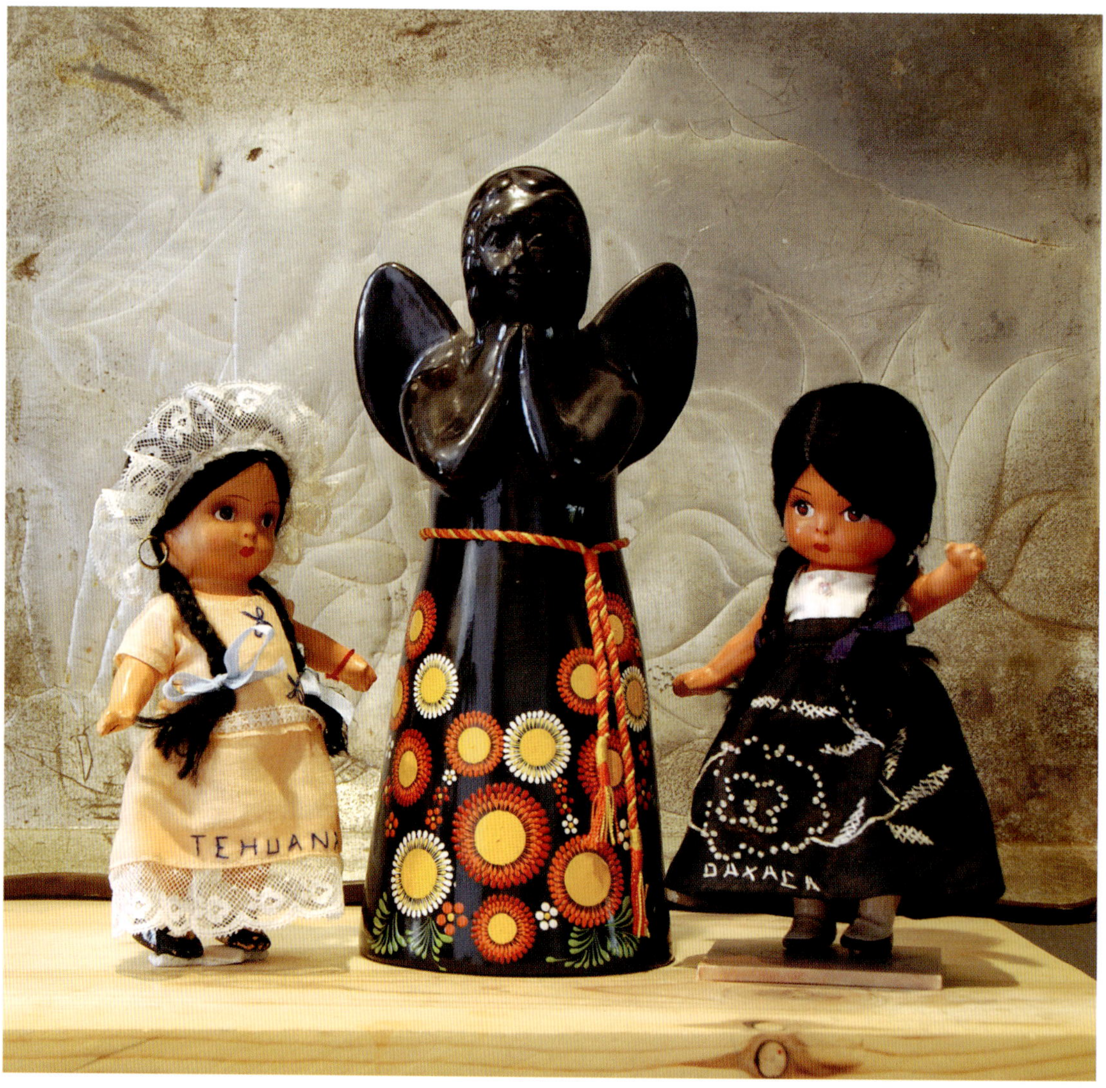

A Oaxacan scene of two popular 9 in. compo dolls from Oaxaca, c.1940s. Made in Mexico, black pottery angel. Stamped and signed. $75 to 100 ea.

Oaxaca

One of Mexico's prized cities, with ideal weather, a rich history, culture, and with more than seventy different regional costumes is Oaxaca. It is home to the *zapotec* and *mixteca* people, with folk art recognized globally and their beautiful costumes. Their celebrated *Guelaguetza* fiesta, also known as *Lunes del Cerro* (Mondays on the hill), is a pre-Hispanic celebration that is enjoyed by Mexicans and foreigners alike. It is a wonderful fiesta at which you can enjoy a parade of many beautiful Mexican costumes.

Oaxaca is also the home of the *Tacuates* and those from the northern forest regions, like that of the *Chinanteca* from the region of *La Chinantla*. The *huipil* of the *Chinanteca* is beautiful in vibrant reds, and is profusely embroidered. Oaxaca and Veracruz are *Chinanteca* towns where the climate is hot and humid. A number of springs and rivers are nearby. In the state of Oaxaca you can truly admire the *zapotecan* women's regional costumes, especially from the region *Isthmus of Tehuantepec* and that of the *Zandunga*. The *Tehuantepec* women, known as *Tehuanas*, are recognized for their picturesque embroidered costumes. Their clothing is bright and colorful and the costume of choice for the *mestiza* woman; it also is worn in other urban cities. The *Tehuana* wears a spectacular wide gathered skirt that is often woven with plentiful, large, satin-stitched embroidery and bordered with a wide, white flounce bellowed with lace at the bottom. Her waist-length *huipil* is made of colored satin, velvet, or other fine cloth embroidered with vibrant flowers. The women wear rich accents of gold jewelry and colored ribbons in their hair. The *Tehuanas* also wear a spectacular headpiece, known as the *resplandor*. It is traditionally worn to church and also during the festivals. Sometimes the headpiece is referred to as a *huipil*, but in fact it is just a wide piece of white bellowed cloth or lace that resembles a short petticoat, with a halo-affect form. It is an absolutely stunning costume with variations of rich colors and fabrics. One of their stately dances is the *Zandunga*. It is a slow dance and great emphasis is on the costumes. They are gorgeous, velvet-embroidered tops with the pleated, bellowed, organdy and lace headpiece and borders. Each of them is different, and together they are like watching a moving garden.

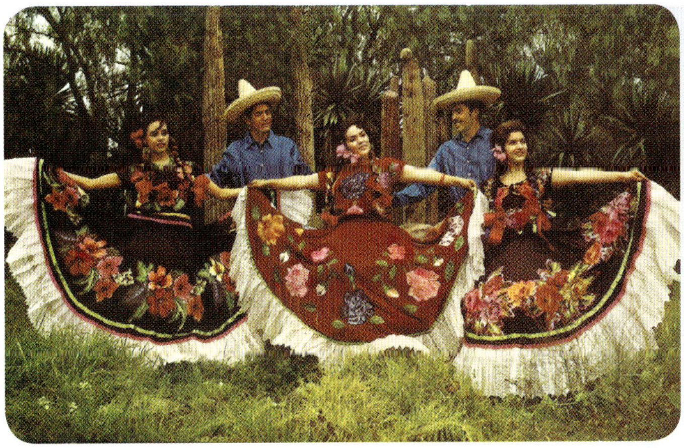

Color Picture Postcard, Tarjeta Postal, "Folklore dance of *Tehuana* from the Isthmus of Tehuantepec" long colorful skirts and flowered *huipils* with elaborate lace borders. Cristacolor, Lito Juventud, c.1950s, Mexico D. F. 4 x 5 in. $15 to 40

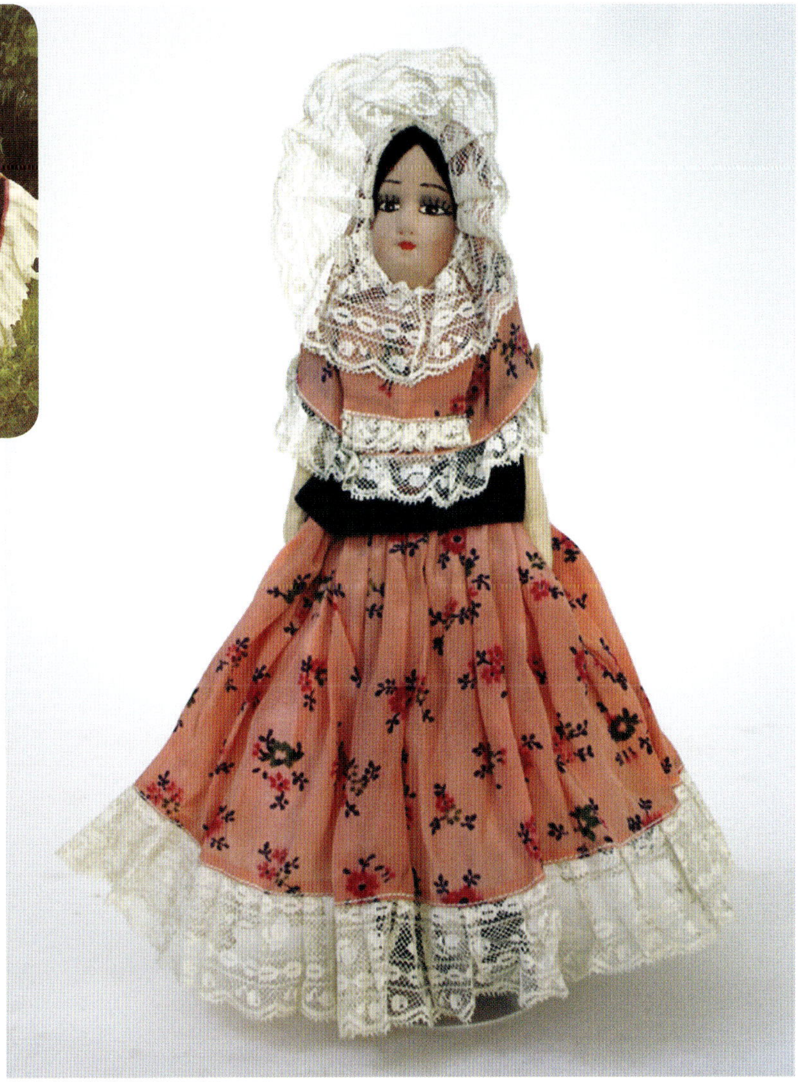

Attributed to the *Tehuana* costume, a 12 in. cloth doll "Christina," molded pressed felt face over papier maché, all hand made. Made in Mexico, c. 1930s. She is a mestiza dress for church as a Tehuana. A silk calico pink print with beautiful sugar lace borders her full skirt and her *resplandor* around her face. She is wearing a black *huipil* and a petticoat underneath her skirt. Her hair is wool braids, her body is hard stuffed with cotton or soft scraps. In excellent condition. $75-150

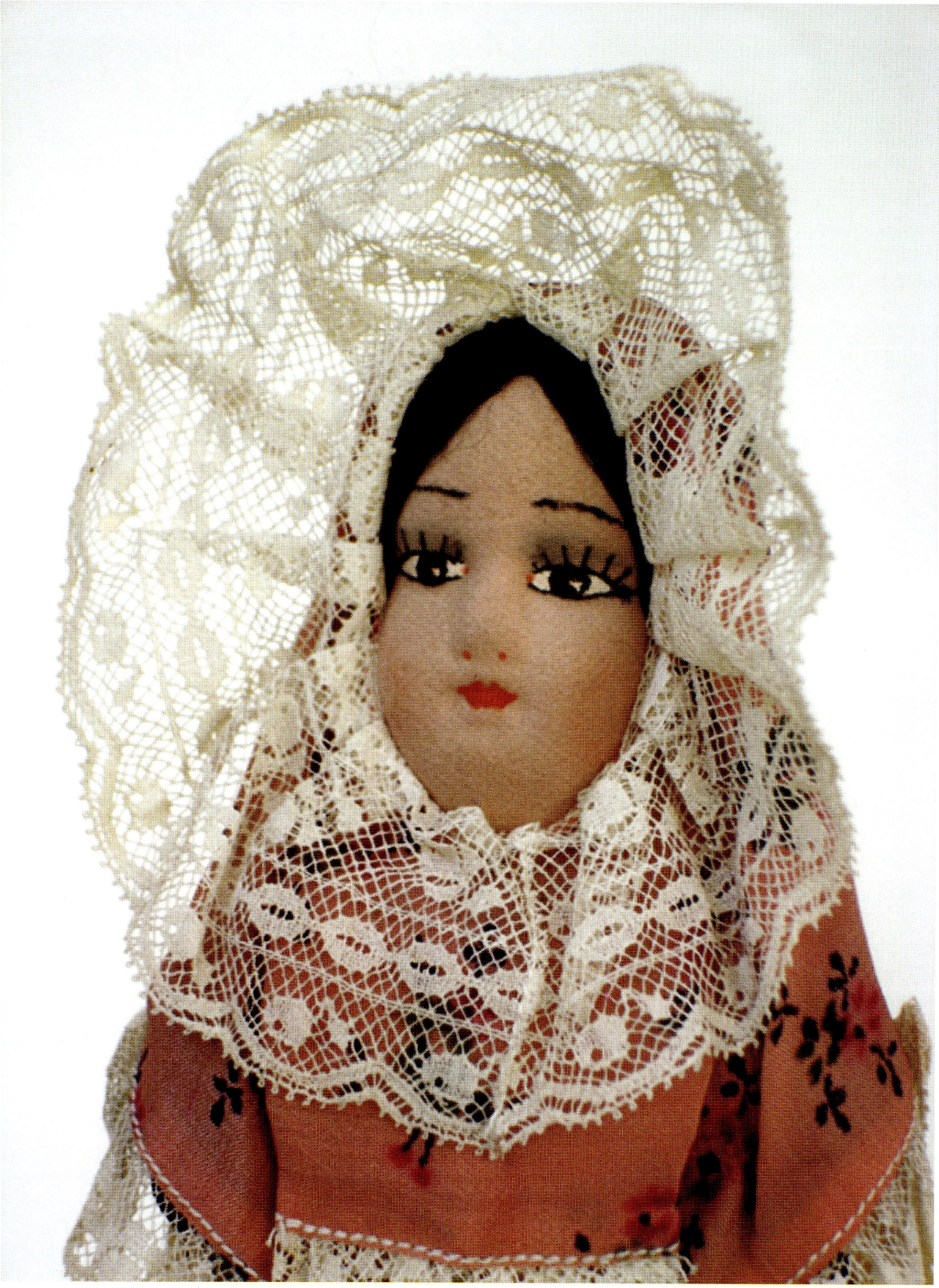

Christina's beautiful face shows careful painting and soft molding. Her *resplandor* hugs her face. $75-150

The back of her dress is carefully rendered, just as beautiful as the front. She is finished with professional touches by an accomplished folk artist.

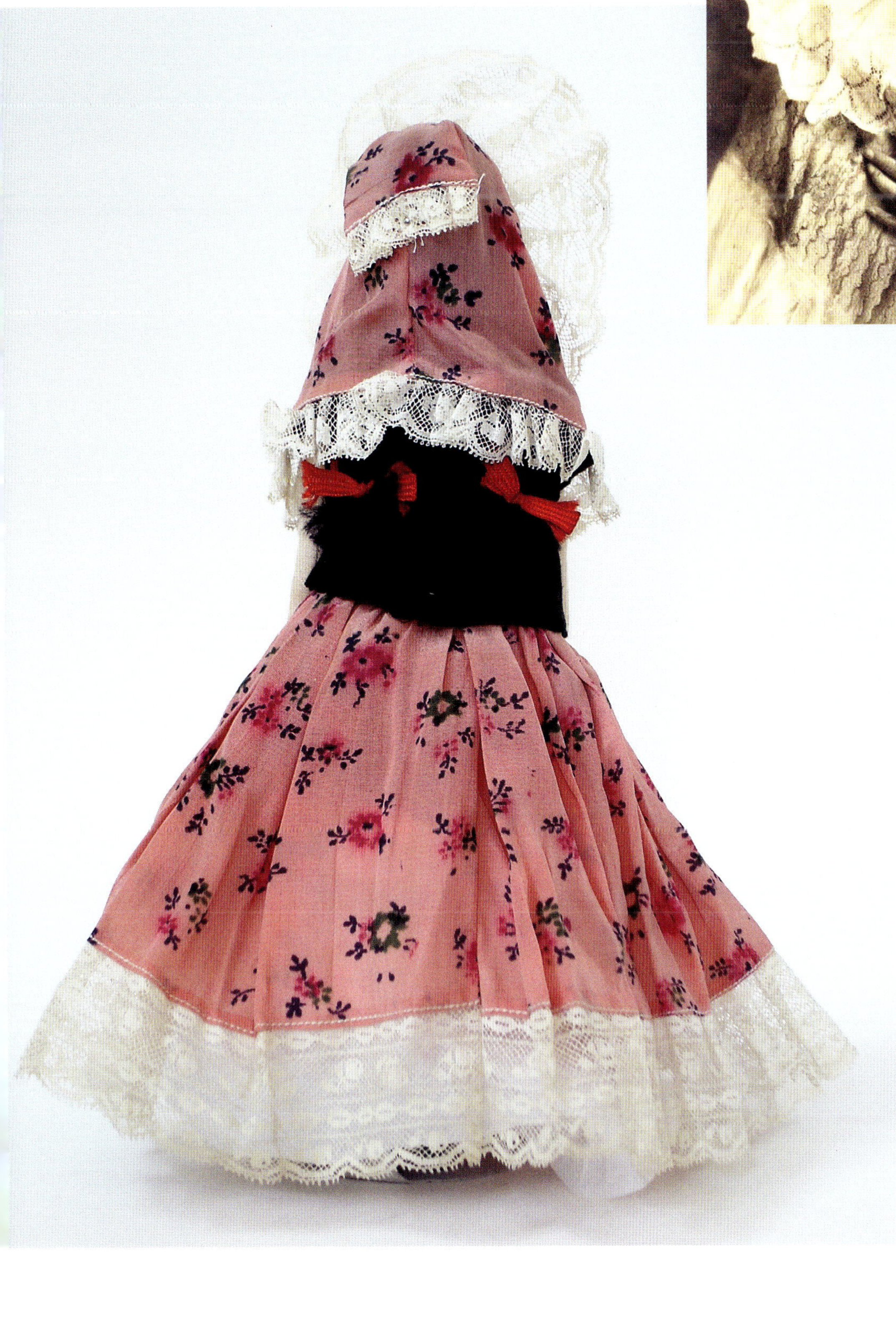

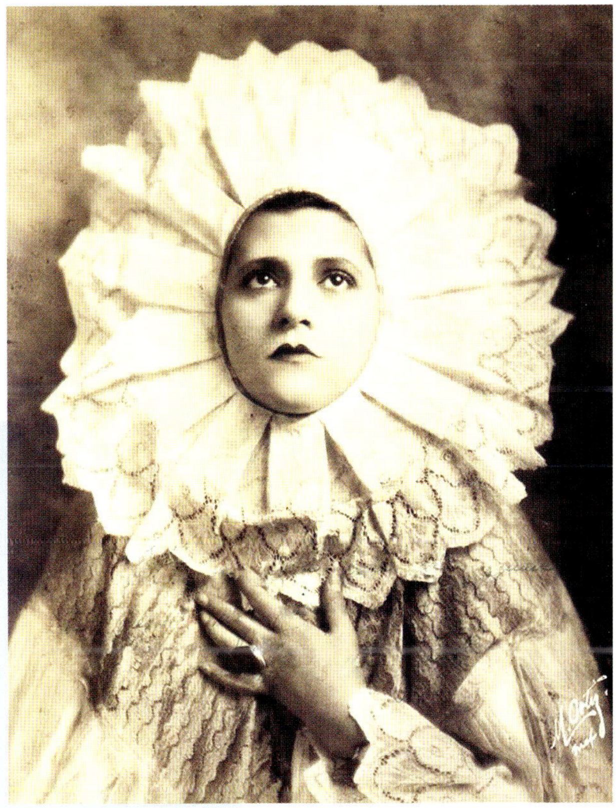

An original sepia photograph of a *Tehuana* woman wearing a cotton linen headpiece, the *resplandor*. Mexico, 20th c. *Private collection of Lydia Colom Delgado*

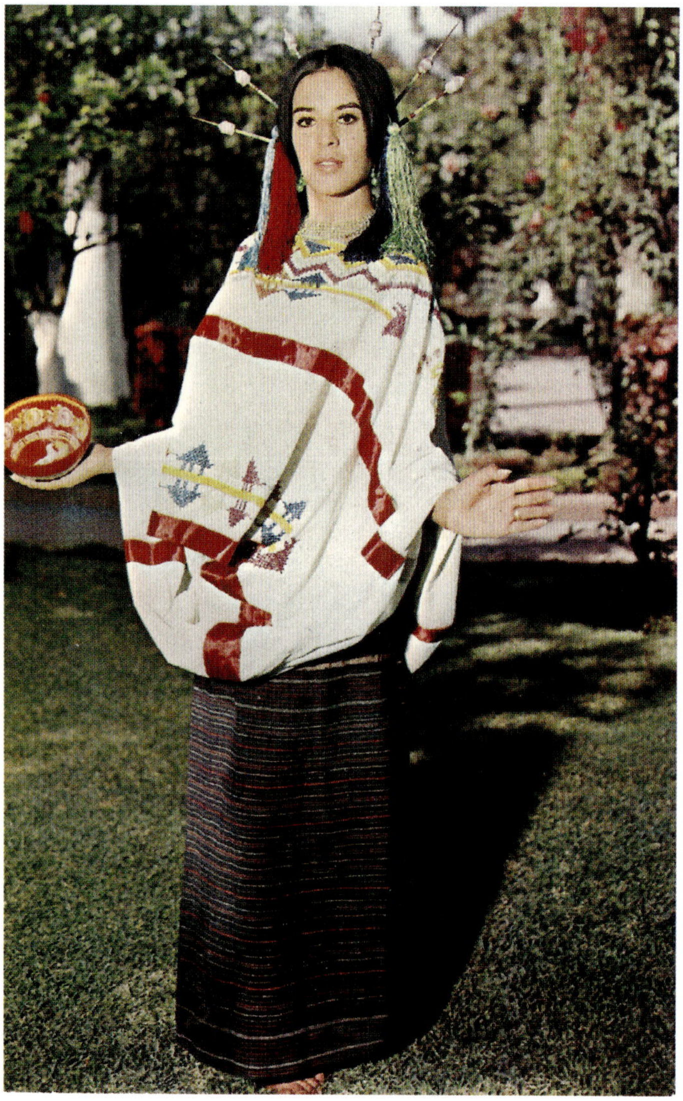

Color postcard photograph, "Tacuate from Oaxaca " long *huipil* with horizontal ribbons and a *enredo* skirt, an indigenous costume of that region. Cristacolor, Lito Juventud, c.1950 Mexico D. F. 4 x 5 in. $15 to 40

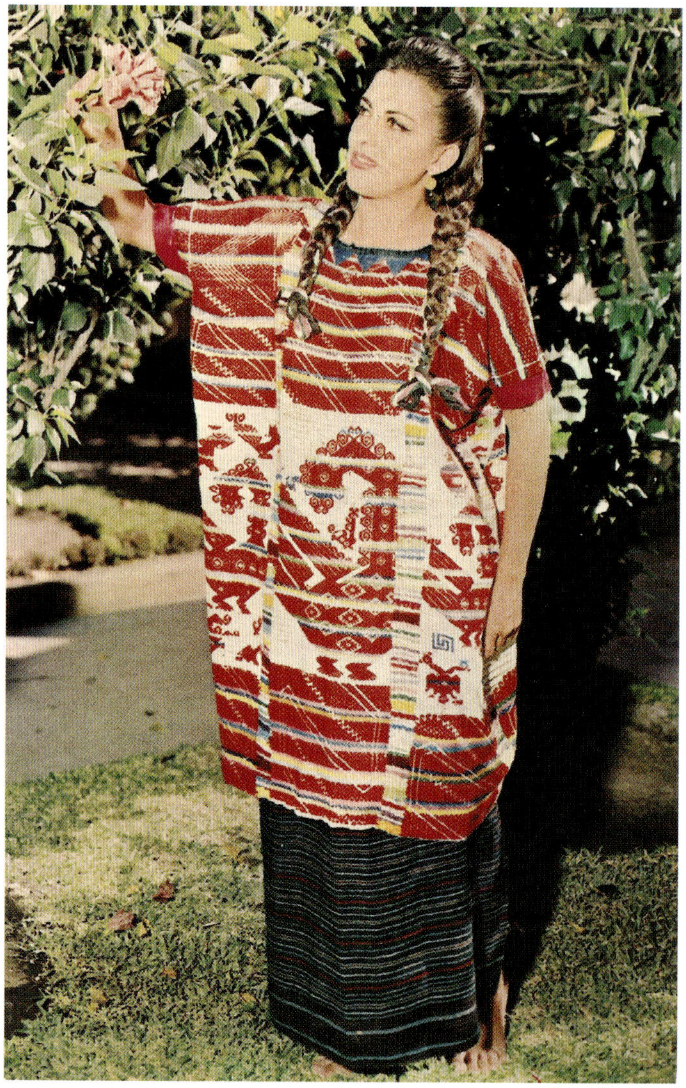

Color postcard photograph, "Chinanteca Indian from Oaxaca," long *huipil* with horizontal dark weave *enredo* skirt. Cristacolor, Lito Juventud, c.1950, Mexico D. F. 4 x 5 in. $15 to 40

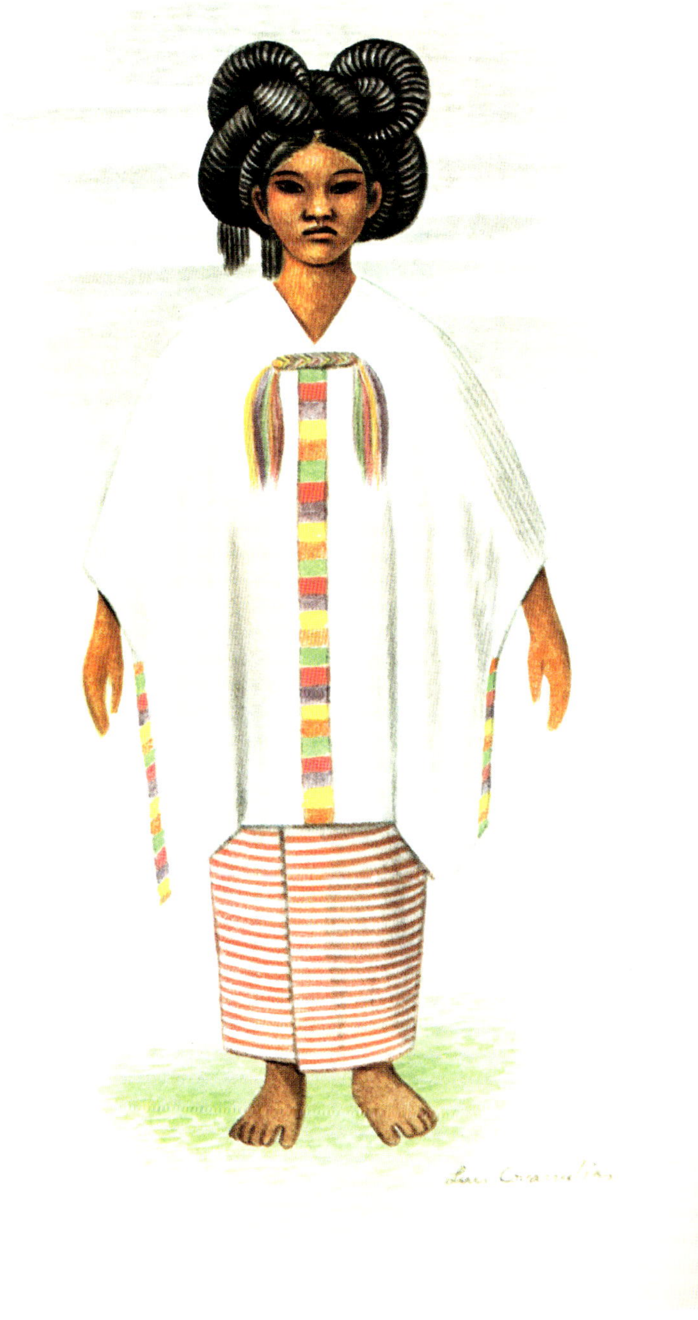

A color chrome reproduction print, c.1940s. From the Mexican Native Costumes booklet, the *Yalalteca*. By Louis Covarrubias, Editor of Modern Art, Fischgrund, Mexico D. F.

In the highlands of *Oaxaca* lies the village of the *Yalalteca* Indians. *Yalalag* sits on the south-western region of *Oaxaca,* and characteristically the Indians still wear modified pre-Hispanic costumes. The traditional clothing of the women is a long white woven *huipil* adorned with a horizontal braid made of unraveled fringed tassels centered below the neckline, at the front and the back. They wear the tightly wrapped *enredo* skirt, that is usually white or with horizontal stripes in orange or brown. Their hair is worn in the form of a turban, twisted into coils and interwoven with black yarn or braided to the back. The men wear the traditional white *manta* clothing, known as the *calzóne blanco*. It is a white full shirt and white pants, that may wrap and tie at the front. It is often accented with a red or other colored sash.

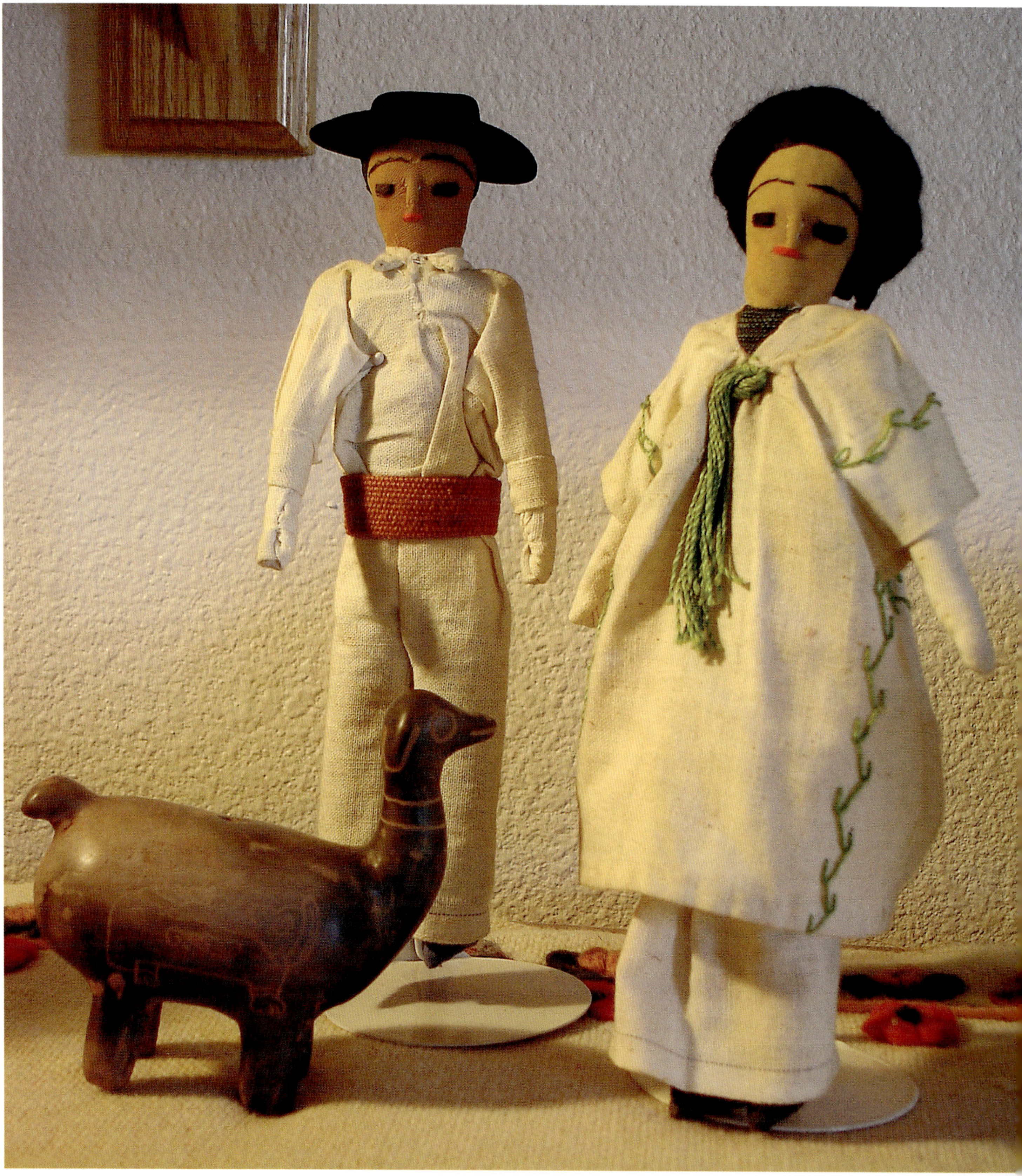

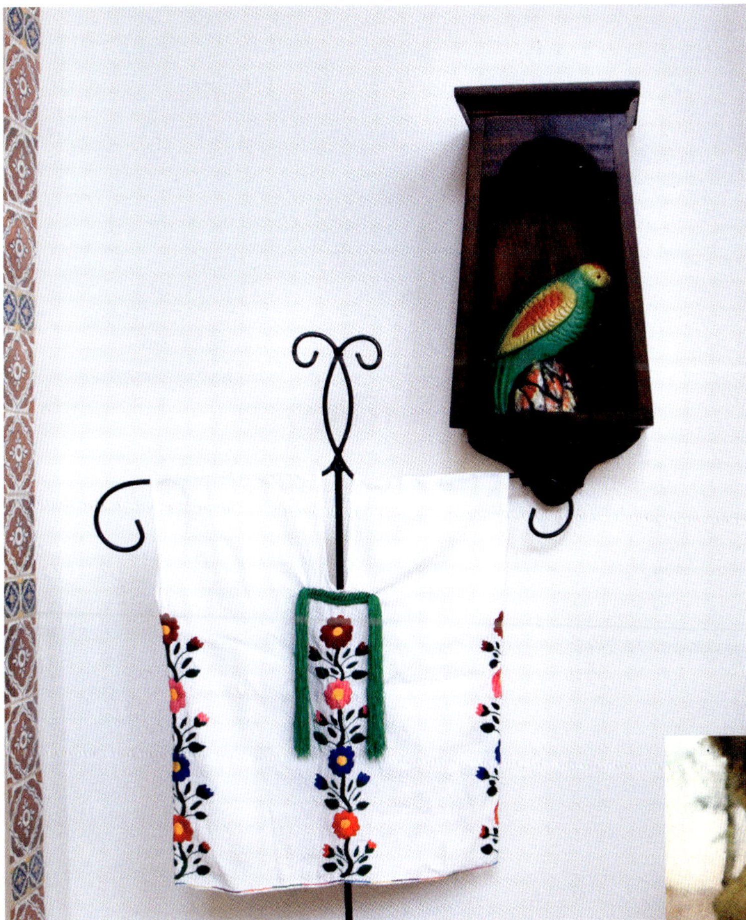

The tunic *huipil* of a Yalalag child, in white cotton *manta* with colorful embroidered flowers down the sides and front, centered tassel is indigenous to this tribe, c.1960s. A parrot tourist pottery bank, Old Mexico. $60

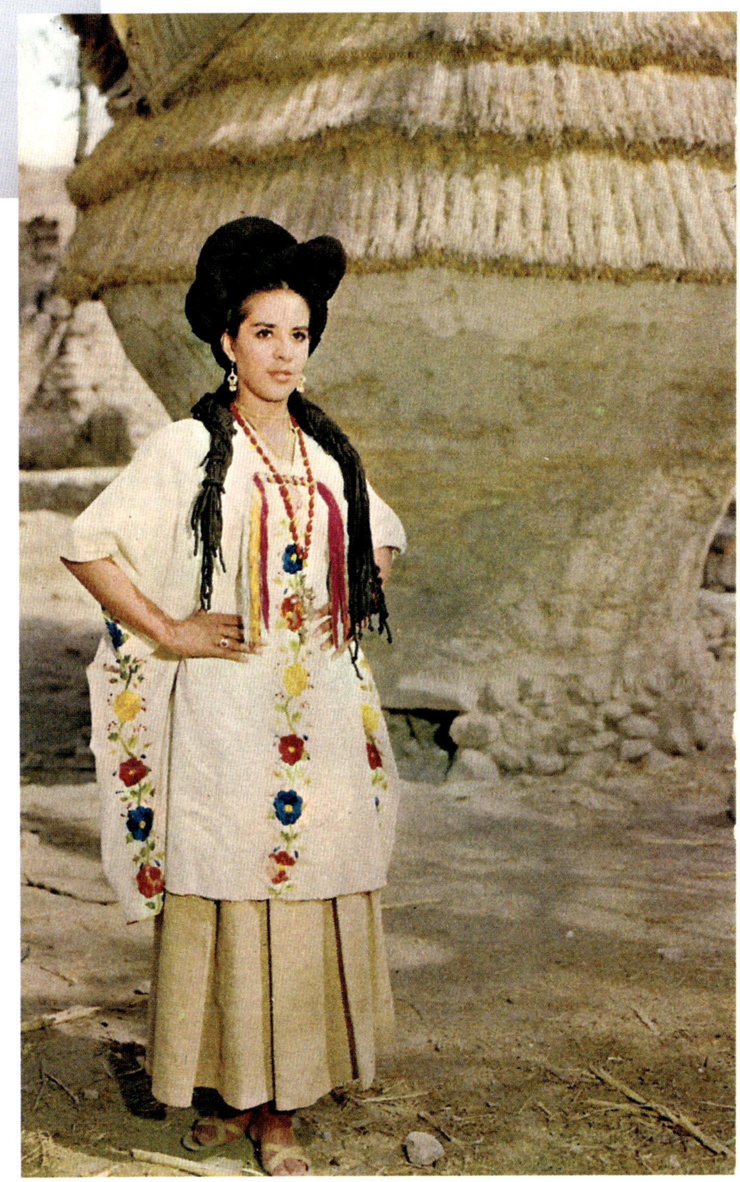

Color postcard photograph, "Yalalteca Costume, Oaxaca," Cristacolor, Lito Juventud, c.1950, Mexico D. F 4 X 5 in. $15 to 40

Opposite page:
Attributed to the Yalalag Indians, this cloth couple, 10 in. from Yalalteca. Very simple and accurate detail, her long *huipil* has a centered tassels and the *caballero* is wearing his *calzone blanco,* white pants, and shirt. Made in Mexico $75 to 150 ea.

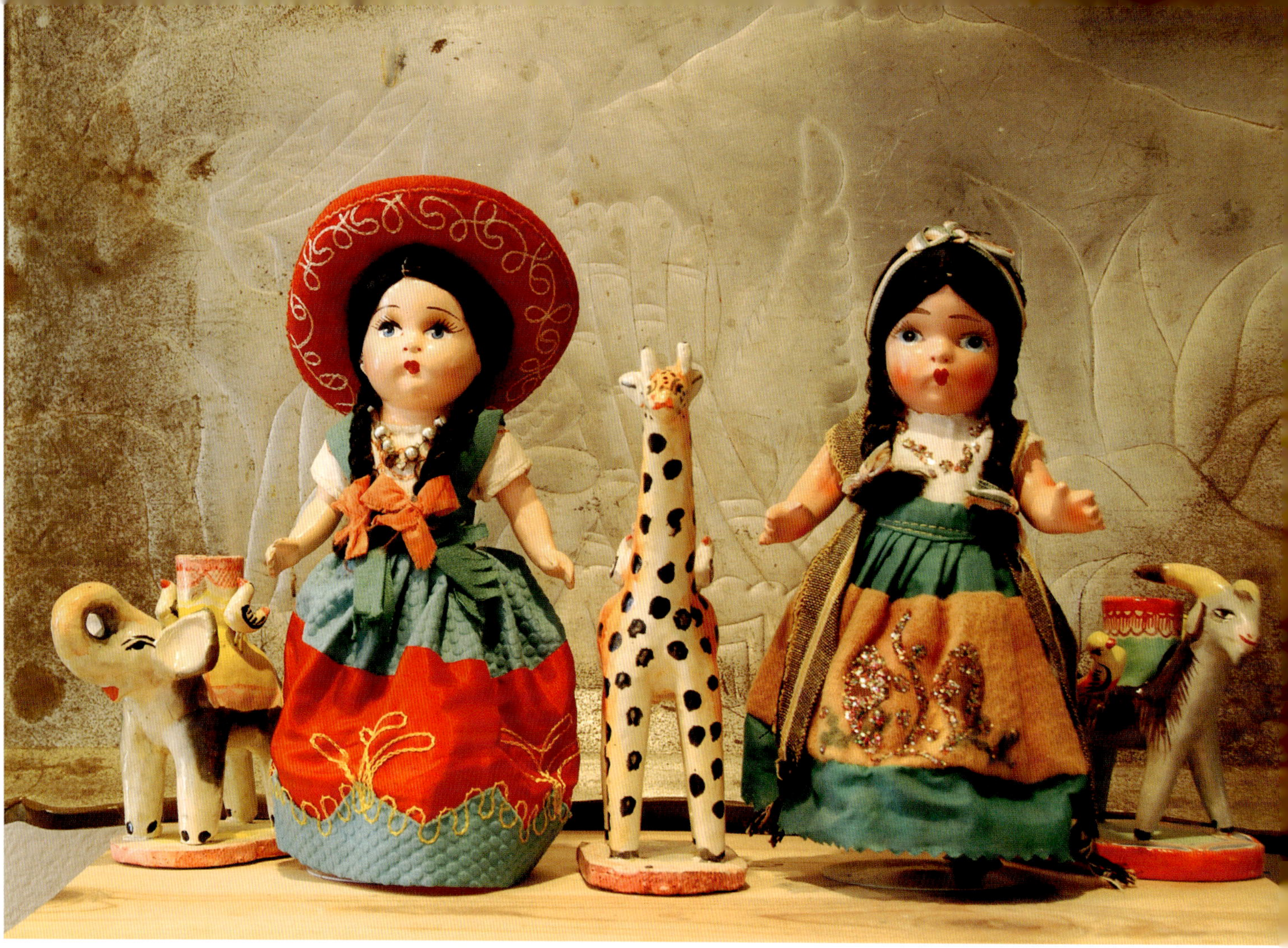

A cute pair of compo Old Mexico dolls, from the district of Puebla. 10 in. souvenir charra has large red bows at the end of her braids, hand detailed painted face and a red felt *sombrero*, with silver beaded necklace, c.1950s. A 9 in. *mestiza* dress with green, red and white. Patriotic and beautiful, surrounded by polychrome whimsical ceramic animals, c.1950s. $75 to 100 ea.

Puebla

The region of Puebla covers a vast variety of Indian *pueblos* (small towns) that produce many types of Mexican popular arts. The townspeople of *Chicontla* and *Huehuetla* are inherently aware of their ancestors and are known as the *Totanacas*. The Indians wear beautiful white *quechquémitls*, some of lace and embroidered skirts with indigenous motifs. Satin and chain-stitched colorful blouses bordered with flowers, birds and vertical arrows are common. Traditional embroidery techniques include those from *Pahuatlan*, where the people have accomplished magnificent embroidery techniques, such as *pepenado* and *pespunteado*, reverse embroidery. Their wrap-around skirts, *enredos*, and a voluminous skirt, the *cueitl*, are usually white or blue and are held in place by a popular wide red sash that is made by the *Otomies*. The 20th century *mestiza* women of Puebla exhibit many European and Spanish influences in their costumes. Resonated from Puebla is "*La China*" (chee-na), affectionately adapted from *La China Poblana* (poe-blah-na), that became México's national dress in the 20th century. The costume is a beautiful tribute to the combined traditions adapted during this period and represented by the *mestiza* women. A white peasant style blouse is embellished in all styles of flora, birds, and flowers in *punta de cruz*, a cross-stitch embroidery. Geometric patterns are applied in various techniques, from embroidery to cross-stitching to satin-stitching. Her red long skirt is finished with a green *bordado*, or embroidered borders, at the waist and hem. The festive full skirt was used as a canvas to flaunt magnificent intricate motifs. The designs were meticulously sewn by hand in small glass beads, gold thread, and opalescent sequins often made from fish or shrimp. The beads were strung, applied overlapping one another, and trimmed with ribbons and embroidery. Mexico's national coat of arms, an eagle clutching a snake, is a favorite theme for the *China Poblana*'s skirt. A beautiful *rebozo* is used in a variety of ways, crossed at the front or worn over her shoulder or head, that compliment the hint of an original indigenous piece. Her hair is usually braided on two sides and tied with red, white, and green ribbons.

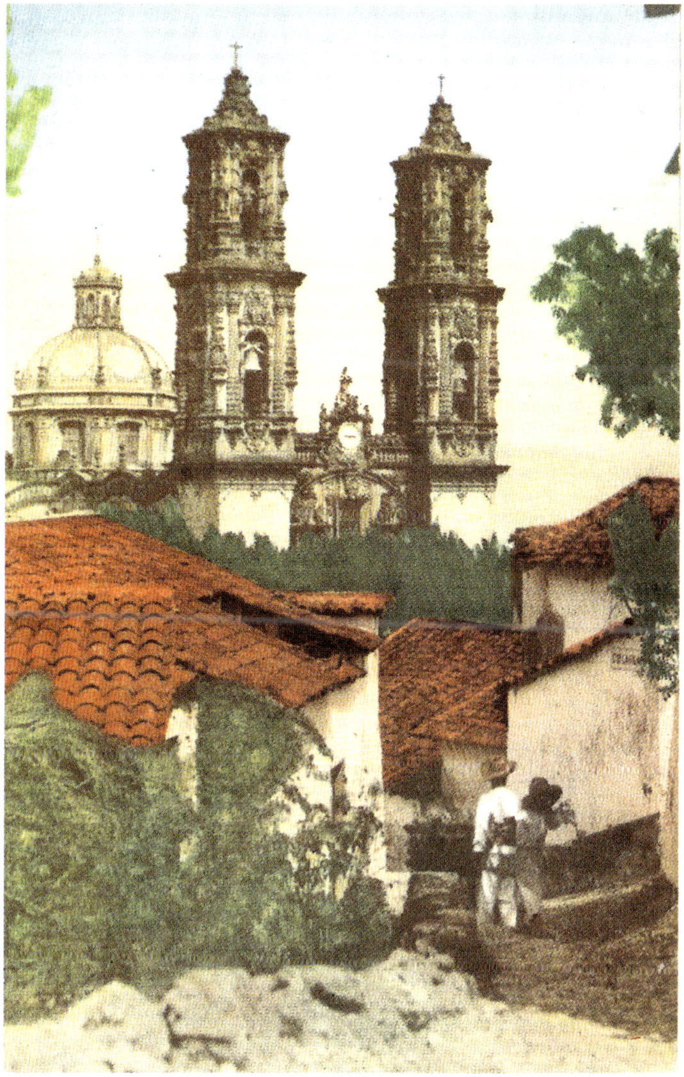

An original postcard, 5 x 3 in., c.1940s, Church and Streets in Mexico, "Fema" S. A., printed in Mexico $15 to 30

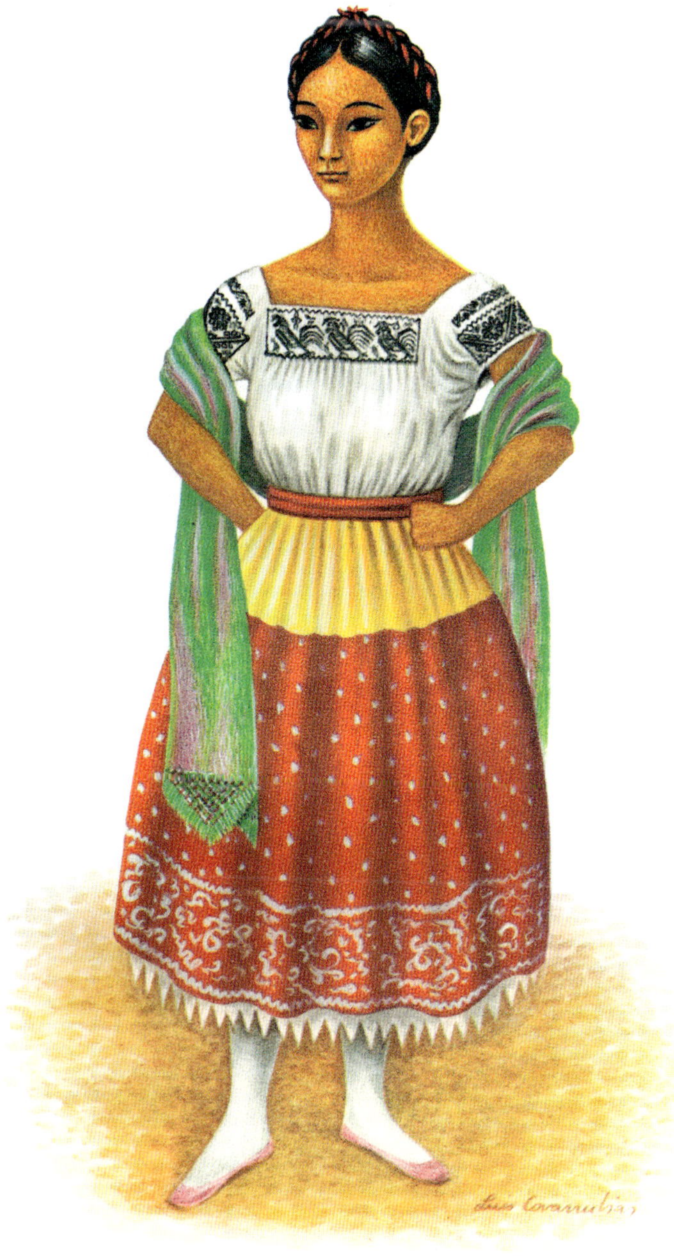

A color chrome print, c.1940s, from *Mexican Native Costumes* booklet, by Louis Covarrubias, Fischgrund, Mexico D. F., the China Poblana.

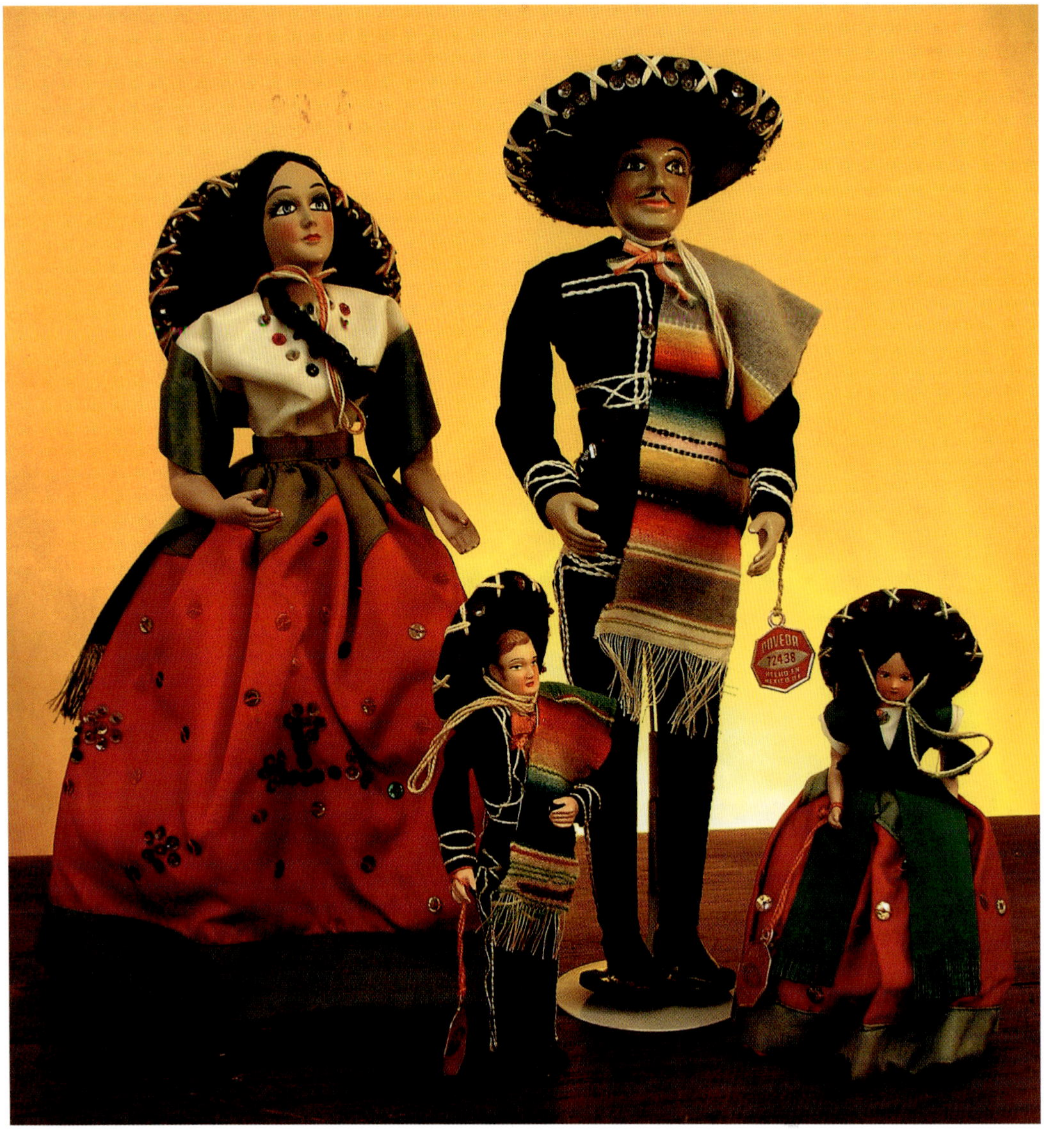

A collection of four rare tourist dolls by a Mexican toy and doll company around the late 1950s. The Poveda Co. made quality souvenir dolls that are highly collectible, especially in excellent condition, such as these. The larger dolls stand at approx. 15 in. tall and the smaller ones are 6 in. tall. Made of a hard composition that was distinct. Hand painted molded features and threads of cotton or silk create the hair on the women. $45 to 125 pr, priced smaller to larger.

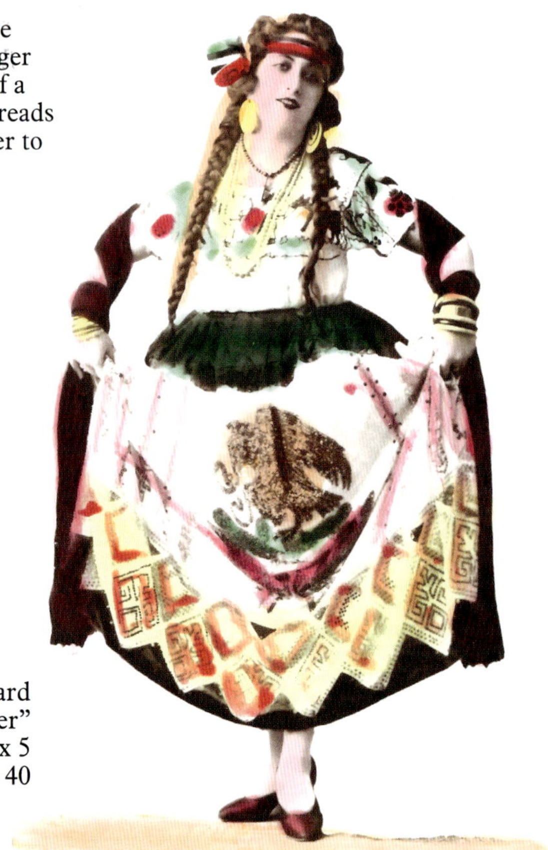

A color tinted postcard photograph, "China Dancer" c.1930s, Mexico D. F. 3 x 5 in. $15 to 40

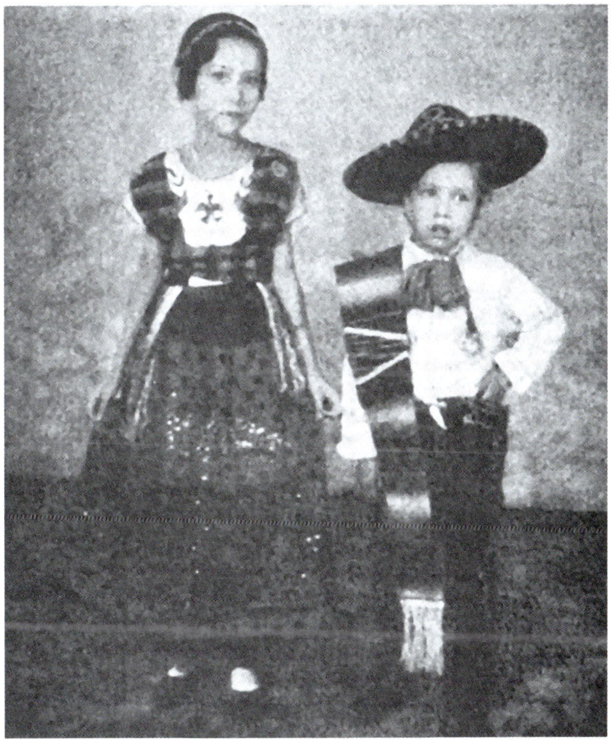

Mexican children in holiday costumes from a print by Stella Burke May, 1936.

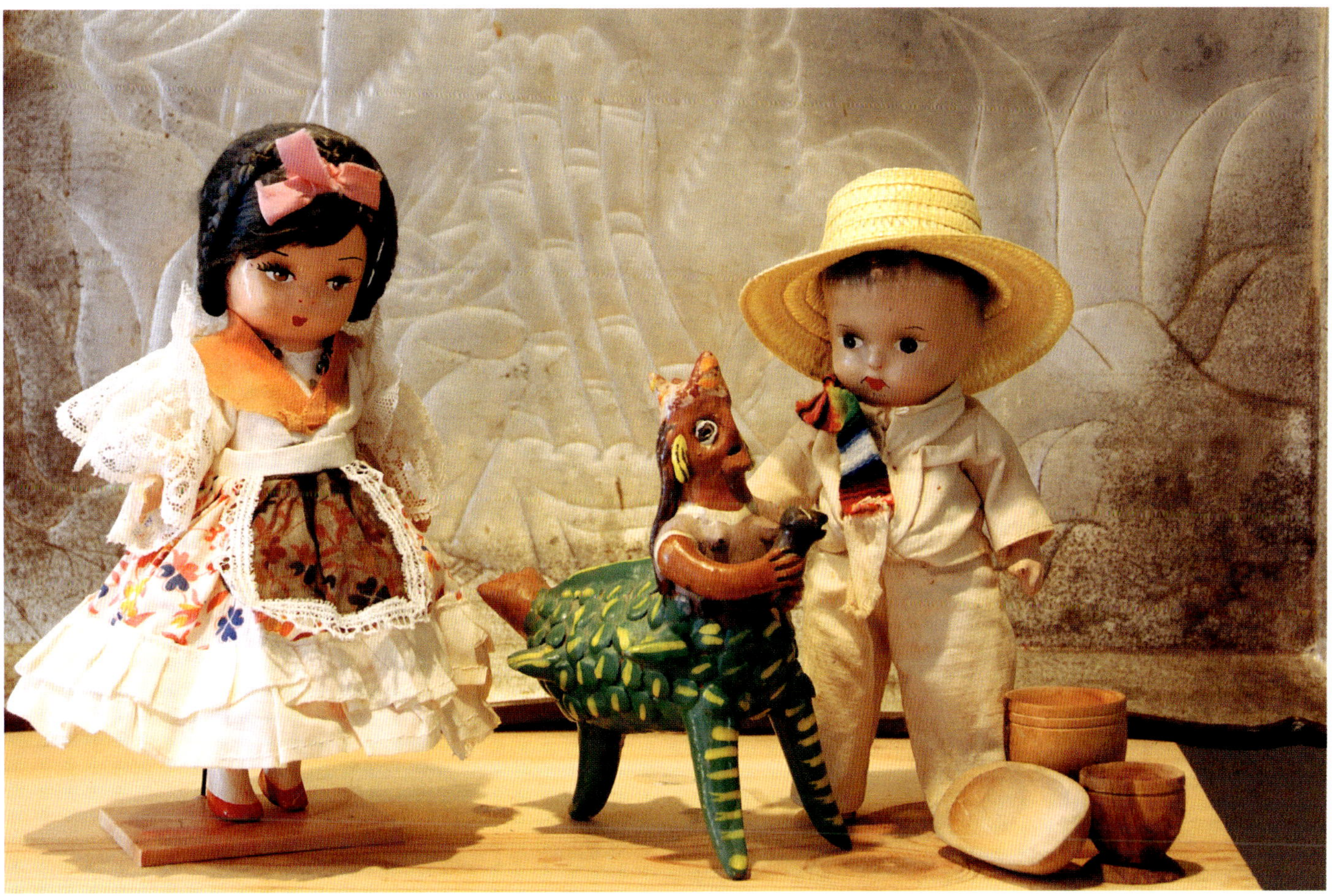

These two locals are attributed to the district of Veracruz, 9 in. compo dolls in popular clothes of the region, c.1940s. Made in Mexico. A sea serpent anamorphic whistle, popular arts piece. Stamped and signed. $75 to 100

Veracruz

A beautiful city that sits on the eastern coast of Mexico, Veracruz is the oldest town on the Gulf of Mexico. It is well known for its rich traditional music that blends Spanish and Caribbean rhythms and for the dance of the "*Sones Jarochos*," with flamenco characteristics. The people of Veracruz are known as *Jarochos*. Those who live near the port are influenced by the many ships that have docked there. Their costumes are light, sheer cotton organdy with full fluffy skirts, chosen to be comfortable and beautiful in the warm climate. The dress of the women of Veracruz is quite beautiful. They

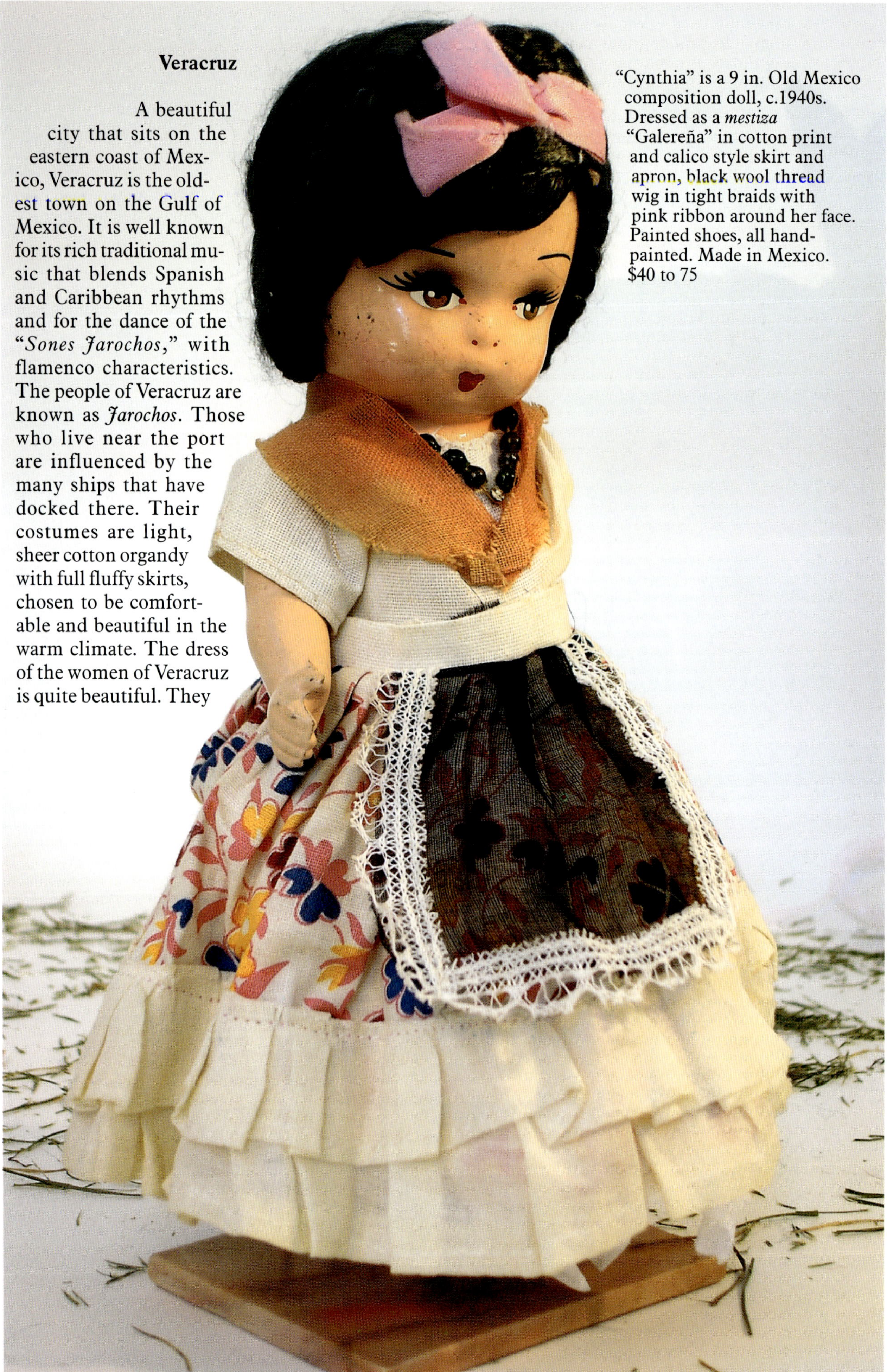

"Cynthia" is a 9 in. Old Mexico composition doll, c.1940s. Dressed as a *mestiza* "Galereña" in cotton print and calico style skirt and apron, black wool thread wig in tight braids with pink ribbon around her face. Painted shoes, all hand-painted. Made in Mexico. $40 to 75

wear a distinct lace shawl or the *quechquémitl* draped over the shoulder and their full skirts have a small black apron. The men are commonly seen in the *calzóne blanco* white garments, with *huaraches*. Veracruz is also home to the *Totonacas*, mainly farmers who still wear many of the indigenous items of embroidered tops and colorful skirts. The local people produce beautiful jewelry with the accessible sea shells.

Three sisters "Diana, Laurita, and Nini," cloth dolls wearing indigenous garments, 20th c. *Mestiza* and Indian costumes with incredible detail, authentic textiles, and inset facial features. Sizes from left to right 14 in., 16 in., 15 in. Made in Mexico. $100 to 250

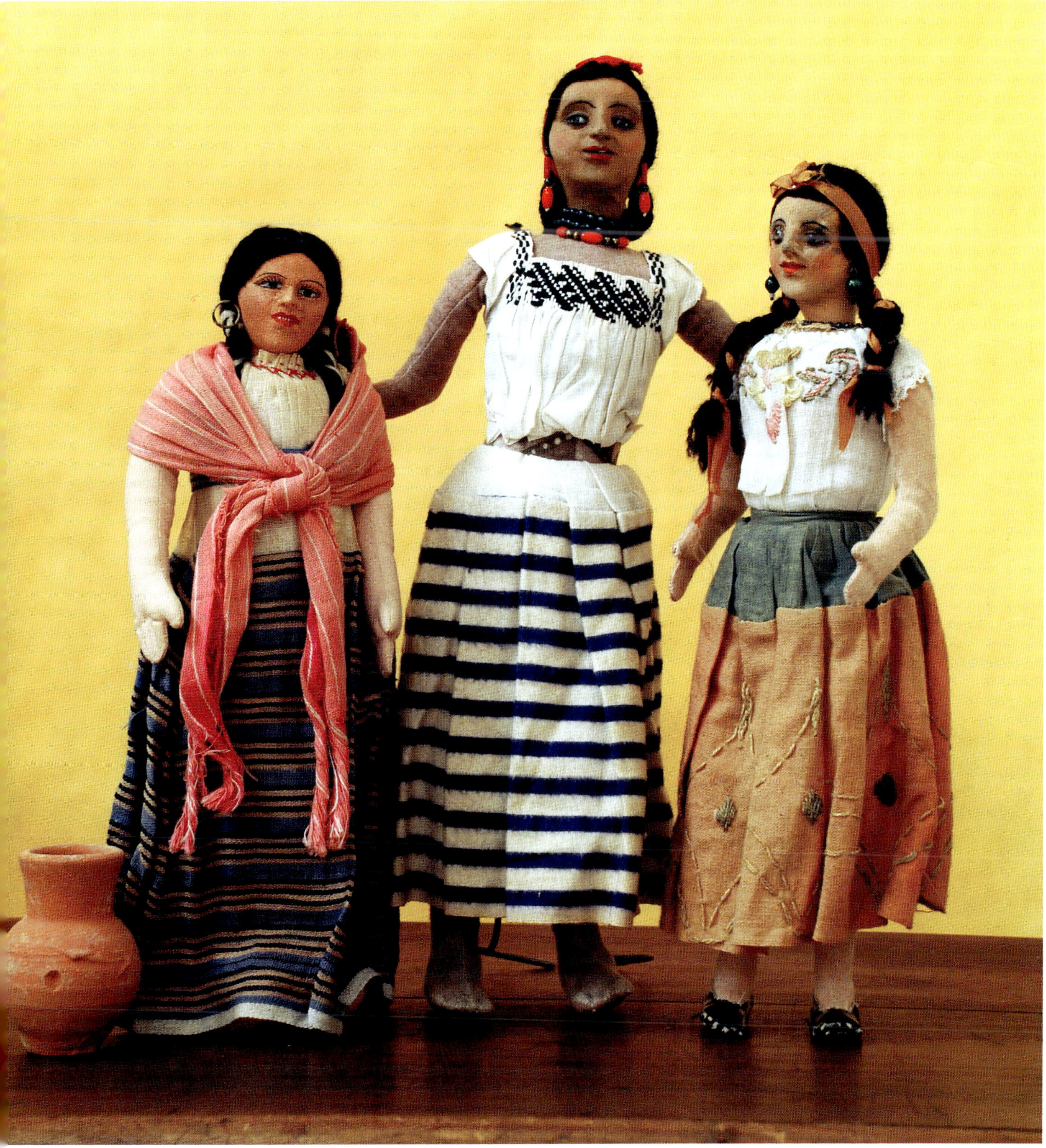

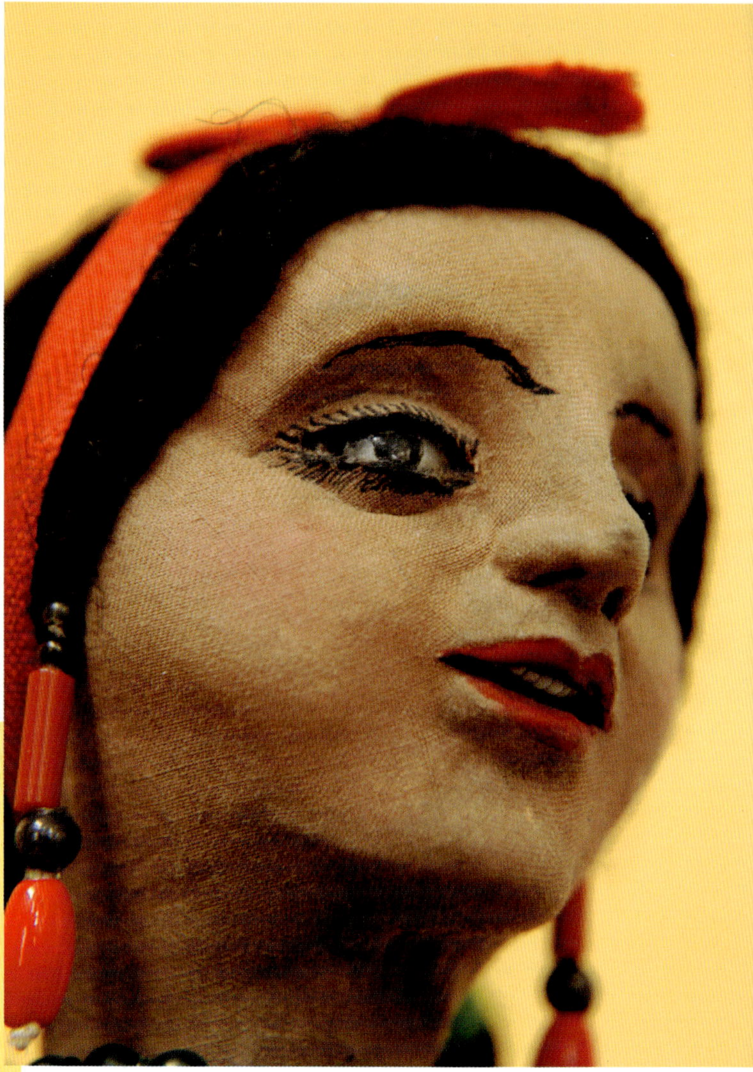

A detailed view of the 16 in. "Laurita" Indian mother with a beautifully molded face. Inset eyes and teeth of seeds and shell, vibrant red coral and *papelillo* glass bead jewelry. Hard stuffed, tinted skin tone with clay slip. Made in Mexico $100 to 200

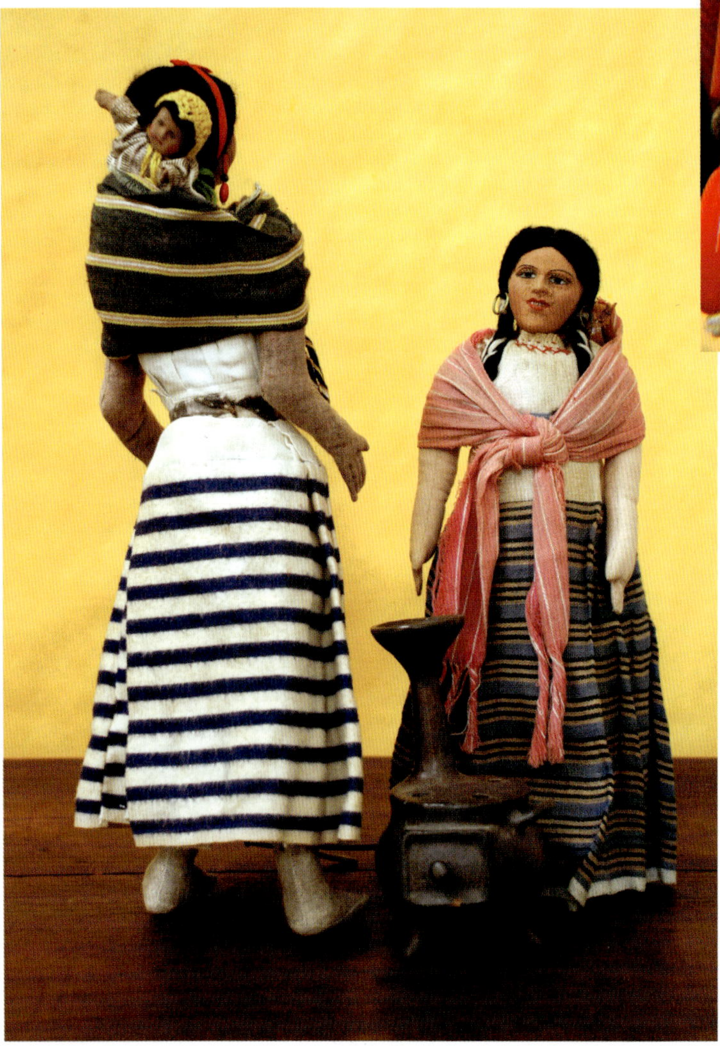

The back of the cloth 16 in."Laurita," an Indian mother with her baby in her *rebozo*, carefully molded of cloth, and a long striped *enredo* skirt, next to a clay 1920s Mexican potbelly stove. The 14 in. "Diana" is wearing a red striped *rebozo*, long *enredo* skirt, and white *huipil*. Made in Mexico $100 to 200ea.

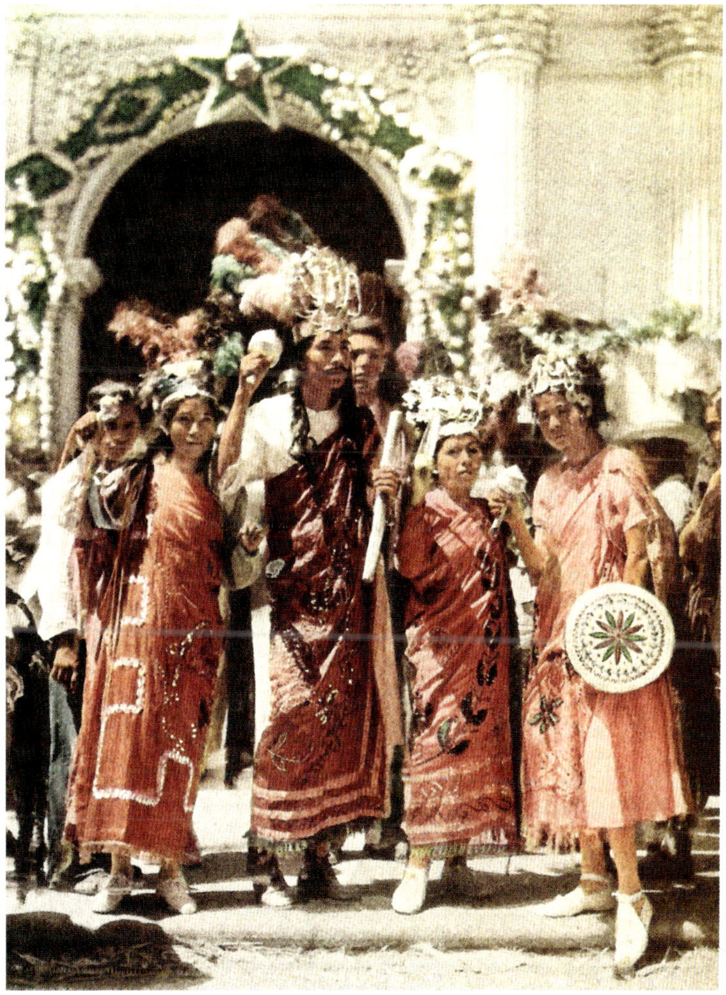

A copy of print showoing the re-enactment in pre-Hispanic costumes for a festival in Guadalajara, 1934.

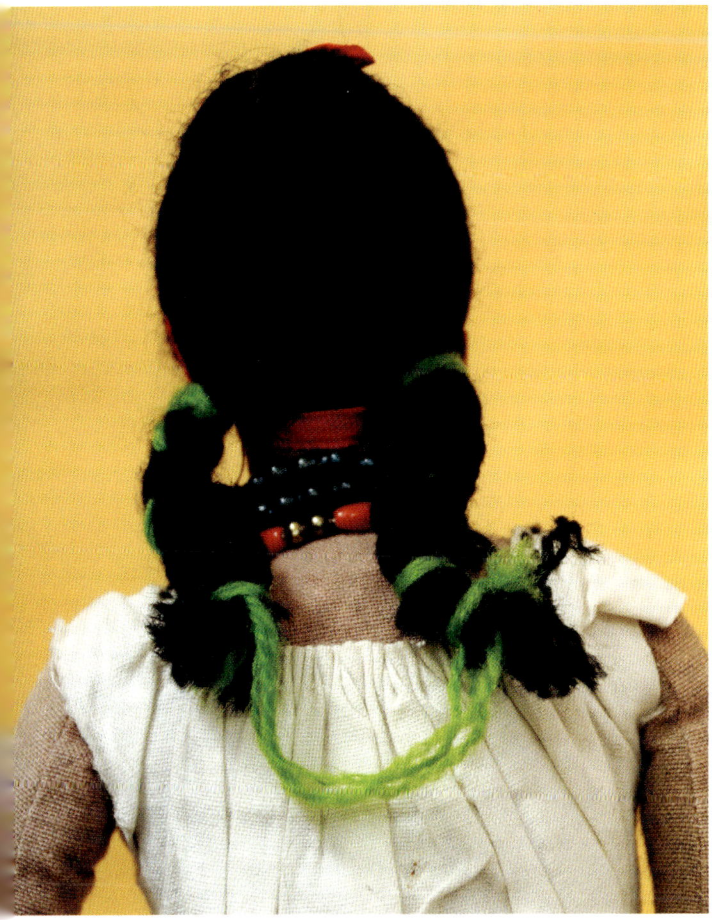

The back of "Laurita" shows her back wool wig braids, her gathered *blusa*, beautiful red coral and *papelillo* glass bead jewelry. Made in Mexico, c.1930s $100 to 200

PART 2
Souvenir and Collectible Dolls

Mexico had a boost in tourism at the beginning of the 20th century, which in turn fostered some of its finest popular arts. Curious foreigners from around the world finally, through means of faster and safer travel, experienced the treasures of its country. The increased tourism enabled a lot of skilled Mexican *artisans* to earn a source of income. Souvenirs were in high demand, especially by the native people of Mexico. Their colorful art, driven by traditional lifestyles, made its way to the market and eventually into the hands of tourists. Like all countries, Mexico offered dolls with many representations of the various regions and favorite costumes. Whether for the wayfarer, collector, or amusement, they were highly coveted from the early 1900s until the 1960s. Just as other talented artisans of Mexico, such as the Oaxacan weaver or the Pueblan potter, the doll makers contributed their splendid skills. As described by Salvador Novo, a contributor to the book *El Arte Popular De Mexico*, "the popular arts were an interbreeding with a dual origin, the Spanish, rich in European tradition, and the Indian." This combination is characteristic of Mexican popular arts and is one the dolls emulate. All souvenir dolls represent an understanding view of any country's costumes and the people that inhabit it. Mexico's costumes are incredibly beautiful, which made the dolls an attractive souvenir. They became popular to tourists as well as doll collectors. Many of the dolls' costumes and textiles were carefully hand applied or woven. The dolls show amazing skills enriched by the techniques and personal traits of the makers. The streets and stores in tourist cities offered an assortment of souvenirs for sale and a certain favorite is always a country's doll. Many also were manufactured by prominent Mexican toy or souvenir makers, such as *Poveda* and *Carselles*. Their dolls were sold in department stores, such as *Sanborns* (well known in Mexico), or in various *curios* (tourist shops) along the border. Several curio, souvenir, and tourist shops were opening and booming, like those owned by Alejandro Savín and Jorge Ibs. Their businesses sold items such as sombreros, silver jewelry, postcards, dolls, clothing, and all types of novelties. There were small *maquiladoras* (factories) in many tourist towns that would make the souvenir dolls. These assembly plants had various methods in making the dolls and were quite prevalent enlisting the talented labor that would provide them with quality. The *maquiladoras* were part of Mexico's Border Industrialization Program, set fourth to encourage foreign trade.

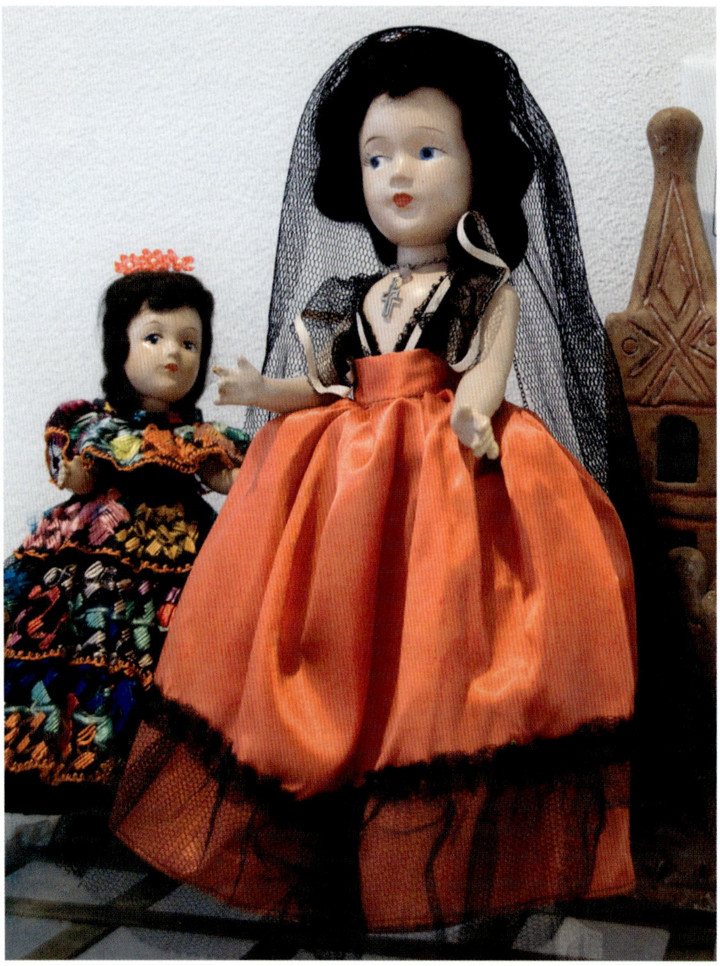

A stunning 16 in. Dream World doll, all composition jointed body, c.1940s. In excellent condition. Dressed as a colonial Spanish maiden. Made in the USA. $100 to 150

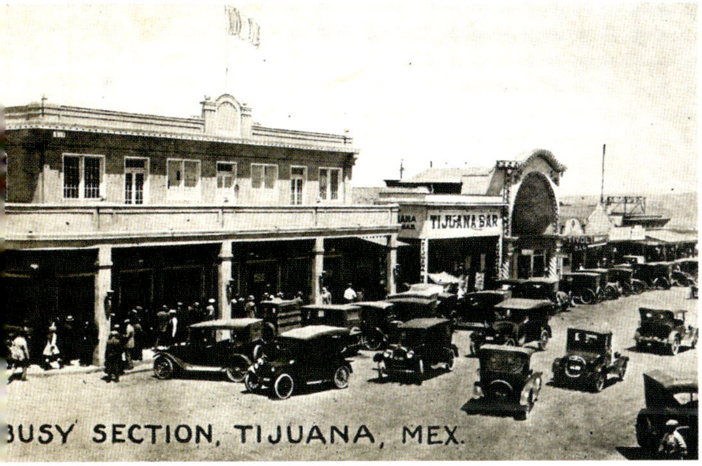

A postcard photograph, 5 x 4 in., c.1927, Busy Section, Tijuana, Mex, published by Lower California Comercial Co. Inc. $25 to 40

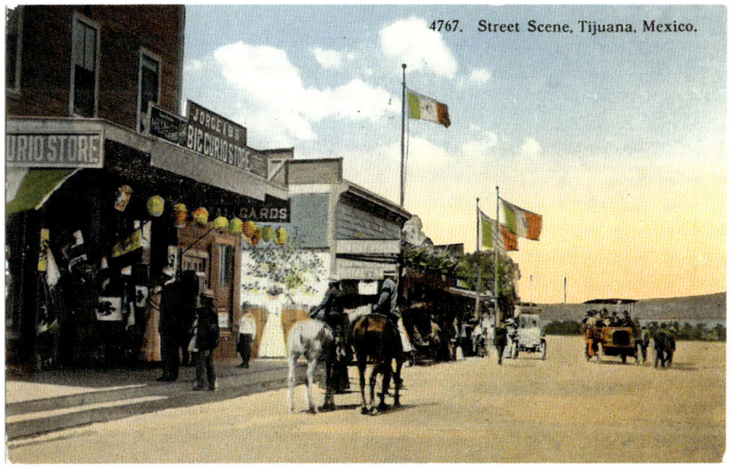

Jorge IBS Big Curio Store in Tijuana, Mexico, c.1919, color tinted postcard 3 x 5 in., USA $75 to 150

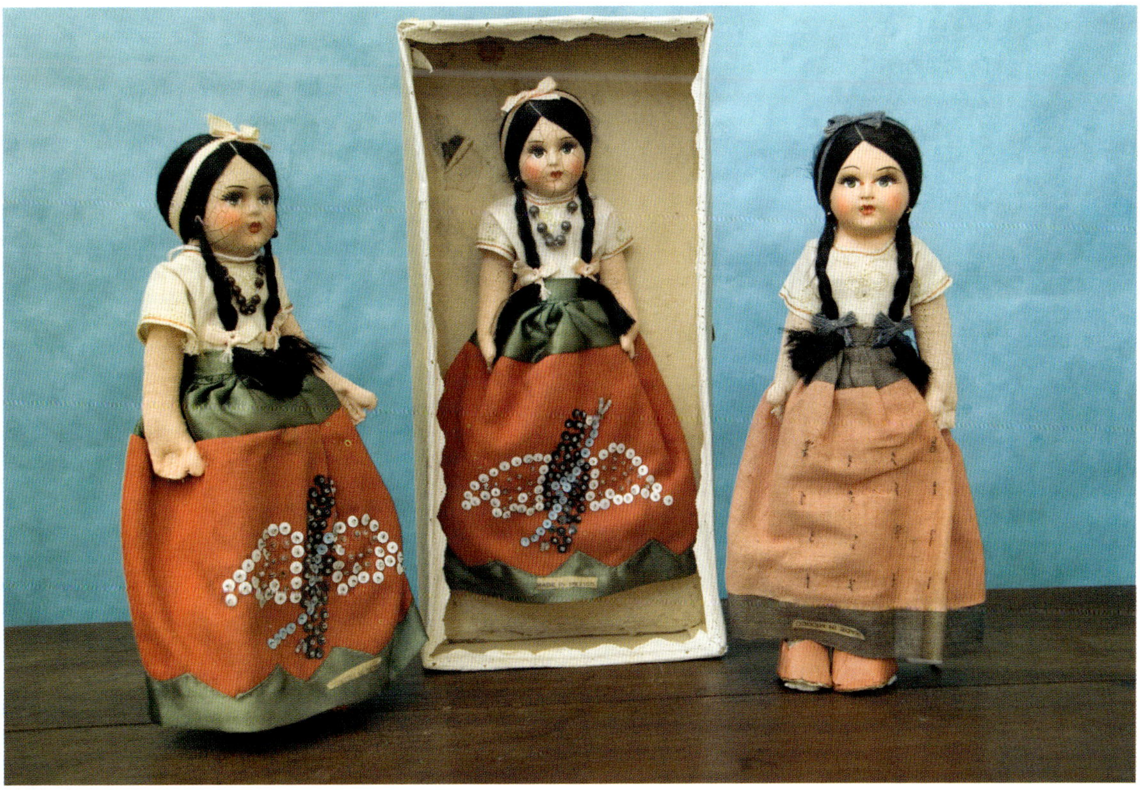

Three Mexican papier maché and cloth dolls, c.1940s.Popular souvenirs sold along the border or in the curios. Long braids and *papelillo* glass bead necklaces, Mexico $40 to 100 ea.

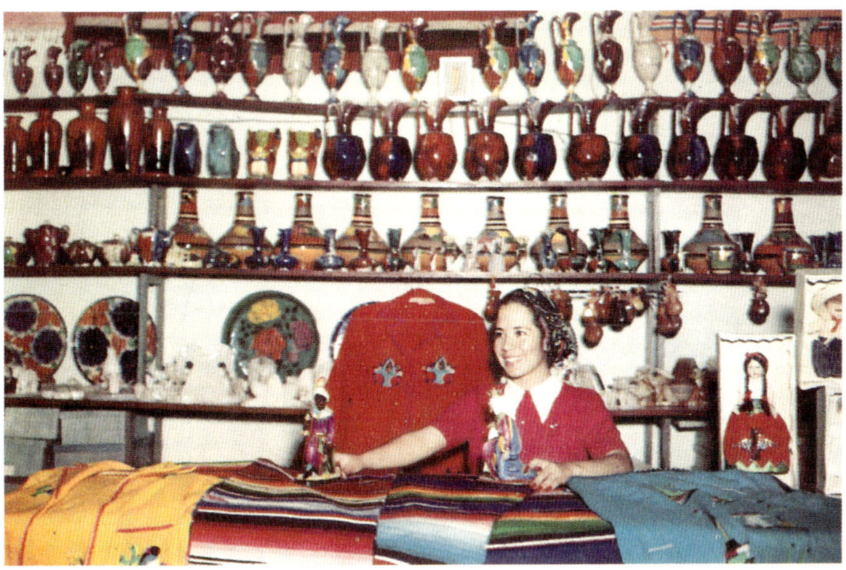

The colorful curio shop in Mexicali, Old Mexico. Notice the dolls and other popular tourist pottery from that period. The color photo postcard photograph is 5 X 4 in., 20th c. Pub. e Dist. by Larry Holland, USA $15 to 30

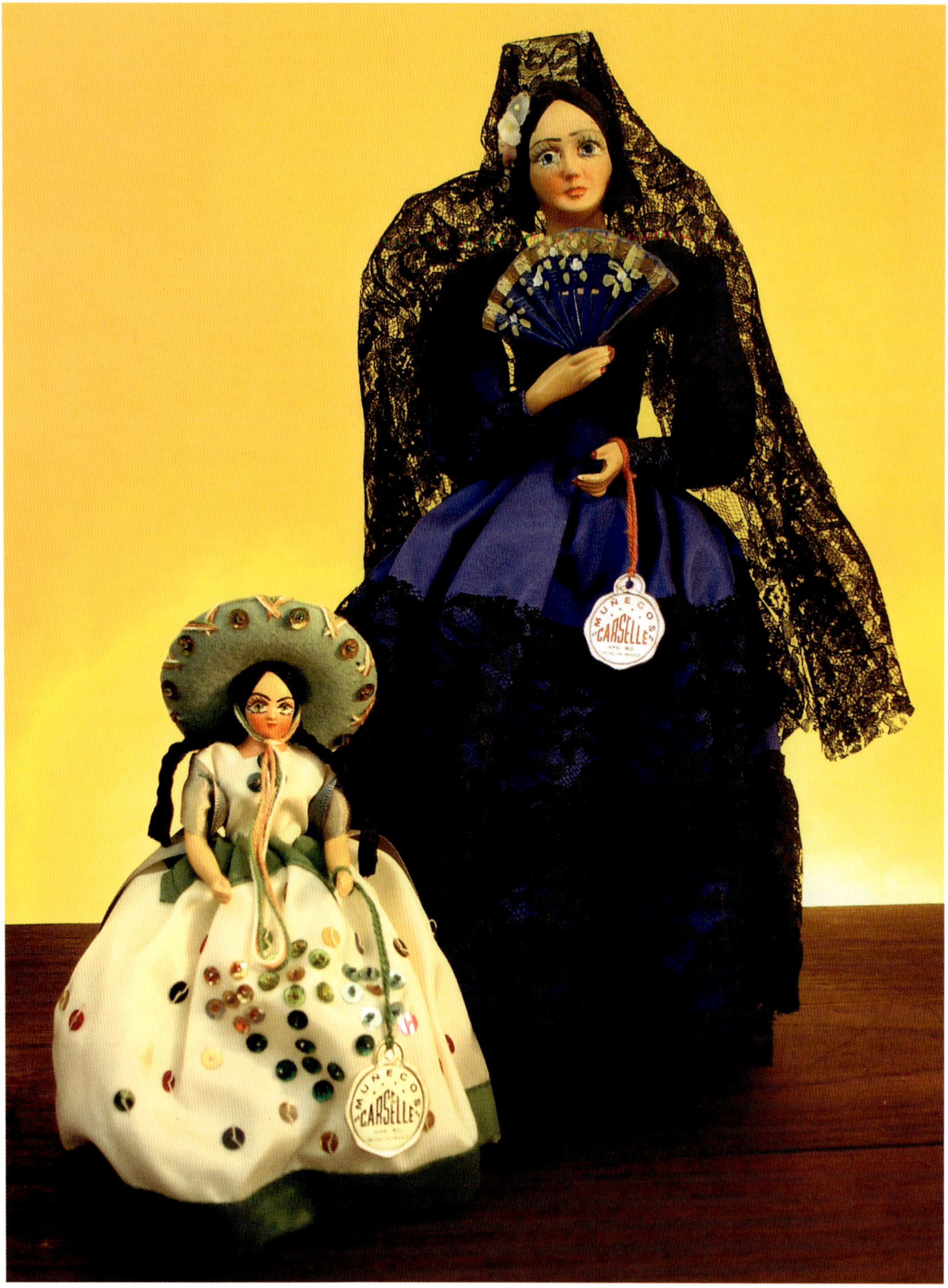

Two resin composition molded tourist dolls by Carselles, Old Mexico, c.1950s. A *Señora* and a *China Poblana* costume. Both were very popular souvenirs sold along the borders and in curio shops. $35 to 80

Composition doll parts from Canada and the United States were also imported and mass-produced from various factories, all with their own distinct composite formulas. They would market dolls all over the world, including to Mexico, such as those from the Ideal Toy Co. The dolls would be clothed, hand painted, and finished with careful consideration to the regions where they would be marketed. These skilled crafters did each one individually, as no two are identical. Whether made from composition, plaster, straw, cloth, or wood, the objective was a souvenir doll, but the results were recognizably a creative path for Mexican talent as a "folk artist."

20th century costume dolls, made by manufactured doll companies or from other countries, were attractive and well made. The quality and costumes were constructed with priority to accurately interpret the Mexican costumes. Whether *hecho en Mexico* (made in Mexico) or made in another country, the dolls reflect the indigenous clothing and possess the essence of *la muchacha* (a girl) or *el muchacho* (a boy).

The doll's clothing can represent a regional costume and its intended purpose. Usually they would be costumed in the style of clothing and textiles from the region where they were being sold. All of the indigenous costumes would have been influenced by the traditions and skills of that town or state and there could often be various mediums of artistry when making them. If they were not manufactured, the dolls would often be molded by hand from wood, clay, and cloth. They would be clothed to resemble the *campesinos* (country men or women) or the Mexican Indian. Finer native dolls were hand painted and dressed with authentic detail, like a *charra o charro* (cowgirl or cowboy) or as an affluent *Señor or Señorita* (gentleman or lady). Some are simply character dolls that may resemble popular or famous Mexican celebrities, such as Mario Moreno Cantinfla, Frida Kahlo, and Dolores del Rios The same characteristics were applied by other doll makers of that era from the United States, Canada, and other countries, such as Eros, Klumpe, Layna, Ravca and others. Better known character doll makers would sell them to finer stores.

There were also doll clubs that sponsored the sale of international dolls, such as Kimport Dolls and the World Wide Doll Club. The dolls would be distributed and sold worldwide as a cultural tribute to Mexico for commercial profit. It was hard for the great doll makers to resist them, as the beautiful Mexican clothing is highly marketable. During the early 1930s to the 1940s, it appears that the popular doll makers studied and researched the most definable Mexican costumes. The quality of vintage

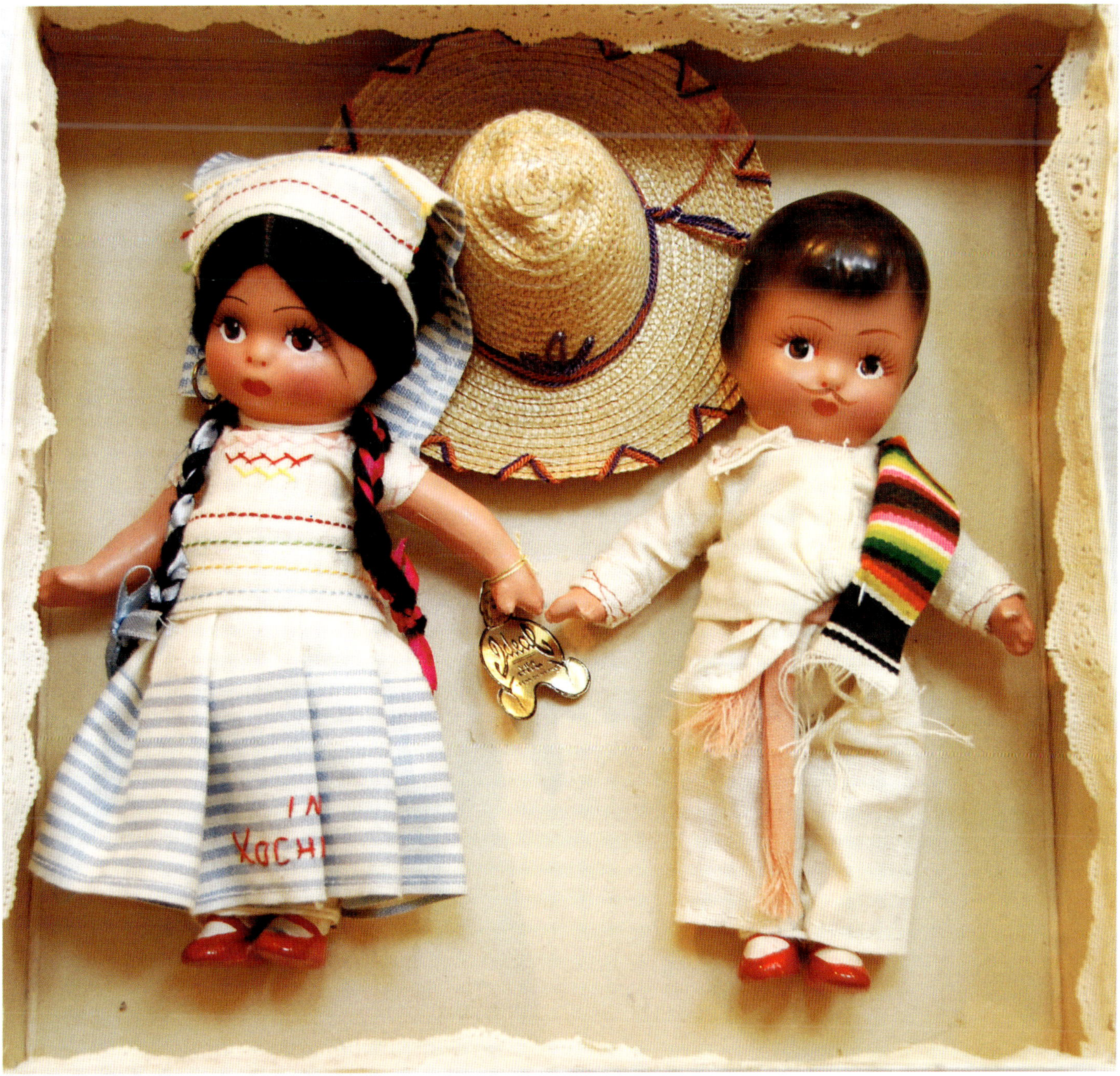

A boxed 9 in. composition tourist doll set made in Mexico by the Ideal Toy Co., dressed in regional clothing marketed for Mexico, c.1950s. A *mestiza* cute couple, on the little *muchachita* her skirt is embroidered at the bottom "Xochimilco." $100 to 175

The interior of The Big Curio Store in Tijuana, Mexico. Color tinted post card, c. 1940s. On the glass display cases note some of the tourist dolls for sale.

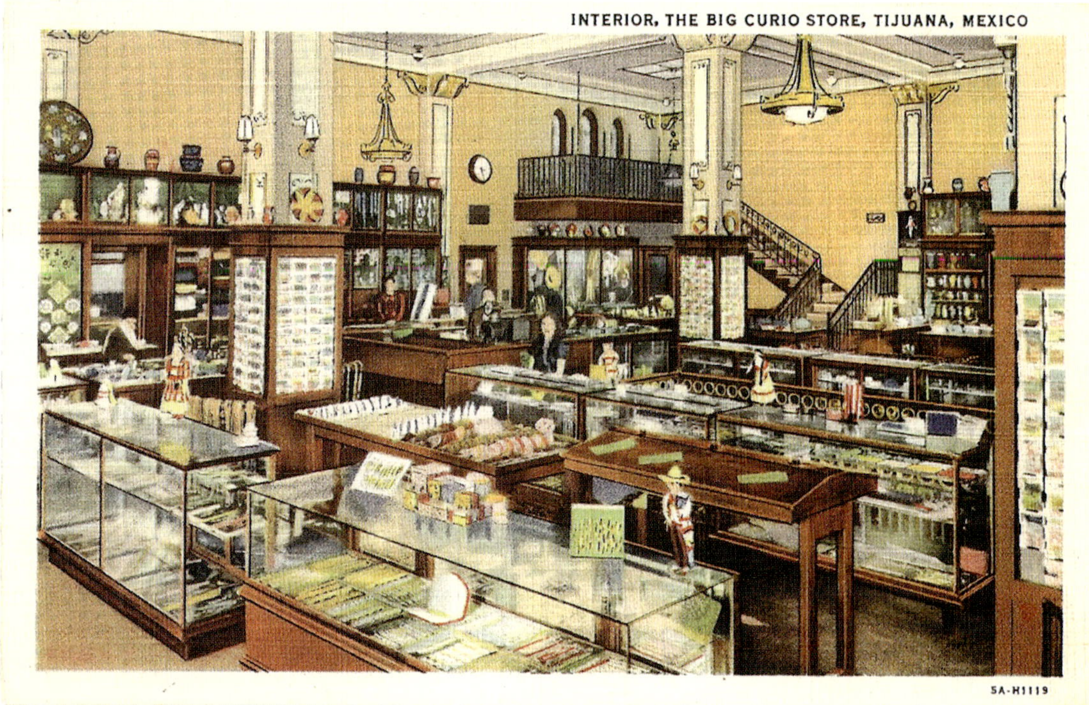

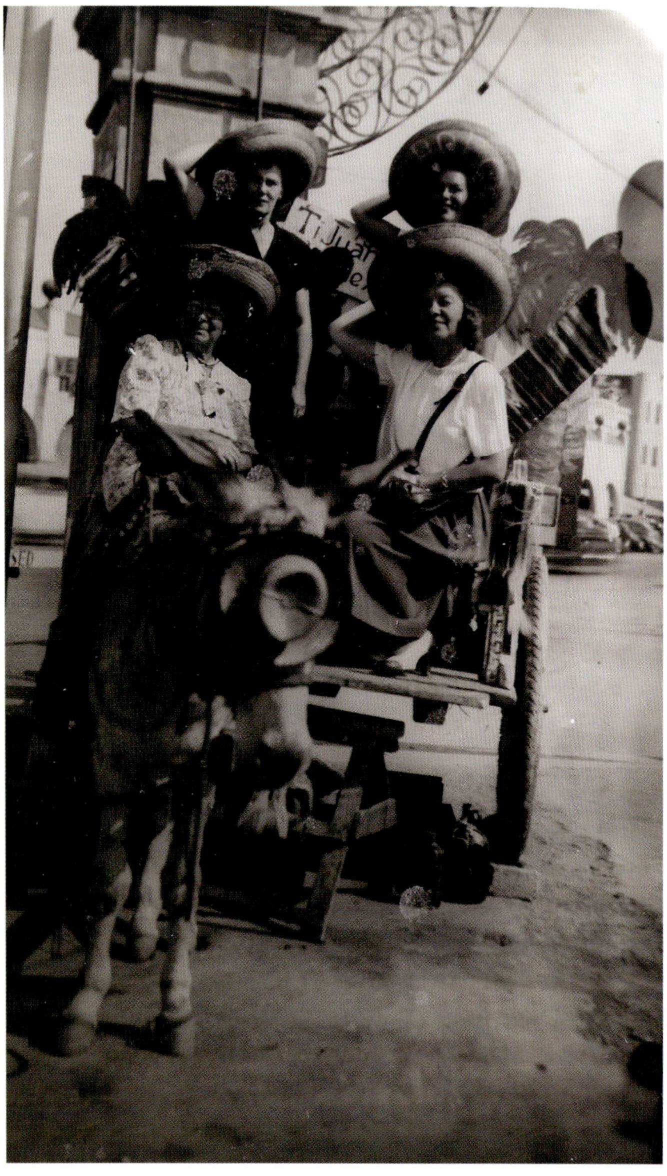

Mexican character dolls is outstanding from this period. They were costly and not considered only tourist dolls; collectors and admirers of the costumes were probably the primary consumers.

It is unfortunate that the Mexican dolls made today have lost their exceptional quality and the handmade skills evident from the past. Economic demands and mass-production has changed its priority substantially. They are no longer made in the same fashion or with the same conscience of pride. Souvenir dolls of today are made with plastic, rubber, and synthetic materials by novelty companies as ephemeral pieces. International costumed dolls have become a national treasure in many countries, and Mexico's dolls certainly merit this level of acclaim. A discerning eye will surely make Mexican costume dolls one of your favorite collectibles.

A popular photograph of tourists on a typical donkey cart along the border towns, c.1950s. 6 x 3 in. $10 to 20

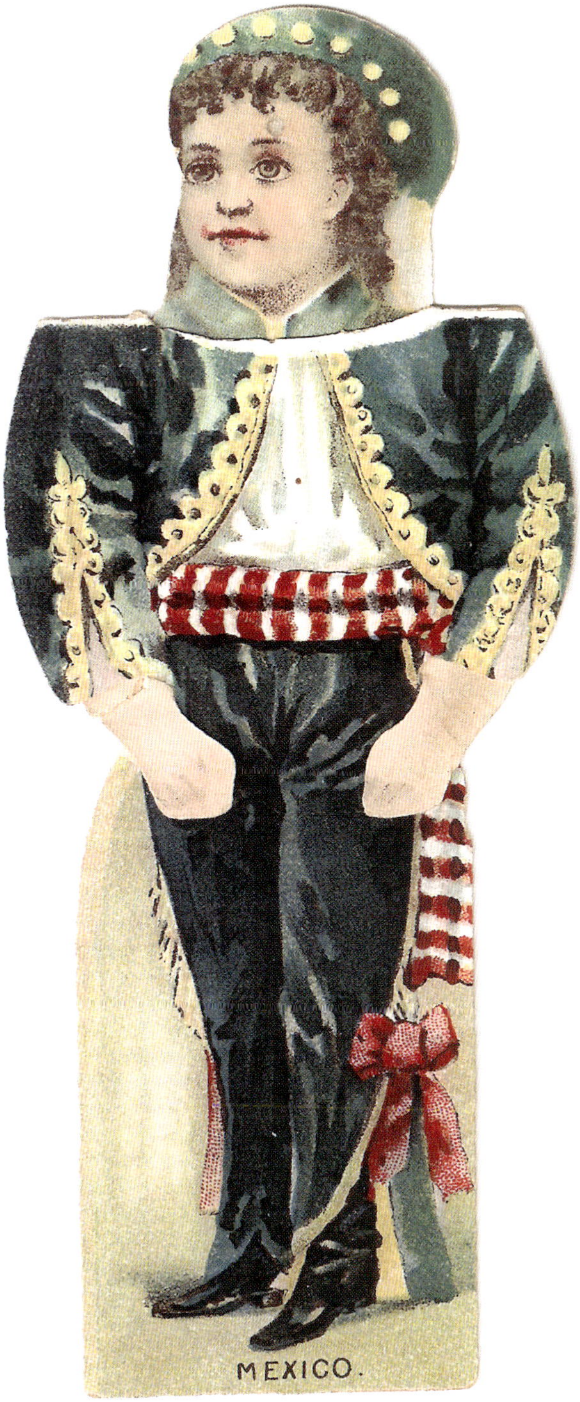

Doll soap advertisement, "Special Offer a set of sixteen of all nations can be had by sending two doll laundry soap wrappers and three two cents," Allen B Wrisley Co., c.1890s, 5.5 in. tall, Chicago $10 to 35

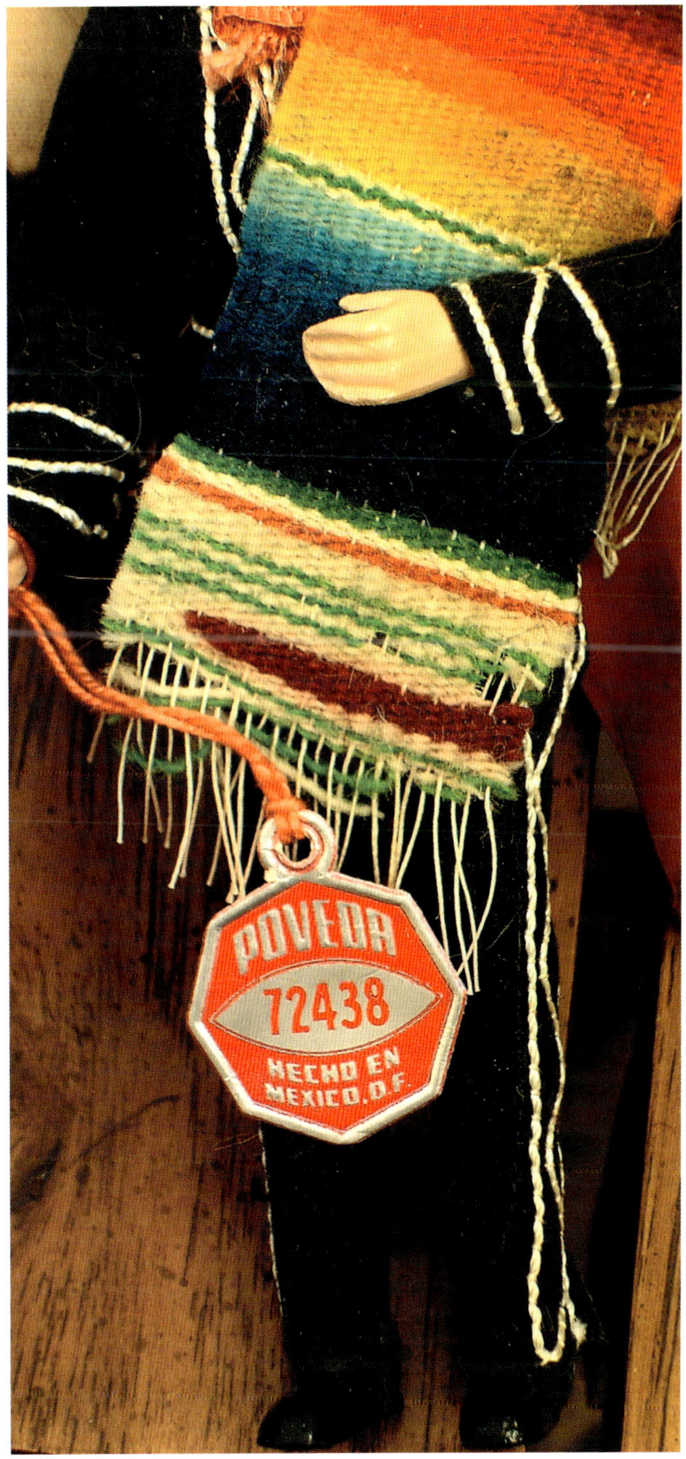

The doll tag Poveda, popular tourist dolls sold only in Mexico, c.1950s.

Attributed to Sanborns store, an original tourist doll bought from Sanborns, 8 in. composition doll dressed as a colonial *Señorita*, c. 1950s. Made in Mexico. Beautiful detail, all original. $35 to 80

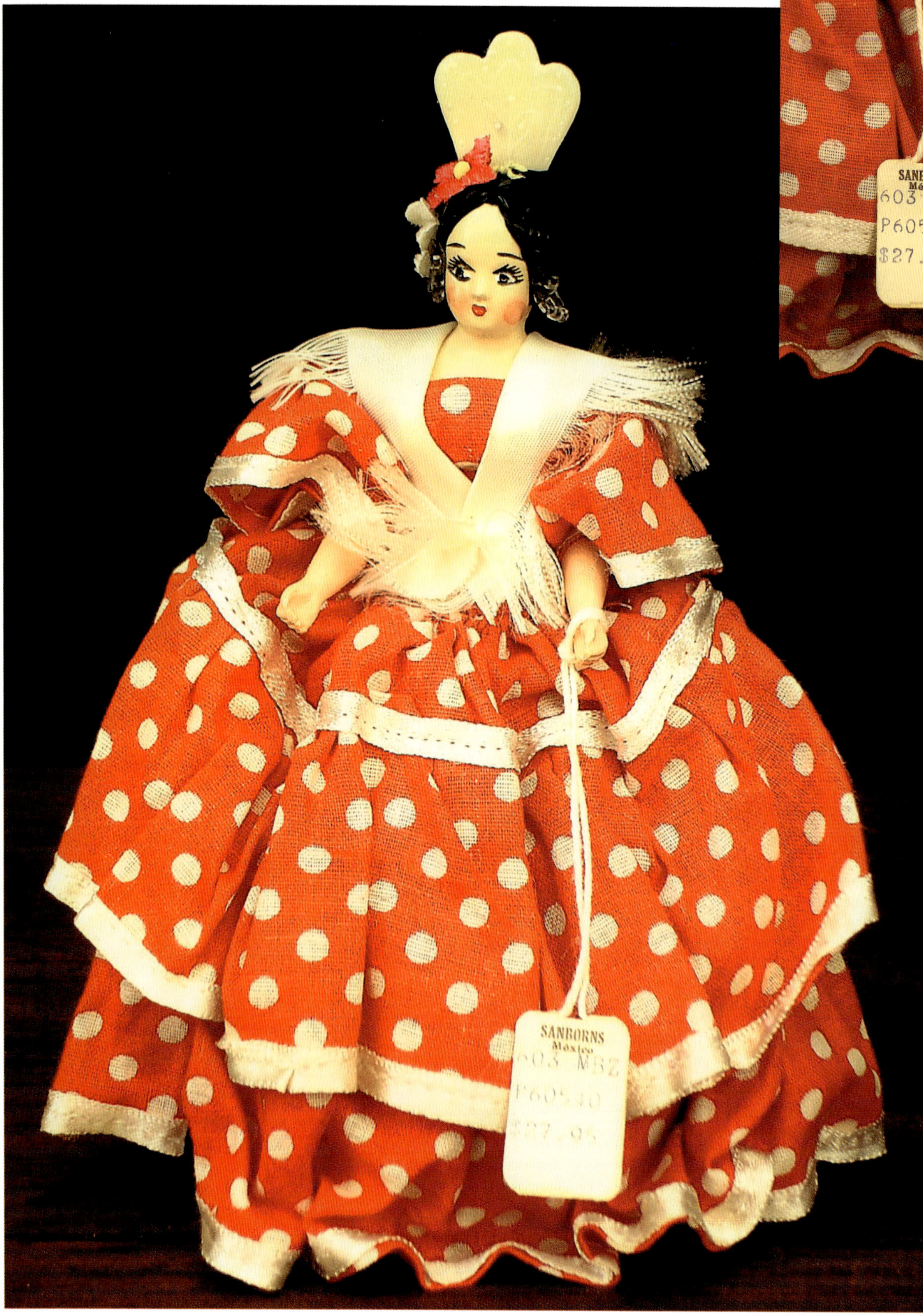

A closer look at the original store tag from Mexico's most well-known tourist store, Sanborns, 20th c. Made in Mexico.

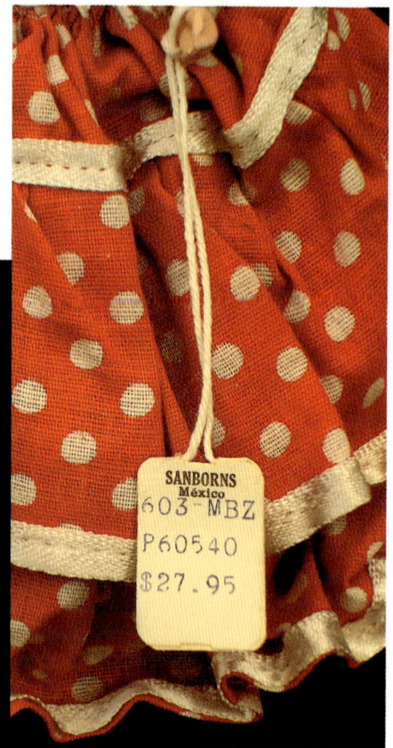

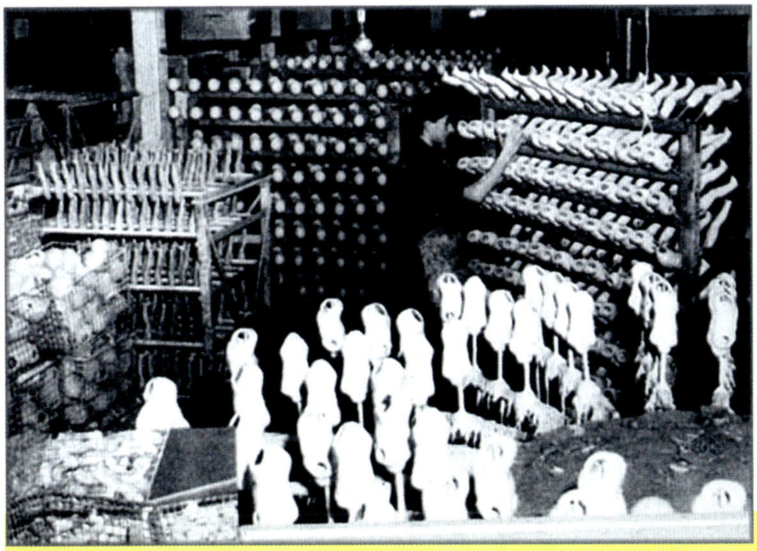

An archived print of "Assembling the parts" photograph of the Reliable Toy Co, Canada, c.1930s. Composition doll molds and racks of mass-produced doll parts for export. *Courtesy of Canadian Museum of Civilization*

A 12 in. cloth doll, c. 1950s. A doll club order with the original box and booklet, named "Miguel." Great authentic detail, dressed as a *mestiza campesino*. Made in Mexico. $40 to 100

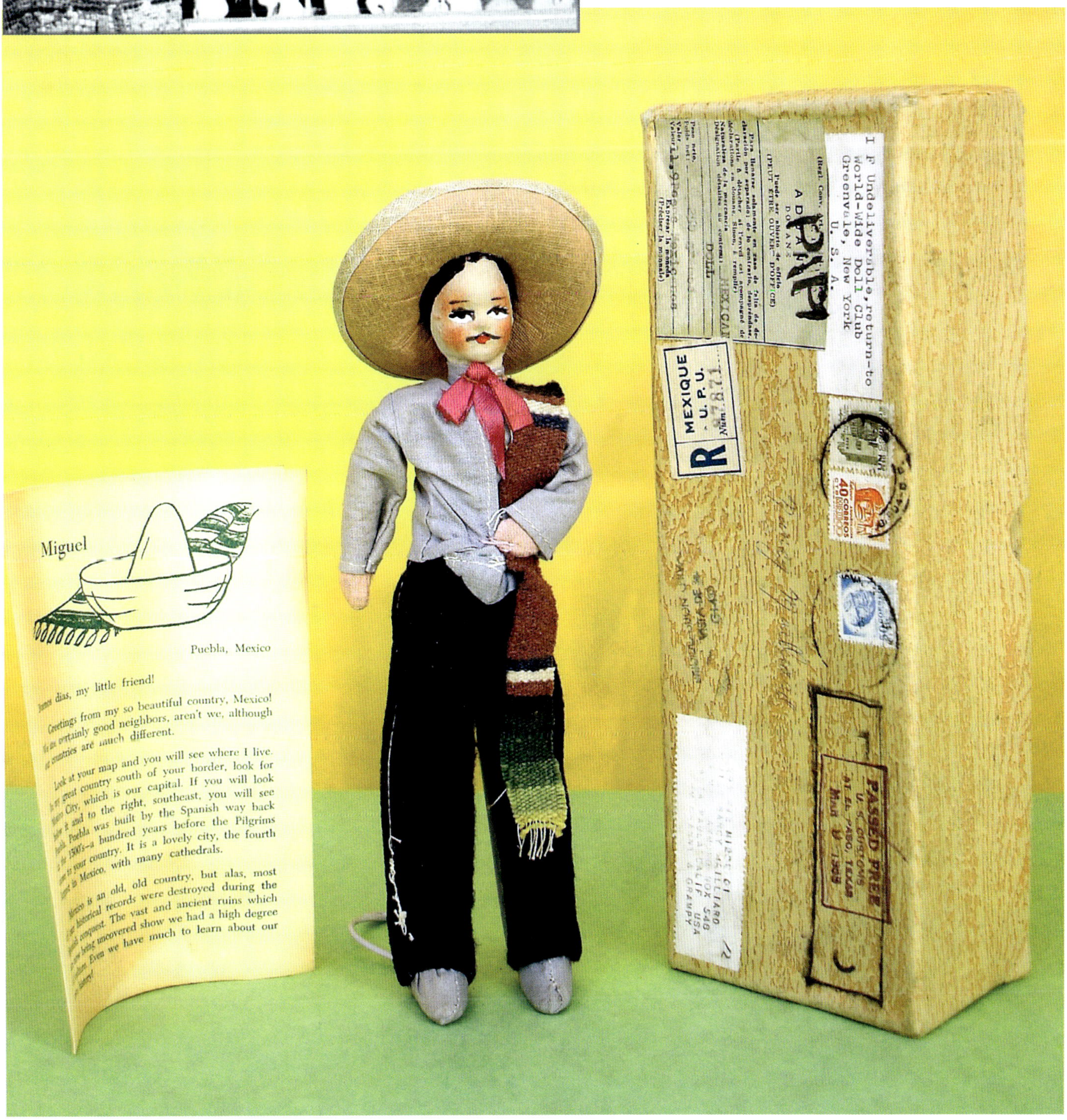

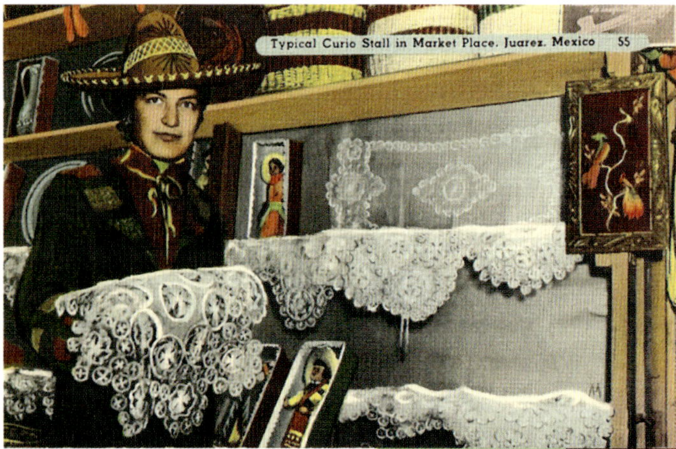

Curio shop in Mexico, c.1940s. An old tourist linen color-tinted postcard depicts popular arts souvenirs and dolls. *Charra* in black *sombrero,* USA $15 to 25

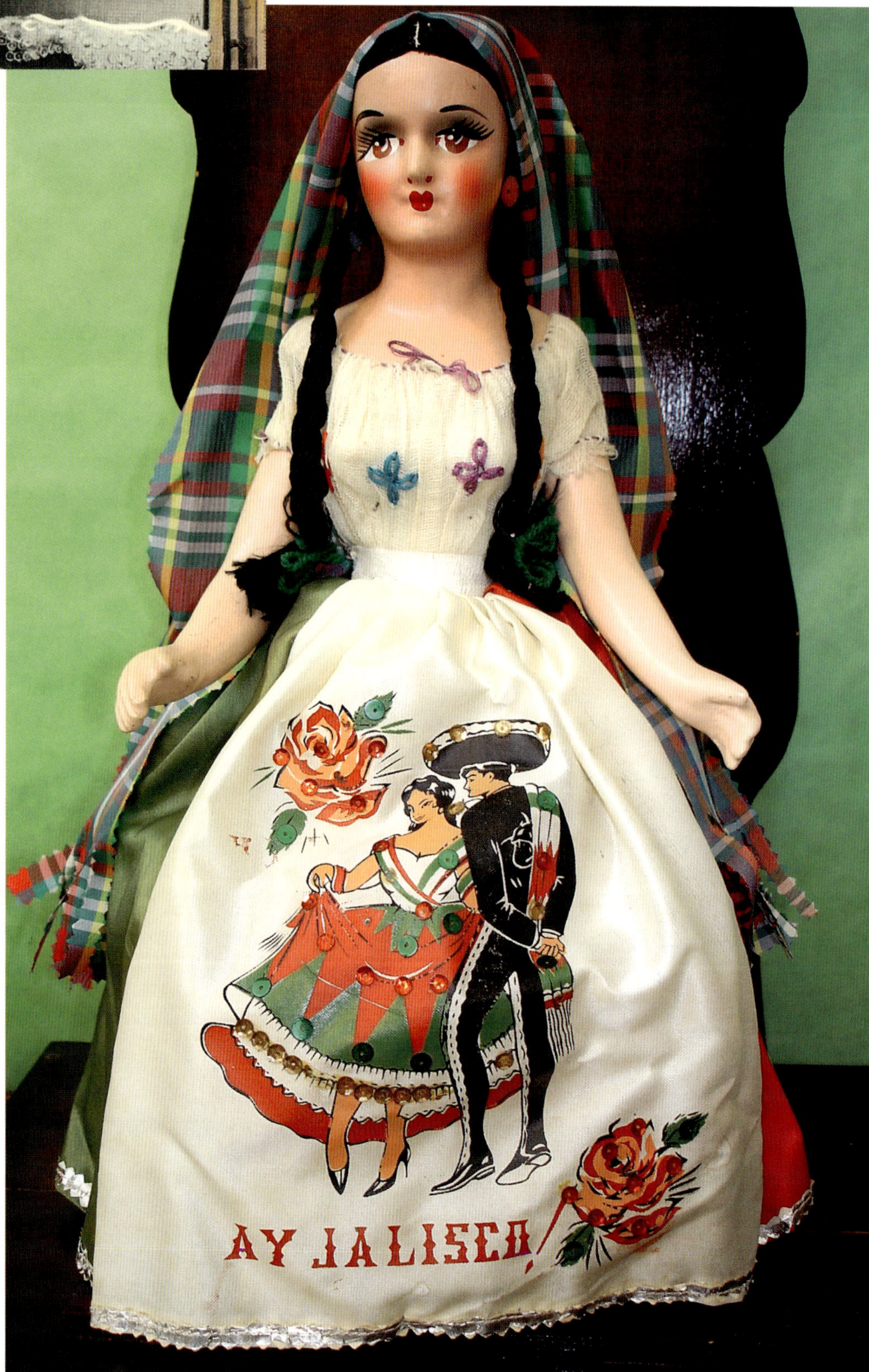

"Ay Jalisco," a souvenir 17 in. Mexican compo doll, c.1940s-'50s. In excellent condition with a green, white, and red skirt, the national colors of Mexico. She has large eyes and a colorful long *rebozo*. $150 to 350

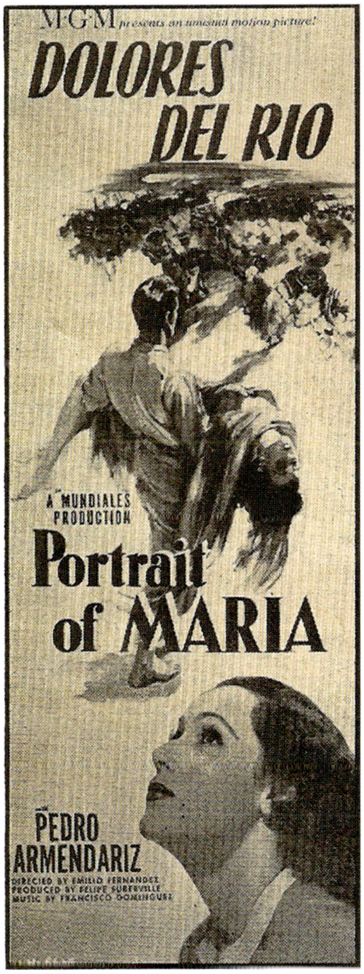

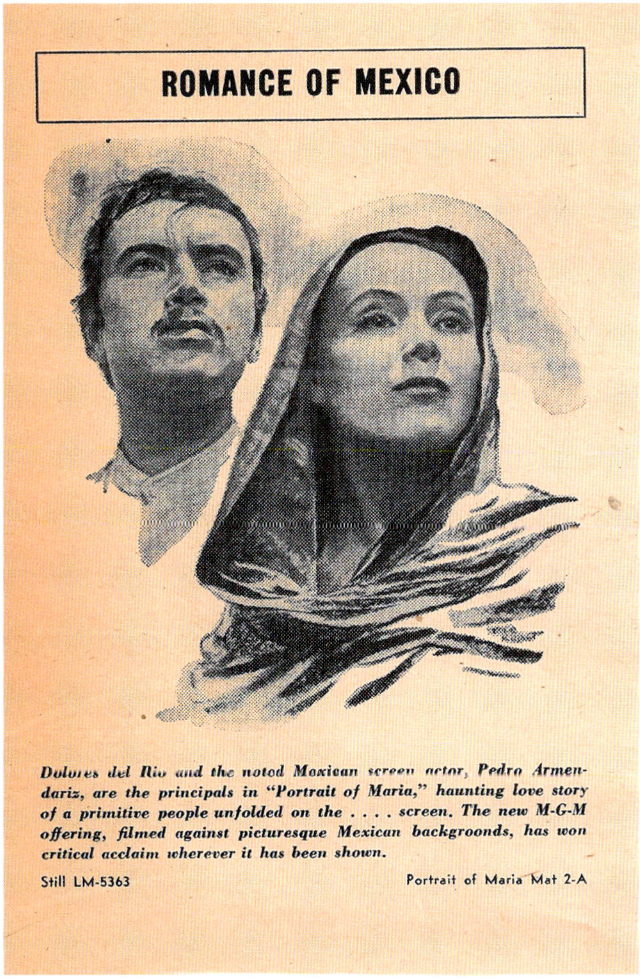

A press release for Dolores del Rio reveals extraordinary resemblance to the larger 17 in. compo tourist dolls. By Mundial Production for Metro Goldwyn Mayer Pictures, 11 x 15 in., 1940s $45 to 75

An original press release for Dolores del Rio in the movie "Portrait of Maria." by Mundial Production for Metro Goldwyn Mayer Pictures, 11 x 15 in., 1940s $45 to 75

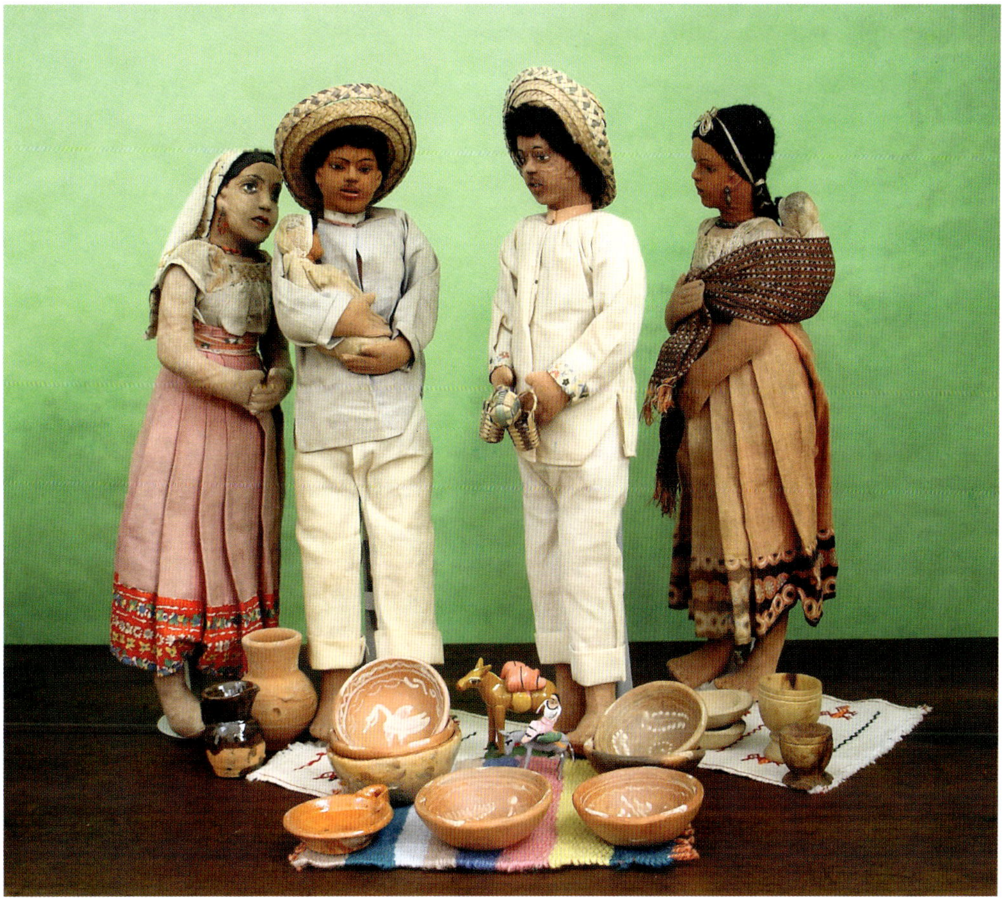

Indigenous Mexican families and their wares on a *petate* woven rug. A group of four large cloth dolls sold along the streets, 17 in., c. 1930s. Fine skill and detail with inset eyes of shell and incised teeth, the face skin has a clay slip over the cloth surface. All are wearing authentic clothing of the period. Personality and quality are portrayed beautifully. Made in Mexico. The two Indian women wear long *enredo* skirts platted and gathered. The *manta* prints have lively patterns. Their *blusas* have tiny embroidered stitching, and fine detail is featured in their expressions. Oversized feet and hands. $150 to 300ea.

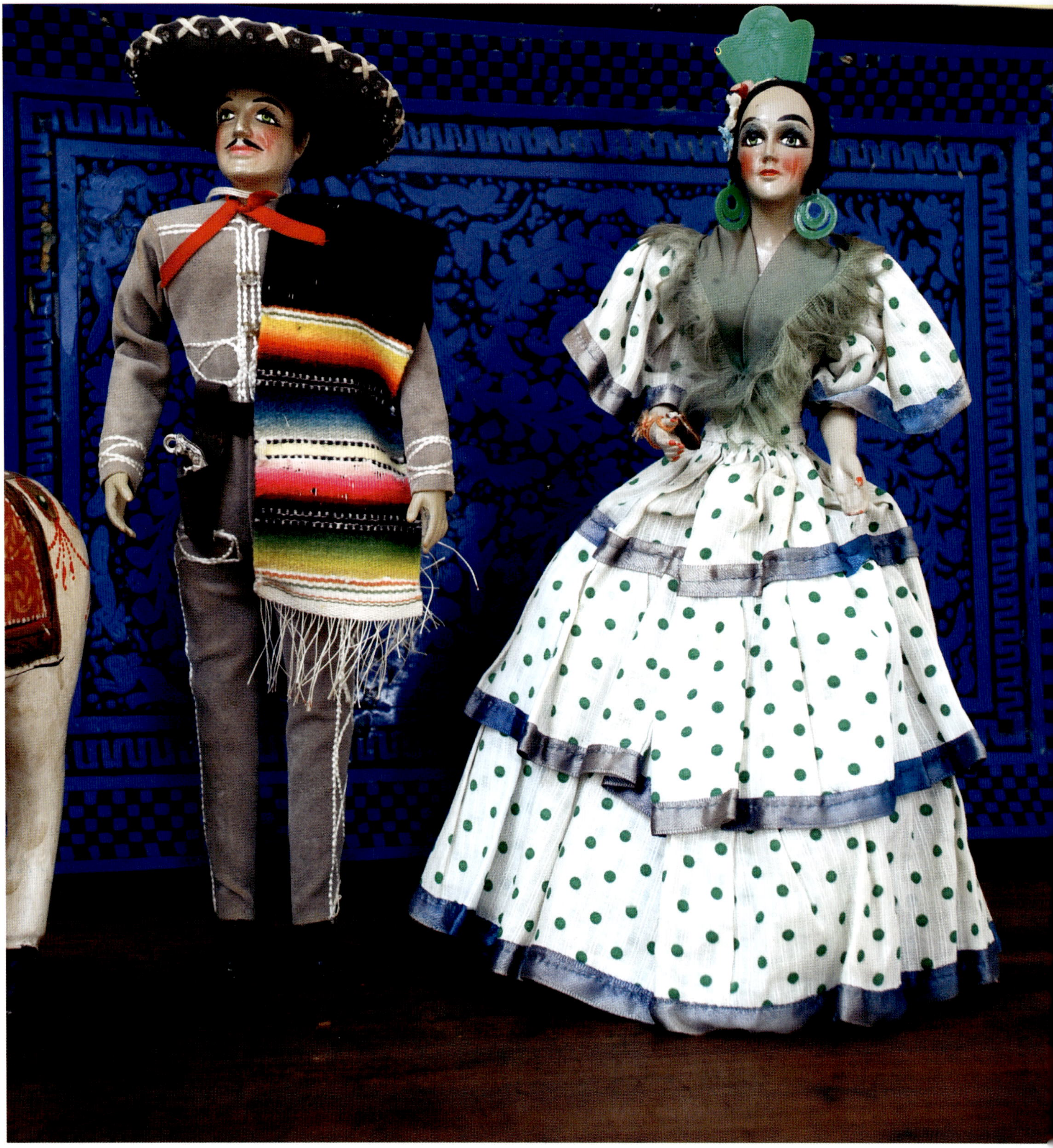

Poveda, Mexican 13 in. tourist dolls, c.1940s. The lovely *señorita* is dressed in a tiered, green and white polka dot *traje*, dress. Her accessories are wonderful: green deco-like tiara and matching earrings. Detail and quality construction in excellent condition. A hard composition resin body. $50 to 100 ea.

Composition *Irromples* Dolls

One of the better classes of dolls was the *muñeca irromples* or *muñeca de pasta*, termed in English as the "unbreakables." This was a popular slogan for early Reliable Toy Company composition dolls. The Mexican composition dolls were different from those imported from the United States or Canada. They hold many of the same characteristics, but their material properties were different. It appears that Mexico's dolls were more resilient, made with a thicker paste that minimized crazing. They have more of a gesso finish than the finer composition dolls that were imported. I discovered this to be a helpful feature when identifying the Mexican-made composition dolls, and it will assist a collector when there is no other source when determining the differences. Mexico's formula was probably developed because of economical, as well, as climatic reasons. The climate would not permit the imported composition formula to withstand long shelf wear. Most of the imported composite doll parts that are marked by exporters demonstrate these flaws, as there is a lot of crazing and peeling in them. It was economically more practical and profitable to make their special composite formula locally in Mexico. This practice provided them with less dependency on importing the parts, it stirred creativity, and it provided local workers with jobs. The labor to dress the dolls locally was cheaper for some importers. Most dolls were dressed with textiles from Mexico. By clothing the dolls locally, in original garments, the dolls provided a more authentic correlation to their country's traditional clothing. They conveyed a more personal connection to the tourist when they were made locally, and certainly they have sustained prestige compared with most souvenir dolls available on the market today.

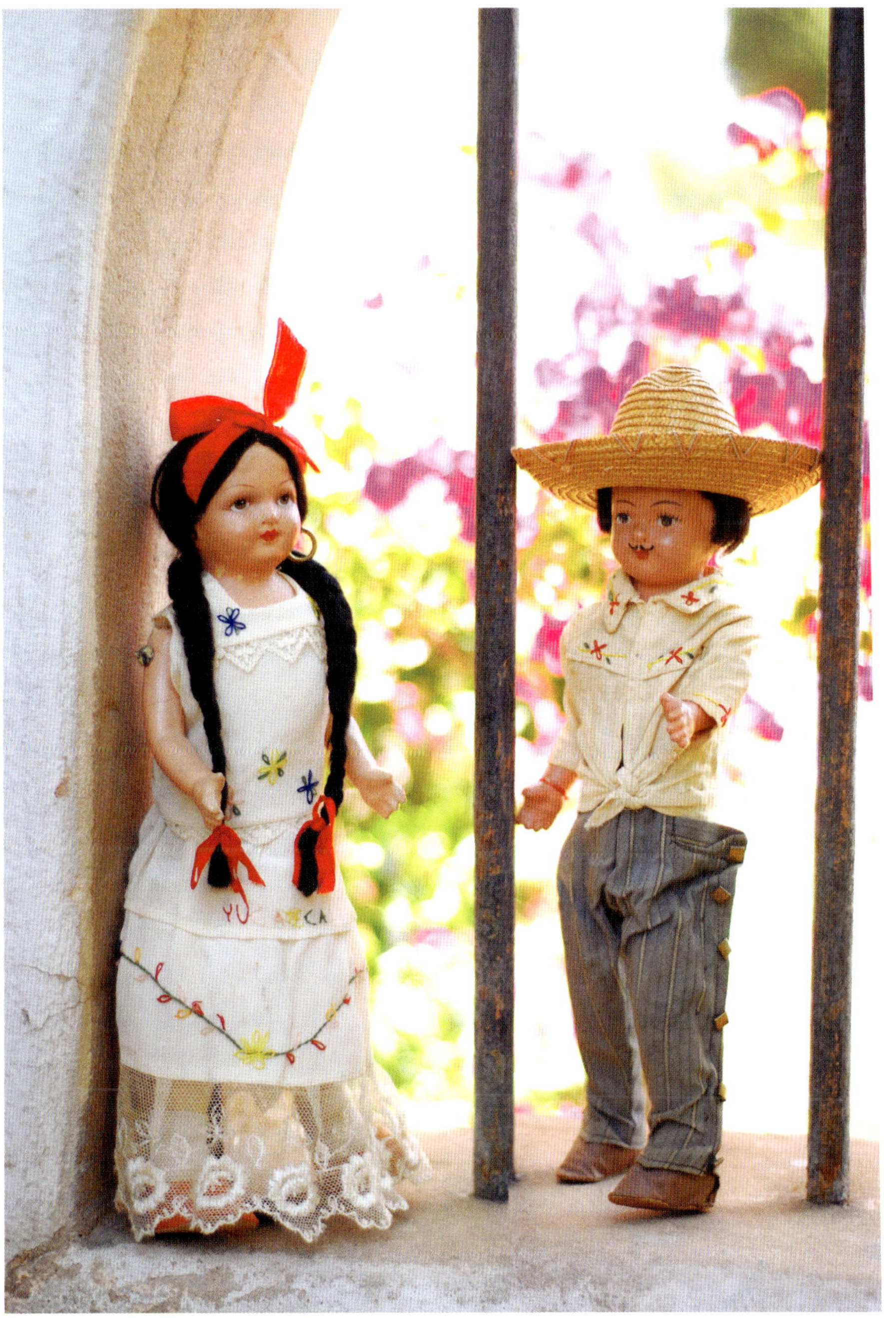

Old Mexico tourist dolls, both with composition and cloth bodies, 15 in., and authentic *mestizo* clothing. Beautiful detailed painted features, mohair wigs and clothing. Her silk dress is embroidered "Yucateca" along the border. No markings. Made in Mexico $80 to 200ea.

A litho print of a Tehuana doll by Luis Hidalgo, 1938.

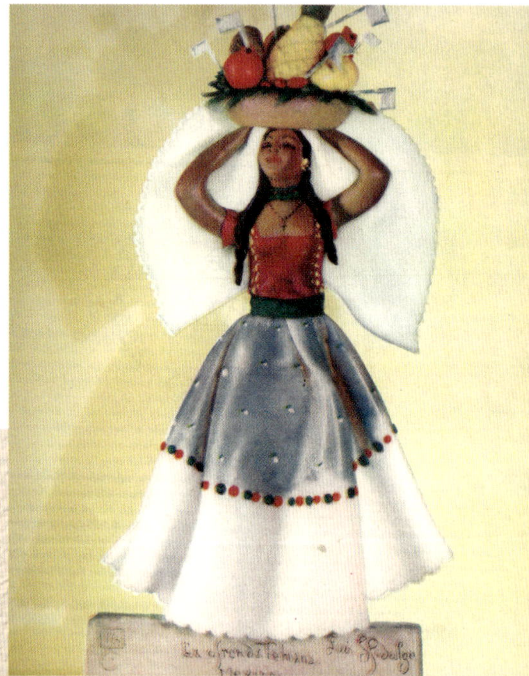

Two 14 in. composition and cloth dolls, wearing traditional *mestiza* garments with all typical accents c1930s, *China Poblana* red *castor* fabric. Puebla red clay potter. Made in Mexico $50 to 125

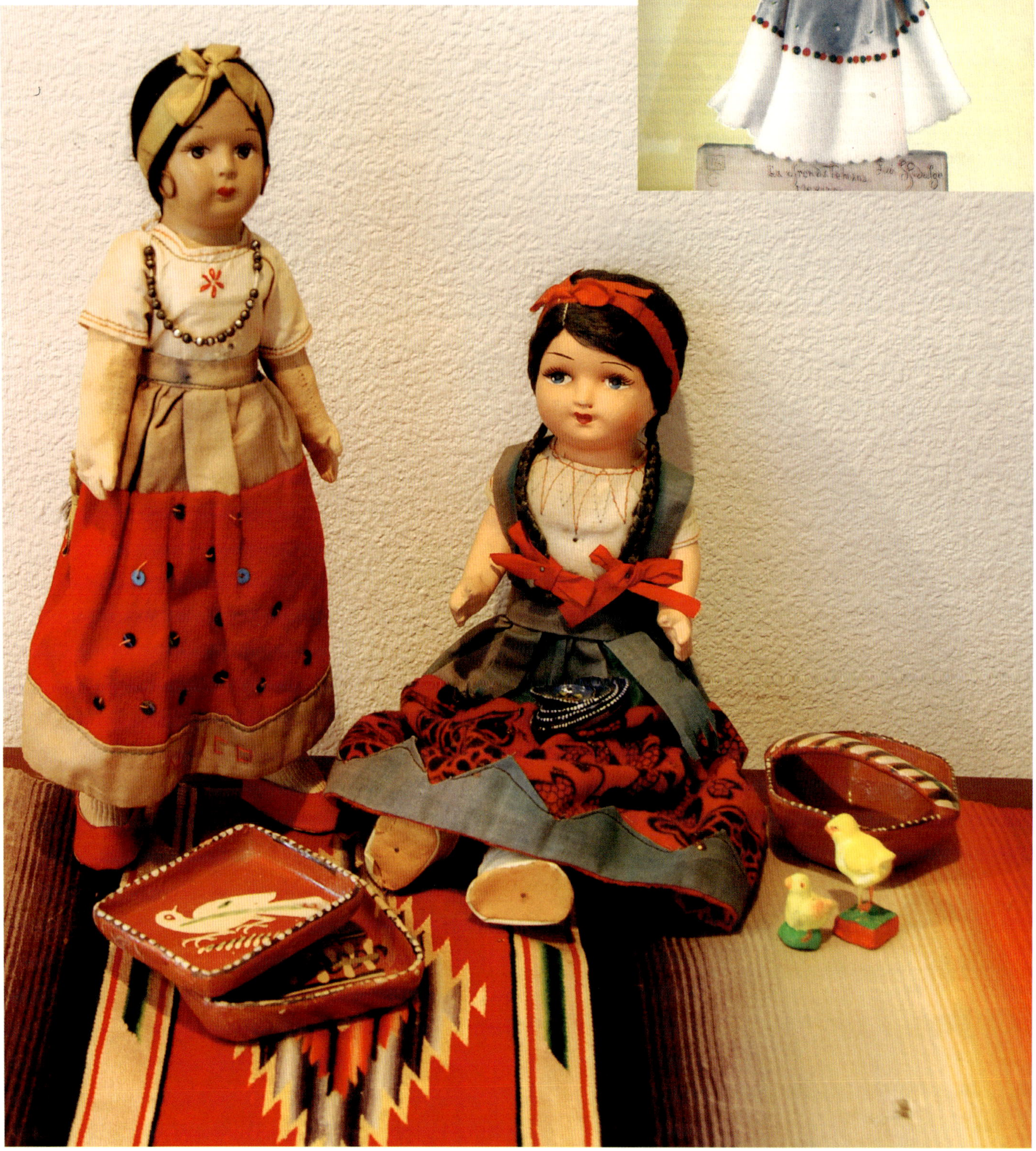

A competitive and thriving tourist market flourished through the 1950s, creating demand for different profitable souvenirs. Mexican composition dolls were certainly popular, and there was an unending production of remarkable beauties. Composition was less expensive and an alternative to wood, cloth, or expensive porcelain import dolls. The paper pulp-based mixture could be pressed into different molds to create parts in a faster and more efficient quantity. This definitely caused a change in the commercial doll industry. Vintage dolls that were imported from other toy companies also were beautiful examples of Mexican costume doll, but. their quality varied depending on the choice of materials, and they were priced higher than Mexican composition dolls. Costume dolls made by large companies in the early 20th century were in high demand. Toy manufacturers were competitive and knew that costume doll production was at its peak. Some imports were prototypes dressed according to their regions by importers to different countries. Mexican import doll costumes appear to be machine made, but many were finished by hand. All of the trimmings and motifs appear to have been chosen carefully and resemble those used on original skirts and blouses.

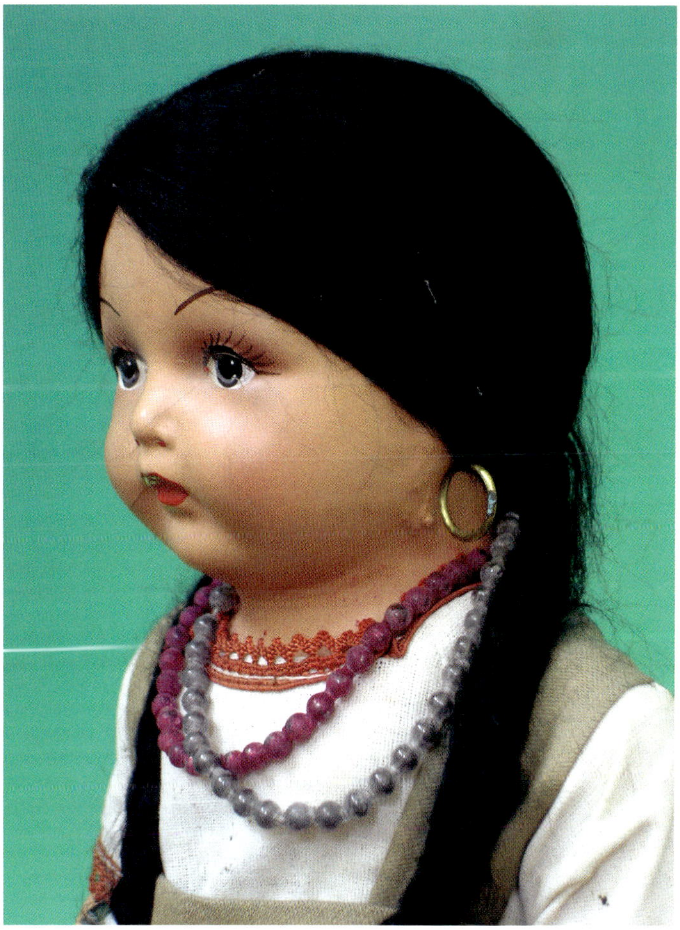

The face of a beautiful old Mexico tourist composition doll made by the E.I. Horseman Toy Co. Molded features, long black braid mohair wig, and painted detail.

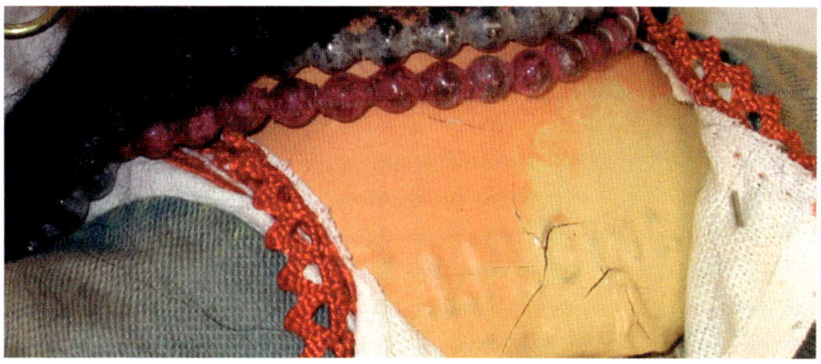

The E.I. Horseman Toy Co. name is stamped on the back of this import composition doll body, but it was dressed in Mexico, 1930s.

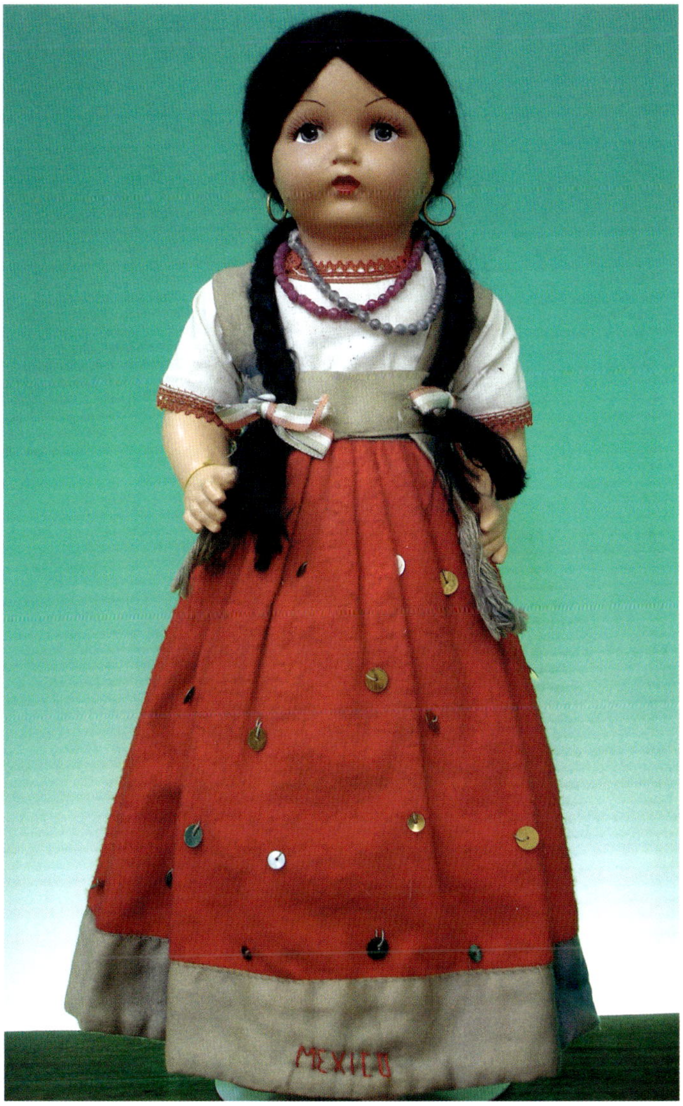

An impressive 18 in. composition and cloth doll made by E.I. Horseman Toy Co. for Mexico, c. 1930s. Marked by maker at the back of the neck. A long *enagua* red *castor* skirt, *huipil* and *rebozo*. Long mohair braids and glass beaded necklace, a treasure. Her body is cloth while her head, arms, and legs are of composition. $150 to 300

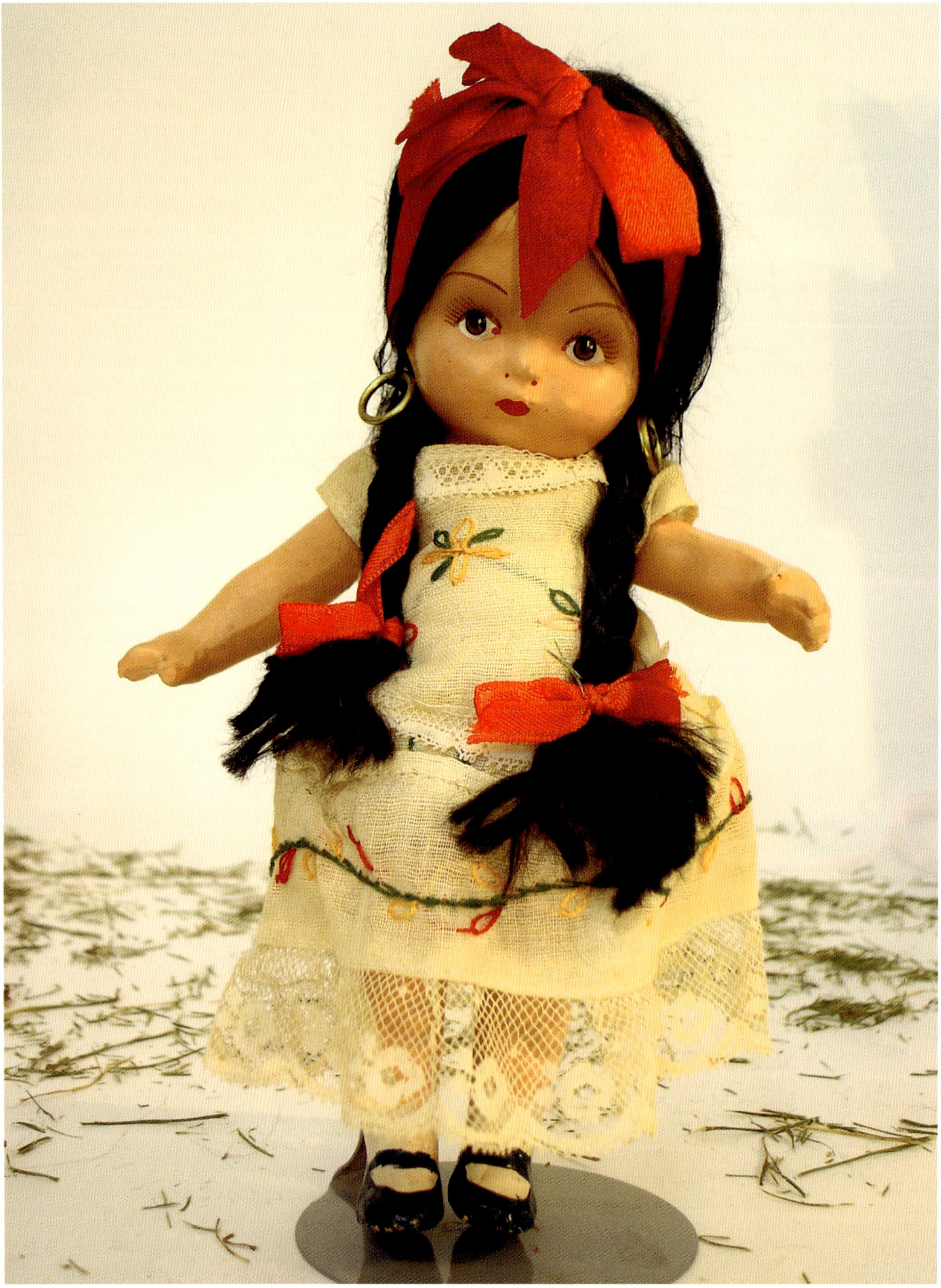

"Nicolilla" is a 9 in. Old Mexico joint-body, composition doll, c. 1940s. Dressed as a *mestiza* in an off-white cotton batiste dress with tiny embroidered flowers and with lace. Mohair wig. Painted shoes and socks. Made in Mexico. $40 to 75

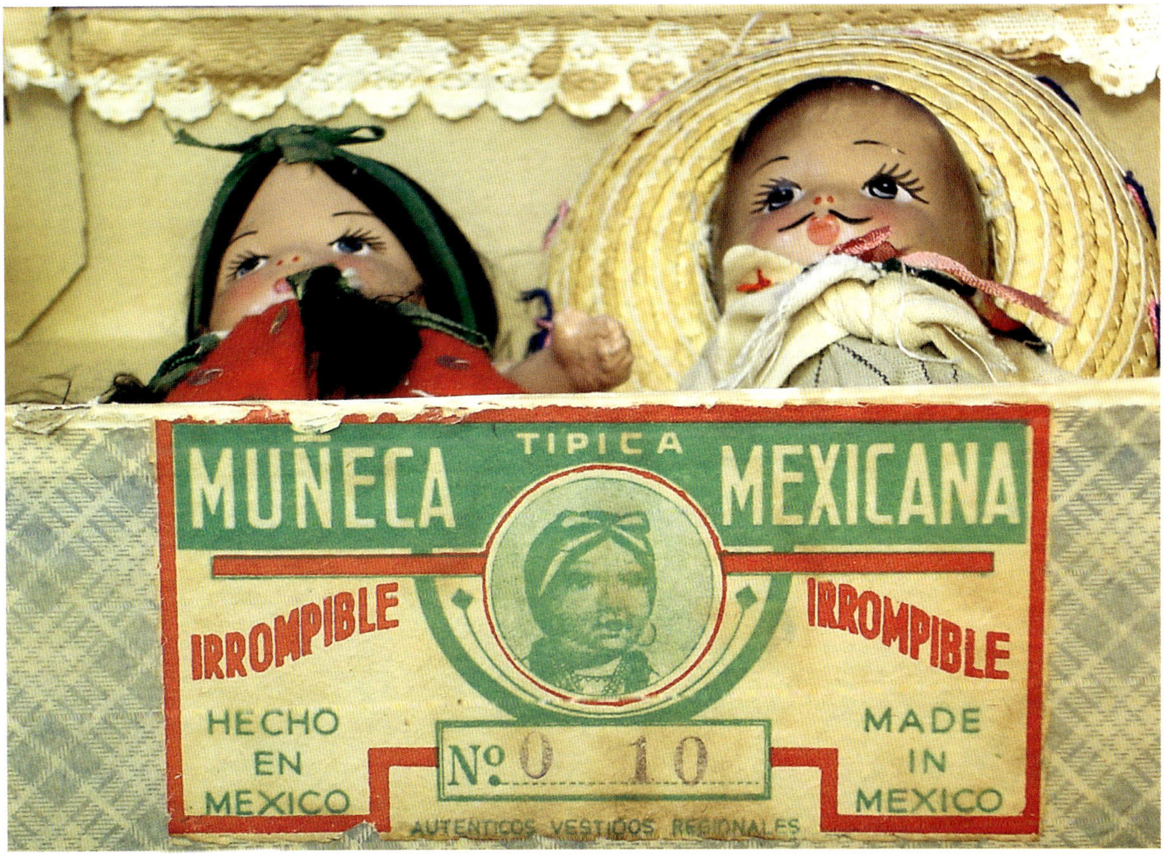

The original packaged Mexican composition dolls, 9 in., typically as marketed in the stores to the tourist, c. 1940s. *Muñeca de irromples*, the same slogan of the Reliable Toy Company in English, translates to "the unbreakables." $75 to 150

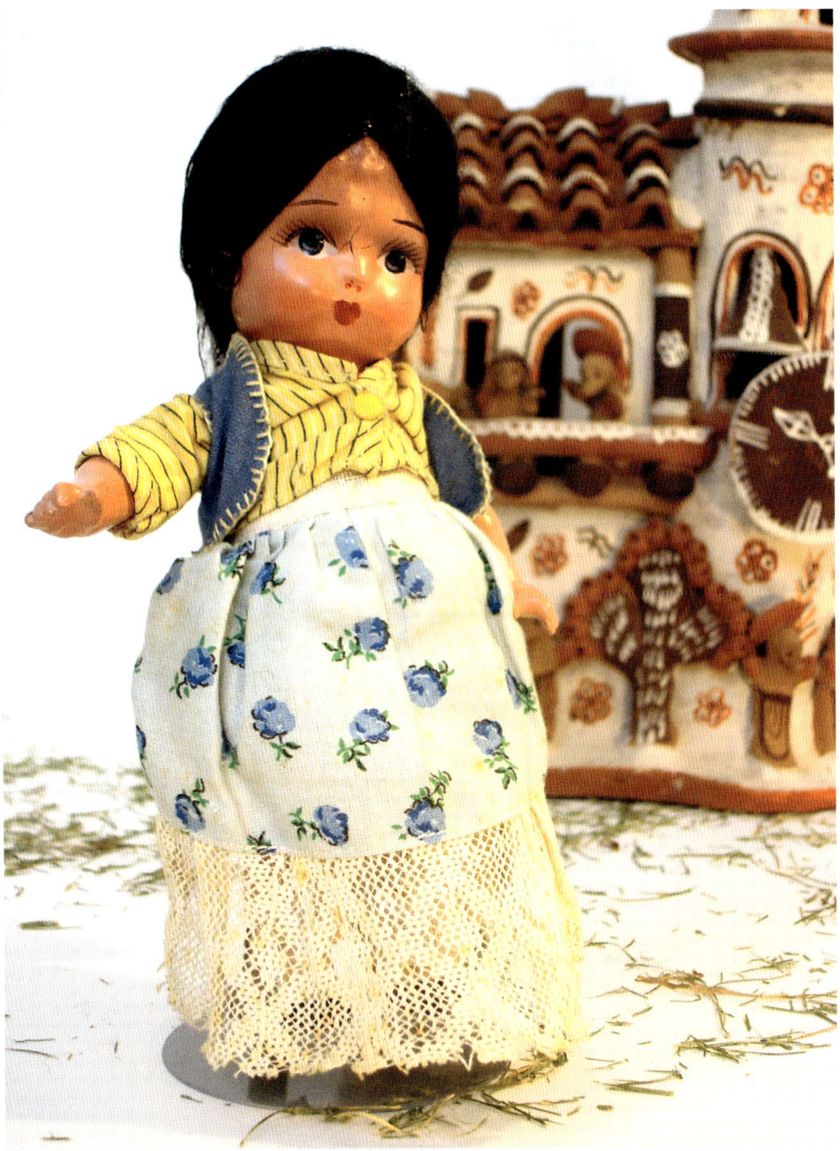

Typical of 9 in. tourist dolls sold in Mexico, a 5-pc. jointed composition doll, c.1940s. Dressed in a cotton *huipil* and calico-style skirt as a *mestiza*, black wool thread wig in tight braids with yellow ribbon around her face. Red painted shoes. Made in Mexico. $40 to 75

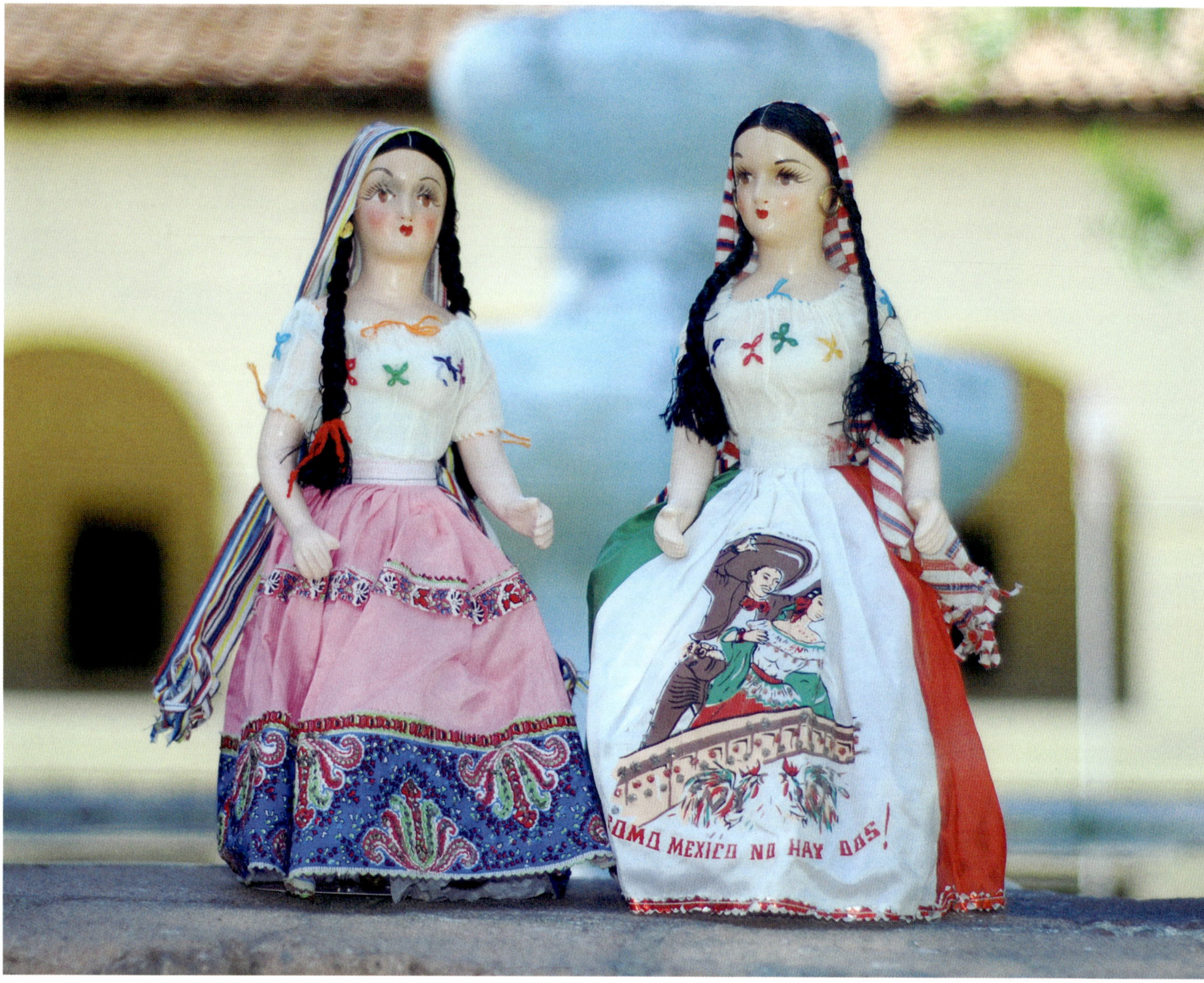

Two 17 in. *señorita mestizas* made in Mexico. A hard Mexican composition jointed doll resembling Dolores del Rio, a famous Mexican movie actress of the 1930s and '40s. $175 to 350

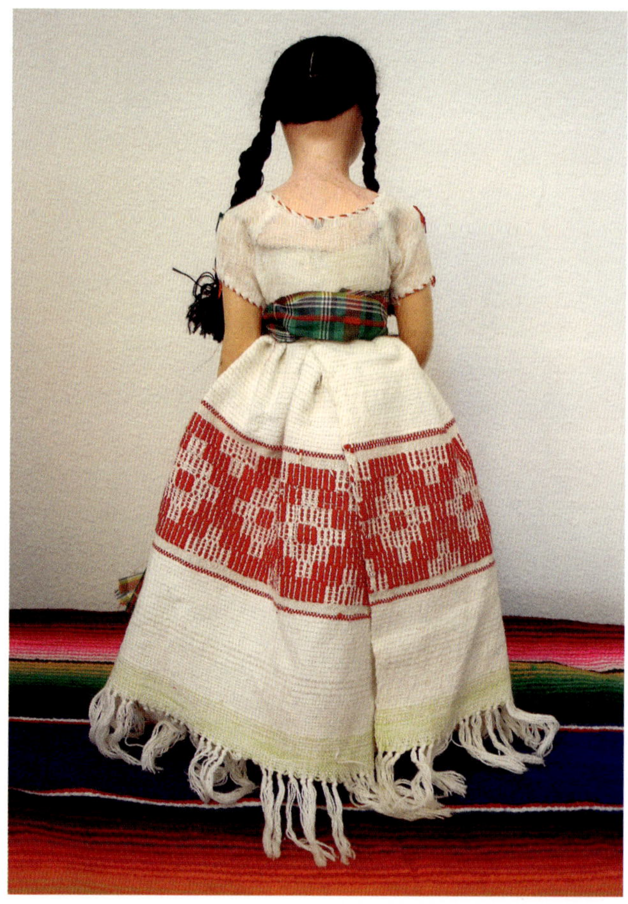

The back of this late 1940s composition doll shows how she is finished. The pattern of the skirt goes all the way around. Hand stitched cotton gauzed wearing a vibrant colored rayon sateen sash. Made in Old Mexico. $175 to 300

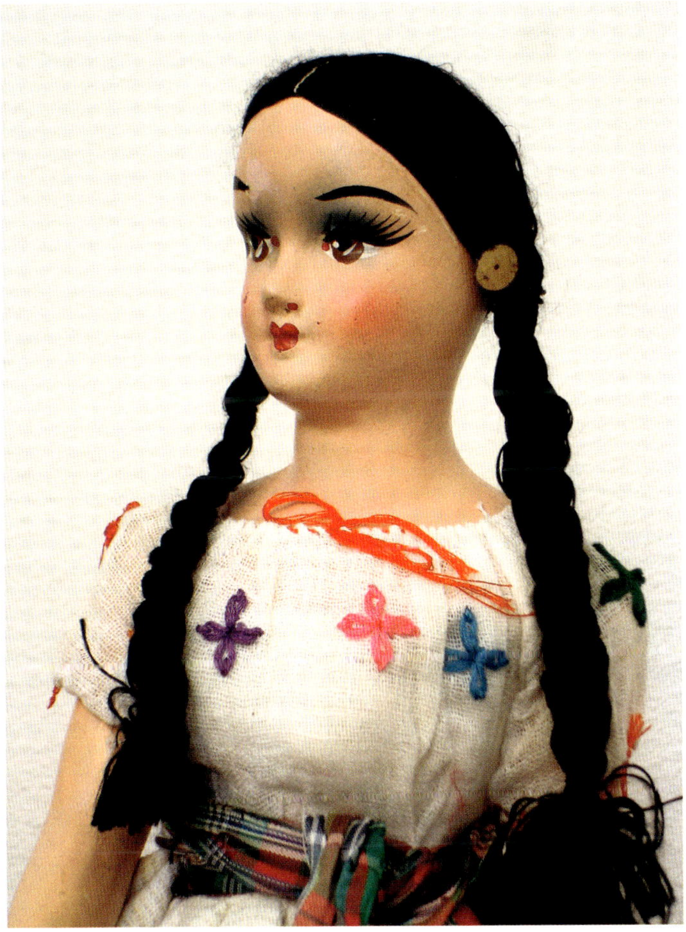

Beautiful black threaded braids, hand painted polychrome detail. Her hands and clothing seem provincial, a folk art quality. Painted gold shoes and white stocking socks.

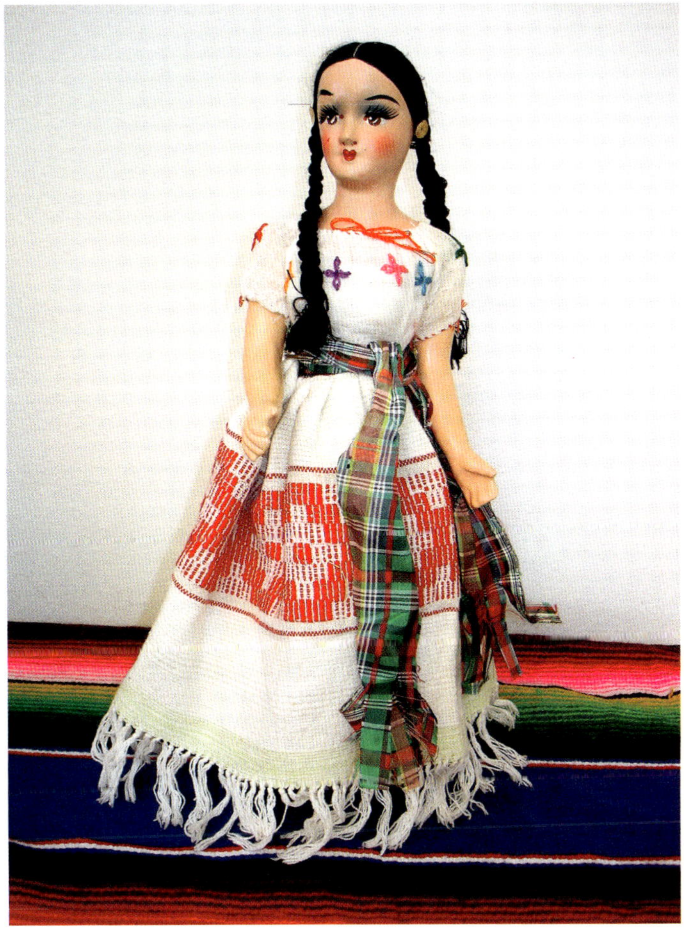

A late 1940s *mestiza* composition doll, dressed in a peasant Spanish top and an indigenous woven skirt. She is approx 16.5 in. tall. A hard stuffed body (saw dust). In excellent condition. Made in Old Mexico. $175 to 300

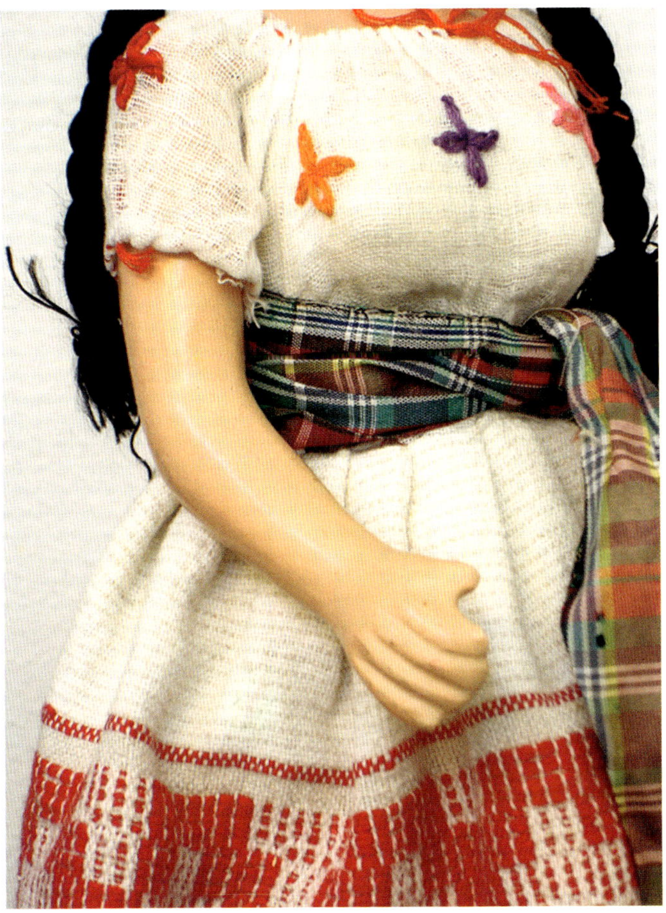

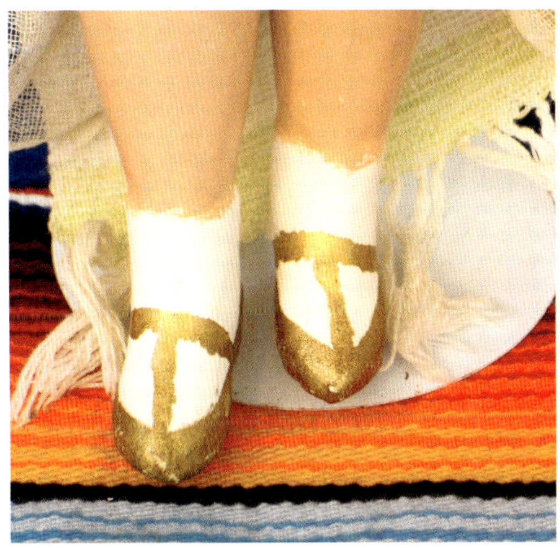

Mexico's composition was different, shoes were hand painted usually in gold or silver. Made in Mexico

The woven textiles and attention to detail on her skirt and *blusa*. Made in Mexico 1940s.

Mexican composition dolls appear to have distinctive differences. Usually the molded hair under their wigs identifies a Mexican original as does the surface of the skin; they are not as polished or smooth as imported composition dolls. Mexican doll eyes are not inset, nor do they have sleep eyes. The Mexican dolls also were strung differently: hooks that were pressed into the mold were strung together with string that held their arms and legs in place. The head was commonly attached to the torso. Mexican composition dolls usually have cotton, silk, or wool threads for hair wigs, accented with accessories that would match the ensemble they were wearing. Their cute molded and painted features often have flirty eyes, and closed red lips were common. Their clothing, though, set them apart. Mexican-made dolls were dressed with authentic clothing of the regions they depict. The Mexican artisan, regarded as a laborer, was a skilled craftsman, and that is reflected in the costumes. Some of the dolls may have been mass-produced in Mexico, but only on a local scale. These dolls could only be bought in Mexico.

Many of the imported composition dolls had heads and body parts made by the thousands by doll companies such as The Reliable Toy Company from Canada, Ideal Toy Corp., and others who produced prototypes. The imported dolls suffer in quality when compared to Mexican-made dolls.

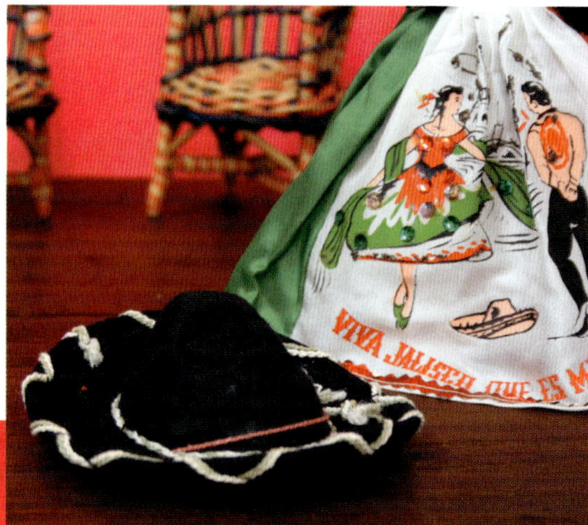

A typical *charro's* wool felt hat and the charra's rayon printed skirt. Colorful attributes of Mexico, c. 1940s. Made in Mexico.

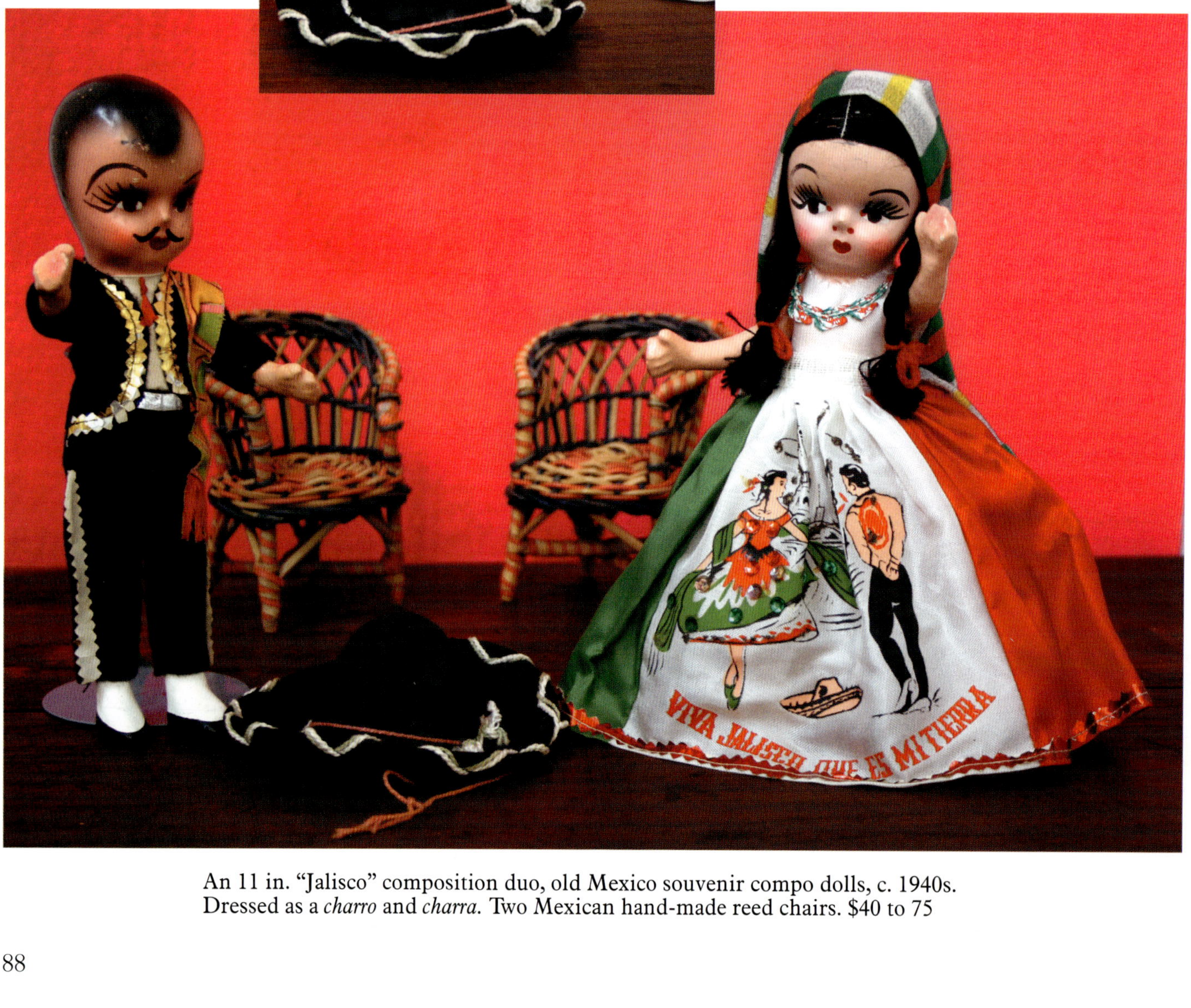

An 11 in. "Jalisco" composition duo, old Mexico souvenir compo dolls, c. 1940s. Dressed as a *charro* and *charra.* Two Mexican hand-made reed chairs. $40 to 75

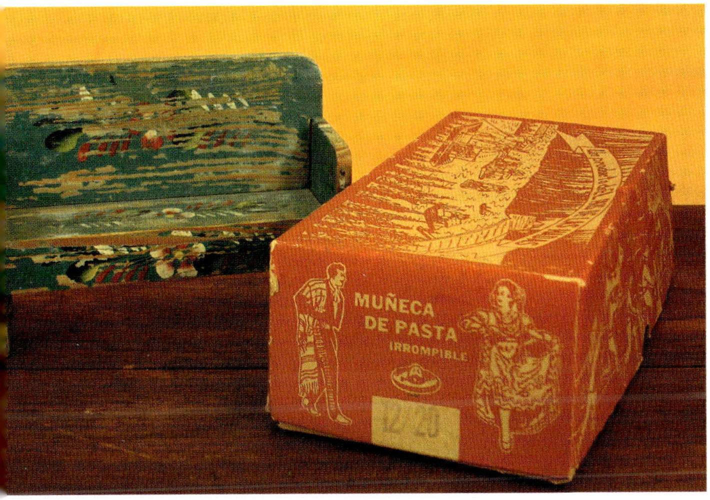

The original box "*muñeca de pasta*" from the dolls made in Mexico, 1950s. Miniature hand-painted Mexican bench, c. 1930s.

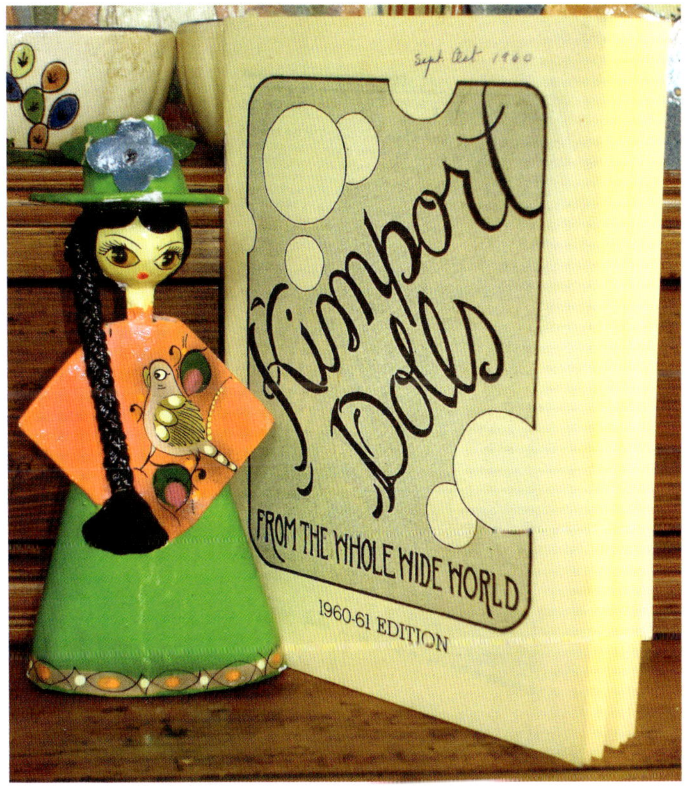

Attributed to the Tonala state, skinny 7 in. doll stands next to the Kimport Dolls magazine/catalog published for doll enthusiasts, 1950s to '60s. $20 to 40

An attributed trio of 9 in. typical tourist dolls, sweet Spanish colonial *mestizas*. Old Mexico souvenir dolls, 5-part jointed and strung bodies. c. 1950s. Made in Mexico $45 to 100 ea.

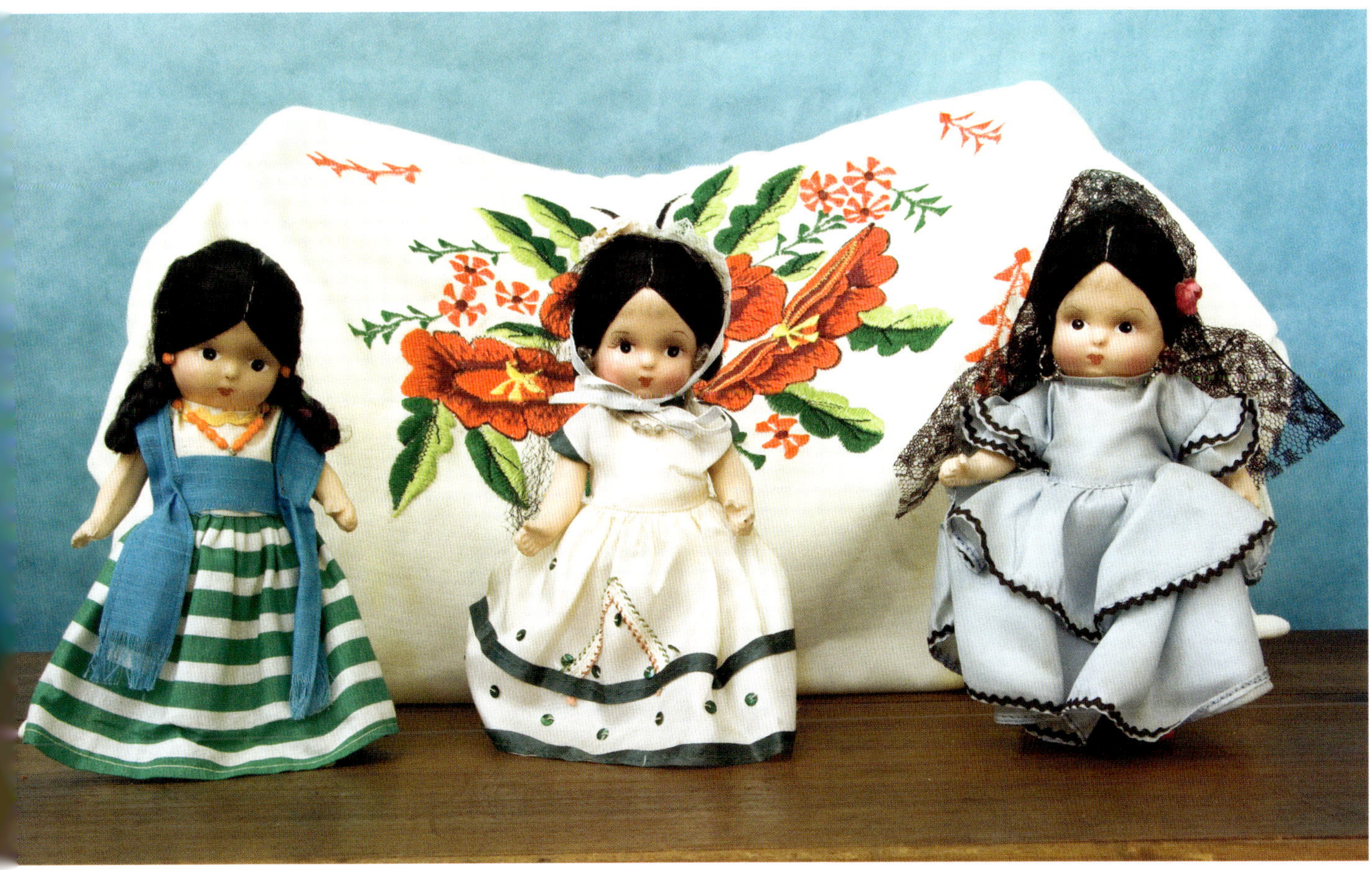

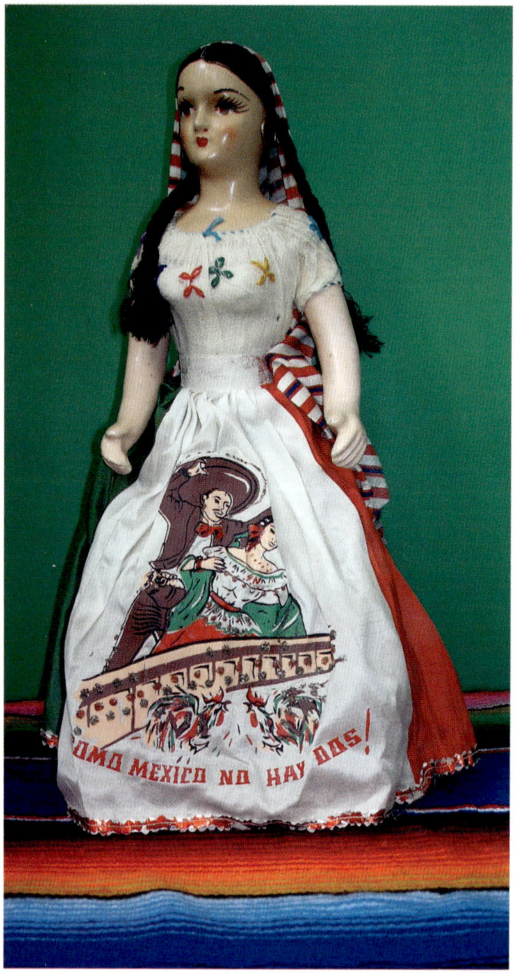

"Como Mexico No Hay Dos," a 17 in. large tourist doll, made in Mexico. Green, white, and red skirt, Mexico's national colors pay tribute to her country, c. 1950s. The Mexican composition doll's face shows a gesso polychrome finish, different than imports composition formula. Excellent condition $125 to 300

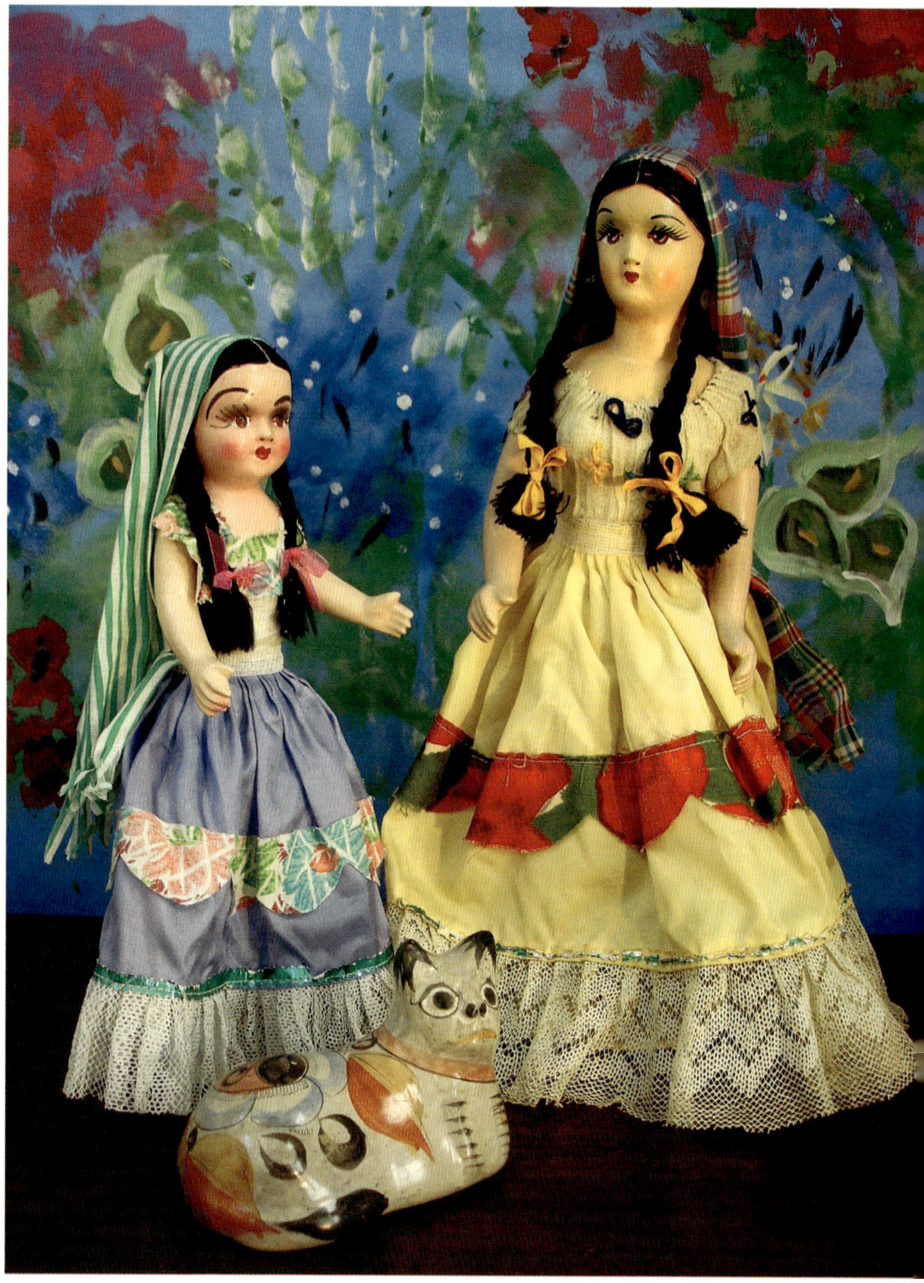

Two *mestiza* dolls, c. early 1950s, 17 in. and 14 in. They were made by different doll makers (notice the molded features), but their clothing is similar. Popular arts Tonala pottery cat. $75 to 300

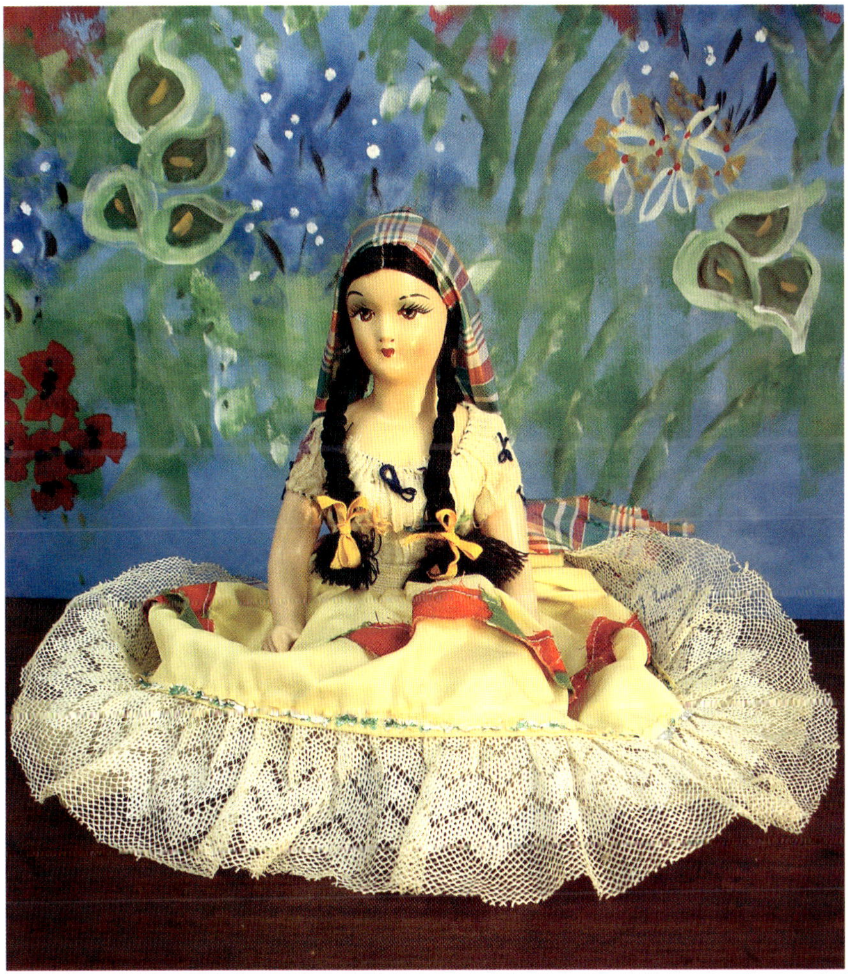

A 17 in. composition doll, made in Mexico, showing the fullness of her taffeta skirt and lovely lace trim, c. 1950s. $125 to 300

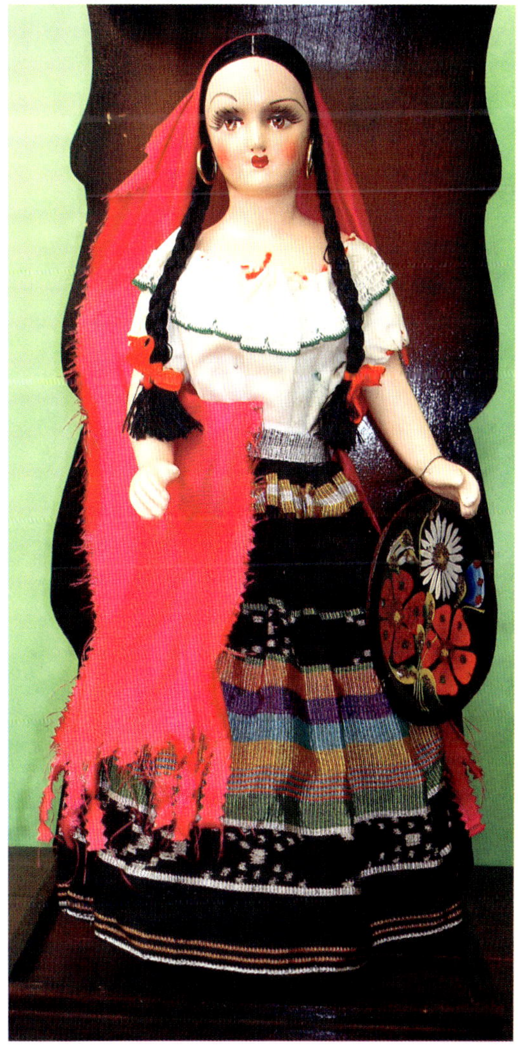

A stunning 17 in. Mexican composition doll, c 1940s-'50s, in excellent condition, all original indigenous detail of a *mestiza*. $150 to 350

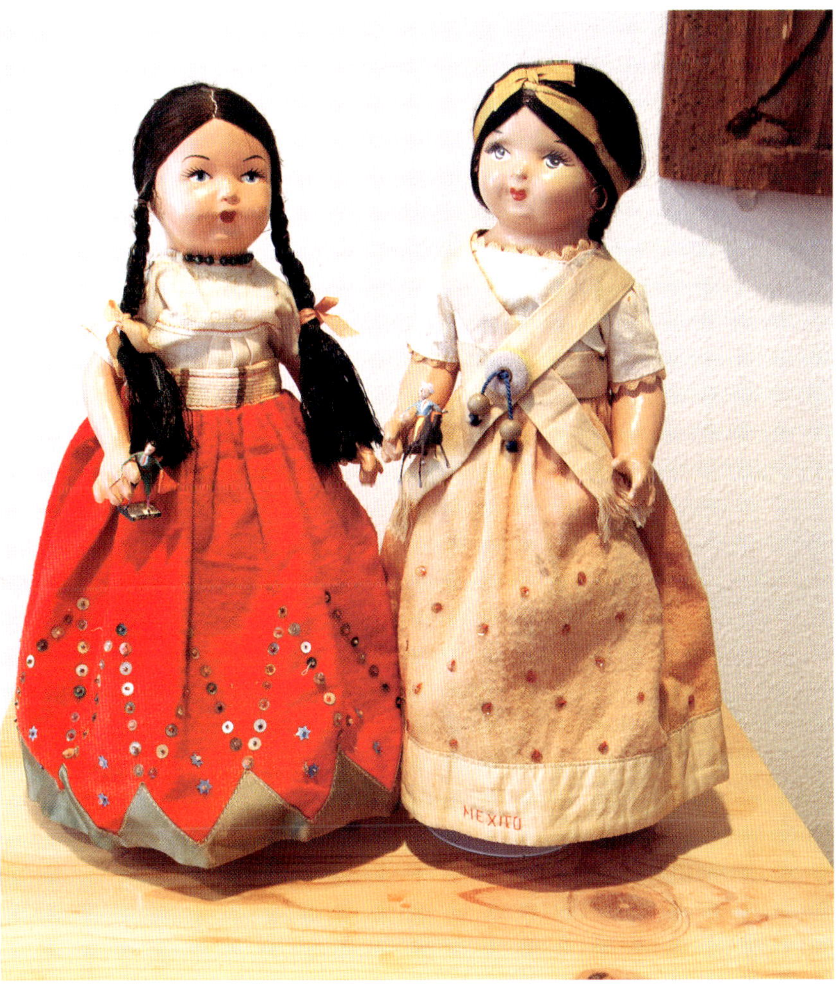

Two 14 in. composition and cloth dolls, both wearing traditional *mestiza* skirts with typical accents, c. 1930s.Both holding tiny wire figures, popular arts. Made in Mexico $50 to 125

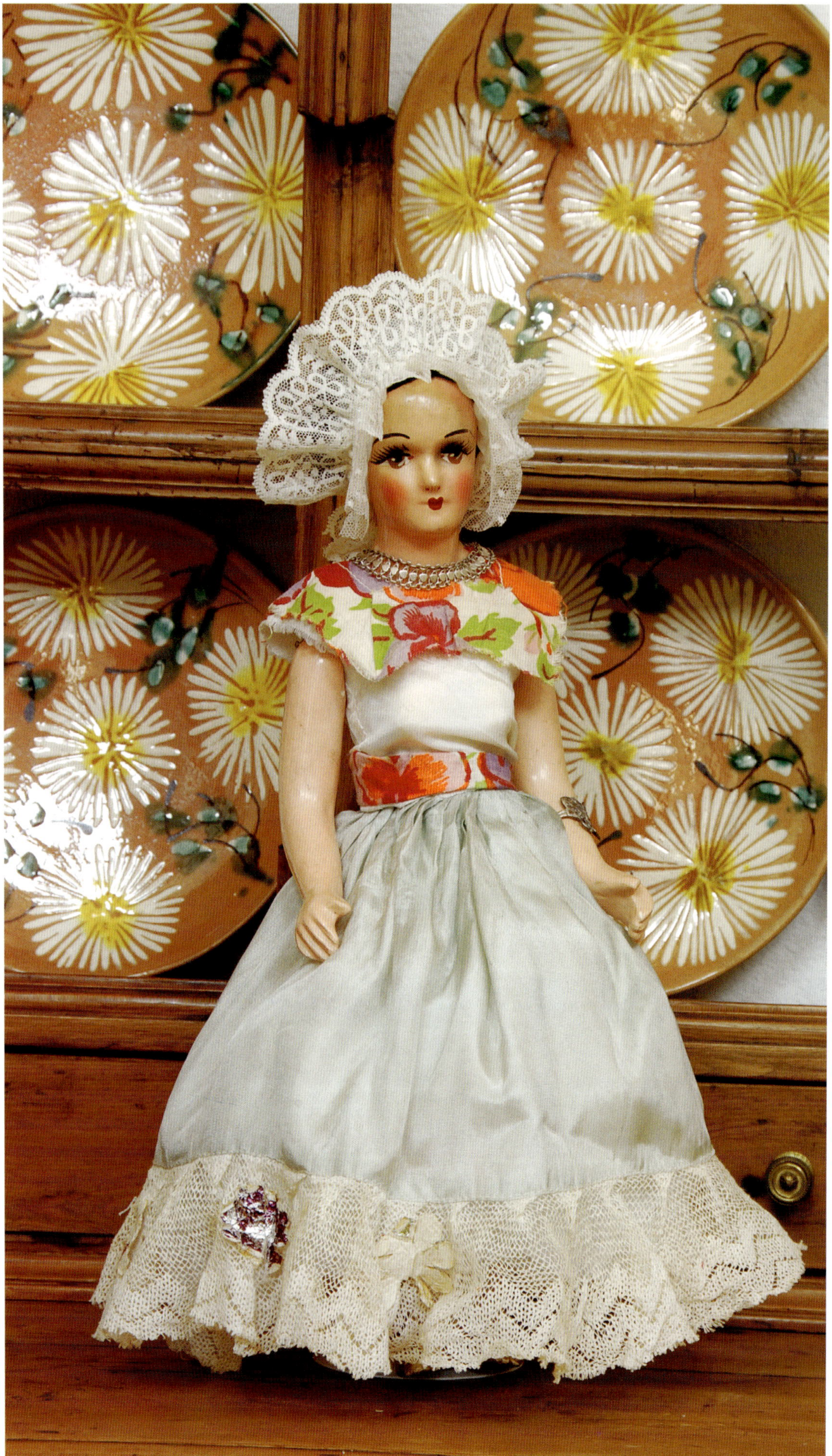

A *Tehuana* dress, a 17 in. composition doll, made in Mexico, c. 1940s. Dress is a rayon taffeta with foil flowers and lace. $150 to 350

Cloth Dolls

Vintage costume cloth dolls reveal many things to a doll collector. The style in which the doll is made, the quality of the materials, and the skill level of the maker determine its value as well as reflect its origin and age. Mexican cloth dolls seem to invoke more personality than composition dolls. A maker's special touch gives the doll variances and particulars that form an essential part of its regional appearance. When you observe the specialties of a cloth doll, you gain a personal experience with which to admire it. You enjoy the characteristics each one possesses, as no two are ever exactly alike. Creating something from bits and pieces of materials, while carefully adding attributes, produces something unique. This is why I greatly admire handmade cloth dolls.

A majority of Mexican cloth dolls were fashioned with indigenous, exceptional detail and were marketed as souvenirs during the height of tourism in the mid-20th century. Like other of Mexico's folk arts, cloth dolls are unmarked and usually lack provenance. If you are lucky, you can trace them to the district they probably came from, but even some of the stores that sold them originally couldn't have told you their source. This fact is even noted in the Cordry's book, in which the authors acknowledge that little in the way of record keeping was ever kept for where the woven textile pieces came from or the origins of their famous, unsigned pottery. Indeed, this important information is the essence of value for many collectors. For this reason, the condition, availability, and quality alone permit the collector to estimate a reasonable value.

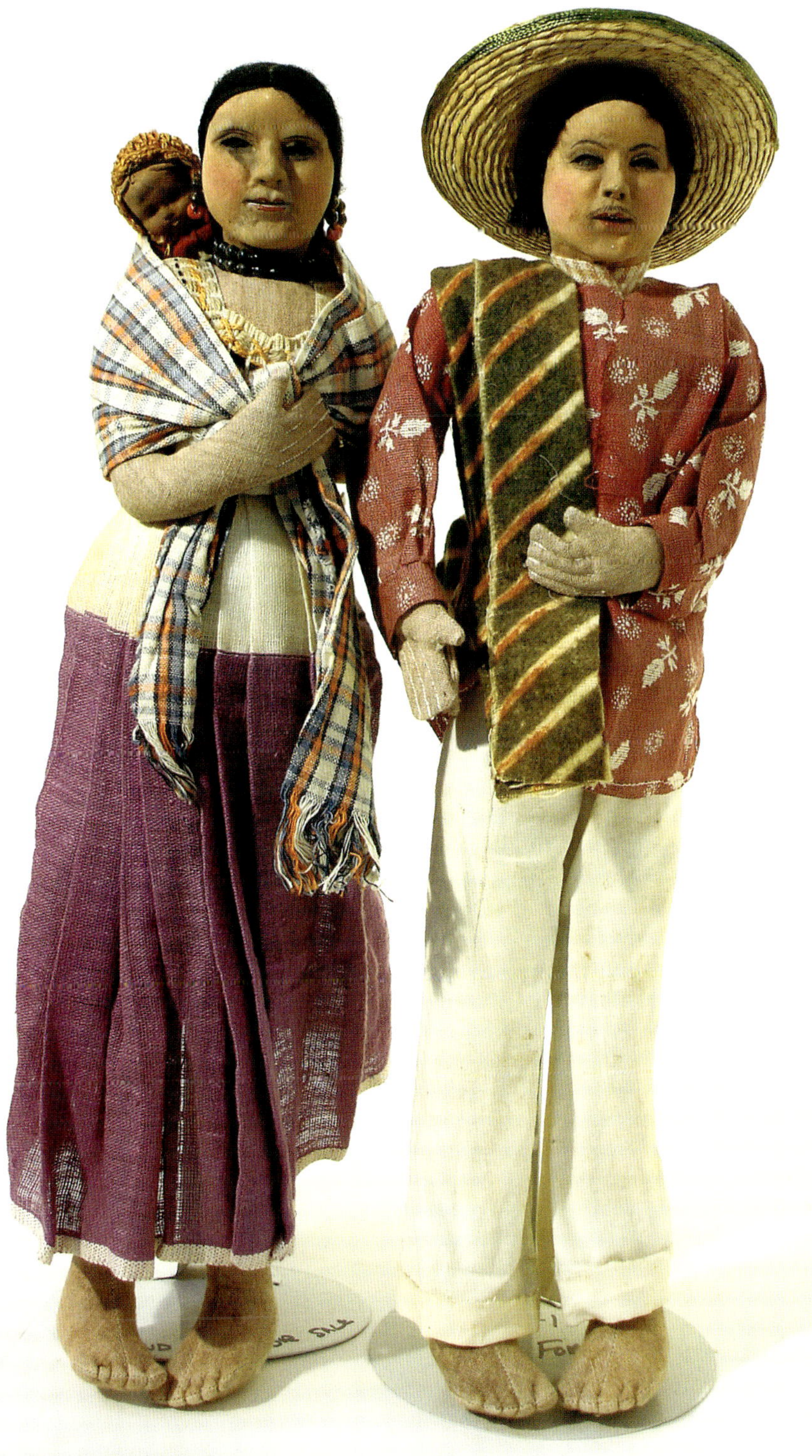

An impressive pair of 18 in. Indian cloth dolls, c1930s. Sometimes referred to as "Diego Dolls," made in Mexico. *Manta* cotton cloth, hard filled with molded features, seeds and incised shells for eyes and teeth. Extraordinary detail sculpted faces. Molded features; a slip clay glaze creates subtle traits to the skin which gives an almost realistic surface. Each one has enlarged hands and feet. *Papelillo* earrings and necklace beads. Mohair wool wigs. The female Indian doll is wearing a white *huipil* with a square neck embroidered with yellow and black, chain stitching. A plaid *rebozo* holds her child, over a white and *enredo* skirt. Both are bare foot. The male doll has a high collared, pleated print *manta* shirt, white pants. A wide brimmed *sombrero* trimmed with green stitching along the border with a *serape*. Extraordinary detail in the faces of these two large cloth costumed Indian dolls reveals how important it was for the artist to authenticate ethnic features. Careful thought and skill interpreted through observation and patience. She illustrates just one of the uses *rebozo*, made of a *manta* cotton, an essential piece that serves a multitude of purposes, tied around and under her arm enabling her to carry her baby throughout the day, protected and close to her at all times. $150 to 300 each

Vintage cloth dolls seem to truly represent the original costumes of Mexico, more so than dolls of other mediums. A maker's creativity, skill, and careful thought was reinvented over and over again when creating each doll. It must have taken days or weeks to make one cloth doll. When comparing them with composition or imported dolls, cloth dolls were less costly to make and resell. Labor was cheaper than the materials used to make the other dolls. Many native artisans could make cloth dolls in the comfort of their homes, with modest supplies, and sell them in the marketplace or to tourist stores for income. The tenacity with which tourist dolls were sold is evident. Makers of vintage Mexican cloth dolls gained popularity for their important souvenirs. This can be verified by the abundance and variety that is still found today.

For the most part, I am unable to substantiate any preferred method by which Mexican cloth dolls were constructed. There was a consistent manner in which each doll was made, and popular "model types," but their characteristics have insightful differences. Most

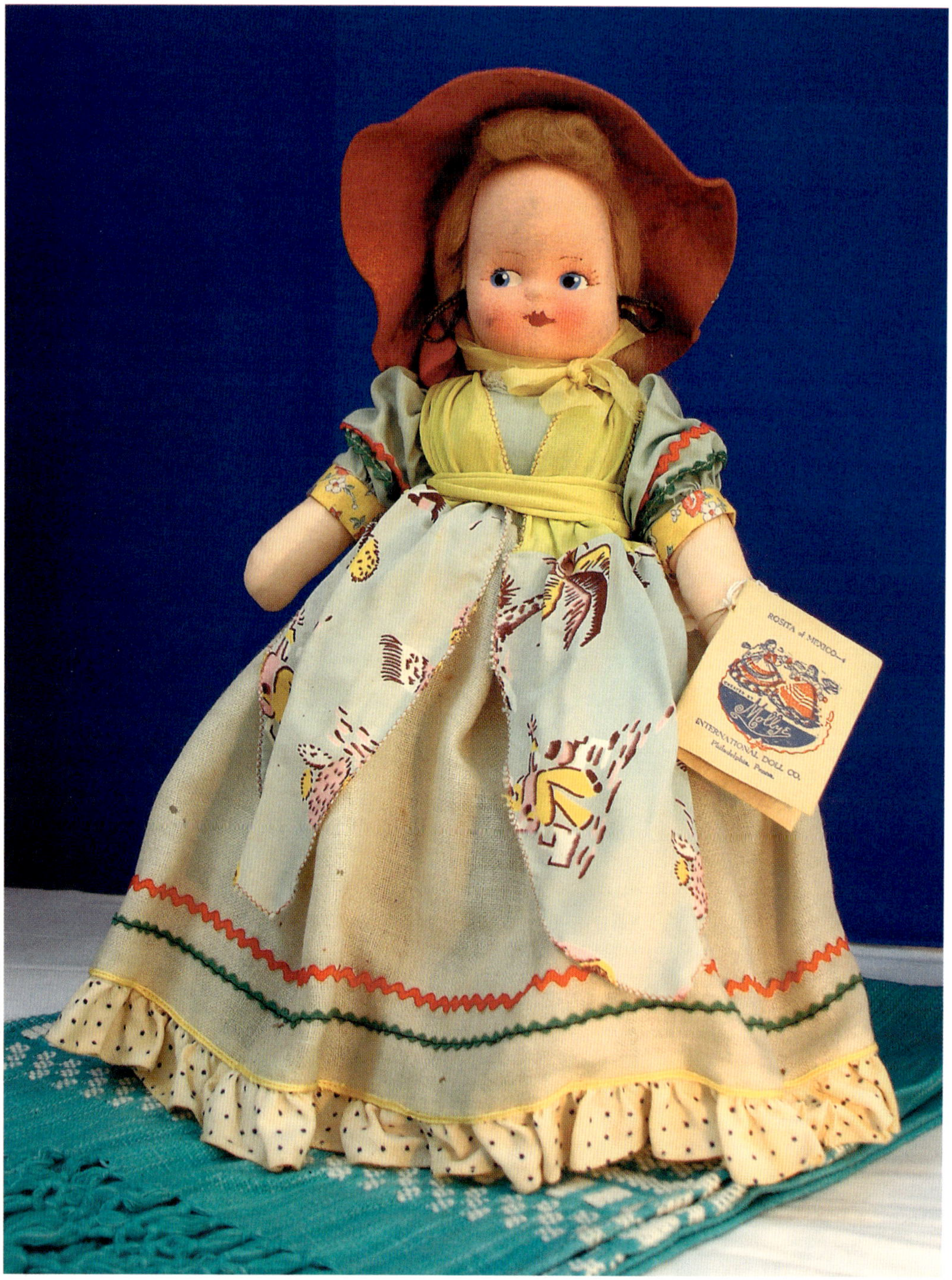

Rosita of Mexico, a Mollye doll, made by the International Doll Co, 15 in. stuffed doll. Her tag states "a skirt of ornate trimming, wide brimmed sombrero and a brilliant sash is the typical Mexican costume." 1940s, Philadelphia, Penn. $60 to 125

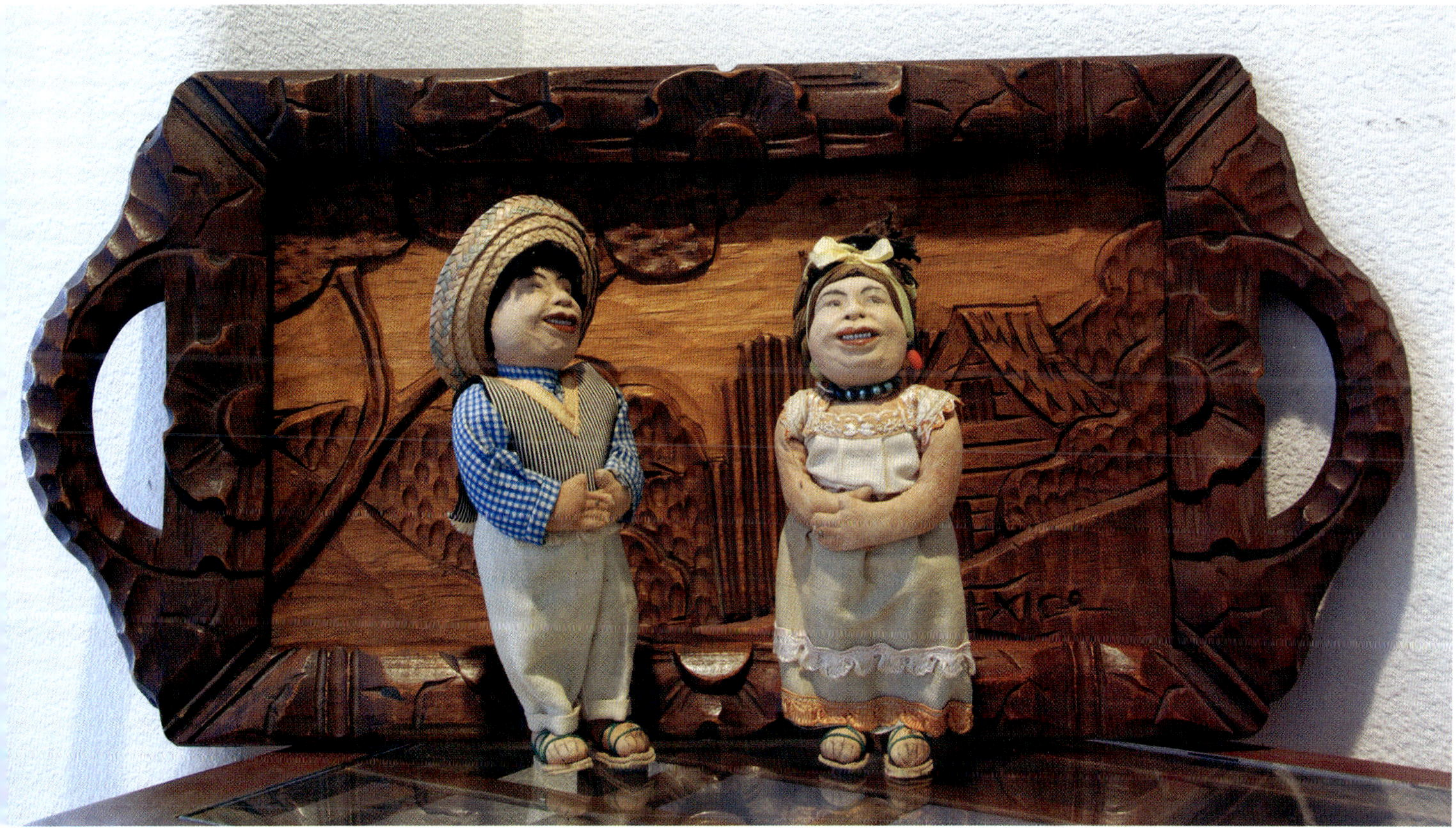

A whimsical, hard, cloth and sculpted 11 in. couple, with over-exaggerated features, c. 1930s. Kimport or doll club dolls. Magnificent detail, with inset eyes and teeth. Behind them is a old Mexico carved wooden tray, c1940s. $75 to 150ea.

of the cloth dolls shown here are over 50 years old and are highly collectible today. Each of them shows unique stitching and embroidery, regional and traditional traits, along with obvious skill of their maker. Although many appear to be entirely hand made, there are just as many in which the bodies where machine stitched with hand-woven cloth. There are also those that were entirely hand stitched with commercial cloth and embroidered details added later by hand. So, quite a few variations appear in their construction.

Most Mexican dolls that have survived over the years are not in the best condition. Cloth and composition bodies were vulnerable to conditions of aging. Unlike European dolls, the materials were not always of the highest quality. Cotton, felt, wool, or other hand-woven textile scraps were often used. Their bodies were often stuffed with straw, wood pulp, cotton, or scraps of any filler material. Hand sewn and machine-made body parts in different sizes and shapes were joined by wire, buttons, nails, or round discs, so they could move freely. Some older cloth dolls have jointed bodies sewn together, and their bodies would be as soft or as hard and stiff as the textiles and the costumes that were used. Usually, they would have mitten-like hands and feet, with just stitching between the fingers and toes.

Their facial features varied from detailed to simple, stitched or painted expressions. Some of the more detailed dolls appear to have been inspired by a real person, as the artisan captured distinctive personalities. They may have molded faces with inset eyes and teeth, tinted complexions, and detailed painted or sewn expressions that would have certainly demanded hours of work. Flatter faces were either painted or hand stitched, with embroidered features being sewn carefully to capture ethnic traits. Some have whimsical expressions, while others were simple interpretations, probably marketed through the tourist trade.

Mexicans utilized an unlimited resource of indigenous materials available to them. They set high standards of quality and it was important to doll makers to document their actual clothing. A wide variety of dolls with their actual indigenous clothing from all of Mexico's regions is hard to find, so it is essential to appreciate those we do find.

Popular costumes, such as the female *China Poblana* or the male *Charro*, were aggressively copied on the dolls. They were the most common costumes worn during the peak of tourism in the 1920s. The cloth dolls shown demonstrate a wide spectrum of variations in popular costumes. They enlighten you as well as document a culture that has passed. Each one discloses strong cultural ties and reveals the conventional clothing worn during a revival of mixed traditions in Mexico.

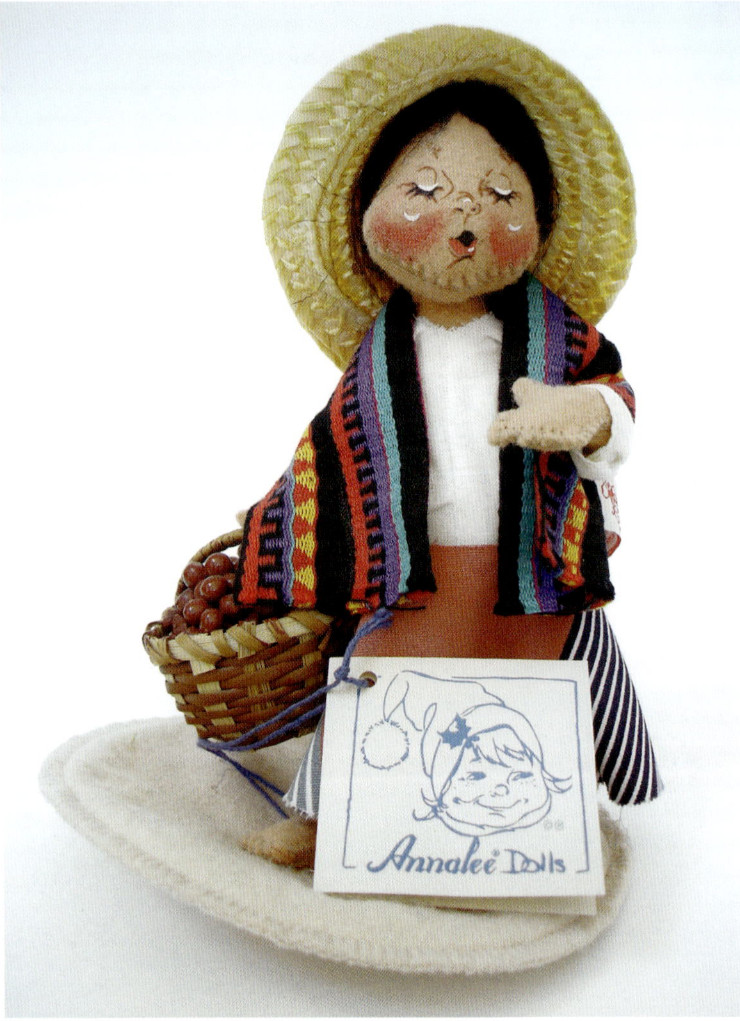

Attributed to the dollmaker Annalee, of New Hampshire, made in the USA, 1995. A 7.5 in. doll, an interpretation of a mousy whimsical Mexican woman, with her basket full of fruit. Hand painted face. Mobililtee Dolls. $25 to 60

A typical tourist doll, 1970s. A more contemporary look at the progression of the cloth dolls, made in Mexico. Note the differences in quality: a *mestiza* in a red full skirt which is painted with glitter glued in various places, no hand embroidery. A crossed *rebozo*, black yarn braids, and a woven *sombrero*. Leather huaraches. $30 to 50

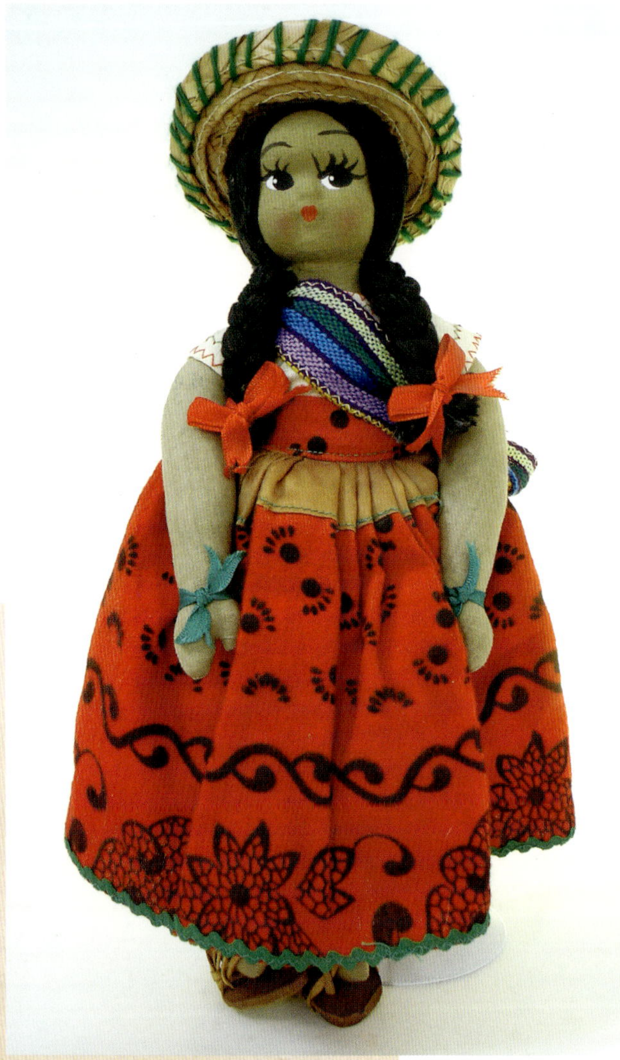

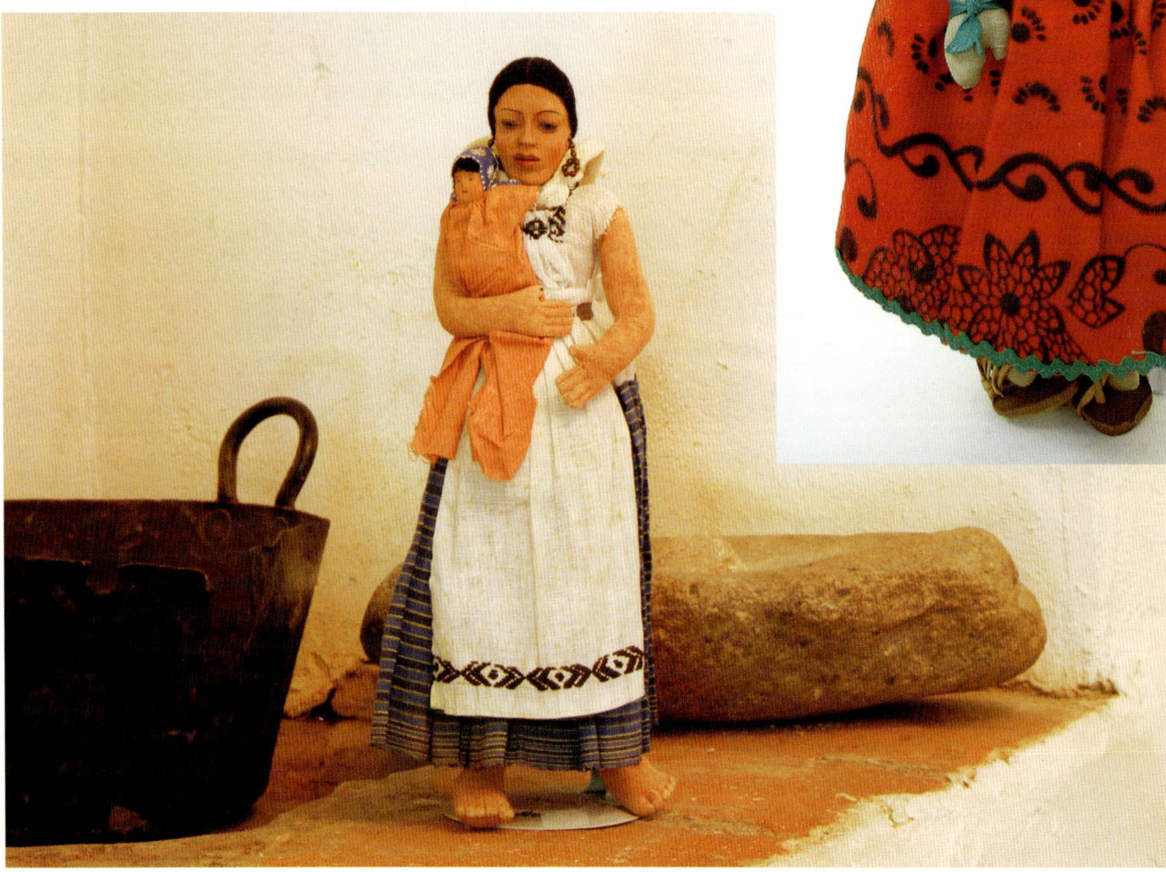

A 16 in. cloth *mestiza* Indian doll with her baby. All cloth body, long *enredo* skirt with *pespunteado* embroidery on her *blusa*. A long apron with glass bead earrings. $125 to 200ea.

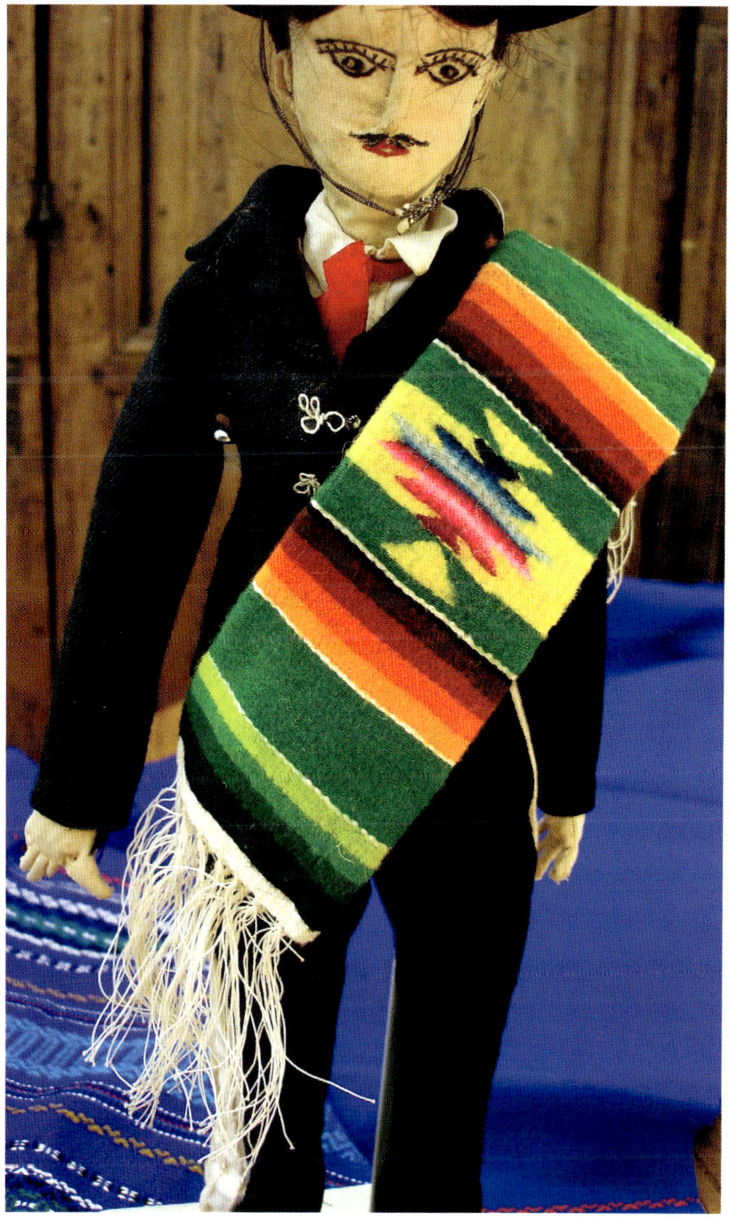

The charro's colorful wool *serape* drapes over his black wool jacket, a pleated white shirt, and his red *moño*. Intricate detail identifies a gifted doll maker.

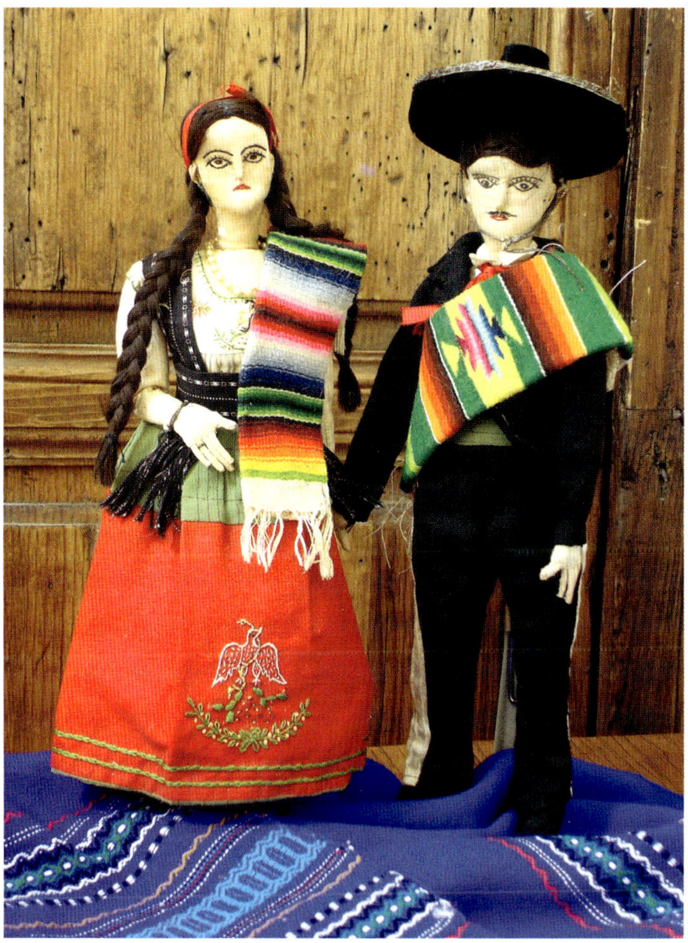

Stunning early 19th c. cloth dolls with definitive clothing of the upper-class *mestizos*.15 in. all-cloth dolls made in Mexico, needle sculpted. Hard stuffed body $300 to $700 pr

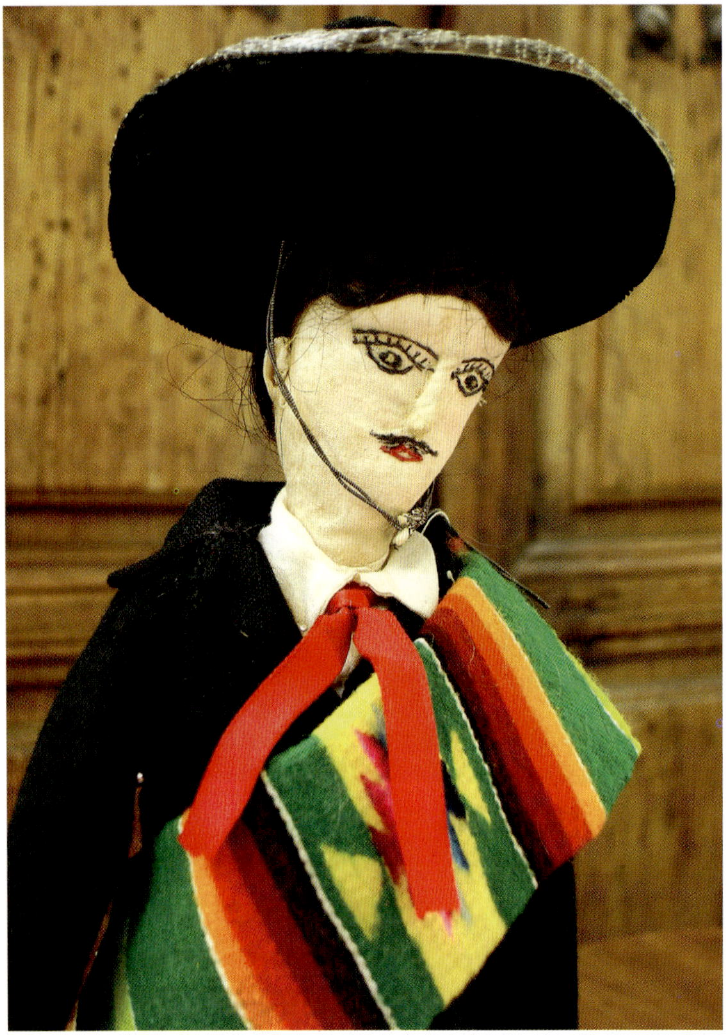

The facial features of this fine 19th c. Mexican cloth doll, clearly show a skilled dollmaker. His *sombrero* ties to his face and his hair is of human or horse hair.

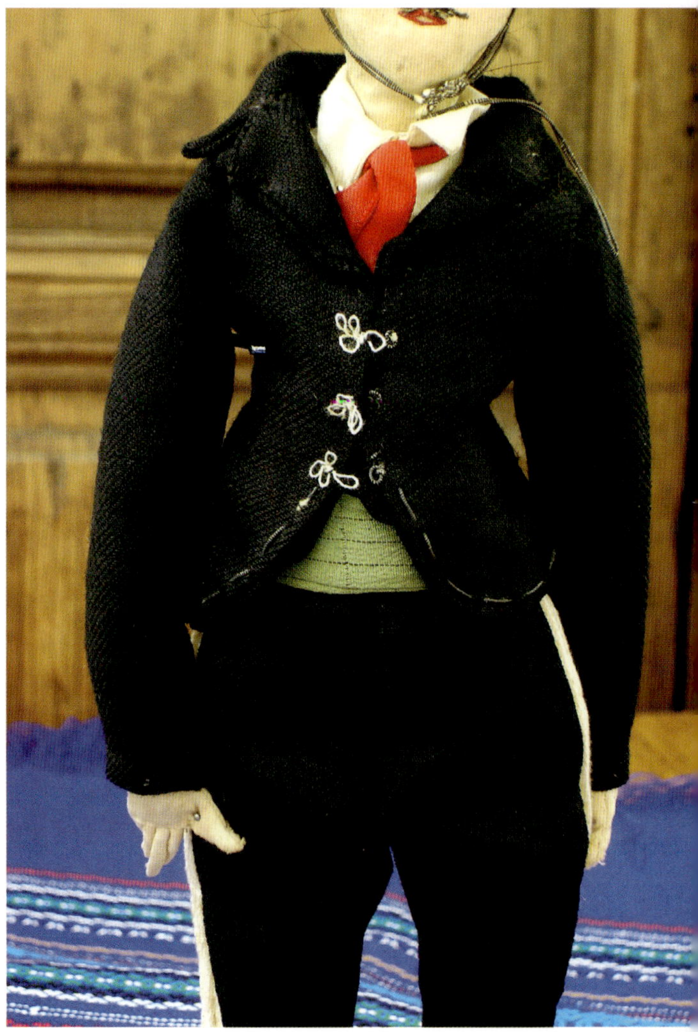

A cropped wool jacket of a *charro* with silver threading mimics *plateado* buttoning down the front. This was only found on upper class *charros* suit.

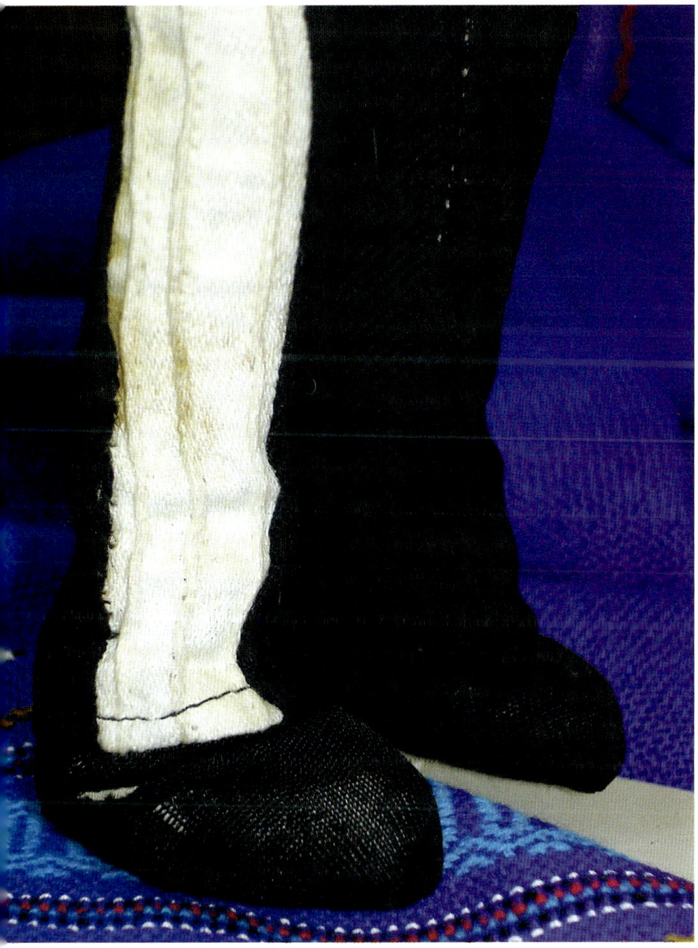

Silver bands down the sides of black wool trousers were common for the urban *mestizo*. Silver threading or with silver *plateado* buttoning all the way down. The black cloth over his feet simulate black boots.

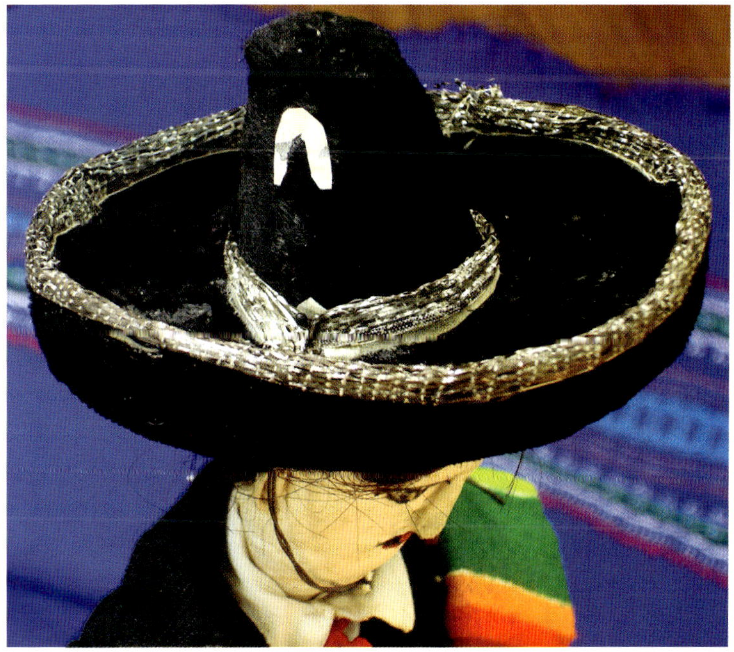

Silver ribbon and trim around his large felt *sombrero*, a status symbol of a fine *charros sombrero*.

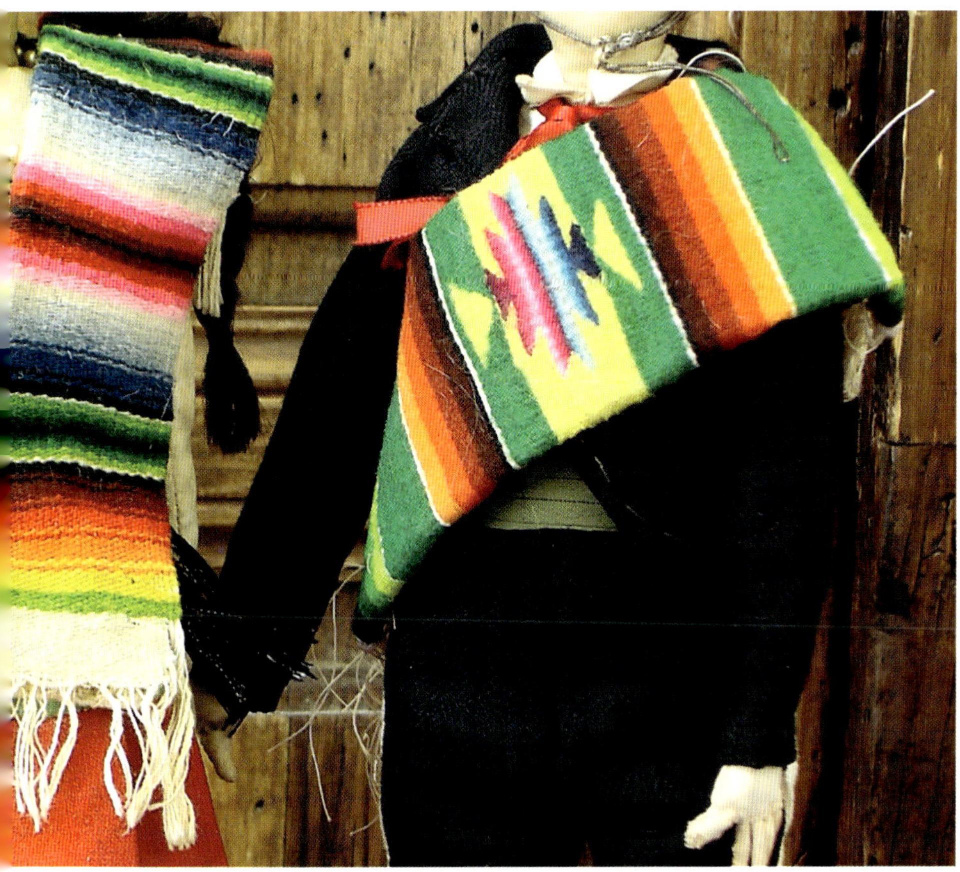

The colorful wool serapes dresses as well as provides warmth to the Mexican *caballero*. The finer the weave and pattern defined his social status, especially those of *Salitillo*.

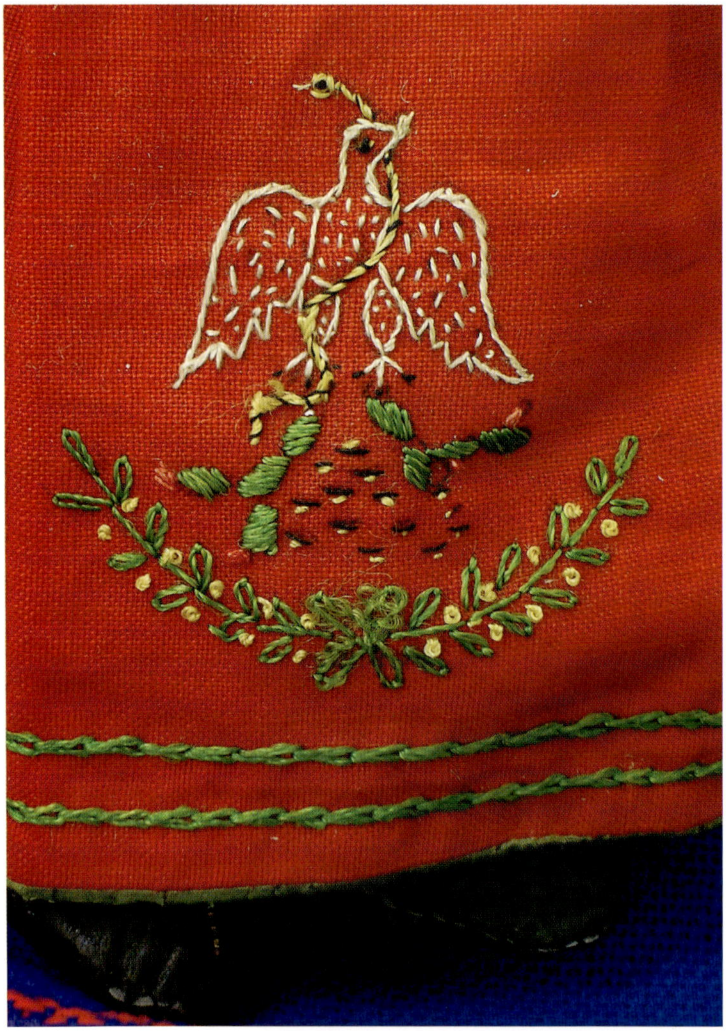

A finely stitched China Poblana red *enagua* skirt 19th c. made In Mexico. This detailed rendition of Mexico's national emblem demonstrates the skill of the doll makers' tiny meticulous petit point stitching with glass beads.

Fine leather shoes of a *mestiza* were custom made for her; hand stitching and a faux buckle adds a refined finishing touch.

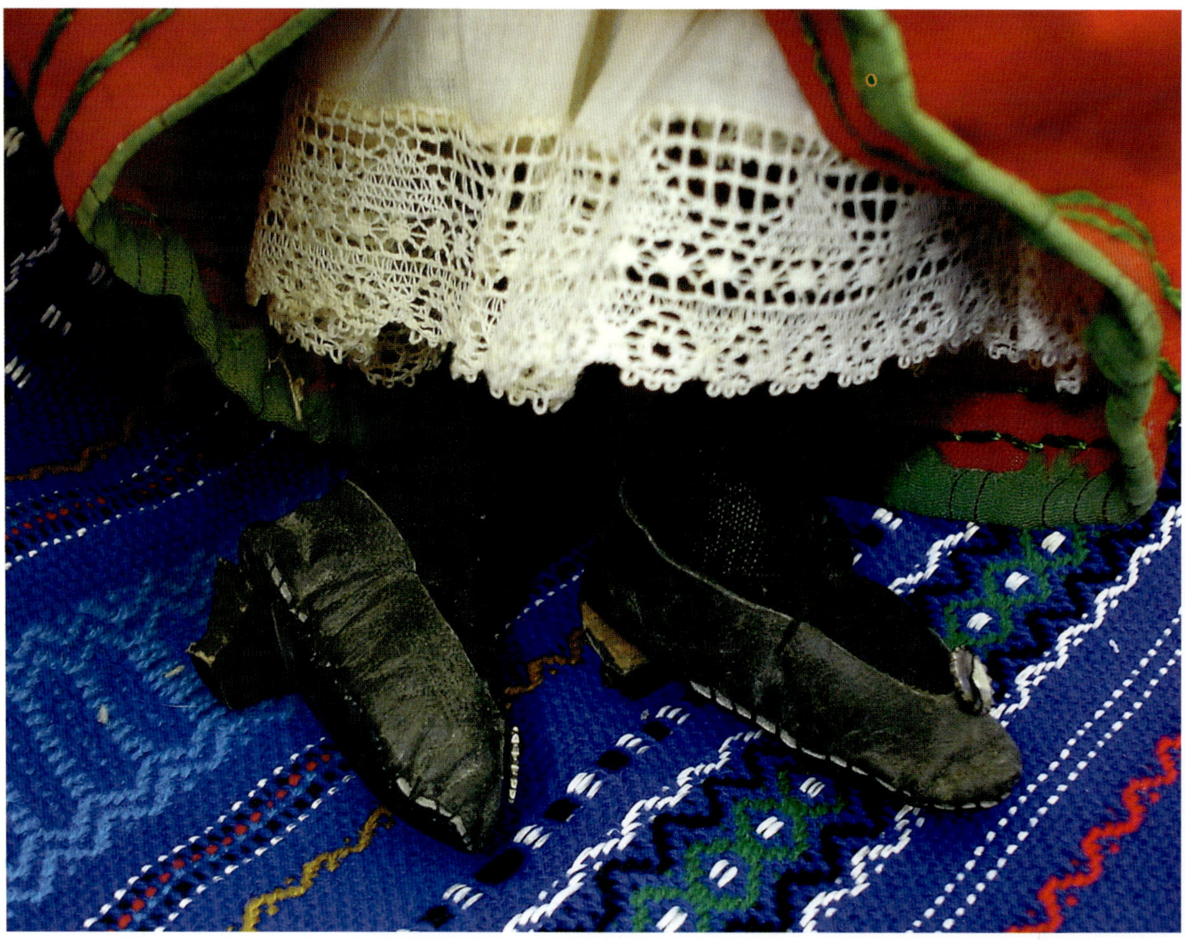

The cloth dolls that come from around the world, outside Mexico, are an impressive genre of period collectible Mexican costume dolls. Those selected for presentation here come from the many doll makers mentioned previously, and more. Toy and doll makers from the United States, Canada, and Europe that produced and exported costume dolls had their own particular styles to interpret Mexican "typical dress." Their materials and trimmings were usually synthetic, man-made pieces, but the detail and expressive way in which they were applied were exceptional. Many have hand-detailed and applied embroidery on the costumes and are of high quality. Some were made of molded felt with painted features and mohair or floss wigs. Their features usually followed the doll maker's traits, like those from Spain by the Roldan or Klumpe makers. With flirty eyes and whimsical expressions, the dolls' only resemblance to a Mexican was the exceptional detail of its costume. The foreign makers took great care and consideration to interpret the dolls correctly. Some other vintage cloth dolls in Mexican costumes were made by renowned doll makers of their era. During the 1920s to the 1950s, a movement among most leading doll makers and toy companies was to make quality exports. Cloth dolls were recognized as a growing trend for children as well as adults.

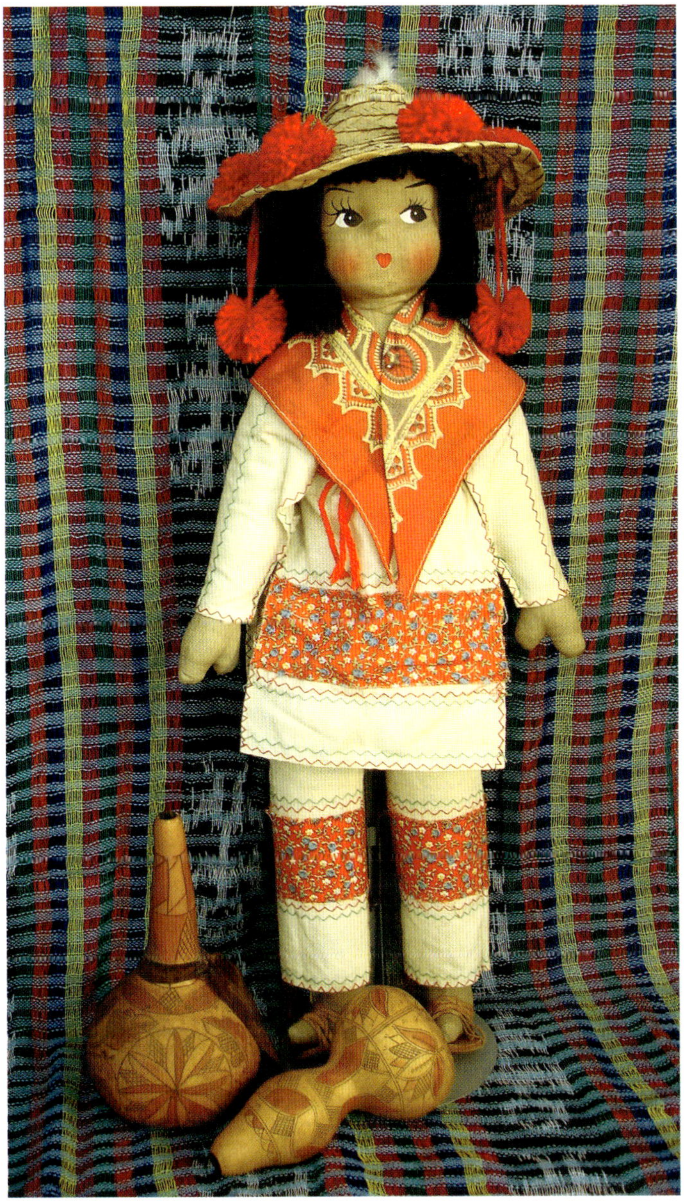

A rare 23 in. cloth *huichol* doll. Georgene or Averill-style cloth doll. Printed cloth with indigenous detail mimics the usual profusely embroidered clothing of the male costumes. Hand painted face, wool yarn hair and colorful poms. Made in Mexico, c1960s. $50 to 100

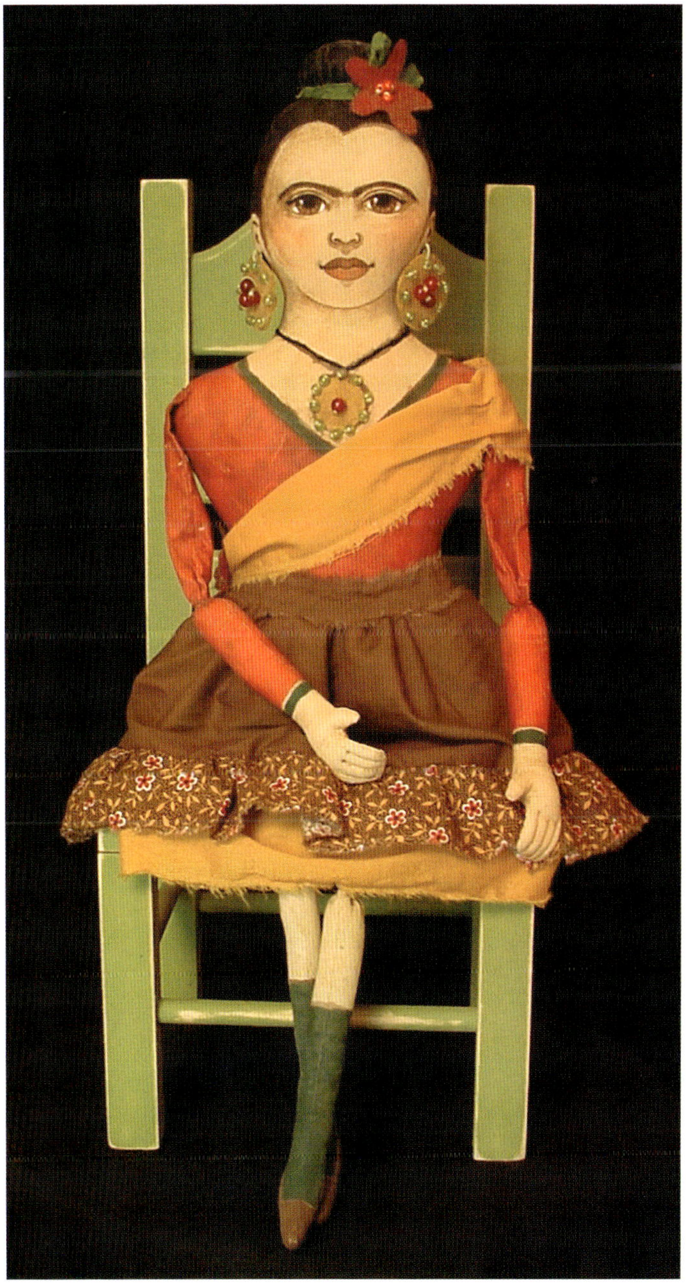

Resembling acclaimed artist Frida Kahlo (1907-1954), an American folk art doll, 20 in. Quality muslin hand-painted and sanded repeatedly in order to create the unique surface that reveals an aged leather appearance. Facial detail captures the essence of her *mestiza* heritage. Accented with earrings and a necklace, and seated in an old green chair. $250 to 500, USA. *Made by Dylan and Jo James Curry*

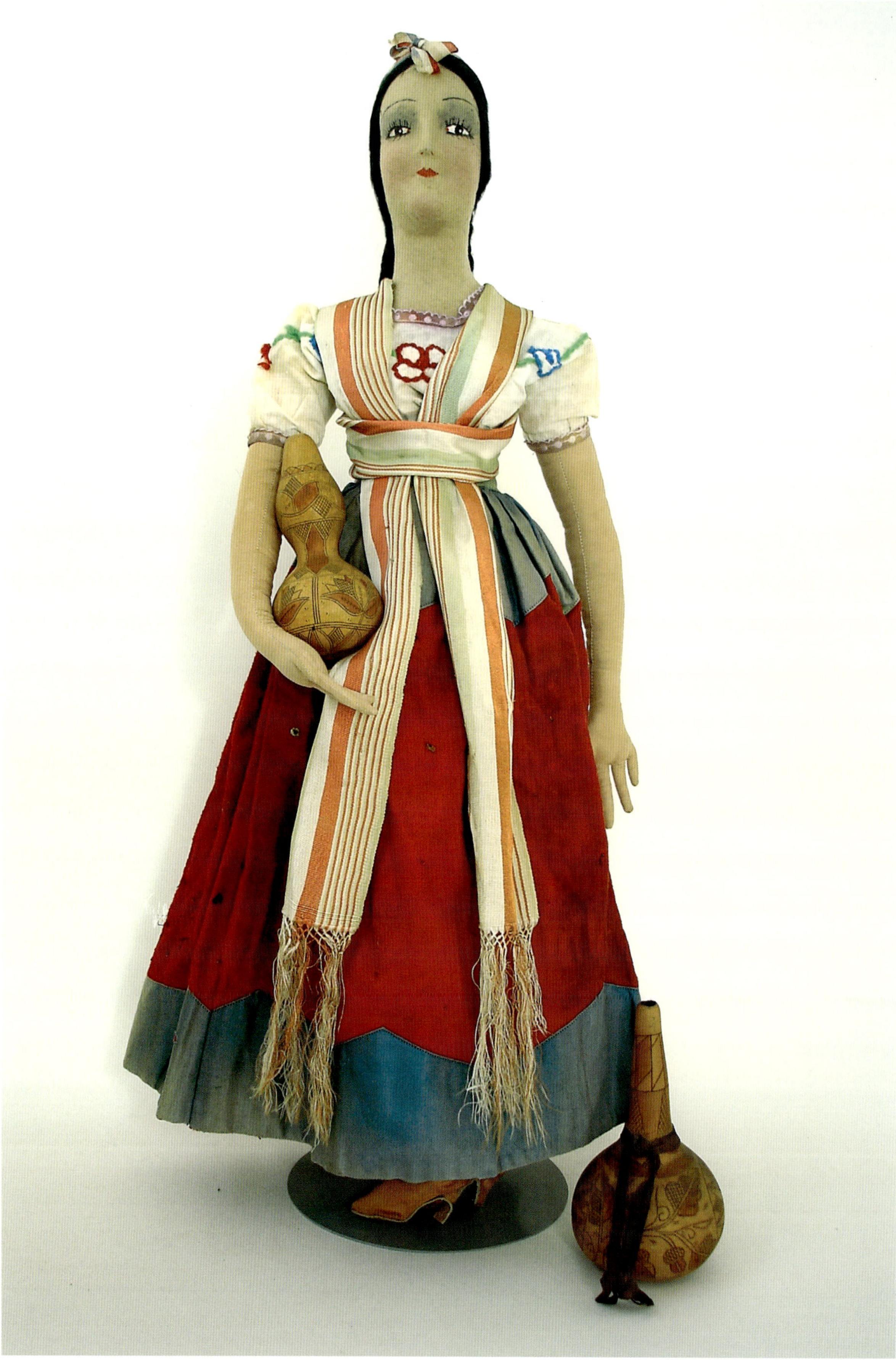

A stunning large rendition of a beautiful *mestizo* boudoir doll "Sonia." Made c. early 1930s, origin and maker unknown, but exhibits the quality of early Lenci dolls. In good condition, wearing a cotton Spanish *blusa* and full red and green *castor* skirt. She is made of cloth, all hand made detail. Her face is felt molded features with wool black braids for hair. A cotton body with molded womanly features. Her striped *rebozo* is made of silk and finished with fringe. $300 to 800

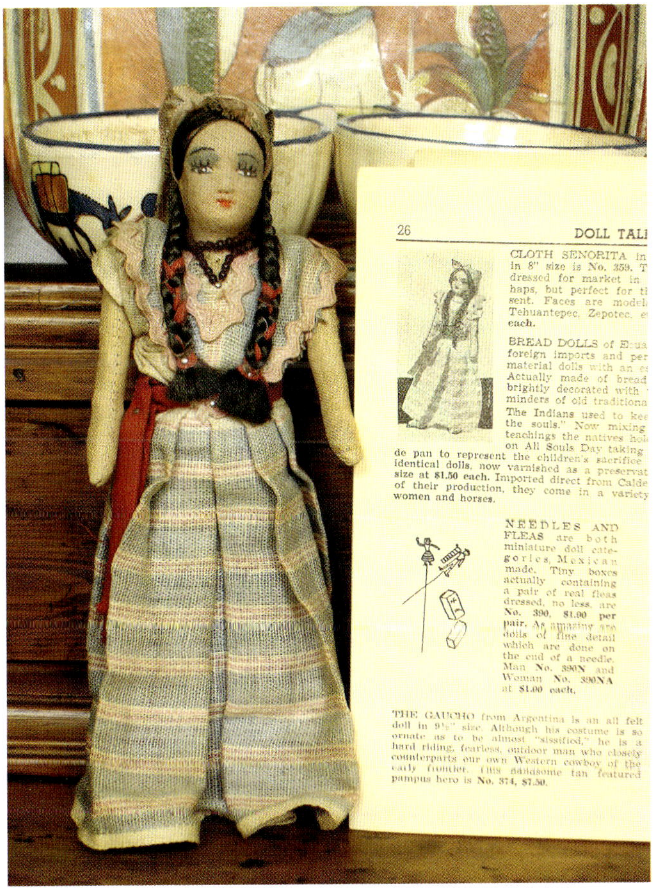

An original Kimport cloth doll, the same as in the catalog. An 8 in. cinnamon-skin girl dressed in the indigenous Indian costume of a citizen of the Tehuantepec, Zapotec, leg stamped Made in Mexico, c. 1950s $45 to 75

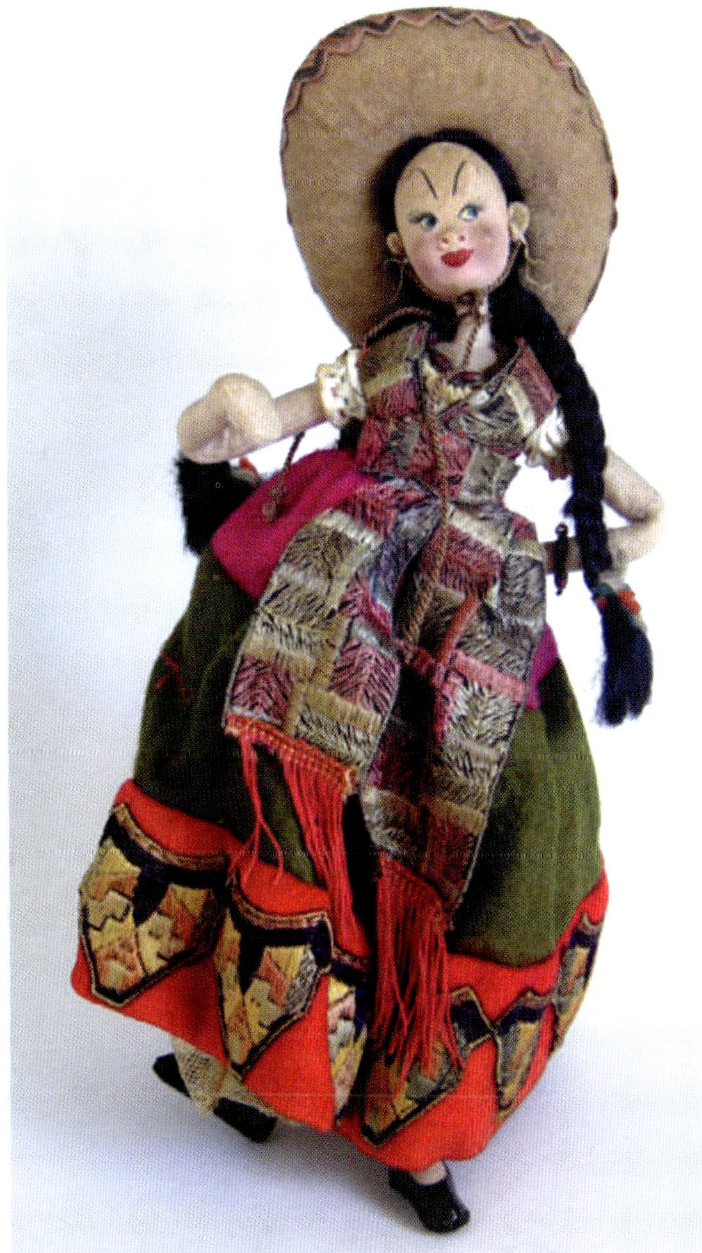

Attributed to the Klumpe Doll Co., made in Spain, c. 1950s, of molded felt, an 11 in. doll costumed to resemble a typical *mestiza*, a mohair wig with whimsical painted features. $60 to 150

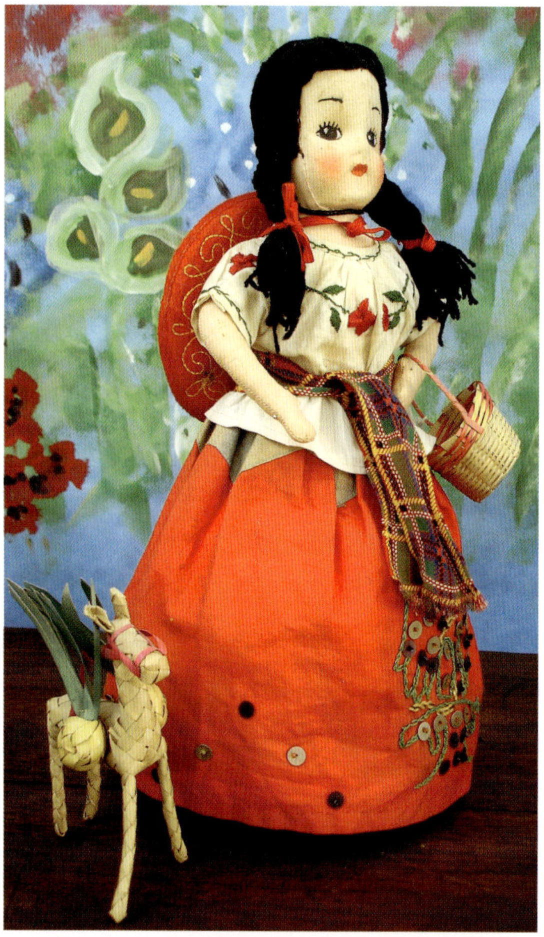

Attributed to a European cloth doll maker, clothed as a *China Poblana* with an embroidered *blusa* in careful satin stitches of typical style, c. 1940s, 18 in., all-cloth body, needle molded features, wool yarn hair. Lovely detail with her *rebozo*, embroidered motifs, and *sombrero*. Woven vintage *petate* toy donkey, c1940s. $75 to 150

A *charro* and *mestiza*, in Bernard Ravca style, a cloth stocking, needled, molded, and tagged 1935 era; wonderful detail to authenticate the clothing of the *mestizo*. $75 to $150 ea.

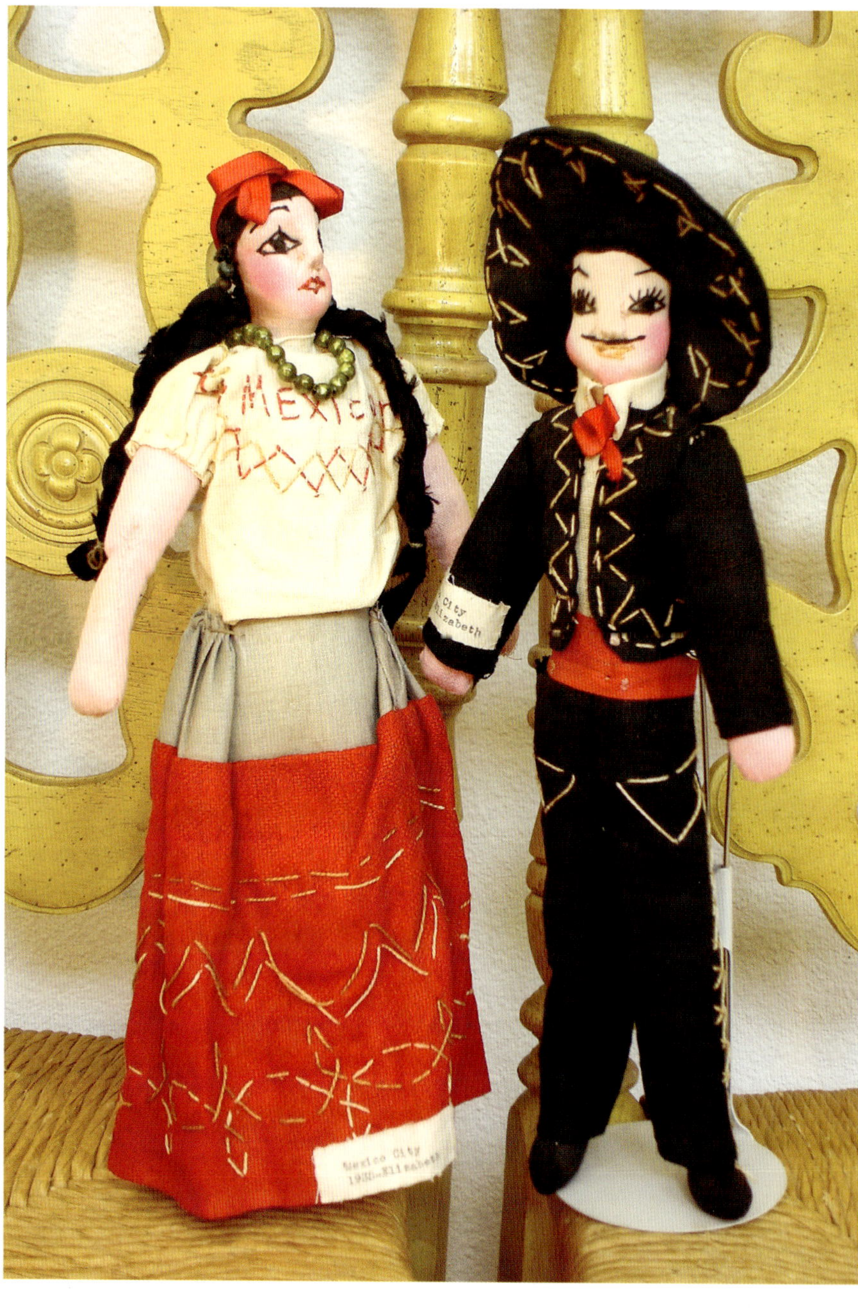

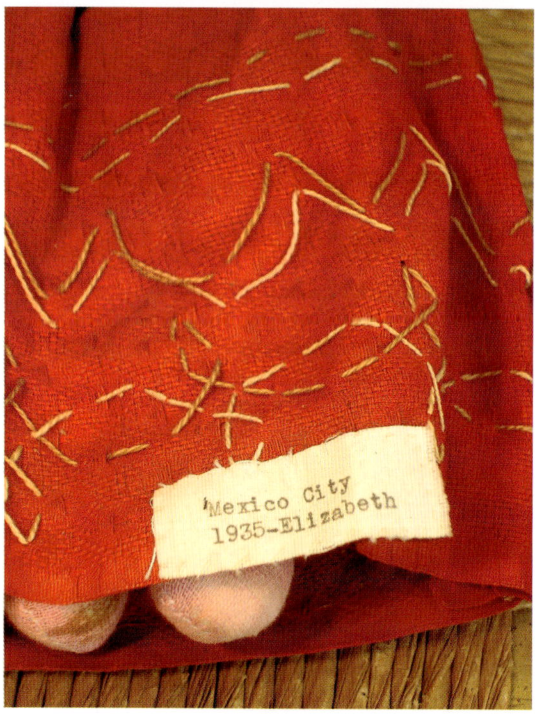

The tag on the skirt of the cloth *mestiza*, "Mexico City 1935 Elizabeth." Ravca cloth dolls $75 to $150 ea.

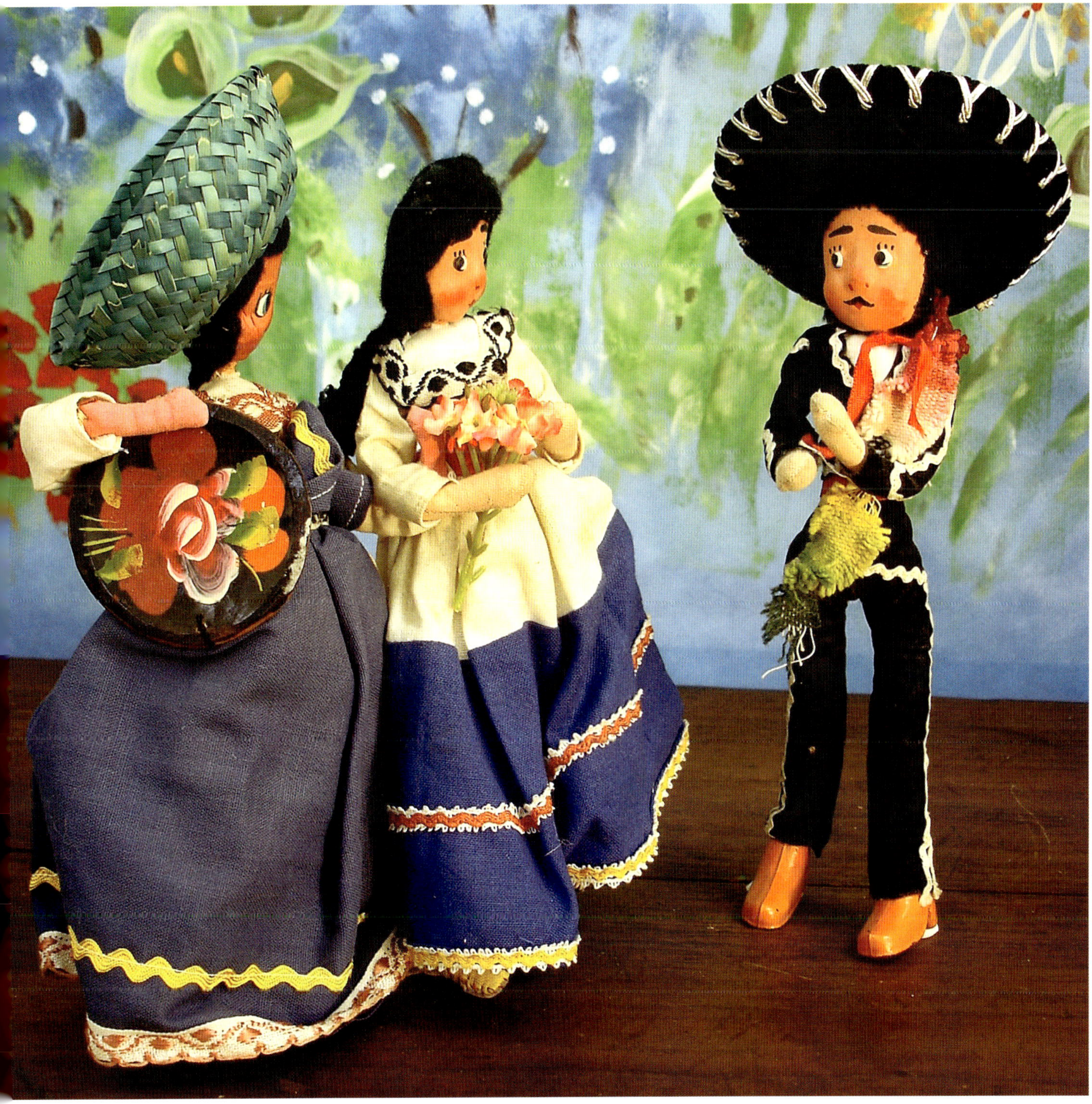

Attributed to Roldan Dolls, three cloth 10 in. dolls from the 1940s. An indicative cloth and wire doll with google-eyes. Whimsical and fun, but dressed in accurate costumes of the *mestizo*. Clothed beautifully, with long black wool hair, painted faces, bendable bodies; colorful and rare, made in Spain. She is holding a *batea* wooden plate, the charro looks worried, does he not? $50 to $100 ea.

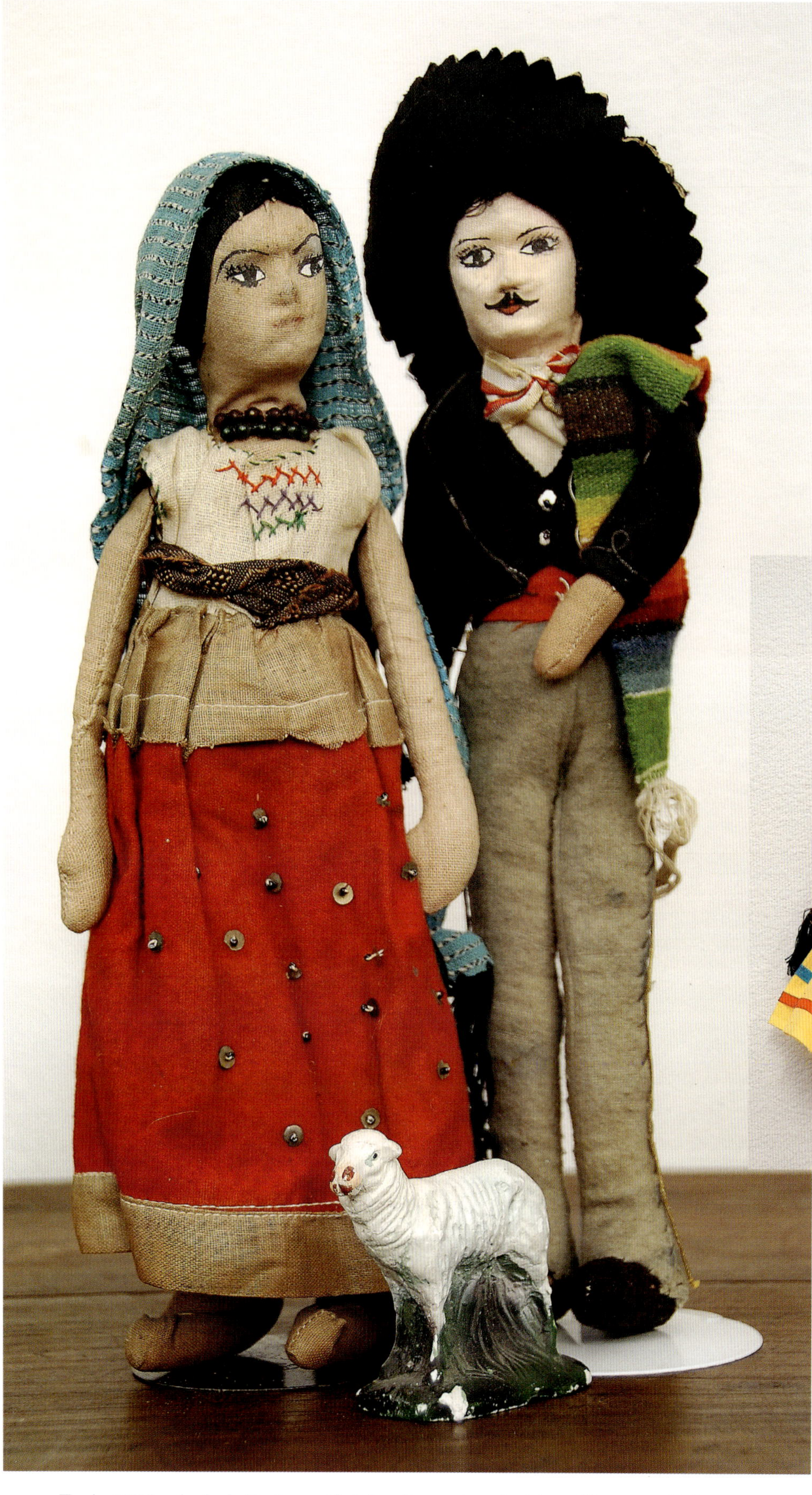

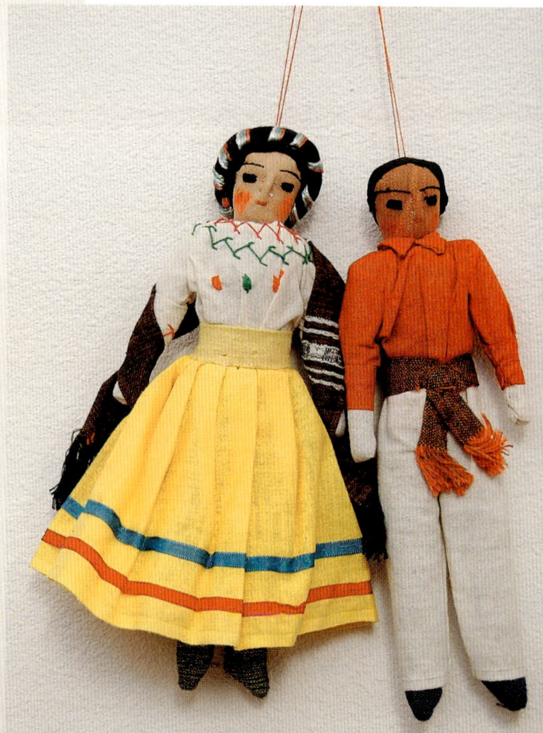

Charming 11 in. cloth dolls, c.1970s. Bright colors and indigenous trim for these *mestiza* Indians from the south of Mexico.

Early 1900s cloth dolls, beautiful detail, *mestiza* clothing. They are 14 in., hard stuffed cloth dolls, with *manta* cloth and wool for his *charro* suit. Made in Mexico

Papier Maché and Mixed Medium Dolls

Papier maché dolls were in high demand in the United States and other parts of the world in the early part of the 20th century. They gained popularity because of the versatility of the material and they were inexpensive to make. Doll historians dictate that the *papier maché* dolls are some of the earliest dolls made for the commercial market. They can be dated as far back as 1540 in Europe, and were composed in various methods. Generally they were prepared from sheets of paper pressed together with rag fibers added to give strength, and binding them with paste and firm pressure, similar to the process of making composition. It is hard to discern Mexican *papier maché* dolls from composition dolls, and they are easily mistaken if they were done by a skilled maker. One of the noticeable differences is in the weight of the dolls. *Papier maché* is much lighter than composition. In Europe there were many types of *papier maché* dolls produced, but in Mexico it was limited to molded features that would be painted and wigged. Their most notable features were authentic costumes and the modest ways in which they were constructed. Usually, the head and arms were the only parts of the doll made from *papier maché*, while the

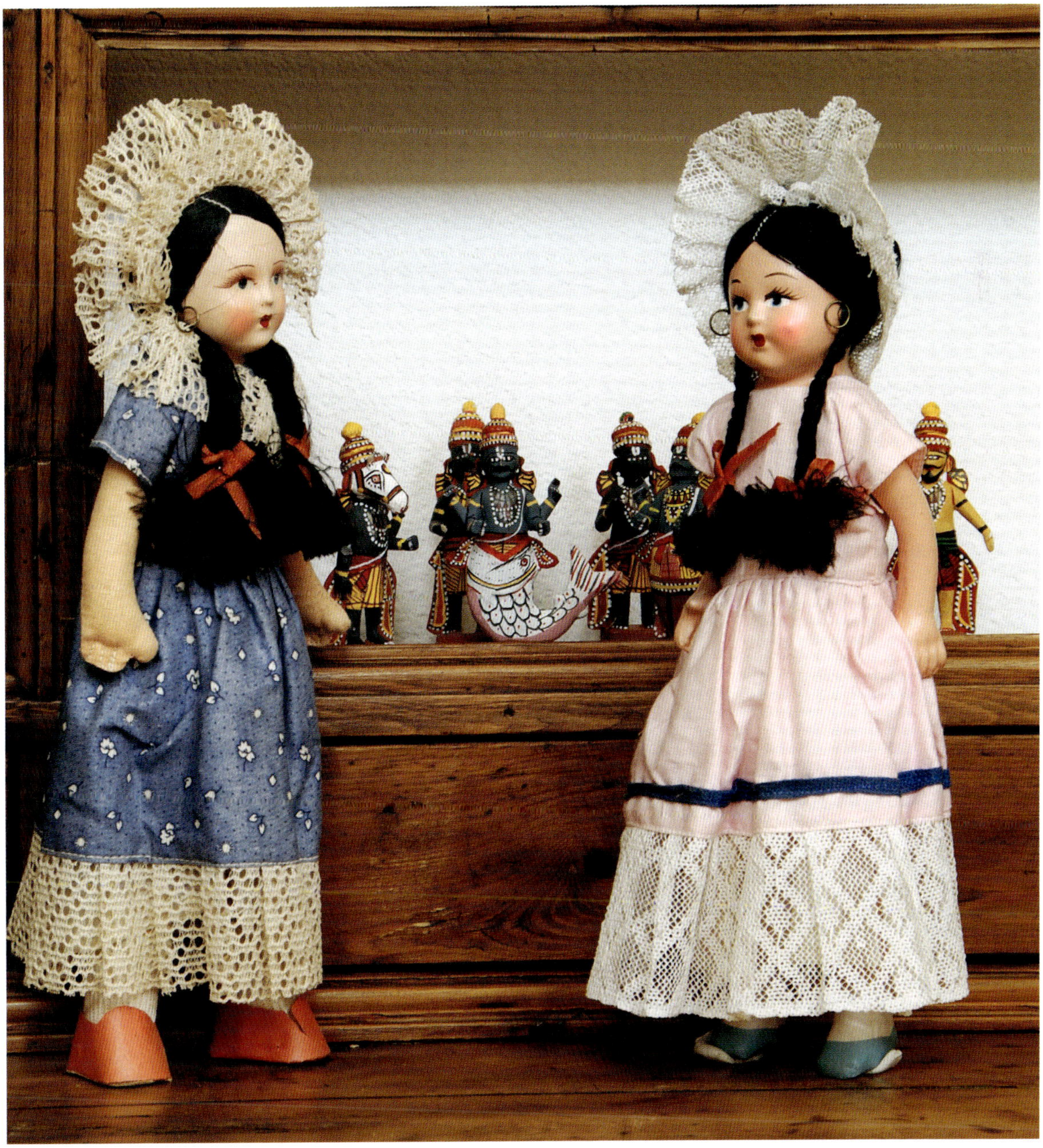

The typical clothing of the Tehuantepec woman, a *mestiza* dress. They are ready to go to church, in a blue dress cloth and *papier maché* face, c.1940s, a pink *Tehuana* is solid jointed composition.They look similar, but are by different makers. Made in Mexico. $75 to 150

body and legs were stuffed cloth. Some of the body parts would be sewn together or joined by a rivet-like button that allowed the legs to move. The face was skillfully hand painted, each one with a different gaze. Their hair usually was long black braids either hung and tied off with bows or twirled around their heads. They came in a wide range of sizes and were typically dress as an Indian or *mestizo*.

Papier maché was a common way in which the Mexicans would create many of their toys and dolls. It was an inexpensive and durable surface that allowed them to use their imaginations, molding and painting them effortlessly. All of the materials were readily available and surely their skills in polychromatic paints were phenomenal.

Beautiful sculpted dolls are a key example of this craft. Although there are many examples of Mexican *papier maché dolls*, those included here are superior in their costumes and represent a recognizable style in which they were painted, such as the "skinny dolls." These beautiful dolls were from Tonalá, Jalisco. They assumed their "skinny dolls label because of their narrow width and linear design. They were introduced in the late 1940s, but other variations evolved during that time as well. Independent *talleres* (workshops) began producing them on a marketable level and many stores in *mercados* (marketplaces) throughout Mexico began to sell them. Imagination is displayed throughout the costumes of these unique pieces. Every step of the manufacturing process took place without the use of machines. The most popular style is a woman with a serene expression and long yarn hair twisted to one side of her head. She was carefully painted with glorious flowers and birds in a paper sculpture, to resemble a modern Mexican woman. She may be wearing an over-exaggerated hat and a skirt, as well as a presumed *rebozo* or *quechquemitl*. Most of the Mexican *papier maché* dolls shown here originated from two regions, Guadalajara (as noted by the signature Tonala style painting) and Mexico City (where one of the renowned artists, Abelardo Ruiz, has been creating them for at least 40 years). They all have similarities, but vary in size from 3.5 inches tall to 34 inch tall, and each artist has their own secret techniques. The special artwork has been preserved by originators known as Sermel, a family-owned business established in the1960s that is still operating today. Not only do they make dolls, but also a variety of folk art animals and birds. Their *papier maché* "skinny dolls" often resemble each other, but are never exactly duplicated.

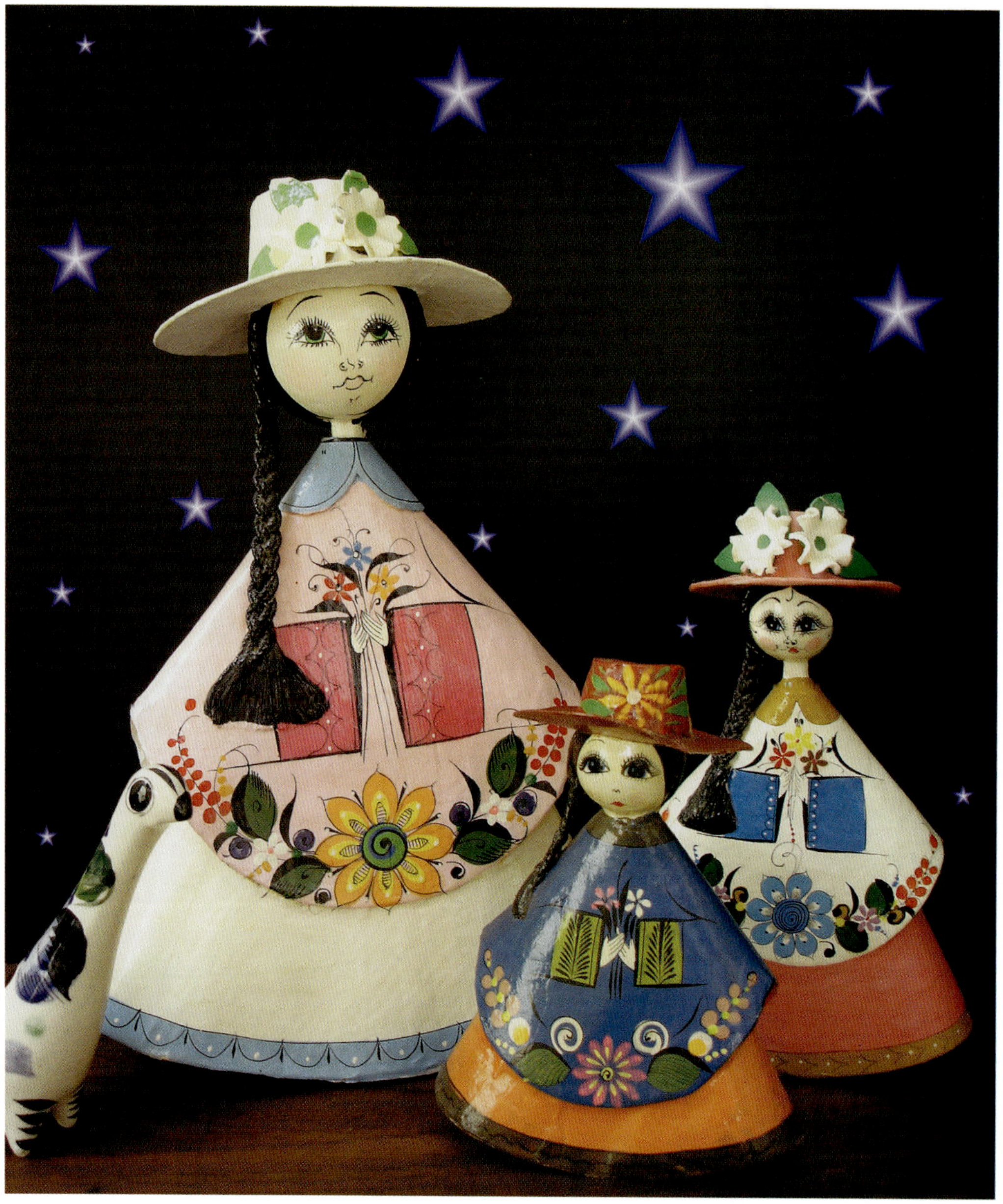

A trio of paper mache Mexican Tonalá tourist dolls, c.1960s. Twilight sparkles this group. Strong traditional patterns that resemble the highly coveted vintage Tonalá pottery. Commonly referred to as "skinny dolls" with their yarn strung hair braided down. Nuño and artist such as those at the Sermel taller. Two are signed, 16 in., 8 in., and 6 in. $100 to 145

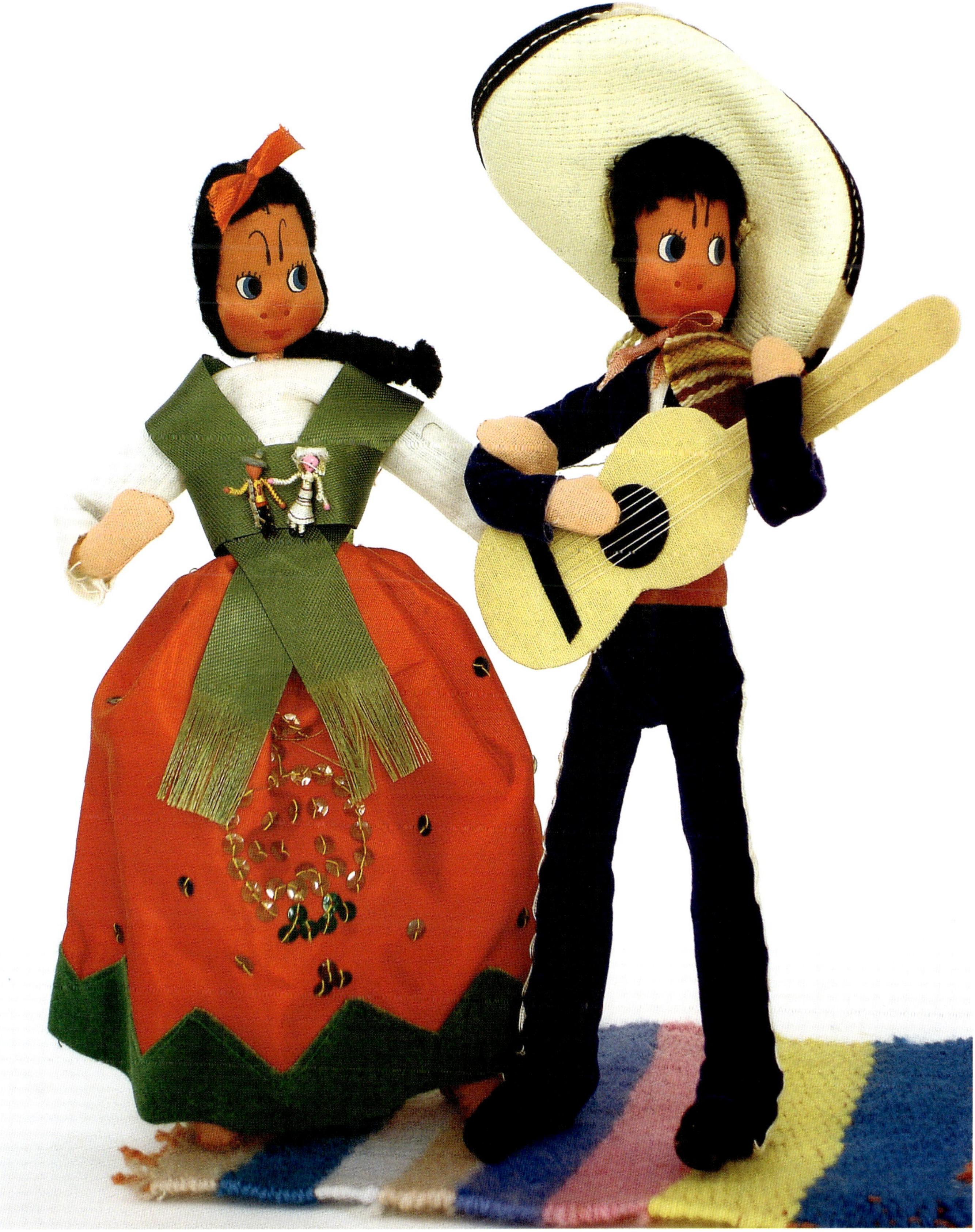

This duo of 10 in. bendable cloth character dolls are by either Klumpe or Roldan, c.1950s. Dressed as a *charro* and a *charra mestizo*. Captured in her China Poblana costume, he serenades with his mock guitar. A lot of detail, painted features and felt clothing. Painted features on the import character doll face is vibrant with google eyes. Her dress is of rayon with sequins and two small doll pins dress her *rebozo*. Made in Spain $40 to 75ea.

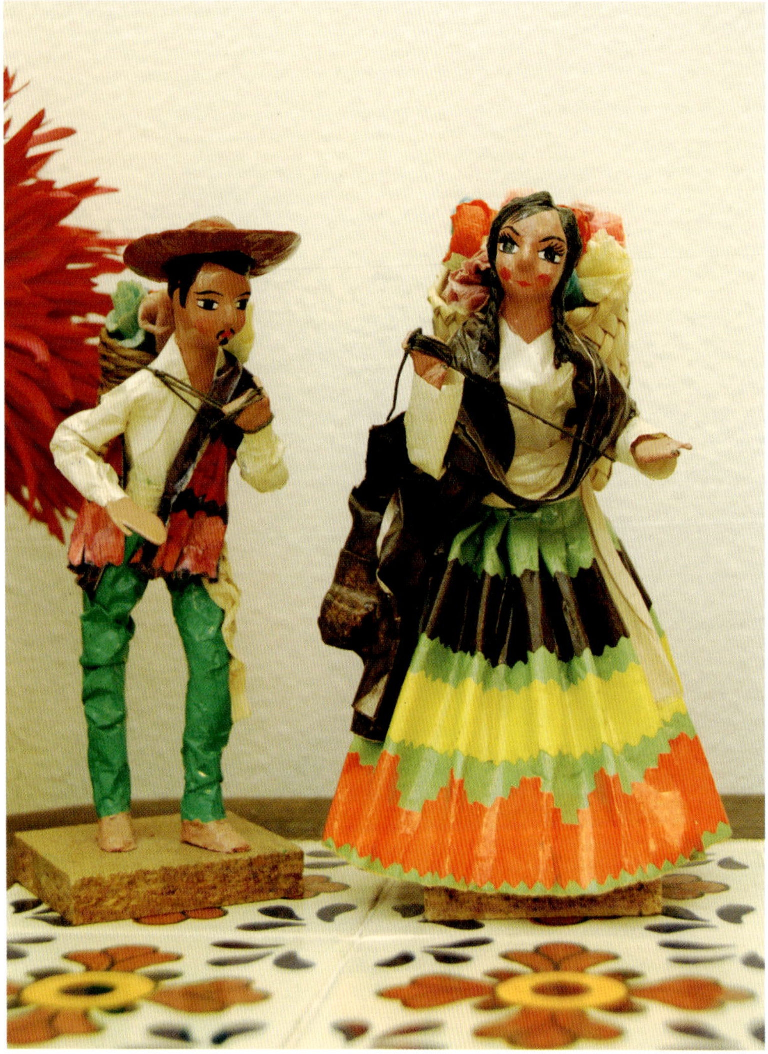

Colorful tourist dolls, an 11 in. couple of *vendadores*, peddlers, selling their wares. *Papier maché* and polychrome painted clothing. c.1960s $45 to 75 ea.

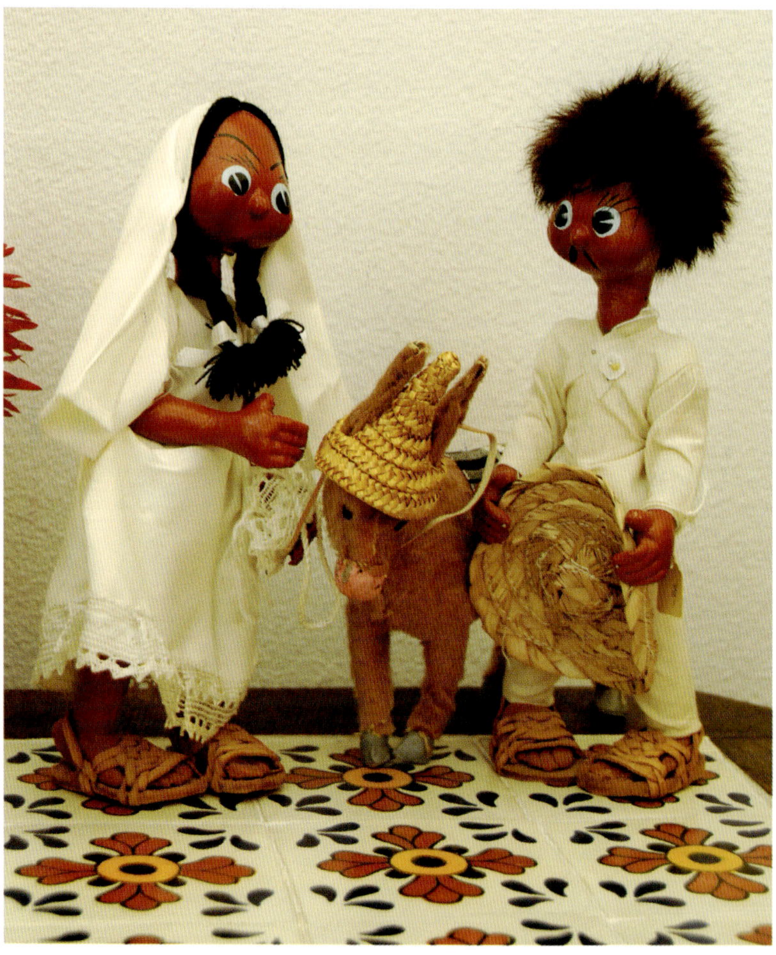

Popular tourist dolls, 10 in. *chicle* often referred to as "La Gente" dolls. Hand-crafted souvenir dolls made in Mexico, early 1960s. A typical *mestizo* Indian and his wife on their wedding day, dressed all in white. These were in the Kimport doll catalog. *Chicle* is a gum-like substance taken from indigenous trees of Mexico. $50 to 100 pair

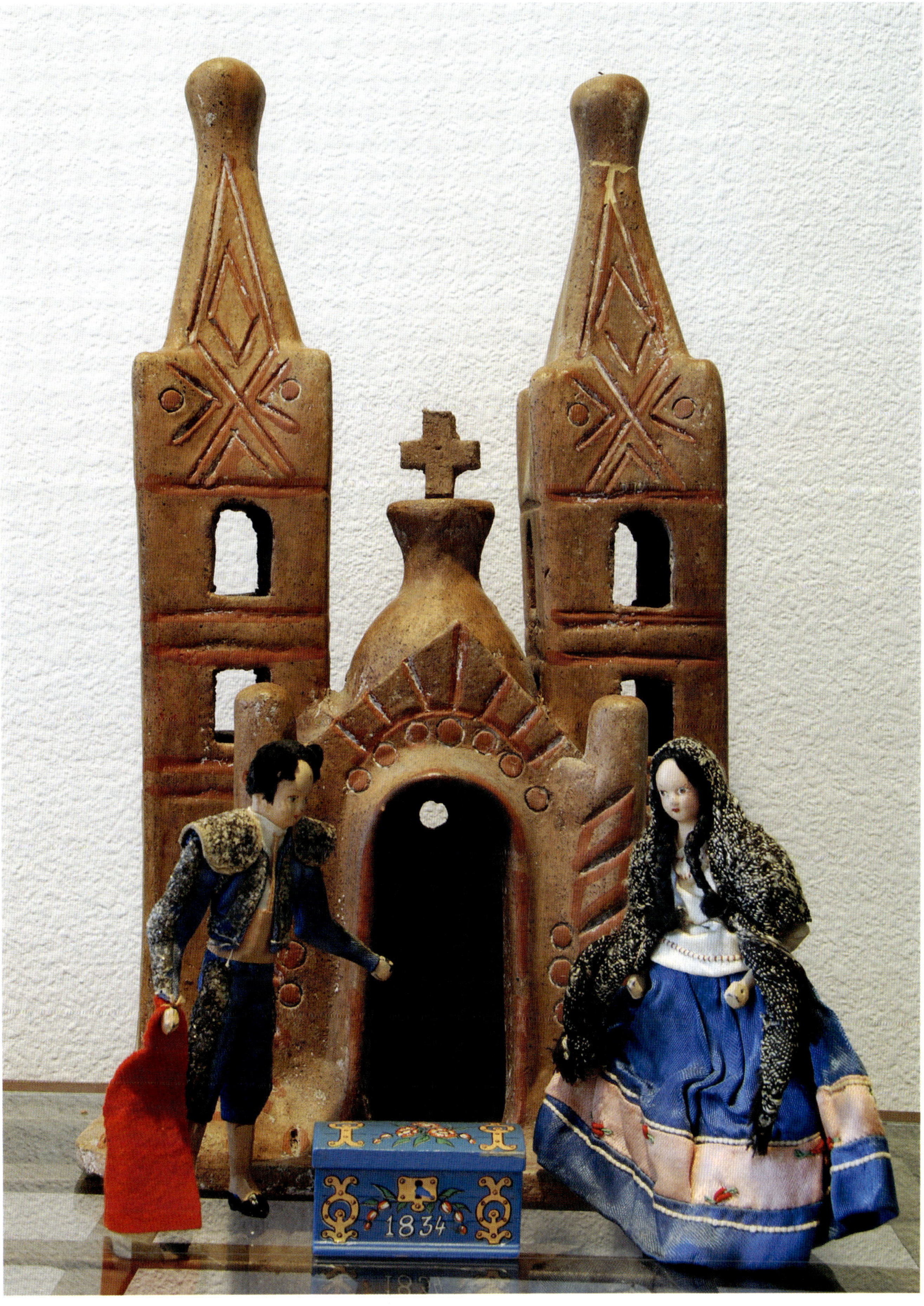

Special 19th c. gunmetal, 6 in. colonial Spanish dressed *matador* and *señorita*. Unique and extremly rare. They stand in front of a Pueblan red clay church. Made in Mexico $200 to 400

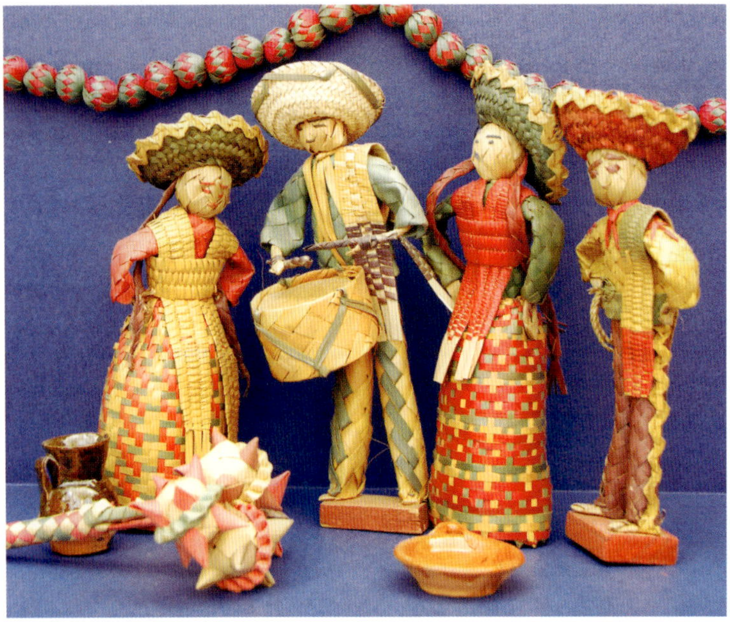

Typical tourist *petate,* 10 in. dolls, most are on wood stands made of straw, reed, or cactus fiber, using every conceivable weaving technique, i.e. basket, herringbone, etc. Dyed colors and different costumes, c.1960s $45 to 75

A duo of finely woven old Mexico dolls, made for the tourist trade, high quality tightly woven reed, 15 in. doll has a basket-weave skirt and body, as a *China Poblana*, even a *rebozo.* The smaller is 8 in. and is a bell that rings, very cute. c. 1950s $45 to 75

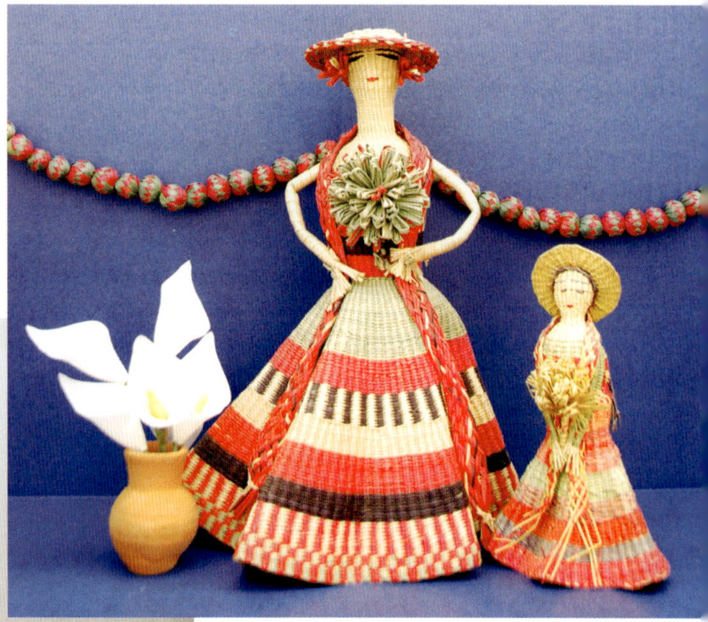

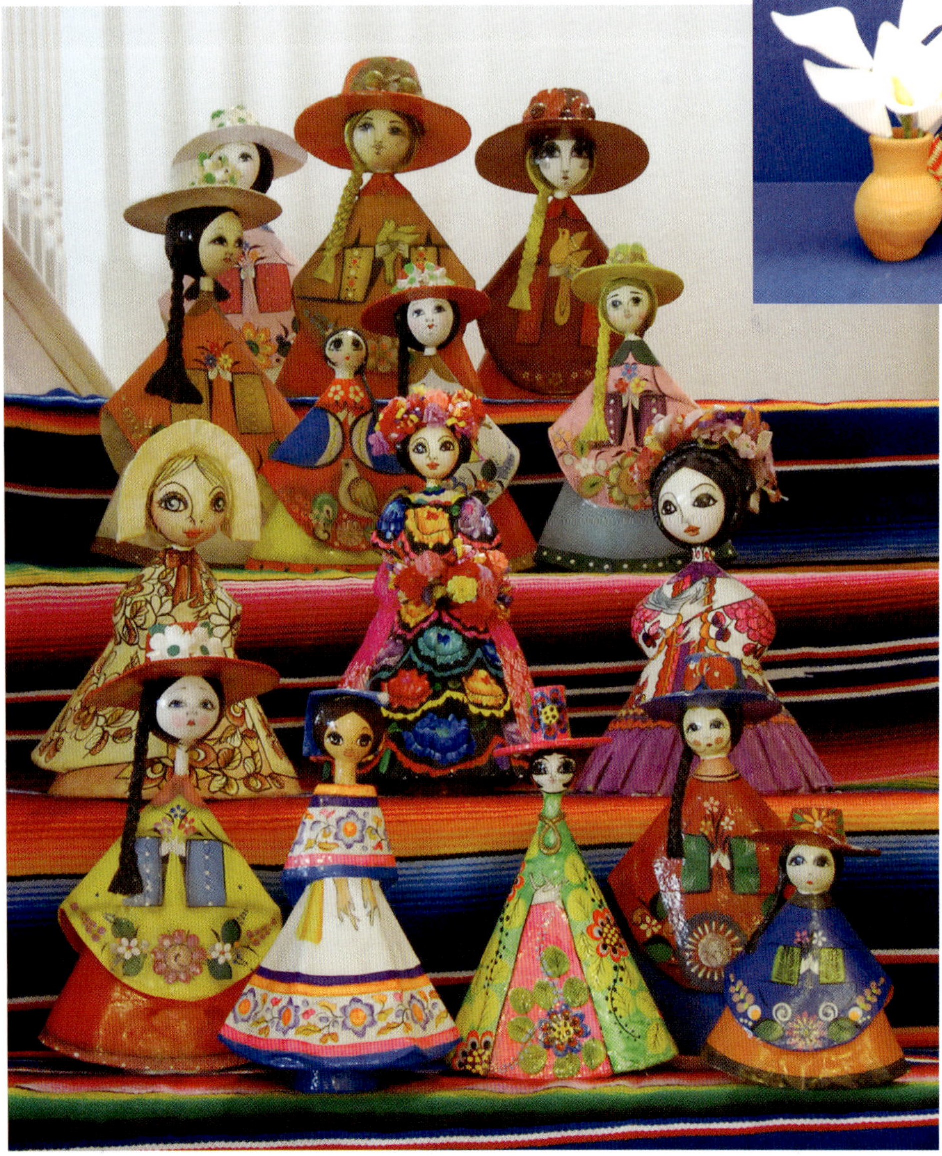

Folk art tole painting on these popular art 13 in. to 17 in. Tonalá *papier maché* "skinny dolls," c.1960s. Bold colors and patterns with shellac shiny surface. Serene expressions, they look similar, but are never alike. Sermel, Nuño, GMS, signed by various *talleres*. $75 to 150

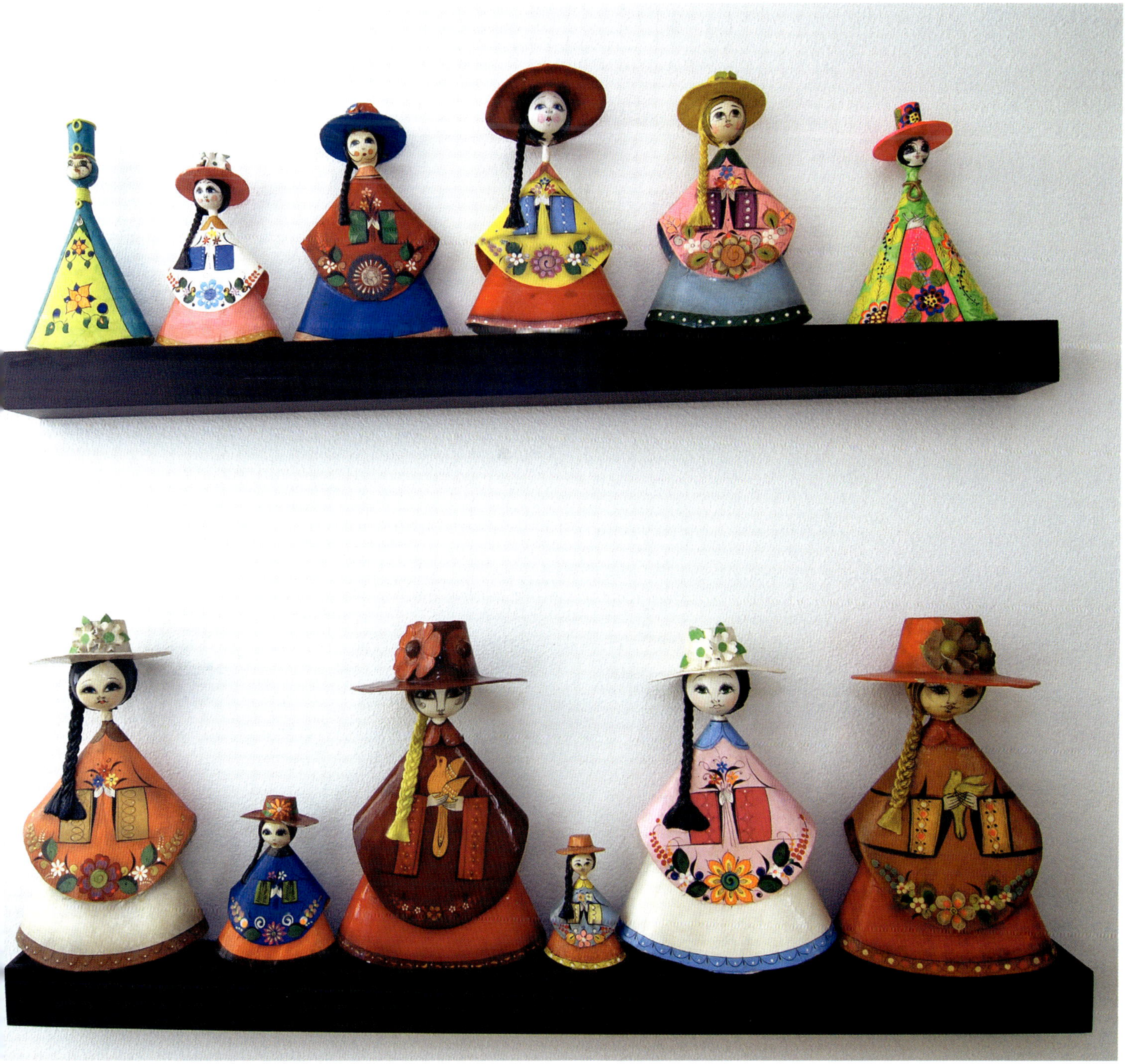

Different sizes and colorful dress on these 6 in. to 17 in. staged Tonalá paper mache "skinny dolls," c.1960s. Hand detail with long braids to the sides, over-sized hats with folk art quality. Long *huipils* and skirts interpreted beautifully for that era. Sermel, Nuño, GMS, signed by various *talleres* and artists. $75 to 200 ea.

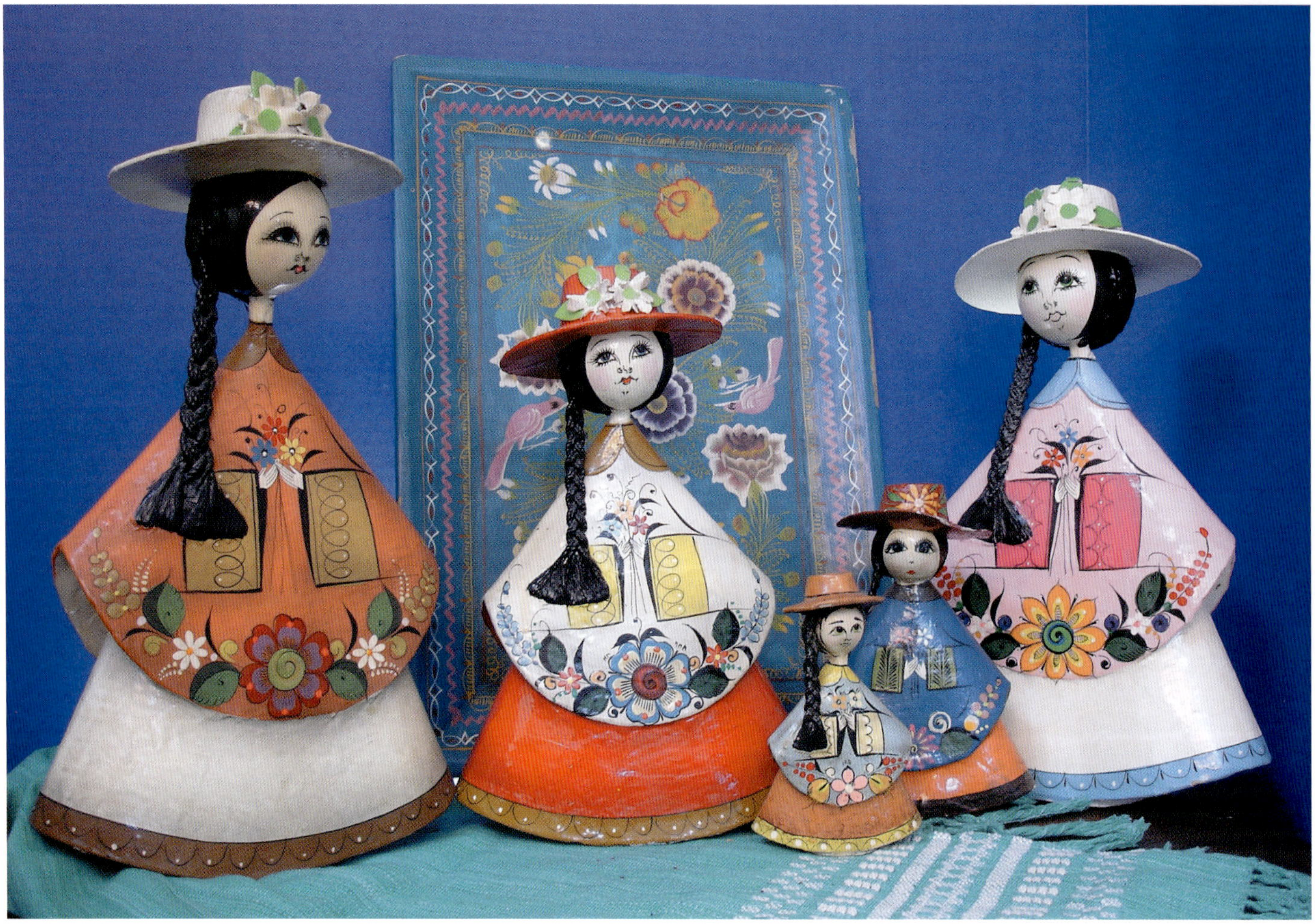

A group of popular arts papier maché, Mexican, Jalisco tourist dolls, made c. 1960s. A smooth surface provides a canvas for the makers of these beautifully painted dolls. Painted in polychrome folk patterns with birds and flowers in vibrant colors. Skillfully rendered with meticulous detail. Sermel taller (workshop), and Nuño, to name a few of the acclaimed artist of this style of work. Some of the dolls are signed and sometimes they are not. From left to right are 16 in., 15 in., 13 in., 8 in., and 6 in. $75 to 150

Among the most interesting dolls are early indigenous sculpted figures, such as beeswax and **monos** (a **Tlaquepaque** style), three-dimensional clay figures. Very few examples are shown here, but you can truly admire them through the book **Popular Arts of Mexico**, by Donna McMenamin. These figured dolls show a concise chronological perception of Mexico and their traditional costumes during the early part of the 20th century. Their clothing was hand applied with painted detail. Wood, clay, wax, and a wide variety of local materials provided the resources for the Indians when creating these figures. Talented artisans captured daily tasks, for example of the fisherman or the humble Mexican peon selling his wares. The incorporated details such as real horse hair as the wig and placed inset eyes and teeth under many layers of material. From the late part of the 19th century, you could find these clay figures in Mexico readily. Many were locally made and sold to tourist or curiosity shops by artisans and their families. Stores such as A. J. Woods Mexican Curiosities, Sanborns, and other shops in Guadalajara or along the border would market them successfully.

Other vintage Mexican costume dolls are constructed from a variety of materials, such as bisque, metal, weavings, and clay. These and other materials can be found occasionally through online auctions, flea markets, or local estate sales, but they are becoming harder to find every day. The Mexican costume tourist dolls that sell on the current market have none or few of the quality and value that their predecessors had. They are usually fiber-filled stuffed toys or plastic molded interpretations, with polyester pre-made costumes. They have little or no authentic hand detail and are often just renditions of Mexico's cherished traditional costumes. Although many were made in Mexico for the tourist trade, other makers from around the globe made them as well. The choice of materials and individual interpretations are original, with overflowing renditions that show a true fondness for Mexico's colorful costumes.

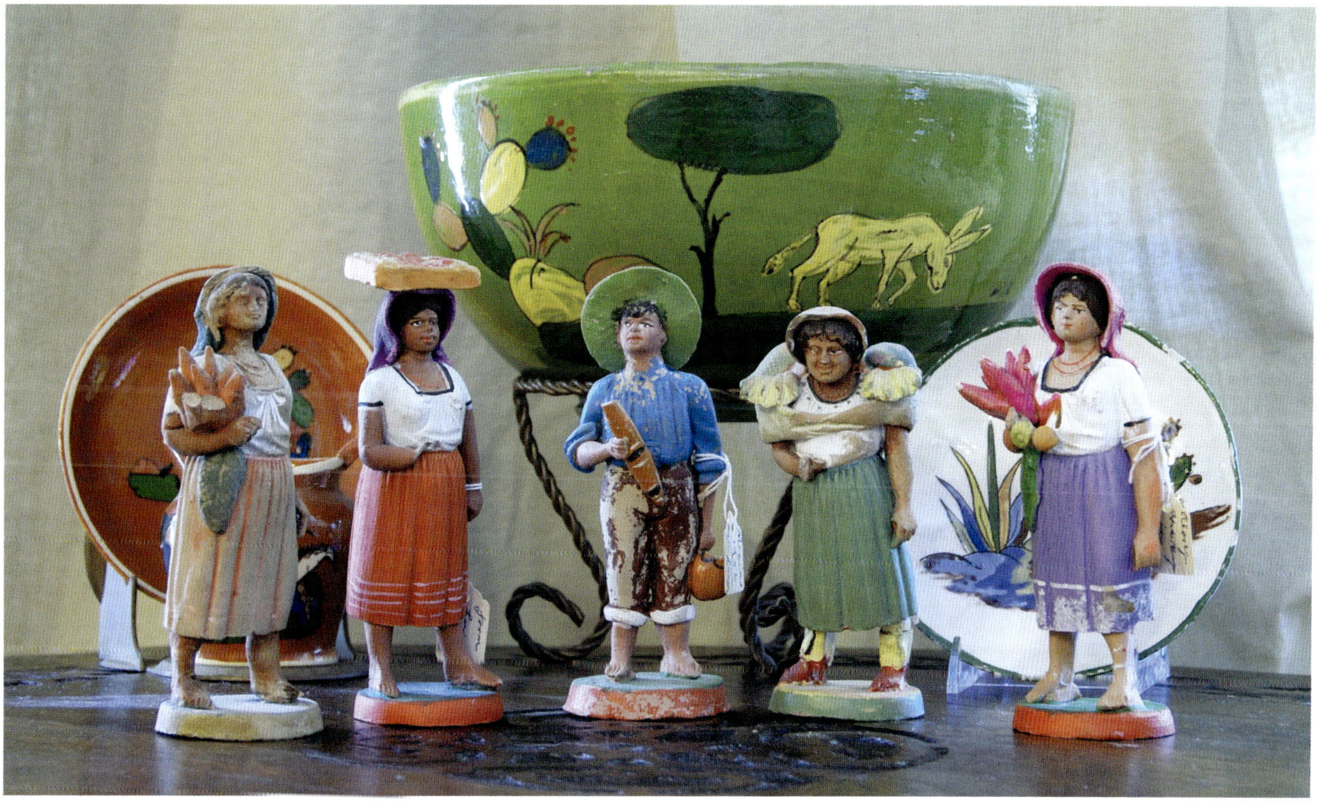

Attributed to the Tlaquepaque clay figures, "monos". Wonderful detail of dutiful people. c.1930s to 50s . Behind is a popular arts Tlaquepaque pottery. Dolls $60 to 150 ea.

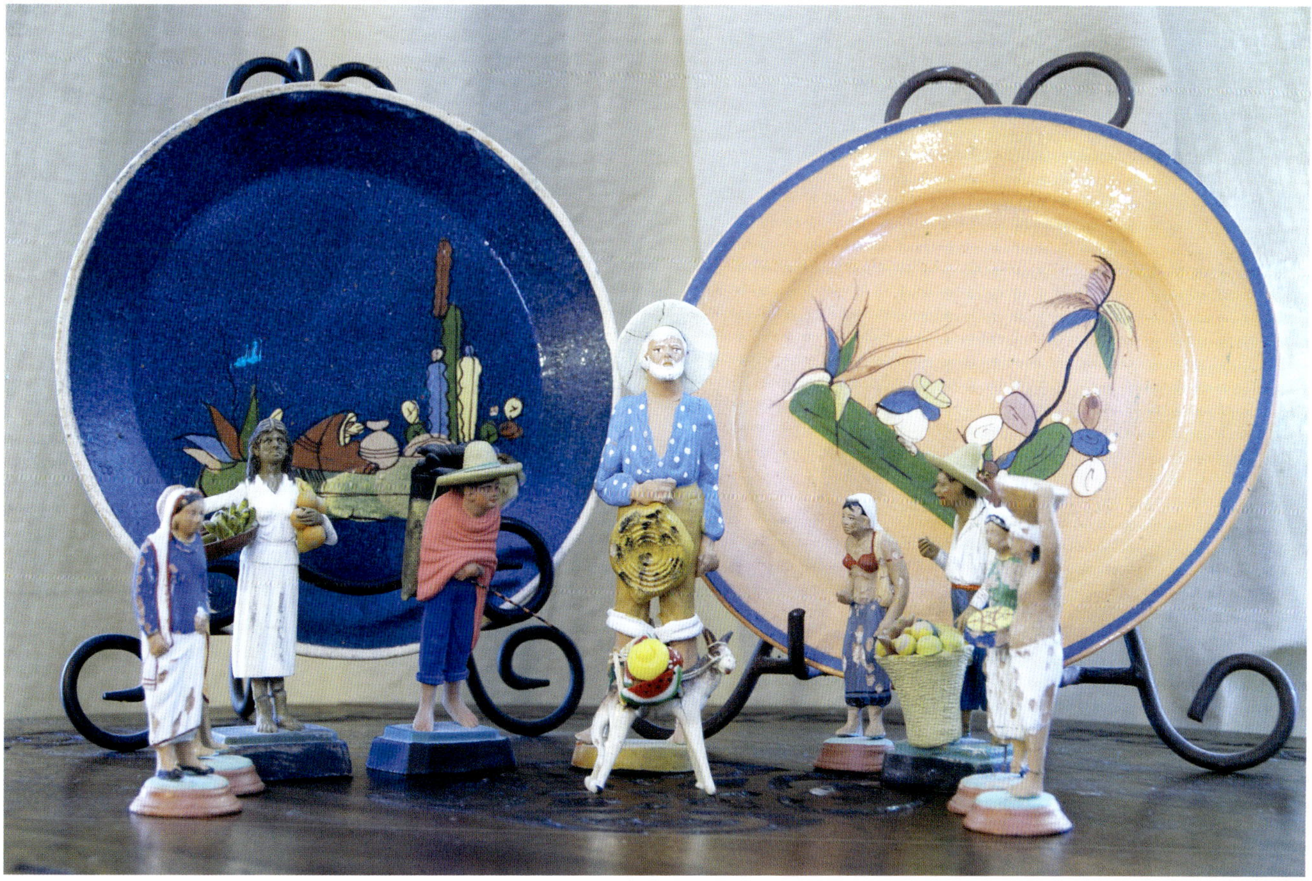

A group of Tlaquepaque style clay figures, "monos." Small realistically rendered local Mexicans interpreted in explicit detail. Hand formed or mold formed and brushed with colorful slips. Tourist pieces sold throughout Mexico Popular arts plates in the background. c.1930s to '50s. $60 to 150 ea.

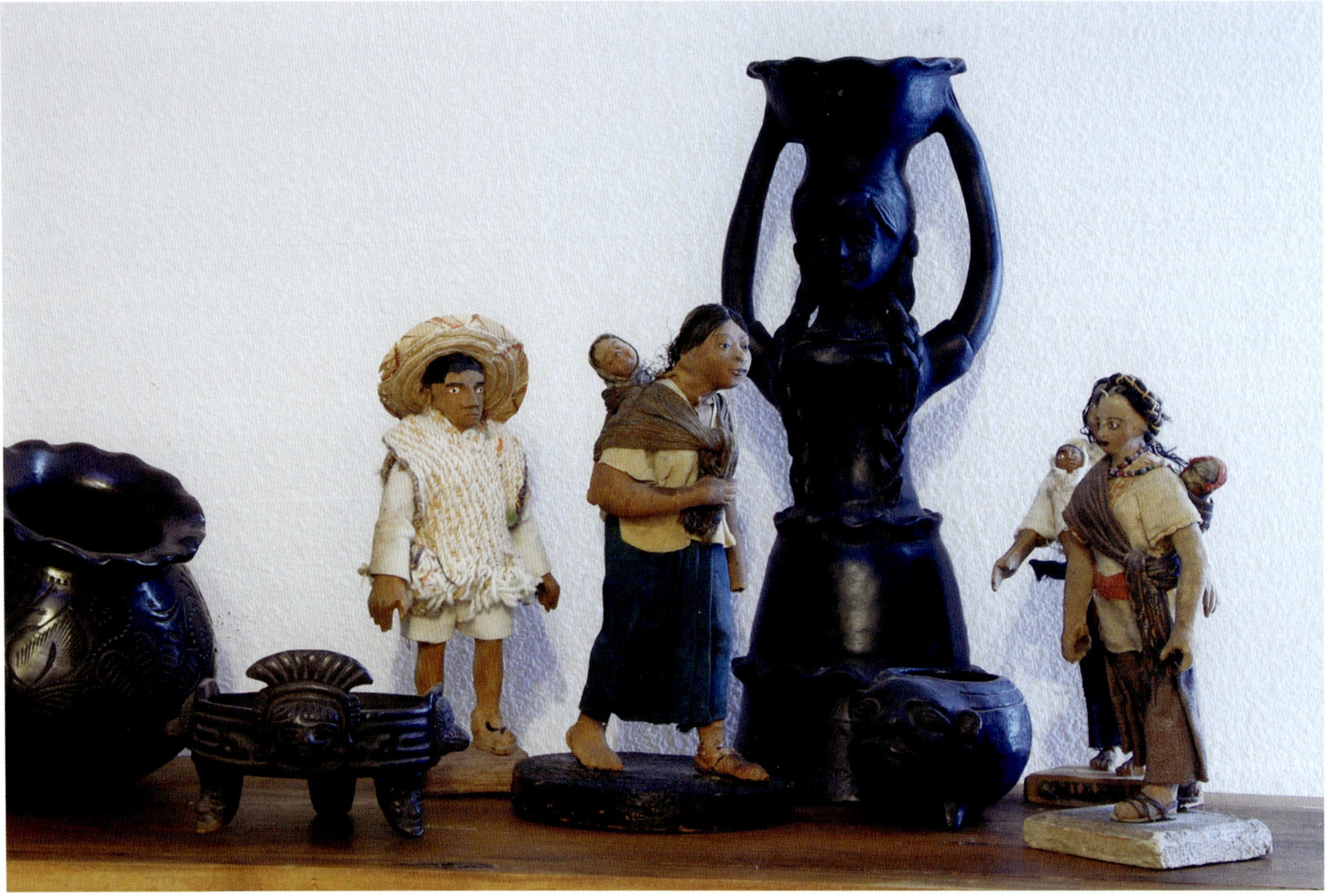

A group of wax and wood figures, extremely rare. The largest is an 11 in. Indian woman with child on a wood base, the original sticker from A. J. Woods, Mexican Curiosities, City of Mexico. The other wax Indian woman and child is 7 in. She has no markings but may be from the W.G. Waltz store. The two Indian men are carved from wood and one is stamped Guererro. Tourist pieces sold throughout Mexico, c.1880s to 1930s $75 to 800 ea.

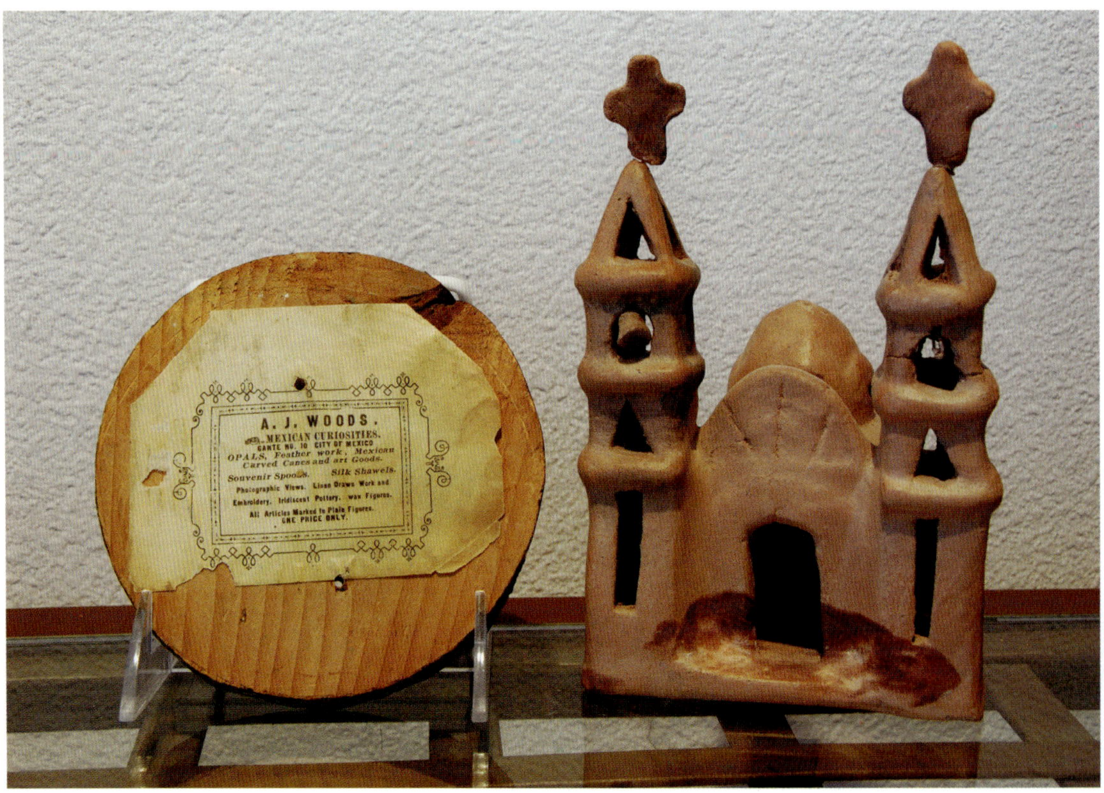

The bottom of the 11 in. wax doll stand from the A. J. Woods Curiosities store, c.1910, Mexico.

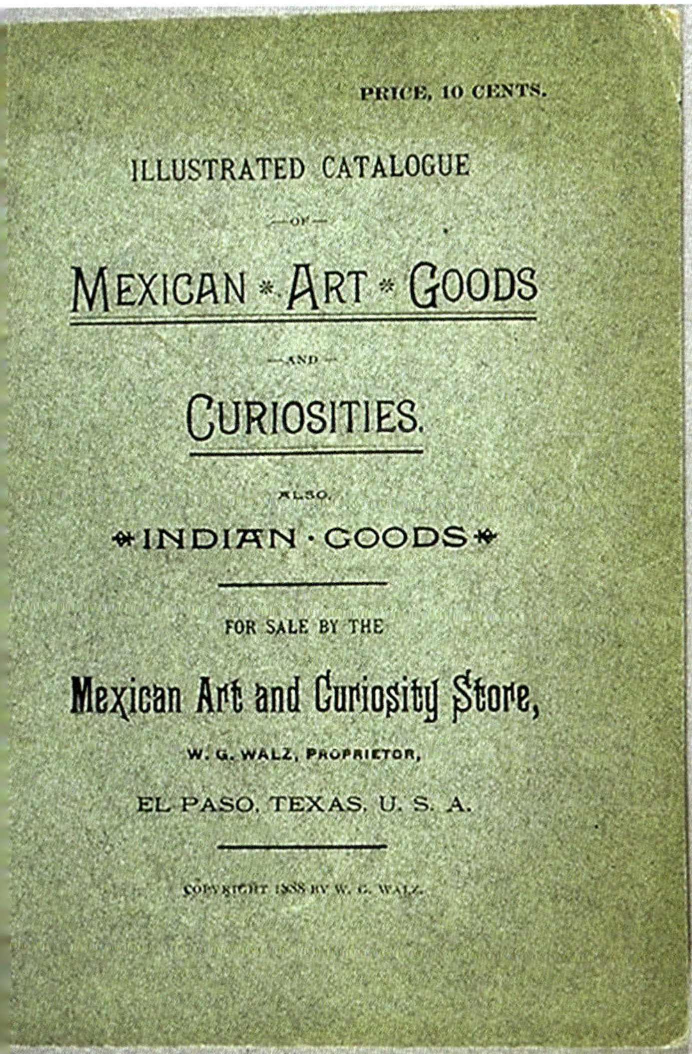

The catalog of Mexican Art and Curiosity Store, W. G. Walz Propictor, El Paso, Texas, 1888. A popular arts seller who handled many items of skilled local crafts.

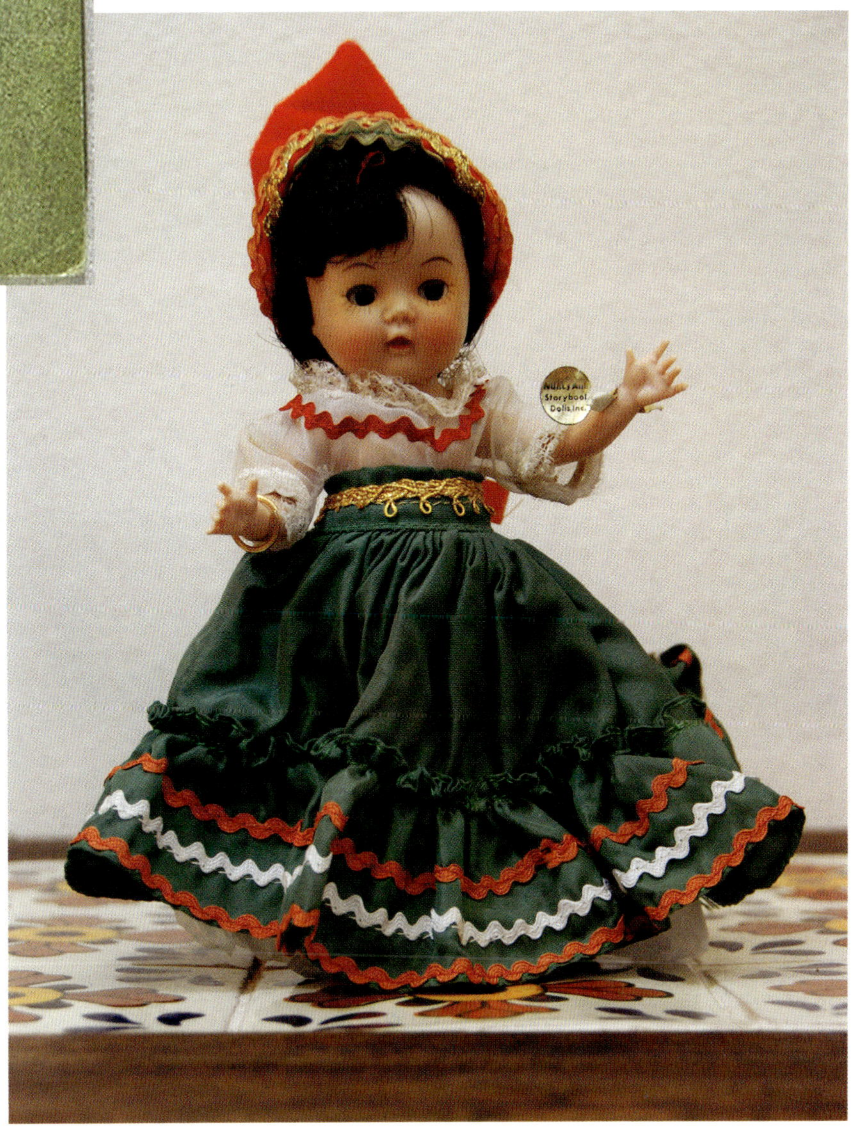

Attributed to the Nancy Ann Storybook dolls, an 8 in. Muffie doll, c.1950s. Her clothes were well made. Jointed body made of a hard plastic, strung. $150 to 200

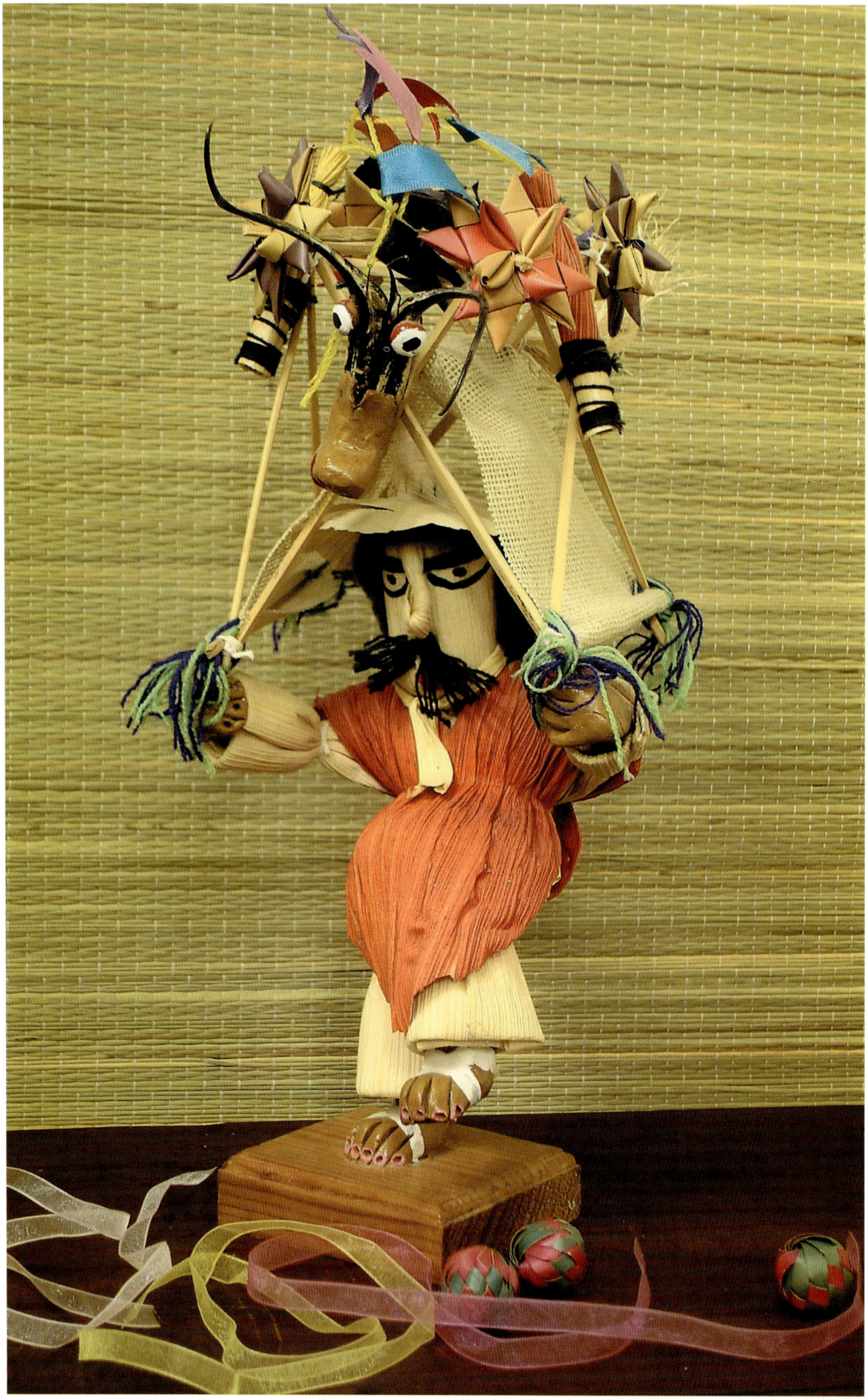

A popular straw and palm woven sculpted doll, carnivals and indigenous beliefs with symbolic origin.Traditional Dance of the Carnivals, c. 1960s, maker unknown, 12 in. tall, dyed straw and wonderful detail. $40 to 60

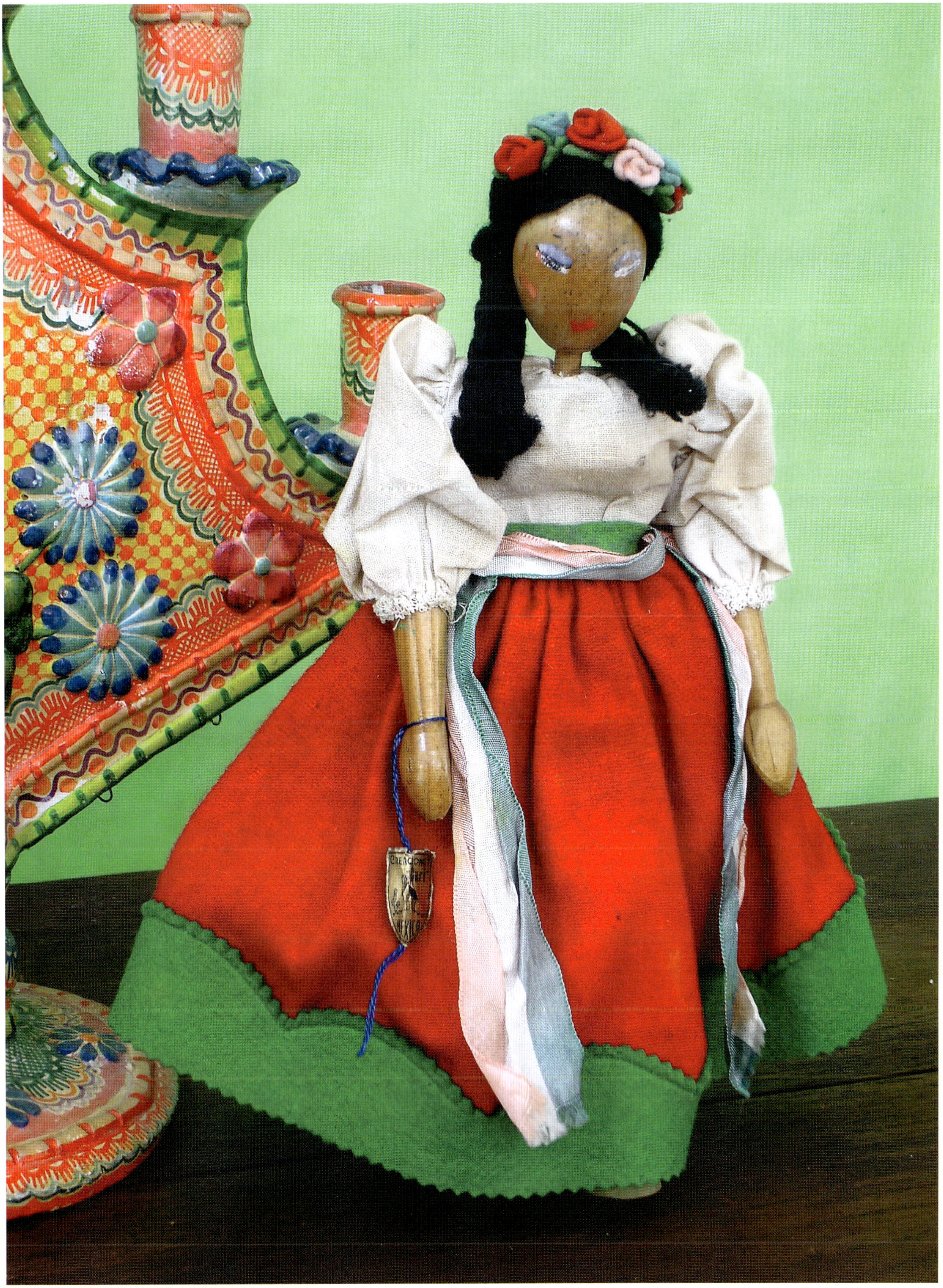

A rare 11 in. spin wooden doll made by "Creaciones Cari," Mexico. Careful consideration to authenticate her clothing was important. $75 to 150

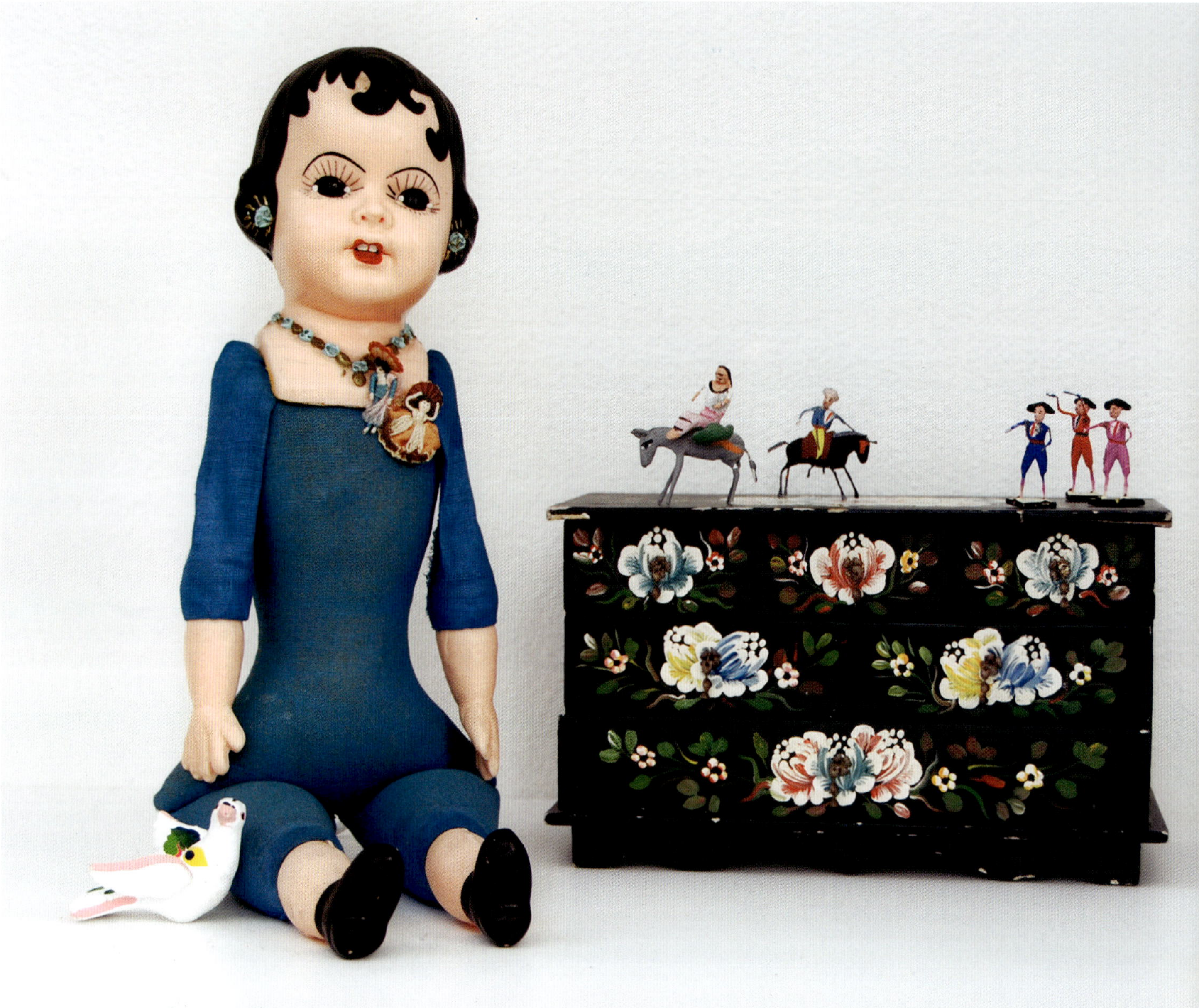

Num. Inventario : 31159
Num. Catálogo : (63)9.156G-1646

Nombre de objeto : MUÑECA
Material : CERA, ALGODON Y PINTURA
Procedencia : ESTADO DE PUEBLA
Uso : LUDICO

Ancho : 7.00 cm
Altura : 17.50 cm

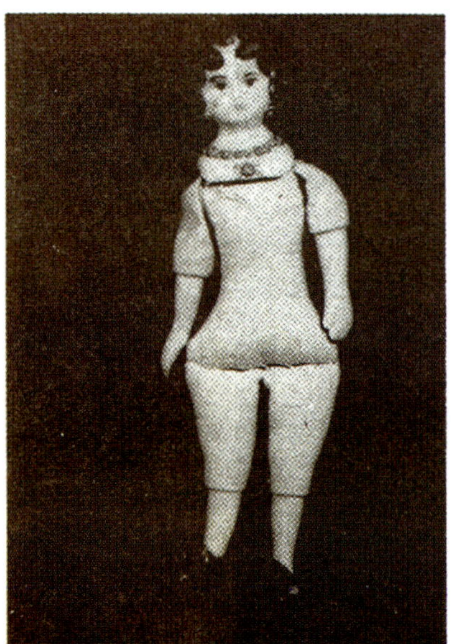

An impressive, 17.5 in. wax and sawdust cloth doll, c.1930s. In remarkable condition, colored layers of wax molded with Spanish traits. Made in Puebla, Mexico $200 to $400

Attributed to the "Muneca Mestiza" catalog by Maria E.S. Santa Ana, for the exhibit of Colecciones Etnograficas del Museo Nacional de Antropologia,1992. Printed in Mexico. A similar doll is from Estado de Pueblo. The year it was cataloged was 1963.

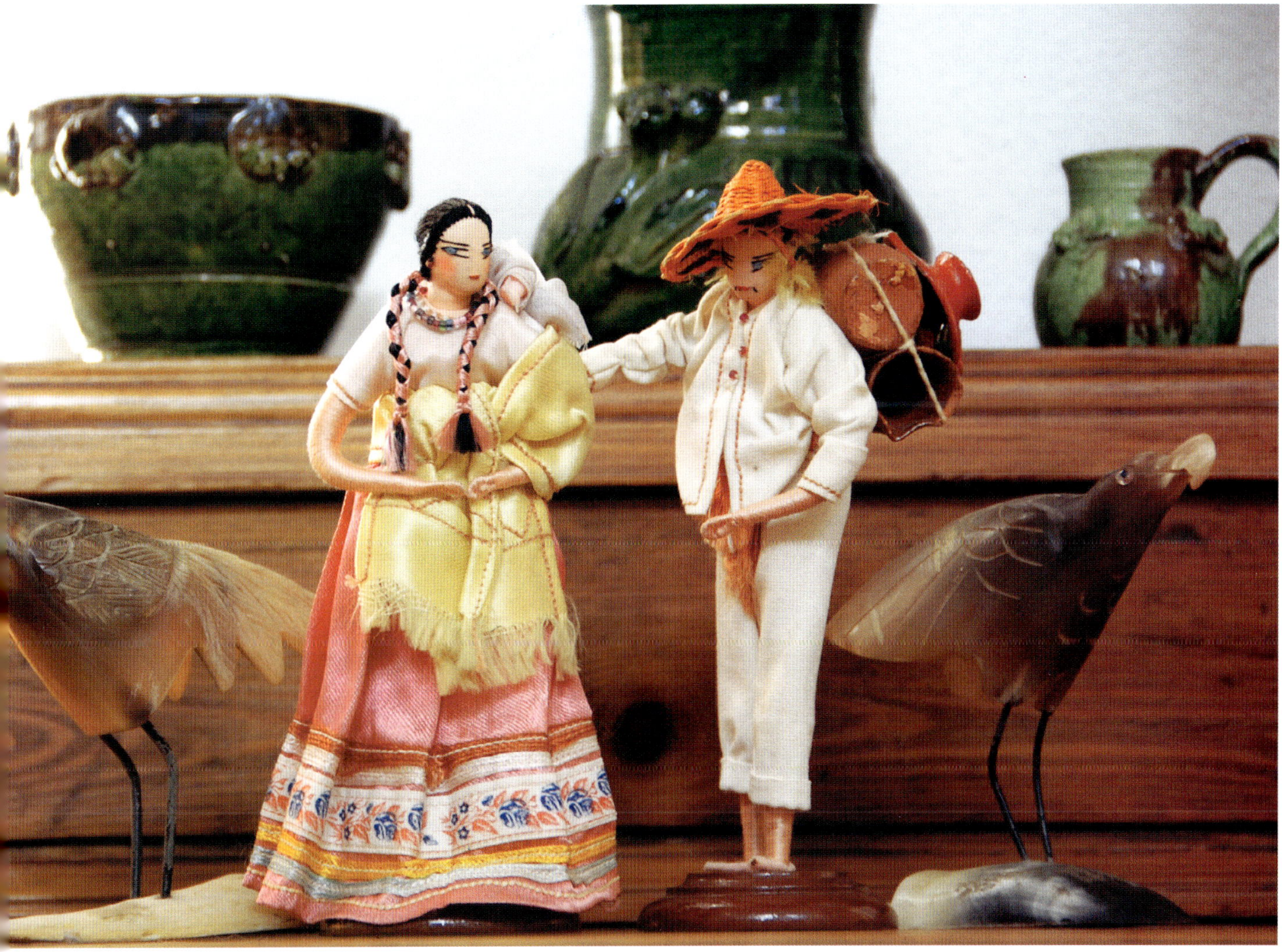

An 8 in. set of miniature *mestiza* dolls, c.1920s. Made of wire, cloth, and horsehair that has been tightly wound, creating the many layers under their clothing. Made in Mexico. Special old Mexico carved birds are from the horn of the "*toro*" (bull).

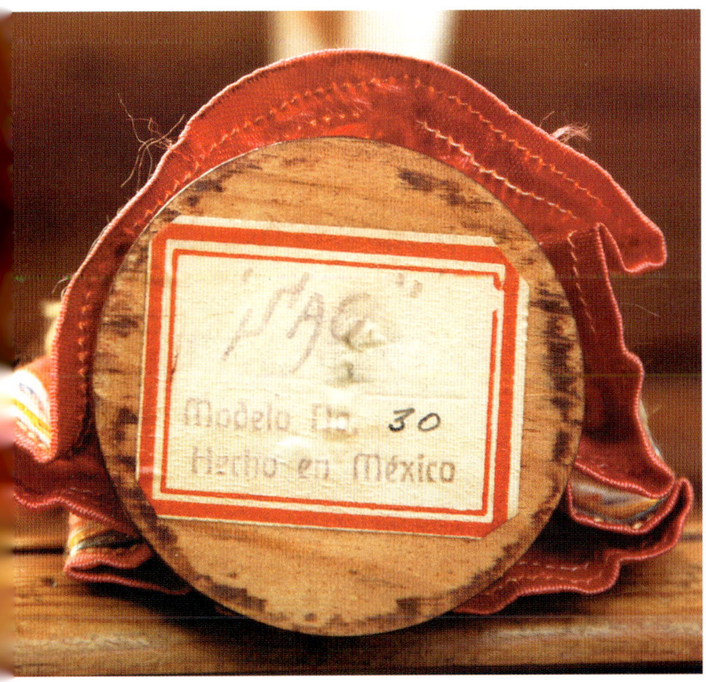

The wooden base of the 8 in. set of miniature *mestiza* dolls, c.1920s.

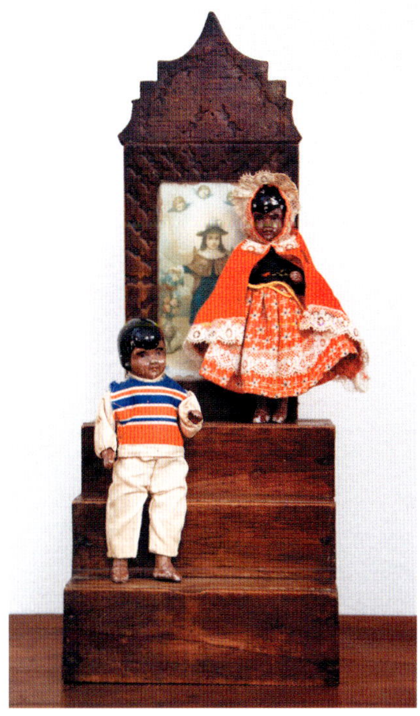

Two 5.5 in., very old molded strung china dolls, European, c.1920. Their skin has been painted for a more ethnic appearance. A *mestizo* couple on the steps of a 100-year-old wooden *retablo* altar. Made in Mexico. $125 to 350 pr.

PART 3
The *Mestiza* and Indian Women

Each state in Mexico has a particular style that underlies fundamental traditions of the Mexican women's dress and their region in the 20th century. Through costumed dolls, they possess an incredible treasure of traditions and hand made textiles. Colonial-era provincial Spanish styles have blended with native Indian customary dress, producing now what is generally described as *la ropa típica*, the typical clothing.

No matter what material they are made with, or from what region they derive, the dolls convey extraordinary examples of Mexican women and their garments. On the dolls, their skirts (*la enagua, la falda* and *el enredo*), their tops (*la camisa* or *la blusa* and *huipil*), plus their beautiful scarf (*el rebozo*) demonstrate compliant traits from the different regions and their inheritance. The diversity in the costumes, be they Indians or *mestiza* women, reflect strong cultural backgrounds. Both symbolize, as well as, identify their distinctive life styles. Just as one costume defines its original Indian Mesoamerica roots the other carries the *mestizos'* definitive influences by the colonial Spanish, as well as Europe and Asia.

The doll costumes illustrate cultural changes that took place gradually. Spanish colonial influences affected the native cultures, which then fused into Mexican traditions. Because the natives worked for the Spanish in colonial times, urban lifestyles became desirable to a majority of the natives. The natives' skills were immediately recognized, particularly their weaving abilities and attention to details. Trading and sharing their talents created new trends in Mexico, with fewer restrictions on the lower class. The ancient caste system (a structured social order), limiting only the wealthy to wearing beautiful embroidered items, became obsolete. Strict laws imposed prior to Spanish conquest had once denied the servant and working class women to wear beautiful clothing, unless it was permitted by the royalty. Of course, this is ancient history, but must be acknowledged as it explains the basis of their costumes and how the clothing has evolved. The wealthy people could afford finer fabrics and elaborate clothing, but it was the skill of the impoverished natives that created them. This liberty entitled natives and lower class people to make beautiful things for themselves, if they could afford to do so. As in any society, the right to wear whatever you want only encourages creativity, which can dictate trends. And that is precisely what is expressed through vintage Mexican dolls and their costumes.

Typical *mestiza* and Indian women's costumes can explain differences that incorporate and underlie a continuity of traditional garments, merged over the 20th century. It has been described as Mexico's "Renaissance," when a revival and recognition of the popular arts was finally celebrated as definitive Mexican art. Simple cultural touches, such as motifs and embroidery or a particular color and trim, exposed a wide variety of influences. The native contributions and the Spanish blend can be supported by a trade industry that allowed import and export to flow freely. There was an increased enthusiasm in the 1930s toward Mexican native dress and style that was considered the *traje tipica.* The intermingling of their cultures was certainly a complementing factor, for both. Indian and Spanish costumes reveal extraordinarily vibrant colors, skills in weaving, and timeless intricate traditional patterns, while the modern urban *mestiza* fashion included luxuries such as silk and wool and encouraged social status and trends.

Opposite page:
Two rare 23 in. composition dolls, c.1930s. "Angelina" and "Christina," in the China Poblana dress and the mestiza traditional dress with indigenous garments. The body is hard cloth, composition head, arms, and legs. Molded features with painted detail. No maker's marks.
"Angelina," a 23 in. composition doll, reveals the special quality of the China Poblana dress. The embroidery technique, fabric and application are accurately interpreted. Angelina wears the red rebozo, a silk blusa and full skirt with a glorious interpretation of the national emblem of Mexico's serpent in the mouth of the eagle on the native nopal cactus. Some crazing and facial features can attribute her body to either an American or Canadian doll maker, but all clothing was made in Mexico. Long braids with entwined red ribbon.
"Christina" is a treasure and tribute to her country's indigenous dress. A hard stuffed body, jointed at the neck, arms and legs. Molded features with hand painted detail. Christina wears a velvet huipil, cotton and lace skirt and a lovely lace rebozo. Her hair is twisted braids entwined with ribbon. $350 to $1100 ea.

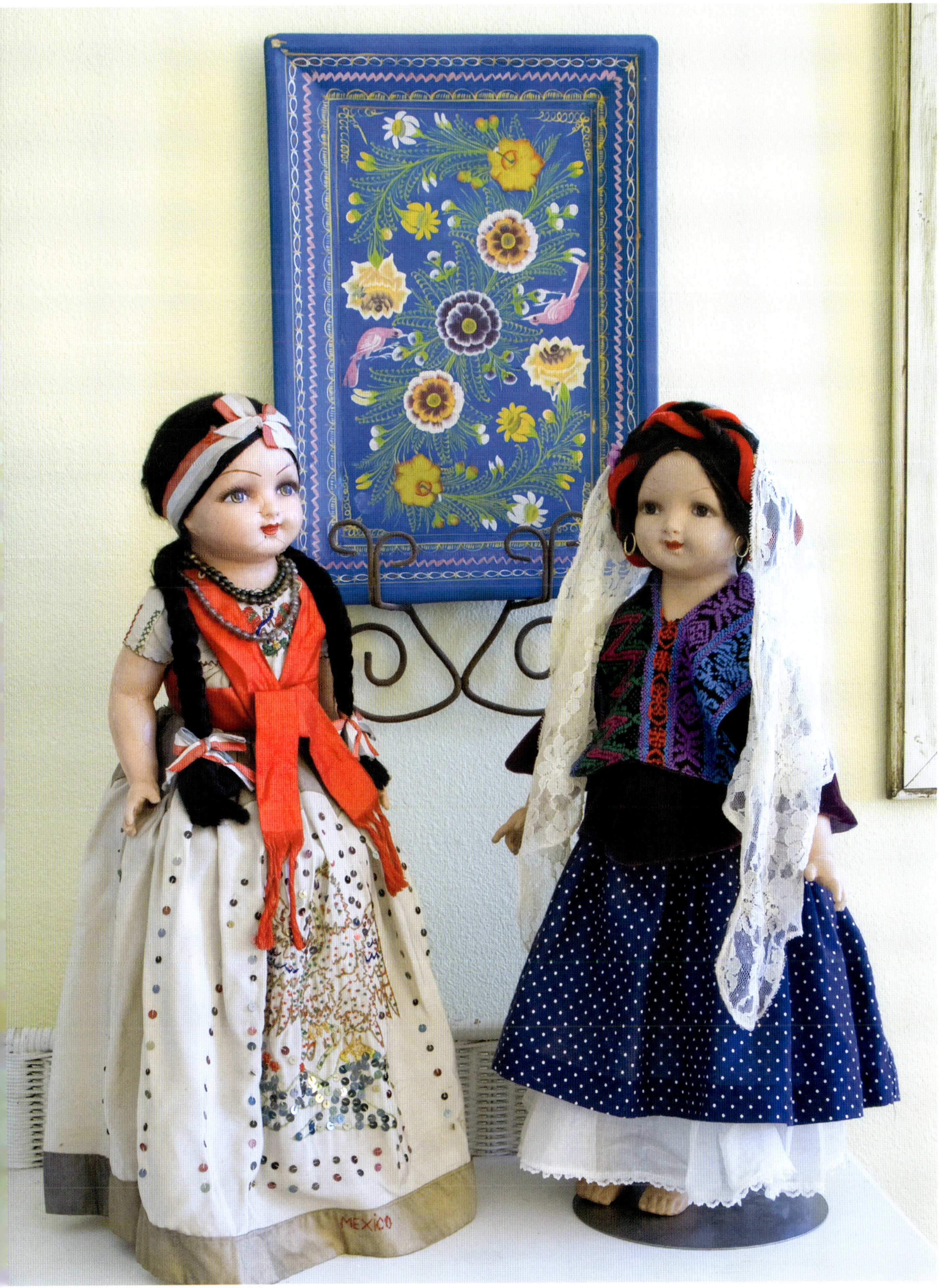
MEXICO

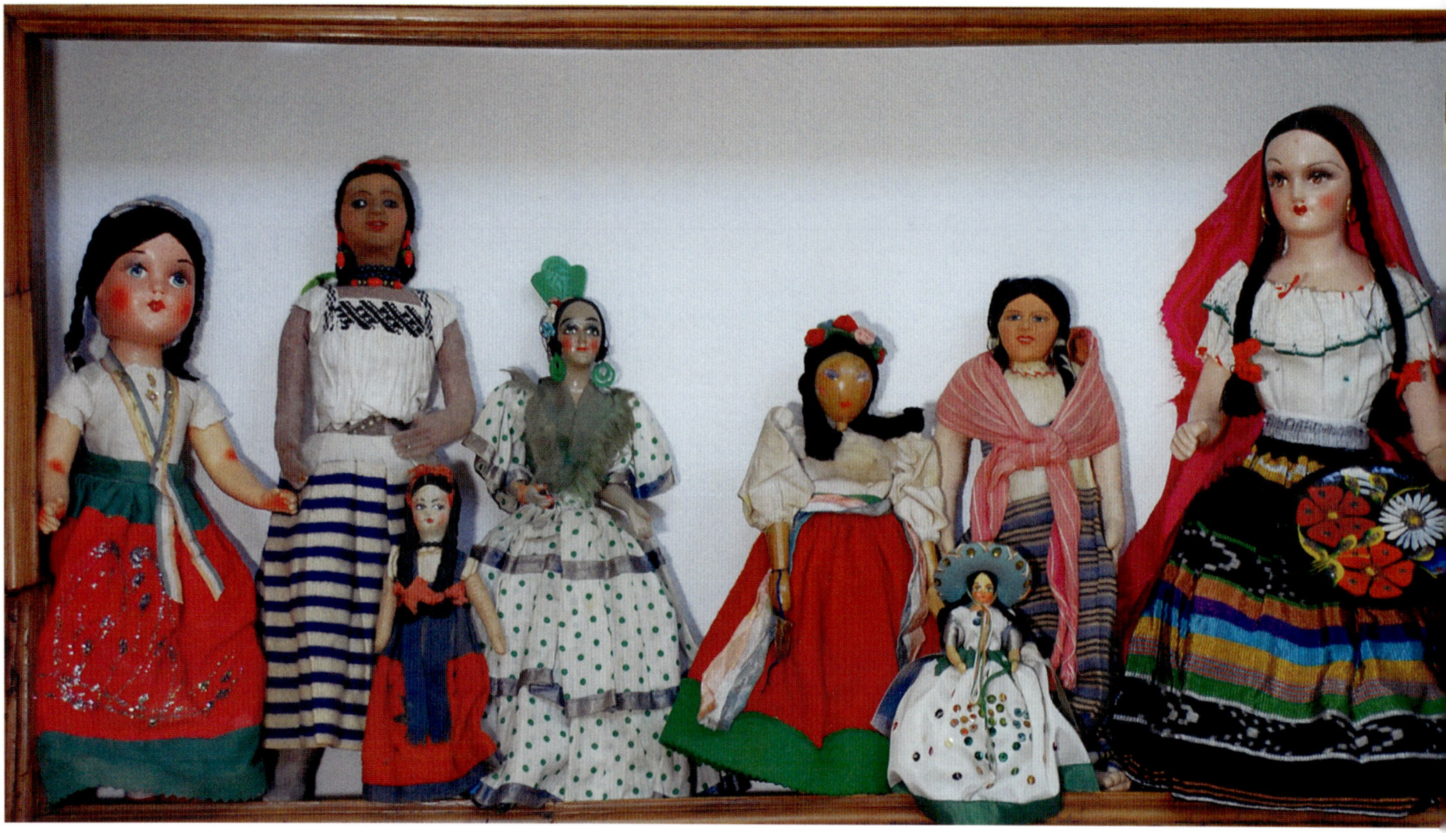

"*Las Muchachas*," a wonderful group of Old Mexico dolls displayed on a colonial shelf, 20th c. $25 to 400 ea.

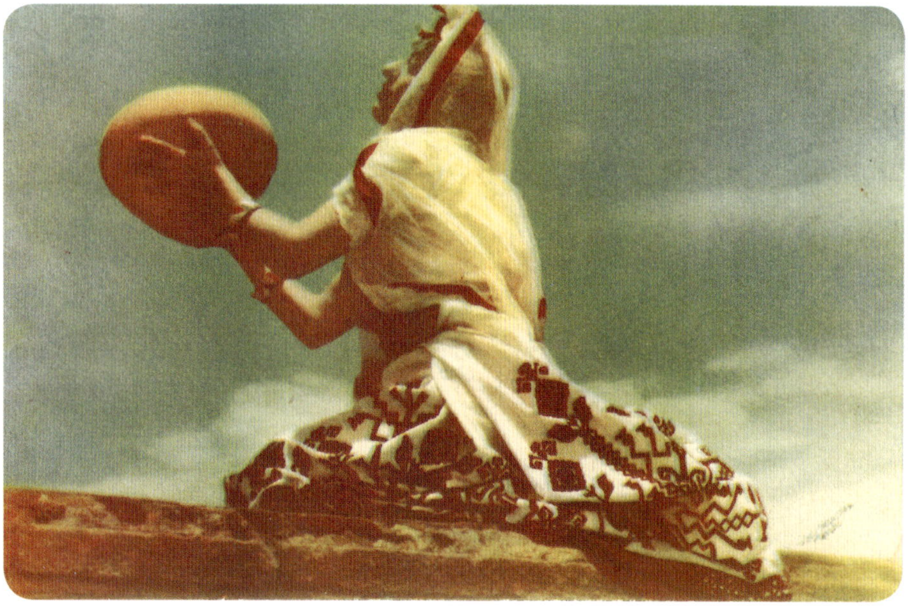

A color tinted paper photo litho postcard, "Tipo de Amatleca," Amatleca maiden from Veracruz, Mexico c.1930s, Mexico D.F

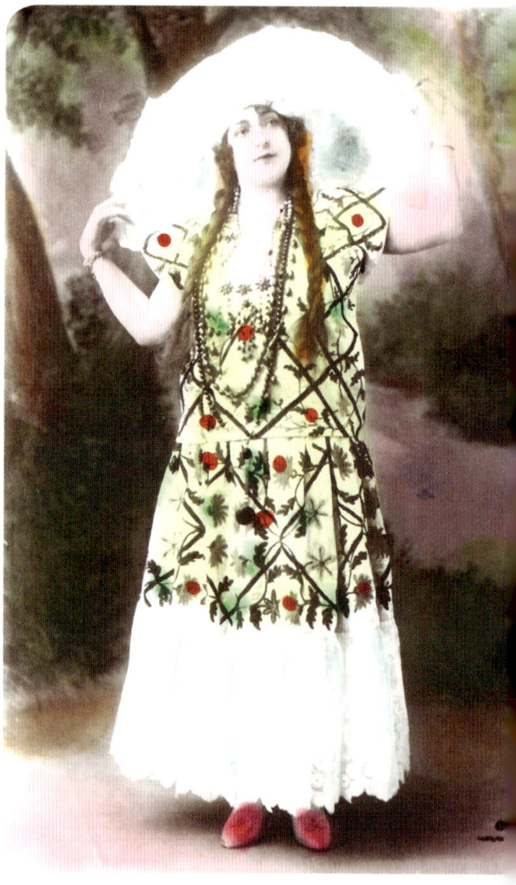

A color tinted paper photo litho postcard, "Tehuana" maiden, c.1930s, Mexico D.F.

La Ropa Tipica, The Typical Clothing

The Mexican Indian woman clothes herself with a piece of landscape. It is not given to everyone, however, to capture scenery and convert it into a garment, states acclaimed Mexican painter and writer, Ramon Valdiosera.

On the Indian dolls, you can interpret these words. His observation of the Indian costume surely acknowledges their textiles and how they were worn. The natural fibers and simplicity in which they were made is never conveyed as plain or uninteresting. Looking closely at the manner in which the clothing is worn, draped, embellished, and woven identifies the many layers of their traditions, no matter how provincial. They are unpretentious yet extremely aware of the detail of their garments. The plain and colorful fabrics, intricate motifs, and trimmings compliment as well as distinguish the different costumes. Although sometimes more somber than those of the *mestiza*, Indian clothing conserves some of the ancestral dignity and amazing weaving techniques. The diverse women of Mexico are distinguished by differences in their clothing as well as their heredity.

La ropa tipica is a common term used in Mexico when identifying distinctive regional pieces frequently admired and identified as the typical clothing of that region. On occasion when living in Mexico, I asked a local woman where I could acquire a lovely blouse like the one she was wearing, and she would respond, *"es la ropa tipica."* Many of the Indian dolls wear the typical pieces of clothing from their regions, but some are combined with other pieces making it difficult to distinguish the origin of their costume. Most of the cloth needed for their clothing was woven, and unfortunately much of it was done in the *obrajes* (forced cheap labor) factories.

On the *mestiza* dolls, you can see clear European influences in their garments. Through their clothing you can really enjoy the wide development of folk art, with native elements transformed into a national Mexican costume. Their vintage clothing is a vestige of how this once-indigenous society embraced new influences, combining them and molding their nationality. Just as the *mestizo* men's economic status is recognizable, so is that of the female dolls. The *charra* or *señoritas* wore silks and rayon fabrics that required special care, while the lower class *mestiza* and the Indian woman wore cottons and wools that were more durable and less costly. In spite of this, each of the doll costumes shows their distinct qualities as they both possess rich color and eye-catching designs. The typical *mestiza* woman used colorful embroidery and indulged in machine-made prints. All of their clothing typifies the *ropa tipica* of the Mexican woman, that which makes them recognizable worldwide.

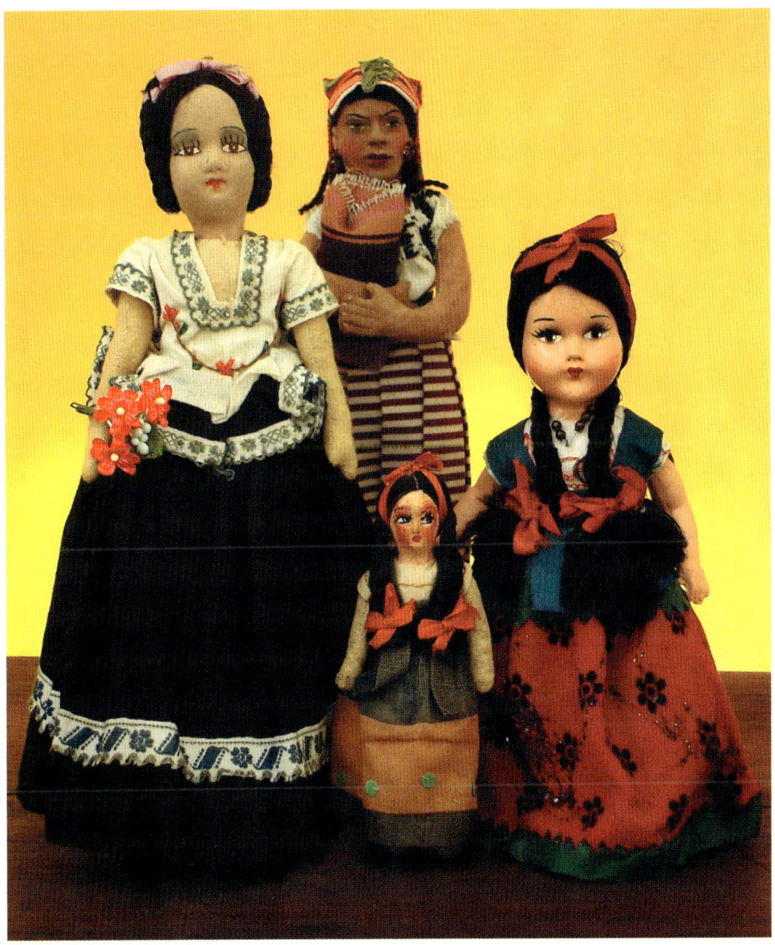

Four popular Mexican dolls dating from the 1940s to the 1960s.
Left to right: A beautiful 13 in. cloth doll, tag states *Tlaquepaque* woman, from the state of Jalisco, c.1940s. The body of the doll is made of a cotton muslin cloth molde face is pressed felt, mohair black wig adorned with pink flowers. Notice the beautiful attributes of this Spanish-influenced costume of the *mestiza*. Lovely red flowers are hand embroidered around the front of the *blusa* following the trim, a full *enaigua* skirt and traditional style in which she wears her hair. Mitten stitched hands and black sewn cloth shoes. No marker's mark.
The indigenous Indian doll behind is also 13 in., made of coarse muslin a hard stuffed body, inset eyes and teeth and molded features, a *servilleta* on her head. No marks, made in Mexico.
The small *mestiza* doll 4.5 in. is made of cloth crudely painted facial features, cotton threads for hair with satin bows.
The 10 in., 5-pc. composition body doll, c.1960s, with hand-painted features and a typical *mestiza* ensemble.
$20 to 125 ea.

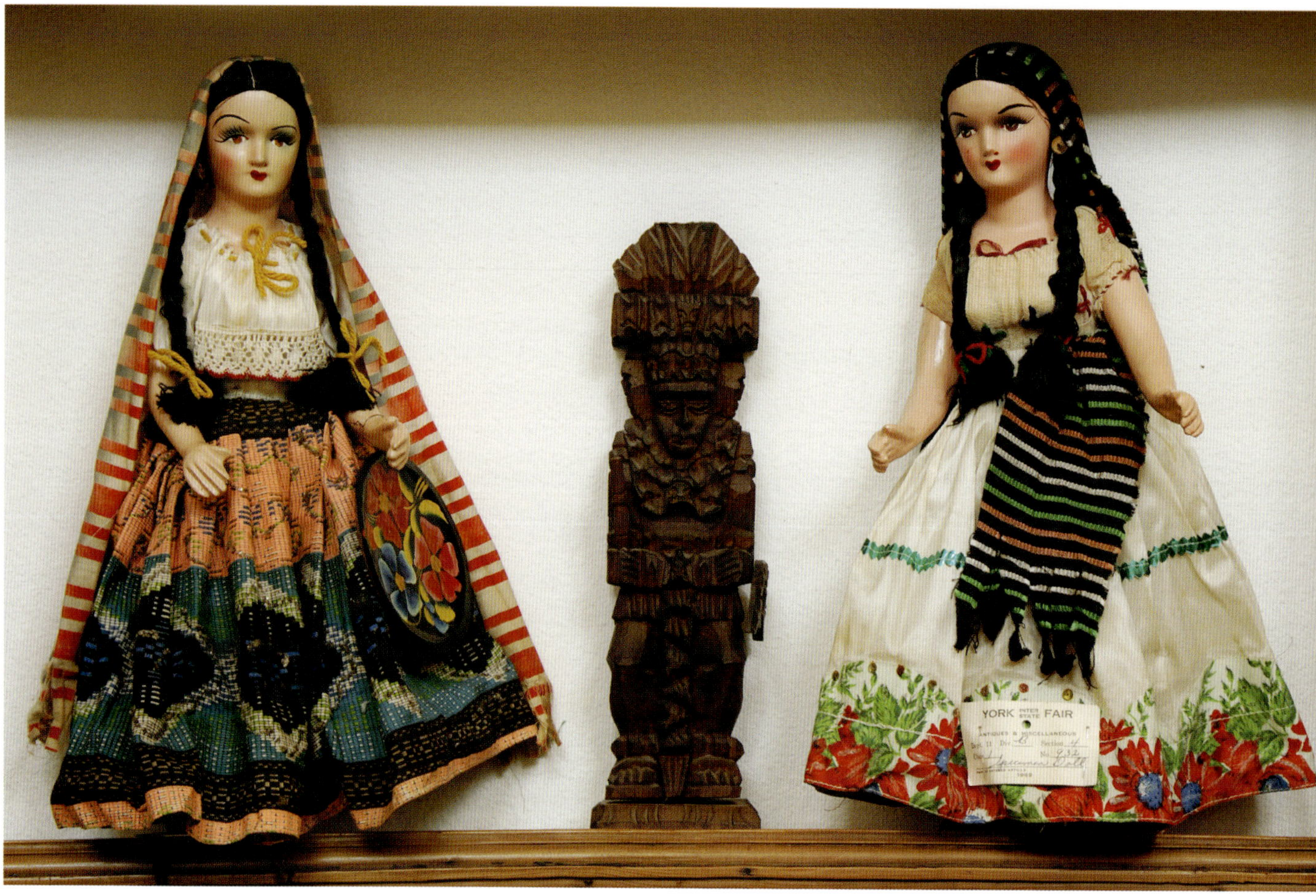

Traditional costumes worn by these 17 in. early composition dolls, c.1940s. The *mestiza,* on the right, has a tag from a USA fair held in 1967, entered in the antique and collectible category, made in Mexico, 1940s. The beauty on the left is wearing a glorious patterned *enagua* full skirt and *rebozo*. In the center is a Mayan Mexican wood figure. $150 to 375 ea.

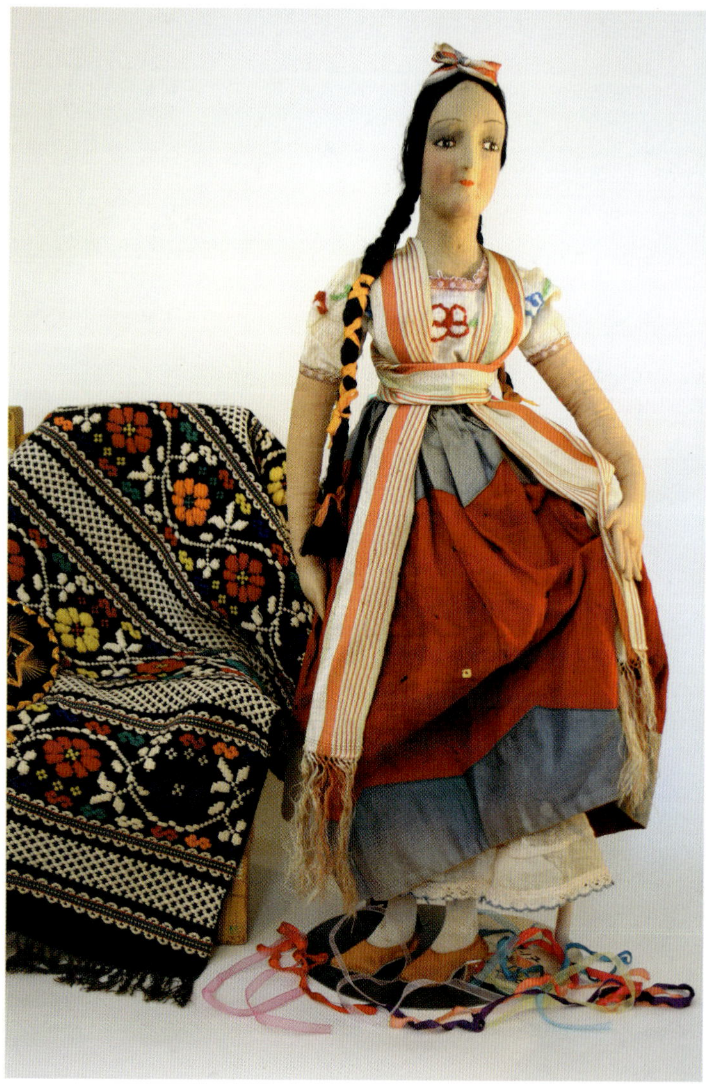

A 28" rare beautiful *mestiza* boudoir doll "Sonia." Made early c.1930s, her origin and maker are unknown, but she exhibits qualities of early Lenci dolls. In good condition, wearing a cotton Spanish *blusa* and full red and green *castor* skirt. Made of cloth, all hand detail. Her face has molded pressed felt features with long wool black braids for hair. Her striped *rebozo* is made of silk rayon finished with fringe. Sonia lifts her skirt to reveal the many layers of petticoats and pantaloons. A formed body with womanly features. Detailed with consideration to the authenticate a typical Mexican dress of her era. $300 to 800

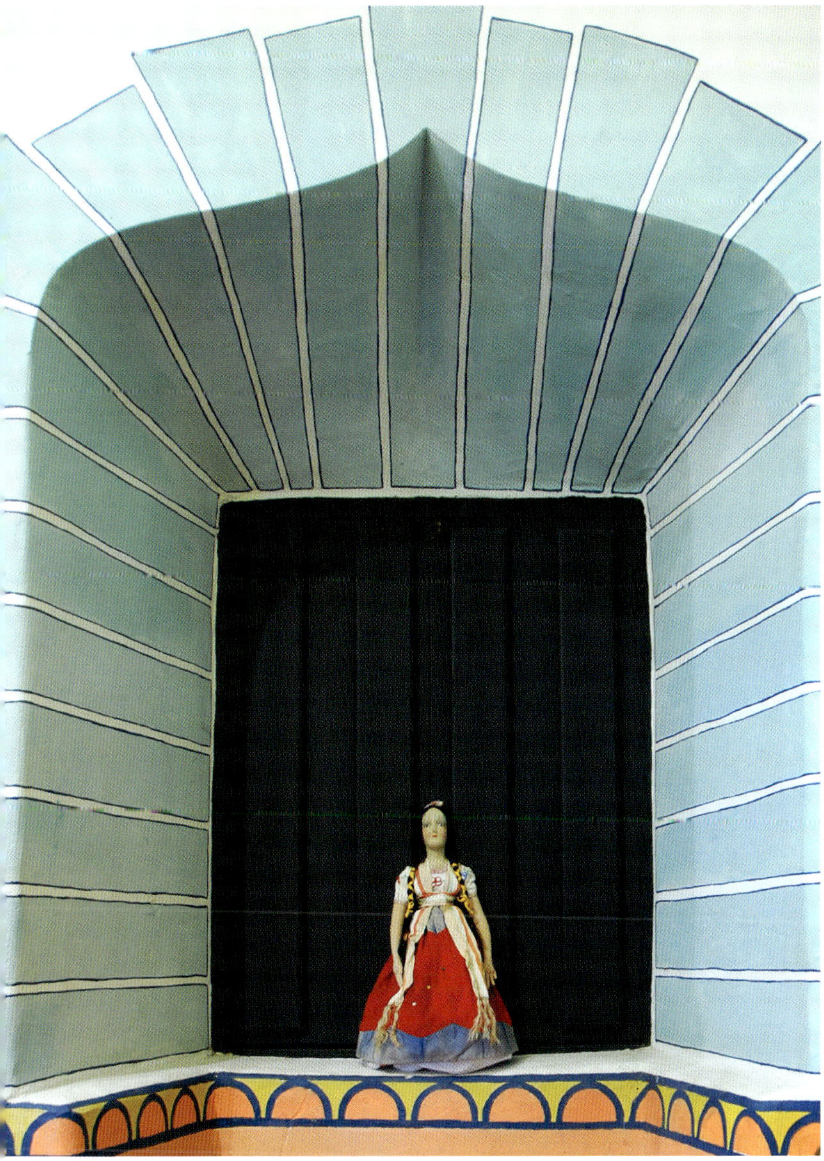

A Mexican missions niche, with Sonia standing in the center.

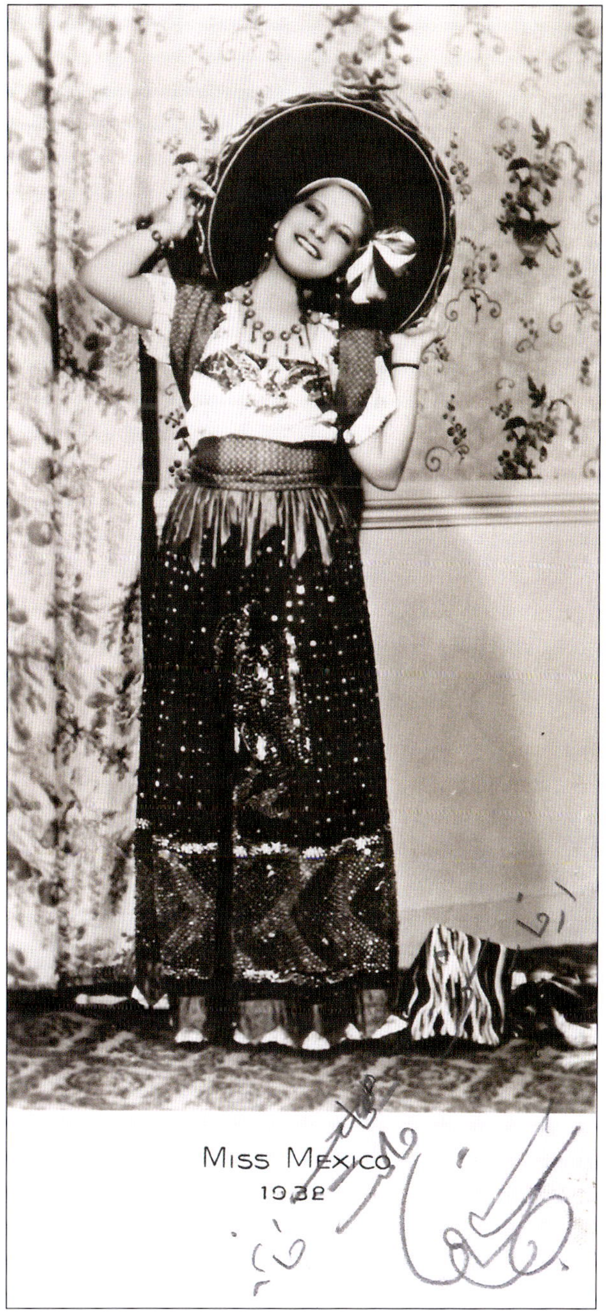

A signed vintage photograph of "Miss Mexico, 1932," 6 x 3 in. $40 to 60

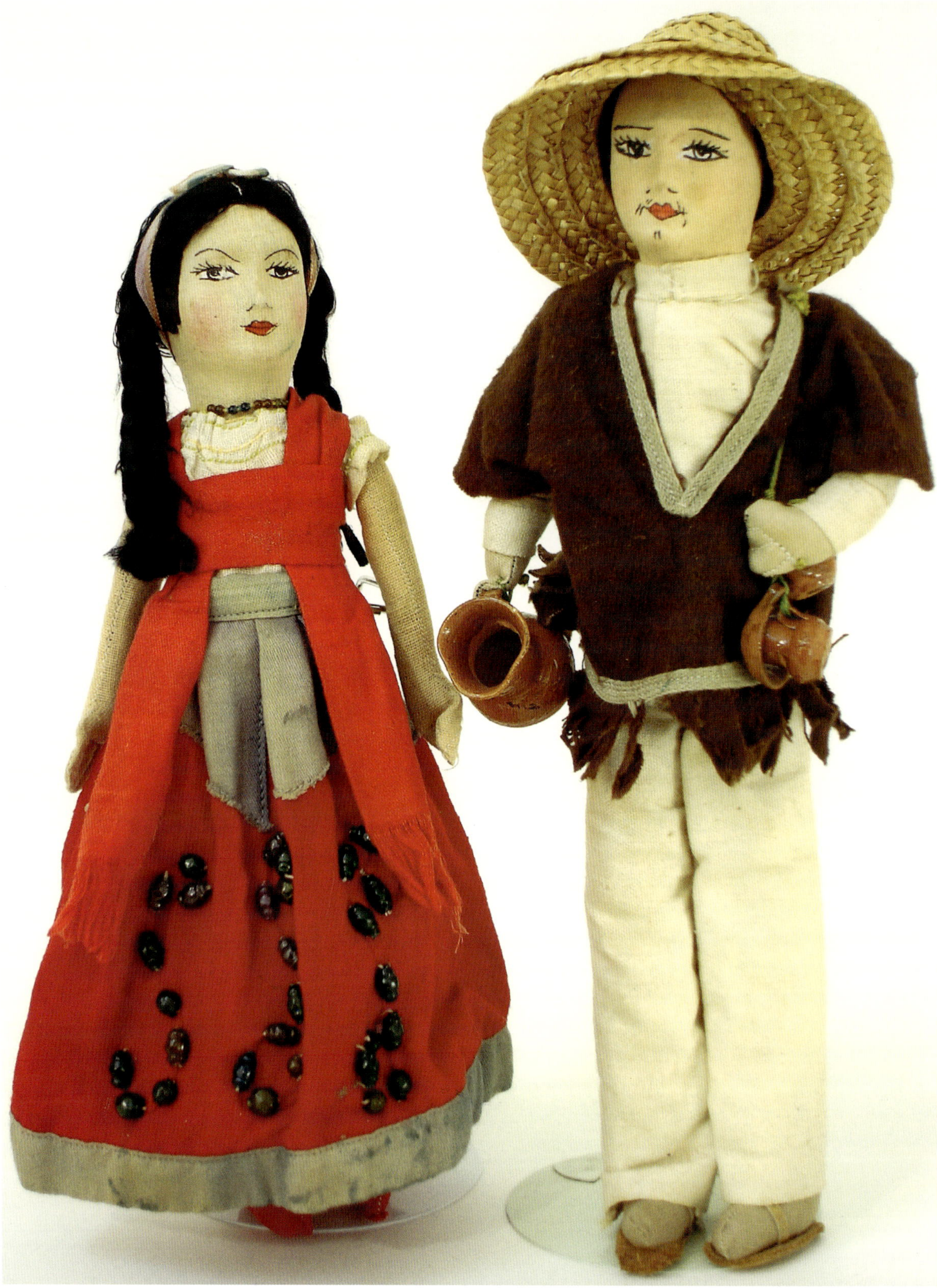

Two 12 in. *mestizos* toting their wares, made in Mexico, c.1930s. A Pueblan potter, with molded cloth, hard stuffed bodies, and detailed clothing. Painted eyes and detail on their faces. She wears a traditional full skirt of red *castor* with glass beading on the front like that of the *zagalejo*. A long red *rebozo* is crossed at the front over a white blouse. They both have mitten hands. He is wearing a *jorongo poncho* in brown *castor* over his *calzón blanco* garments. The Pueblan couple was made for each other. Their accessories are a woven palm *sombrero* and *papelillo* necklace with a colorful Mexican ribbon in her wool hair. $75-150 ea.

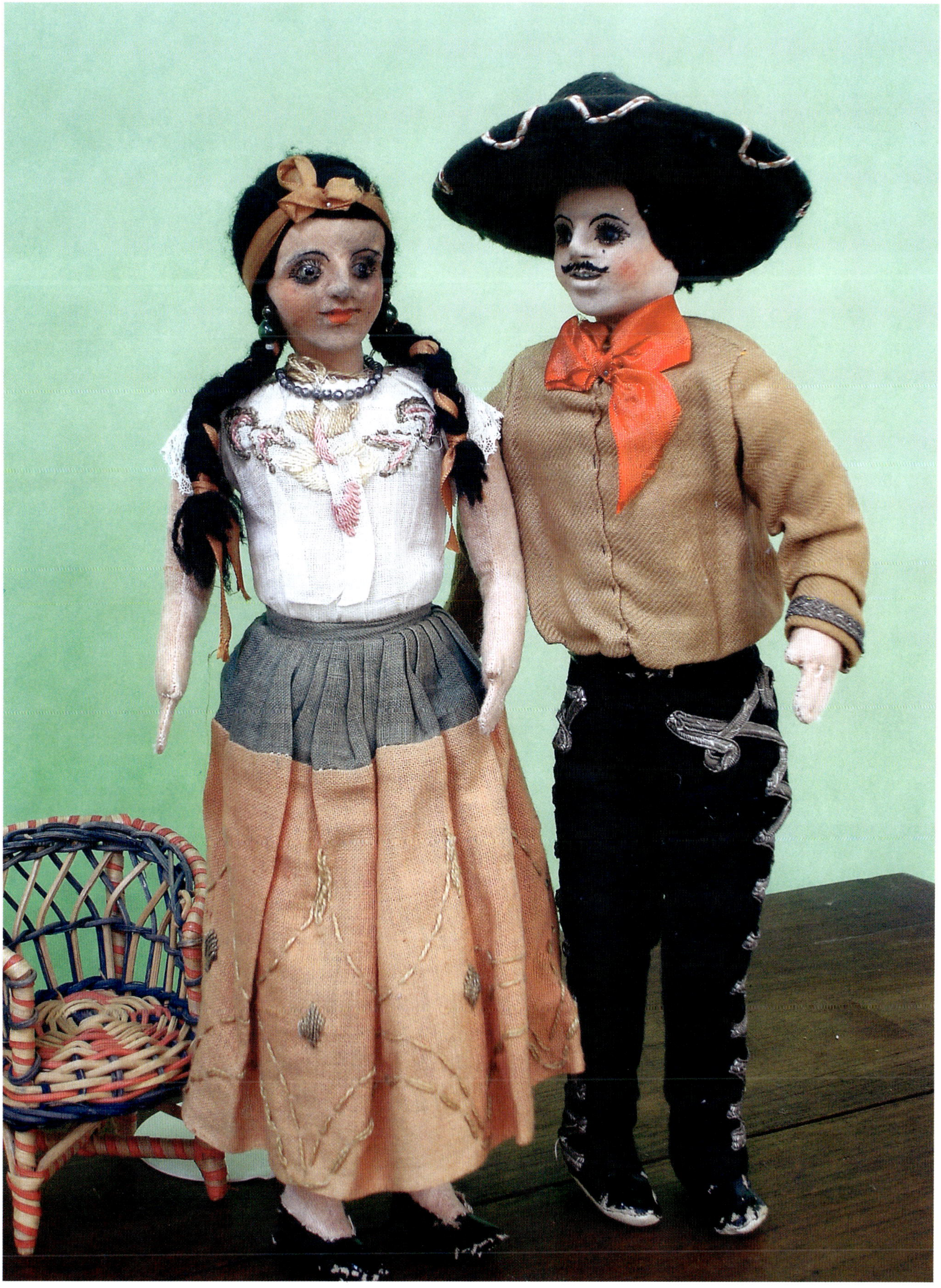

Rare and distinctive 11 in. cloth dolls, made in Mexico, early 1900s, constructed of cloth and careful detail. *Mestizo* couple, *manta* cotton, mohair wigs. All hand-made with inset eyes and teeth. $150 to 300 pr.

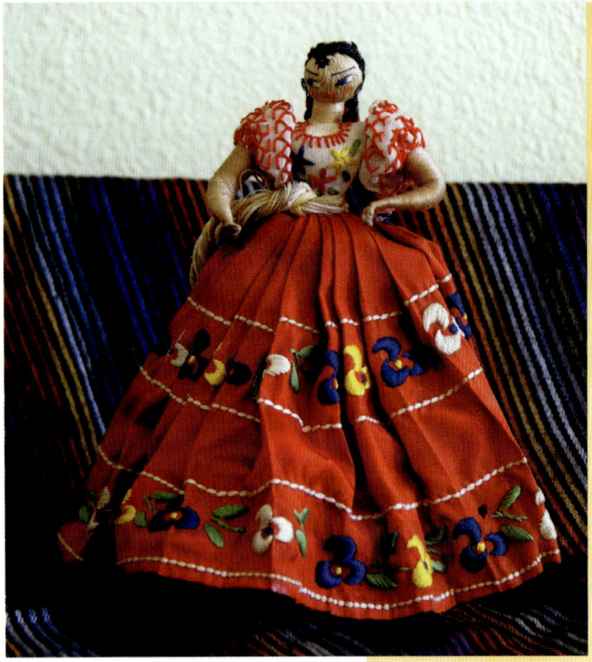

A rare of a *mestiza* made of silk threads tightly spun around wire, sculpted with needle molding. Profusely embroidered skirt and top. Maker unknown $50 to 100

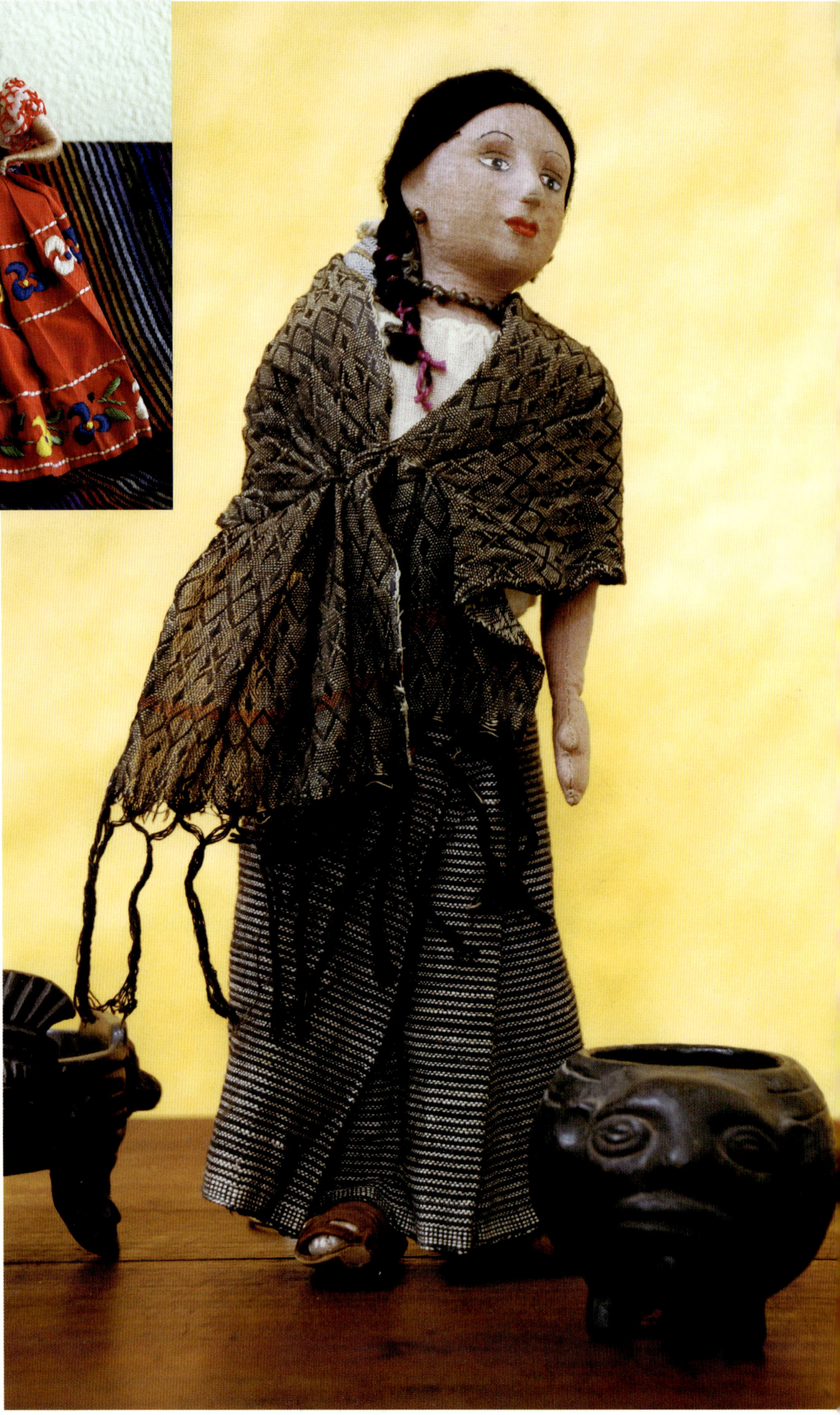

A 13 in. Indian woman, most probably Santa Maria, with a dark *enredo* skirt and woven *rebozo* in beautiful *paloma de bolita* pattern, from the district of *Michoacán*, c.1930. Beautifully sculpted of cloth, leather *huaraches*, accessories, made in Mexico. She stands with antique black Oaxacan pottery. $100 to 200

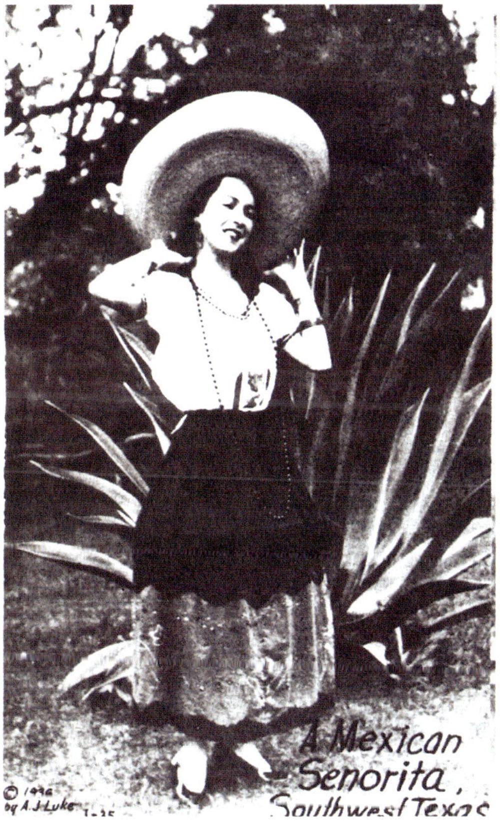

Postcard, Old Mexico photograph, "A Mexican Senorita, Southwest Texas," Made by Luke and Co., Texas, 4 x 5 in.

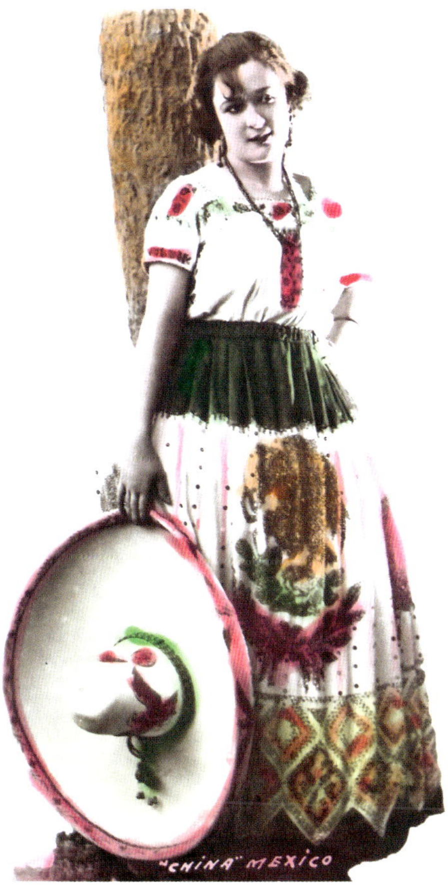

A color tinted photograph postcard, "China," Mexico, early 20th century, Mexico D.F. $10 to 15

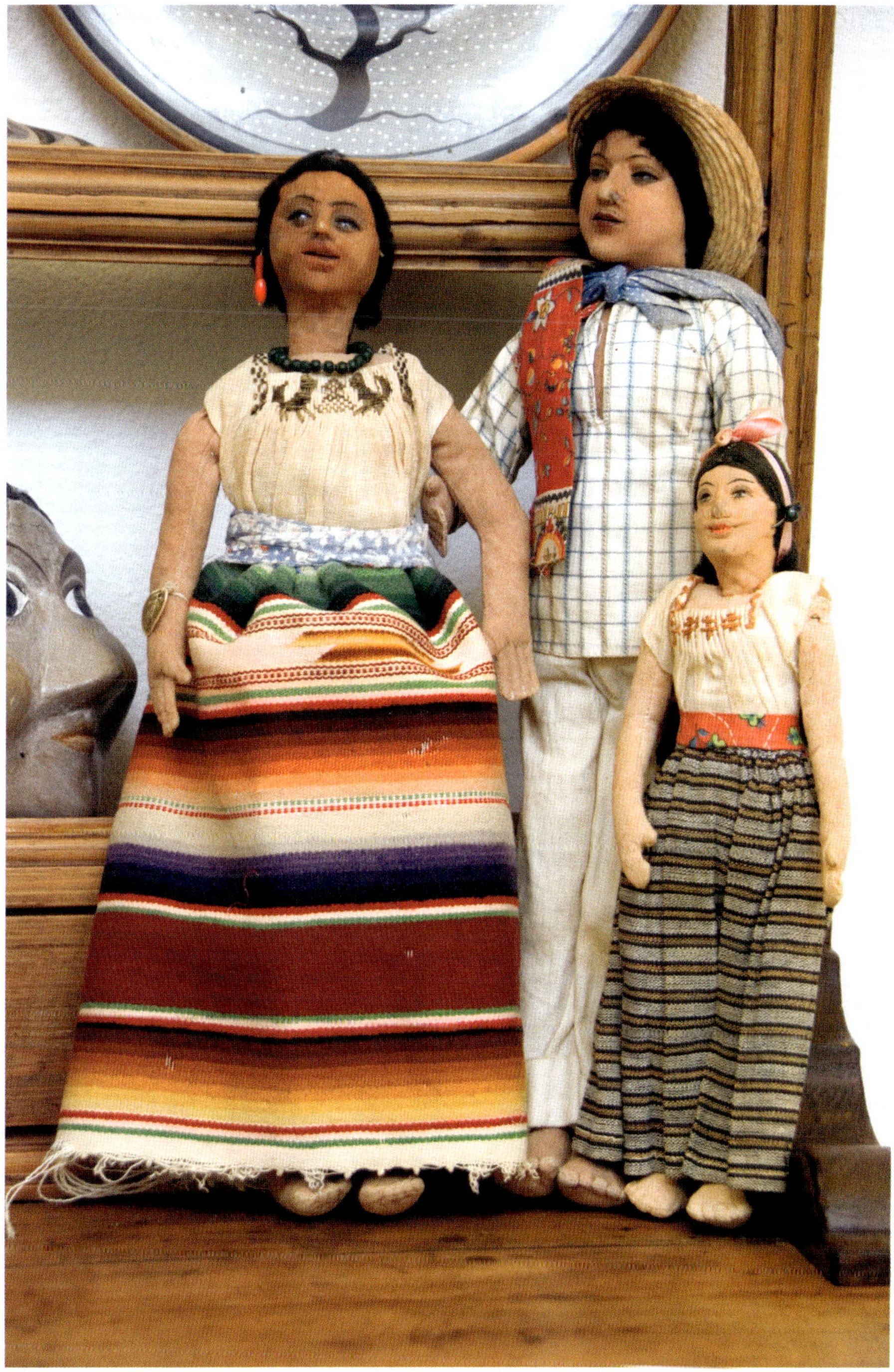

A trio of 20th century cloth dolls, 18 in. to 16 in. cloth bodies stuffed with sawdust or fine straw bits. Inset features with amazing personality. Clothing is all authentic indigenous pieces. The tallest Indian woman's skirt appears to be from an old *serape*, and animals are embroidered on the top of her *blusa*. The tall *caballero* has beautiful eyes deeply inset under the red clay-tinted molded skin, with wool hair and *petate sombrero*. The smaller *mestiza* Indian has lighter skin with special features. Made in Mexico $100 to 400 ea.

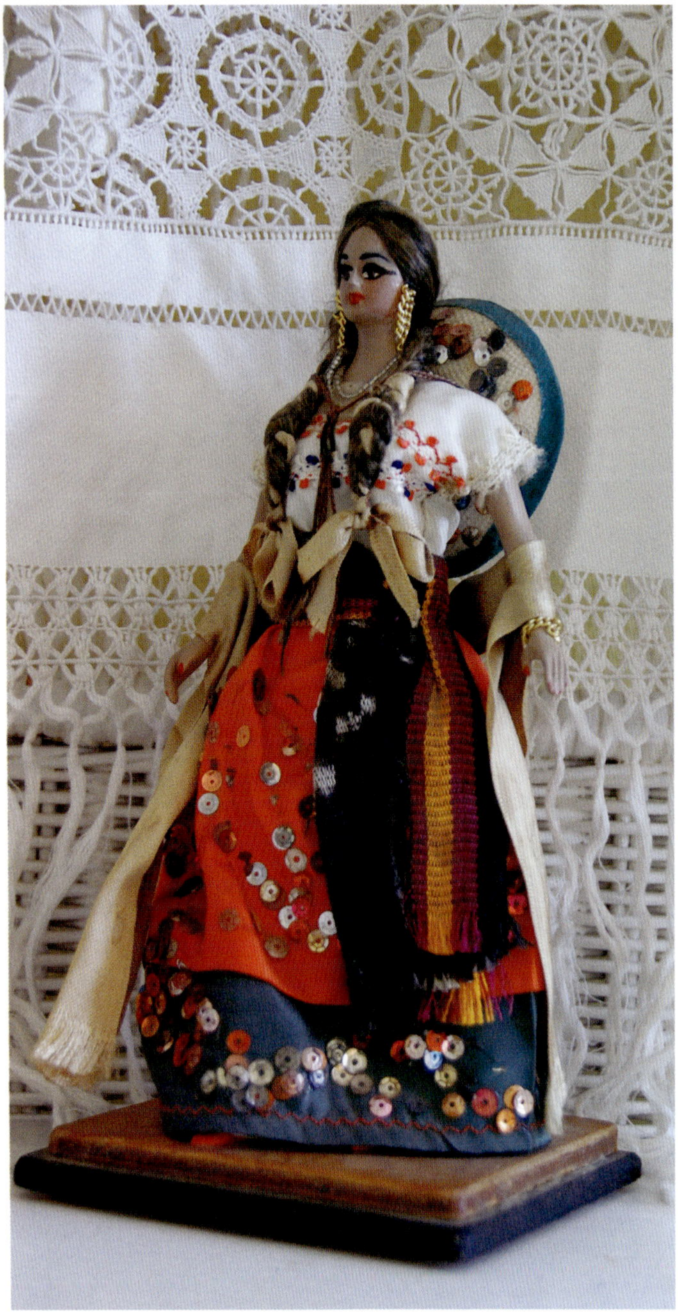

A typical tourist doll from the district of Veracruz. A commercial interpretation of a 10 in. *China Poblana* doll. A composition resin on a wood base, c. 1960 – '70s. A tourist purchase, stamped on the base, Made in Mexico $35 to 60

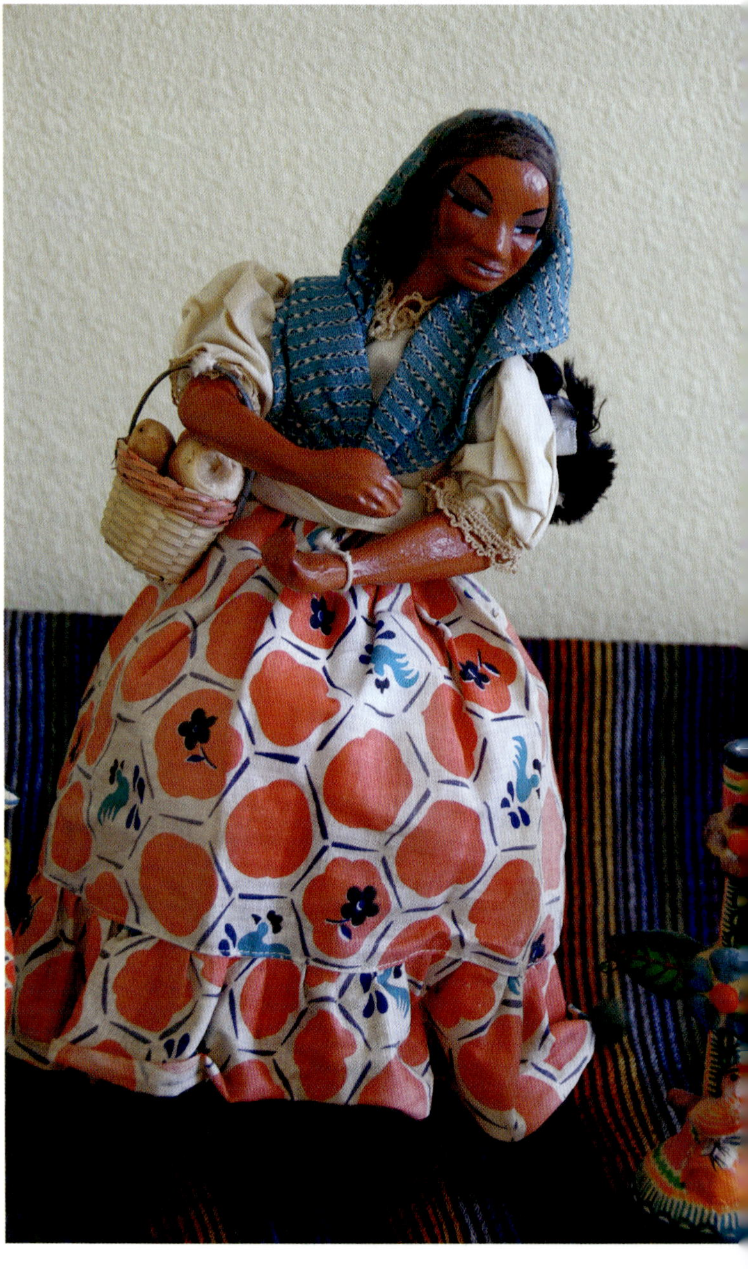

A stunning 14 in. *mestiza*, c.1940s, with a calico print skirt and peasant top. Body is made of a unique red clay composite material set on a wire body, large feet enables it to stand, wonderful hand-painted detail. Made in Mexico. $60 to 100

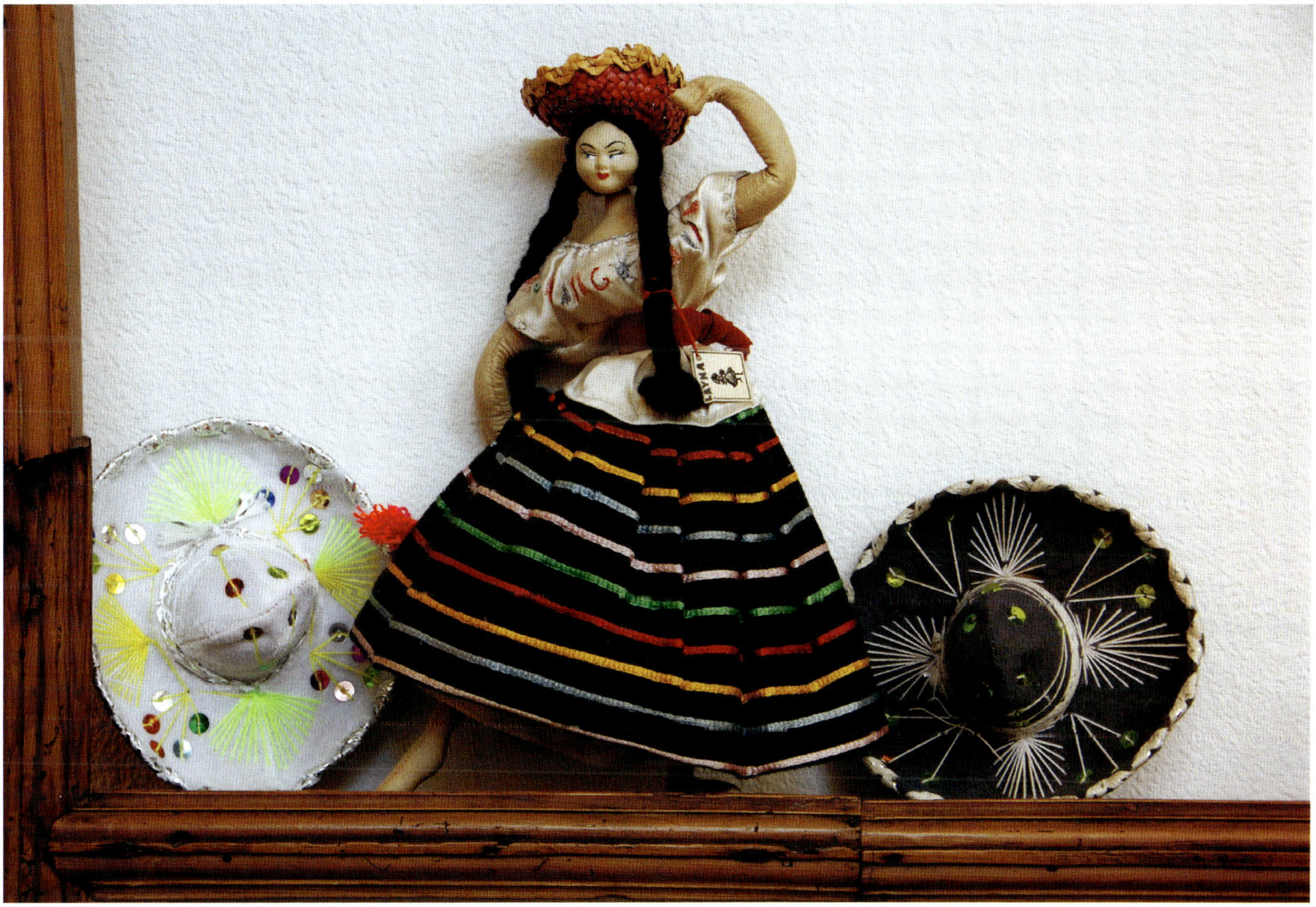

A unique 12 in. cloth and wire doll by Layna, c.1940s. She has a vivid expression and exceptional detail. A bendable form body is well constructed and her head moves. Made in Spain $75 to 125

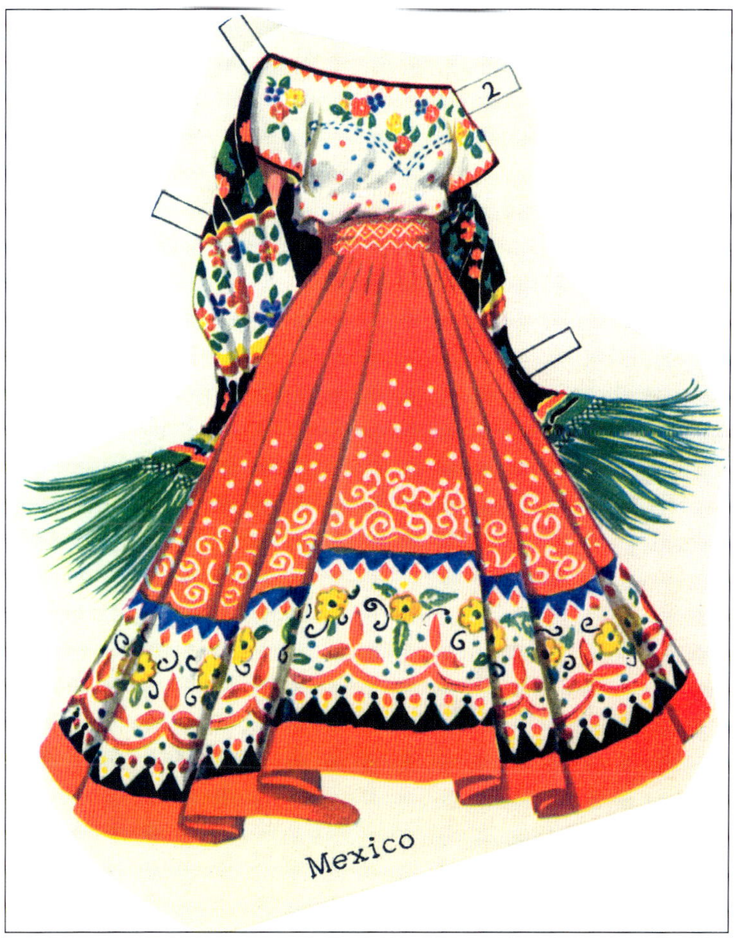

A typical dress worn by the urban city *mestiza* of the 1940s, in colorful prints with indigenous accents. From a paper doll, 1944, USA

El Rebozo, The Shawl

The Mexican women's quintessential garment is the *rebozo,* or shawl. This long rectangular cloth is normally about 30" wide and 2 yards, long but it can vary in length and width. Of course on the dolls, they are proportioned to their interpretive size, with many variations and uses. The shawl is worn by both Indian and *mestiza* woman dolls. It is a prized piece of clothing for Mexican women, always properly stored to keep its beauty.

By the late 19th century, the *rebozo* had become the symbol of Mexican womanhood, just as the native *huipil*, or tunic, was in the 20th century. Their color, design, cloth, and fringe vary, just as they do on other garments. It is a utilitarian textile as well as a beautiful item of clothing, and can even indicate a woman's availability by the way in which it is draped. Hanging and knotted tightly, it is used to carry many things, including their babies. In some regions it is twisted and knotted around the head to balance a jar.

On the Indian woman, shawls are used for a multiple of these purposes, but on the *mestiza* woman it is more likely worn over the head. around the shoulders, or folded on the shoulders and crossed in the front for adornment. It can define her by the way in which it is draped. Just as the men's *serape* can define his status, so can the *rebozo* define the women.

The most common types of *rebozo* are made from cotton, rayon, or silk. They are generally woven on horizontal looms and are finished with tied fringe. There are many variations in shawls' weaves and dyes. One style in particular is a knotted dye process known as the *paloma de bolita* pattern in which the *rebozo* shimmers or looks as though it has been sprinkled with sugar. Moorish, Chinese, and influences from India, with elaborate fringed borders and lavish embroidery, imply a mixed inheritance. The origin of the *rebozo* has an indistinct past, but most likely it was developed as a religious prerequisite, a head covering to enter the church. Mexicans are very religious and their Christian foundation suggests that the Spanish woman's *mantilla* was used in a similar manner. Their traits include lavish embroidery and festive finishes, with a *guilloche* (a braided effect) patterned fringe. These can be extraordinarily fine, with knotted tasseled designs in the fringe woven as birds and flowers, taking months to make. It is a typical folk garment to admire on the Mexican woman's costume and one that will surely sustain priority. On the dolls, shawls do not show all these outstanding qualities, but they do possess the beauty and usefulness for which they were created.

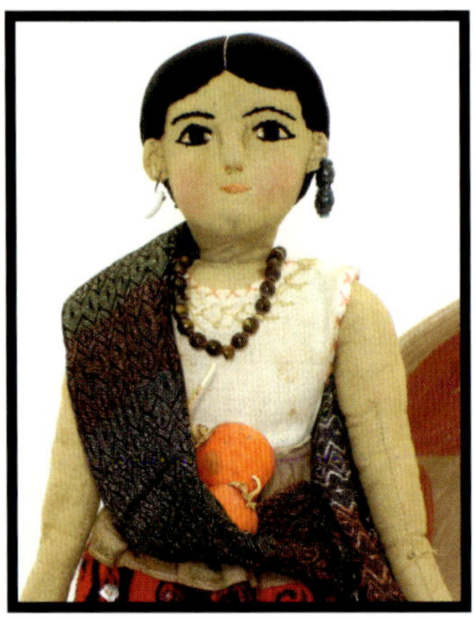

A close view of the cloth doll Zulma, her beautiful accents on her clothing and accessories. Needle molded embroidered facial features. Artist unknown.

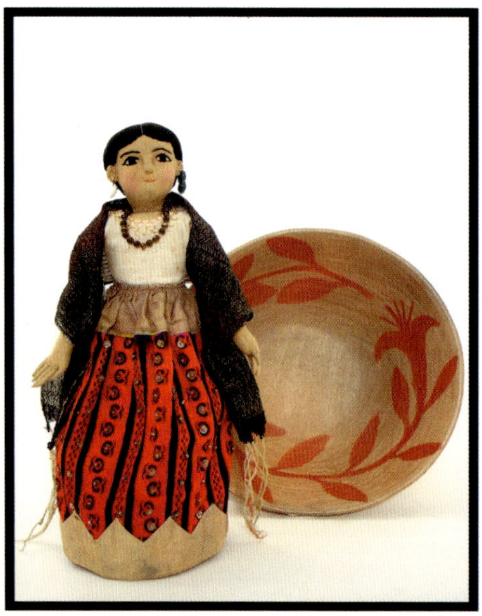

"Zulma" is a 15 in. cloth doll, c.1920s, a wonderful example of an original, early 20th c., Mexican doll, with strong *mestiza* and Indian traits. Her *rebozo* is beautiful, and serves many uses to the *mestiza* and Indian women. Worn crossed and wrapped around the bodice for beauty, over her head to enter the church, around her shoulders as a shawl for warmth, around the waist as a sash, and wrapped and knotted over their shoulders to carry a child or items. The multi-purposes of the *rebozo* is extraordinary, and with patterns such as the *paloma de bolita*, it is a beautiful as well as an essential piece of their clothing. $125 to 350

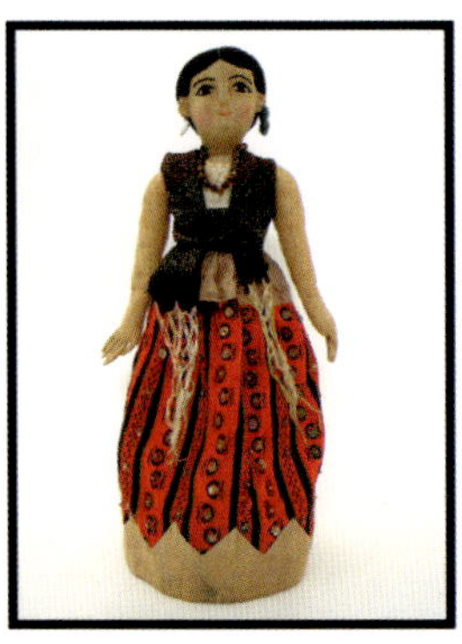
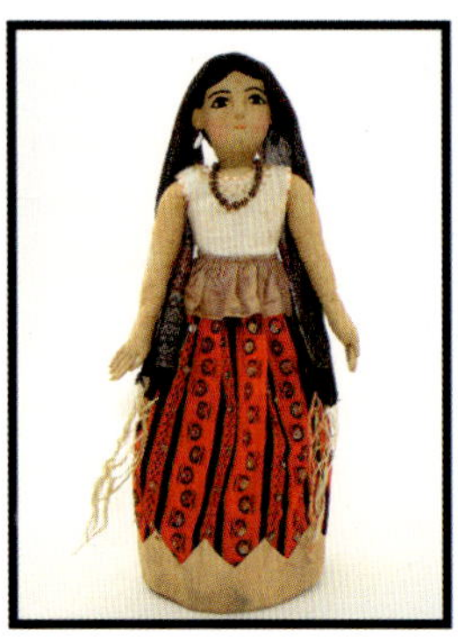
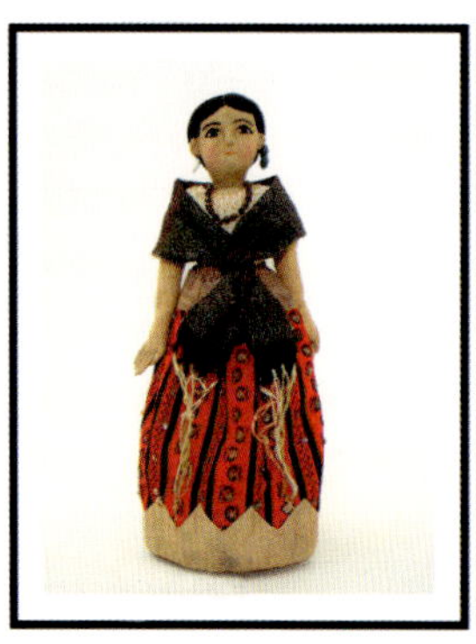
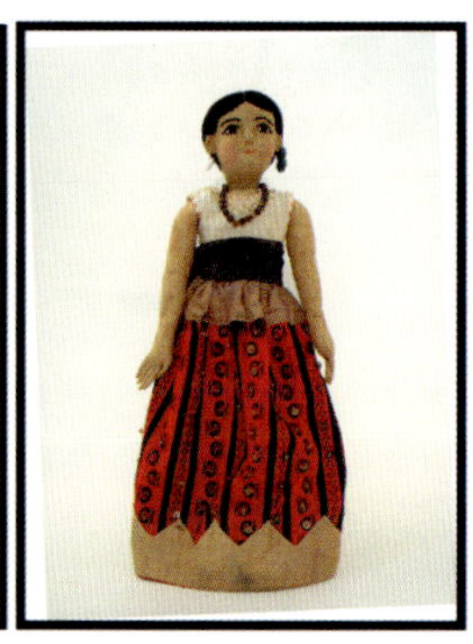
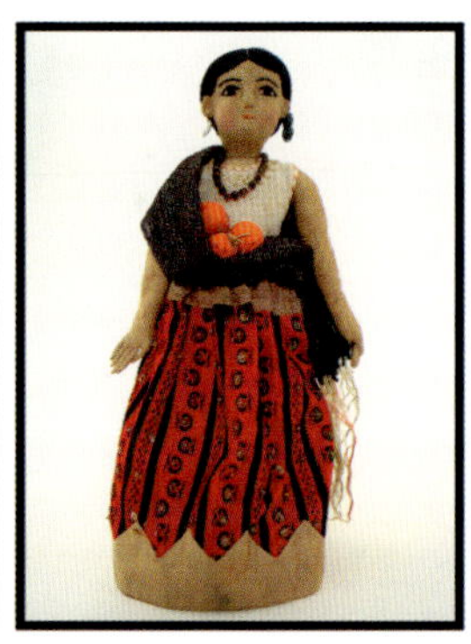

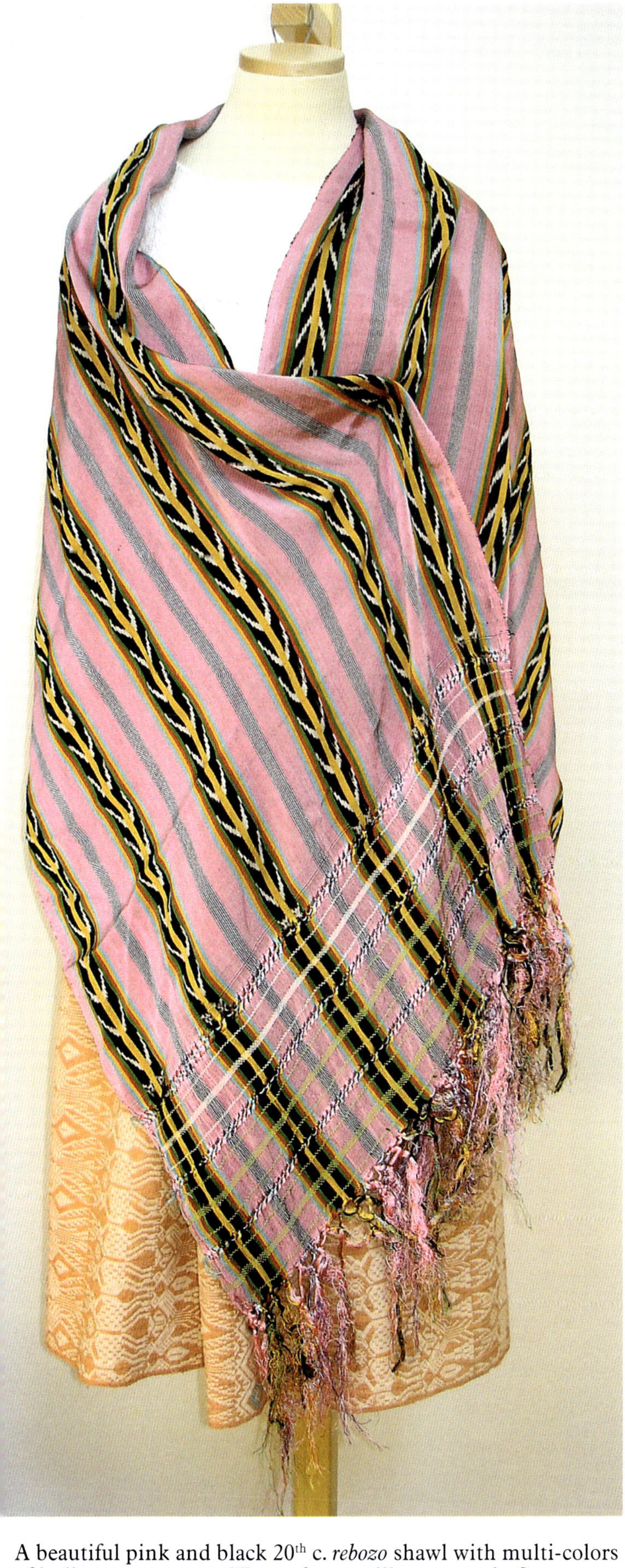

A beautiful pink and black 20th c. *rebozo* shawl with multi-colors of indigenous pattern. Woven from a silk or rayon in Santa Maria del Rio, San Luis Postosi. This has an *ikat*-pattern and demonstrates beautiful Mexican patterning and color. *Author's collection* $100 to 200

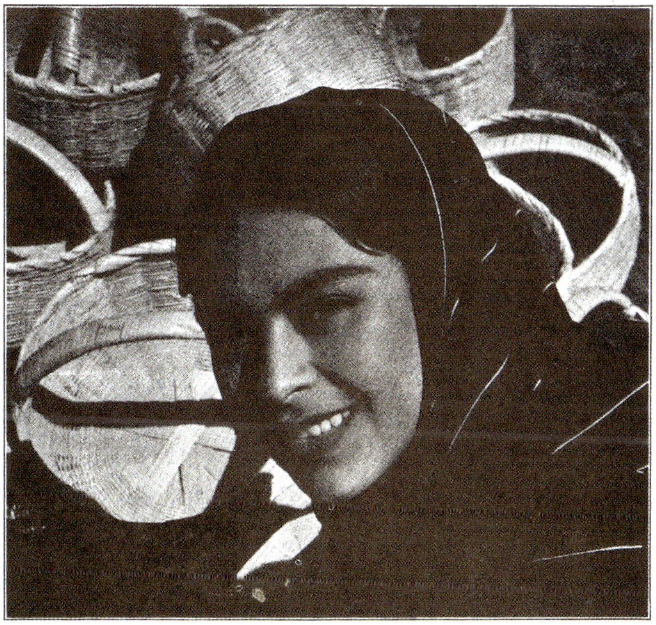

A smiling *mestiza* with a *rebozo*, 1936.

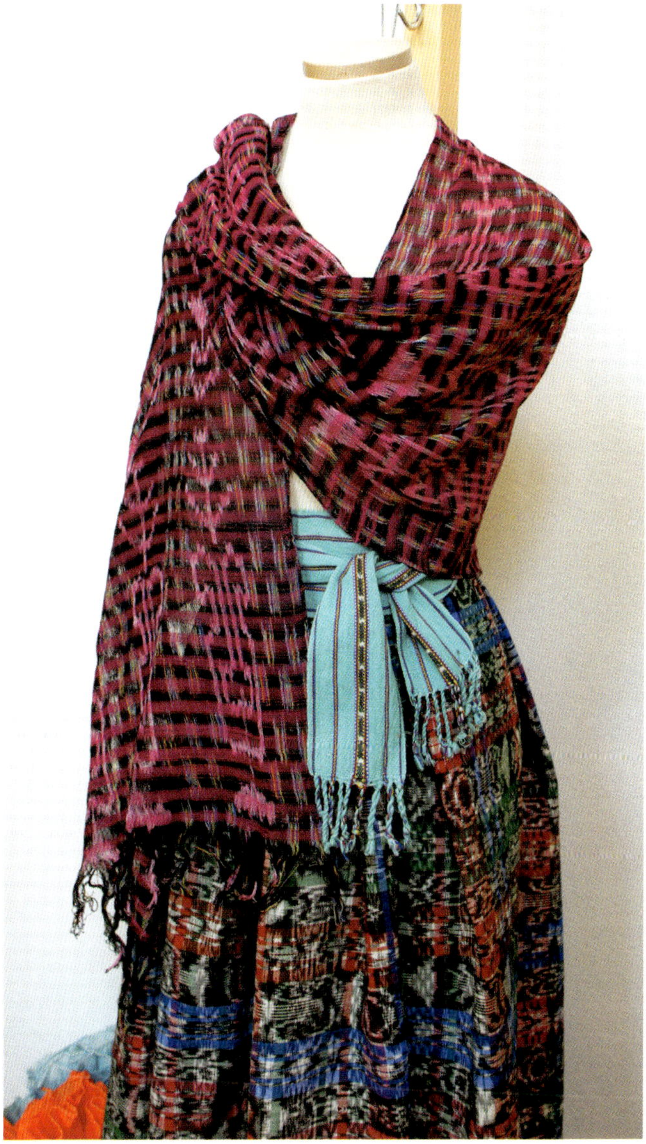

A beautiful cotton, open-weave *rebozo* with magenta and black design, and knotted fringe, c.1950s. Made in Mexico. $40 to 60

La Falda, The Skirt

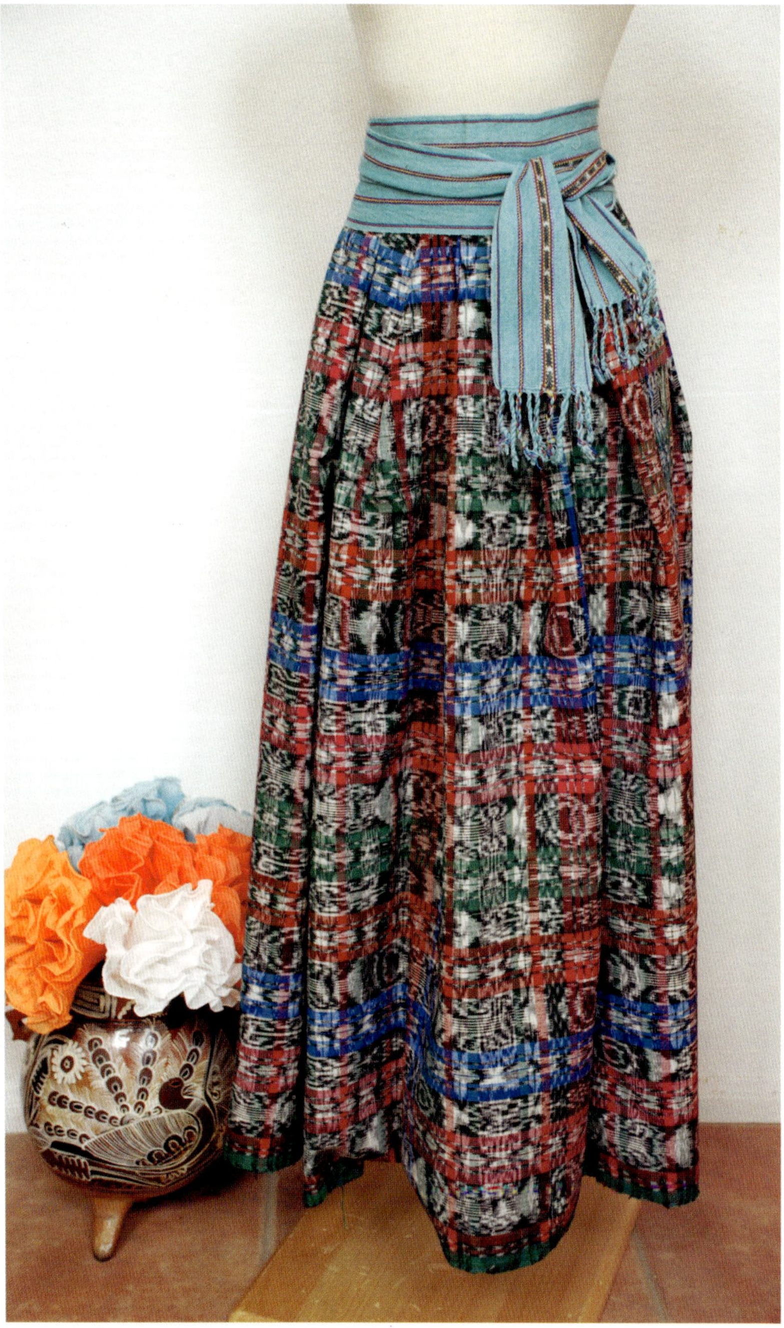

An aqua *ikat*-dyed *faja* (sash) wrapped, tightly woven, and tied-off at the ends with knotted tasseled. An *enredo* skirt in a multi-colored woven pattern with a crotch-hatch design 20th c. Made in Mexico

One of the most fascinating items of clothing worn in a variety of ways is the Mexican skirt. There are various styles that include *la falda, la enagua, el zagalejo,* and el *enredo.* The dolls show some of the true ways in which the many different skirts were originally worn. Social class, tribal customs, and the climate were influences that would dictate the choice and style of their skirts. Also influential were urban trends that were constantly threatening the traditions, from decade to decade. Generational cultural skills were passed down diligently by the elders, but by the 19th century weaving their own clothing began to lose importance. The law of supply and demand was so overwhelming that many traditional woven garments once made by the Indians were substituted with machine-made cloth, *manta.*

Mestiza woman in communities closer to towns and urban life wore a fuller skirt fashioned with more of a European influence; it had a tighter waist and a little higher hemline. On the dolls, the *mestiza* trend mimicked the same sort of clothing the Spanish women wore. It may exhibit less hand woven textiles but more detailed embroidery on *manta* (machine-made cloth). Many skirts were made from the textile *castor*, a solid-color, muslin cotton that was sold in bolts. The machine-made cloth, *manta*, bought in the marketplace, came in solid colors and calico prints that were bright and lively. Their skirts were long and full, usually gathered at the waist with a tie-cord that adjusts the fit of the waist at the back; they also were secured with a belt or sash. Lace trimmings, ribbons, ric-rac, and layers are also a favorite addition to *mestiza*-inspired skirts. Depending on their *pueblo* (town), their skirts can also define their origin and class. Usually the higher social class had the fancier skirt .The skirts of *señoritas* and the urban *mestiza* have colonial Spanish characteristics.

For example, the skirt of a typical Guanajuato person, *Galereña*, is made from cotton and can have up to four layers, very similar to European peasant skirts. Under the skirt is an A-line design, over which another skirt, known as the *zagalejo* (a red flannel with green triangular design on the waist and hem), is worn. The third layer is a white cotton poplin petticoat accented with ribbons over the *zagalejo.* Finally, the fourth skirt is a floral calico print made of cotton organdy (sheer stiff muslin) and finished with a short train at the back, similar to those on Flamenco style dresses. This was a traditional dress worn by the *Galareña*.

The principal skirts worn by the Indian's dolls are the wrap-around style known as *los enredos* and as the *pazujongo*, or "tube" skirts, a more indigenous style. They would also wear *enaguas*, a fuller skirt that was worn by *mestiza*, such as the China Poblana skirts.

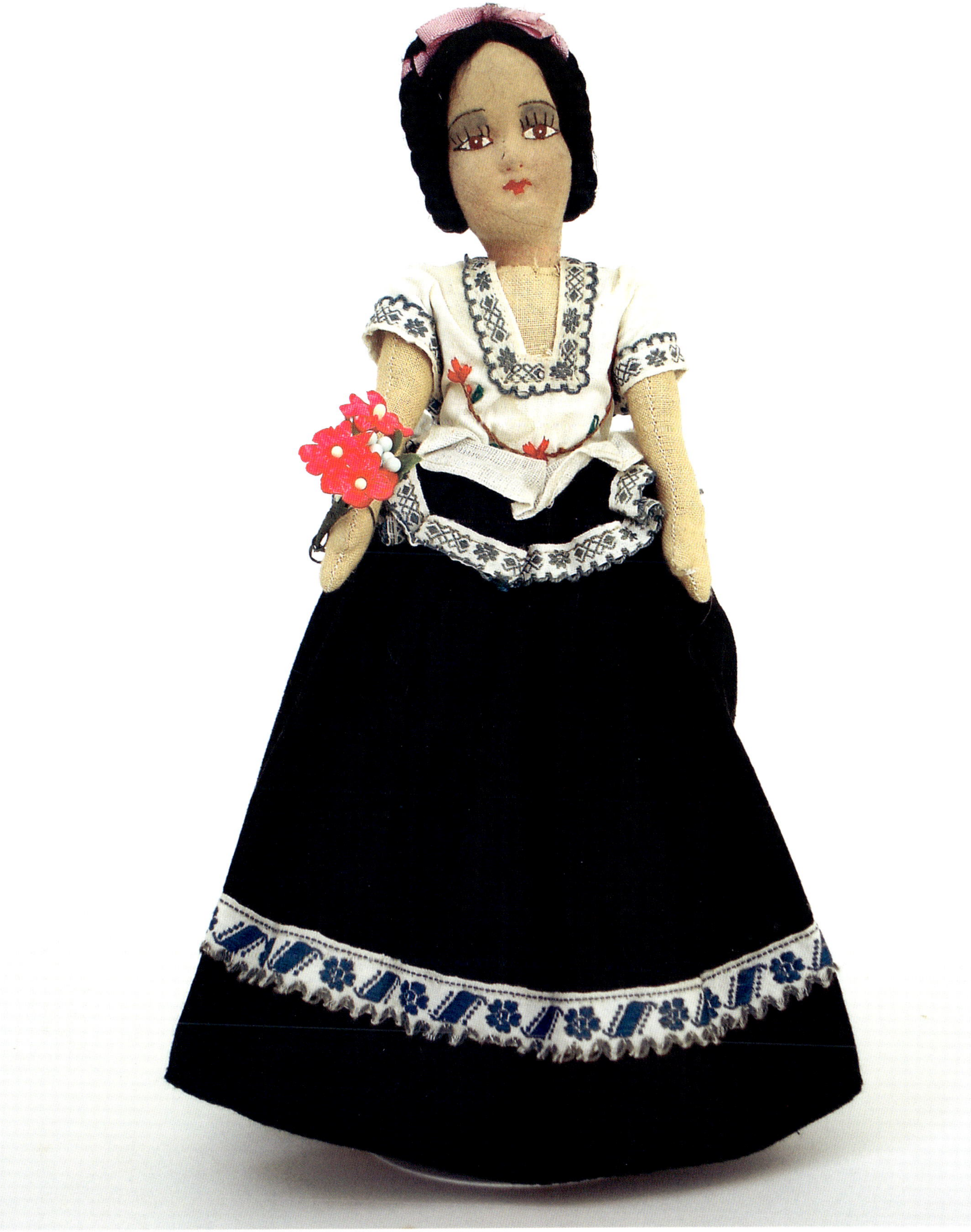

This is a proud *mestiza*, labeled from Tlaquepaque, Mexico. A 12 in. cloth doll, with pressed *papier maché* face and molded features, hand-painted detail. Dressed in a traditional long, black *enagua* full skirt, trimmed at the bottom. A white *huipil*, a chignon-braided wig. $75 to 125

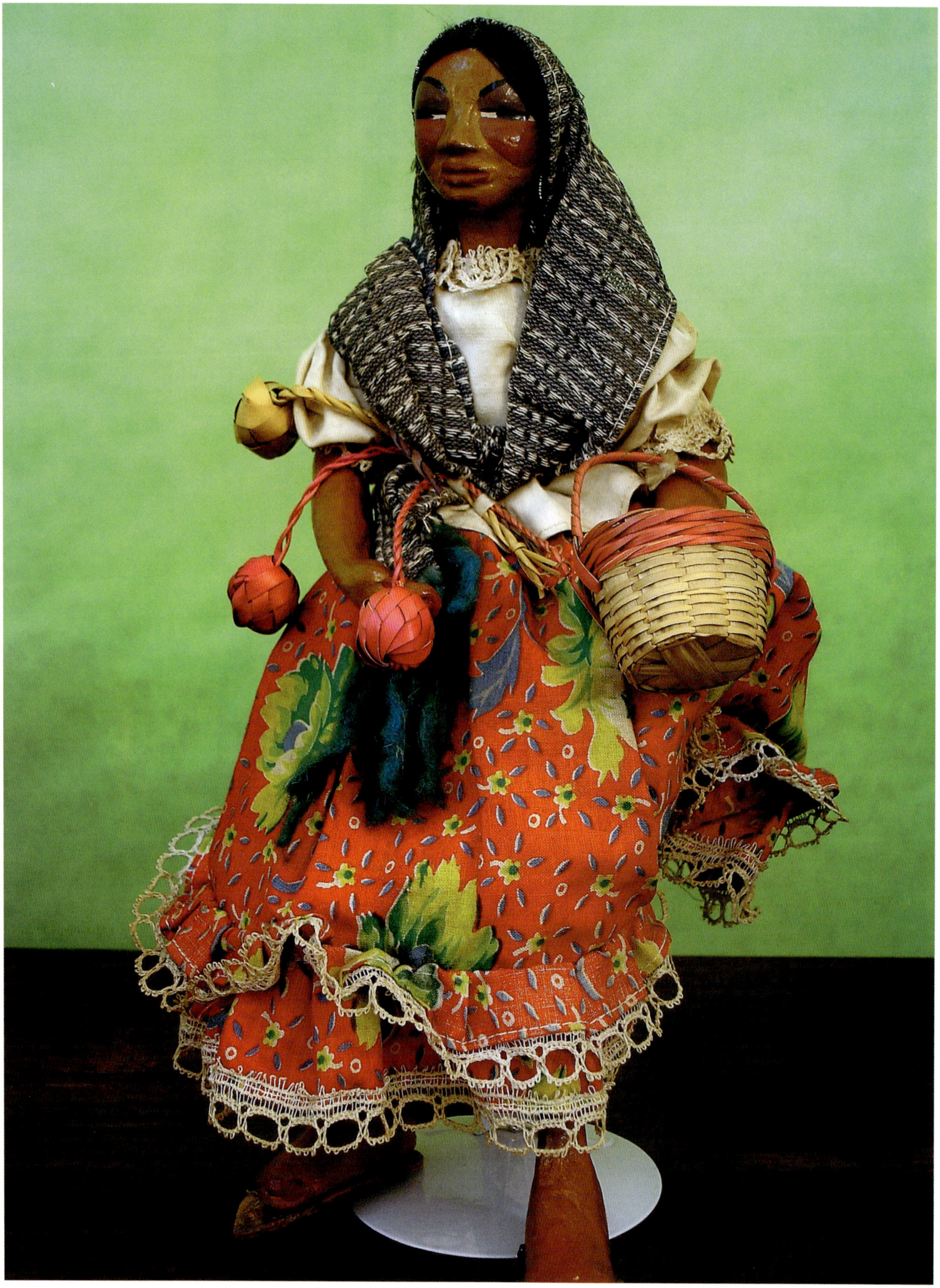

A large 14 in. clay-body *mestiza* with her basket and wares, bendable wire through the body, made in Mexico, c.1940s. Molded features and painted detail. A full skirt made of printed *manta* with colorful rickrack, c.1950s. Typical clothing of an urban *mestiza galareña*. $75 to 125

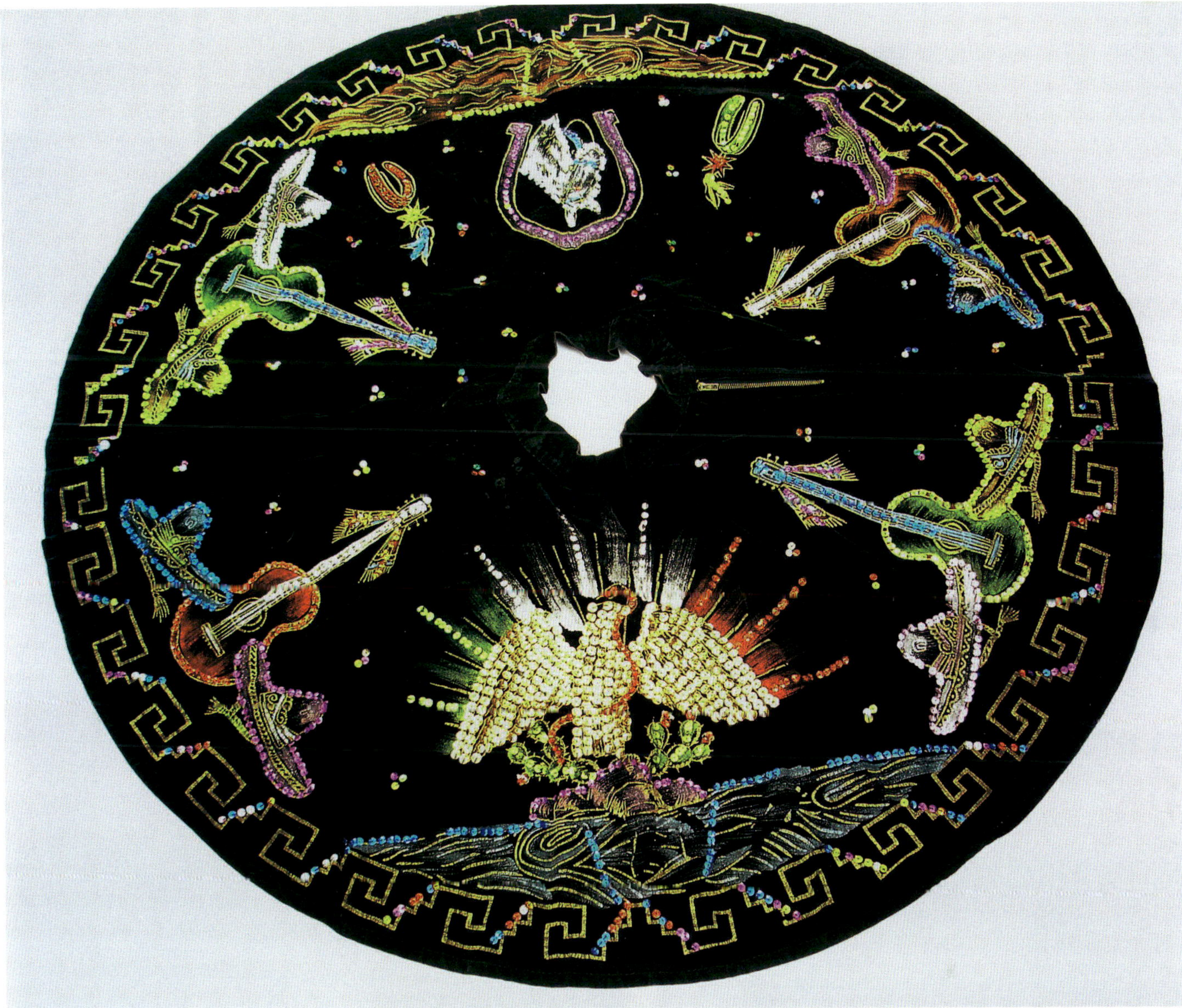

A small, black velveteen, festive round skirt, c.1955. Hand-painted with sequins and spangled designs. Wonderful local motifs.

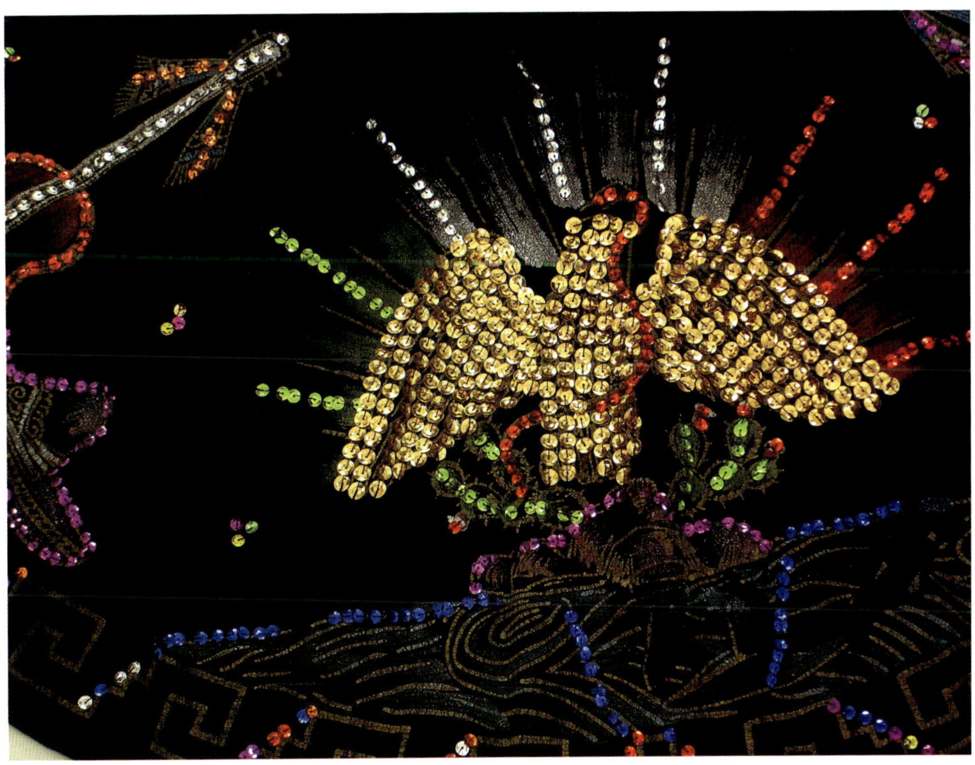

A detail on the black velveteen skirt always included their prized Mexican emblem, the eagle.

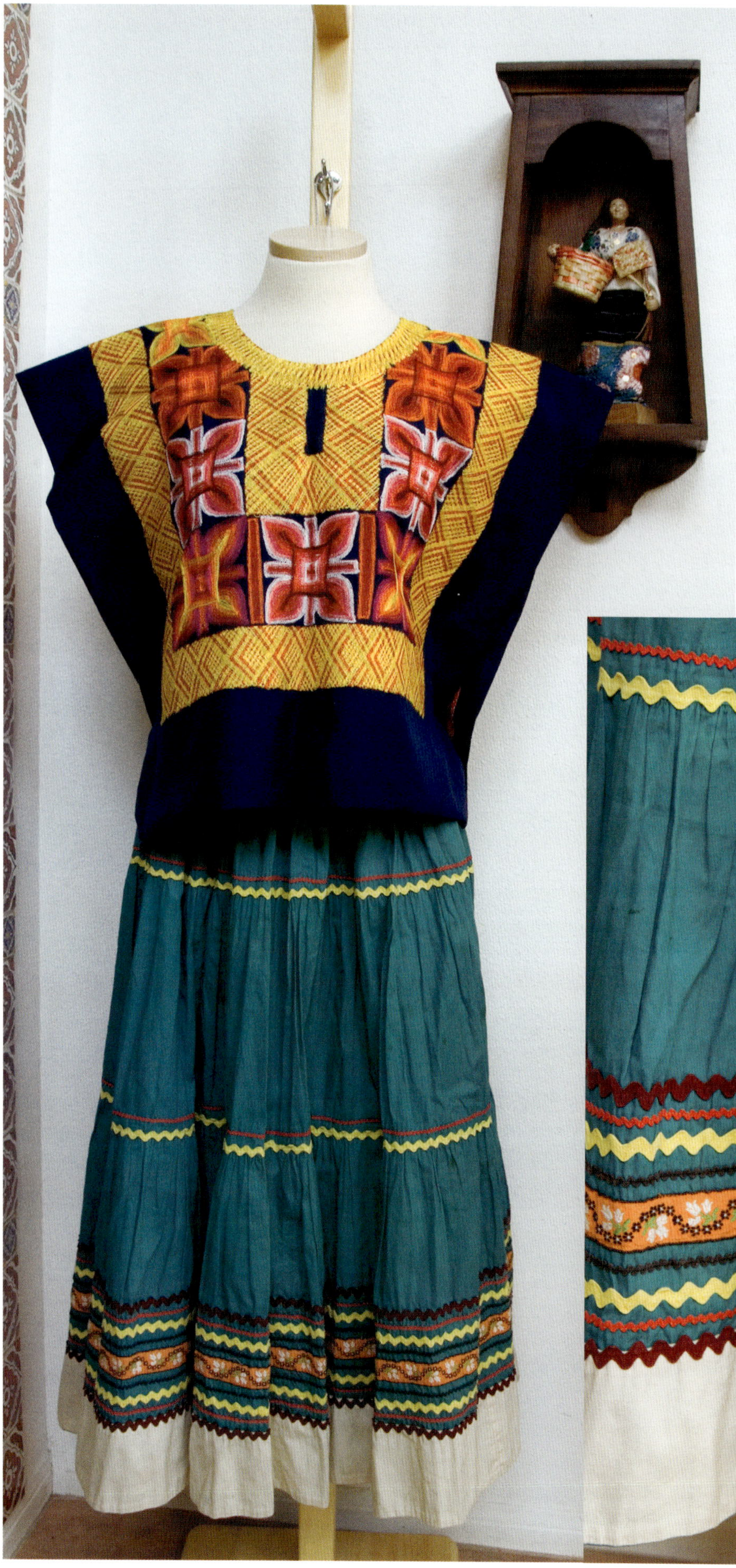

A *huipil* from the district of Oaxaca, matched with a traditional *enagua corte* (short full skirt) made of *manta* cotton with colorful rickrack trim, c.1940s. Made in Mexico

Below:
The lively trim of the *corte* skirt exhibits beautiful detail that was popular on mid-20th c. skirts.

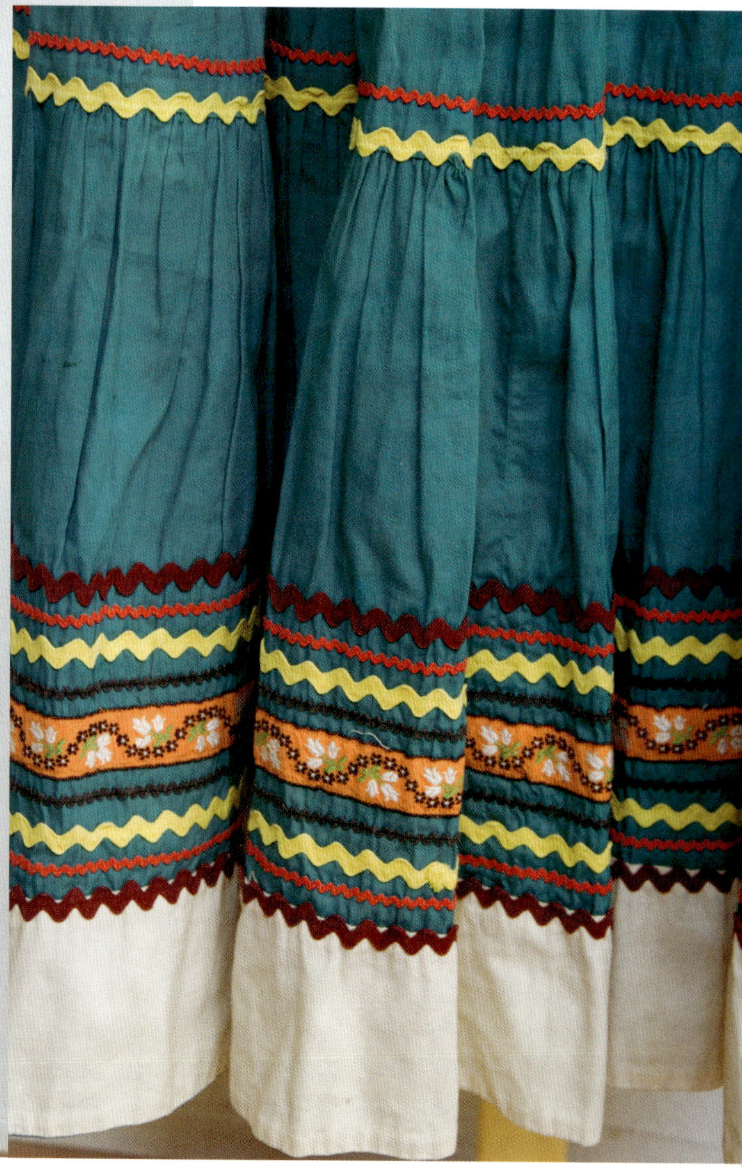

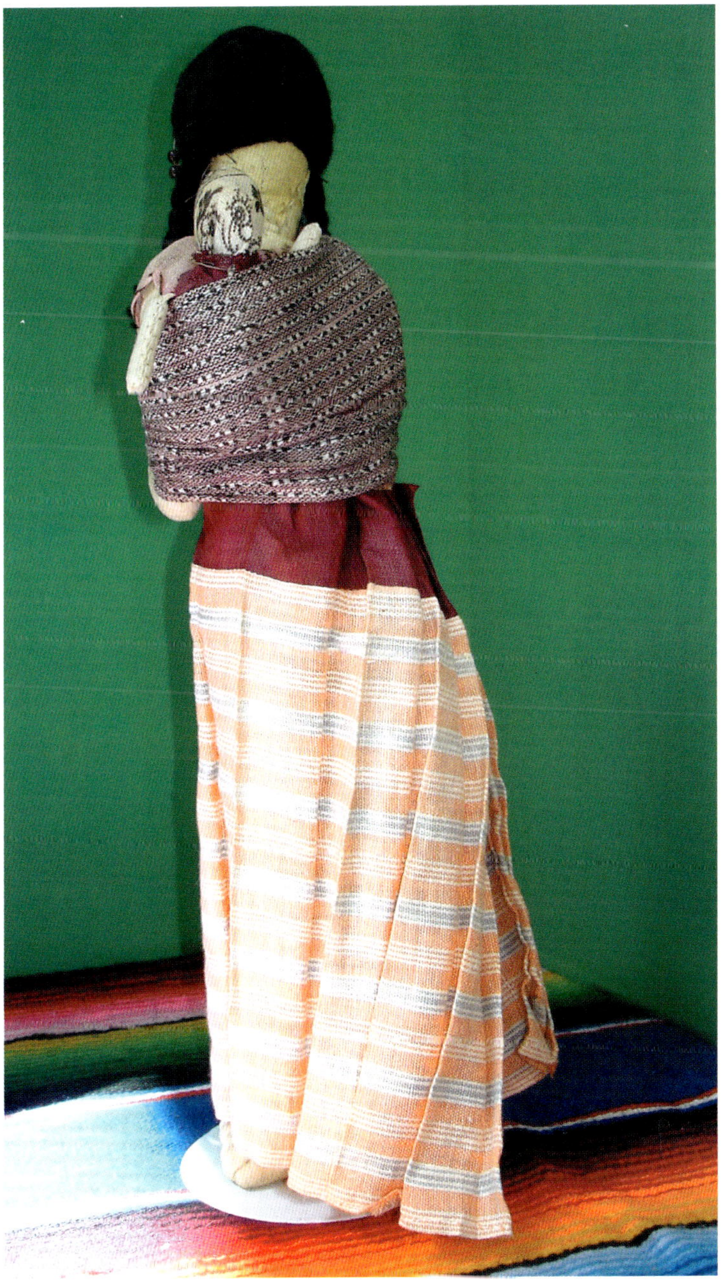

The back of the Diego woman's woven *enredo* skirt. Notice how the *rebozo* holds the baby securely, and the voluminous folds of the skirt.

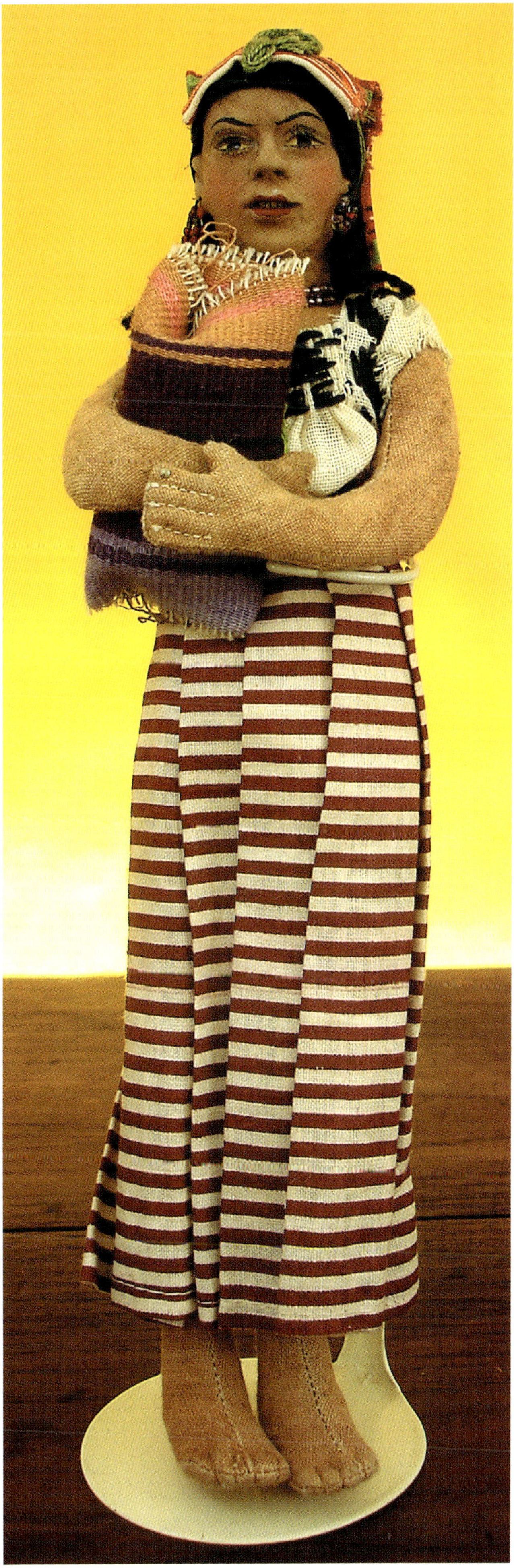

A 14 in. indigenous Indian cloth doll, made in Mexico, c.1930s. Molded facial features, painted detail, embroidered blouse, and *castor* striped *enredo* skirt. $75 to 150

The skirts worn by indigenous Indian dolls appear traditional as well as practical. The *enredos* are made from long strips of hand-woven cloth or bolts of *manta* (muslin) and wool, fashioned in a variety of ways. The Indian women dolls confirm the grounded customs with more identifiable qualities on their clothing than the men. There was greater emphasis specific to their regions, as the men usually wore the plain white *manta* shirt and pants. The skirts' hand-woven wide strips were wrapped around the body lengthwise, layered with deep pleating that would give it a full look. The pleats can be worn in the front, all around, or at the back. These gathered pleats will be held together with a sash or belt with color variation. Decorating the sashes is important, bright colors and motifs define its surface. Although plain white *manta* skirts were used a lot, you will also admire colorful striped skirts. The layered items of their clothing over the skirts add interest as well as function. The wide sash is a beautiful finish to the waistline and their colorful width holds the voluminous folds of the cloth. Their *fajas* (sashes) are also prized for their decorative motifs, as well as for their purpose.

An interesting as well as informative 1912 publication, *New Trails in Mexico,* by Carl Lumholtz, identifies the use of sewing machines in making some of their garments, especially by those who lived near or in the cities. This surely suggests documentation that sewing machines were probably used to make some of the commercial cloth dolls as well as their clothing. Documentation through the dolls entails an appreciation of the styles of their skirts, the cloth of the skirts, and how they were assembled. Though some do appear to be pieces of loom-woven cloth, there are some that were made of commercial fabric, either hand sewn or machine sewn. The specialty of the dolls is their hand finishing and detail, with borders and trims of embroidery.

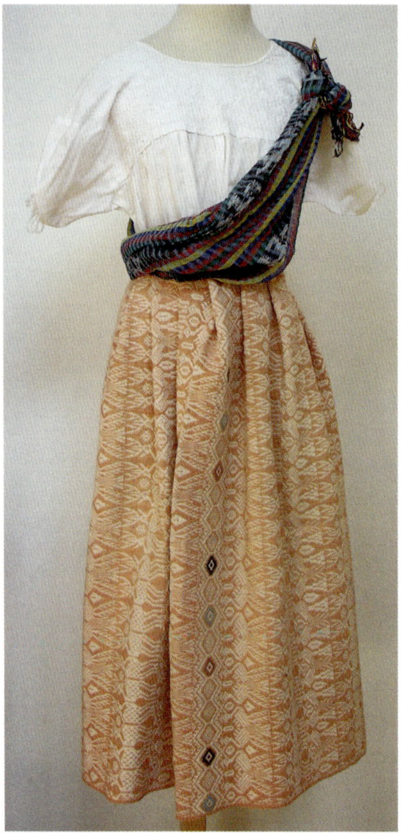

La ropa tipica worn by a local *mestiza*. White on white cotton embroidered *blusa* in satin stitches, with a heavy woven *enredo* skirt and a slung *rebozo* ready to carry what she needs. Made in Mexico, c. 1950s.

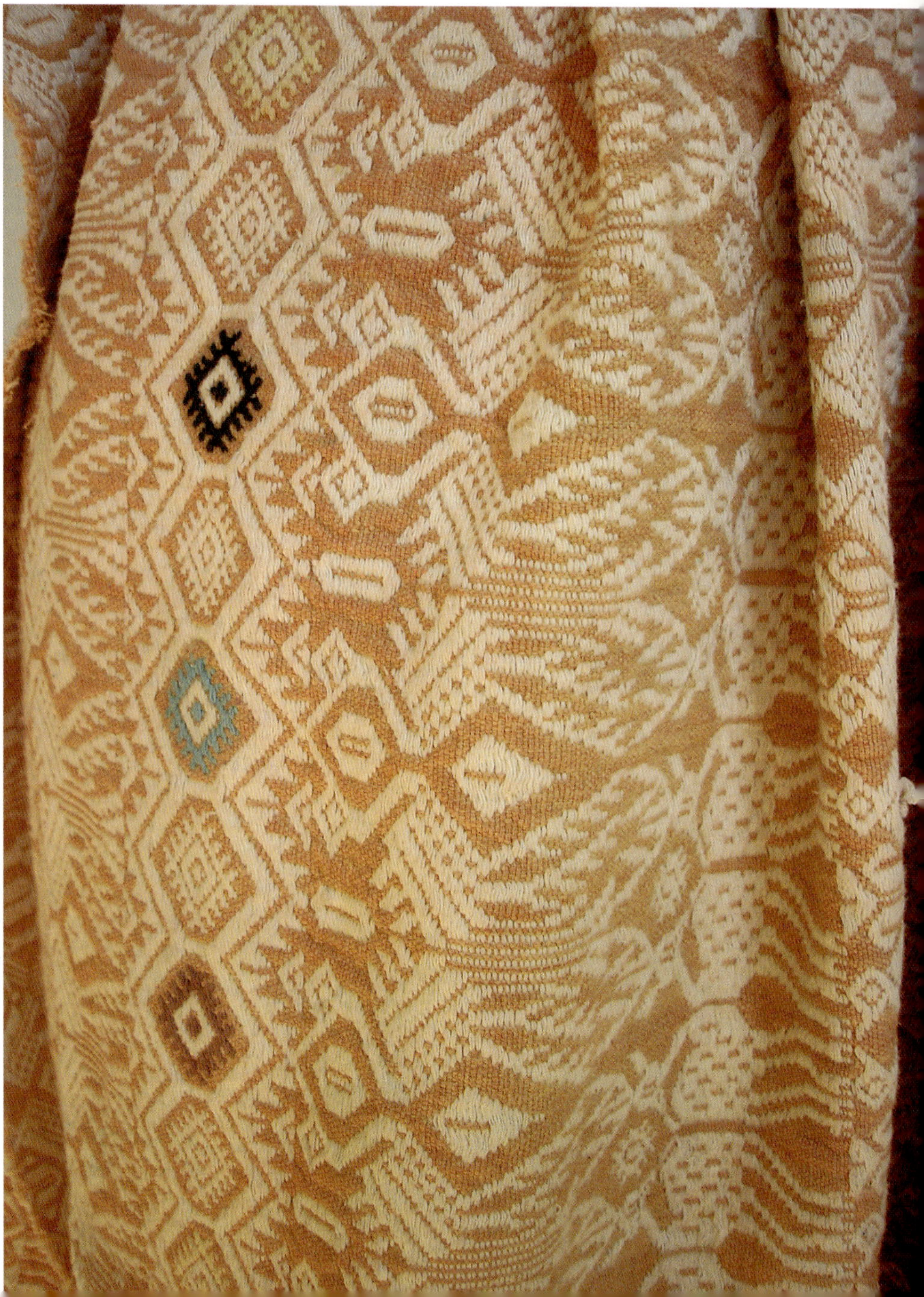

A close view of the skirt's heavily woven texture, with colored diamonds, indigenous detailed motifs, and brocade-like embroidery. Puebla, c.1950s.

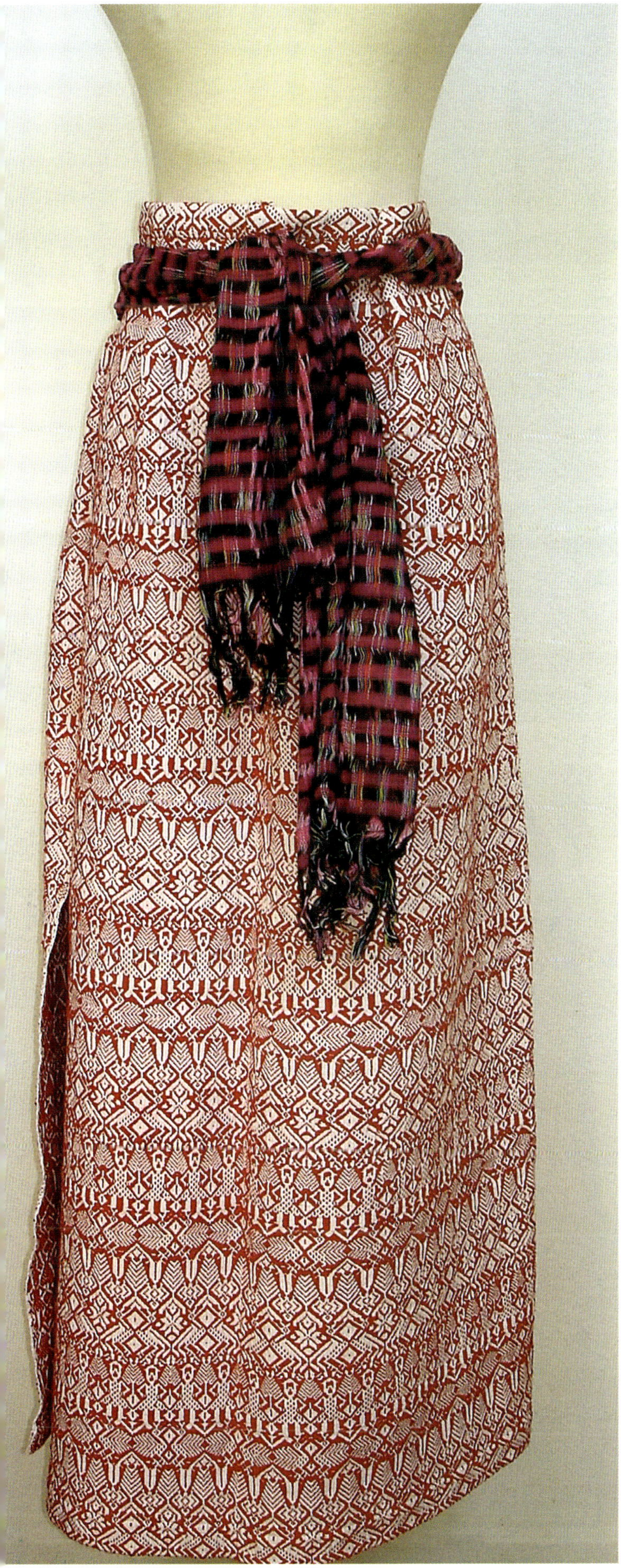

A beautiful *enredo* wrap skirt, c.1950s, homespun cotton of red and white reverse weave with profuse design throughout. Puebla, Mexico.

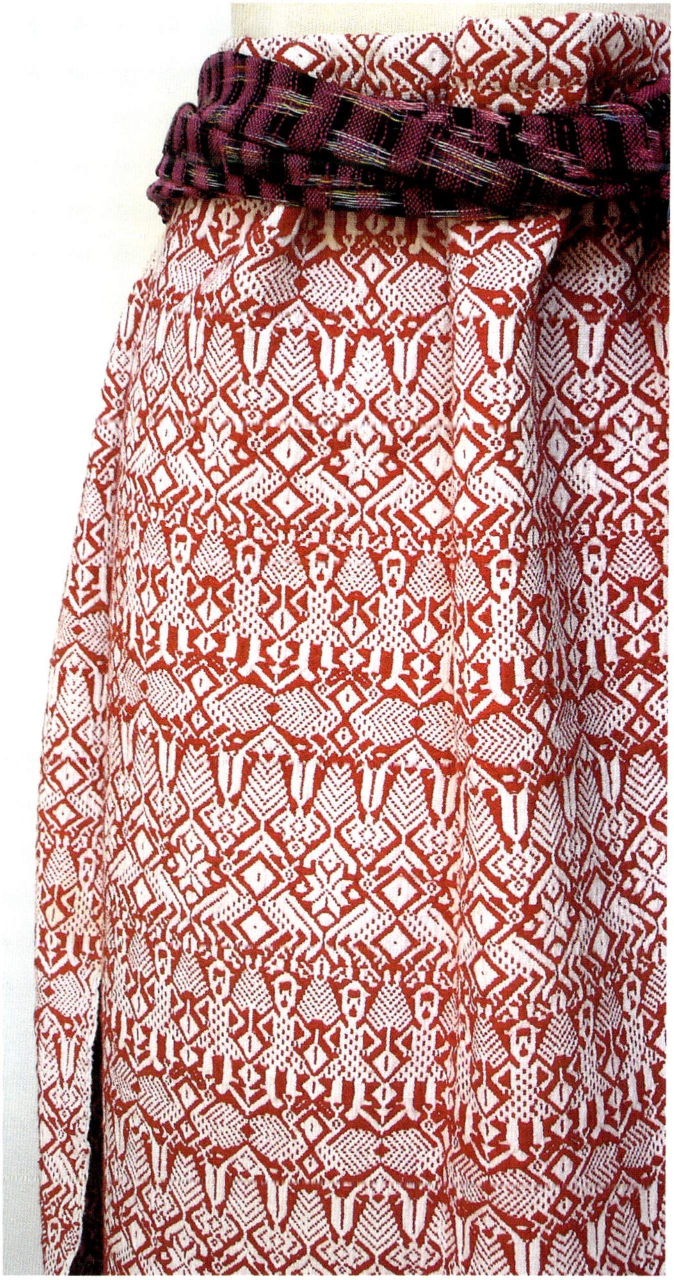

A close view of the *enredo* wrap skirt, c.1950s. Double woven, features a woman with trees, another row is birds and diamonds repeated. Made in Mexico

A detail of the skirt of the *China Poblana* costume, 20th c. The National emblem of Mexico is embroidered on the front in spectacular sequined spangles. $125 to 250

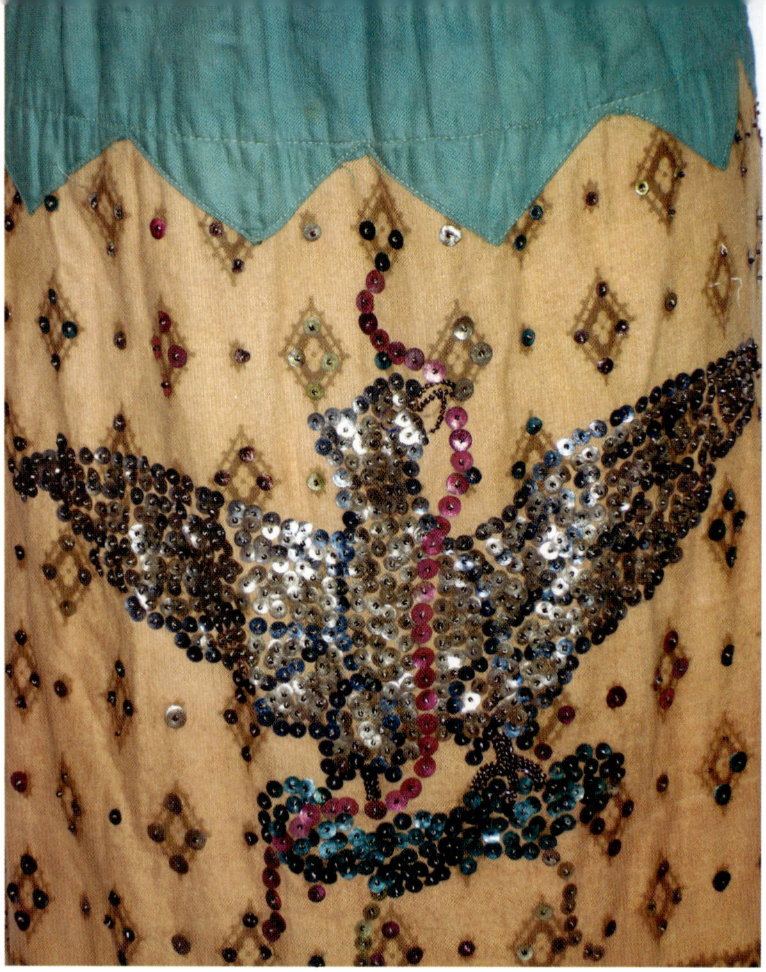

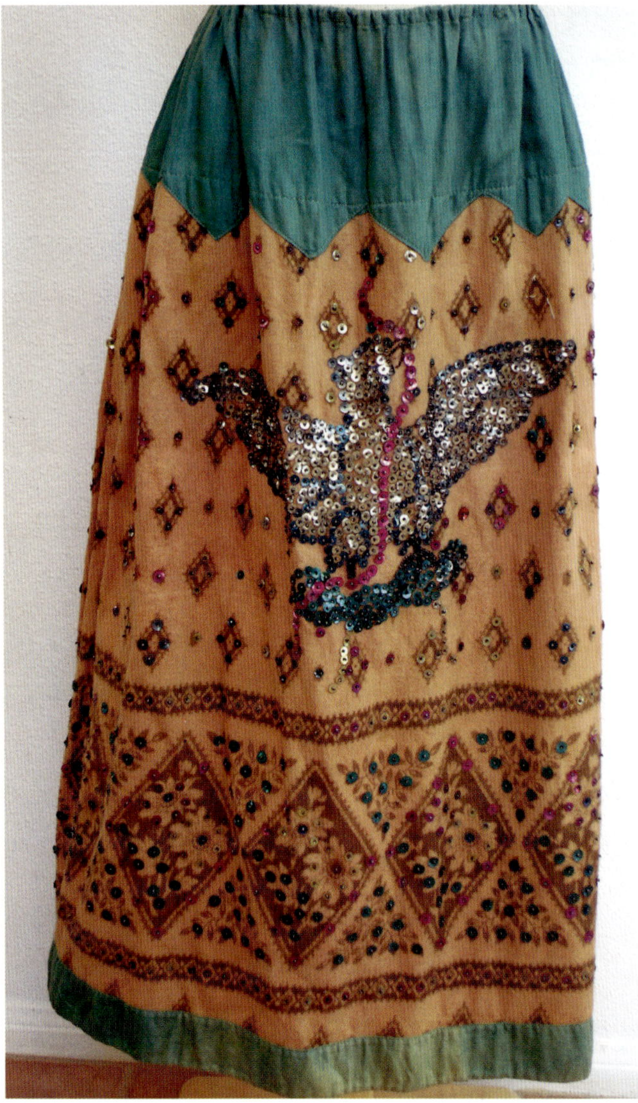

An Old Mexico festive skirt of the *China Poblana* costume, 20th c. Green and faded red flannel *castor*, with embroidery and sepia-ink tinted, stenciled motif, sequins, and beading, with a draw-string waist line. Worn in festivals and dances. $125 to 250.

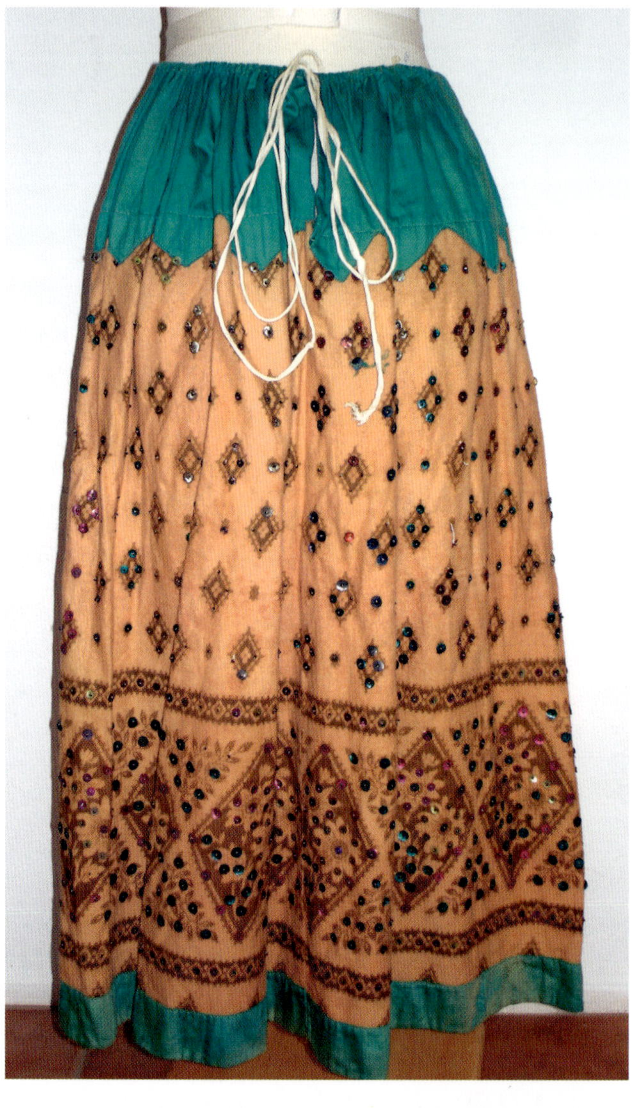

The back view of the *China Poblana* skirt. 20th c.

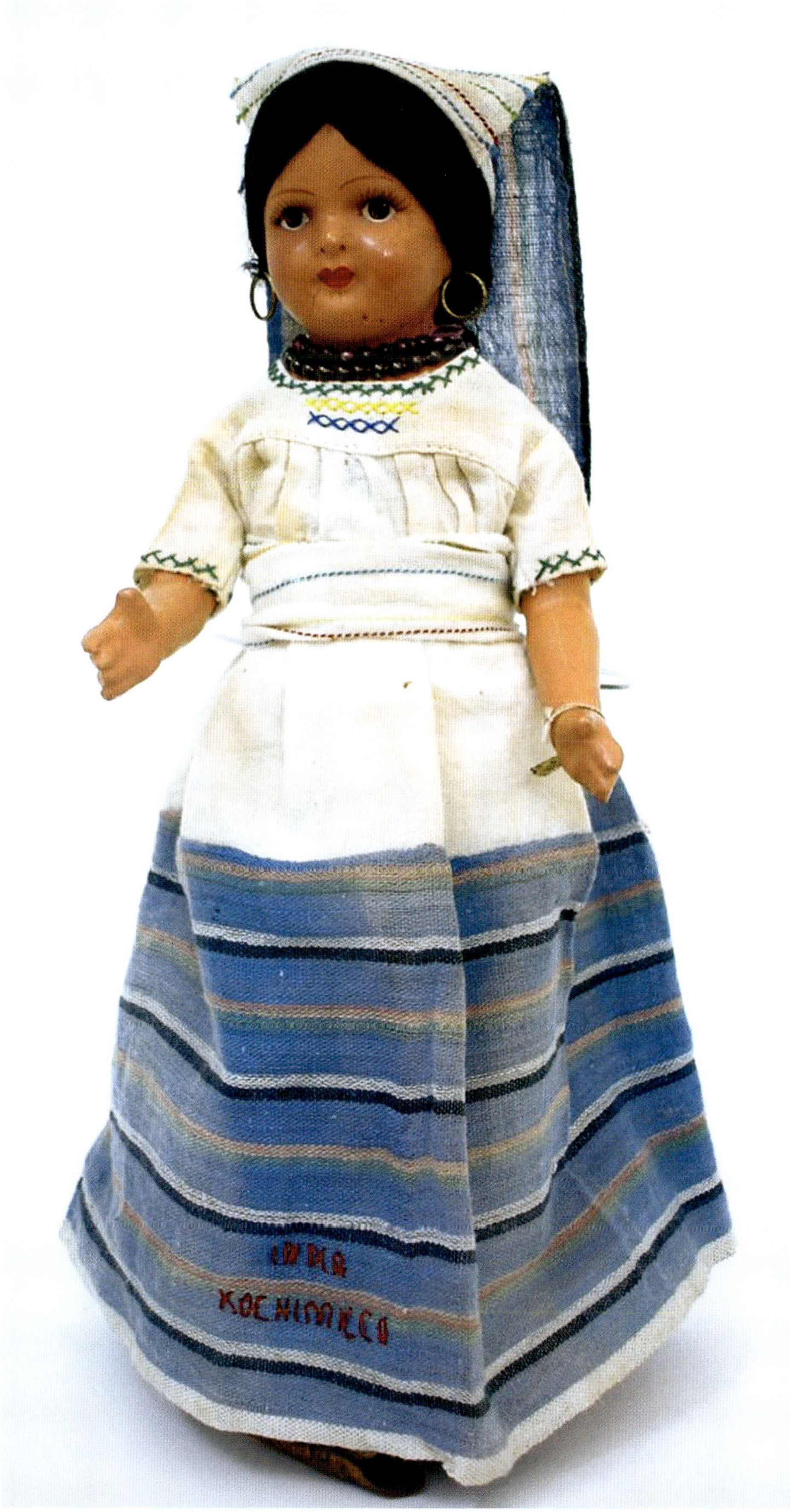

Attributed to Xochimilco, Mexico, a 14 in. composition and cloth doll dressed as an indigenous Indian, c.1940s. Tag on wrist reads "*muñeca irrompible.*" Embroidered on the border of her skirt is "*Xochimilco.*" Made in Mexico. A white and blue *manta* cloth embroidered top and a matching *servilleta* (hair scarf). Long black wool braided hair. $75 to 175

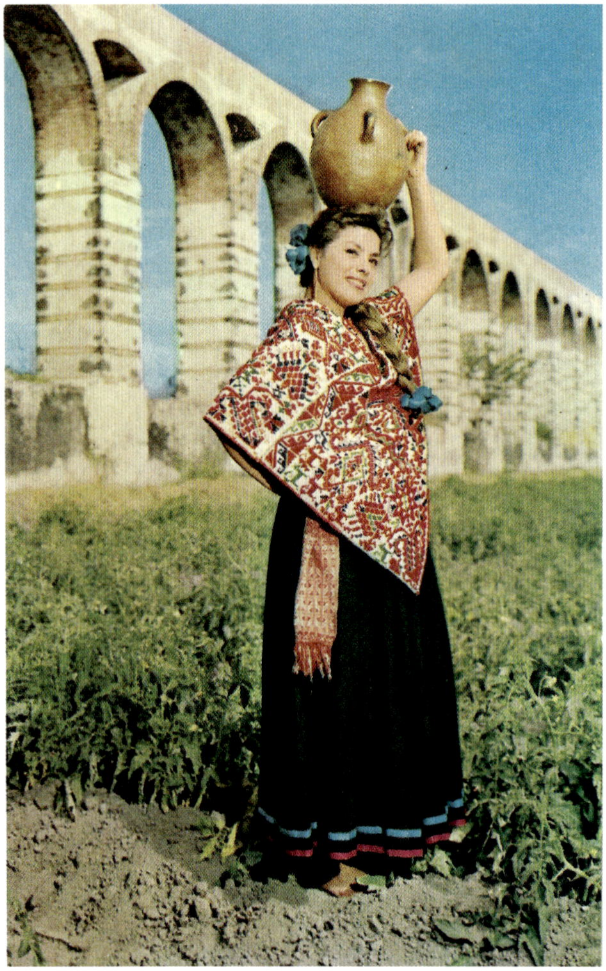

Color postcard photograph, "Acaxochitlan, Hidalgo," Cristacolor, Lito Juventud, c.1950 Mexico D. F. 3 x 5 in. $15 to 30

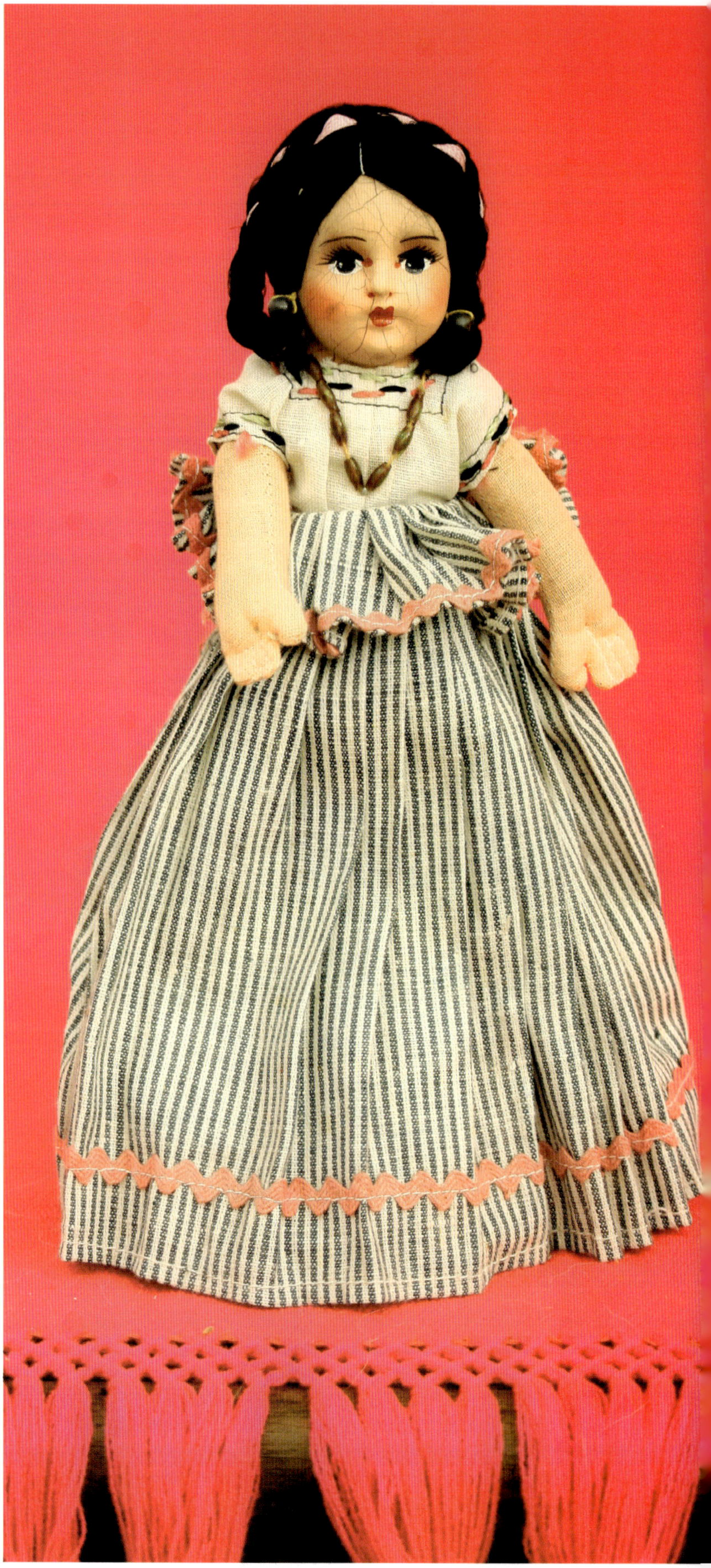

A 12 in. cloth doll with a *papier maché* compo face, she is from Tlaquepaque, c.1945. White and blue with pink trim, full skirt and *huipil* top. $60 to 100

El Huipil, La Blusa and *Quechquemitl*, The Tops

The *huipil* (pronounced wee-pil) and the Mexican *blusa* are the typical blouses that the Mexican Indian and the *mestiza* dolls are wearing. They are an essential part of their costumes that has sustained an ageless style recognizable worldwide. The blouses have always remained an important piece for the woman. To be comfortable as well as beautiful was important without compromising their traditions. One can admire a mix of the varieties of the *mestiza* and the indigenous Mexican Indian *huipils*. Beautiful floral and birds motifs are a favorite pattern, with rich detail and color that is often made of light or heavy cotton. They hand apply embroidery, appliqués, or cross stitch patterns that mimic favorite symbols and motifs from their lives or were simply created from a vivid imagination.

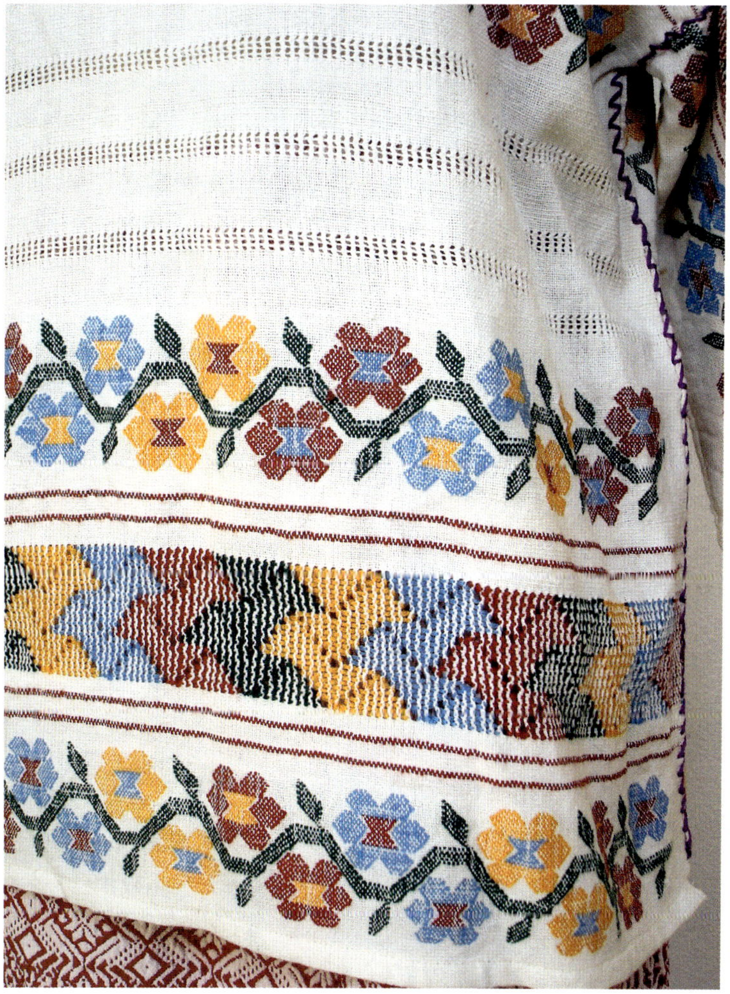

White cotton with detailed flowers and bands of stylized zigzag lines in multi-colored embroidery, made in Mexico

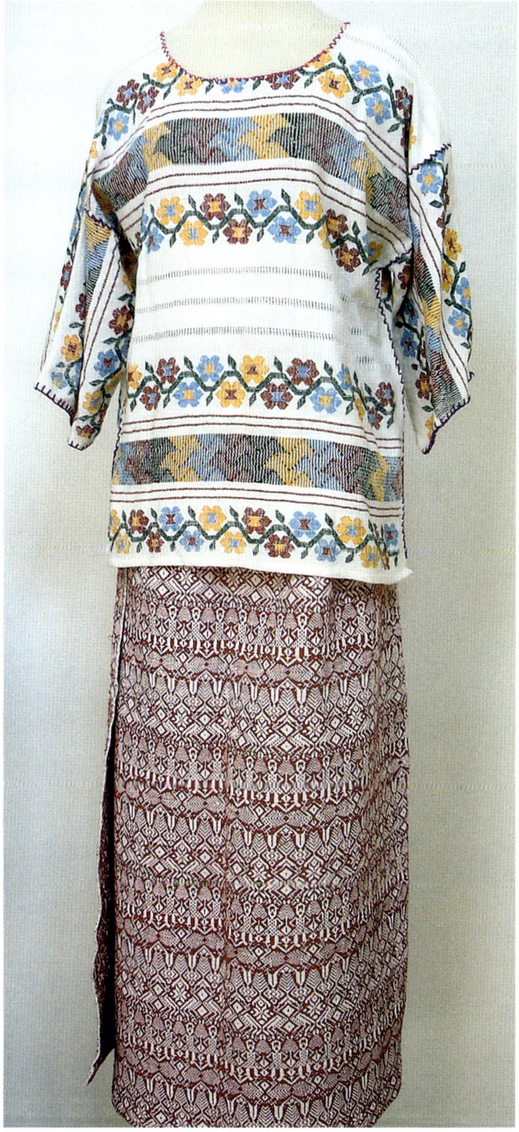

Indigenous *huipil* tunic woven in gauze and brocade technique, c.1950s. Homespun cloth and cross-stitched design, red and white reverse embroidered *enrdo* wrap skirt, Chinantec, Oaxaca.

The differences between the *blusa* and *huipil* are traced to their cultural influences as well as trends that pushed a more urban look in the 20th century. Distinctions between the two types can be made, and they will be noticed on the dolls. The indigenous *huipil* derive from ancestral Mayan influence. They are often more spectacular than the *blusa* in that they can be a profusely embroidered and woven in various patterns with dyed threads. They are a tunic style that exhibits more tribal and traditional themes. A short-sleeved top, usually with a square neck, they are cut straight in the body and loose fitting. It is generally embroidered around the neck, folded in half, and stitched at the sides with space allowed for the arms. The length may vary, either short or ankle length. It is also worn as a dress or over a skirt that is then tied with a woven sash belt (*faja*) or just left open. Most *huipils* are hand woven on looms with combined weaving techniques and applied embroidery. The *huipil* is a heavier woven top; the skill involved in creating them is passed down from generation to generation. On the dolls you will see a wide variety, where some of them are longer, shorter, or worn tucked in or out of the skirt.

I want to reiterate that I am not an expert on woven textiles, as some of the doll clothing may appear to have Guatemalan traits. This is valid because of the integral ancestry of both of these cultures, and it is highly conceivable that patterns and symbols cannot be locally discerned. The facts remain that the dolls were purchased in Mexico or as Mexican costume dolls, and any misinterpretation was not intentional. *Huipils* are a prized piece of clothing for the Guatemalans and deservedly so, but those from Mexico surely remain a favorite on the dolls or on me! They are vivid and expressive canvases of art that display skill and traditional motifs you can wear proudly.

On the other hand, the Mexican *blusa* is reminiscent of the beautiful Spanish woman's blouse. It is a more feminine garment with strong traditional influences from Spain and Europe, similar to a peasant blouse in style and design. It accentuated and enhanced the urban Mexican woman and soon became very fashionable. It has a squared or rounded neck line at the front, with short finished sleeves; it also has a more feminine form than the *huipil* only because it is more proportioned to the female body. They can be made from a light cotton fabric that is loomed or woven, or from commercial blends bought by the bolt. They are almost always embellished with colorful embroidered necklines and gorgeous floral and bird motifs that include silk threading and beads in various styles of stitching and techniques. They were constructed similarly to the *huipil*, except the *blusas* have attached sleeves. They were almost always pieced together on a sewing machine, but then all the embroidery and trims were hand applied.

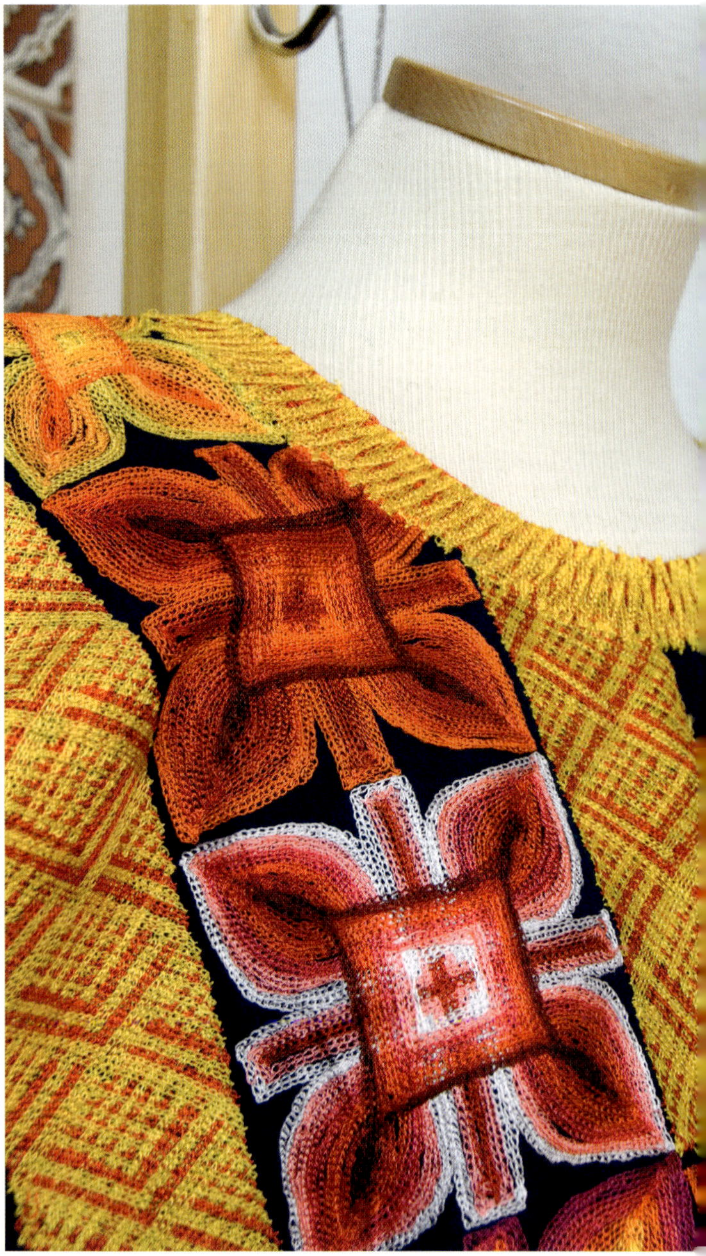

A detail of the indigo sateen *huipil*, c.1950s. Oaxaca, Mexico

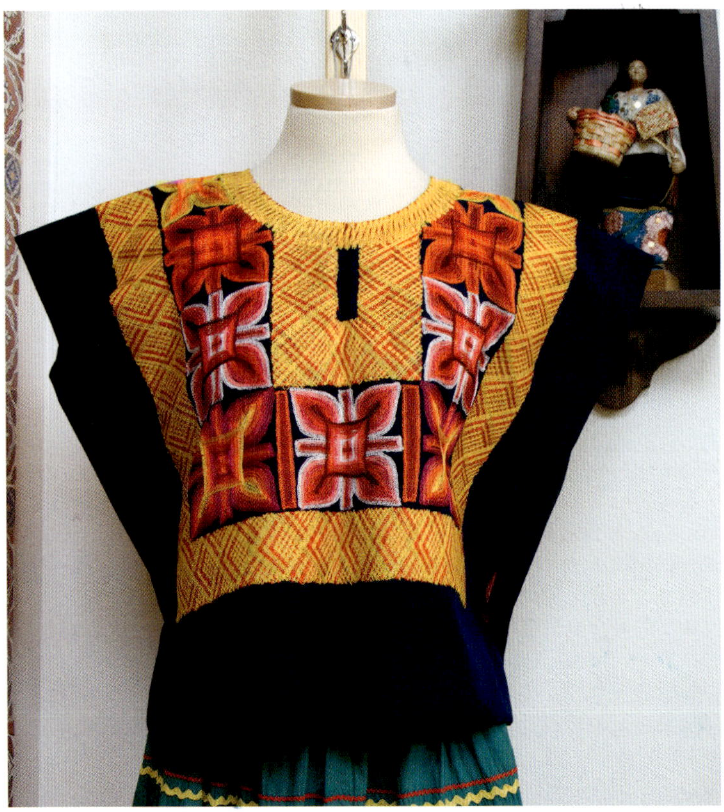

A *huipil* of a Zapotec, indigo sateen, with an amazing technique of machine embroidery in chain stitch, cotton, gold and yellow threads. A tedious process, even though machine done, in an interlocking geometric pattern, c.1950s. Oaxaca, Mexico

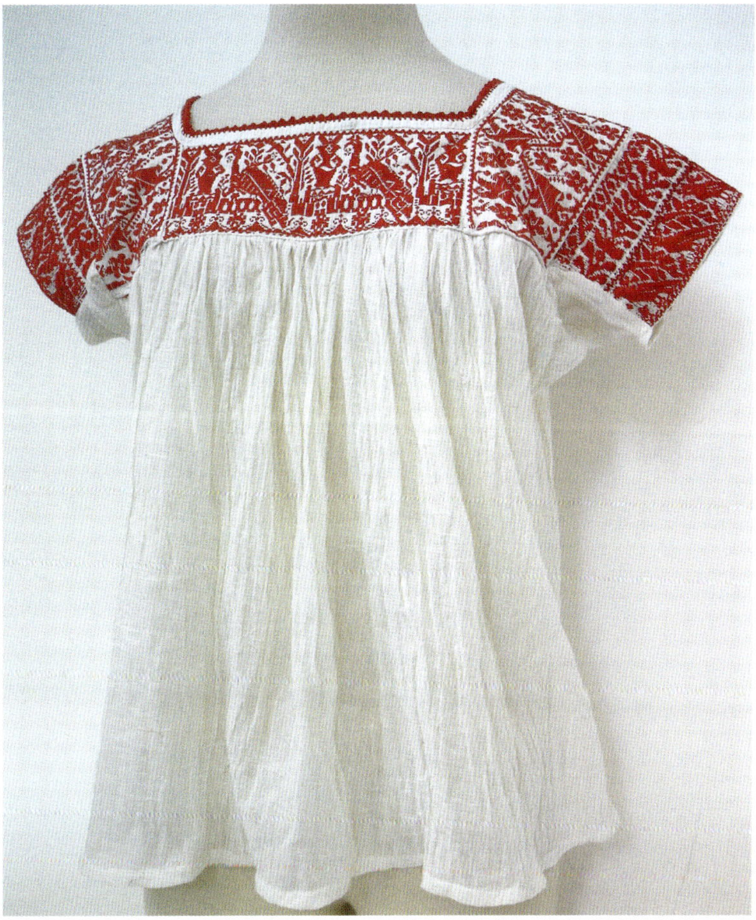

A typical Mexican *blusa* c.1950s, made of a cotton *manta*. Hand-embroidered in bright red *anthromorphic* patterns. A squared neckline with careful detail and short sleeves. Puebla, Mexico

A closer view of the Mexican *blusa*. Small stitches in red wool or cotton threads create a negative pattern, in excellent condition. Maker unknown.

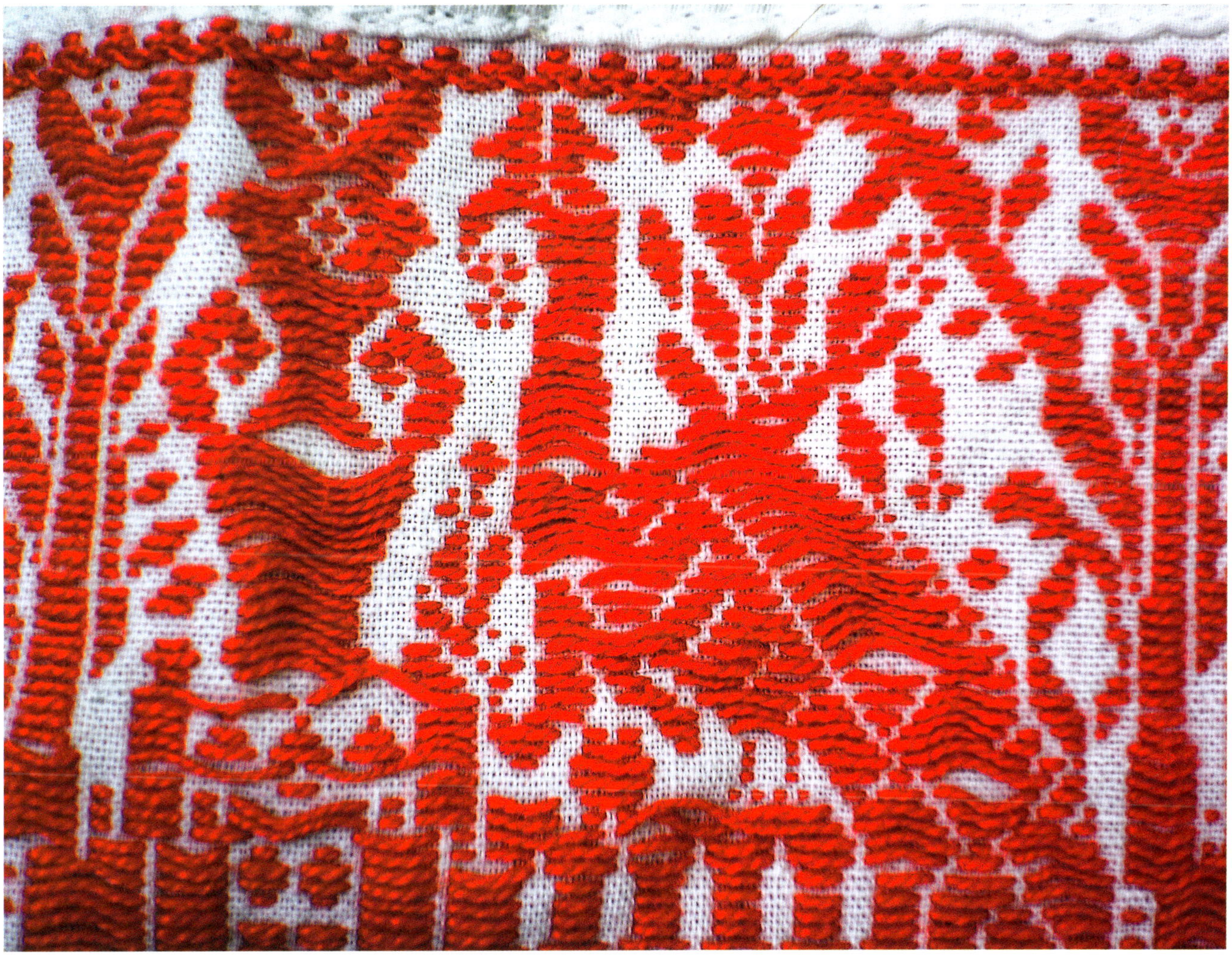

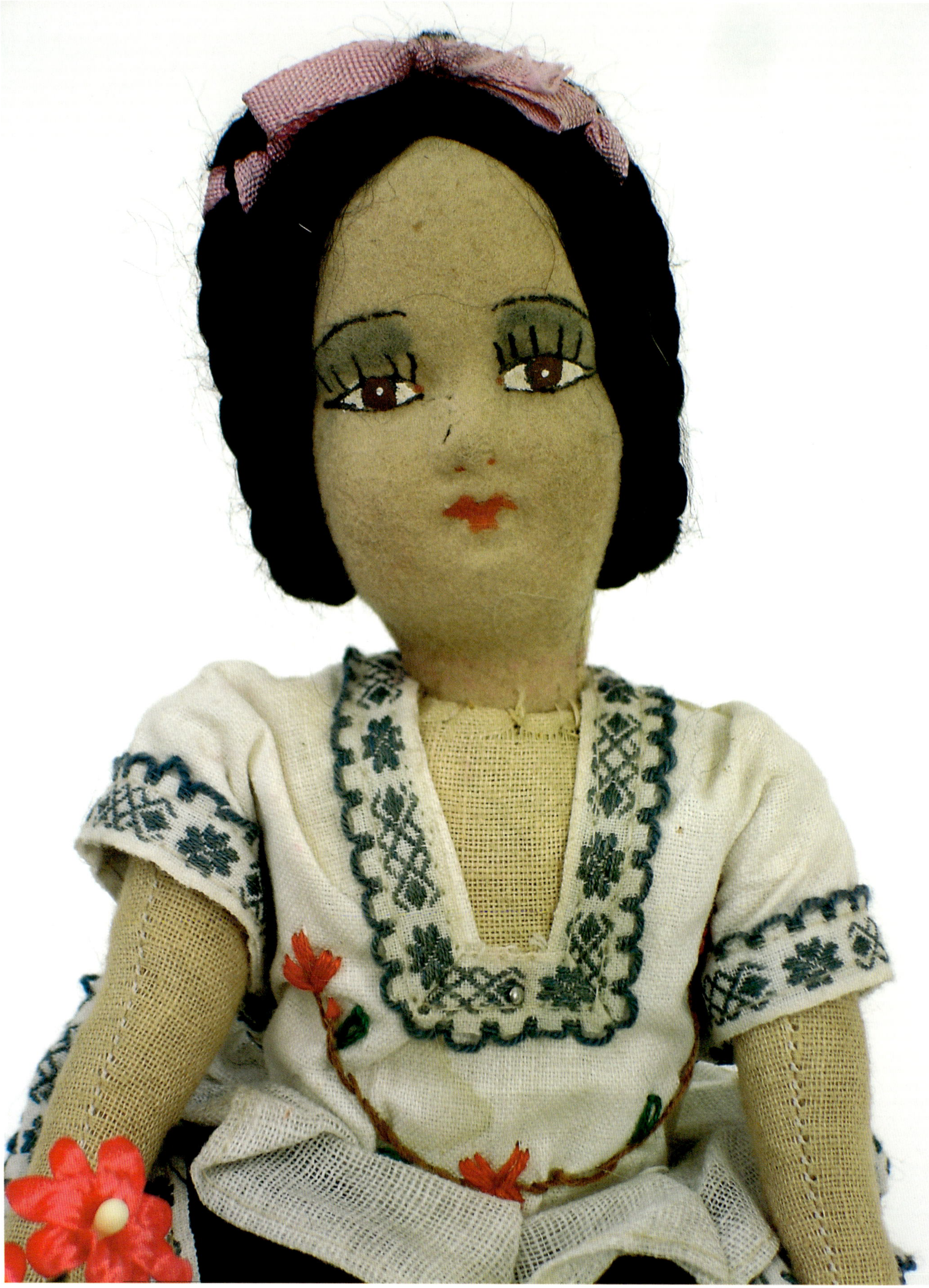

Notice the embroidered detail in this homemade *huipil* on a 12 in. cloth doll from Tlaquepaque, Mexico. Pressed paper mache face, with molded features and hand-painted detail, c.1950s. $75-125

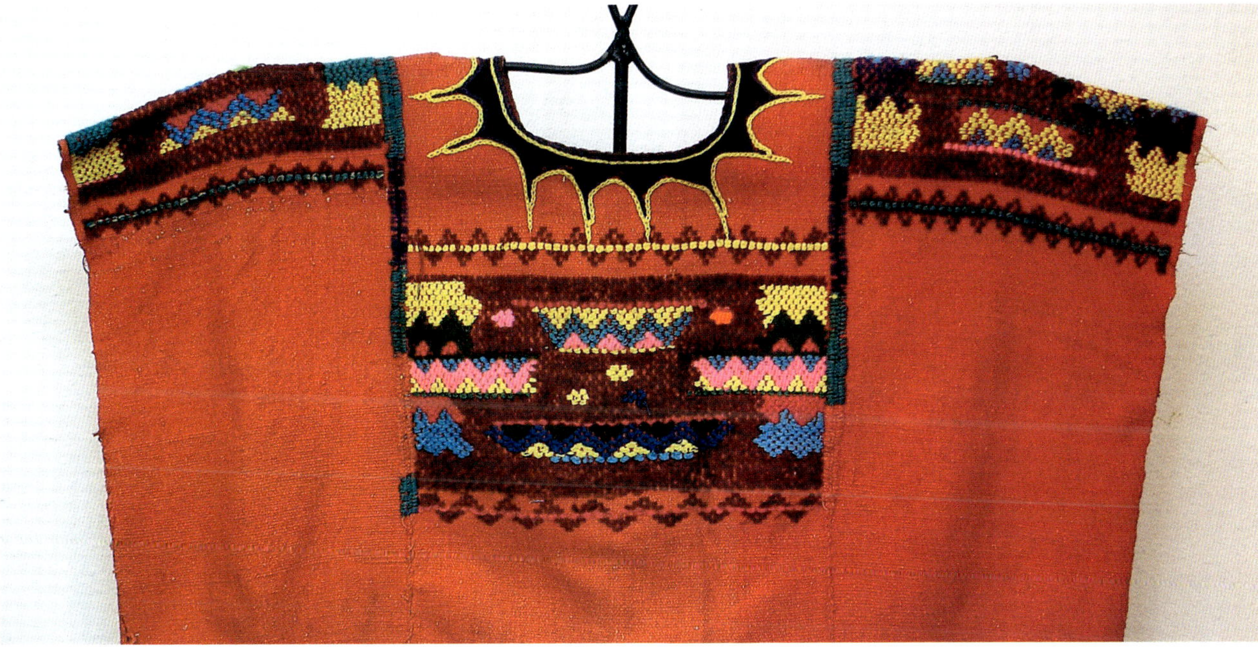

Brocade vertical-band pattern on a woman's *huipil* tunic, woven from homespun cotton, diamond hook motifs, cross stitch pattern running with chain stitch, satin stitch, rich details, and vibrant color, c.1950s. Mixteca community, Oaxaca.

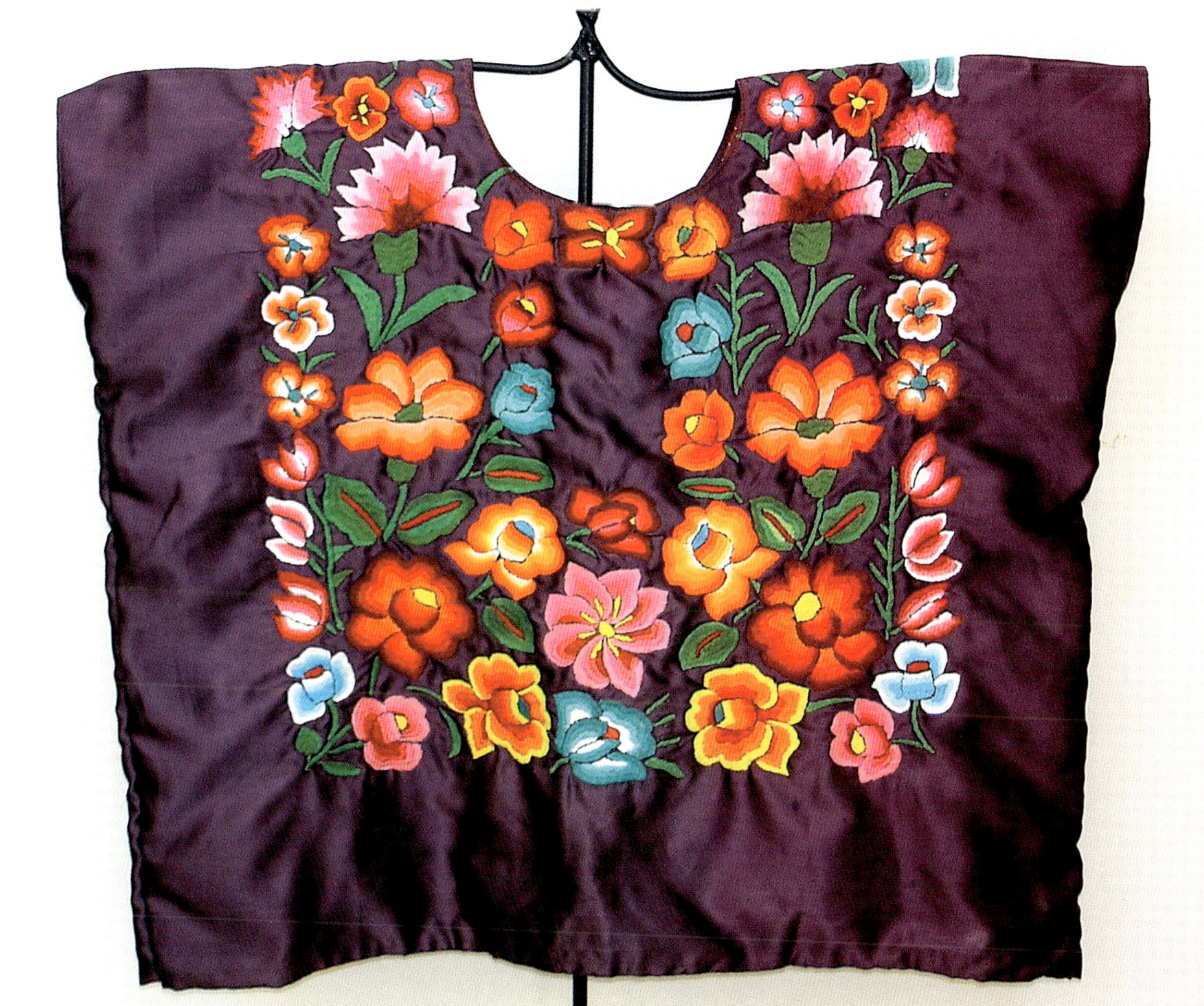

Made from satin silk, a Tehuantepec *huipil* adorned with large satin-stitched flowers in colorful pattern. Rich detail presents a work of art. Made in Mexico

The *huipil* and the Spanish style *blusa* were both favorite tops of the acclaimed artist *Frida Kahlo*, the wife of the artist *Diego Rivera* (famed Mexican muralist). She was definately a credible *mestiza* of her time, in the1940s. Frida adored her country's clothing traditions and she often combined indigenous items that clothed the *mestiza* Mexican woman. One of her favorite styles was that of the *Tehuana of Tehuantepec* (described in Part One) from the state of Oaxaca. Although these costumes are very expensive, you can still buy beautiful examples of *huipils* throughout Mexico quite reasonably.

The *quechquémitl* is a classic piece of clothing worn by the indigenous Mexican Indian and *mestiza*. This ancient poncho or shawl-like garment has been around

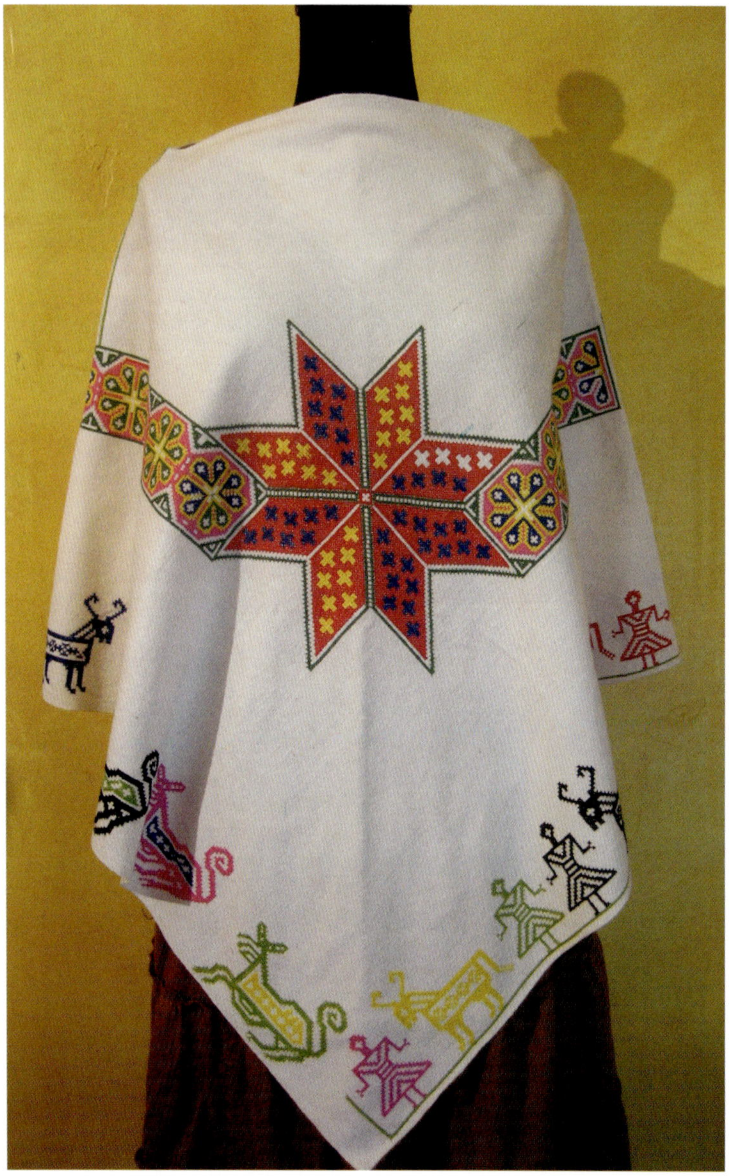

Attributed to the Huichol, a beautiful *tuarra* cape, c.1930s. An authentic cape worn by the Huichol Indians, indigenous people descendants of the Aztecan. The 8-petal flower and decorative elements always include nature's treasures. Homespun cotton and complicated detail. *Courtesy of Kathleen Morales, Santa Barbara, California*

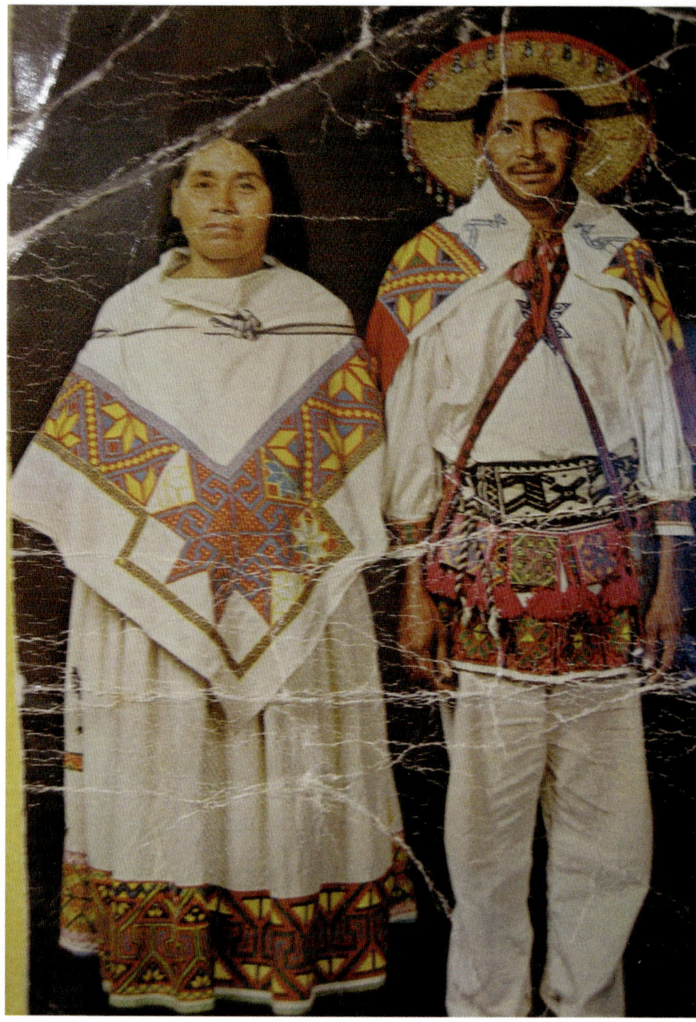

A color photograph Huichol couple in traditional garments, 20th c. *Courtesy of Kathleen Morales, Santa Barbara, California*

for thousands of years and serves as not only a cape over a top but also as the top itself, sometimes even worn on an Indian's head. The shape is of a rhomboid, with a hole in the middle for the head to go through. In the central and northern regions of Mexico they are still worn to keep warm or for their aesthetic beauty. There are variations in the assembly of the *quechquémitl*, but it is a fairly simple design created from two rectangles to make a square. It has two points and is sleeveless, and is generally worn with the points facing front and back, but can also have the points to the sides. These are very vital pieces to the wearer, as it is an identifiable item from region to region. Often profuse embroidery covers the surface, with beautiful designs or simple cross stitches of different colors. Their beauty is sometimes the woven fabric itself, colorful and with diverse patterns that demonstrate their skill and origin. The methods used to decorate the present-day *quechquémitl* include embroidery and brocading. Some of the examples on the dolls appear with very little embroidery when compared to the actual *quechquemitl* worn. One of the most extraordinary *quechquemitls* is from the *Tepehuas* of Veracruz.

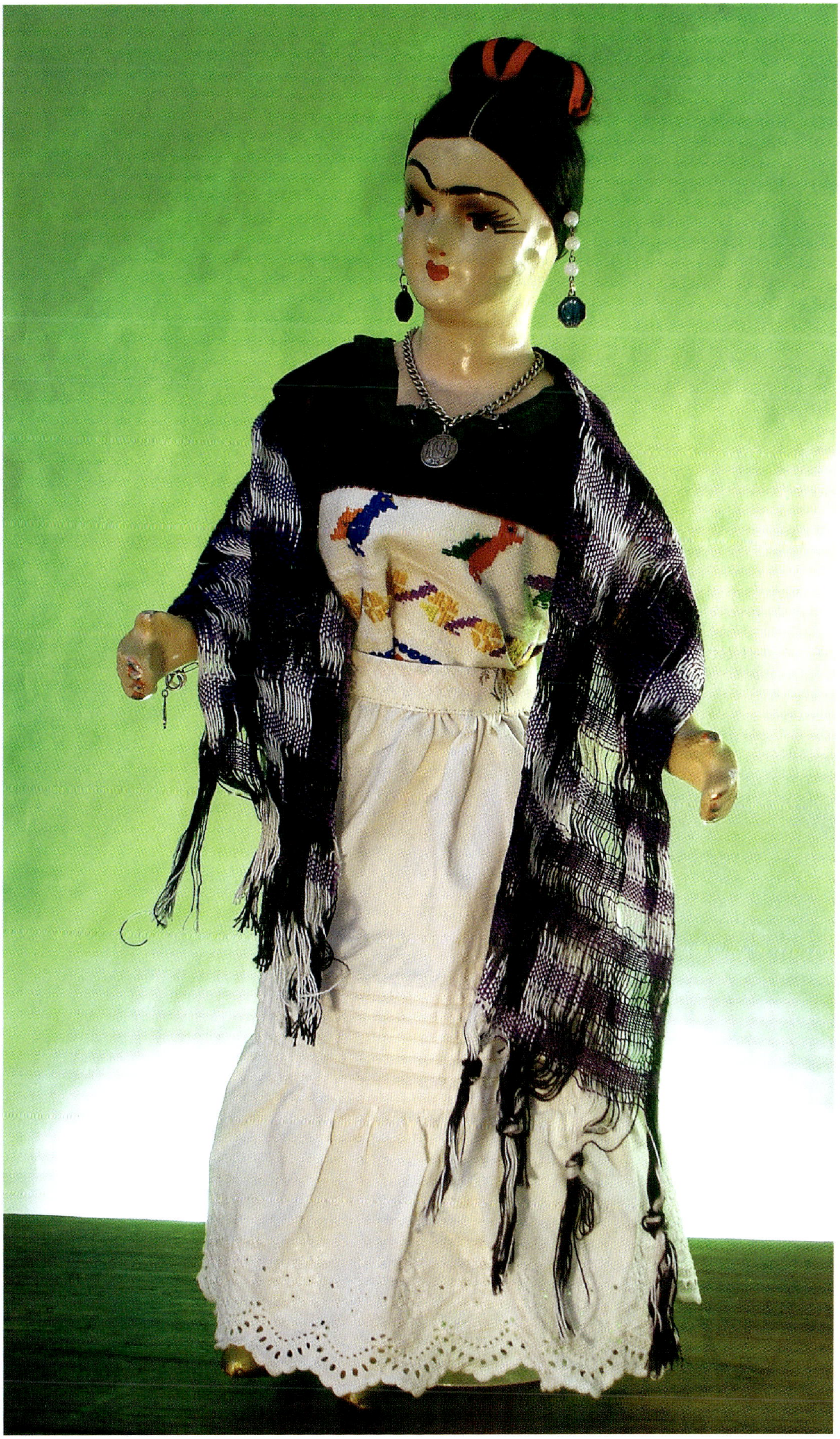

A lovely interpretation of a Frida Kahlo 17 in. composition doll, c.1940s. She is wearing a colorful *huipil*, a white colonial skirt, and an indigenous woven *rebozo*. Sterling necklace and accessories. Her hair is prepared in a traditional Spanish chignon bun. $200 to 500

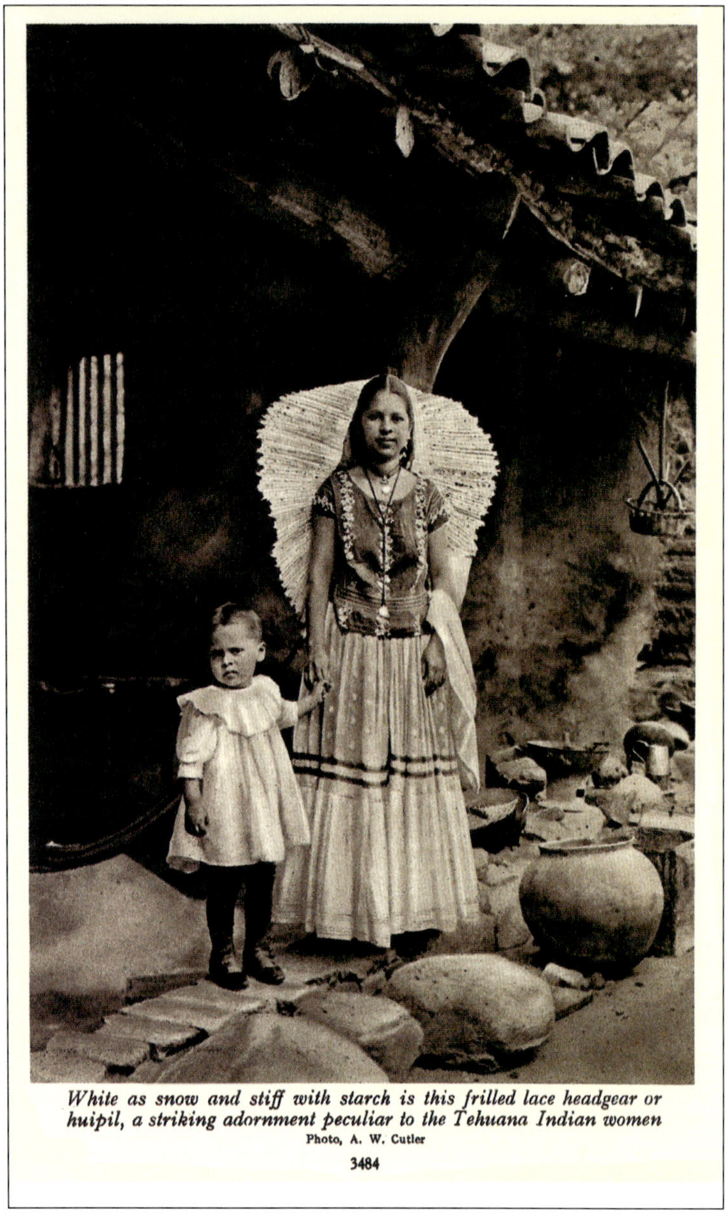

A sepia photogravure of a Tehuantepec woman with a *huipil* and her child, c.1920s.

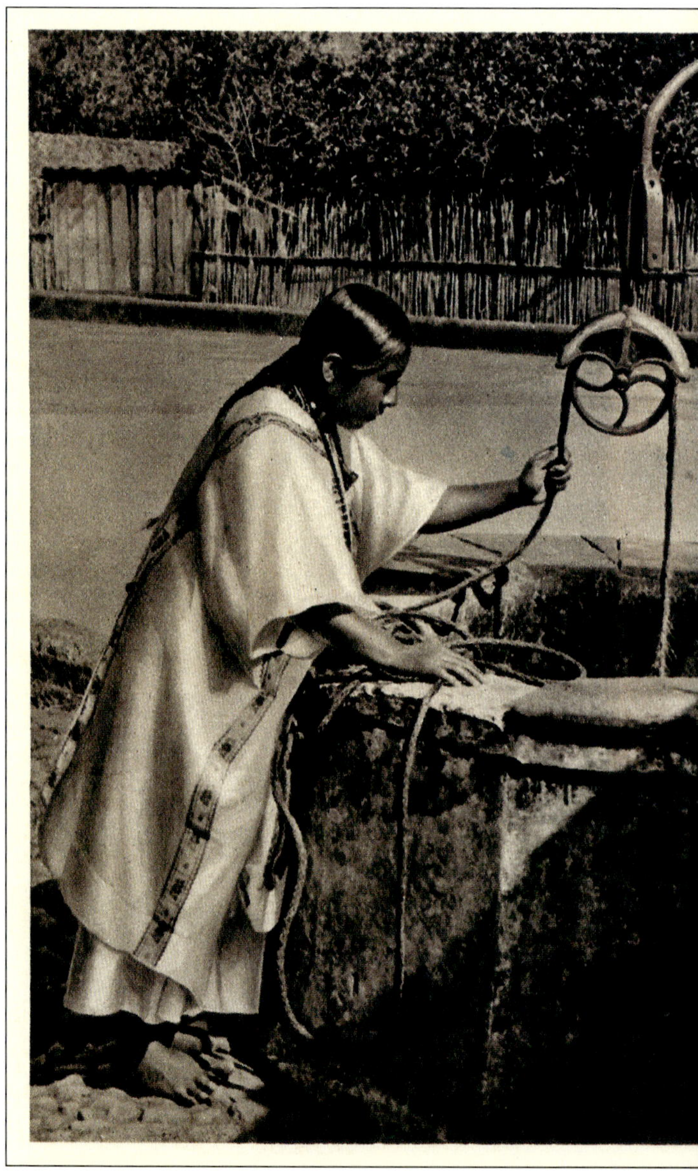

A Mexican Indian woman in a long tunic, 1922, photogravure print.

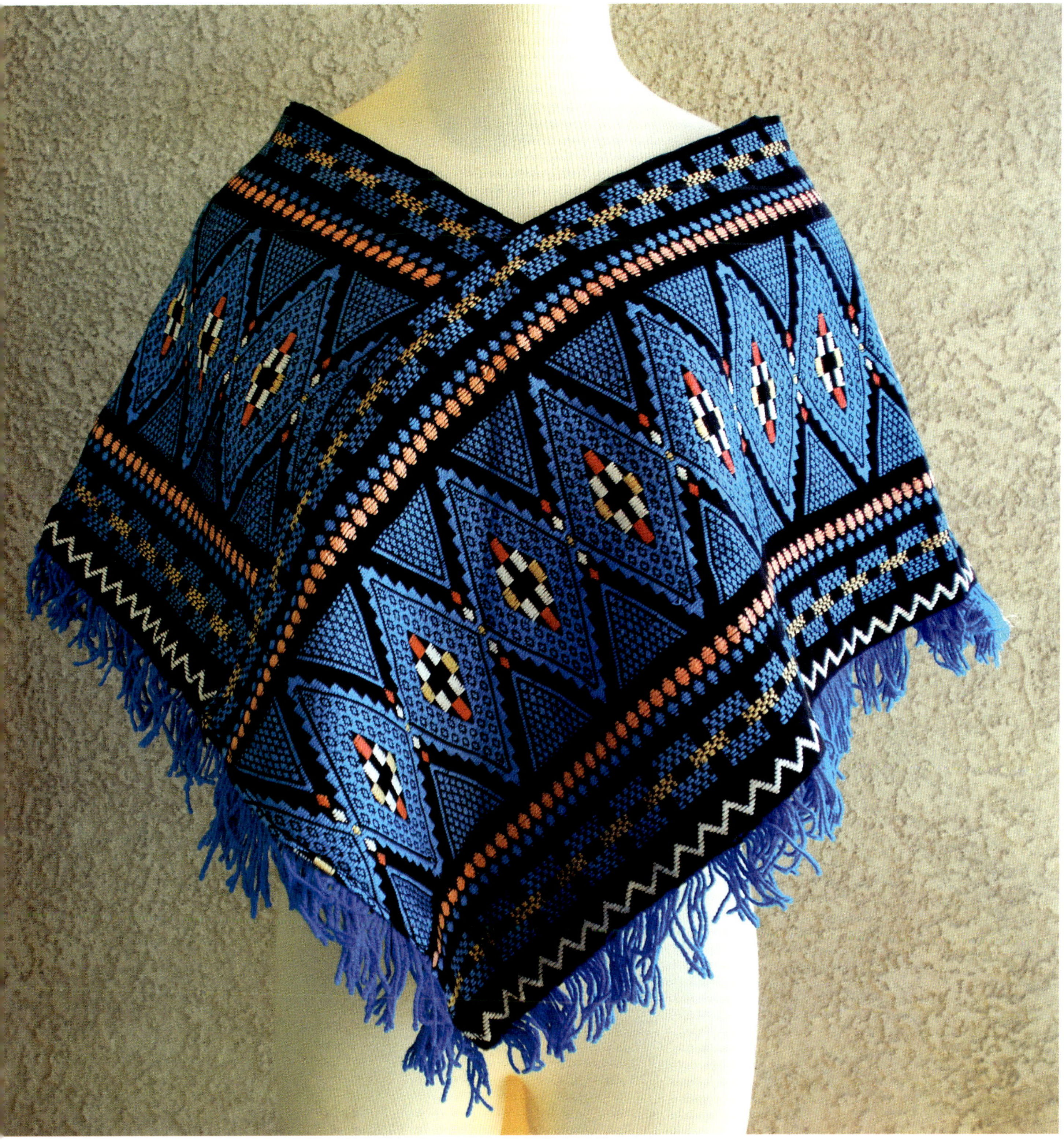

The *quechquémitl* (kes-ke-met), closed shoulder cape. Made from commercial cloth with brocade woven geometric shapes and fringed border. An essential piece for the indigenous natives, 20th c, made in Mexico.

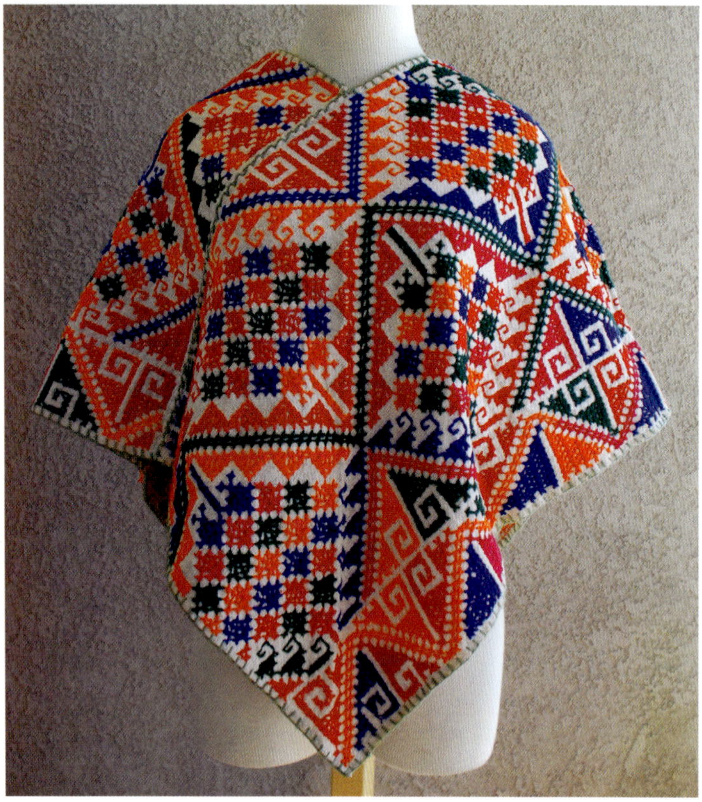

A spectacular Huichol *quechquémitl* (kes-ke-met) with bold wool threads, cross-stitched flowers and geometric shapes. It is worn with the point at the front or to the side, 20th c, made in Mexico.

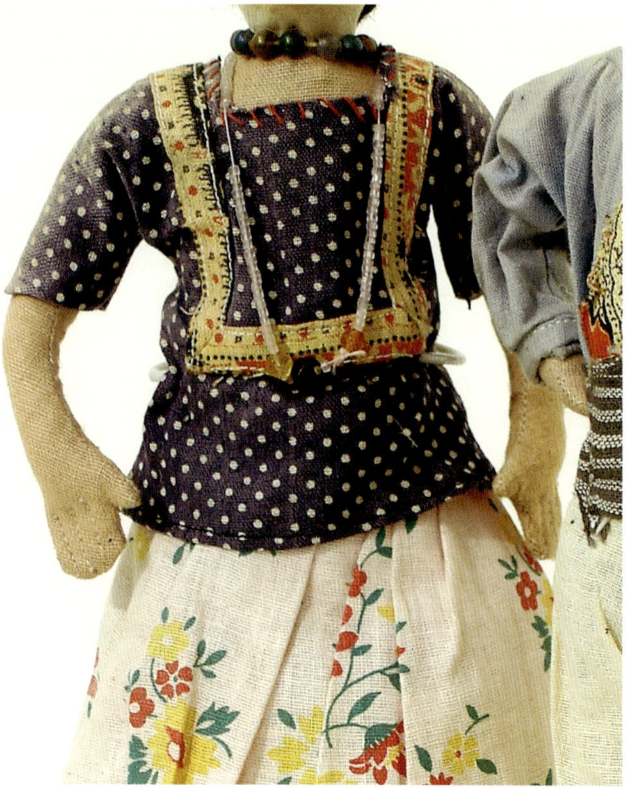

The *huipil* (tunic) is printed *manta* cloth on an early 20th c. cloth doll with glass beads for jewelry. Oaxaca, Mexico.

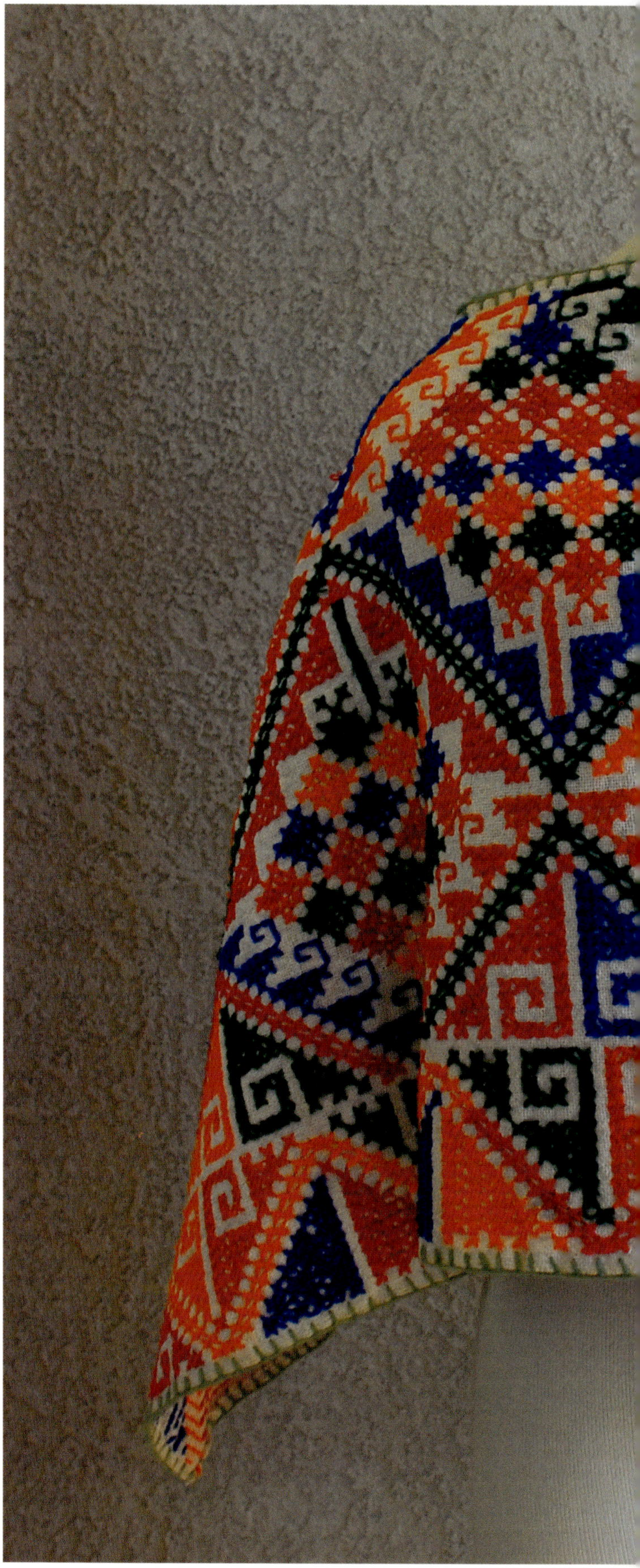

The cross stitched Huichol *quechquémitl* (kes-ke-met) worn with the points to the side. Made in Mexico.

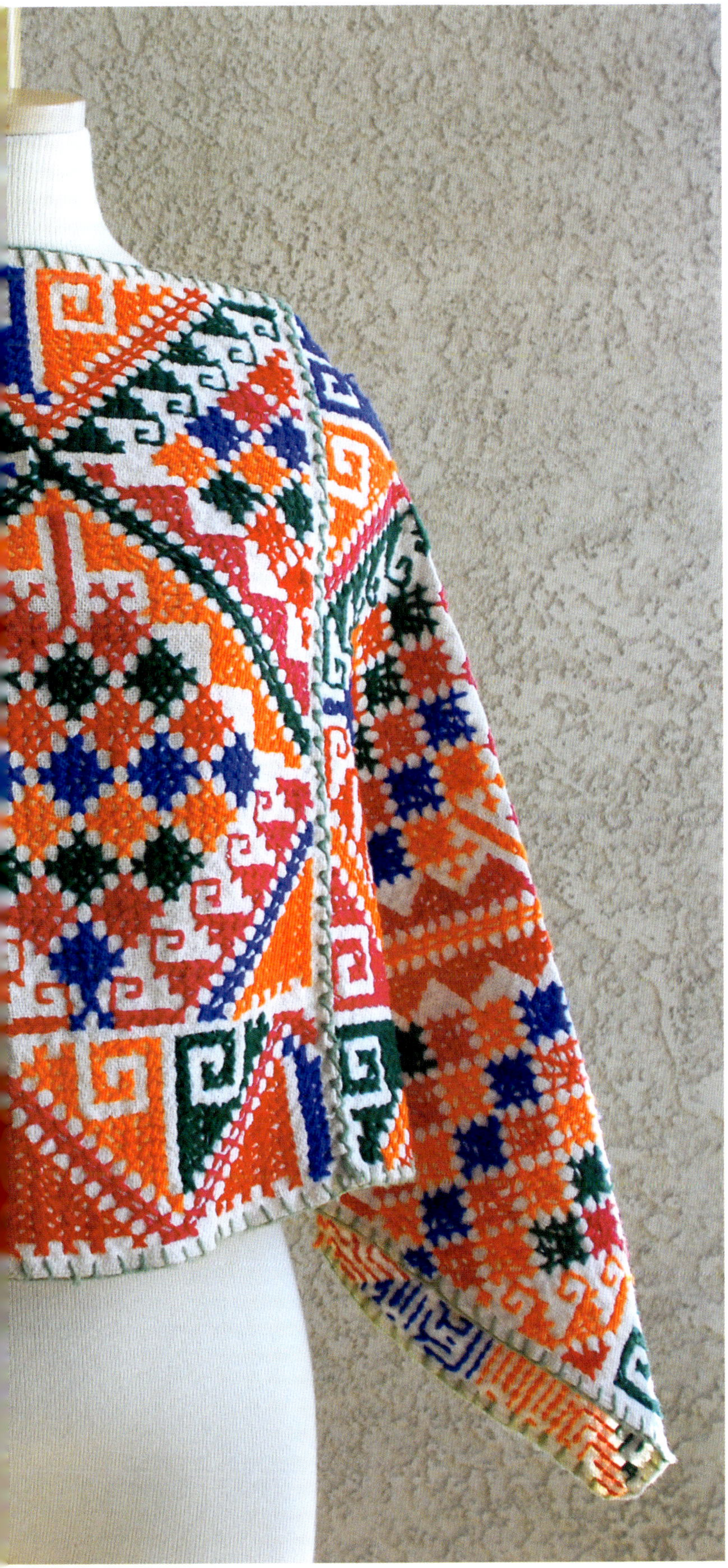

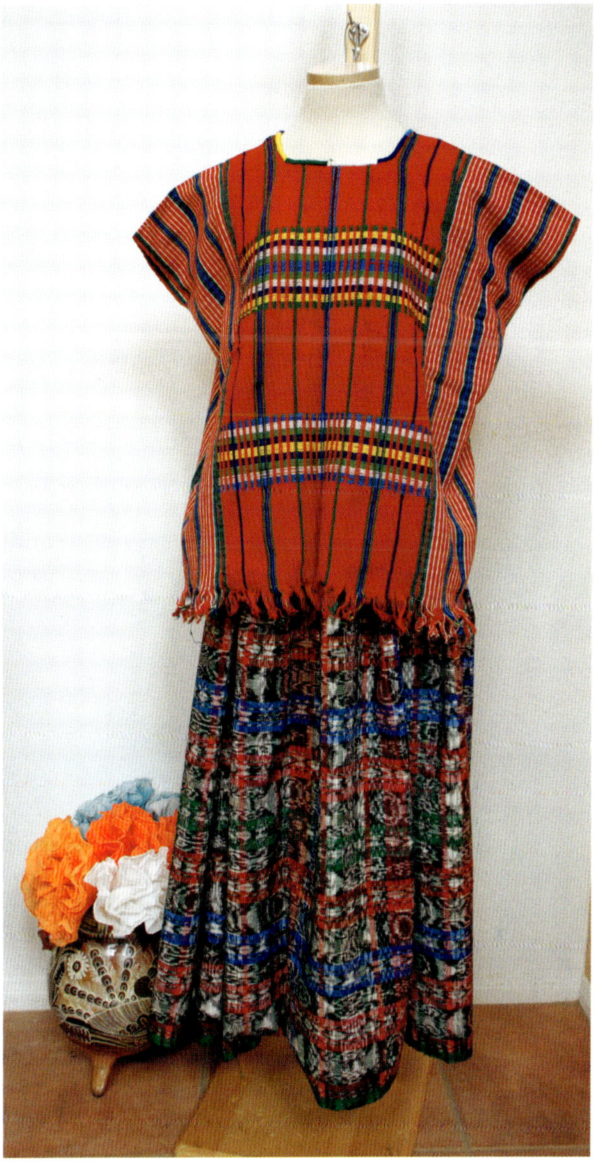

The red *huipil,* Oaxacan tunic, is a beautiful example, with cloth webs, woven and patterned with vertical and horizontal decorative stitching and frayed hem. It is worn with a typical *enredo* skirt in vibrant multi-colored woven pattern with a crotch-hatch design and feathering similar to the *rebozos*. 20th c.

Colonial Dress of the Mestiza

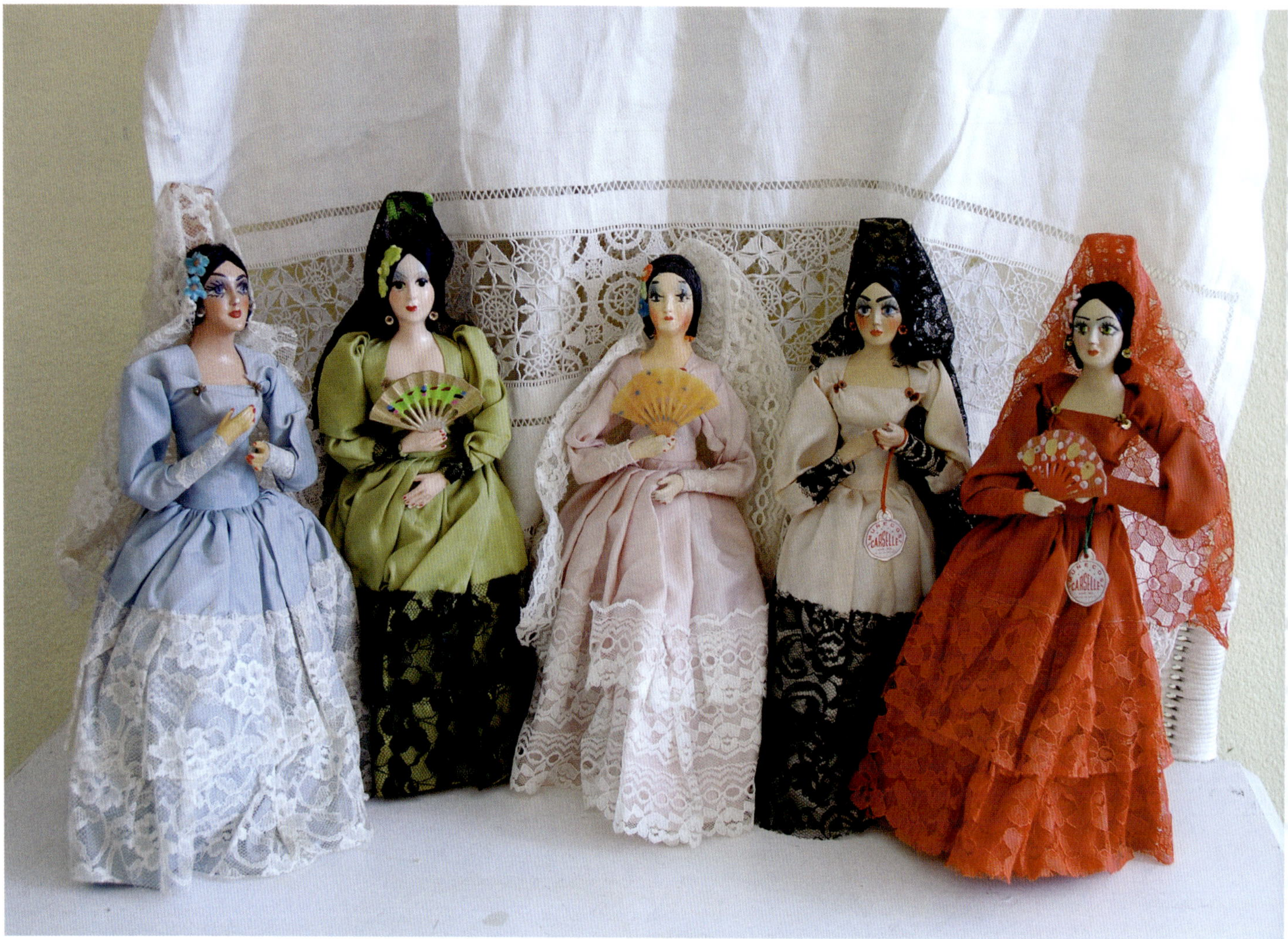

Attributed to Poveda and Carselle, these are Spanish *Señoritas*, 12 to 13 in., composition resin tourist dolls, sold c.1940s to 1960s. Their satin rayon dresses, lace, and accessories truly exemplify their Spanish influences, made in Mexico $45 to 100

The Spanish style of dressing influenced Mexico's noble and upper level urban citizens during the colonial days (16th c. to 19th c.). Mexico had endured three centuries of Spain's domination and it left them with beautiful ornate churches, *palacios*, and traditional Spanish garments. The growing Spanish society in the New World encouraged the development of a thriving textile industry. They had established influence in the architecture, religion, and social structure long before the 20th century, and therefore traditional progressive Spanish women and men inspired clothing trends for many Mexican aristocrats. Women's dresses, such as the rich gowns of the beautiful Señoritas, and the fancy suits of the *Charro* were always imitated on Mexican costume dolls.

Spanish-style gowns were worn for galas and important events and were made usually from imported fabrics. They were made of the finest fabrics with layers of rayon or silk trimmed with gold and silver threading and embroidery. The bodice was fitted with fanciful accents, and would fall to a full skirt with tiers of wide ruffles. It was supported underneath by a wired petticoat and a corset to accentuate the waist and bust line. Around her shoulders she would have a lace *rebozo* or shawl, and even a *mantilla* as a headpiece with a *tiara*. Her shoes, which matched the gown, were slippers of various materials, cloth or leather, that she would wear with pantaloons and knee-high stockings.

The *caballeros* (gentlemen) would wear the *traje* of the *charro* or their military suits. They wore flamboyant tailored suits of fine wool and silk shirts. The suits were trimmed with *soutash greco* style silver cording and *plateados* (silver buttons), and would display any credits merited by his social level. His *sombrero* and *serape* were present and always a part of the ensemble. All of these distinctive items of Spanish-influenced clothing were defined traditional garments for the upper class. They have remained as a recognizable costume historically on the upper-class *mestizo* dolls and one that is a favorite souvenir.

"Carmen," 15 in. early 20th c cloth elite *mestiza* doll, wears Spanish lace with rosettes. An ivory silk dress with lace ruffle and tiny black beading around the sleeves. The body is hard stuffed with mitten hands and heeled shoes of cloth. Glass beads in red and green around her neck and earrings, she also has a cotton lace petticoat with pantaloons. $80 to 200

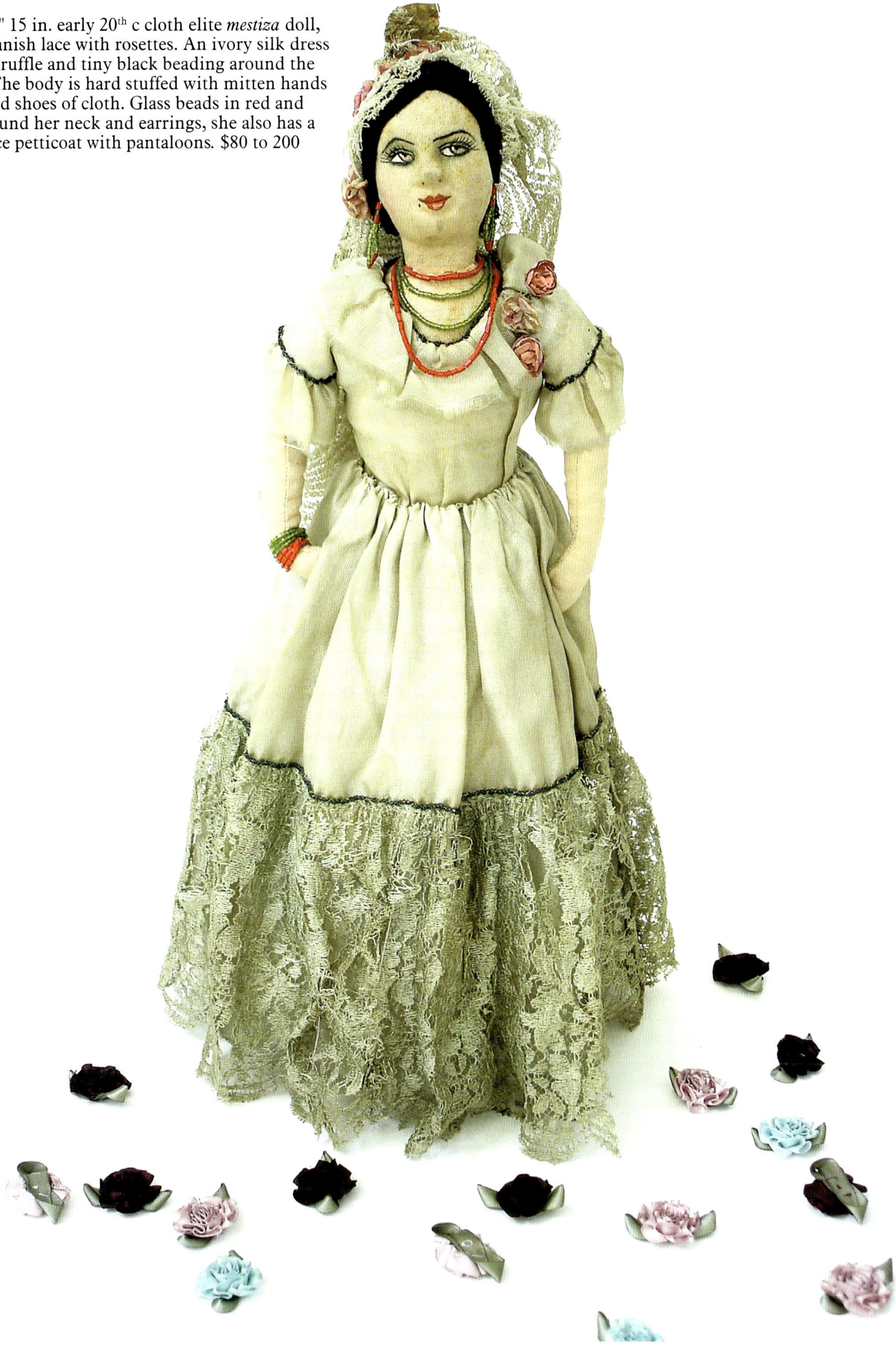

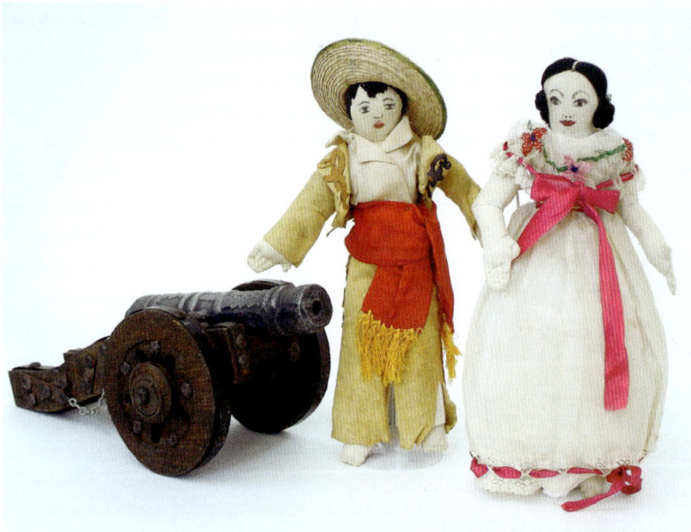

Representative of Spanish Colonial Mexican costumes is this cloth couple, 19th c., with extraordinary details on the 12 in. dolls including hand-applied facial features and silk thread wigs. The Señorita is wearing a batiste cotton dress with lace trimmings, red ribbons, and embroidered flowers, and she has a petticoat and pantaloons under the skirt. The *charro* wears a spectacular leather, short *bolero* style jacket with *greco* detail and pants with a red *faja*, sash. Made in Mexico. $225 to 450pr

An original photograph postcard, c.1920, showing Spanish Californian Dolls, from the Museum Inn, Riverside, USA.$25 to 35

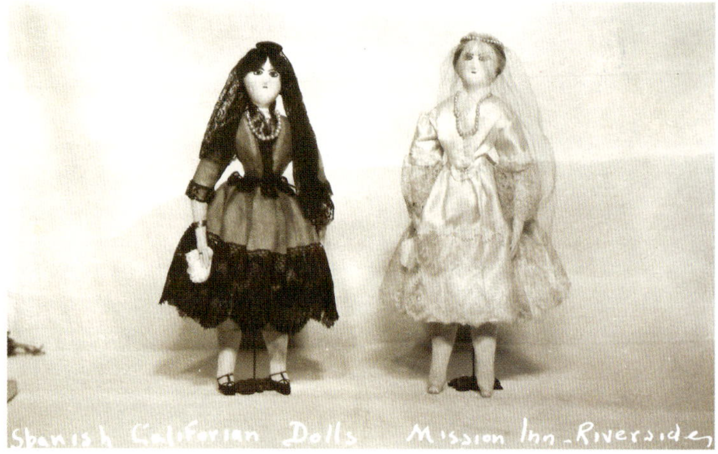

Below:
La Señoritas, two 11 in. hard cloth dolls, made c.1950s in Europe, maybe Italian. Molded features, hand-painted faces, and wonderful detail. Their clothing is carefully made with quality trimming. No markings, white linen ruffles with trailing mantilla. *La Señoritas* have jet black, chignon-styled, wool wigs tightly woven into a back bun. Felt pressed flowers and poms of wool. $75-150

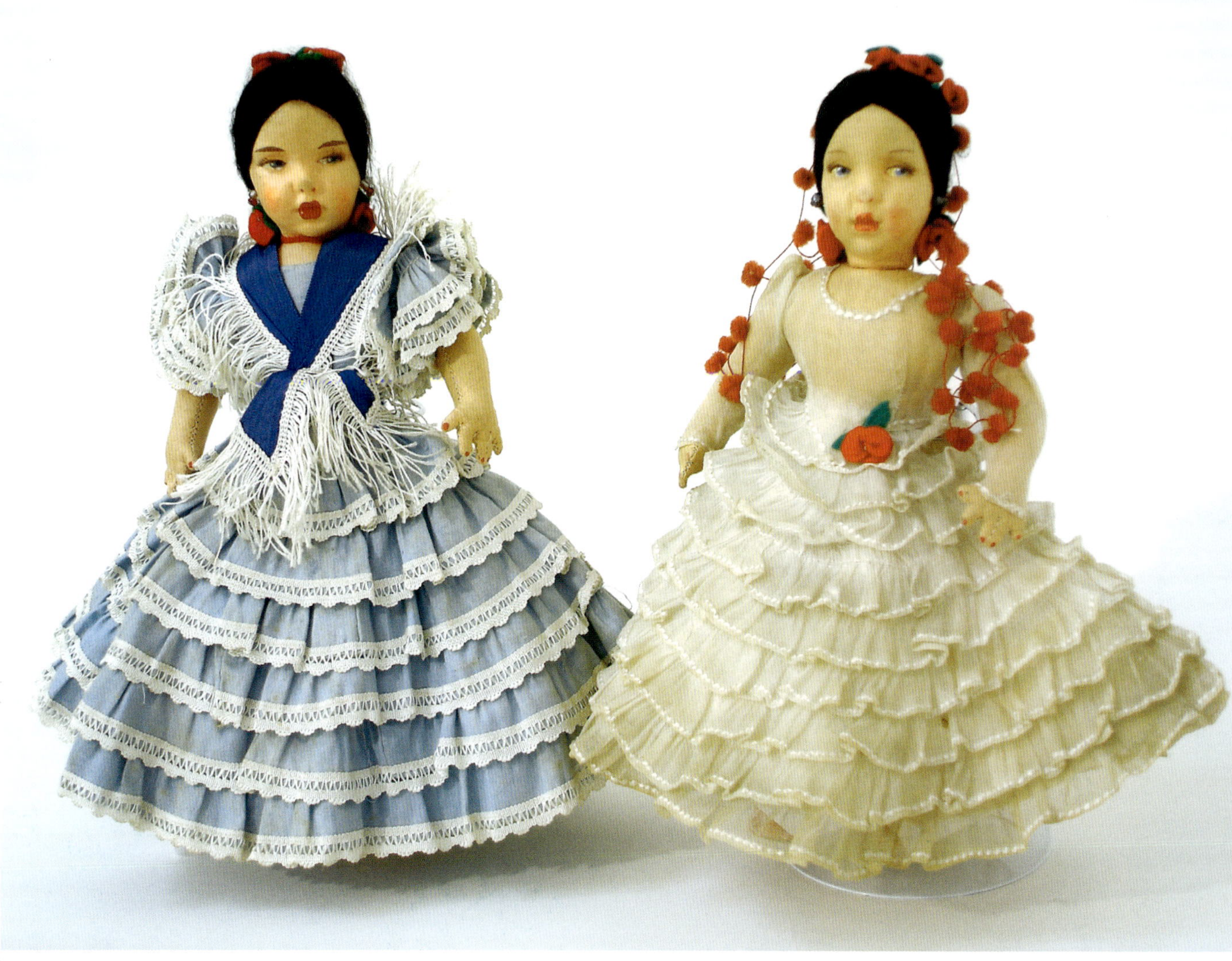

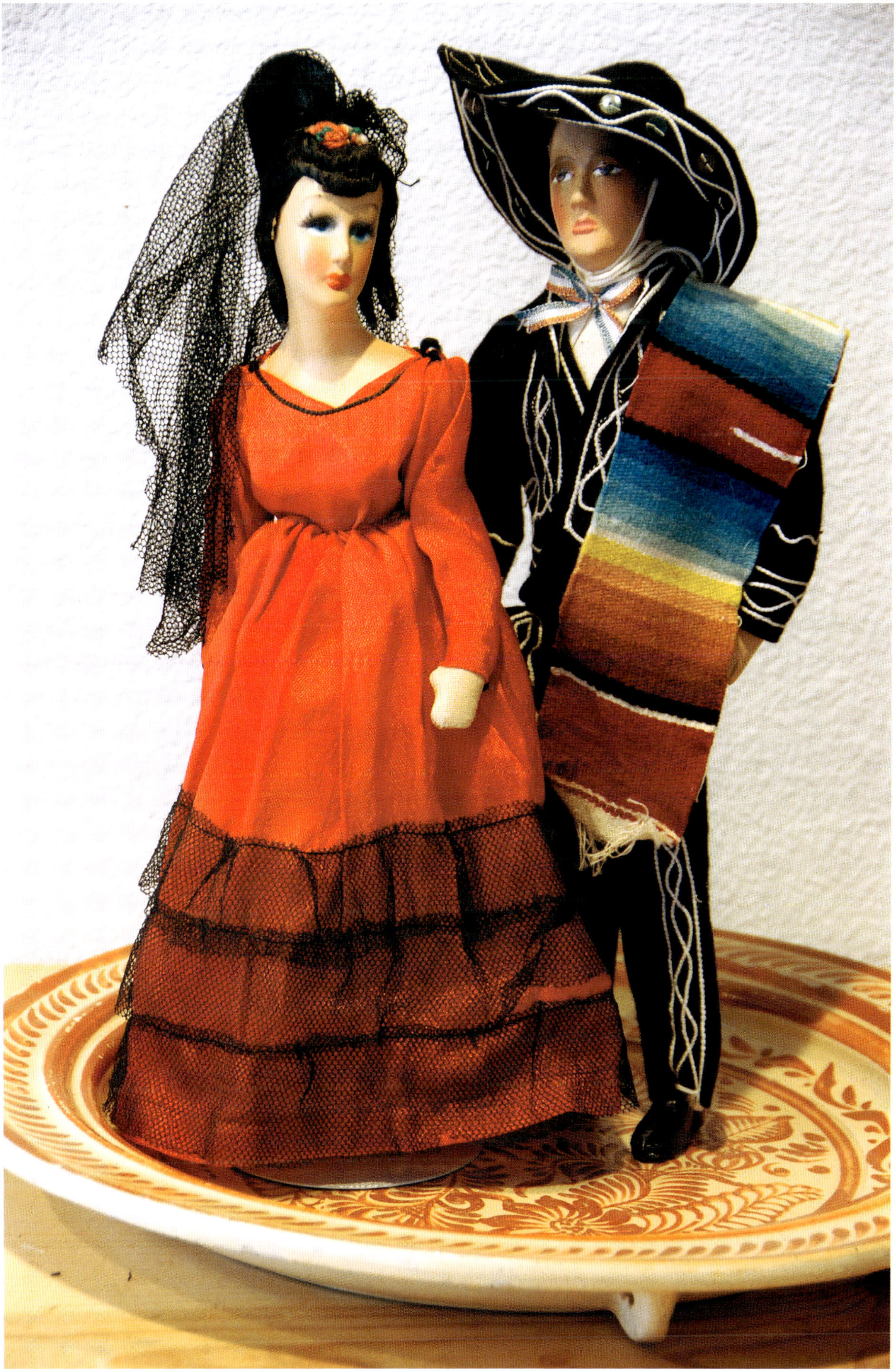

This Spanish *mestizo* couple illustrate the colonial influences: her black and red dress with a traditional *tiara*, and his black suit with all the glorious trimmings of a grand *Charro*, c.1940s. $75 to 150 ea.

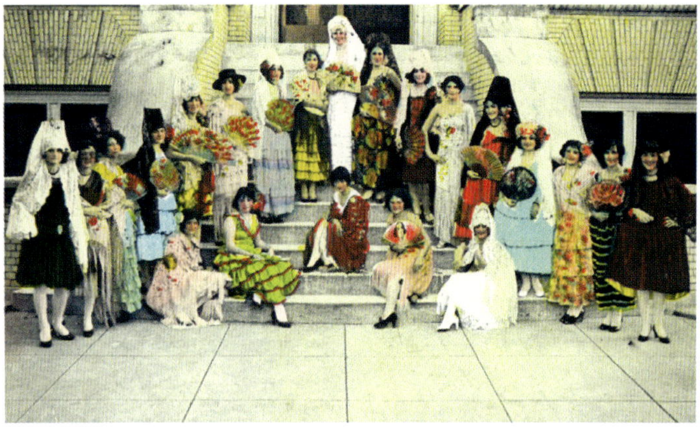

Glorious urban *mestizas* dressed for a party. Tarjeta Postal, Mexico City, 1934, dated on the 3 x 6 in. postcard. Made in Mexico

Below:
A stunning *Señorita* with a lovely Spanish dress, tiara, *mantilla*, and fan, a 17 in. composition doll that resembles the *mestizas* on the postcard. 1940s, made in Mexico.

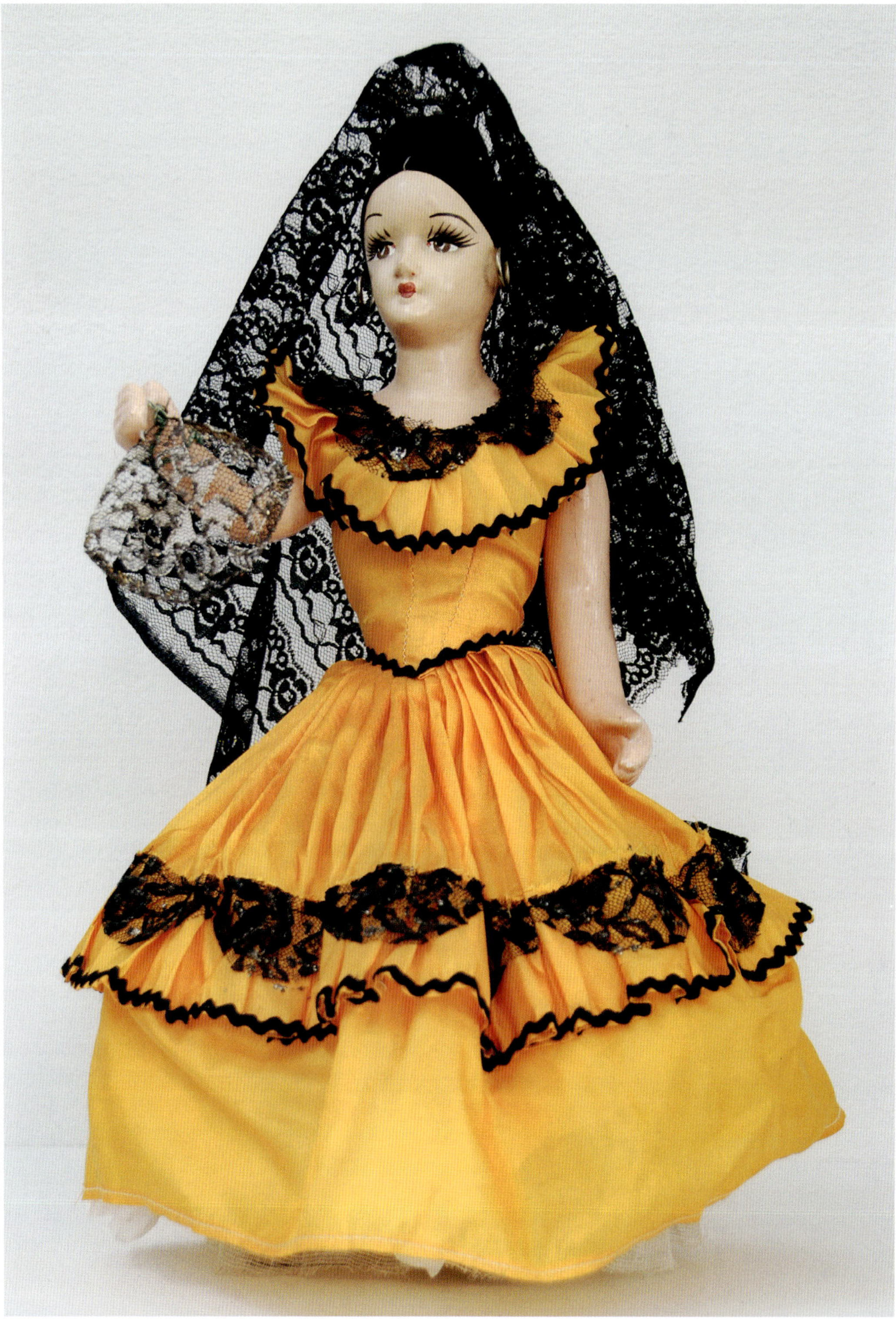

The *China Poblana* Costume

The most striking female *mestiza* costume is that of the *China Poblana* . It is the most common costume found on vintage Mexican dolls and undeniably one of the most beautiful dresses worn by Mexican women. It translates the *mestiza* and Indian blend, that is admired throughout the world, into a glorious festive ensemble. The many different ways in which it can be interpreted are represented by the dolls.

Although the costumes show modifications, you will always know they are dressed as a *China Poblana*. Their dress is ornate in red, green, and white, which are the national colors of the Mexican flag. The *China Poblana's* colorful costumes offered doll makers an opportunity to show their talents, so you will see many different ways in which she is dressed. She wears an elaborate costume with profusely embroidered sequined skirts and a *huipil* or *blusa* made with gold threads and beads. She could also be less presumptuous as a modest country *mestiza señorita* by wearing all the colors and style of the dress with minimal embroidery. You see her dancing to the *Jarabe Tapatio* (Mexican hat dance), the national dance of Mexico, or proudly celebrating one of the many Mexican holidays.

Her costume includes a peasant style white *blusa* made of either silk or cotton. The neckline is usually bordered with extraordinary embroidery of flora. The long shawl around her shoulders, crossed in front or worn as headpiece, is her colorful *rebozo.* Sometimes she will wear a large women's' *sombrero* that is trimmed with gold or silver threading and embroidery. The most beautiful item is the skirt, referred to as the *zagalejo*. It is a full-bodied red skirt accented with profuse embroidery, often with a contrasting green colored, saw-tooth trim along the border of the hem and at the waist. The material of the skirt is rayon, silk, or a less expensive red *castor*. Chinese sequins, spangles, and *papelillo* glass beading, called *pepenado,* in patriotic themes will adorn the skirt as well as the blouse.

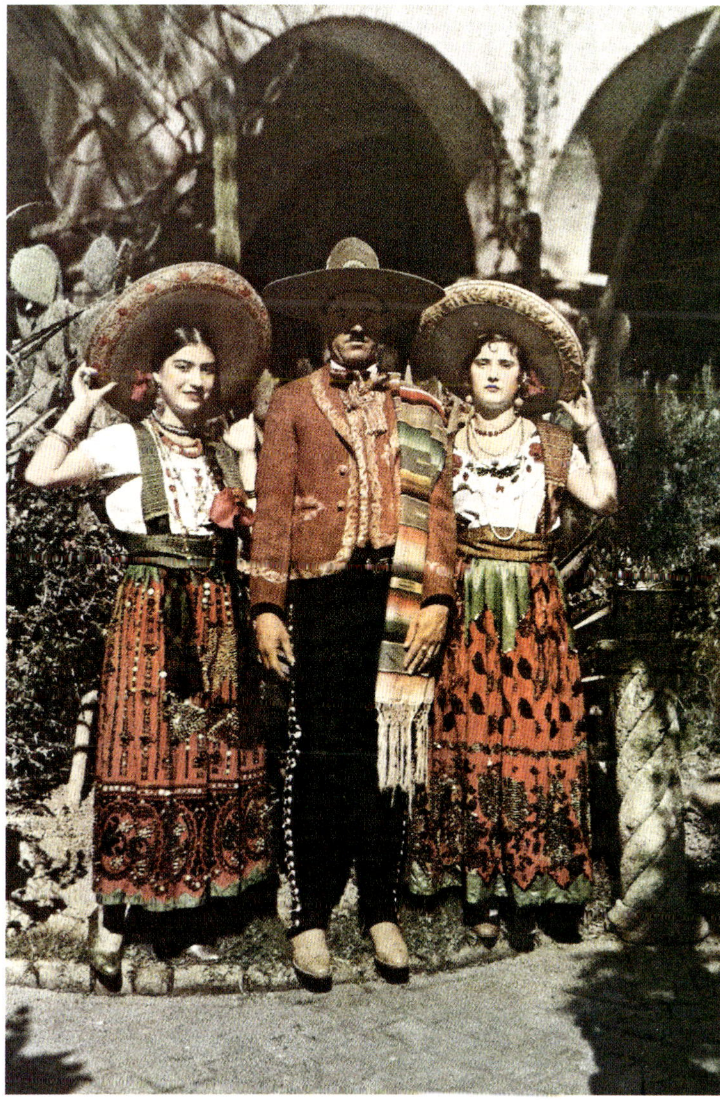

A color print, *China Poblanas* and *Charros,* 1934.

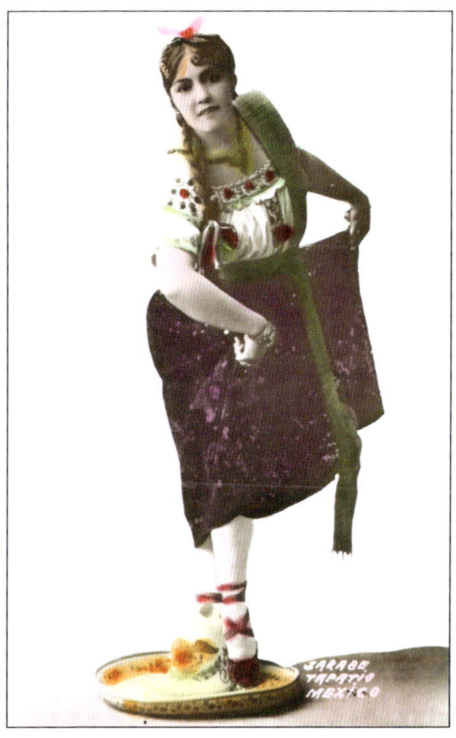

A color tinted photograph postcard, "Mestiza Dancing the Jarabe Tapatio," Mexico City, early 20th century, Mexico D.F $10 to 15

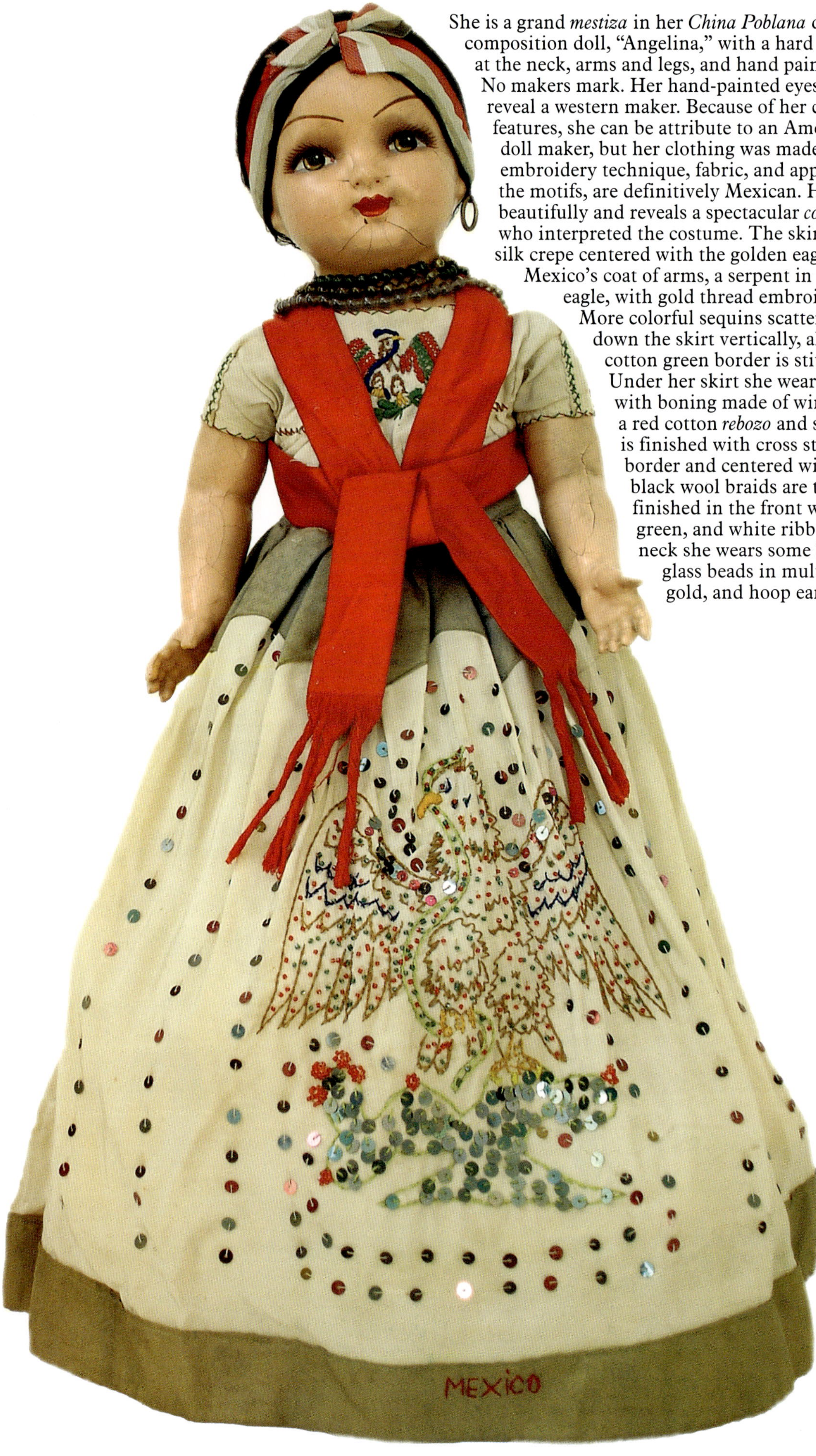

She is a grand *mestiza* in her *China Poblana* dress, this 23 in. composition doll, "Angelina," with a hard stuffed body, jointed at the neck, arms and legs, and hand painted detail, c.1930s. No makers mark. Her hand-painted eyes and fair complexion reveal a western maker. Because of her crazing and facial features, she can be attribute to an American or Canadian doll maker, but her clothing was made in Mexico. The embroidery technique, fabric, and application, along with the motifs, are definitively Mexican. Her full skirt opens beautifully and reveals a spectacular *costurera* (seamstress) who interpreted the costume. The skirt's fabric is a fine silk crepe centered with the golden eagle on the cactus, Mexico's coat of arms, a serpent in the mouth of the eagle, with gold thread embroidery and sequins. More colorful sequins scatter in the front and down the skirt vertically, all around. On the cotton green border is stitched "MEXICO." Under her skirt she wears a cotton petticoat with boning made of wire hoops. He wears a red cotton *rebozo* and silk *blusa*. Her *blusa* is finished with cross stitches along the border and centered with an eagle. Long black wool braids are tied at the back and finished in the front with Mexico's red, green, and white ribbons. Around her neck she wears some beautiful *papelillo* glass beads in multi-tones of green and gold, and hoop earrings. $550 to 1100

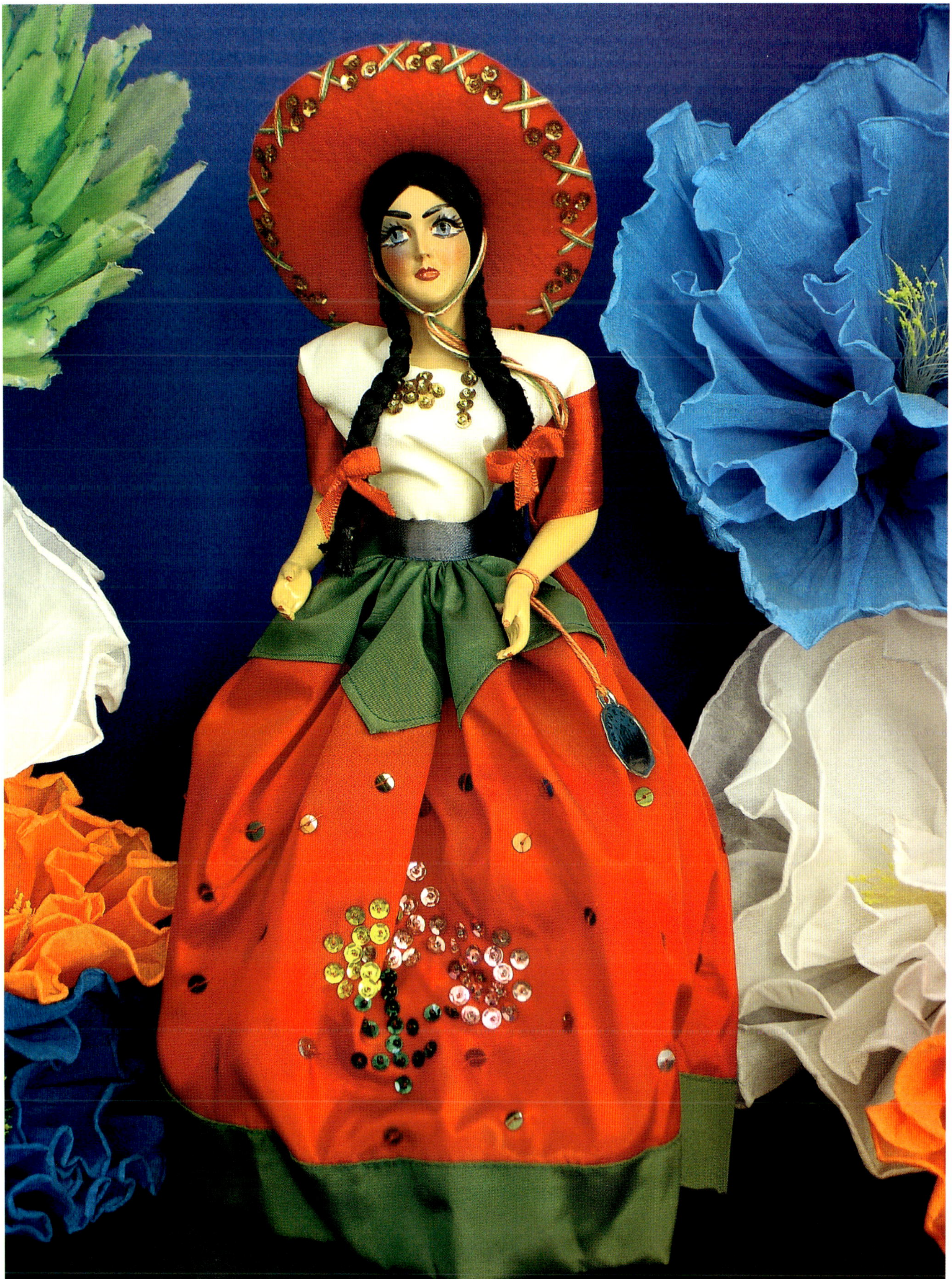

A typical 13 in. Mexican *China Poblana* doll from the 1950s, made by Carselles; she is also a *charra* dressed in traditional green and red rayon from Mexico City. She wears a sequined skirt and top with *rebozo*, a red felt *sombrero,* and has detailed, hand-painted features. Mint condition in box. $50 to 125

The *China Poblana* costume was adopted from a folklore legend of a captured exotic princess. There are many versions of this folkloric tale, but in spite of the discrepancies all of the many stories depict her as a fascinating woman.

A book, written in 1960 by Louise A. Stinetorf, *La China Poblana*, is a fictional rendition of this mysterious woman of the 17th century and it created an even more mystifying evolution of this costume. She is presented as the spiritual "Joan of Arc of Mexico," with added theory as well as decades of research on who she may have been. The story depicts a harem princess who becomes one of Mexico's national heroines. The choice of white on her costume represents snow-capped volcanoes, the green represented palm trees, and the red was for spilled blood of others who had suffered heroic endeavors. Coincidentally, the same colors were chosen for the Mexican national flag for the same reasons, and its design is often credited to *La China.* The story of to this costume is charming, but the nebulous history of its origin only adds intrigue. It is a costly costume for the wearer and became so elaborate that it could only be worn for special occasions. In honor of *La China Poblana*, a monument was built in Puebla over a large tiled fountain at the northern end of the city.

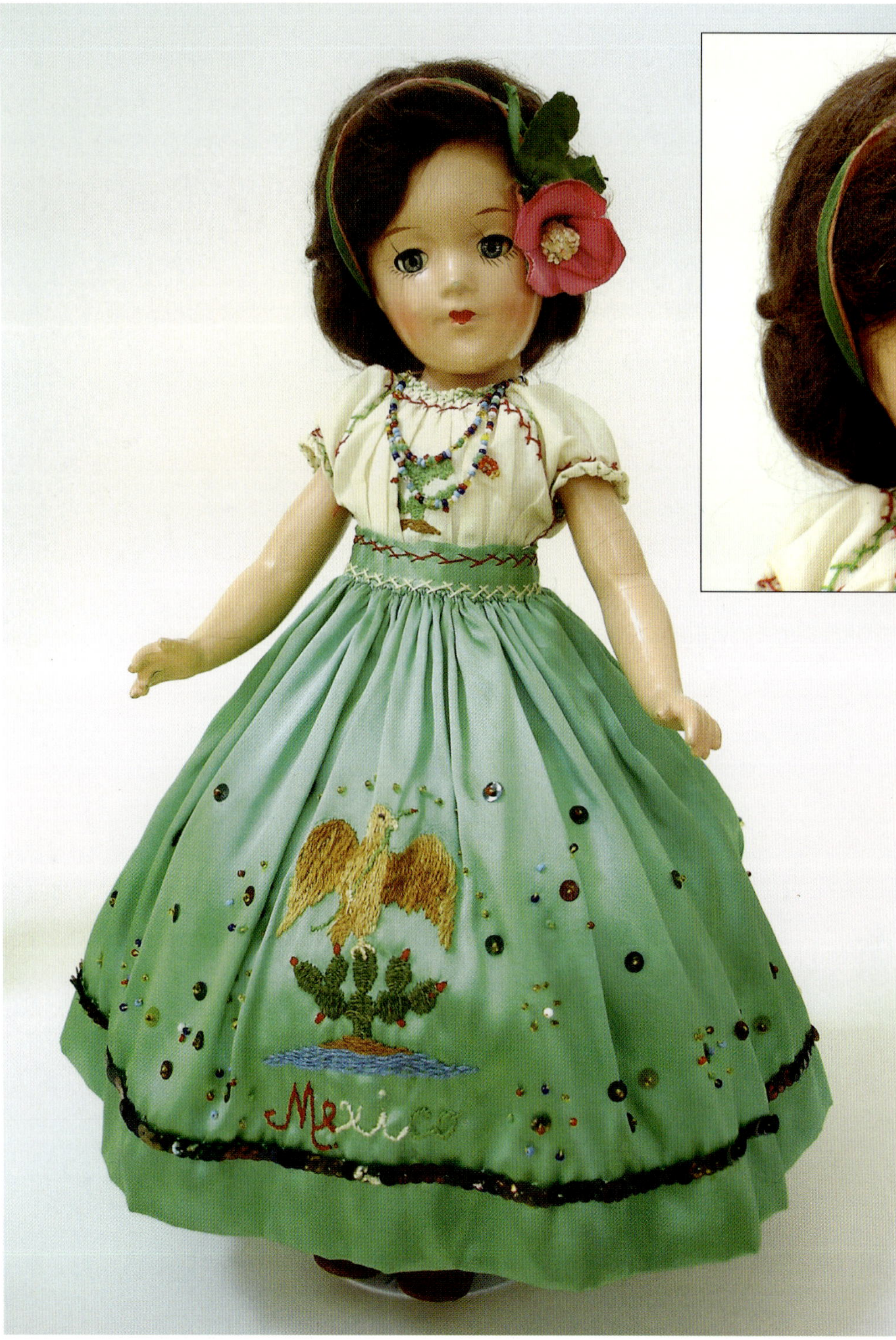

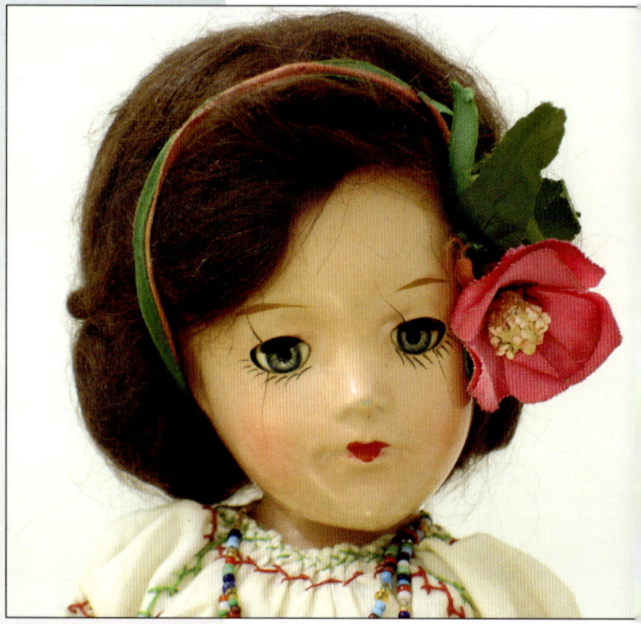

"Tonita's" smooth composition face has little crazing and wonderful detail with blinking eyes, and she resembles many favorite American character dolls from her period. Colorful margarita flowers in her hair accent her blushed complexion. Made in the USA. (See Dedication for more of Tonita.) $150 to 400

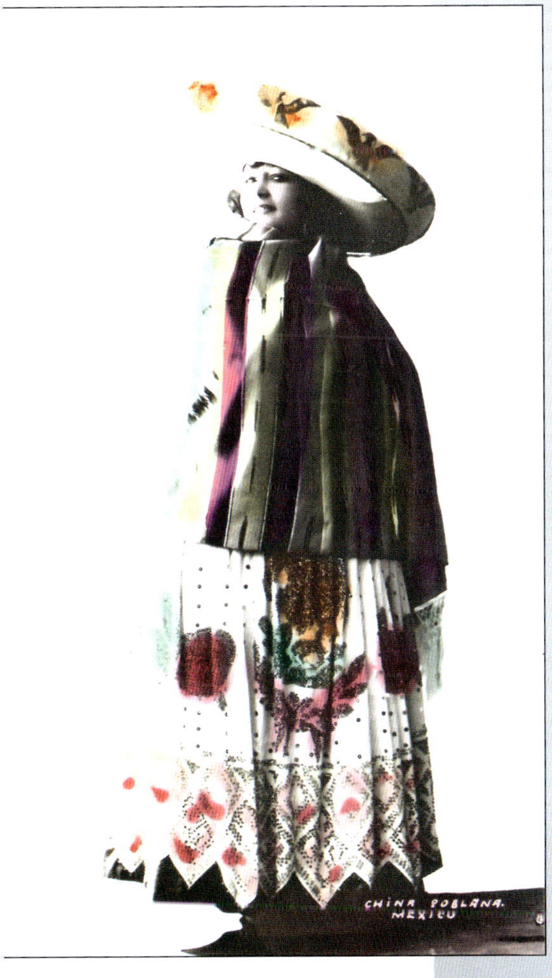

A color tint photograph postcard, "China Poblana Mexico," 20th century, 3 x 5 in., Mexico D.F. $10 to 15

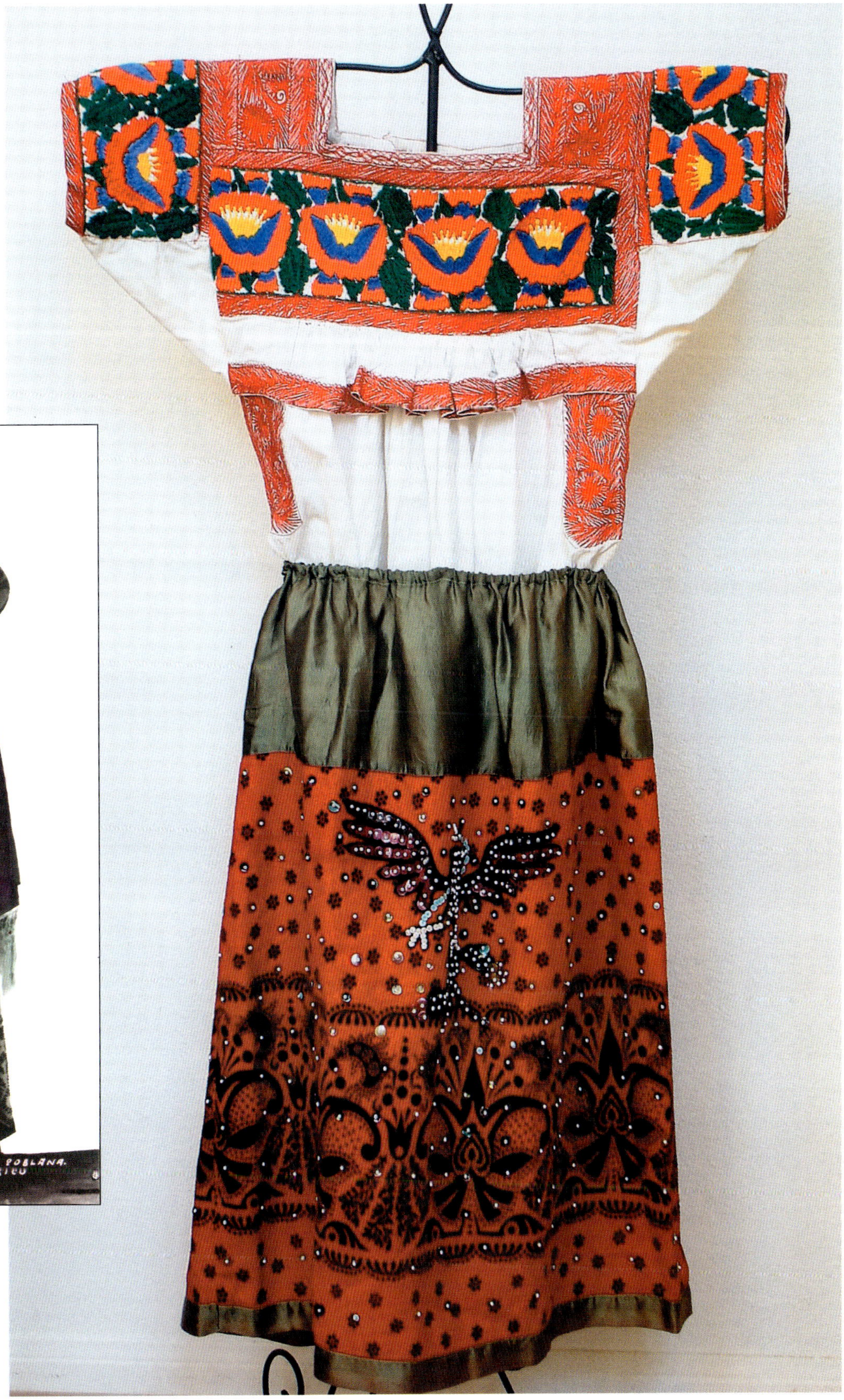

An original *mestiza China Poblana* costume, c.1940s. The Mexican blouse has geometric interlocking machine patterning combined with hand applied satin stitch borders at the neckline and sleeves. Oaxacan inspired, it has bold colors and beautiful detail with additional ruffle above the breast bone,.The skirt, in calf length, is made of red *castor* flannel with green silk satin. The waist is adjusted with a string. A combination of embroidery and black ink tinted stenciled motif, sequins, beading, and classic embroidery trims this garment that is still worn for festivals and dances. $250 to 500 set

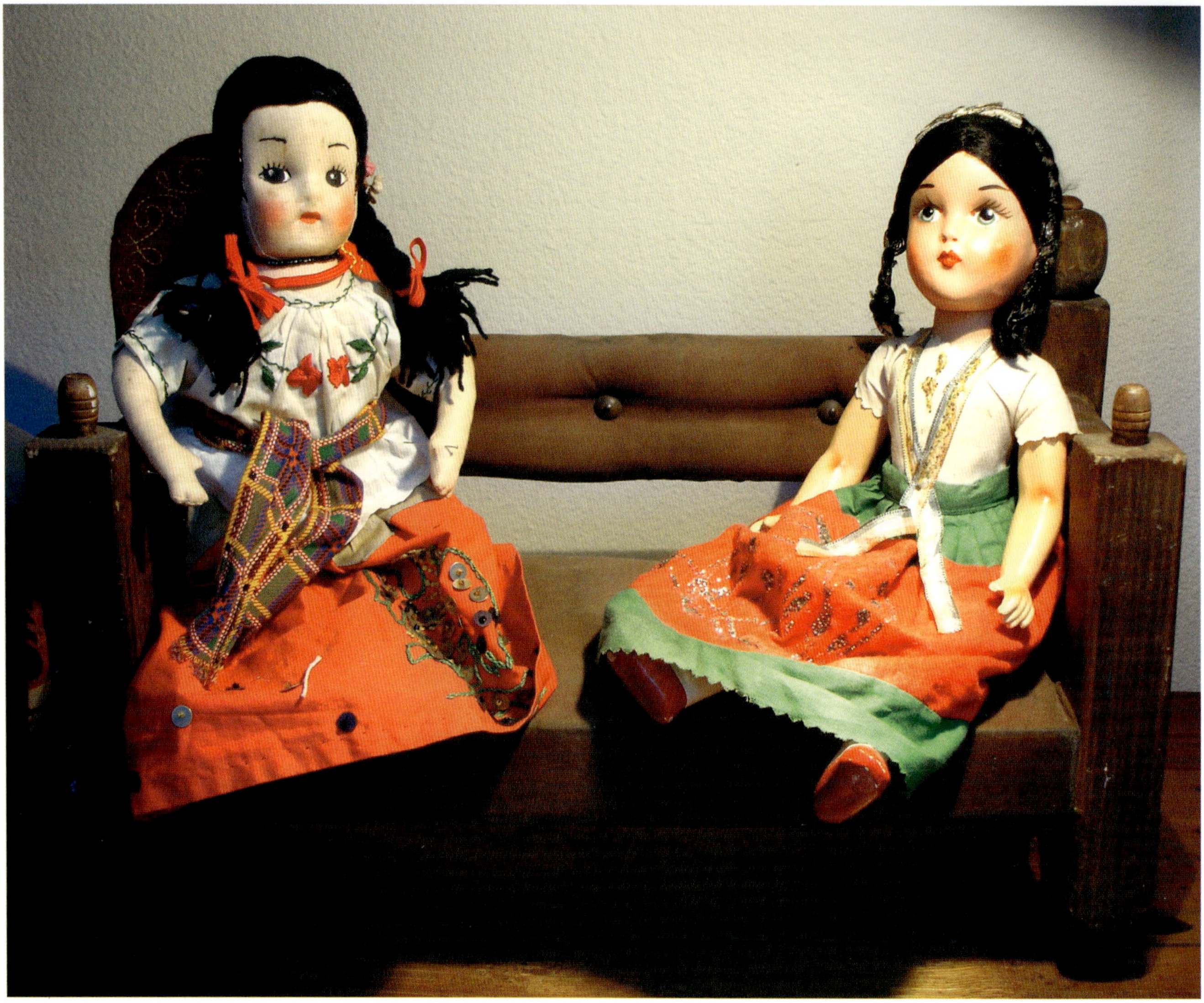

An Averill-style, 17 in. cloth doll, c.1940, hard body dressed as a *mestiza* with beautiful detail, black wool yarn hair, USA. She is with her friend a solid 16 in. composition doll, strung and jointed, hand painted detail like that of the China Poblana,c1950s,made in Europe (Italy). Mexican leather and mesquite bench,c1930s. Dolls $75 to $200

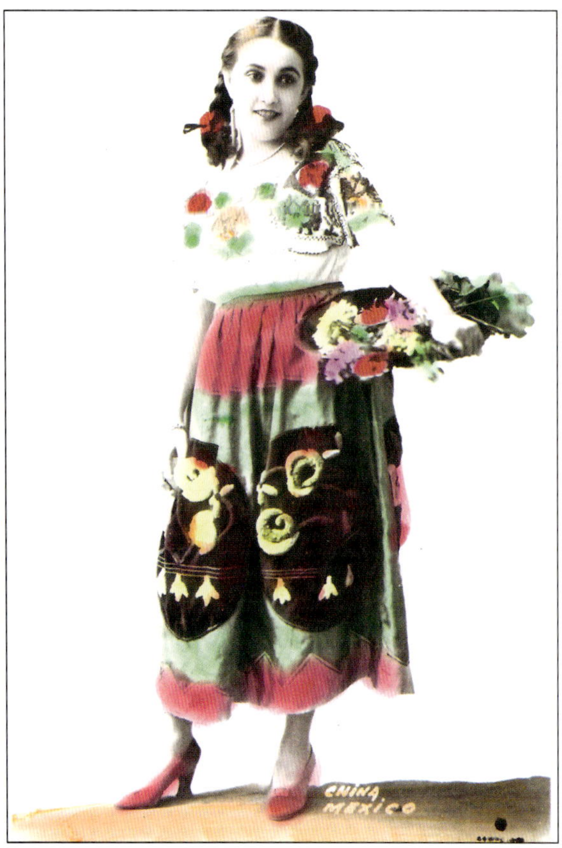

Left:
Color tint postcard photograph, "China Joven" with her large basket of flowers, c.1930s, Mexico D. F. 3 x 5 in. $10 to $15

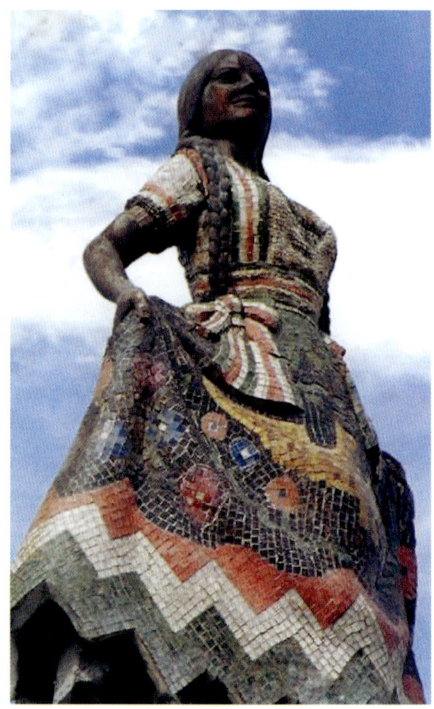

A statue built in honor of the *China Poblana*, in Puebla Mexico. A colorful tiled tribute to the costume rests on a large tiled fountain, 2005.

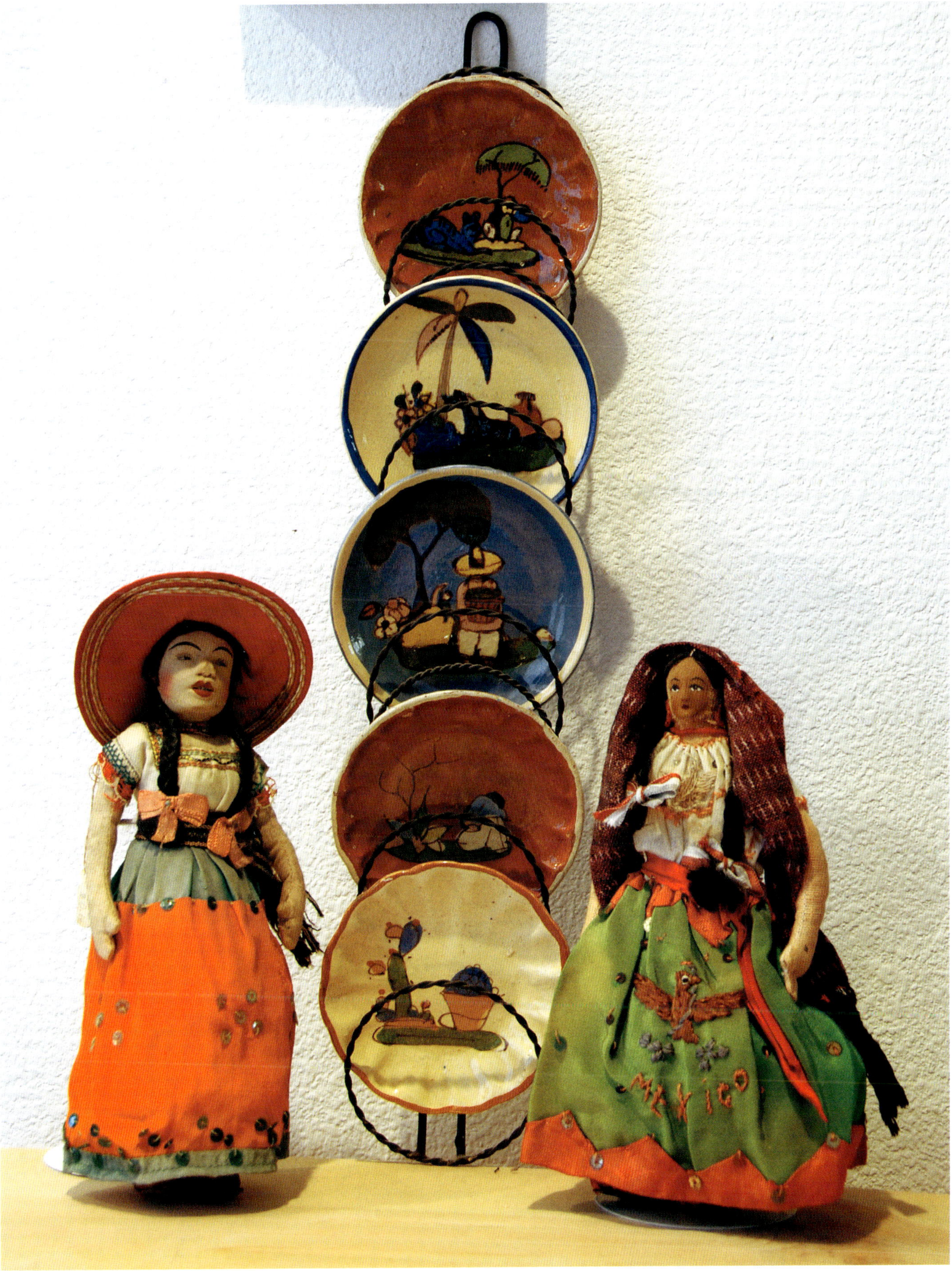

Two dazzling cloth *China Poblana* dolls, 1920s, with meticulous details. They are small, 9 in. dolls, but their costumes are phenomenal, of rich detail, and thier faces are tinted darker. They stand in front of Tlaquepaque saucers in various colors and styles. $60 to 100 ea.

Accessories

Mexican skill in textiles, shown through their clothing, is a brilliant example of diversity in the Mexican culture. But you must also admire the magnificence of their accessories, which include many items of nature transformed into wonderful pieces of jewelry, hairpieces, and sashes. The ingenuity of Mexican jewelry makers is exemplified by the materials they used.

Mexico's abundant resources furnish many materials for making needed accessories that have never been frivolous. The hills of Mexico hold silver and gold, and its shores and oceans are filled with shells and pearls. Nothing of beauty went unnoticed by Mexican artisans. Shell, seeds, stones, and fibers could be transformed into marketable jewelry, just as well as silver. The Indians discovered numerous ways to convey beauty through nature, instrumentally as well as aesthetically. Natural dyes turned hardened seeds of the cocoa, squash, sunflower or other indigenous seeds into wearable art. Gemstones such as amber and lapis were shaped *en cabochon;* quartz, jade, and so many semi-precious stones were worked Cut red coral, incised shells, pearls, and fish vertebra were just a few of the choice materials available, and iridescent fish scales sequined their skirts. Necklaces, earrings, bracelets, encrustations, ribbons, and yarn would adorn their necks as well as their hair. Glass beads were introduced by the Spaniards in trade and were prized by indigenous people. The Indians mix and blend glass beads of opaque color as well as tinted tones. Their beaded necklaces vary. Symbolic significance as well as visual beauty grounds their jewelry to their definable heredity. They wear beautiful beads made from paper-thin glass with an enameled finish and known as *papelillo.* They come in brilliant colors and are usually of four or more strands and finished with satin sash streamers at the end.

The world has acknowledge the Mexicans' talent in silver jewelry. Oaxacan silver mines contributed greatly to the abundance that was available and much of its silver jewelry from the late 1930s to the 1960s is still highly in demand. Silver *tallers* (workshops) of Taxco are surely the most famous today and since they were established in the 1940s. A few of the dolls shown here have some Mexican silver jewelry pieces, but by no means do they include the fabulous silver of Taxco.

The skirts were held in place with waist sashes that would secure the often voluminous folds of cloth. One type of sash is the *soyate,* named for a flat woven twill reed. It is a highly functional sash still worn by many women in the states of Puebla and Oaxaca. Many beautiful sash styles are worn by almost all of the Indian women. Prized for their decorative value, sashes sometimes enhance an otherwise somber skirt and top. Mexican sashes also hold a medicinal value and old customary beliefs, so they are an essential part of the clothing that a woman would not be without.

In her hair or around her head, Mexican women wore traditional costume pieces. The *resplandor,* worn by *Tehuana* women, is a unique headdress for special occasions that is made with stiff white lace. The folklore that explains from where this piece originated is quite fascinating. It is told that there was a young Indian woman who found a white cotton item of clothing floating in the ocean tide. It was actually a European child's petticoat, but to the native woman it was so beautiful that she wore it on her head and tied it at the back. It was then copied by others and adapted as part of their costume.

Women also wear woven headband sashes or colorful ribbons that are braided into their hair in a variety of ways. Incorporating designs from their ancestors as well as using continental inspiration, they have always ornamented themselves with items that are important to them. Complimenting their clothing with jewelry and accentuating their garments was customary in Mexico, but not an extravagance.

The most common shoes for the Mexican woman in the 20th century were *huarache* sandals. There were various types of *huaraches*, and they were used in every home. The *huaraches* were easy to make, comfortable to wear, and fairly inexpensive, so all classes wore them. In some of the rural regions, if the people could not afford sandals they would go barefoot; sometimes because it was preferred. Many Indian women went without shoes. In the early 20th century, shoes were not a priority for the poor women; they would rather have had a rebozo or ribbons for their hair. The *mestiza* and upper class *senoritas* wore slippers and soled shoes or boots. They would be store bought or made by a local *zapatero* (shoe maker).

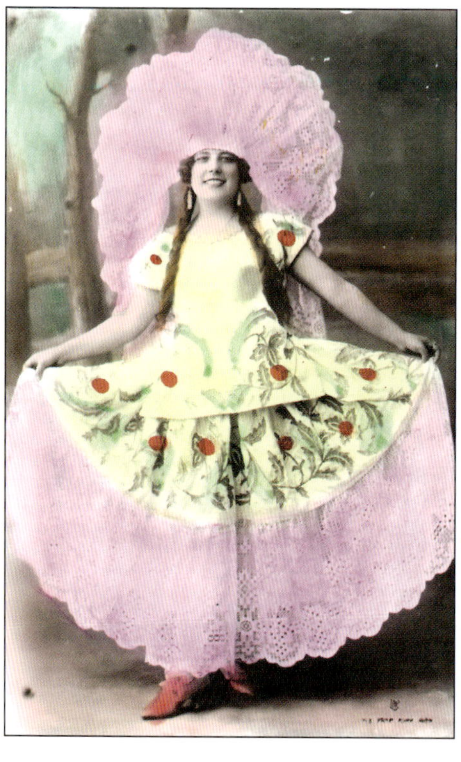

A color tinted photograph, "Pink Tehuana" maiden, Mexico, 1930s, 3 x 5 in. $15 to 40

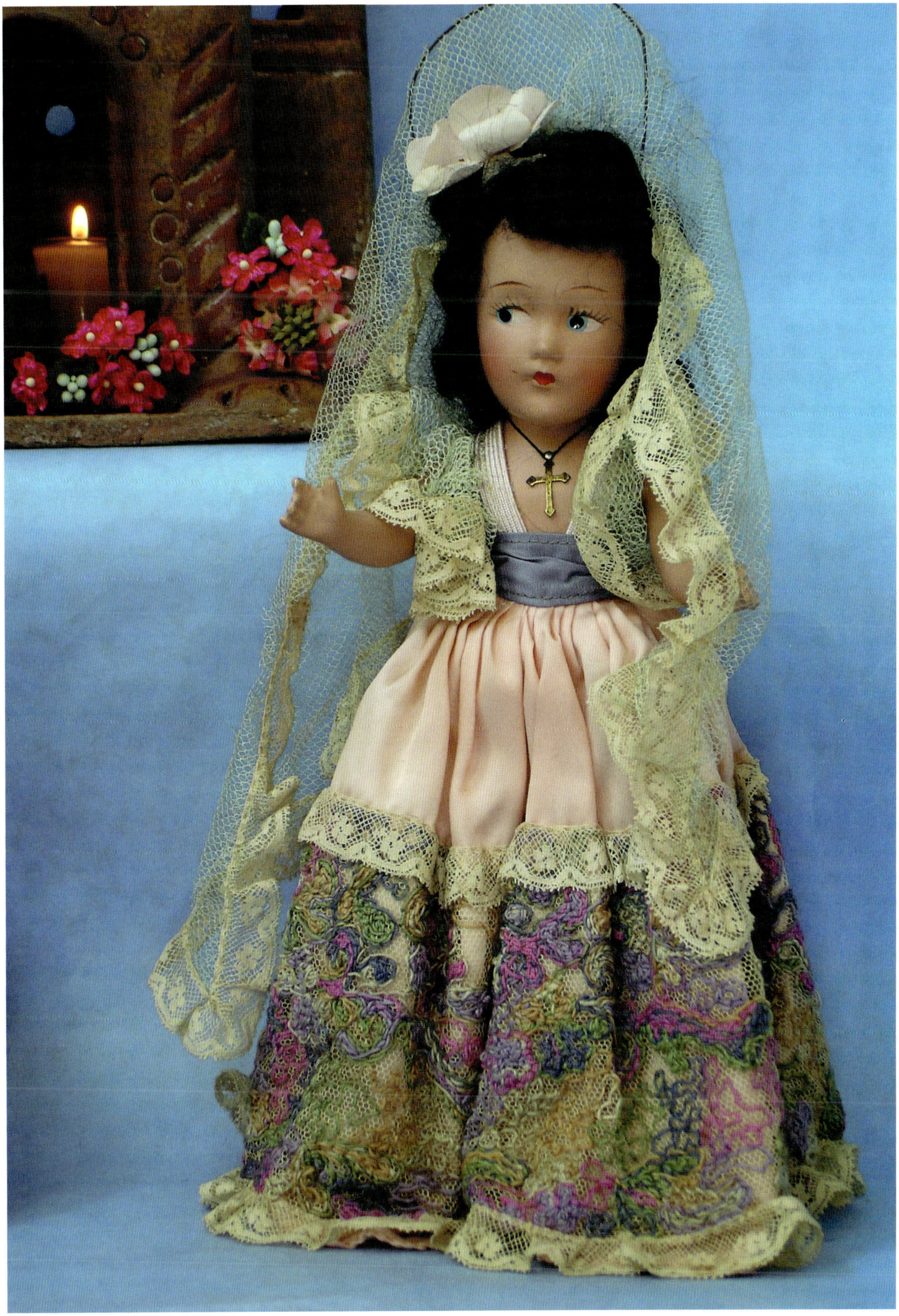

A stunning, 14 in., Dream World doll, all composition strung body, c. 1940s. She is dressed in a festive yellow and lavender lace dress with a Spanish *mantilla* over her head. Made in the USA. $75 to 125

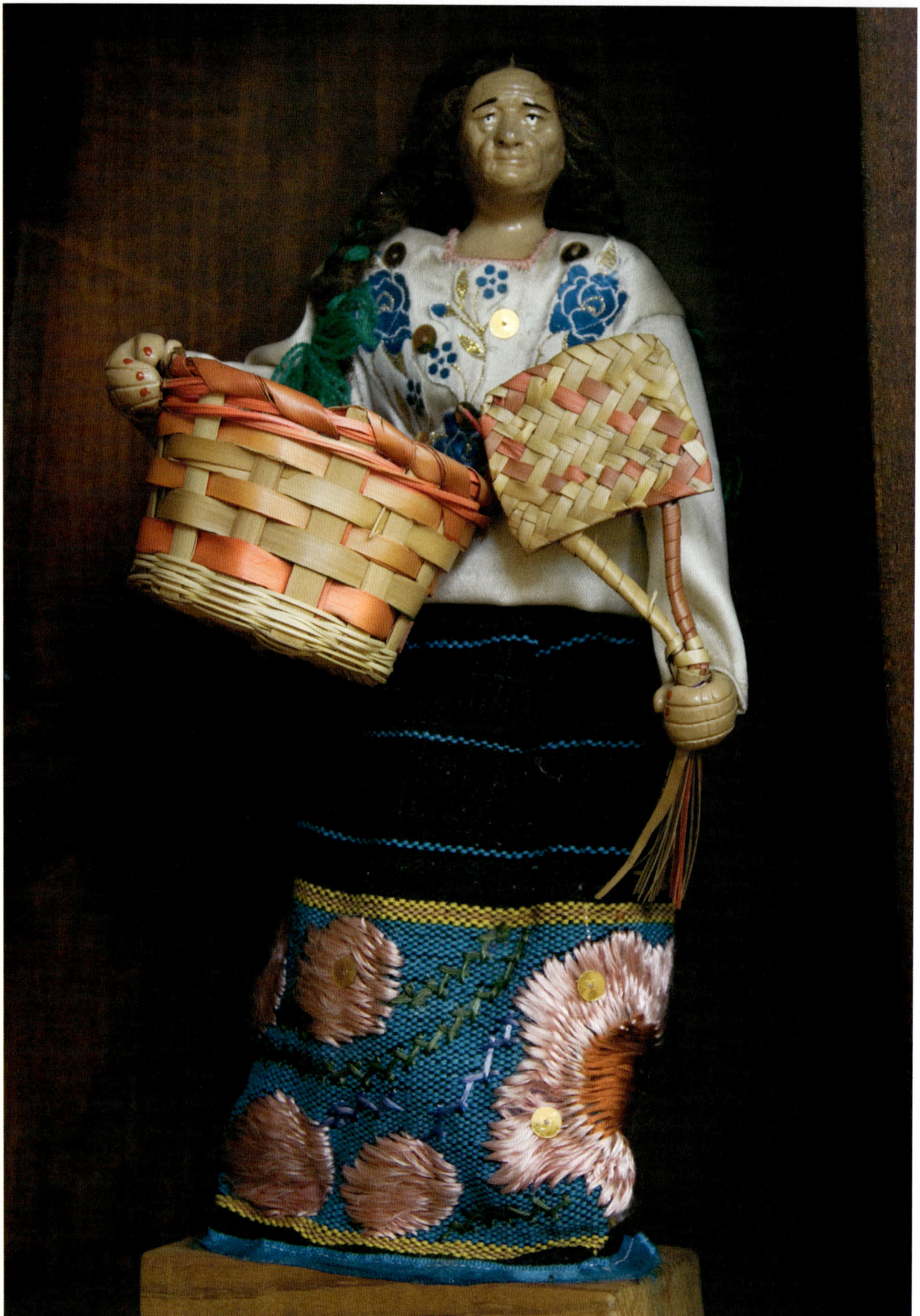

The old Nahua woman from Guerrero, c. 1950s. A 14 in. doll made of molded composition resin on a wooden base. Her facial features reveal an older Indian woman, and she wears beautiful hand-made garments. Made in Mexico $50 to 100

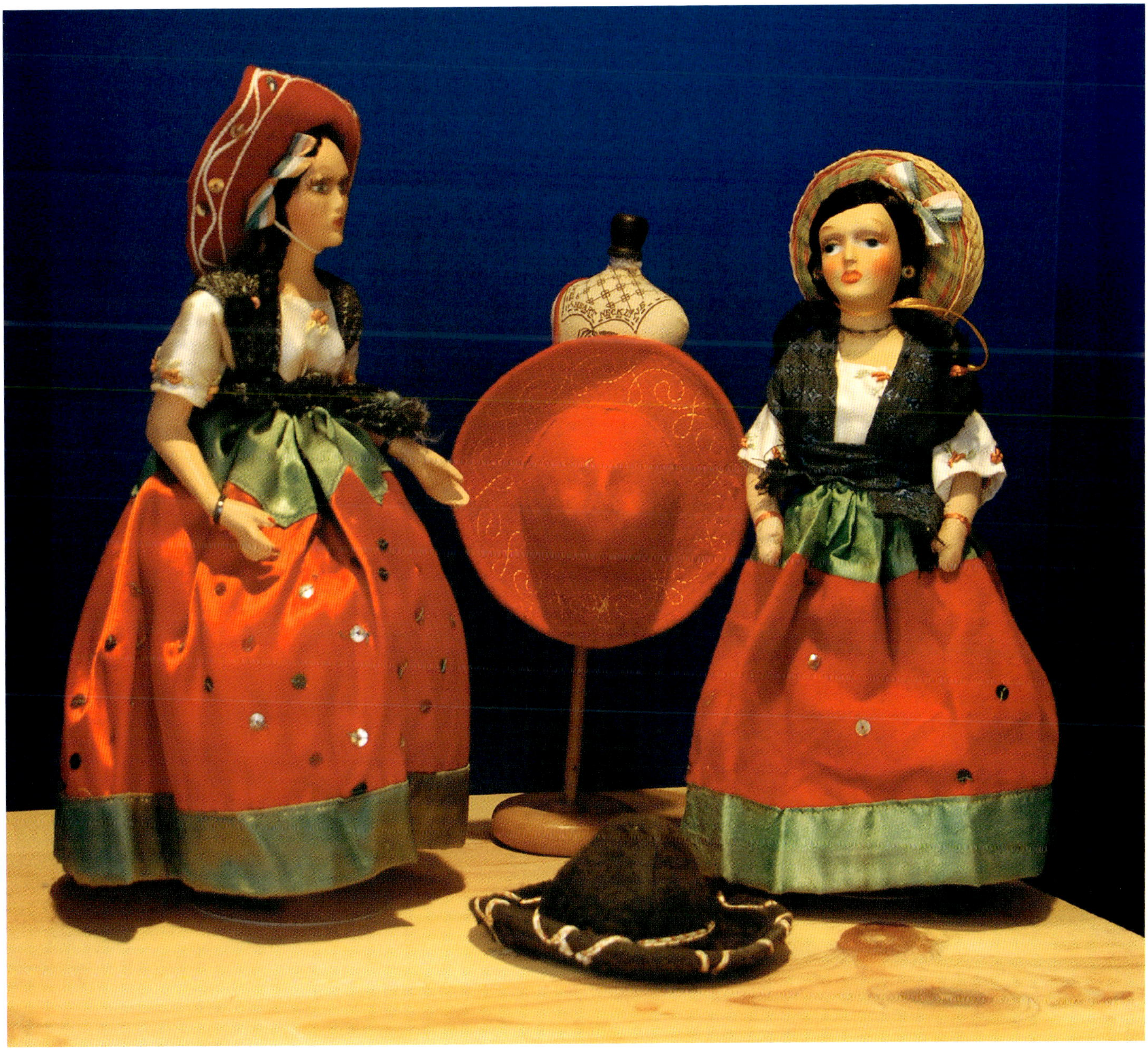

The sombrero is an essential part of the women's *charra's* costume. She loves them to be as beautiful as her dress. Two *China Poblana*, *mestiza* costumed, composition doll.s with lovely detail, airbrushed faces, mohair wigs, 12 in. and 10 in., c.1940s. $75 to 150

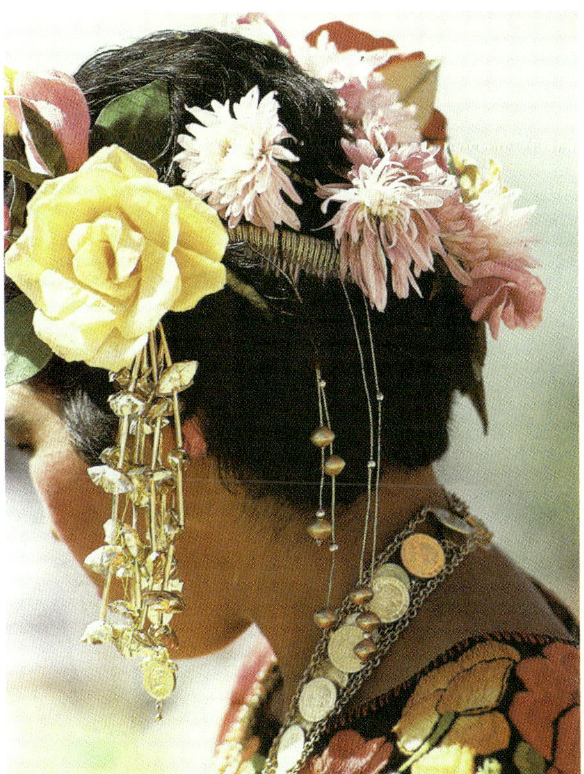

A color postcard, 5 x 4 in., 1985. A Tehuana dancer, with an abundance of beautiful accents in her hair, from Oaxaca, as seen during the Guelaguetza Festival. $5 to 15

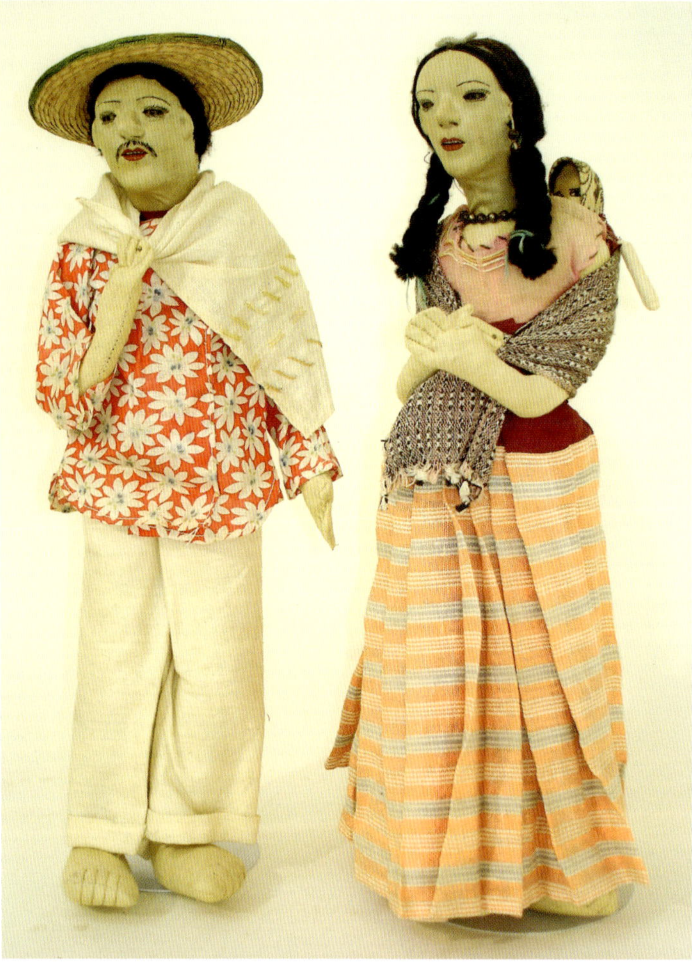

A large Indian couple, made of cloth body, hard stuffed with straw or horsehair scraps, 17 in., sometimes referred to as "Diegos" dolls, stamped Mexico, c. 1920s. The female carrys her baby in a woven indigo and white *rebozo*, and she has a black wool braided wig and glass beads for earrings. A pink *huipil* and an indigenous *enredo* skirt pleated fully at the back, and bare feet. Inset features under molded sculpted faces with painted eyebrows, eyelashes, and lips. Glass beaded necklace and a woven *rebozo*.
He wears *manta* clothing, with a colorful shirt and white pants, a white *quechquémitl* cape knotted around his shoulders, with mitten-stitched hands and feet. He has a vintage flower print on his shirt and cross stitching on his *quechquemitl tuarra* cape, painted eyebrows, moustache, eyelashes, and lips. On his head are a black wool wig and a finely woven *sombrero* accented with a green border. Mint condition. $150 to 300

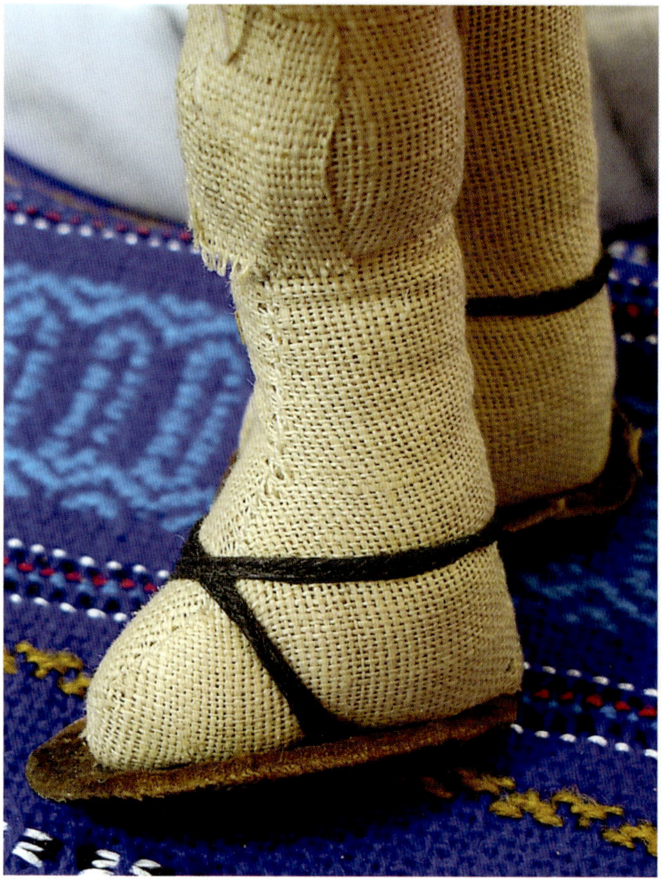

A leather strap *huaraches* sandal on a cloth doll's foot. The sole is a simple cut-out with thin leather strips for the straps. The legs show the porous fiber of the *manta* cloth.

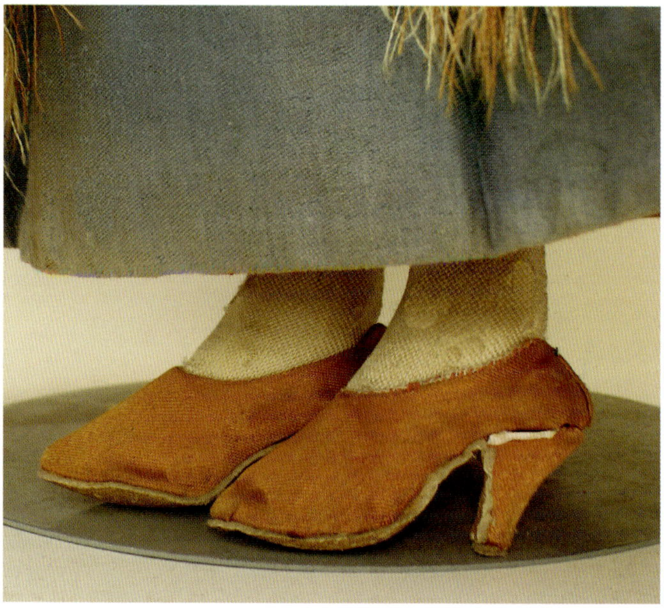

A closer look at "Sonia," the large cloth boudoir doll's sateen slippers with card heal. Made in Mexico, see Sonia again in the "*La Ropa Tipica*" section of this book.

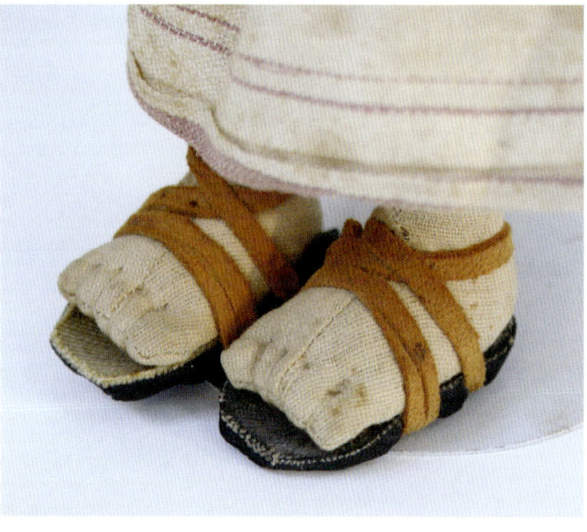

The *huaraches* sandals are the most popular shoes for the Indians and *mestizos*, these are stamped Mexico, c.1920s. Leather and cloth are stitched and glued together under the inner sole.

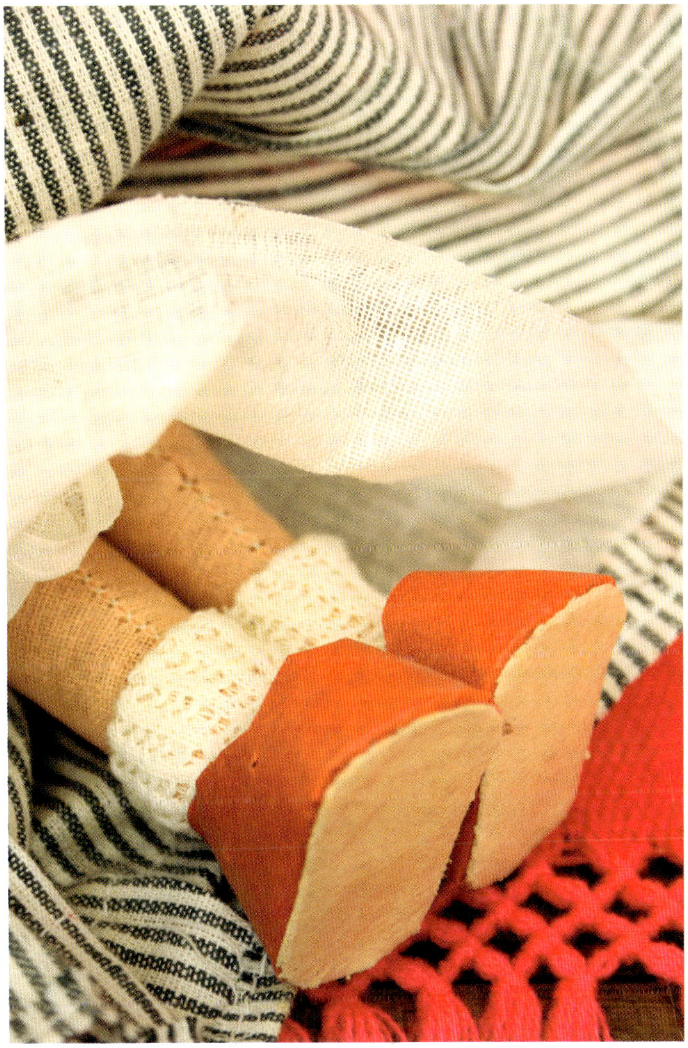

The red paper shoes on a cloth doll and her knitted socks, c.1940s, made in Mexico. See the doll again in the " La Falda" section of this book.

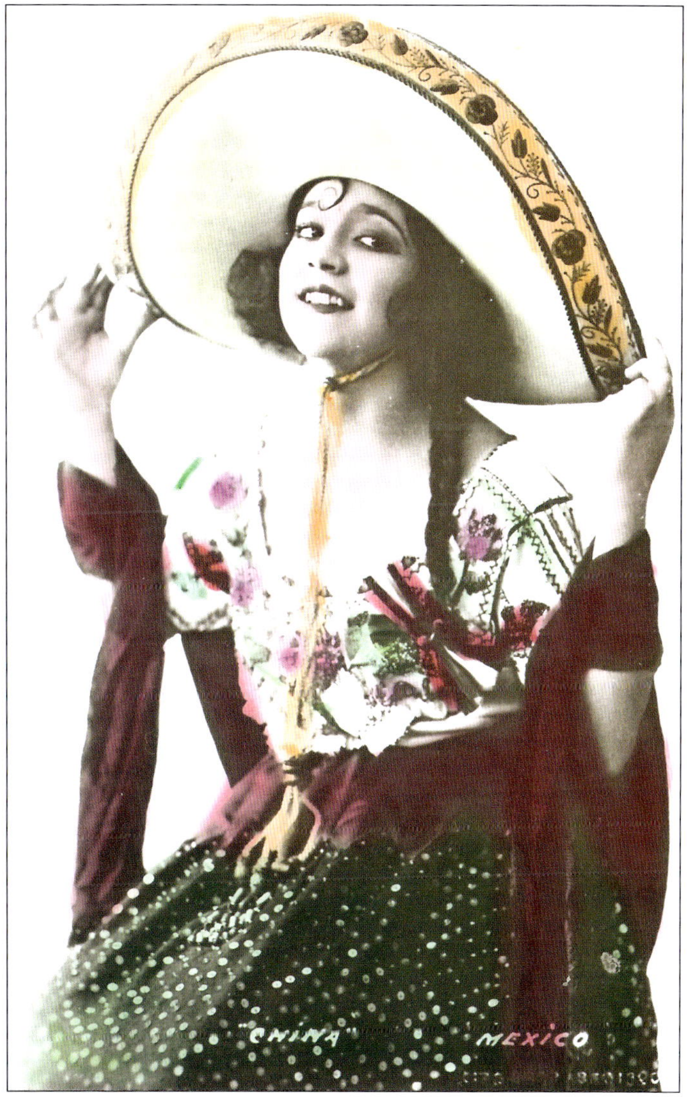

A color tinted photograph, "China" maiden, Mexico, 1930s, 3 x 5 in. $10 to 15

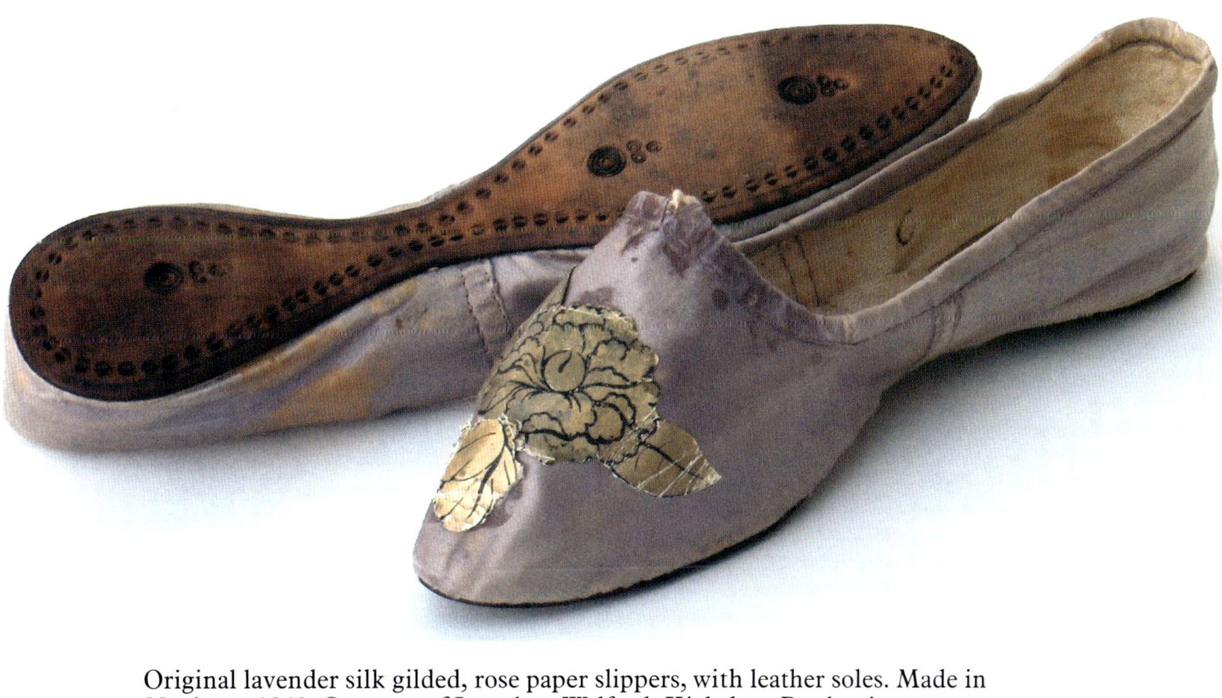

Original lavender silk gilded, rose paper slippers, with leather soles. Made in Mexico, c 1840, Courtesy of Jonathan Walford, Kickshaw Productions

Part 4
The *Mestizo* and Indian Men

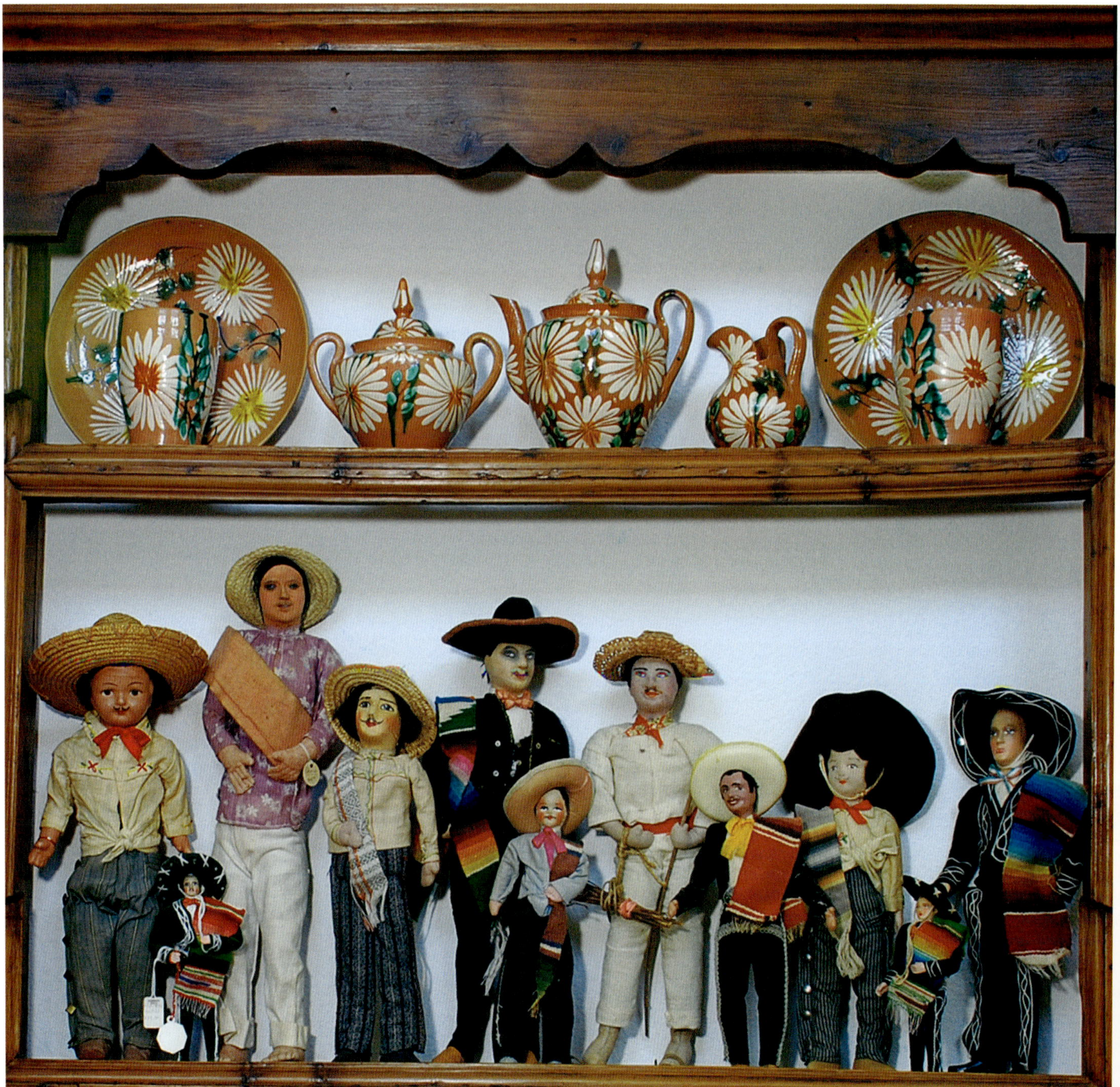

Los Hombres, a group of old Mexico dolls portraying men, displayed on an early 20th c. colonial-style shelf.

A typical Mexican *hombre* (man) during the 20th century always wore a *sombrero* (hat) and carried a *serape* (blanket). They would wear *huaraches* (sandals) and a sash belt to hold up their white pants. These garments are recognized worldwide as Mexican. The costumes of the male dolls reveal differences between indigenous Indians and the *mestizo* in Mexico.

Spanish colonists and urban life had strong influences on Indian men's clothing. The men were the family members most likely to travel outside the village, so it was they who adapted to changes in order to feel accepted in the larger towns. The Indians lost the use of many of their indigenous costumes, but they were the obvious contributors to Mexican costumes that we know and love today.

Mestizo dolls demonstrate this influence and change. Commercial cloth sales escalated in the early 20th century and replaced many of the traditional woven textiles. Trade and economic responsibility within the city limits encouraged changes that filtered to the villages. The convenience of buying commercial cloth became preferred, but demand was high for hand-woven textiles for both export and trade. Intricate motifs, colorful application, and weaving skills were outstanding; these increased the sales of traditional woven textiles, making them high in demand. In retrospect, the *mestizos* living near urban areas actually sold some of their traditional garments so that they could feed and support their families, and in turn they bought commercial cloth to wear. But in the more remote areas they would adhere to their indigenous clothing. By the mid-20th century, unbleached cotton muslin (*manta*) and machine made shirts and pants became the most common clothing of the Mexican man. The distinctive items mentioned earlier would help to define their origin to some degree, but not always. Although both the *mestizos* and the Indians would buy and wear *manta*, the native Indian men would always wear an indigenous garment, such as a sash, *quechquémitl*, or *serape*. Indian women took great pride in dressing their husbands and sons, so they collectively honored their traditional colors, motifs, and embroidered traits on their attire. Noticeable differences between *mestizo* and Indian doll clothing is, for the most part, expressed by the style in which the clothing is worn and its accessories. Indian men wore pants made of solid white muslin cotton, or sometimes dyed a color, that was tied with string at the waist or held up by a sash. The pants were cropped or rolled and gathered at the ankles. Pleating their shirts was common, and on occasion some embroidery identified their village. At their waist, they would tie their sash to the side. Many of the Indian's sashes had colorful motifs that held legendary as well as medicinal purposes for the wearers.

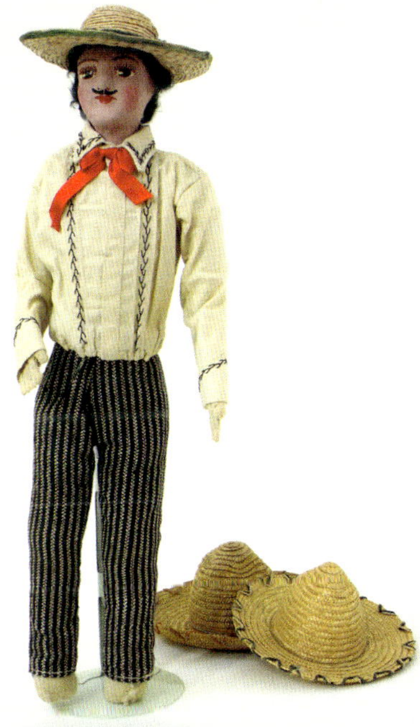

This impressive 16 in. young urban *mestizo* is wearing a typical pleated shirt with hand embroidered trim down the front, a red *moño*, wool herringbone weave print trousers. Made of hard filled cloth, his face is cloth over paper mache, with painted detail. His hair is wool and a beautifully woven *sombrero* trimmed in green. Made in Mexico $150 to 250

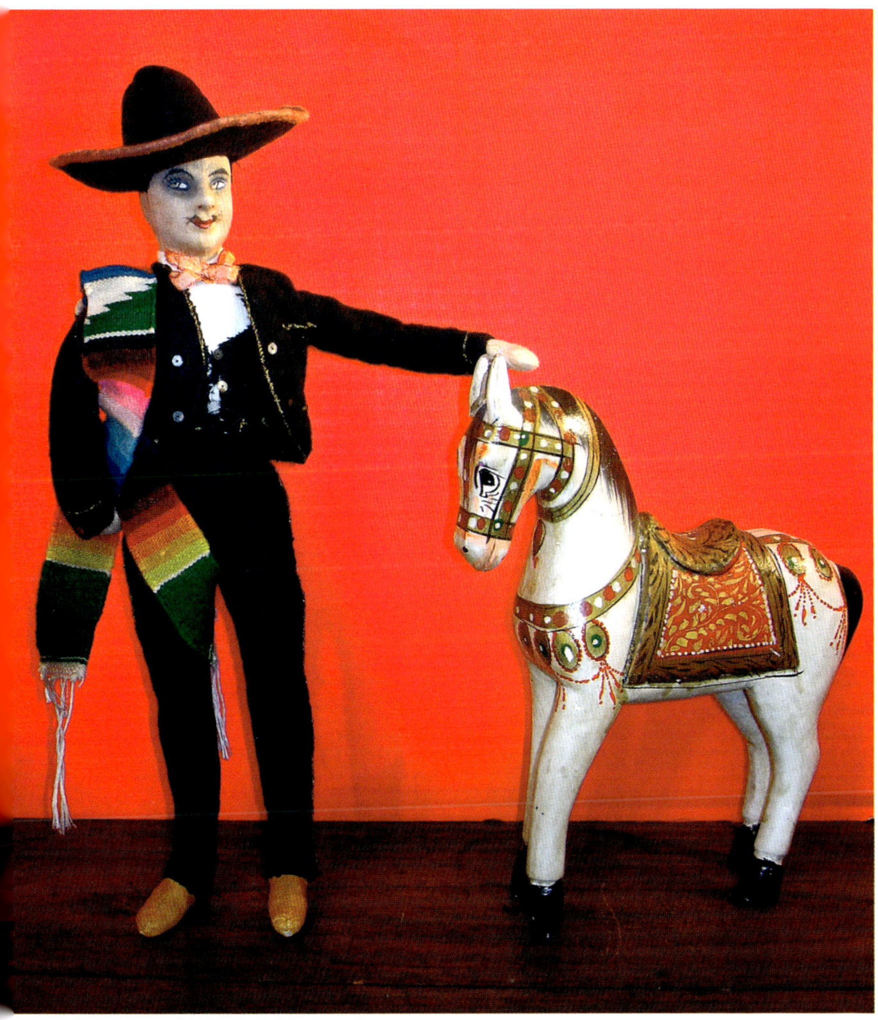

A rare Mexican *charro*, an 18 in., hard cloth doll made in Mexico, c.1930s. Molded features hand-detailed with real horse hair mustache. A side glance expression of excellent quality with black wool *charro* suit, white shirt, red *moño* (cravat), a large *sombrero*, and leather shoes. $100 to 250

Many centuries ago, the Indians of Mexico were masters of their own land. Spanish conquest imposed new laws, which altered thousands of years of traditions. The development of urban lifestyles caused the garments of the Mexican Indian to change, although ceremonial and social importance are among the few glimmers that suggest a future for indigenous clothing styles. One of the Indian costumes that prevails is that of the *Huichol* (wee-shawl) tribe, from high in central Mexico's Sierra Madres mountains. They wear the unbleached white muslin cloth, almost always decorated. Embroidered cross-stitched sacred motifs of animals and colorful stories border their pants, making them identifiable. *Huichol* Indians decorate their hats with similar color and they can be flamboyant with ribbons and pom-poms. Dried cactus woven *sombreros* with simple patterns are transformed into works of art. Many tribal differences are demonstrated by cultural influences, such as embellishing their clothing with customary skills from their past. Symbolic myths and legends influence the motifs that are embroidered on their clothing. They are a highly religious tribe who regard their folklore as truth, not myth.

A traditional costume for Indian men is the *calzón blanco*, a pair of loose pants with slits and sashes at the hem to keep them in place around the ankles. Their muslin, pleated top is oversized and collarless, and the men tie a red sash, or *faja* (long wide sash), around their waists for color and later they may be used to carry things.

Indian doll shirts are also made of *manta*, they are themselves fashioned as a *huipils*, loose fitting, buttonless, and worn outside of the pants. Like that of the *calzón blanco*, the many styles and traits vary from village to village. Their serape is a treasured possession, made to last the man many years. Some of them have openings for the head, like the poncho and the *jorongo*, and are shaped with open sides or cut to give a round or square neckline. Both wool and cotton are used, but wool is preferred. The same careful detail and beauty of their serapes can also be appreciated in their *morral* (shoulder-bag, satchel). The *morral* is a utilitarian piece, as their actual clothing usually had no pockets; their possessions are kept in their *morrals*.

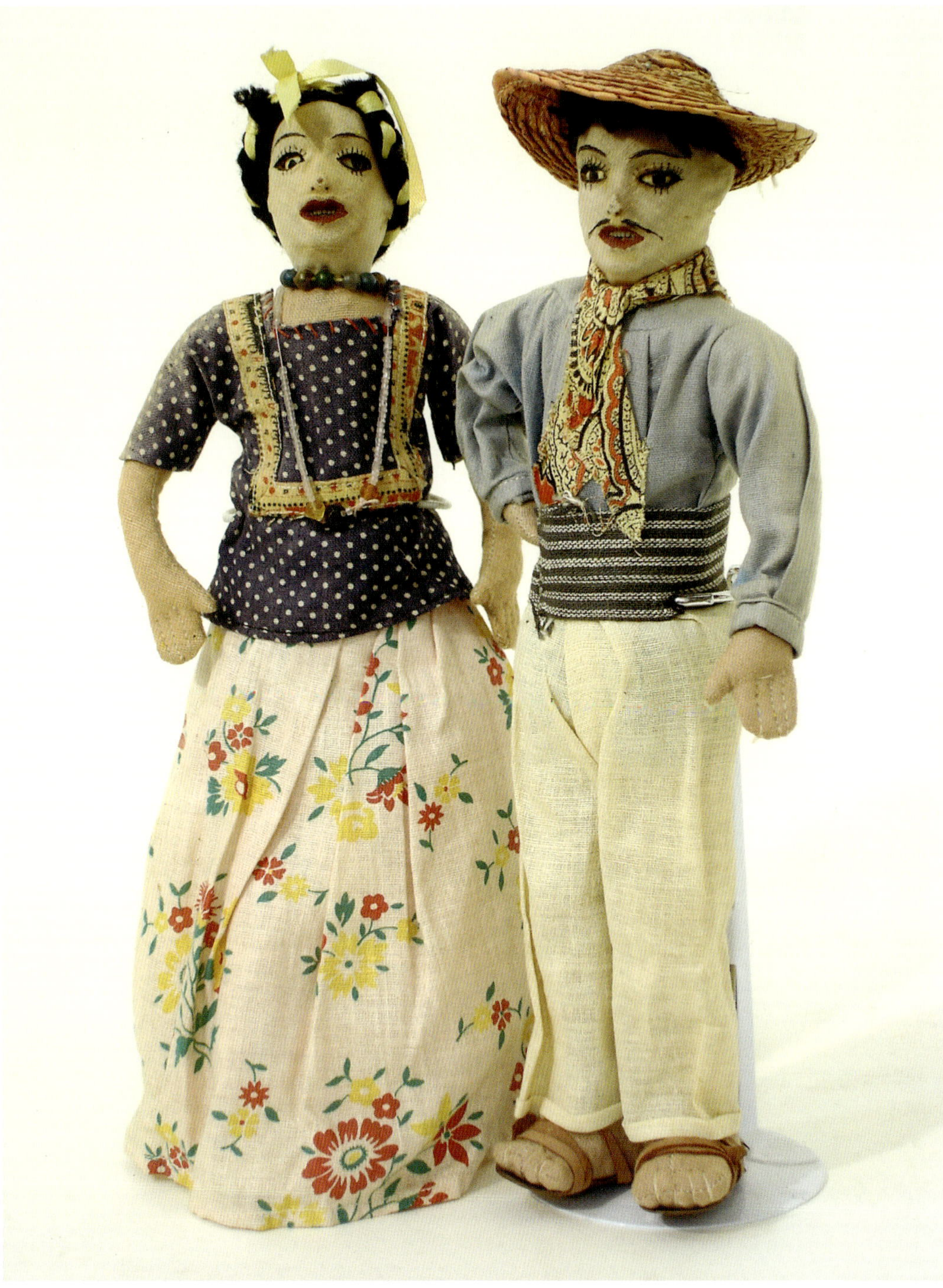

The provincial 13.5 in. Diego-style couple, "Lourdes and Pablo," stamped Mexico, c. 1920s. Inset features under their molded faces with an almost mummy-like, pasty complexion, with eyelashes, moustache, and eyebrows, incised shell teeth, aand molded ears. Lourdes is wearing a black and white polka dot cloth *huipil* with embroidered bordering, a calico *enagua* skirt of cotton and *huaraches*, glass beads, and braided hair entwined with yellow ribbon. Pablo has on a blue *manta* top and white pants, *huaraches* and smaller woven *petate* straw hat over his black wool wig. $75 to 150

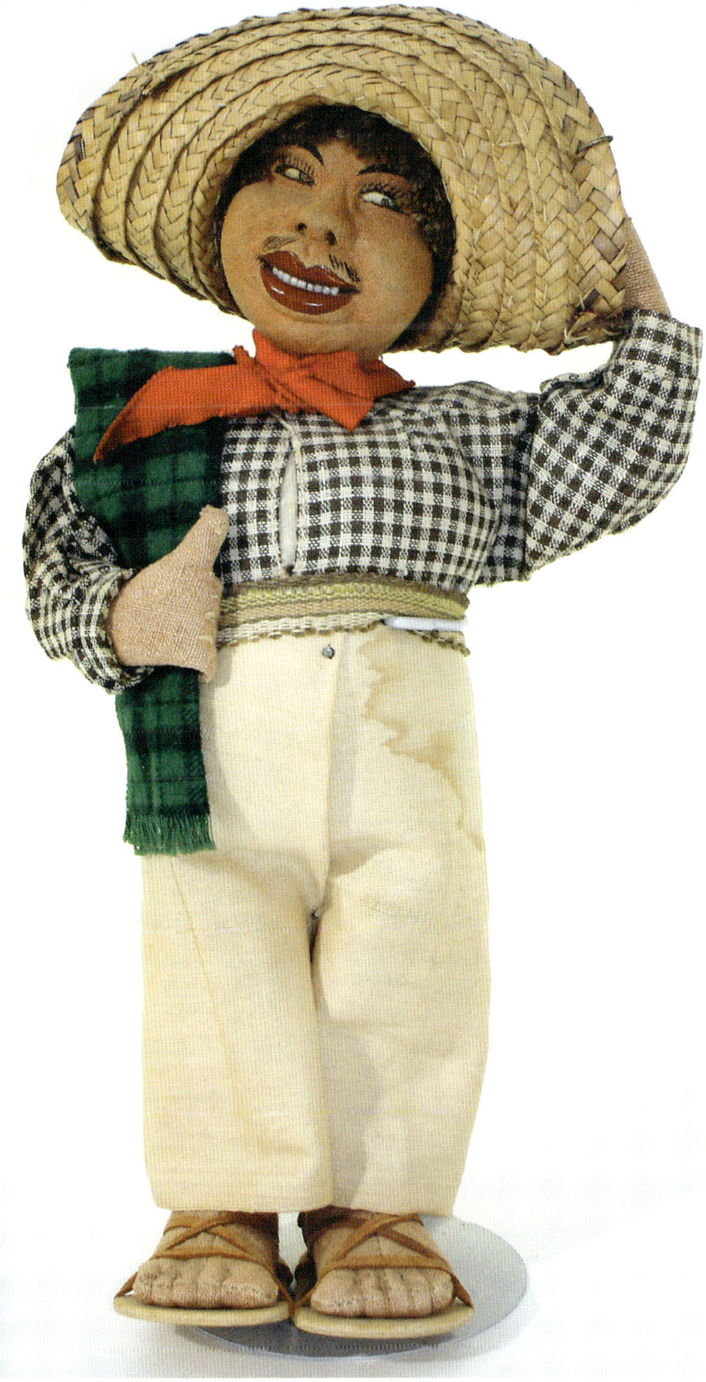

"Pancho" doll resembles "Cantinfla," a well-known Mexican character actor of the 1940s. Cloth 11 in. doll, hard-filled body with over-exaggerated feet and a very colorful appearance. He is wearing white pants, with a black and white checkered *manta* shirt, and a red *moño* with a wool serape over his right shoulder. He holds his oversized straw sombrero. and has extraordinary facial features, molded with inset eyes and teeth incised. He wears *huaraches* on his large feet. Truly a special piece of folk art. $75 to 150

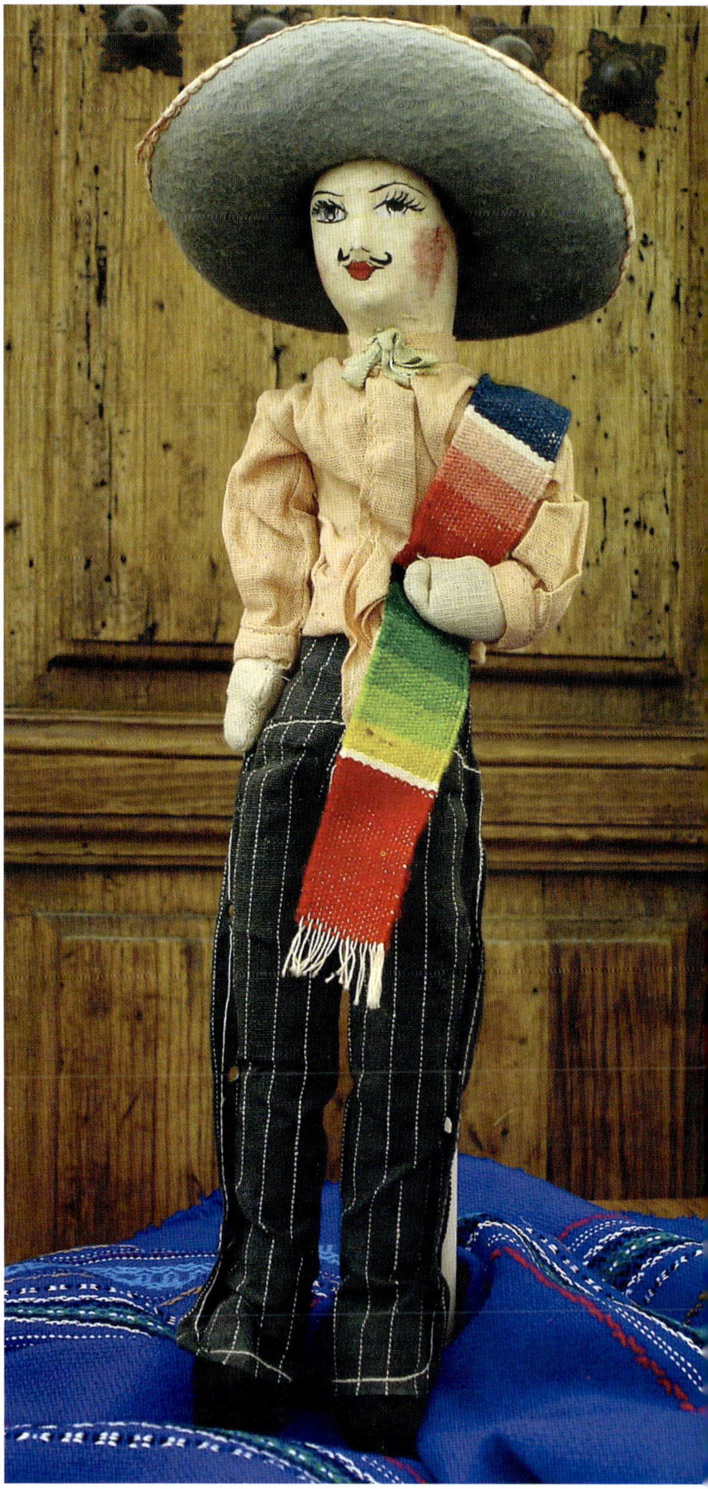

A 16 in. cloth doll of a *charro*, c.1940s. He is wearing a *manta* shirt with a colorful *serape*. His cotton or wool trousers, tighter around the legs, loose at the crotch and waist, are in a black and white tic striped pattern, a common cloth for Mexican trousers, and are riveted on the side. An oversized felt *sombrero* in blue has red and gold trim. $50 to $100

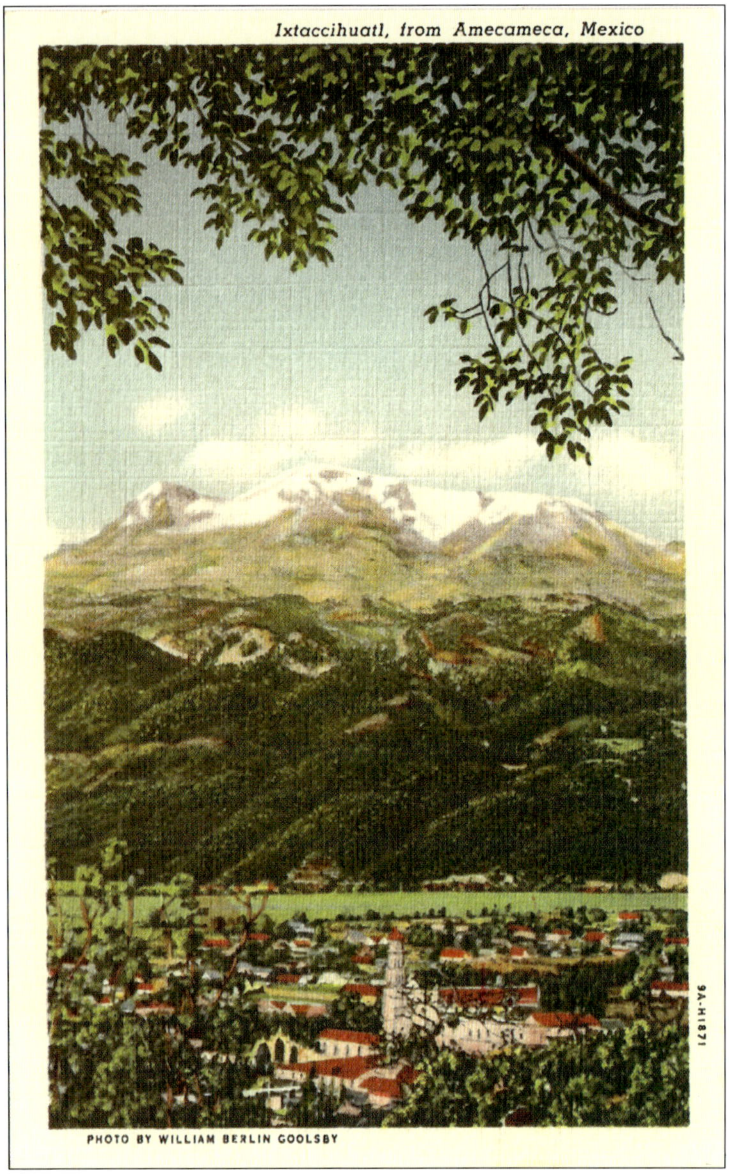

A color tint-tone postcard, 5 x 3 in., c. 1954, "Ixtaccihuatl," from Amecameca, Mexico, Genuine Curtreich-Chicago. $15 to $30

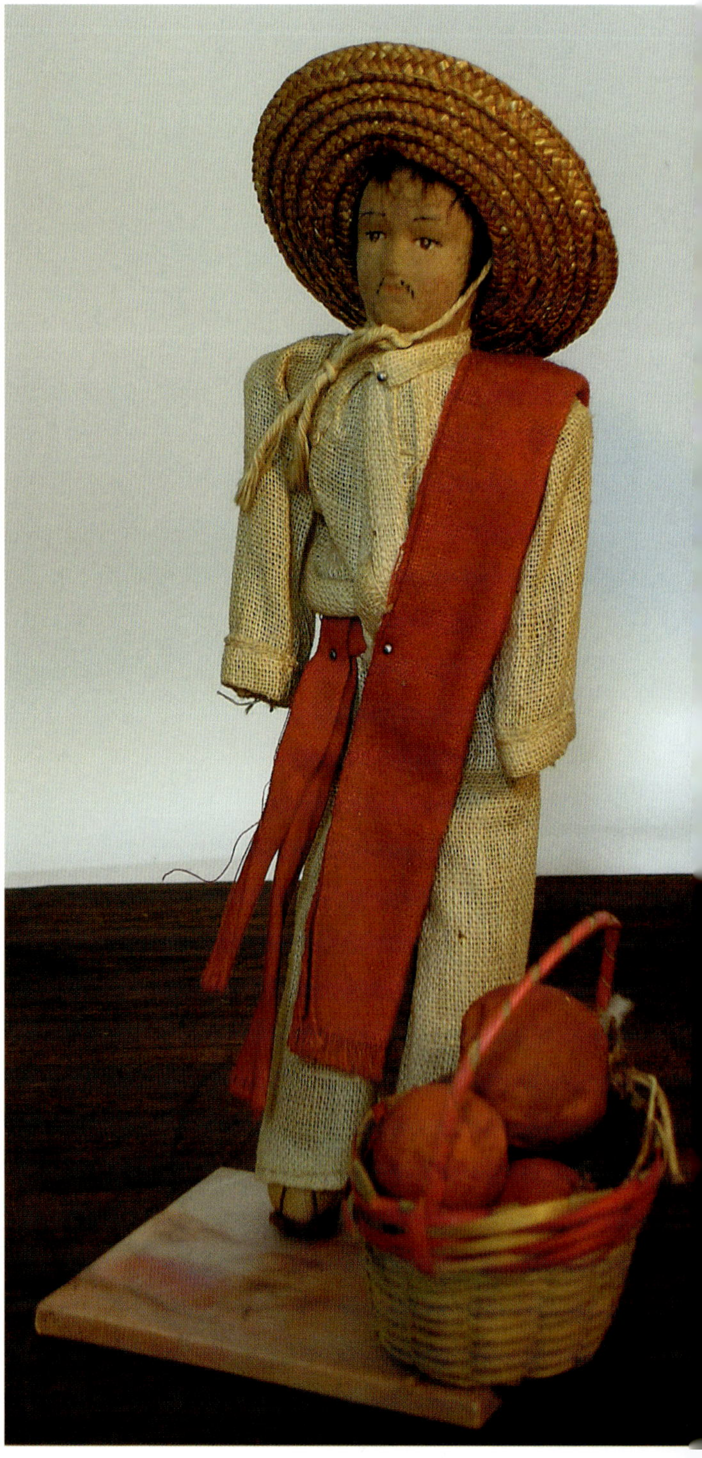

Typical Old Mexico clothing includes the white *calzóne blanco* pants and shirt on this 12 in. cloth doll with red *faja* sash, c.1940s. All cloth, painted features, and a sewn thread wig. $40 to 75

There are also common accessories. The *ayate of ixtle* (waist sashes) are decorative strips of woven wool or cotton. The *manga* (wool woven cape) or the *tilmatl* (rectangular cotton cloak) sometimes are made of *maguey* (a coarse woven fiber). These were alternatives of the serape, depending on the tribal customs.

Natural dyes were prepared very carefully and favored over synthetic dyes. Their original clothing was entirely of genuine materials, not only in respect to variety and subtlety of the colors but also in their choices of wool. Their newly-learned looming techniques enhanced the Indians' clothing. These distinctions of their laborious talents demonstrate how important their clothing is to them.

The Indians' choice of footwear is the *huaraches* and they are essential when working or walking long distances. But many of the Indians went barefoot and bare feet are still common in the remote regions. Foot apparel varied as well among the classes. Leather boots, deerskin moccasins, woven shoes, and *huaraches* (sandals) were clearly their choices. The male dolls express all the diverse ways in which the Mexican costume evolved, from the colonial times through the end of the 20th century. Widely worn palm hats are an essential piece of their costume as well, and you will rarely see them without one. Their *sombreros* could have been trimmed with leather, wool, colored ribbon strips, or poms of wool.

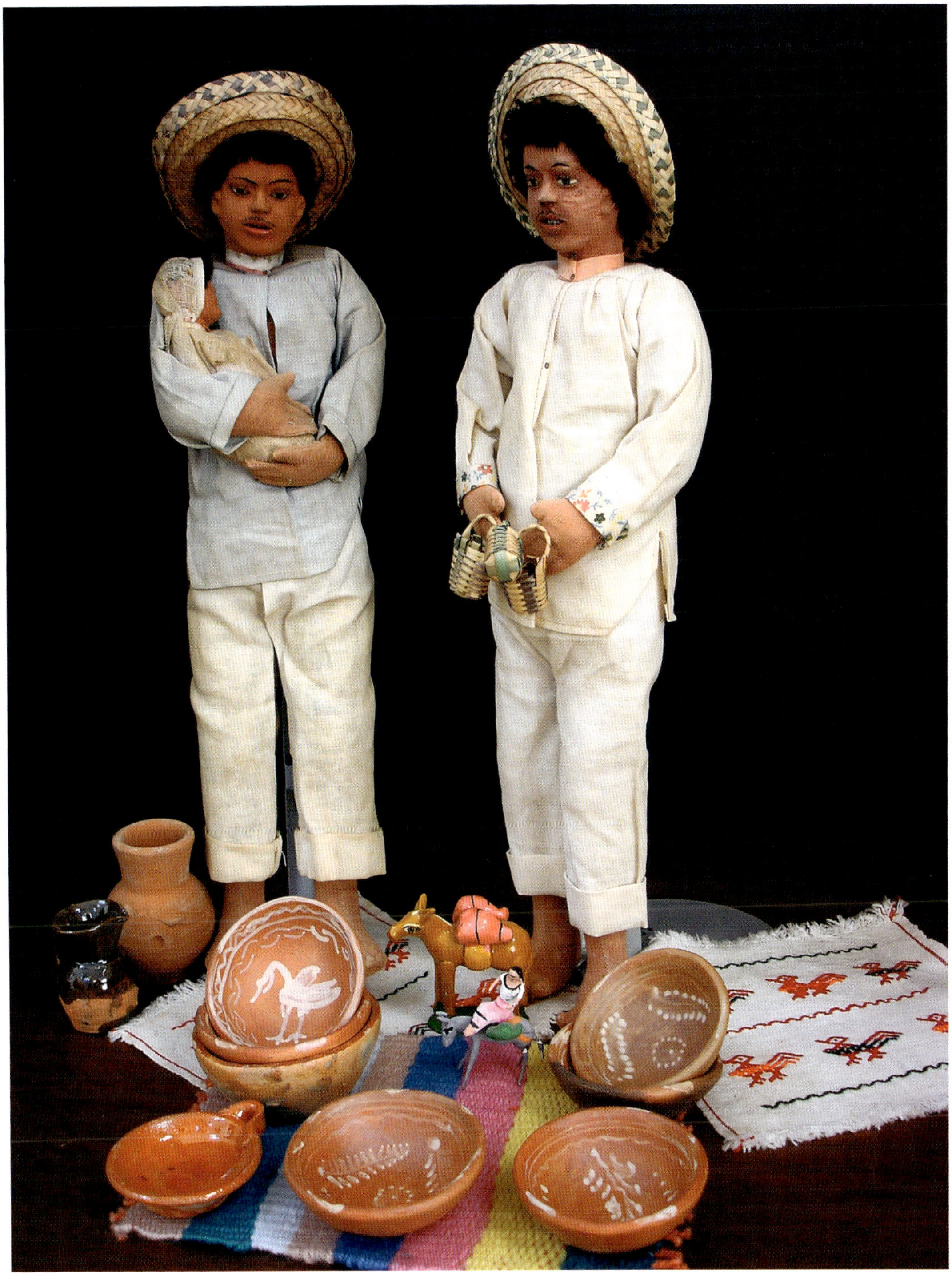

Two large 16 in. cloth *caballeros* (men), c. 1930s, made in Mexico. They are selling their wares on a *petate* rug and holding a baby, and are dressed in *calzóne blanco*, a white and light blue cotton *manta* cloth. Faces are detailed with inset eyes and teeth. The skin is tinted brown, the wool hair is very detailed, and the bodies are hard stuffed. $125 to 200 ea.

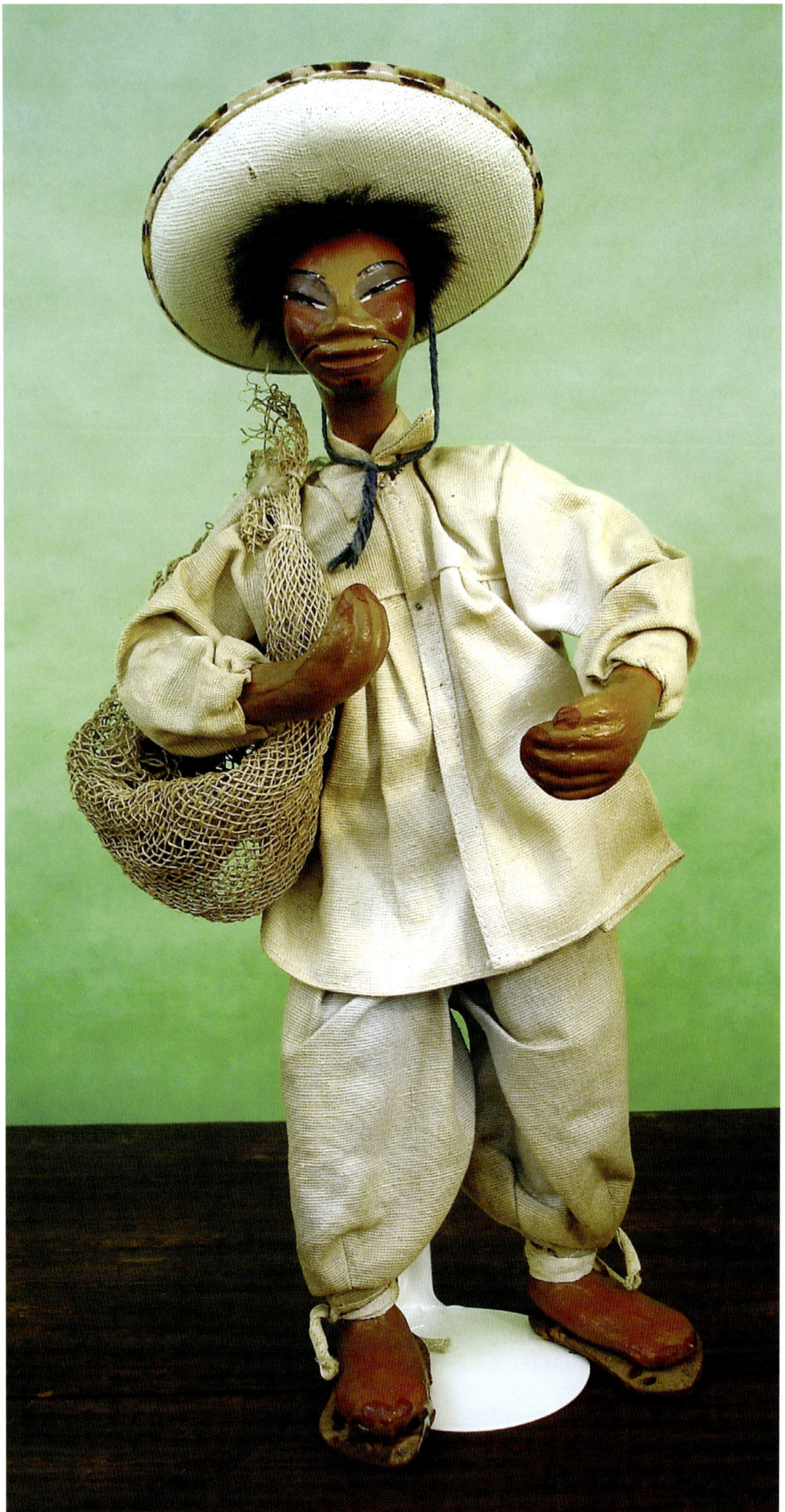

A 17 in. clay and wire sculpted doll, c. 1940s depicting an Indian fisherman holding a net and wearing traditional *calzóne blanco* garments, cropped pants tied at the bottom, which was common, and *huaraches.* Made in Mexico. $60 to $100

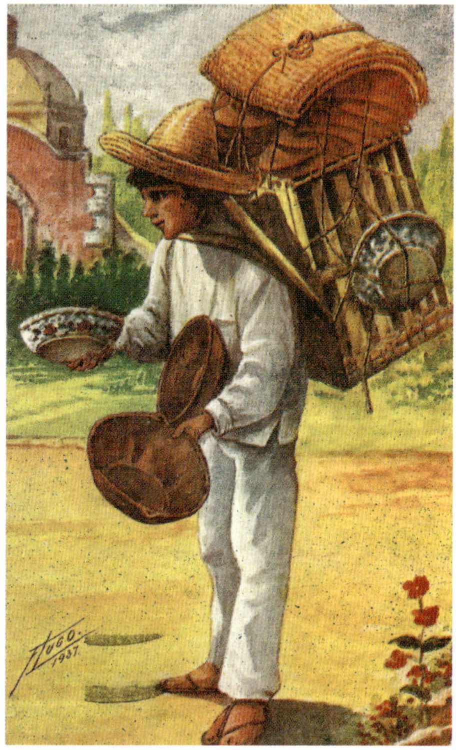

A tinted litho postcard, 5 x 3 in., "Mexico en Colores, an Indian selling his wares on the streets," signed by HUGO, 1937, Mexico, published by Frederico Liebig. $15 to $30

The *mestizo peon's* or *campesino's* daily attire, however humble and less elaborate, served its purpose. He was a worker, a common man who dressed to his social class limits. Although a lot less flamboyant than that of the *charro*, his clothing was certainly more functional and comfortable and it evolved with some western as well as native influences. On male dolls, their clothing appears plain, with particular attention always drawn to the *serape* or sash. Their hats are woven from the different materials available from their regions and are more affordable. Cotton shirts are loose and comfortable, worn over the pants, tucked in, or knotted at the front. Open collared shirts with wide cuffs had wide tails so they eres multipurpose. He could work easily with comfort or tuck the tail in. Sometimes he would wear the *moño*, a tied cravat around his neck; for it would also serve to clean the sweat from his face. His sash or belt supports his loose pants, but often it has beautiful motifs and colored stitching. The pants are wide at the top, so that they cross in the front and tie around the waist. They are made in solid muslin or wool, sometimes with vertical stripes. The *serape* is woven with bright colors and traditional traits that add status or dress to the Mexican *peon* or *campesino*. His shoes were *huaraches* or boots, and a woven palm *sombrero* often had colorful attributes. While his clothing may have been dirty or aged, the serape would conceal these imperfections and he could feel proud. His wife would dutifully mend and weave his clothing.

During the colonial period, the wealthy *charro* or *haciendados* (land owners) had clothing that showed strong influences from Spain. His horses and riding attire were represented as grandiose and functional. The *charro* doll is dressed in a broad-brimmed *sombrero* that is ornamented and banded with distinctive markings and held with a chin strap.

The Mexican military operated with required standards in the late 19th century, so much of their clothing was uniform. A military soldier would wear a linen or cotton shirt tucked in, loose and comfortable but formal. Around his neck he would wear his *moño* (cravat bow tie). A woolen or leather waist-length coat fastens with silver buttons, *plateados* (silvered ones), and with a frog closure like a piece of jewelry on the front of their coat. The *mestizo* men wore *pantalones* (pants) with particulars for comfort and dress. Their pants were loose fitting, similar to those of the *campesinos*, comfortable or tightly fitted to mimic the Spaniards and because they were regarded as fine looking. The special breeches or pants had elaborated borders that would overextend along the outer sides and be studded with the silver *plateado* buttons along the outer flap. He wore leather shoes or boots, often worn over the trousers. He would wear his *chaparreras*, (chaps), similar to the American cowboy. Another accessory was his belt, whether an elaborate sash or tooled leather it was part of the ensemble. Their clothing was detailed and display special traits indicative of the Spanish military, such as the *plateados* buttons and the waist-length coats, often tailored and made to order of fine wools and cottons. They would also wear capes or cloaks with oversized black hats decorated elaborately. This was their clothing, but now it is just a costume.

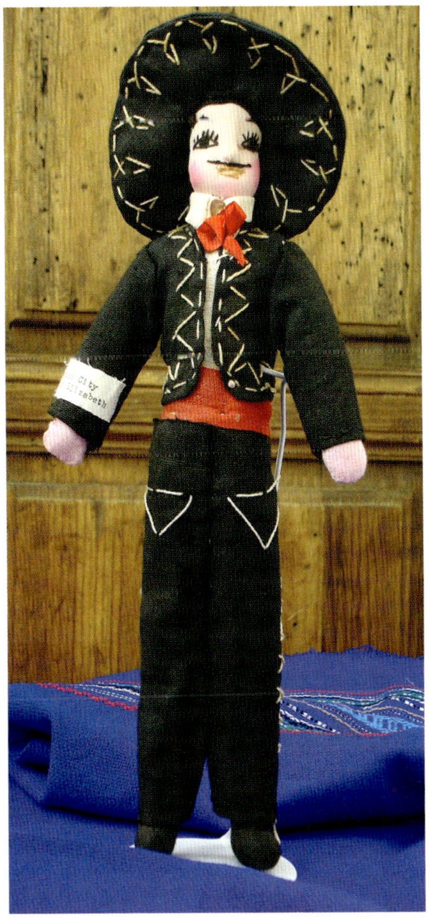

Attributed to the Ravca doll maker, a 15 in. cloth *charro*. A characteristic Ravca stocking body with needle formed features and tinting. He is wearing a white shirt with a black wool *charro* suit and a large black cloth hat. The suit is accented with gold stitching and black cloth makes his shoes. The label sewn to his arm reads, "Mexico City Elizabeth 1935." $75 to $100

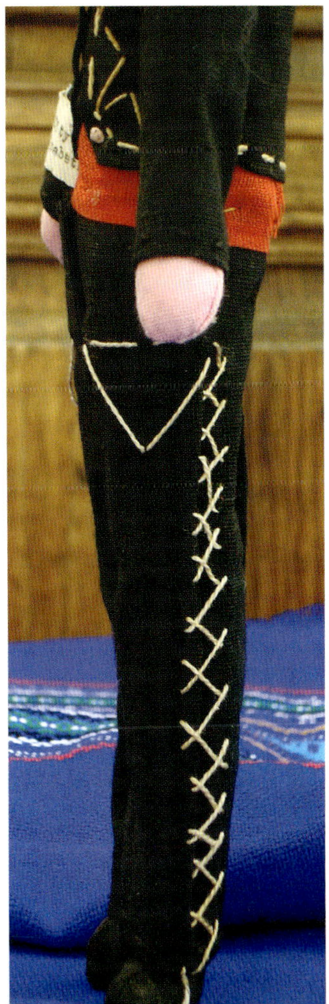

The trousers of the grand *charro* cloth doll in black wool with gold stitching and an extended outer seam flap with rivets. c. 1930s. Made in Mexico

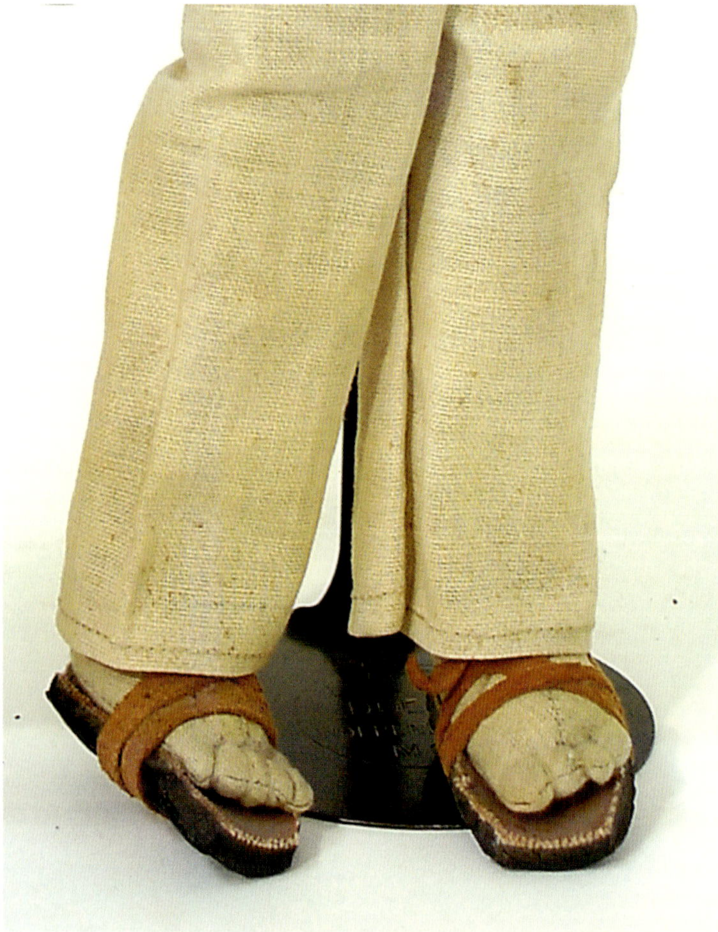

Typical cloth doll's leather *huaraches,* c.1940s. Made in Mexico.

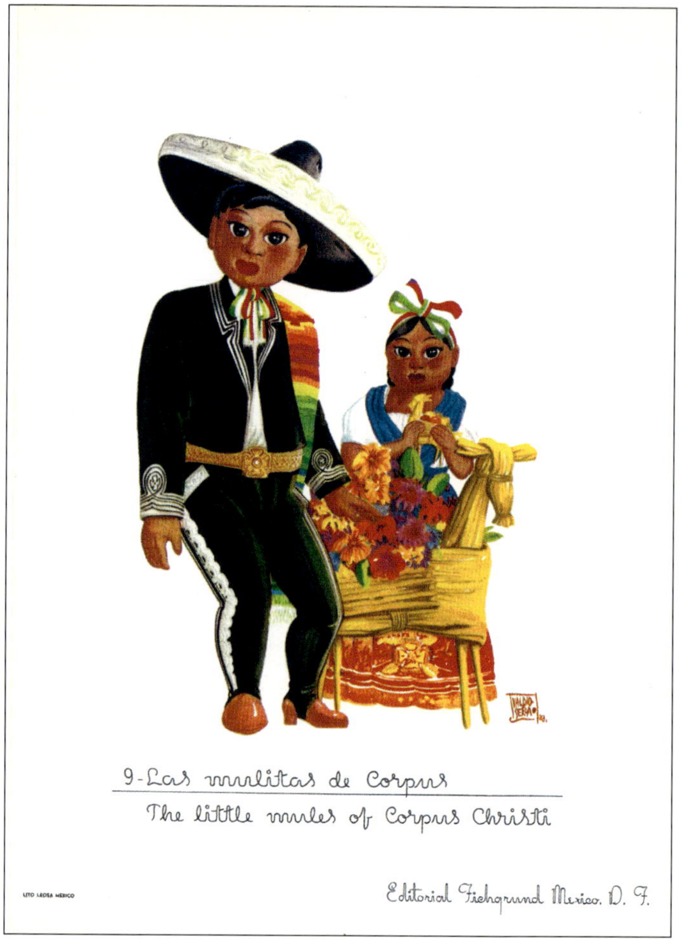

Color litho print, Ramon Valdiosera, titled "Mexican Children and Toys," made in Mexico, 1949. Editorial Fischgrund. $35 to 55

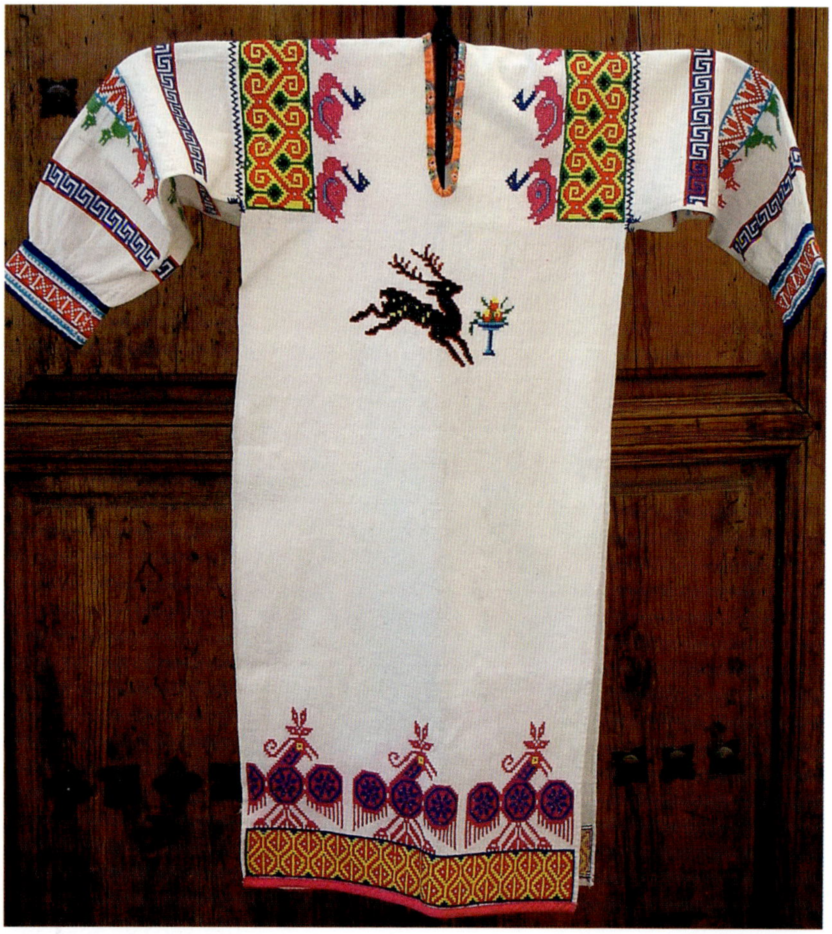

The front of a traditional *huipil* shirt of the Huichol tribe, c. 1940s. White cotton with rich natural dye colors in elaborate indigenous motifs that are spiritually inspired pre-Hispanic, with Mayan stepped fret patterning. Designs brocaded with wool or cotton threads, Jalisco, Mexico. $300 to 400

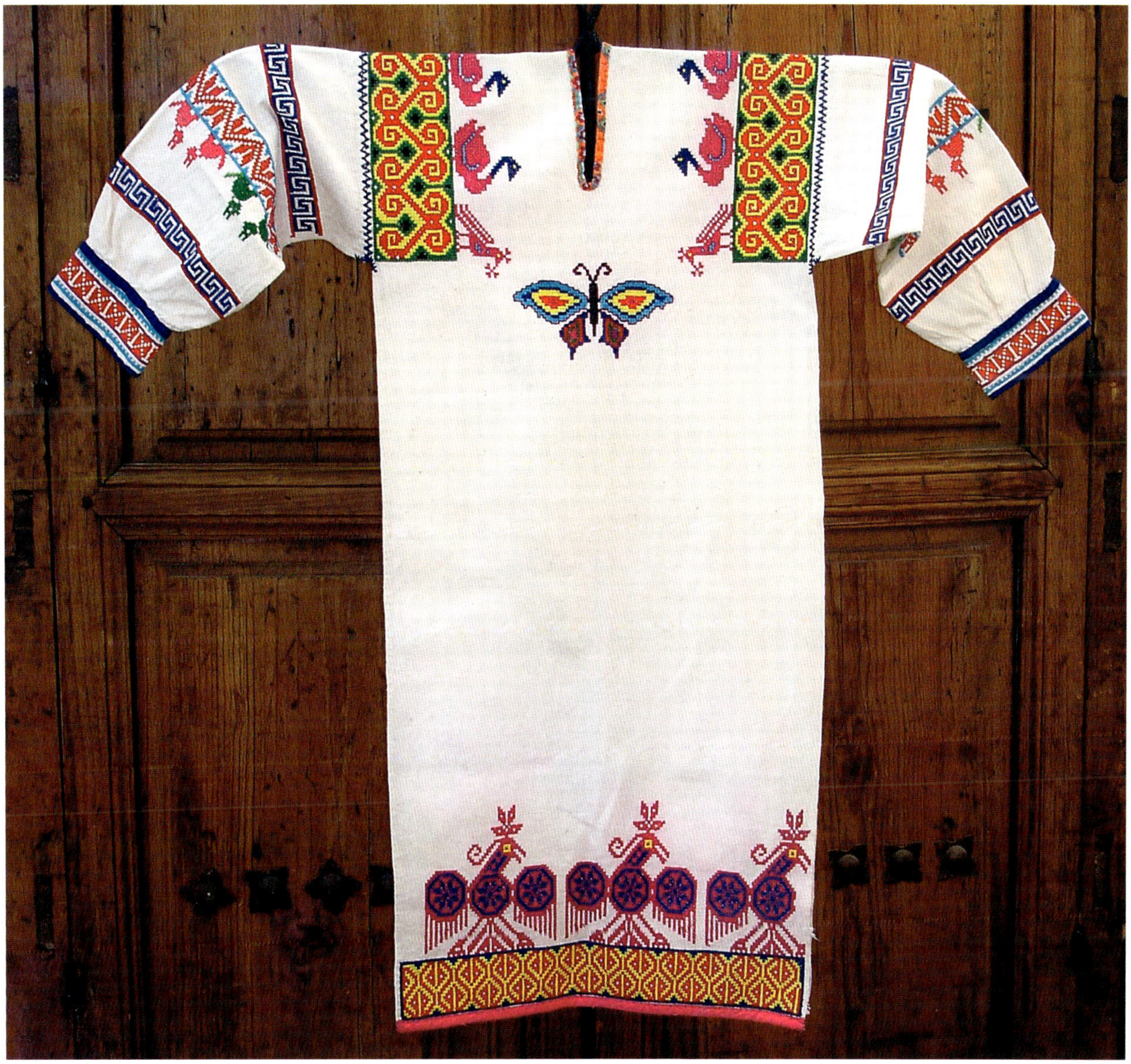

The back of the Huichol *huipil*, c.1940s. Center is a beautiful embroidered butterfly.

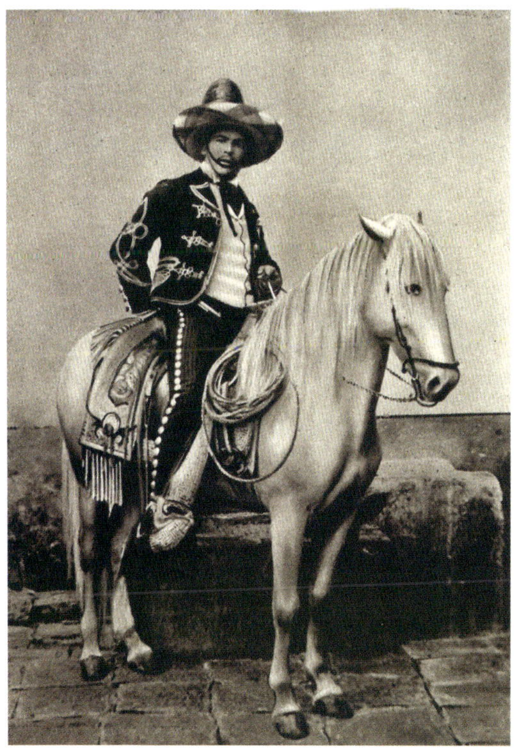

A grand *charro* on his horse, 1920s.

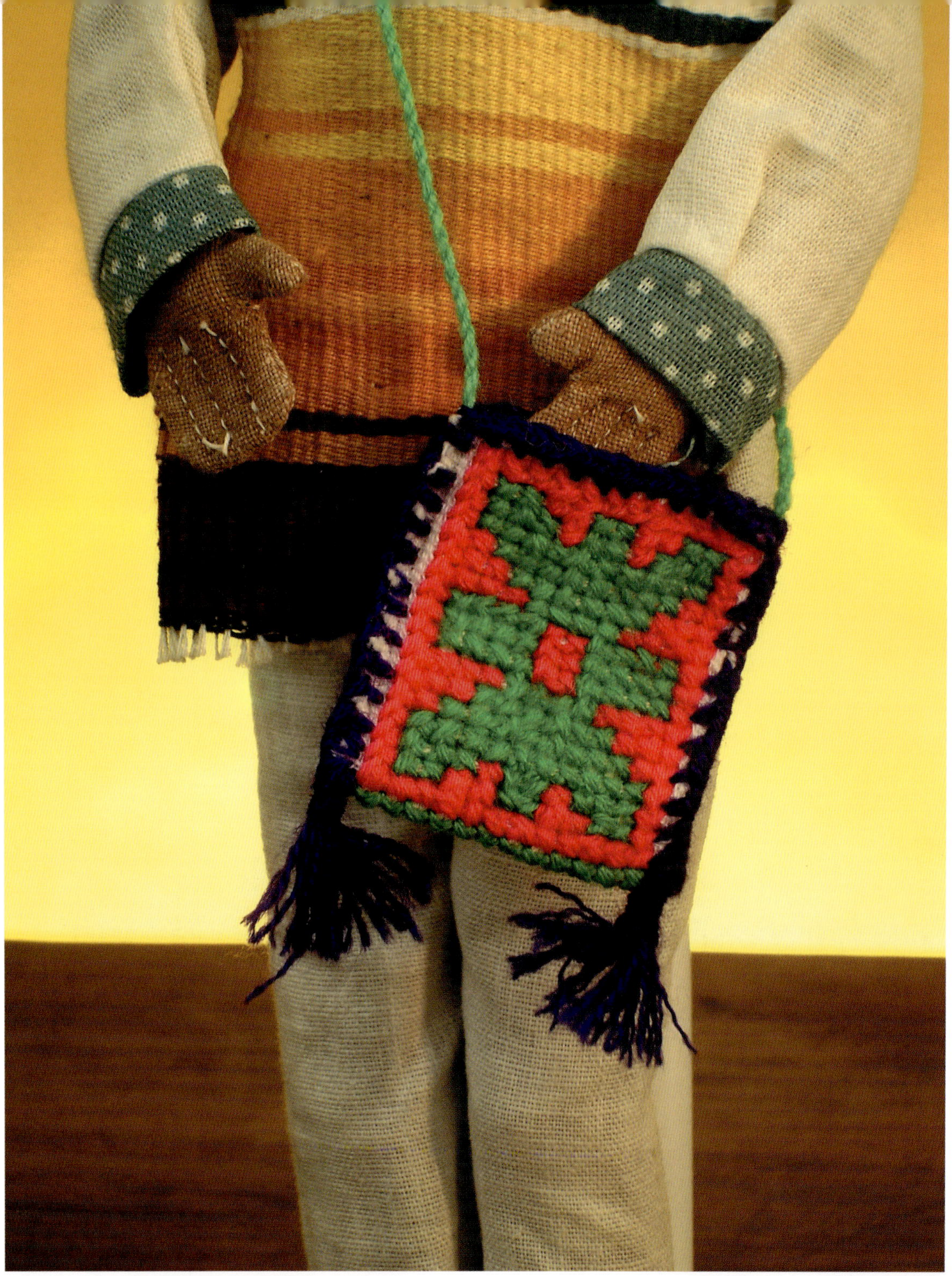

A detailed view of a small miniature *morral* bag. The 8-star flowers are fret stitched, c. 1950s.

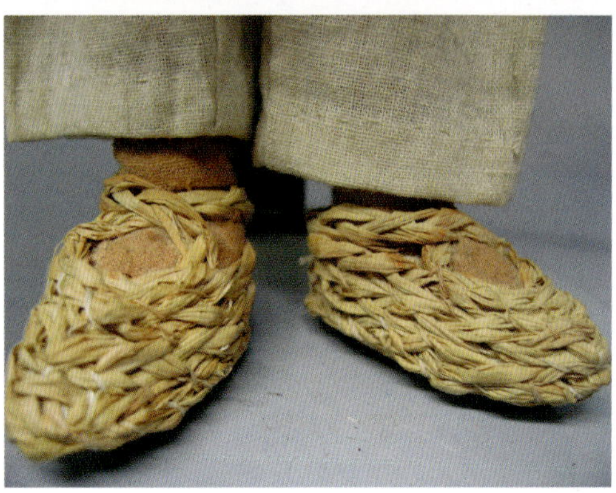

Woven shoes on a 14 in. Kimport cloth *caballero* (male) doll made in Mexico, c. 1945.

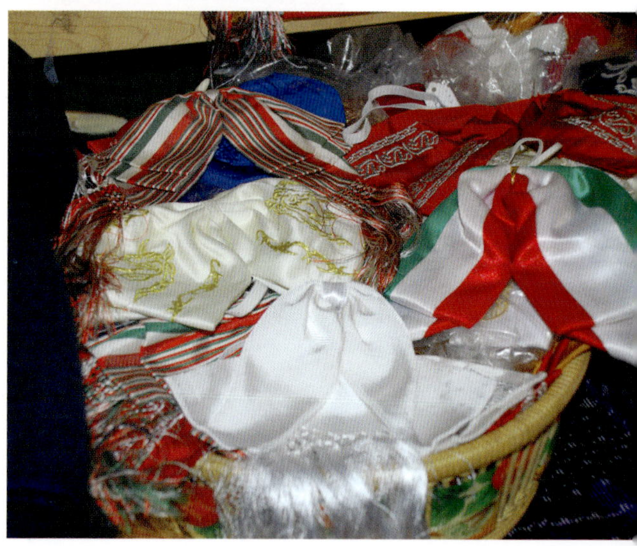

A contemporary basket full of varied Mexican *moños,* cravats for the *charro* or the *mestizo*, on Olvera Street, Los Angeles, California, 2007.

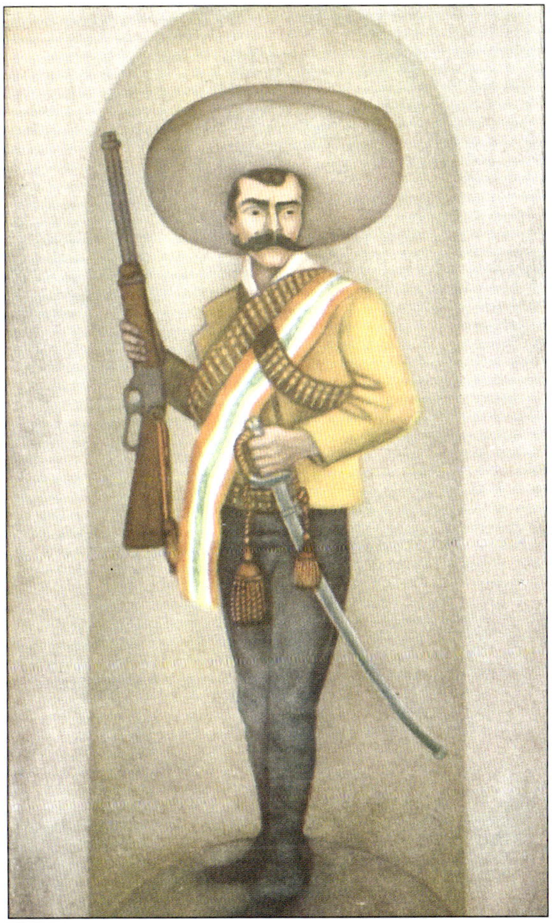

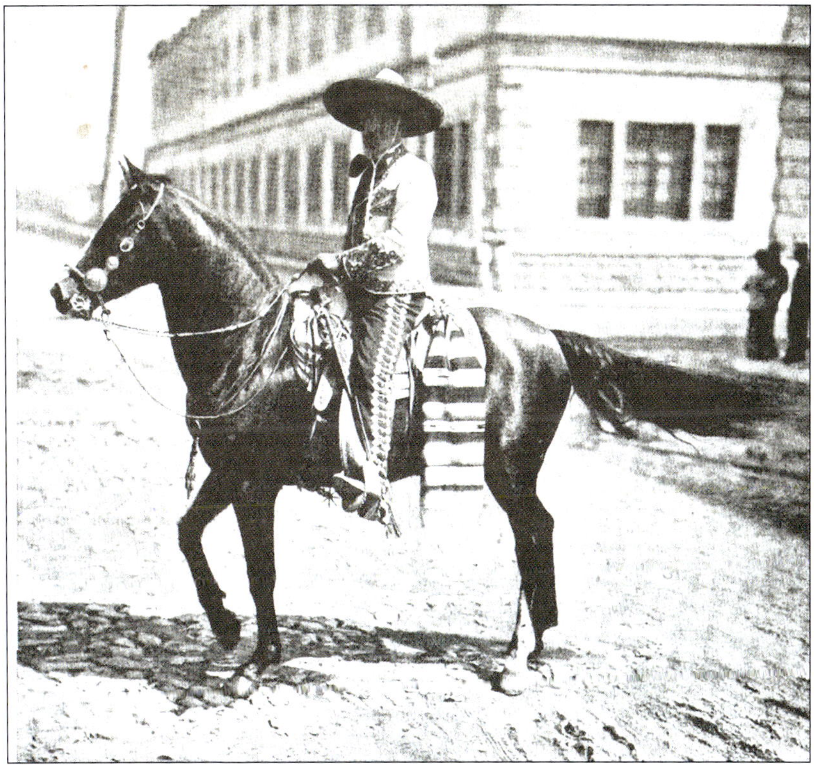

A Mexican *charro* on his horse, 1930s.

An original postcard 5 x 3 in., c. 1940s, "General, Emilio Zapata," by Diego Rivera, published by Fishgrund, Mexico. $25 to 40

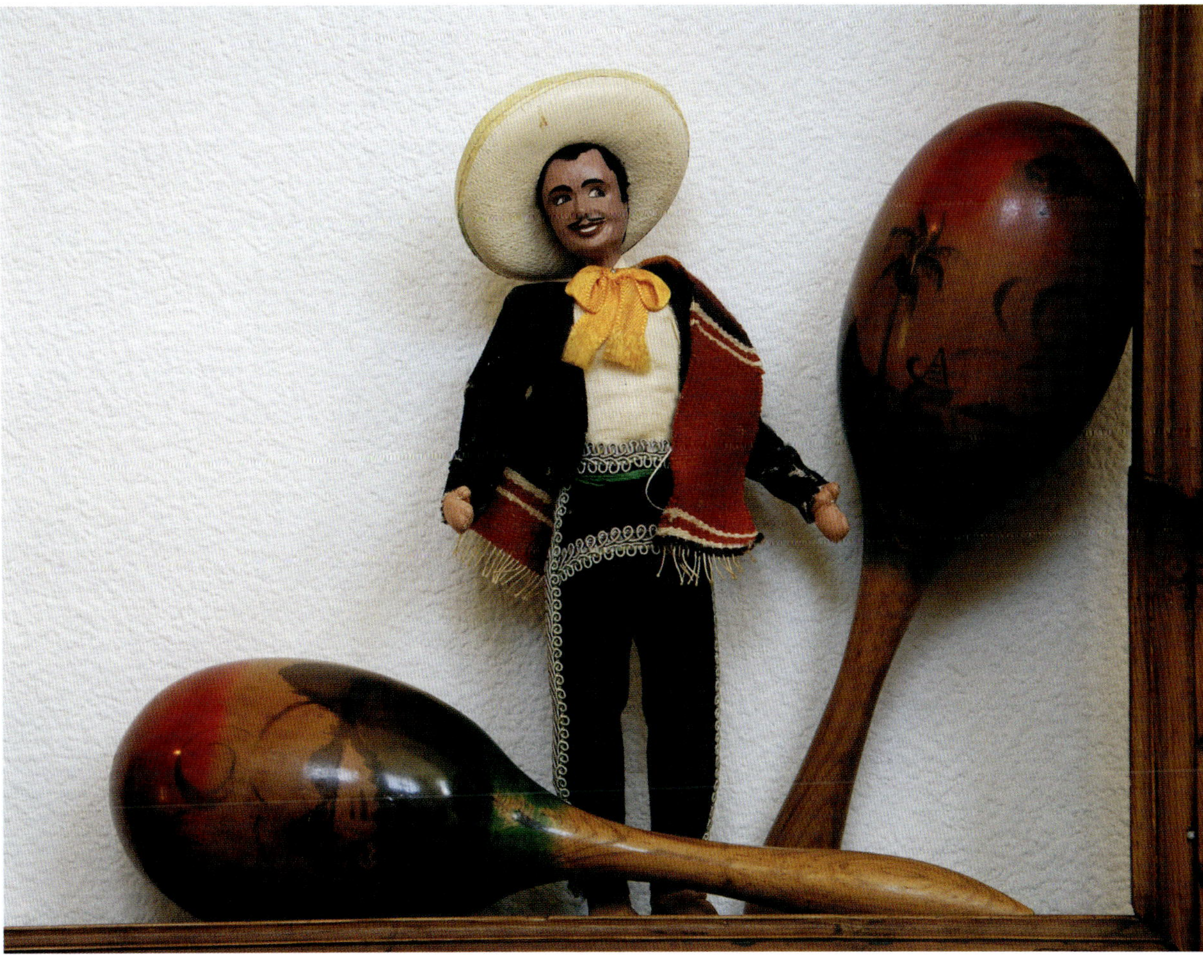

A flamboyant 10 in. compo *charro* doll wearing the typical wool *traje* (suit), c. 1940s. Shown with a pair of old Mexico maracas. $50 to 75

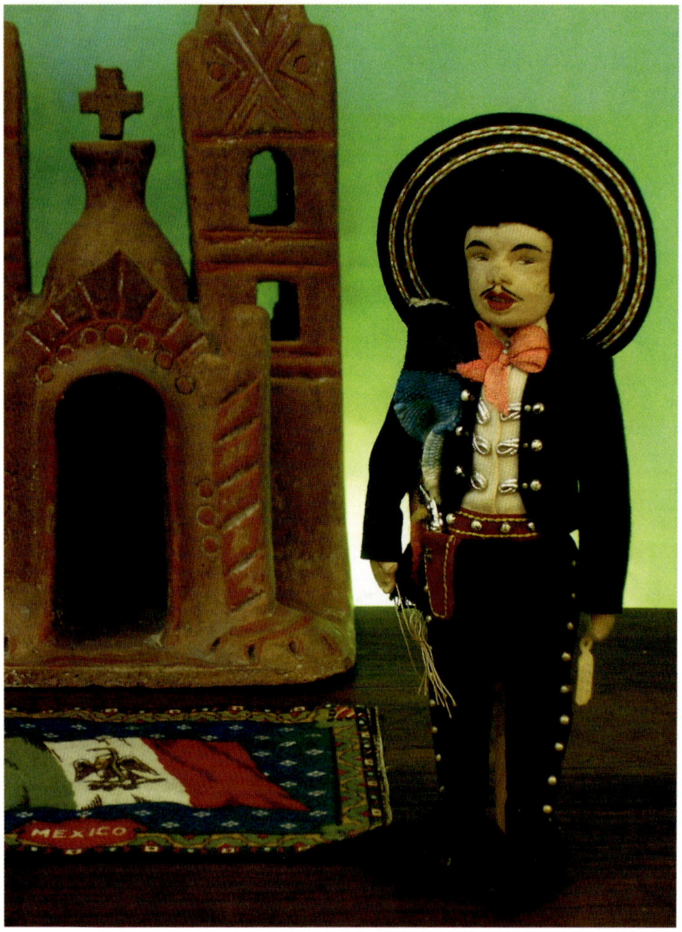

A *mestizo* Mexican soldier 13 in. cloth doll, made in Mexico, c. 1940s. Molded *papier maché* face, black wool wig, very detailed clothing. Wool *charro* suit with silver threads and silver studs down the sides of the trousers and jacket, a wool *serape*, large *sombrero*, a pistol with holder , and black boots. Shown with an old Pueblan clay church, c.1940s. Doll $150 to $250

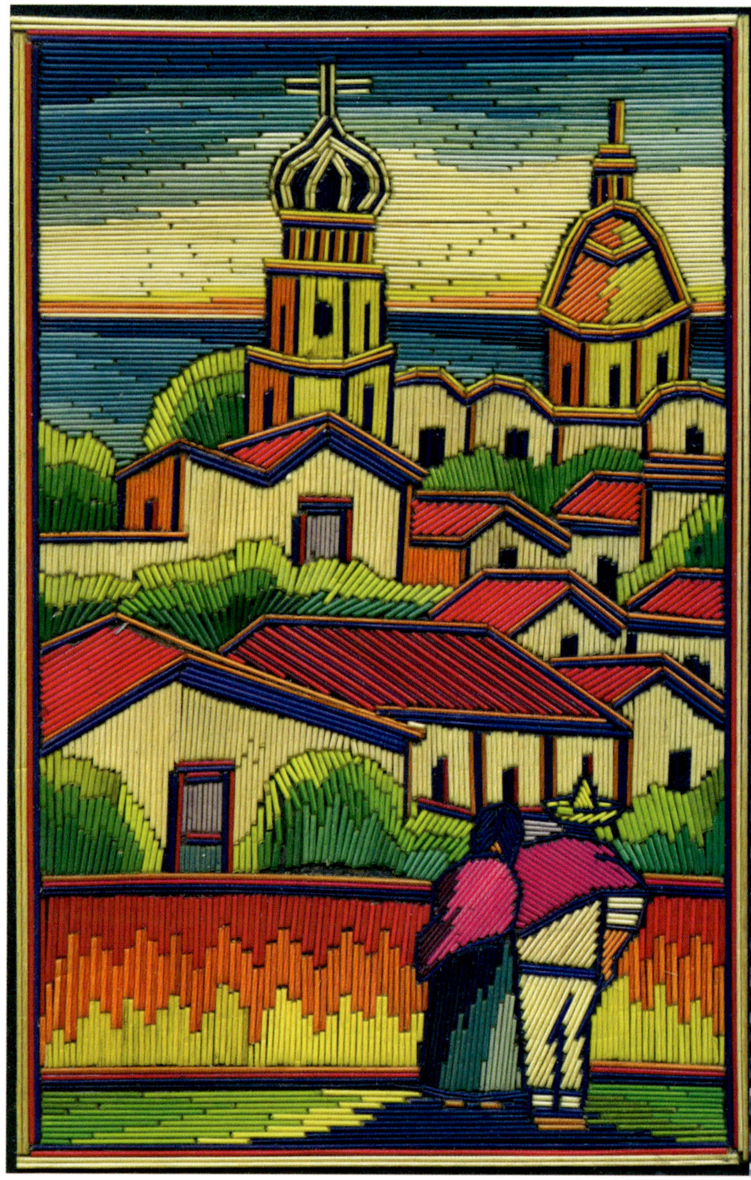

A colorful mosaic straw scene of Puebla, Mexico, c.1980. 8 x 10 in.

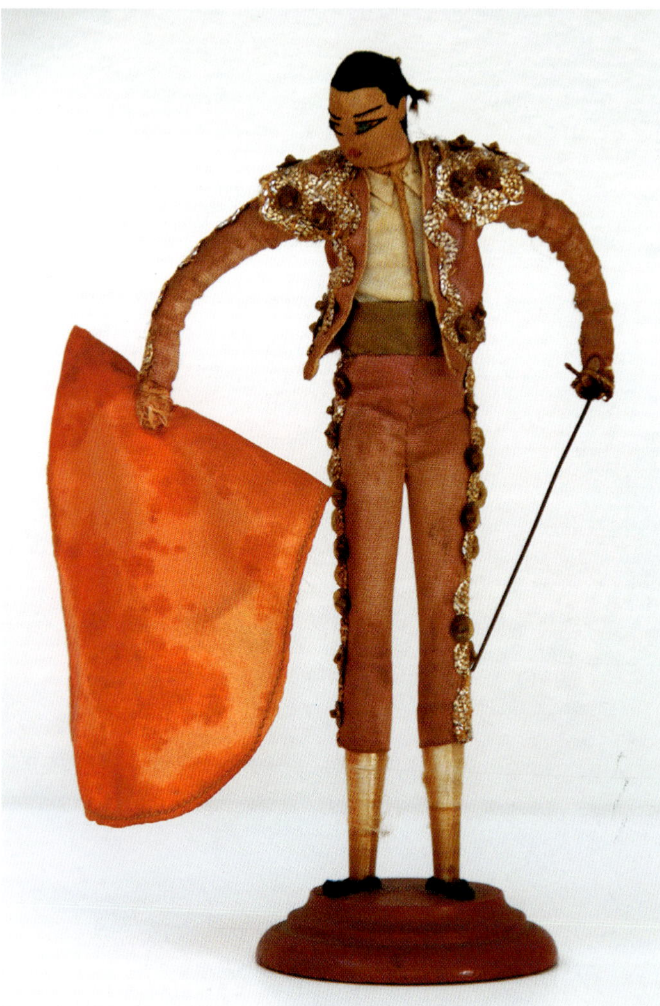

A *matador*, 8 in. wire and horsehair, cloth doll, showing great accents and detail, early 20th c., made in Mexico.

El Sombrero, The Hat

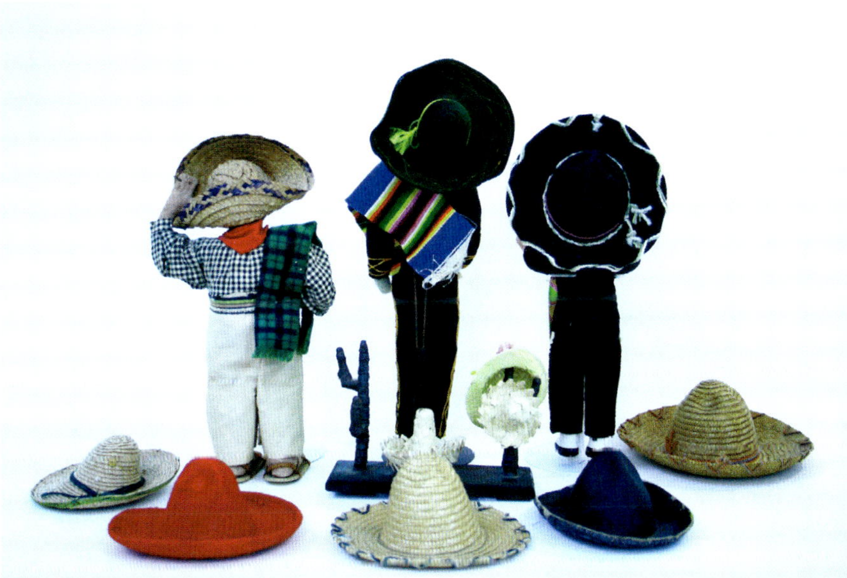

Los caballeros and their many *sombreros*, c. 1920s to 1950s. They are found in various colors and materials, such as felt, velvet, leather, palm, and reed and from 3 in. to 9 in. wide, shown with folk art, cast iron cactus, c. 1920s. All made in Mexico.

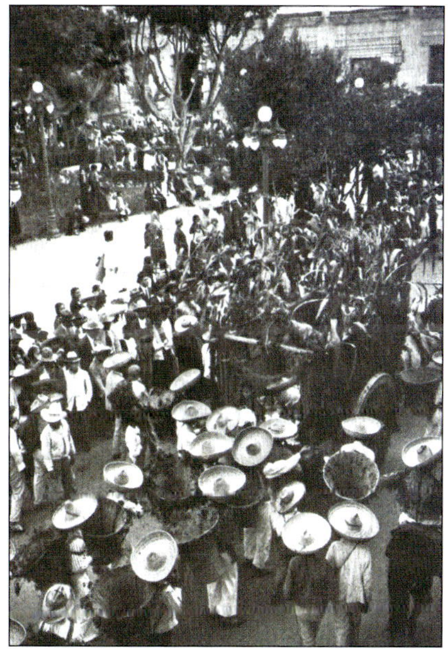

A photograph of busy Guadalajara, 1934.

In Mexico, the *sombrero* is not just an accessory; it is one of the most important items of the Mexican man's attire. On dolls you can define the wearer's purpose, status, and origin by correctly reading from his hat, and it serves as a functional part of their costume. Although the *sombrero* is usually noted as an exaggerated wide brimmed hat, there are Indians who wore hats that had narrower brims and a lot or no decoration. Function was the *sombrero's* priority, but it was also a component of his whole ensemble. On many of the indigenous men dolls you see interpretations of the Mexican *sombrero.*

The word was adapted from the Spanish word *sombra*, meaning "shade" or "shadow." They were made with a wide high tip and an extra wide brim with the intention of keeping the head cool and protected from the sun. The tallest part points to the back, while the longest part rests on the front to protect the face from sunlight. There are many varieties.

The *sombrero* can be made from leather, cloth, felt, reed, straw, or palm. The straw or palm *sombreros* are commonly known as *petates*, like woven mats, as this is what they are made from. They are hand woven in all shapes, texture, and sizes. Some are made of fine, thin straw in designs intricately woven or dyed in different colors. The *campesinos* and *peon* men, as well as Mexican Indian dolls wear dozens of different types of these straw hats, with each region having its own special traits. Turned up or curled brims can have tall or small crowns, in all widths and heights. In Morelos, the crowns of the hat are large and the brims wide; sometimes the wearer must take his hat off or tip it to pass through a doorway. They are finished with a woven chin cord that is worn under the chin to keep the wind from blowing it from his head and to keep it hung around the back of his head. These hats also could include different trims, like bands of ribbon, balls of wool yarn poms, and strings.

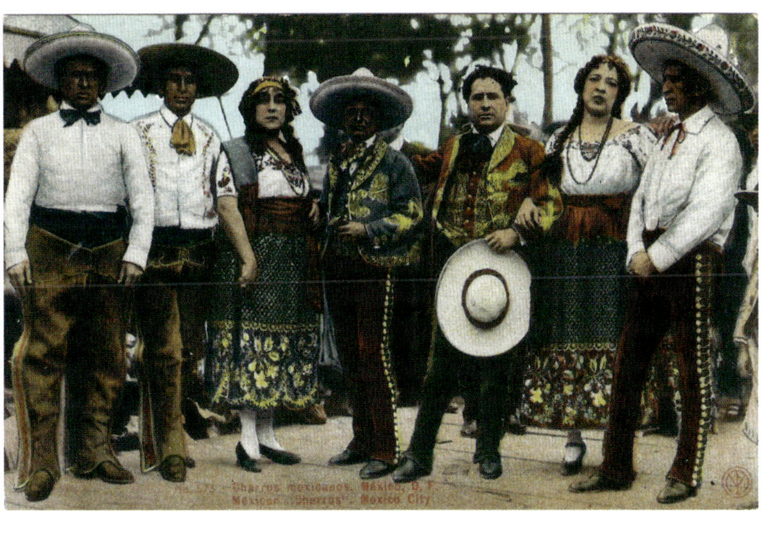

A tinted photograph postcard, "Republica Mexicana Tarjeta Postal," *Charros* in Mexico City, c. 1920s, Mexico D.F $15 to 30

For the upper levels of society and those of the *charros*, the most elaborate varieties of *sombreros* were made. They can be found of woven dyed reed, wheat fiber, felt, leather, or wool. Tooled and refined *sombreros* were for the *charro*, for a more urban flare. *Sombreros* of the wealthy or the *mestizo* were a status symbol. Some *sombreros* were overwhelmingly gaudy and their only purpose was their flamboyant flare. They were decorated with elaborate finishes of silver, tooled leather, braided cording with sequins, and be lined in satin or velvet and sometimes be padded. Most often they were made to order for the wearer by the best *sombrero* makers in Mexico. The *charro* dolls have magnificent examples of Mexican *mestizo sombreros*, do some of the "female" *charra mesitza* dolls.

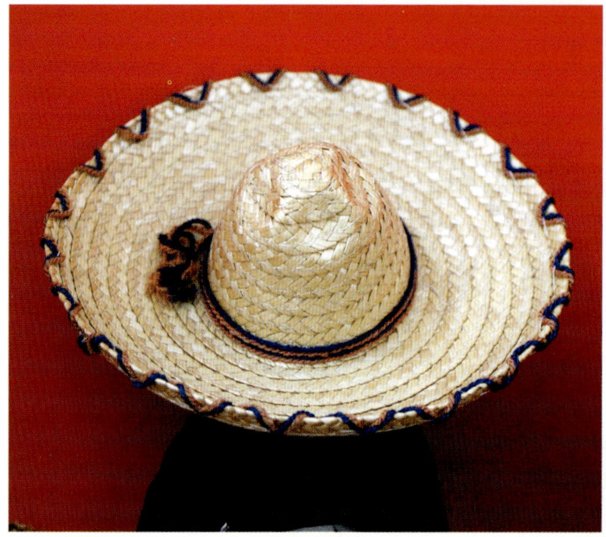

A miniature reed-woven *sombrero* trimmed around the crown and rim, c. 1950s, made in Mexico. $5 to 20

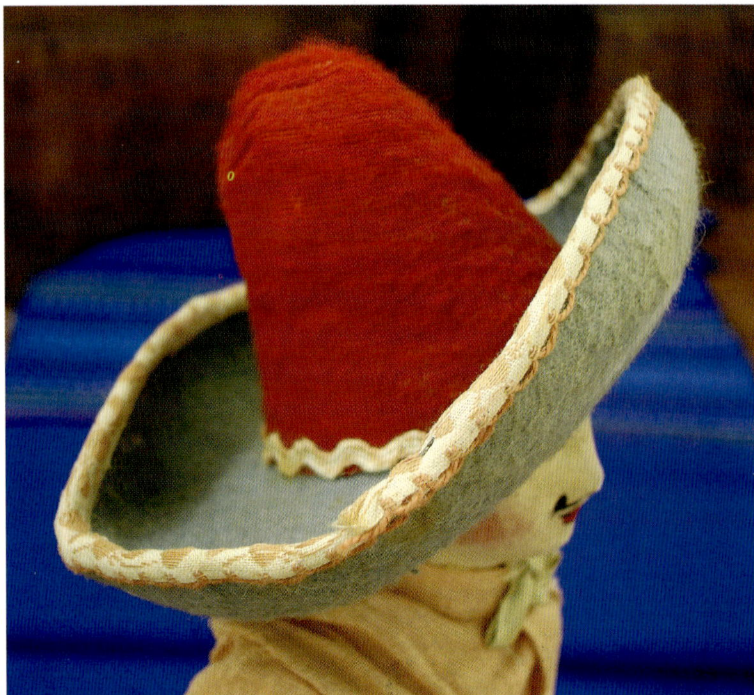

A wool felt *sombrero* in red and green, trimmed with gold rick rack, made in Mexico.

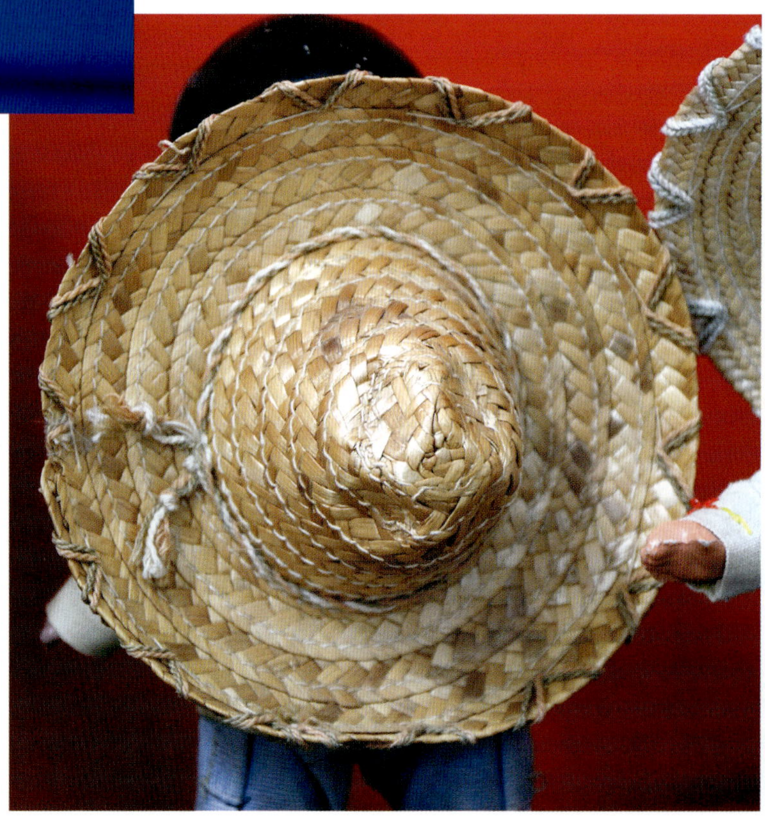

A palm *petate* woven *sombrero*, 20th c., made in Mexico. $5 to 20

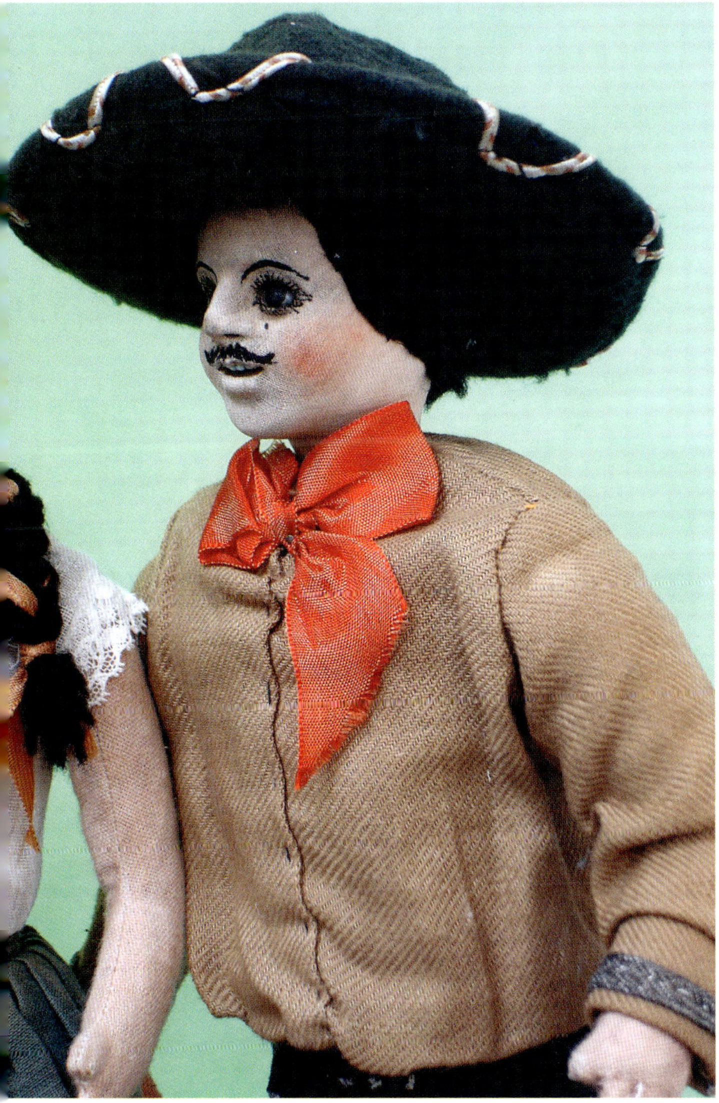

Wool felt *sombrero* on a rare, 11 in., cloth *caballero* doll made in Mexico, early 1900s. He is a proud *mestizo*. $150 to 300

A stunning 20th *maguey* woven Mexican *sombrero*. Leather tooled band around the crown, lined with leather and velvet. Chin strap in a tight reed weave. Some aging, but condition is overall good. $50 to 125

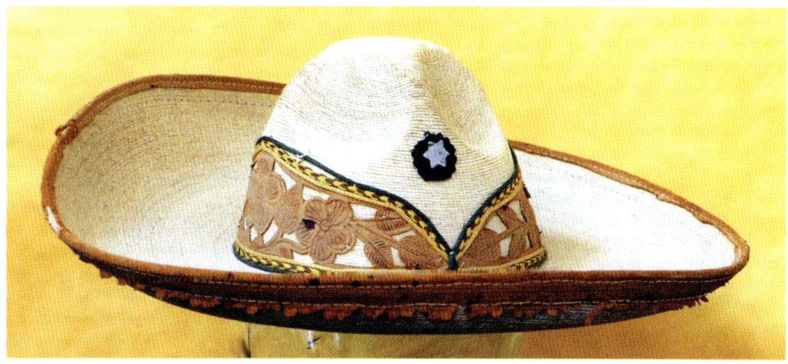

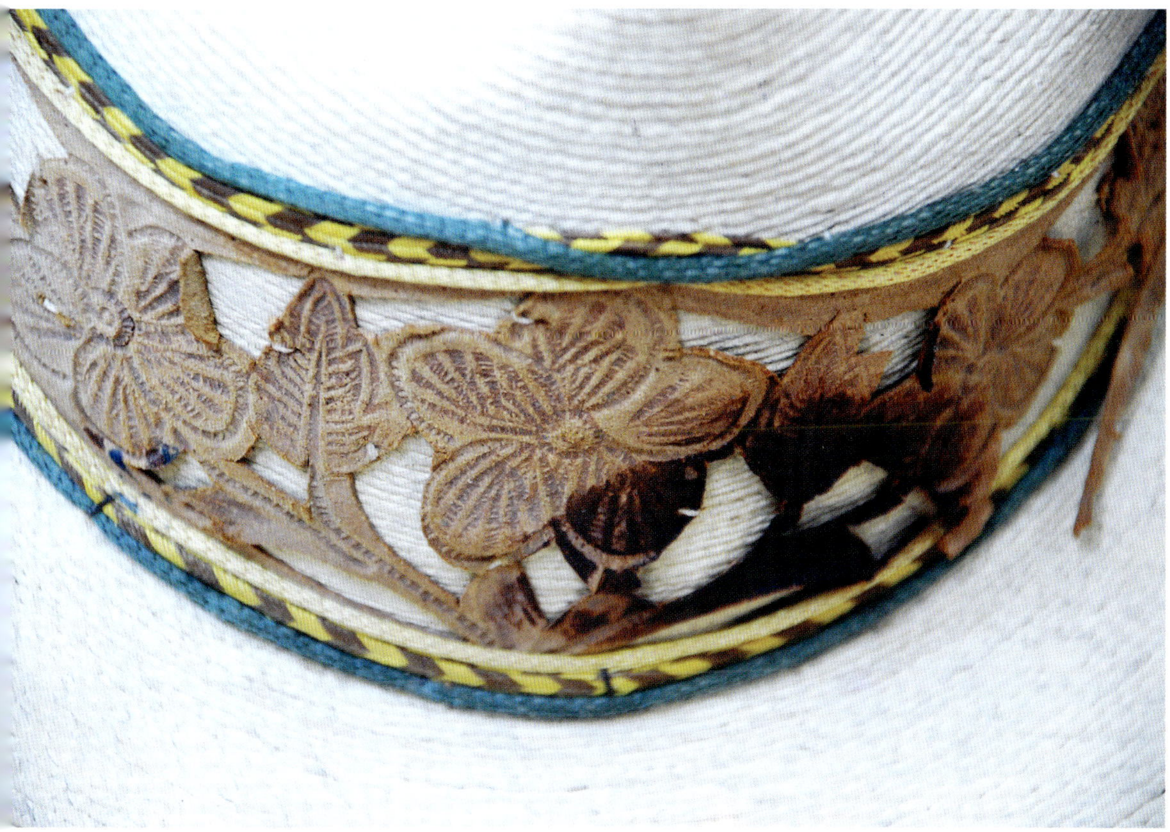

Detail of the tooled leather band.

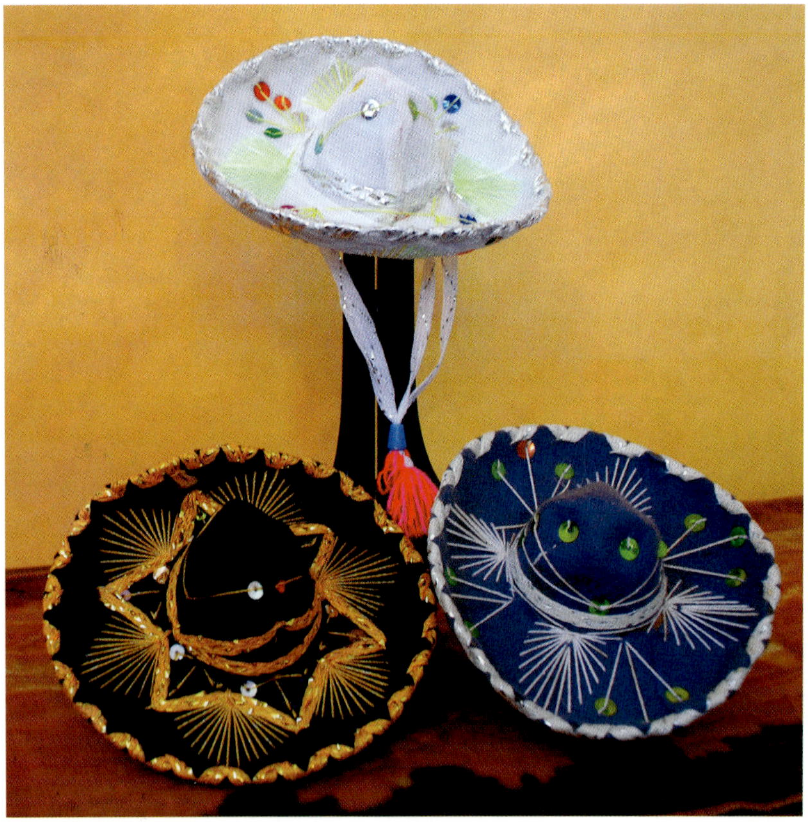

Three miniature *sombreros*, *charro* made by Pigelle style, c. 1960s in Mexico. Velvet and felt constructed with real chin straps, 12 in. to 14 in. diameter. $15 to 50 ea.

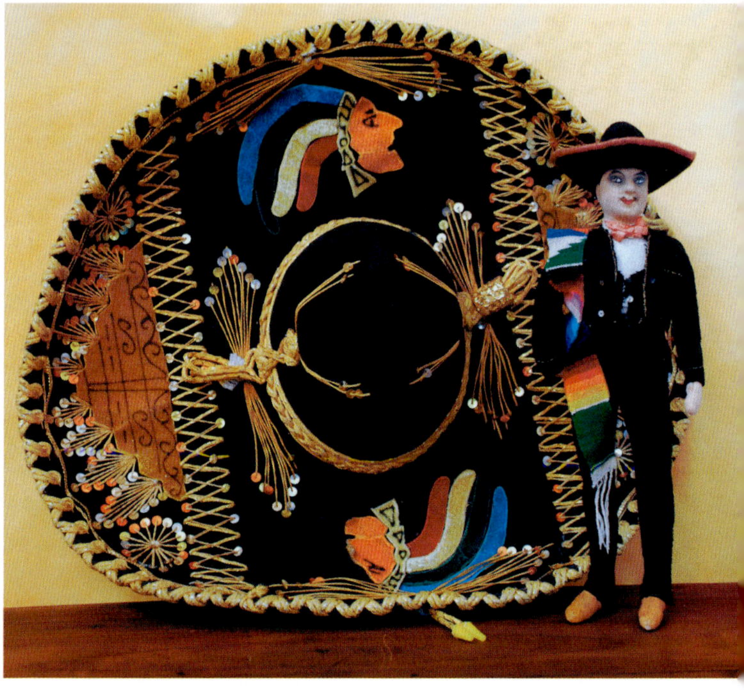

A large and flamboyant Mexican *charro's sombrero*, c.1950s, worn in parades and the charrerías, 28 in. diameter, made in Mexico. Impressive black velvet, leather, and cloth *sombrero* has appliqués and indigenous embroidered detail covering the surface. An early 20th c. *mestizo* doll. $150 to 250

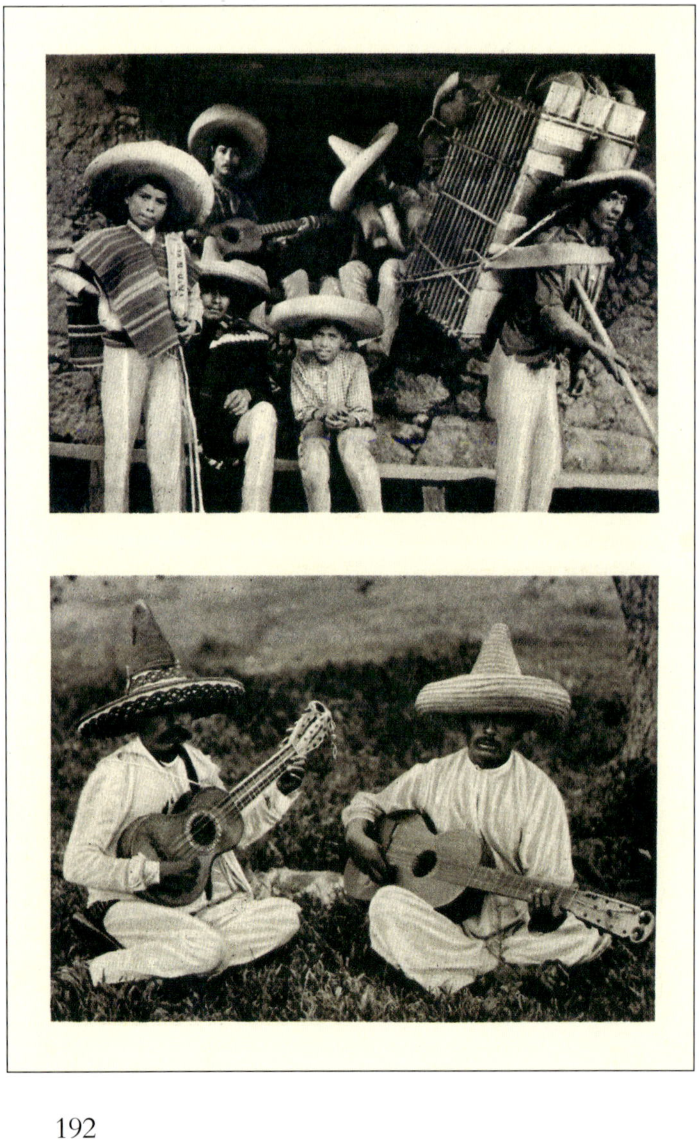

Mestizos and Mexican Indian, 1922, a photogravure.

A *maguey* woven Old Mexico miniature *sombrero* with colorful strips of ribbon, c. 1940s, diameter 9 in. $15 to 20

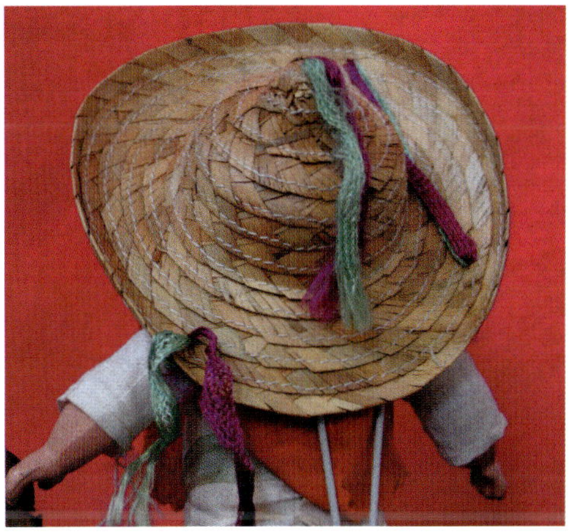

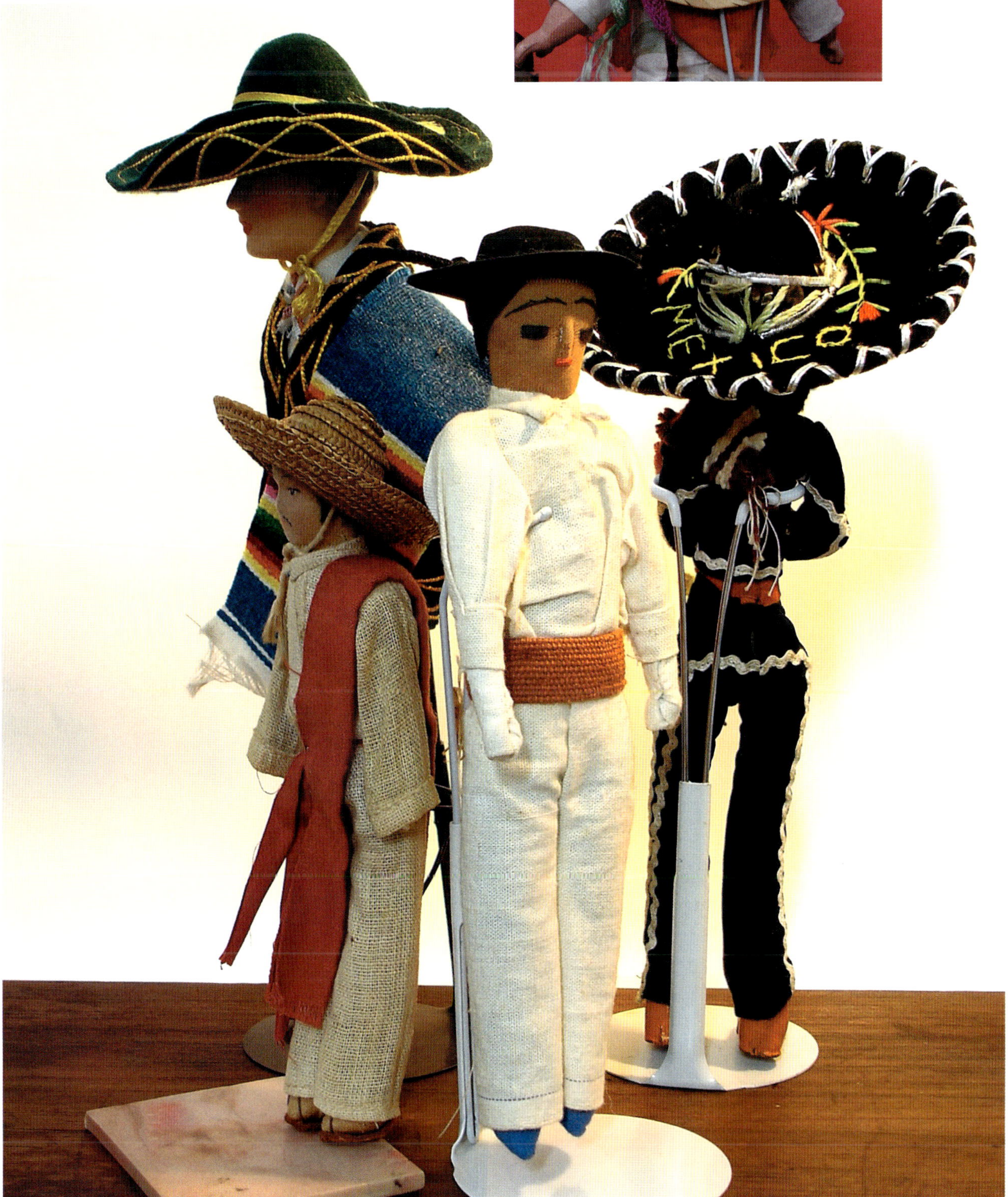

Mexican *caballeros* and examples of their *sombreros*, c.1920s to 1940s, in sizes from 3 in. to 11 in. diameter. All made in Mexico. *Sombreros* $10 to 20 ea.

El Serape, The Blanket

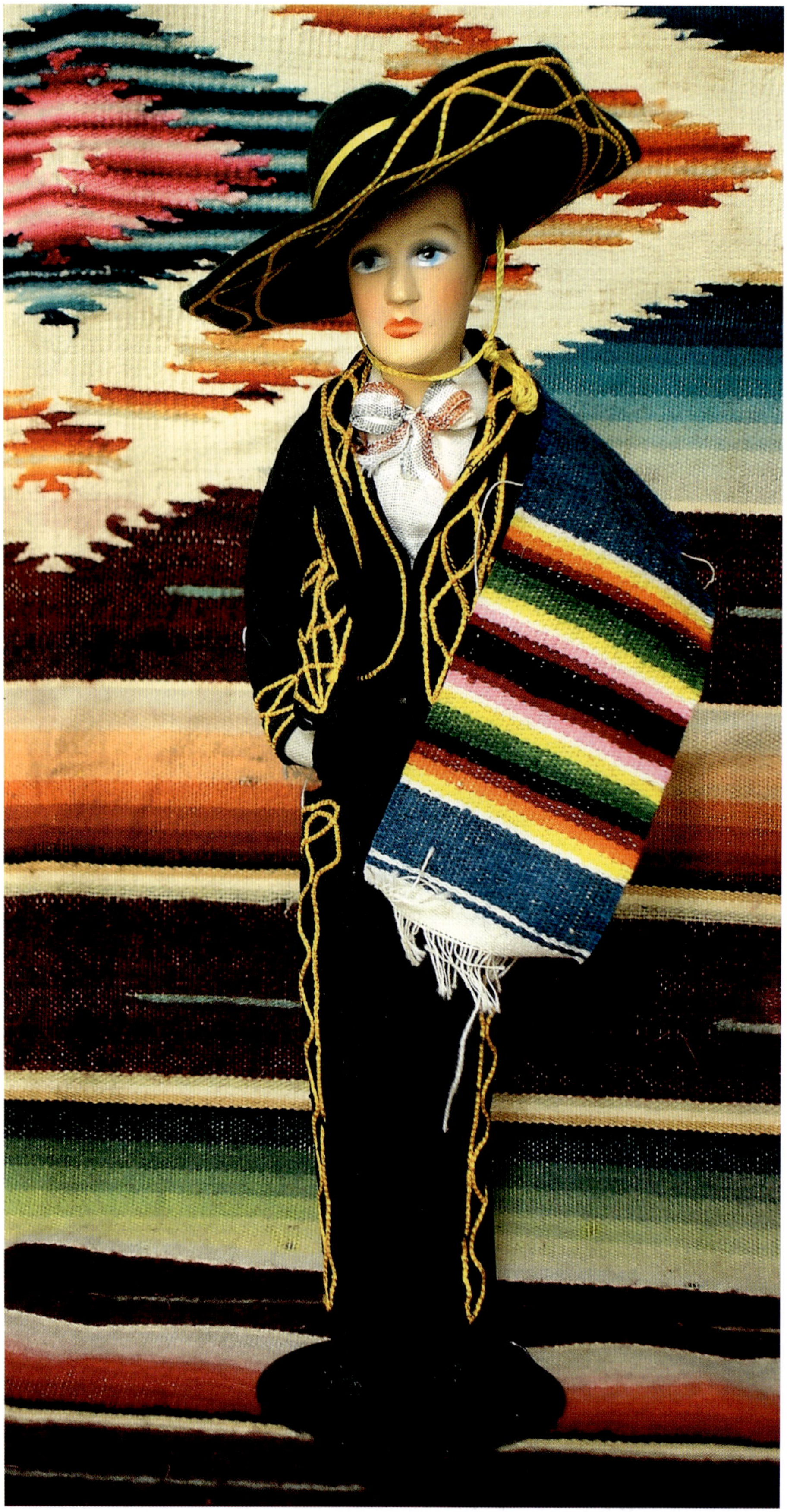

A picturesque, 12 in., composition *charro* wearing a colorful wool *serape*. He stands in front of a Saltillo *serape*, c.1930s. $75 to 150

The colorful wool or cotton blanket (or shawl) worn over the Mexican man's shoulder is recognized as the *serape*. It is a long rectangular shape of woven homespun cloth, with the width wide enough to cover the shoulders and down the arms. All the types have fringe along both ends. It was a suitable and multi-functional item of clothing that was utilized by the men of every social level. The *serape* has been adapted for many uses, such as a cape or cloak for warmth and for purposes of status and identity of the wearer.

Serapes were woven from fine wools as well as ordinary wool and cotton. The *serape de Saltillo* is widely known worldwide for its mastery of treadle-loom techniques. Often the special *serapes* from Saltillo were made with cotton warp and wool weft and dyes. These specialized tapestry woven *serapes* gained such acclaim that *Saltillo serape* patterns were adapted in other regions of Mexico as well. Diamonds, small triangles, rhomboids, and other shapes grouped in areas seem to mimic a number of early native *serapes*. The *serapes* from Tlaxcala, Oaxaca, and Michoacán include strong traditional decorations with indigenous themes applicable to their regions. Their continuous creative quality, colors, and designs define their purpose and importance.

Otomi men, in the state of Mexico, also wear a cape-like piece called the *ayate* that is made from the maguey plant or finely open-woven cotton. It is tied over one shoulder asymmetrically with a multi-purpose use, such as for carrying items. They can have *bordado* and are hand woven.

There are other different interpretations of the serape, such as the *poncho* (a wool or homespun cape with opening at the head), *el quechquémitl* (a triangular cloth shawl), and the *jorongos* (similar to a large poncho).

A colorful wool Saltillo *serape*, made in Mexico, c.1930s.

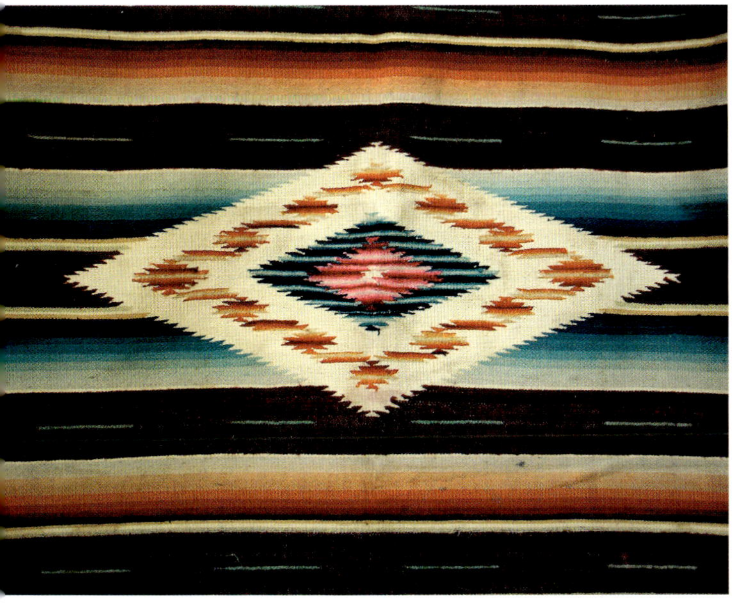

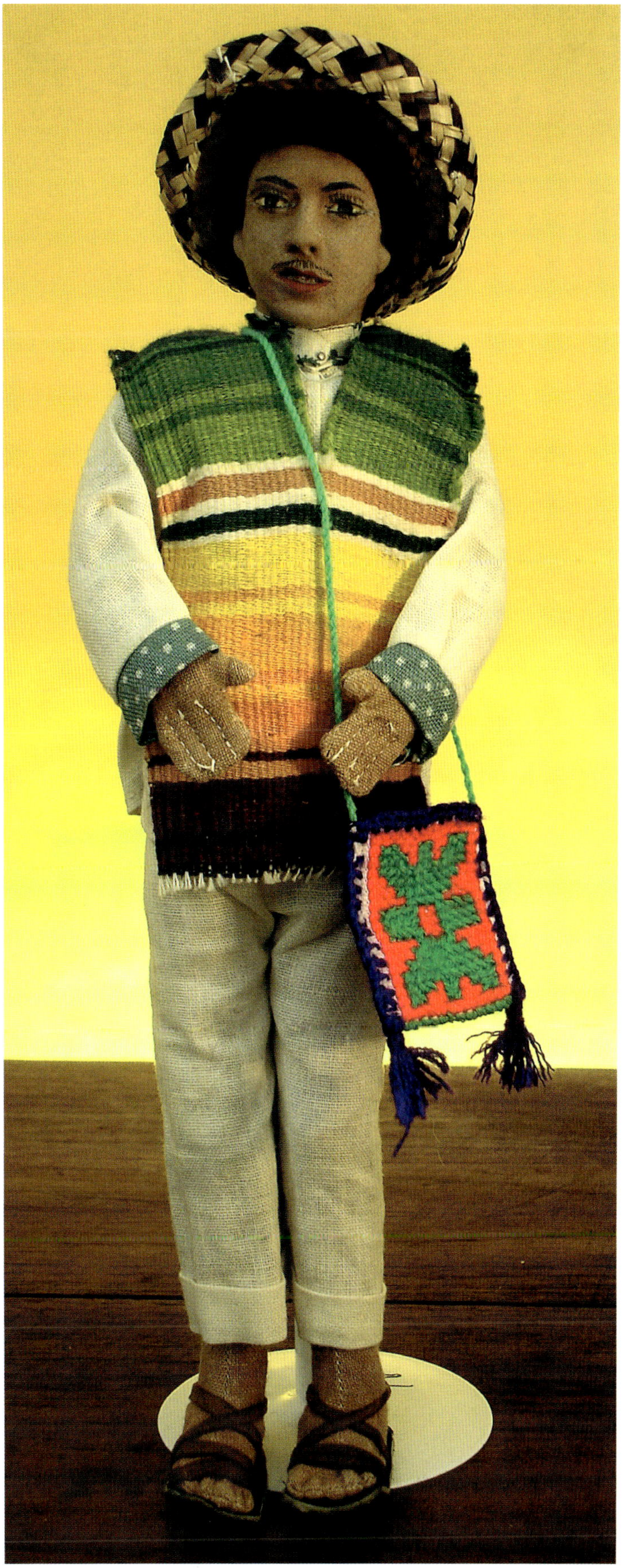

A *mestizo*, 14 in. Indian cloth doll wearing typical clothing, the *calzóne blanco* pants, wool poncho, *huaraches*, and a small *sombrero*. Made in Mexico, c.1930s. Molded facial features with painted detail. $75 to 150

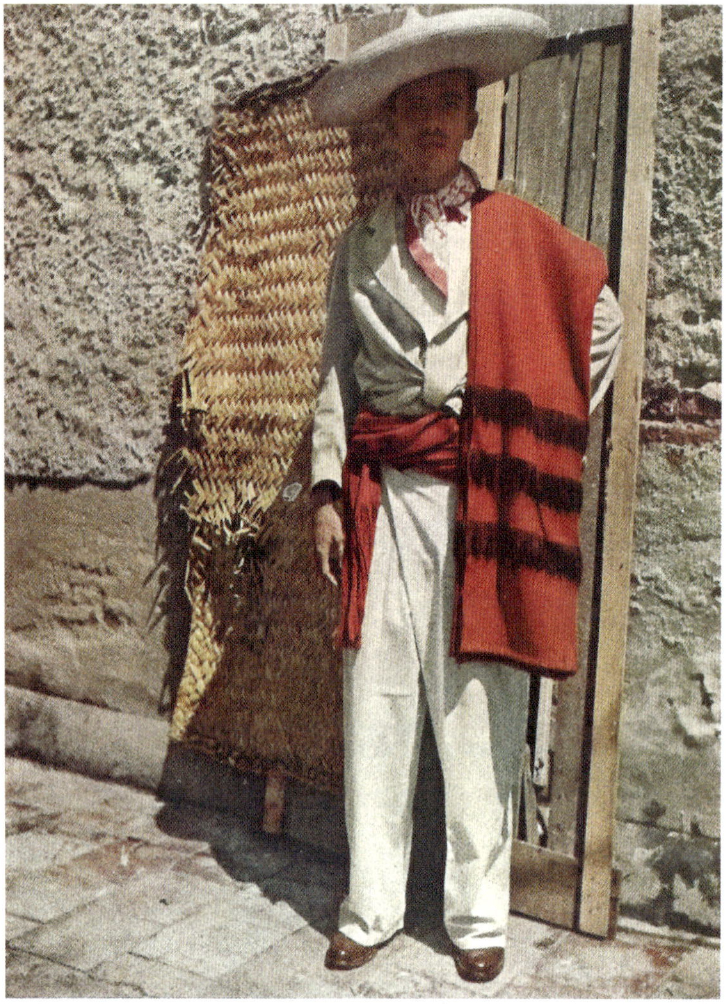

A young *mestizo* stands in front of an adobe house, wearing the typical *calzóne blanco* pants and top, spectacular wool red *serape*, and straw *sombrero*, 1934.

A variety of tourist *serapes* in brilliant colors, made of wool, cotton, and synthetic blends, 20th c., made in Mexico.

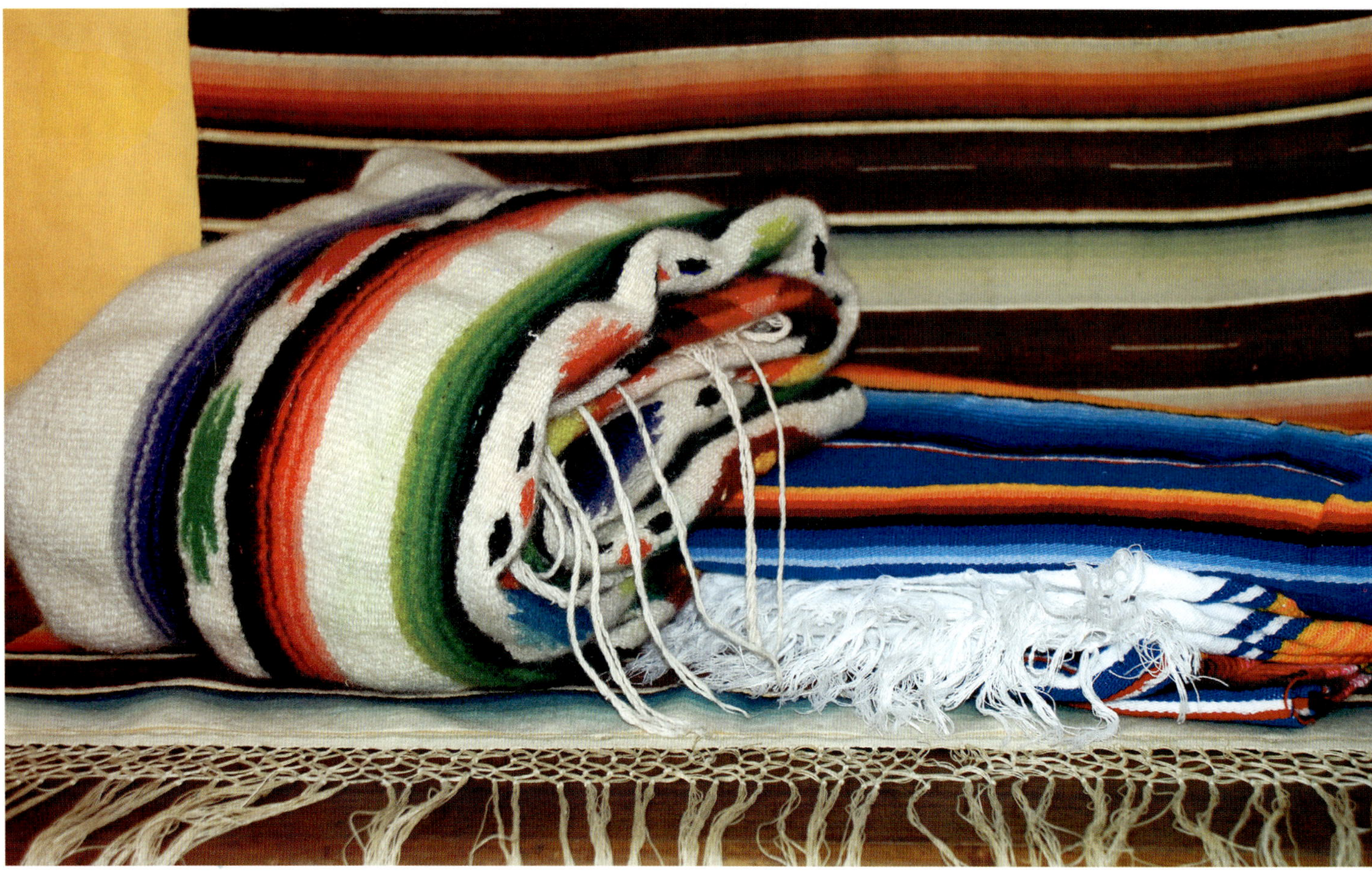

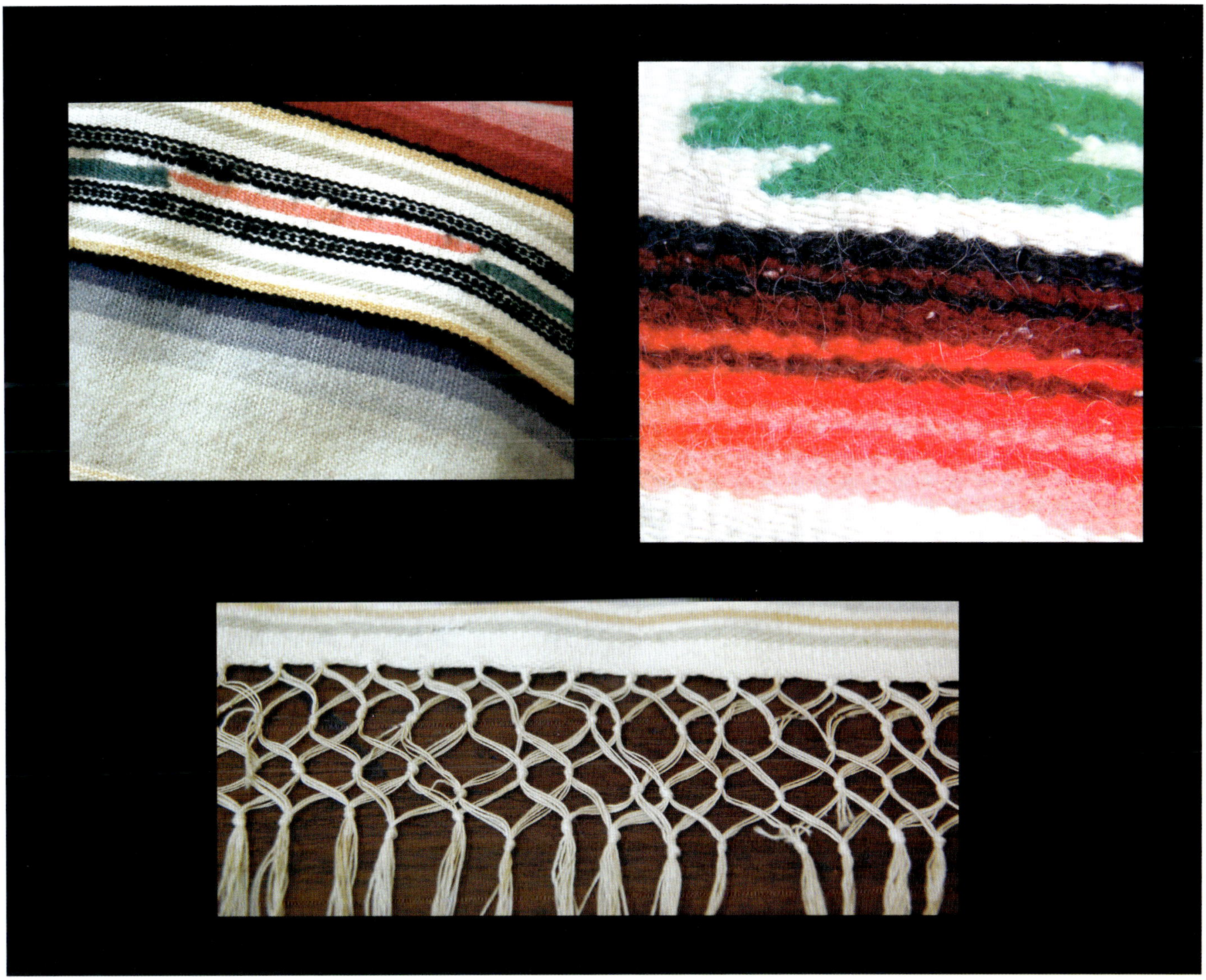

The different weaves of the *serape*, popular designs in a multitude of colors, made in Mexico.

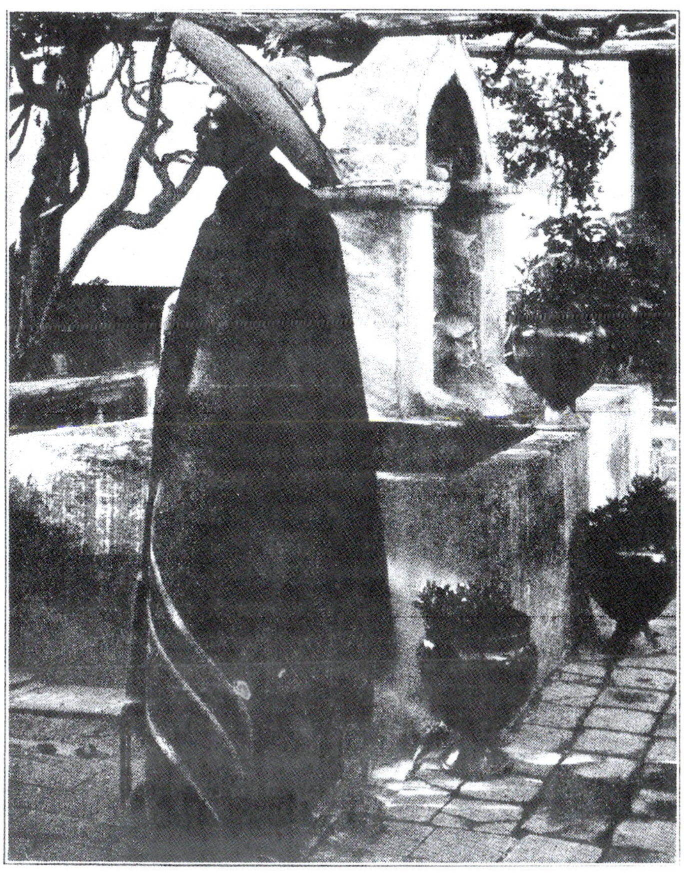

"*Serape* Man" print, 1936.

The male dolls display some of these styles, and while they do not compare with the outstanding detail of authentic *serapes*, they give a broad idea of their use and beauty. A few are actual miniature versions of real *serapes*, but others are merely general replicas.

The *serape's* popularity and high trade demand has made it an industry for Mexico. They provide a hefty source of income for Mexico's export trade and tourist industry. The most prized, finely woven *serapes* take months to make and are very expensive. Today, the *charro*, for example, wears elaborate woven *serapes* in the *Charreda*, a Mexican horsemanship exhibition and notable festive event that incorporates equestrian competitions with demonstrators wearing spectacular flamboyant costumes. There are also costumes of the *mariachi*, which is similar to the *charro* as they both feature fancy suits, *serapes*, and large *sombreros*.

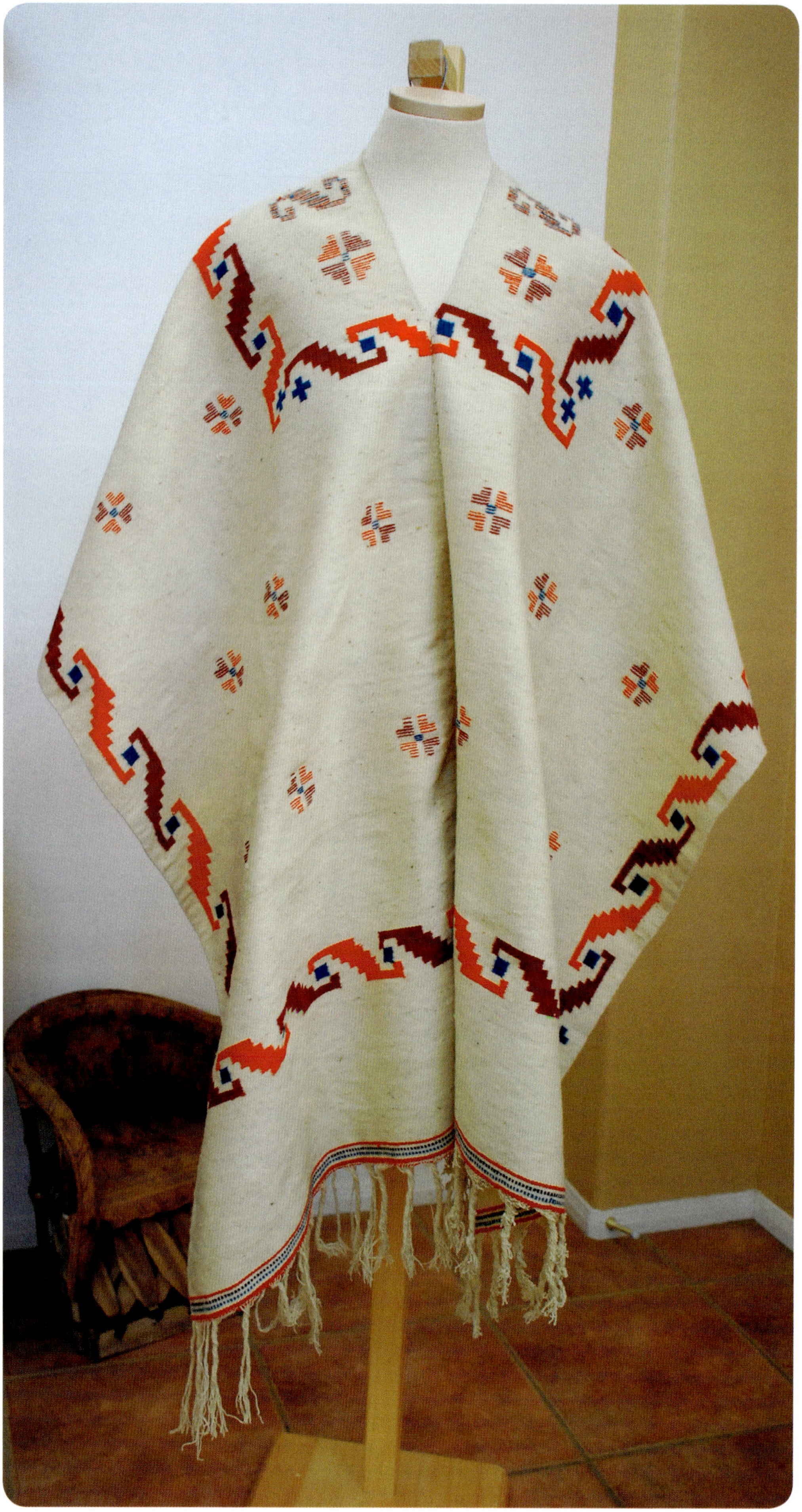

A large, wool, Old Mexico poncho with traditional patterns, c.1940s, in excellent condition. $150 to 300

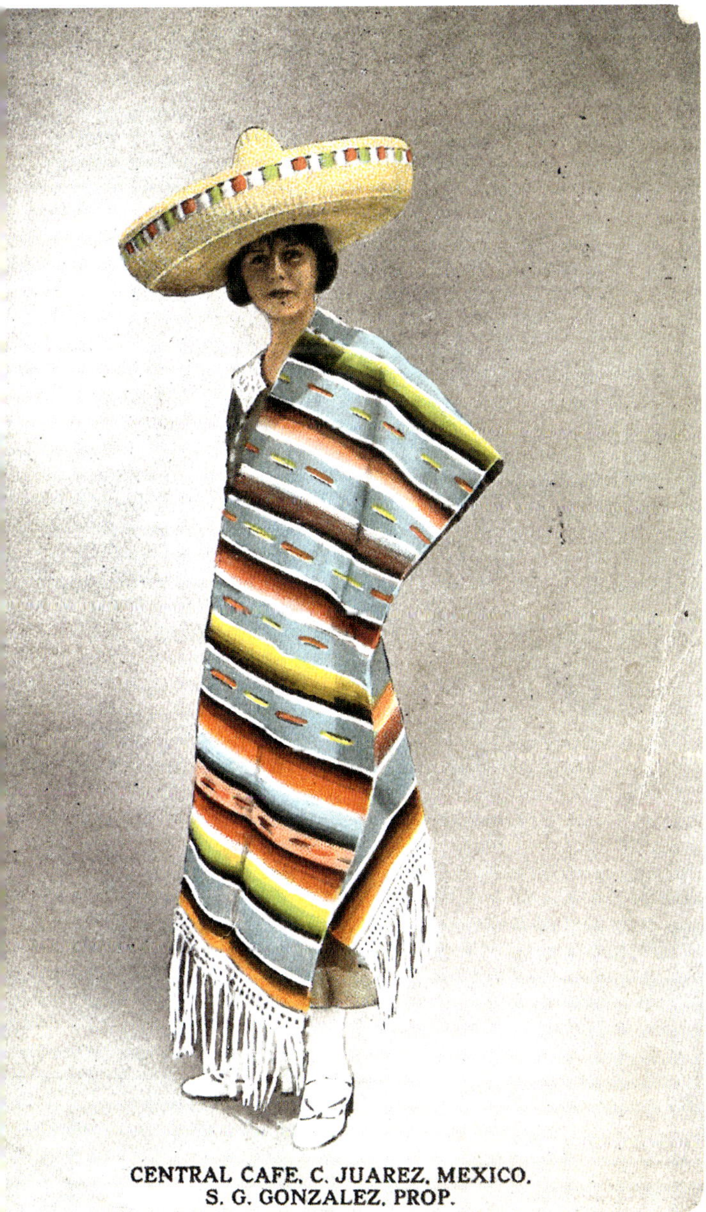

Postcard, color tinted, "CENTRAL CAFE," C. Juarez, Stamped 1927, 3 x 5 in., S.G. Gonzalez, Prop. Mexico. $15 to 30

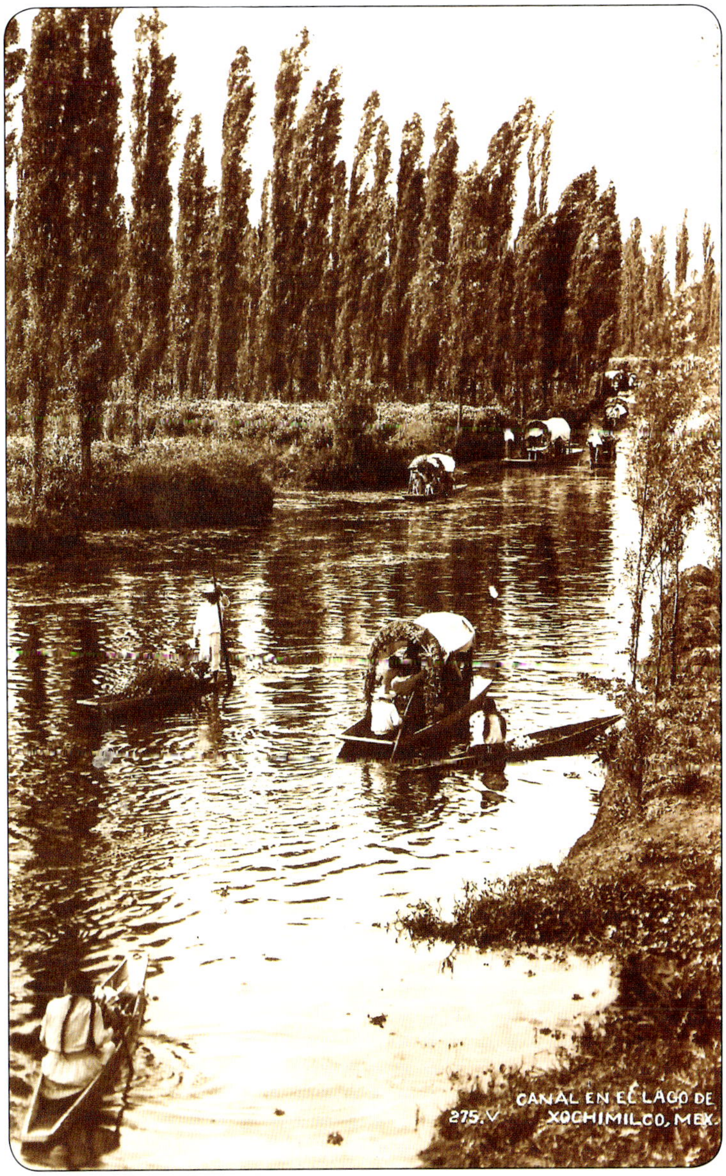

The Xochomilco canal in Mexico city, postcard photograph, 1930s.

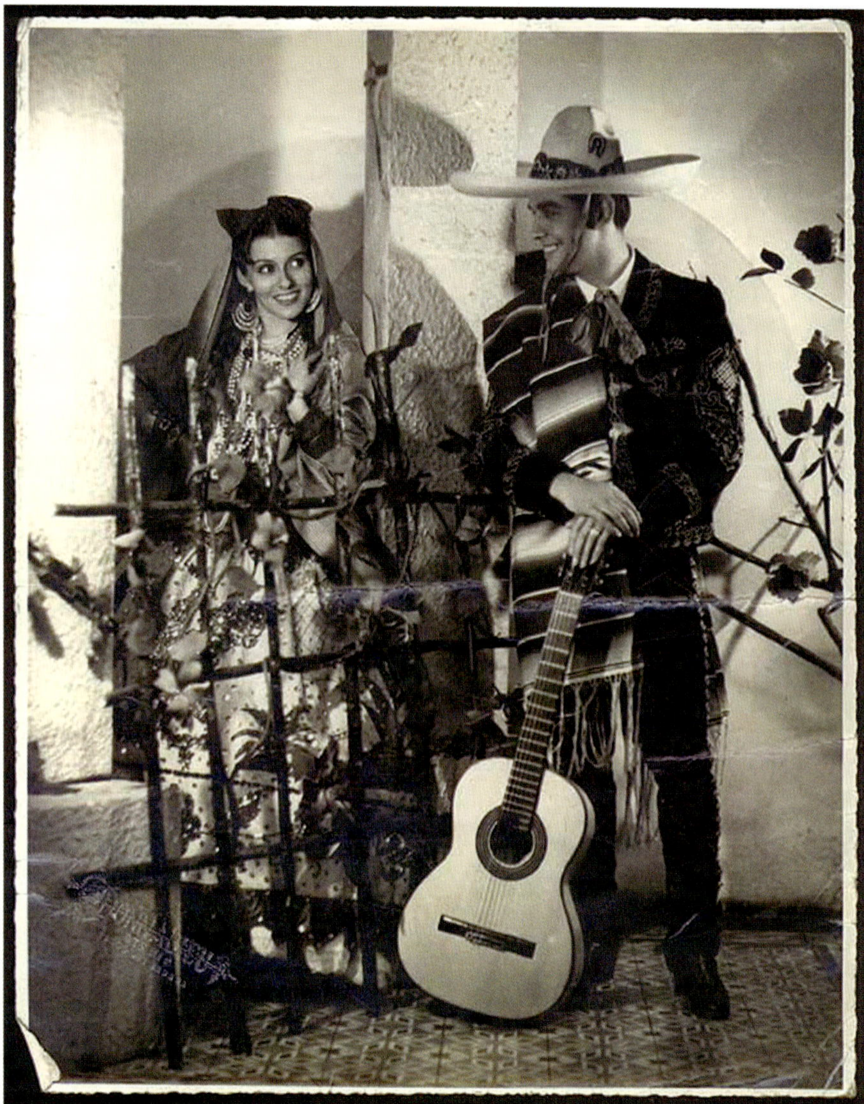

Serenading his lady, an 8 x 10 in. glossy publicity photograph of a *charro* and a *charra*, 1942.

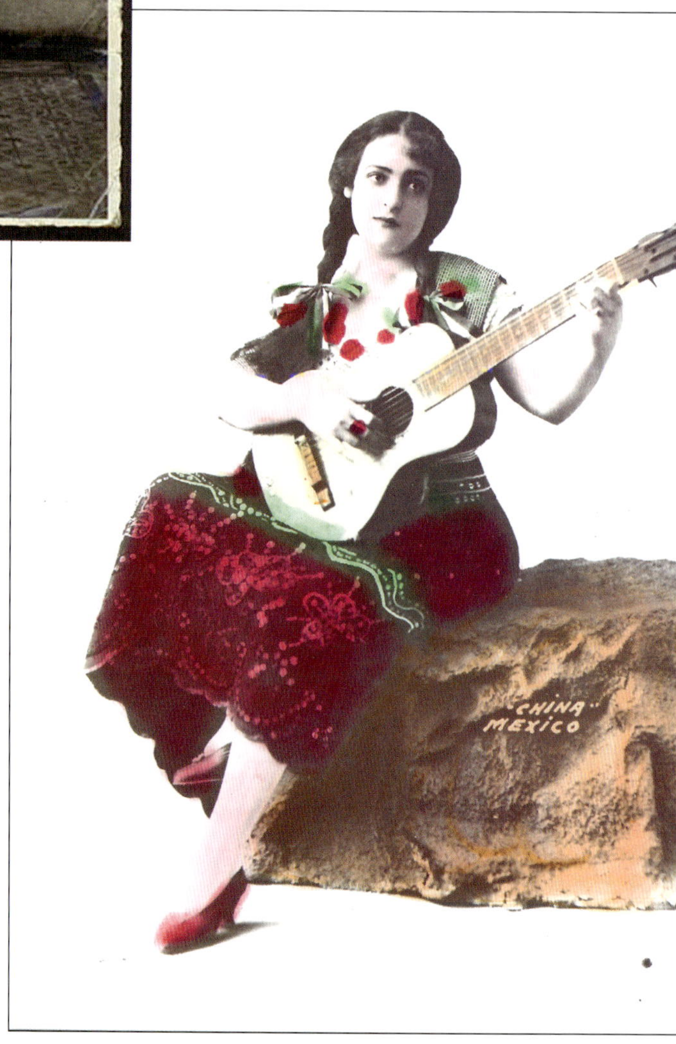

Postcard photograph, "China Guitara," a somber mestiza with her guitar, c. 1930s, Mexico D. F., 4 x 5 in. $10 to 20

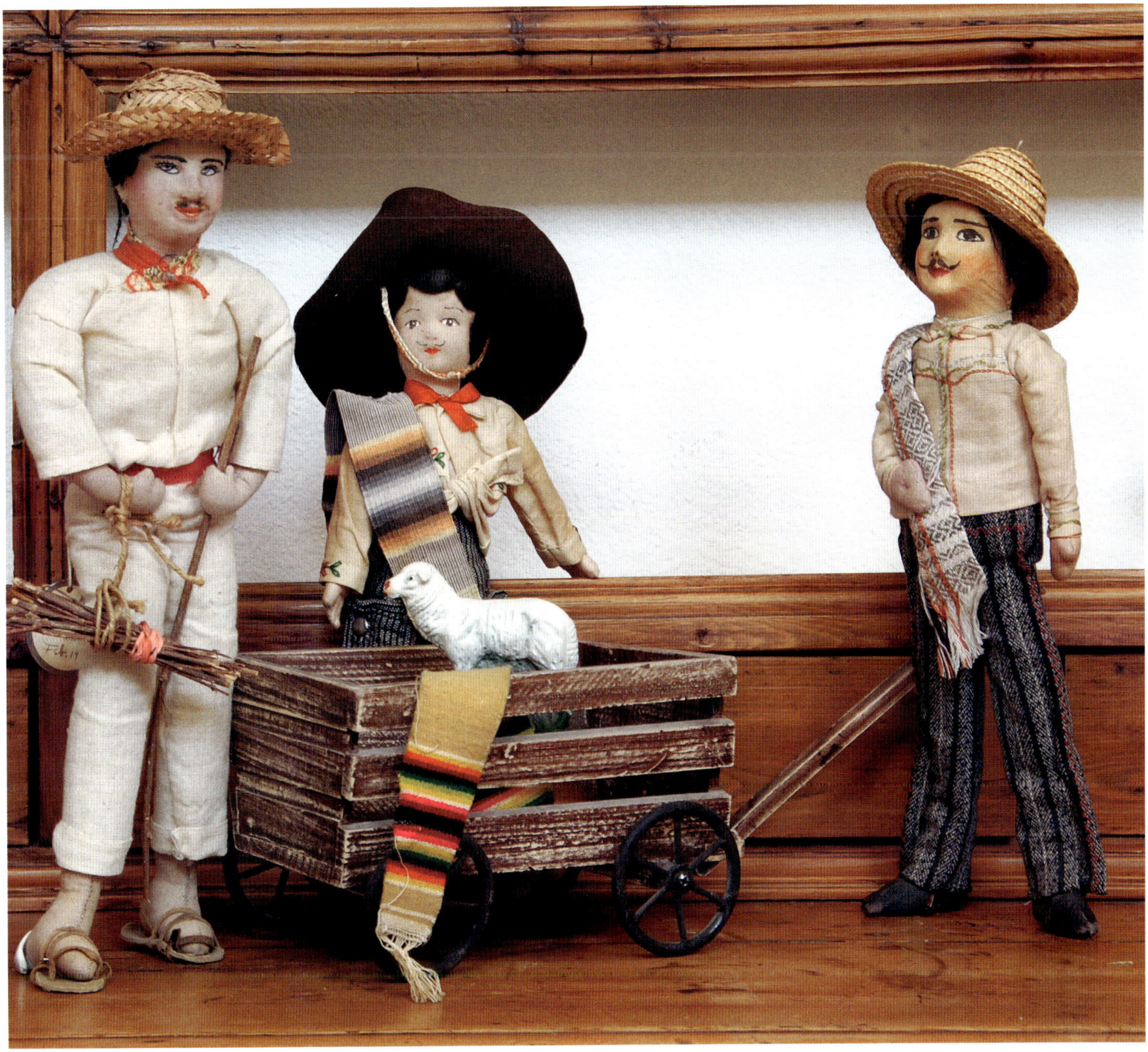

A trio of typical Mexican *mestizos*, 20th century. A large cloth 16 in. doll with molded facial features and a bundle of wood. In the center is a 13 in. cloth doll with felt painted face, striped serape, and large *sombrero*. The 14 in. *caballero* pulls the cart and wears a *serape*. All original, made in Mexico with authentic detail. $65 to 125

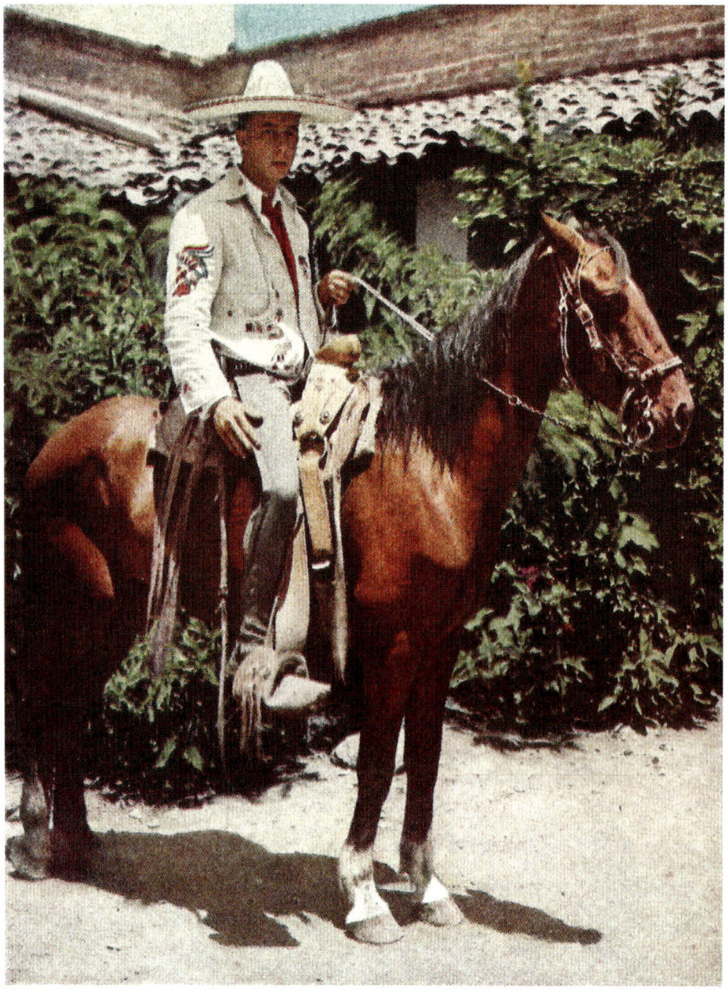

A young urban Mexican on a horse dressed in a white *charro* suit, 1934.

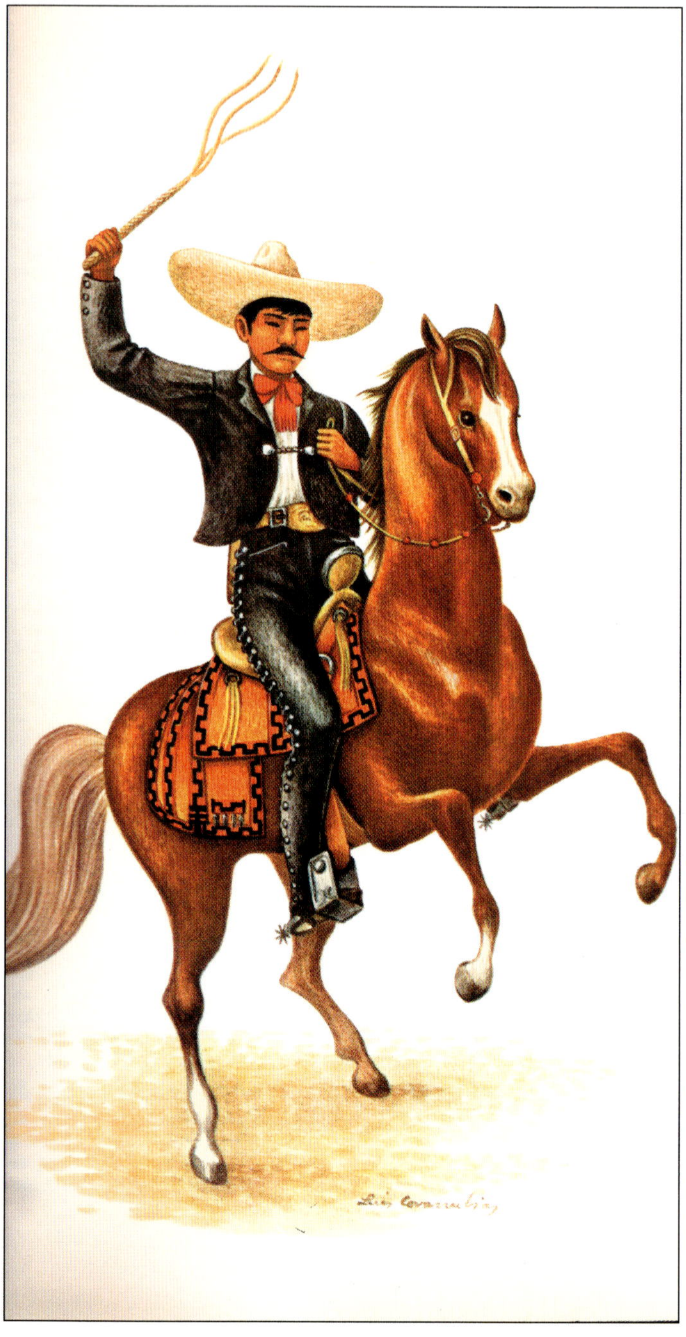

A grand *charro* on a horse, mid-20th century, a color print by Louis Covarrubias.

Glossary

Adelita (ah-day-lee-ta): a colonial influenced dress that has many layers or ruffles. Used in most festivals in Mexico because of its flamboyant appearance.

Abelardo Ruiz: a Mexican papier maché artist in Mexico City

Anthromorphic: human and animal attributes interpreted in their folk art

Arte Popular (are-tay pa-poo-lar): Popular Arts interpreted as Mexico's folk art

Aqua (ah-goo-a): water

Arbol de la vida (are-bowl de la vee-dah): the tree of life

Artisan: a folk artist or craft maker

Ayate (ah-ya-te): a porous fiber woven from the Maguay agave used to make a woven cape used by the men, Otomi and sashes.

Backstrap Loom: a loom tied around the weavers' waist with tension than can be adjusted by leaning back

Batea (bah-tay-a): a wood bread making bowl

Blusa (blue-sa): a top or blouse, peasant style with Spanish influences

Bordado (bore-da-doe): the embroidered border edge at the top or bottom

Border Industrialization Program (BIP): a program developed in the 1960's that contributed to the establishment of industries along the United States-Mexico border. The primary intentions of the BIP were to encourage industrialization in Mexican border regions.

Bolero (bow-lay-ro): A popular Spanish dance also popular in Mexico

Caballero (ka-ba-yeh-row): Mexican or Spanish men

Caites (ka-it-ez): a more ancient sandal worn in Chiapas highlands, a high heel piece back, hard sole, strung between the toes and around the back heel piece for support.

Calzoncillo (cal-son-see-yo): long underwear, drawers

Calzóne Blanco (cal-so-ne blank-oh): traditional white tunic shirt and pants worn by the mestizo and the Indian men in the region of Mexico.

Campesino (camp-pey-see-no): the worker, country farm peon

Cantaro (can-ta-row): a pitcher used to carry water

Carselles (car-seh-yes): a novelty Mexican doll and toy maker

Castor (kah-store): a cotton fabric, only available in Mexico today.

Cazuela (cah-soo-ay-la): pottery bowl used for cooking

Chamula (cha-oo-la): a tribal group predominantly in the state Chiapas

Chaparreras (cha-par-rey-rax): leather over trousers, chaps

Chaquira (cha-key-rah): glass or plastic beading

Charra (char-ra): a Mexican cowgirl or charrita (little cowgirl)

Charreda (char-red-ah): a Mexican rodeo

Charreria (char-rey-ree-ah): artisan of the charro and charro

Charro or **Charra** (char-ro(a)): Mexican mestizo cowboy or cowgirl which wear the traije suit & typical attire of that style.

Cholula (cha-loo-la):a city in the district or state of Puebla in central Mexico, east of Mexico city.

Chiapas (chee-ah-pas): a district state in southern Mexico

Chiapaneca (chee-ah-pa-necka): citizens of Chiapas and also referenced to their typical mestiza lace & colorful flowered folkloric dress from that region.

Chicontla (chee-con-tla): Chicontla is a small Totanacan village located in the state of Puebla

China Poblana (chee-na po-blah-na): a name given to the particular costume "Chinese of Puebla;" a Mexican costume for women inspired and adapted by the legend an Asian girl Catarina.

Chinampas (chee-nahm-paz): the floating gardens, Mesoamerican crops state of Mexico

Chinanteca (chin-an-teka): indigenous people from the state of Oaxaca

Chincuete (chin-coo-et-tay): a skirt worn that is wrapped and fashioned around the waist, often with a striped horizontal weave or solid color.

Chinelas (chi-nay-las): satin slippers shoes

Chulita (o): little cute, usually in reference to a child, male or female

Colonial: the colonial period 1520s to 1820s, New Spain controlled Mexico after the conquest up until Mexico's independence.

Colonias (ko-low-knee-az): the colonized neighborhoods of large metro areas

Composition: an early century mixture of glue & sawdust or any type of filler that would be molded in making dolls body parts.

Corriente (ko-ree-en-the): moving, the movement or flow, idiomatic expression as well that expresses a common use.

Corte (core-the): short, also use to identify a shorter skirt style

Costurera (coss-too-ray-rah): seamstress, tailor or someone that sews

Cueitl (coo-ett-il): a volumous skirt worn by an indigenous group in the state of Puebla

Enagua (in-ah-goo-ah): a full gathered longer skirt worn by the mestiza and the Indians.

En Cabochon (in-ka-bow-chon): a stone that is shaped and polished not facetted, flat bottom

Enredo (in-ray-do): a long & wide wrap around skirt, fashioned in a variety of ways.

Escaramuza (es-ka-rah-moo-sa): an event that displays usually 8 women and their horsemanship skills during a charrería

Equipale (eh-kee-pa-leh): a pig skin hide leather piece of furniture

Faja (fa-ha): a sash or belts worn around the waist

Falda (fal-da): womens skirt, gathered and to the ankle or calf

Frijoles (free-hole-es):Mexicos brown beans, cooked and smashed

Galareña (gah-la-rey-ni-a): a distinctive costume of the mestiza women of Guanajuato

Greco: an elaborate baroque technique used with ribbon or cord, i.e. soutash, to create a design

Guadalajara (gua-da-la-har-a): the capitol of Jalisco, a state in Mexico.

Guerrero (goo-air-o): A state in Mexico, where Taxco and Alcapulco

Guilloche (n.): A braided effect. In ornamental art, any pattern made by interlacing curved lines, seen on rebozos

Haciendados (ha-see-end-dah-dos) ranch or land owners, with workers

Huaraches (who-ah-raw-chez): Mexican sandals

Huehuetla (wu-wu-ett-la): a town the state of Puebla

Huichol (witch-all): indigenous group of Mexican Indians who live in the central regions of Mexico including Nayarit, Jalisco

Huipil (wee-pil): a traditional Indian top or blouse, woven and often indicative designs from the villages it is from

Ikat: a dye technique made of fish used in making garments

Irrompible (ear-ohm-pea-bleh): unbreakable

Isthmus of Tehuantepec: an isthmus the shortest distance between the Gulf of Mexico and the Pacific Ocean. Santa Maria Tehuantepec is in the state of Oaxaca and is referred to in this name as well.

Ixtle (ist-lee): a strong fiber made from the maguey plant

Jalisco (ya-lis-co): the second largest city in Mexico, the capital is Guadalajar

Jarabe Tapatio (hah-rah-bay tah-pah-tee-o): the Mexican hat dance that is the national dance of Mexico.

Jorongo (ho-ron-go): a serape made on a back strap loom with slit for head

Kahlo, Frida: 1907 – 1954, an internationally acclaimed female Mexican painter.

La Chilena (la-chee-ley-na): A dance done in Guerrero with handkerchiefs

La Placita (la pla-see-ta): from "plaza", a smaller area, usually the center of the town where the church sits North. A colonial city was usually planned around the placita.

Manta (man-ta): an unbleached muslin cloth or colored cloth, or sometimes referred to as a cloak or covering

Mantillas (man-tea-yas): Spanish rayon, silk and lace scarves

Maguey (mah-gay): made of a plant, a strong coarse woven fiber, also used for drink

Mariachi (ma-rea-ah-chee): Mexican musicians that wear flamboyant costumes and wide brim sombreros

Mestizo (mess-tee-o (a)): the term of choice for European & Indian decent, with the connotation primarily that of the Spanish

Mesoamerica: the geographical regions of Mexico, Central America, Guatamala to Beliz, and the southern regions that extend from Mexico and their indigenous cultures.

Metepec (meh-tay-peck): the Nahuatl people, a municipal in the state of Mexico

Mixteca (mees-tay-ka): an important group of Indian tribes living in the northern and southern regions, shared by the states of Puebla, Oaxaca and Guerrero.

Moño (moan-e-o): a cravat like bow tie

Morral (more-rahl): woven carry all bags worn usually by the men

Muñeca de concreto (moon-echa de con-crea-to): plaster of Paris doll

Muñeca de tela (moon-echa de tay-la): cloth dolls

Municipios (moon-e-see-pea-ohs): a municipality, a term used to define the different sub national entities.

Nahua (nah-wah): a tribe and or city, also the term meaning a dance done with the hands entwined, to move in tempo that may describe embroidery.

Oaxaca (wa-ha-ka): one of the 31 districts (state) of Central Mexico, southern region

Oaxacan (wa-ha-kan): a native of Oaxaca

Obrajes: textile factories set up by the Spaniards, exploited native workers

Olinalá (lh-leen-ah-la): the name of a town in the state of Guerrero, Mexico. Known for their laquerware, glossy painted on wood.

Olla (oh-ya): a pottery earthenware jar, many used to store water

Otomi (o-tom-ee): indigenous people from Central Mexico
Pahuatlan (pa-who-at-lan): the indigenous people of Puebla, Otomi and Nahua
Paloma de bolita (pa-low-ma de bow-lee-ta): a special woven rebozo that shimmers or glistens because of the weave and threading
Palacios (pa-la-see-oz): palaces, ornate large buildings or structures
Papelillo (pa-pe-lee-yo): paper thin glass beads
Papier maché: a substance or material made of paper or other textile with glue or paste
Peon (pea-on): the poor urban dwellers, mestiza or Indian
Pepenado (pe-pe-na-doe): reverse embroidery, the stitches emphasize the background fabric outlining a motif.
Pespunteado (pez-poon-tea-ah-doe): embroidering while simultaneously gathering the cloth in fine tucks, producing a negative pattern. Similar to pepenado
Petatate (pe-ta-te): a woven mat, used to sleep on as well as many other purposes, made of reed, palm and other materials
Pintor (pin-tour): painter, some one who paints
Plateados (pla-the-add-os): silver ones referring to their silver buttons or jewelry
Puebla (poo-eh-blah): a state in central Mexico, east of Mexico City. Puebla is also the name of the capital.
Puerpécha: an indigenous group of Michoacán
Pueblan (poo-eh-blan): a native of Puebla
Poveda (poe-ve-dah): Mexican toy and doll maker
Quechquémitl (kes-ke-met): triangular cape poncho style garment worn over the huipil, elaborate weaves, northern region
Rebozo (rey-bow-so): a long strip of cloth: scarf like shawl usually with fringed border, widely used in south eastern Mexico for many purposes
Resplandor (res-plane-door): the Tehuanas woman wide white head piece, made of a pleated fabric and lace.
Retablo (ray-tab-low): small paintings of miracles or stories that are made in offering to Christ or the Virgin in performing miracles. A painted alter piece in churches.
Ropa tipica (rope-ah-tip-ee-ka): typical clothing
Sanborns: well known tourist border department store
San Miguel de Allende (san- me-gell de ah-yen-day):a city in the state Guanajuato
Señor (sin-yor): a man, "mister", before a mans name like Mr. but not capitalized
Señor del Rebozo (sin-yor del ray-bow-so): Patron saint of the rebozos
Señora (sahn-yor-a): a woman, "Mrs."
Señorita (sin-yor-ree-ta): a young lady or woman, "Miss" but can be for a young married woman
Serape (seh-rah-pay): a woven blanket, most specifically worn by men's as a cloak.
Sierra Madres: central mountains region of Mexico to the US border barrier to east and west
Skinny Dolls: long necked paper mache dolls, painted Tonala style.
Sombrero (some-bra-row): a woven hat with usually somewhat of a high tip and a very wide brim, used for protection from the hot sun in Mexico. Peasant sombreros are usually made of straw, while wealthier mestizo wear sombreros made of felt that are very ornate.
Soldadera (sol-dah-dare-a): a Mexican woman soldier
Soutash: a cord ribbons, used in making into floral or patterns like the "greco patterns"
Soyate (so-yah-te): a twill reed woven sash
Syncretism: the blending of traits from two different cultures to form a new trait that is innately its own.
Tacuates: indigenous group from Oaxaca that has their own distinct language
Taller (tah-ye-air-es): work shop, artisan centers or informal factories of creative work.
Talavera (tah-la-veh-rah): a Majolica-like style of pottery made in the state of Puebla, Hand painted and beautiful Spanish patterns.
Tarascan (tar-ask-can): an indigenous group of Michoacán
Tehuantepec (te-who-an-the-peck): in the southeast state of Oaxaca
Tenochtitlan (te-knock-tlan): the Aztecan capitol now known as Mexico City.
Tilmatl (tecl-ma): A Nahuatl word, which was their name of the cloak worn by the Indian men before the conquest, like the serape serves today.
Tlaquepaque (te-la-key-paw-key): the Indian meaning for "a place above clay land," a city in the state of Jalisco known for beautiful folk painting
Tonala (tone-al-ah): a part of Guadalajara in the state of Jalisco, also a style of pottery with characteristics of detailed brunido style painting that adorns their work.
Traje (tra-hey): an outfit or dress
Trajineras (tra-he-nea-ras): a taxi boat that is decorated if flowers along the canals in Mexico
Tuarra (too-ah-row): a triangular style cape worn by the men
Valdiosera, Ramon: a prolific Mexican artist and writer of the 20th c..
Vaqueros (va-care-rows): Mexican Cowboy
Yalalag (yah-la-lag): an indigenous Indian of Mexico, Hidalgo Yalalag, particularly in Oaxaca
Zagalejo (saga-ley-ho): a full gathered skirt, usually red flannel, bordered with a traditional cotton triangular border at the top and bottom of the skirt.
Zandunga (san-dune-gah): traditional dance
Zapatero (sah-pa-tear-oh): a shoe maker
Zapotecan (sah-poe-tek-an): an indigenous group from the state of Oaxaca and Guerrero

Bibliography

Books

Campbell, Reau. Complete Guide and Descriptive Book of Mexico. City of Mexico, Press of Thos.Knapp Printing and Binding Co..1899

Chase, Stuart. *MEXICO,A Study of Two Americas.* New York, The MacMillan Company, 1931.

Cordry Donald & Dorothy. *Mexican Indian Costumes.* Austin & London, University of Texas Press , 1968.

Covarrubias, Luis. *Mexican Native Costumes.* Mexico, Fishgrund. No date, presumed 1930's.

Edward, Linda. *Cloth Dolls From Ancient to Modern Collectors Guide.* Atglen, Pa, Schiffer Publishing, 1997

Judd, Polly and Pam. *Americas, Australia and the Pacific Islands Costumed Dolls.*3rd Series, Maryland, Hobbie House Press, 1997.

Gutierrez, Elektra and Tonatiuh. *El Arte Popular De Mexico.* Mexico D. F., Artes de Mexico, 1970-1971.

Lanks, H. C.. *Otomi Indians o Mezquital Valley.* Hidalgo Mexico,Economic Geography, Vol 14, 1938.

Lechuga, Ruth. *El Traje Indigena de Mexico su evolución, desde la epóca Prehispánica hasta la actualidad.* Mexico, Panorama Editorial,S.A., 1987.

Lechuga, Ruth.*Arte Popular Museo.* Mexico Publication: Artes De Mexico, 1998.

Lewis, Oscar and Ruth. *A Day in he Life of a Mexican Peasant Family, Marriage and Family Living.*Vol. 18 No.1, Illinois, University of Illinois, 1959.

McMenamin, Donna. *Popular Arts of Mexico 1850-1950.* Ltd..Atglen PA. Schiffer Publishing, 1996.

Ross Fent, Patricia. *Made In Mexico, The Story of a Country's Arts & Crafts.* New York, Alfred A. Knopf, 1960.

Sayer, Chloë. *Mexican Costume.* London, England, The British Museum Publications Ltd., 1985.

Sayer, Chloë, *Textiles from Mexico.* Seattle, University of Washington Press, 2002.

Sayer, Chloë. *Mexican Patterns.* New York, Portland House, 1990.

Shipway, Warren and Verna Cook. *The Mexican House Old & New.* New York, Architectural Book Publishing Co.Inc..1960

Smith, Susan. *Made In Mexico.* New York, Alfred A. Knopf, 1930.

Smith, Patricia R. *Modern Collector's Dolls, Identification & Value Guide.* Kentucky, Collectors Books, 1995

Stinetorf, Louise A.. *La China Poblana.* New York,The Bobs Merrill Company Inc..1960.

Toneyama, Kojin. *The Popular Arts of Mexico.* N. Y. WeatherHill, Inc., 1974.

Toor, Frances. *Mexican Popular Arts.* Mexico, Frances Toor Studios, 1939.

Valdiosera Ramon & text by Salvador Echeverria. *12-Mexican Native Costumes.* Mexico D.F., Eugenio Fischgrund, 1951.

Valdiosera Ramon & text by Hector Ventura Castro. *Mexican Children & Toys.* Mexico, D.F., 1949.

Winter, Nevin O., *Mexico and her People of To-Day.* Boston, L.C. Page & Company (Inc.), 1923.

Internet

Castillo, Marko. *The China Poblana*, Mexico, Universidad Veracruzana.Website: PopulArte, 2006.

Ergau Production.*OaxacaOaxaca.com, Textiles.* Mexico, 2000-2005. (accessed 7/2006)

Freund, Bob, *www.mexicantextiles.com.*An informative website that contributes to the slow extinction and preservation of the indigenous textiles of Mexico.2006 (accessed 9/2006)

Houston Culture. www.houstonculture.org/mexico/ website. The Traditions of Mexico project is an effort to feature many of Mexico's unique customs and cultural celebrations. Texas (accessed 7/2006)

Mexico Desconicido. Mexicodesconocido.com. A website dedicated to the distribution of informative up to date cultural changes in Mexico with interesting articles and history that is enjoyable and easy to understand. Hidalgo, Mexico. (accessed 12/2006)

Millán, Saúl. *The Comisión Nacional para el Desarrollo de los Pueblos Indígenas.* A website and organization developed with objectives to protect, inform the communities as well as develop new programs and contribute to all the needs in protecting the indigenous people. In Spanish only. www.cdi.gob.mx/, Mexico D. F. 2003 (accessed 5/2006)

Tulane University. www.tulane.edu.com. This website is sponsored through Tulane University and displays many examples of Mexico's older costumes and clothing. (accessed 2/2006)

INDEX

References in italics to other information